RICHARD SCHULZ
UNIVERSITY OF PITTSBURGH

ROBERT B. EWEN

Adult Development and Aging

Myths and Emerging Realities

MACMILLAN PUBLISHING COMPANY

NEW YORK

Collier Macmillan Publishers

LONDON

Macmillan Publishing Company
866 Third Avenue, New York, New York 10022
Collier Macmillan Canada, Inc.

LIBRARY OF CONGRESS CATALOGING-IN-PUBLICATION DATA
Schulz, Richard, 1947–
    Adult development and aging.
    Bibliography: p.
    Includes index.
    1. Adulthood—Psychological aspects.   2. Aging—
Psychological aspects.   I. Ewen, Robert B., 1940–
II. Title.
BF724.5.S38   1988   155.6   87-20239
ISBN 0-02-407770-4

Printing; 1 2 3 4 5 6 7   Year: 8 9 0 1 2 3 4

(Continued on page 483 which constitutes a continuation of the copyright page.)

ISBN 0-02-407770-4

To my grandmother Jullianna Voth and to my
father Adolf—R.S.
To Judy and Meredith—R.B.E.

Acknowledgments

We would like to thank Lynn Reder, Joan Rogers, William Sauer, Jim Staszewski, Connie Tompkins, and Ann Yurick for their comments and suggestions.

Preface

The study of adult development and aging is a young but rapidly growing science. Although we know a great deal more about this topic today than we did a decade ago, many of us still subscribe to unfounded myths about adult development and aging. One of the major goals of this book is to contrast existing myths about adult development with the best available data, whenever possible, to separate fiction from fact. Accordingly, we have attempted to summarize and synthesize the most current empirical literature available at the time of writing.

Much of what we know about adult development is emergent: that is, we have some understanding of this complex process, but definitive answers are not always available. Indeed, we will never have definitive answers to some questions because the answers change along with the technological and social environments within which individuals develop. As a result, throughout this book we identify many important questions for which the existing empirical data are still speculative. New information may quickly alter existing conceptions of the field.

Writing a book on adult development and aging inevitably raises the question: Should individual chapters be organized by chronological age or by topic? We have opted for the latter strategy because age *per se* is not necessarily a good marker of adult development and because we believe that the complexity and diversity of the material covered in a text such as this is easier to comprehend when organized in a topical fashion. Although our choice of topics is heavily influenced by our backgrounds in psychology and gerontology, we have not ignored important biological, sociological, and medical contributions to our understanding of adult development and aging. This book covers traditional psychological topics such as sensation and perception, memory and learning, intelligence and creativity, and psychopathology, but also includes separate chapters on such topics as stress and coping, social relationships, and work and retirement.

Our approach differs from existing topical treatments of adult development in that we place a strong emphasis on providing the reader with both a fundamental understanding of a particular topic as well as the most current age-related data. For example, in discussing memory and cognition, we provide sufficient background information on relevant theories and research methods to enable the reader to appreciate how research on age-related changes has evolved and understand the significance of the most current findings on this topic.

We have also included a number of valuable aids designed to make this complex, interdisciplinary body of knowledge accessible to the reader. Each chapter contains a glossary of key terms, a summary of central concepts, and a section called myths vs. data that highlights key issues within a topic and contrasts old with current views. An extensive reference list will enable students and instructors to pursue in depth topics of special interest. Finally, an *Instructor's Manual* is available to all instructors who adopt the text. It includes an extensive list of multiple choice and discussion questions for each chapter, cumulative exams, learning objectives, and suggested readings rated by level of difficulty.

In sum, this book is designed for individuals who value textbooks based on the best available current data and who appreciate that knowledge about adult development is in a state of flux, with new data becoming available almost daily. This book will especially appeal to those instructors who want to encourage critical thinking skills in their students and who want to encourage students to understand and use research-based knowledge along with conventional wisdom as the basis for thought and action.

R.S.
R.B.E.

Contents

PART III *Personality and Social Development*

PART IV *Crises and Problems*

PART I

Introduction

CHAPTER 1

Introduction

This book is about adult development and aging. Let us consider each of these terms separately:

Adult implies that we will not be concerned with such periods of life as infancy, childhood, and the early teens. Although the law specifies minimum ages for certain behaviors (driving an automobile; military service), there is no clearly identifiable age at which human beings leave adolescence and enter adulthood. As a general guideline, we will be dealing with events that occur after about age 20.

Development means that we will be studying changes that occur over time. Adult humans are not static entities; they change as they grow older, often substantially. However, it is also important not to exaggerate the magnitude of these changes. Many common beliefs about the negative effects of aging have proved to be mere myths when investigated scientifically. In this book, therefore, we will: (1) *Describe* important differences and similarities between younger and older adults, basing our observations on data derived from empirical research. (2) Suggest likely *explanations* for those age-related differences that we discover. (3) Indicate how this information might help us to improve adult life. In addition to describing various phenomena and identifying the underlying causes, behavioral scientists also strive to apply their findings in ways that will *modify* our environment for the better.

The developmental approach focuses on changes within the individual across the adult life span (**intraindividual changes**), and on the extent to which such changes occur at different rates among different adults (**interindividual differences**). (See Baltes, Reese, & Nesselroade, 1977.) If the typical adult shows a moderate loss of hearing between ages 40 and 70, this is a significant *intra*individual change. Having described this phenomenon, we next face the task

3

of explaining why such auditory declines occur. For example, a specific part of the auditory system might degenerate with increasing age. If we correctly identify the cause, we may then be in a position to devise appropriate corrective methods (e.g., a mechanical device that takes over the function of the impaired organ).

Alternatively, we might find significant *inter*individual differences in the amount of intraindividual change. That is, some adults may experience much greater auditory declines than do others. Further investigation might then reveal that these hearing losses are caused primarily by frequent exposure to extremely loud noise. This would suggest such corrective measures as protective earmuffs for those who work with loud machinery, and greater caution by those who enjoy listening to rock music on personal headphones.

Some theorists define adult development in terms of a series of distinct stages, ones that are presumably experienced by most or all adults. According to one such model (Levinson, 1986), the period from age 17 to 22 is a bridge between preadulthood and early adulthood; the period from age 22 to 28 is a time for building and maintaining an adult mode of living; the period from age 40 to 45 is the time of midlife transition or "crisis," and so forth. If this model were supported by substantial research evidence, it would provide an appealing framework for discussing adult development. In our opinion, however, the available data do *not* support the concept of universally applicable stages of adult development. (We will have more to say about this issue in Chapter 7.) Therefore, the chapters that follow are organized instead by substantive area: physiological aspects of aging, sensation and perception, learning and memory, personality, and so on.

Lastly, *aging* indicates that we will be paying considerable attention to the behavior of older adults. This is currently an extremely popular research area, for reasons that will be discussed in the following section.

Human Aging and Life Expectancy

Journey back for a moment to the dawn of civilization. During this chaotic era, primitive humanity tried desperately to survive with rudimentary knowledge and few tools. Not surprisingly, very few achieved the age of 40; in fact, the average life span during these prehistoric times was in all probability a mere 18 years! Those who did succeed in reaching their mid-twenties or early thirties were regarded as unusually wise and capable because of this great accomplishment (Dublin, 1951; Lerner, 1976; Schulz, 1978). As civilizations grew and living conditions improved, however, longevity

Chapter Glossary: Introduction

Aging	Changes that significantly decrease the probability of survival, and that are caused by processes within the individual which are universal, inevitable, and irreversible.
Cohort	A group of individuals that has experienced the same event at the same time; frequently, a group of people born in the same year or in adjacent years. (For example, the baby boom cohort is usually defined as all those persons born between 1946 and 1958.)
Geriatrics	An area of specialization within the field of medicine that deals with the scientific study of the diseases, debilities, and care of aged persons.
Gerontology	The scientific study of aging and the special problems of the aged.
Interindividual differences	Differences between different people or groups of people, as when some individuals show greater age-related declines than do others.
Intraindividual changes	Changes that occur within a given individual over a period of time.
Life expectancy at birth	The number of years that will probably be lived by the average person born in a particular year.
Life expectancy at a specific age	The number of additional years that will probably be lived by the average person who reaches the specified age in a particular year.
Maximum life span	The extreme upper limit of human life.

increased. There are now more than 23,000,000 people in this country age 65 and older, including more than 100,000 over 100 years of age—a phenomenon that has been referred to as "the graying of America."

Definitions

AGING. Human **aging** consists of changes that are caused by processes within the individual, and that significantly decrease the probability of survival. These changes are universal and inevitable.

They cannot be avoided or reversed; no one can escape growing old, nor can a middle-aged or elderly person become young again (although some have tried, as we will see in Chapter 3). Thus aging differs from illnesses and diseases, which are evitable, may have external causes, and may be cured or alleviated.

LIFE EXPECTANCY.   **Life expectancy at birth** refers to the number of years that will probably be lived by the average person born in a particular year. In 1970, for example, the life expectancy at birth for women in the United States was 74.9 years. This means that if you are an American woman who was born in 1970, and if the course of your development should prove to be neither more nor less favorable than the average for everyone born in that year, you will live approximately 75 years. You might instead be more fortunate than the average woman born in 1970, and live to be 80 or even 90. Or you might be less fortunate, and be struck down by an accident or illness at an early age. The life expectancy figure is an average: it represents the best guess as to your life span, but it could easily be wrong in any one instance.

Alternatively, we may ascertain an individual's **life expectancy at a specific age.** In 1970, the life expectancy for American women age 65 was 17.1 years. That is, the average American woman who reached age 65 during 1970 could reasonably expect to live to about age 82. The *at birth* life expectancy figure (which was only 51 years) no longer applies to these women, because they have demonstrated a favorable course of development by avoiding fatal illnesses or accidents during infancy, childhood, adolescence, and early adulthood.

MAXIMUM LIFE SPAN.   The extreme upper limit of human life is known as the **maximum life span.** This figure is typically inferred from the greatest authenticated human age on record: a Japanese man, Shigechiyo Izumi, died of pneumonia at age 120 on February 21, 1986 (*Newsweek*, March 3, 1986, p. 71). Some individuals claim to have lived considerably longer, but this has proved to be one of the many myths that pervade the field of adult development and aging.[1] (See, for example, Schulz, 1978.)

Life Expectancy, Past and Present

HISTORICAL TRENDS.   It has been estimated that the average ancient Roman lived for only about 22 years, settlers in the 1620 Mas-

---

[1] Throughout this book, we will highlight common myths and the corresponding empirical evidence in chapter boxes for ready reference.

sachusetts Bay Colony survived for approximately 35 years, and the average resident of the United States born in 1900 lived for some 47 years. By 1983, however, the life expectancy at birth in this country reached a new high of 74.7 years. (See Table 1.1.) The largest gains since 1900 have been demonstrated by females of all ages, infants, children, and young adults. Conversely, life expectancy at birth tends to be somewhat lower for males. (See Table 1.2.) From 1970 to 1983, the life expectancy at birth for blacks increased by slightly more than five years but is still lower than the corresponding figures for whites (United States Senate Special Committee on Aging, 1985; see also Table 1.3).

The data in Tables 1.1 and 1.2 appear to reflect an amazing increase in human longevity. But as we will see throughout this book, appearances are often deceiving. Because of improved medical procedures (e.g., vaccinations that prevent infectious diseases) and better standards of public health (living conditions, nutrition, sanitation), the mortality rates for American infants and children have dropped sharply since 1900. More people are living into their 60s and 70s, so the average life expectancy at birth has increased ac-

TABLE 1.1   Human life expectancy at birth from prehistoric to contemporary times.

Time Period	Average Life Span (in Years)
Prehistoric Times	18
Ancient Greece	20
Ancient Rome	22
Middle Ages, England	33
1620 (Massachusetts Bay Colony)	35
19th Century England, Wales	41
1900, USA	47.3
1915, USA	54.5
1954, USA	69.6
1967, USA	70.2
1971, USA	71.0
1983, USA	74.7

SOURCE: Lerner (1976, p. 140); National Center for Health Statistics (1984).

TABLE 1.2   Life expectancy at birth and at age 65 as a function of sex and calendar year (United States).

Year	Life Expectancy at Birth		Life Expectancy at Age 65	
	Male	Female	Male	Female
1900	46.4	49.0	11.3	12.0
1910	50.1	53.6	12.1	12.1
1920	54.5	56.3	12.3	12.3
1930	58.0	61.3	12.9	12.9
1940	61.4	65.7	11.9	13.4
1950	65.6	71.1	12.8	15.1
1960	66.7	73.2	12.9	15.9
1970	67.1	74.9	13.1	17.1
1980	69.9	77.5	14.0	18.4
Net Gain, 1900–1980	23.5	28.5	2.7	6.4

SOURCE: United States Senate Special Committee on Aging (1985, pp. 20–21).

cordingly. To clarify this point, suppose that we obtain one small sample of people born in 1900 and a second small sample of people born in 1915, and we ascertain the life span of each of these individuals:

Group 1—Born 1900 (1900 Cohort)		Group 2—Born 1915 (1915 Cohort)	
Person	*Years Lived*	*Person*	*Years Lived*
James	2	Robert	50
Mary	58	Jane	47
Ellen	60	Jeffrey	62
Steven	56	Alma	60
Thomas	61	Louise	64
Mean:	47.4	Mean:	56.6

(A sample of only five cases is, of course, far too small for any valid scientific conclusions to be drawn, but will serve for purposes of illustration. Also, for convenience, we have rounded off years lived to whole numbers.) All members of Group 1 were born in 1900; this group is therefore referred to as the 1900 **cohort.** Notice that James succumbed to an illness early in childhood, and lived for

TABLE 1.3 Life expectancy at birth as a function of sex and ethnic group for the United States in 1982.

	Males	*Females*
Whites	71.4	78.7
All Nonwhites	66.5	75.2
Blacks	64.8	73.8

SOURCE: National Center for Health Statistics (1983, p. 4).

only two years. The members of the 1915 cohort had the good fortune to be born at a time when a method for preventing this illness had been discovered, resulting in a decrease in childhood mortality rates. If we look only at the means for each cohort, we might incorrectly conclude that between 1900 and 1915, a way was found to increase everyone's life span by about nine years. In actuality, however, those born in 1915 *who reached old age* did not survive a great deal longer than did members of the 1900 cohort *who reached old age*. Much of the difference between the group means is due to the fact that more people born in 1915 survived the perils of infant and childhood diseases, and reached old age. That is, the life expectancy *at birth* increased substantially.

To be sure, life expectancies at older ages have also increased significantly during the past century. To illustrate, consider the life expectancies at age 65 shown in Table 1.2. In 1900, the average 65-year-old man lived for an additional 11.3 years. A man who reached age 65 in 1980 had a further life expectancy of 14 years, or 2.7 years longer. Although this increase is smaller than the corresponding gain in the life expectancy at birth (23.5 years), it is important; many people would willingly spend a considerable amount of money to add almost three years to their lives. The data for women reflect an even greater increase: life expectancy at age 65 rose by 6.4 years between 1900 and 1980, while the life expectancy at birth gained 28.5 years.

Adults past age 70 are also living longer. The life expectancy at age 85 has increased by 24 percent since 1960, and an additional 44 percent increase is projected by the year 2040 (United States Senate Special Committee on Aging, 1985). On the popular morning television show *Today*, the names of persons who have reached their 100th birthday are often announced. If this were done for everyone in this country, rather than just for those who elect to write in, some 42 names would be announced every morning!

Because more people are living into their seventies and eighties than ever before, today's families are more likely to span three generations. This development has created many new and important issues, such as the nature of grandparenting and the problems of adults who must care for both their own children and an elderly parent.   *Nancy Durrell McKenna/ Photo Researchers*

In sum: much of the apparent increase in human longevity is due to substantially greater life expectancies at birth. That is, many more Americans are reaching old age than ever before. (See Figure 1.1.) There have also been smaller but significant increases in life expectancies at older ages, indicating that those of us who do survive until old age are likely to live a few years longer than did our counterparts of a century ago.

IMPLICATIONS FOR OUR PRESENT SOCIETY.   Currently, the population of the United States is approximately 236.5 million. The distribution by age is shown in Figure 1.2. Two important facts can be gleaned from this figure. The generation of baby boomers, those born in the decade after World War II, will dominate the age distribution in this country well into the next century. And the "old-old," those age 75 or more, represent a relatively small proportion of the over-60 age group and of the population as a whole.

Since 1940, however, the percentage of elderly Americans has increased markedly. This is due only in part to the aforementioned

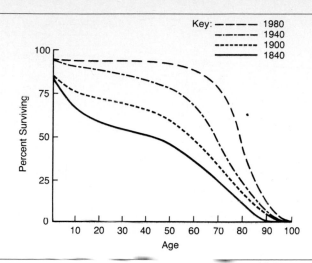

FIGURE 1.1 Percent surviving as a function of age, 1840–1980 (United States). United States Senate Special Committee on Aging (1983, p. 57).

gains in life expectancy. The annual birth rate in this country rose significantly just prior to 1920, and declined dramatically after the mid-1960s. As a result, the proportion of Americans age 65 and older is now larger.

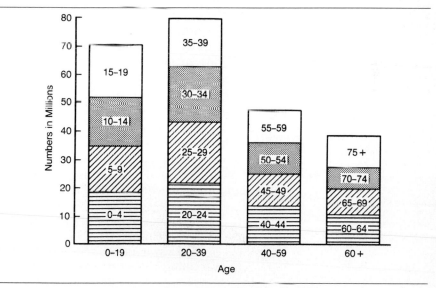

FIGURE 1.2 Distribution of the United States population by age (1984). United States Senate Special Committe on Aging (1985, p. 8).

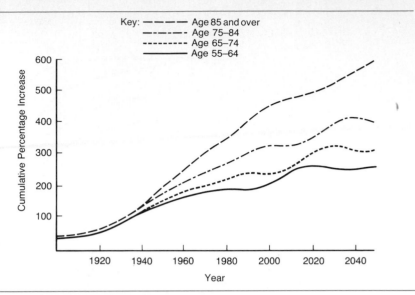

FIGURE 1.3   Percentage increase of older adults by decade (United States.) United States Senate Special Committee on Aging (1985, p. 14).

Barring some highly unexpected development, the number of elderly Americans will continue to increase for the next half century. (See Figure 1.3.) The gains will be greatest among those over 85, who constitute the most rapidly growing segment of the American population (Brody et al., 1983). By the year 2050, it is estimated that the proportion of Americans age 85 and older will jump from about 1 percent to over 5 percent of the total population, and that approximately one of every four Americans over age 65 will be 85 or older.

Dramatic increases are also projected for the over-65 age group as a whole. During the past two decades, mortality rates have declined by 1 to 2 percent per year. If these declines continue, almost two fifths of the American population will be above age 65 by the year 2080, with the number of centenarians approaching 19,000,000 (Vaupel & Gowan, 1986). These demographic changes may portend major social changes as well:

> Will increased life expectancy be accompanied by increased healthy, productive life expectancy? . . . Who would wish to live to age 120 in, as Shakespeare wrote, 'mere oblivion, sans teeth, sans eyes, sans taste, sans everything'? The evidence [pertaining to this issue] is weak . . . In any case . . . it would seem to be prudent to place a very high priority on the development of ways of delaying or alleviating debilitating conditions [in the elderly].

Myths About Aging: Life Expectancy

MYTH

Some human beings have lived to be 130, 140, or even 170 years old.

BEST AVAILABLE EVIDENCE

Empirical evidence has failed to support these claims. A man from the Ukraine who supposedly was 130 years old had falsified his date of birth in order to escape military service during World War I; he actually was only 78 years old (Medvedev, 1974). A convenient fire destroyed the records of an Ecuadorian man who claimed to be 130 years old. Further investigation revealed that he died at age 99. And an American man who allegedly died in 1979 at age 137, and who was at one time noted in the *Guinness Book of World Records* for this reason, was later found to have died at age 104 (Meister, 1984). Apparently, the notoriety that comes with extreme old age offers a strong temptation to exaggerate the truth. The greatest authenticated human ages are 120 years (a Japanese man), 113 years and 273 days (a California woman), and 113 years and 124 days (a Canadian man).

As the proportion of the population over age 65 begins to approach the proportion between ages 20 and 64, delayed retirement will almost certainly be required to save Social Security from bankruptcy. If more of the elderly hang on to their jobs, however, promotional opportunities will diminish for the young, and whatever gain there may be in wisdom and experience in an organization may be offset by a lack of fresh thinking and new blood. In addition, the increase in the proportion of the elderly might result in a further shift of political power, and even greater governmental focus on the needs of the elderly and inattention to the needs of the young. A major challenge to society will be to develop career patterns and societal norms that enable the elderly to contribute while simultaneously giving the young a chance.

When lifespans reach or even exceed a century, the division of life into three successive stages of education, employment, and retirement will undoubtedly have to be rethought. Not only to contribute productively to society but simply to understand society, octogenarians will have to have learned about the advances and changes that have occurred since they finished high school or college. Delaying the age of retirement to age 80 or 85 might permit periodic leaves from work—a year, say, every decade, for ongoing education.

In addition, a reduction in the hours worked per week and an increase in the number of weeks of vacation per year might facilitate part-time education on a more or less continuous basis. The 64,000 hours or so of lifetime work under the emerging system of 35 hours per week . . . from age 22 to 62, could alternatively be arranged so that a person works 28 hours a week, with two months' vacation per year and a year's leave every decade, from age 22 to 82. If [the] median lifespan approaches a century, that would still leave 18 years of retirement. (Vaupel & Gowan, 1986, p. 433.)

Because so many more of us are living longer than ever before, the past few decades have seen a considerable growth of interest in the study of adult development and aging. Researchers, policy makers, educators, and lay persons alike have become increasingly concerned with the scientific study of aging and the special problems of the aged **(gerontology),** and with the medical study of the diseases, debilities, and care of aged persons **(geriatrics).** Among the problems and issues of current importance are:

- Will our physiological, sensory, and cognitive processes sustain us as we grow toward old age? Or should we expect serious deterioration in our physical abilities, vision, audition, memory, and intellectual capacities?

- Are most elderly adults so ill and helpless as to require extensive medical care or institutionalization, or do most remain self-sufficient and independent?

- Should we expect to undergo significant changes in personality during the lengthy course of adulthood? Or is personality most likely to remain relatively stable?

- Are social relationships typically satisfying after middle age? Or are most older adults ignored by their families and peers?

- Because life expectancies are greater for women than for men, the American population includes significantly more older women than older men. This discrepancy is particularly large in the upper age ranges. (See Figure 1.4.) What problems does this cause for older women who become divorced or widowed, and what can be done to improve matters?

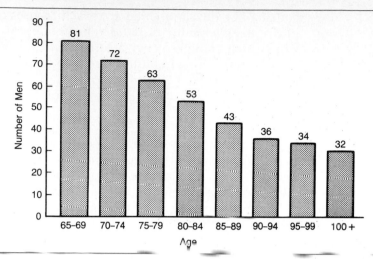

FIGURE 1.4   Number of men per 100 women by age group (1984).
United States Senate Special Committee on Aging (1985, p. 17).

- Should we expect retirement to be a rewarding or a traumatic experience? What, if anything, can be done to make the former outcome more likely?

- Will we have considerably more difficulty dealing with our stressful environment in middle and old age? Or will our greater experience in living make us more adept at coping with such problems?

- Are certain kinds of psychopathology more likely to afflict older adults? If so, what can be done to treat these disorders?

- While some theorists would disagree (Fries, 1983; Fries & Crapo, 1981), the preponderance of data indicate that older adults now live longer after the onset of a terminal illness than ever before (Myers & Manton, 1984a; 1984b; see also Chapter 12). That is, dying is often a lengthy process. How may terminally ill patients and their loved ones be helped to cope with these traumatic months, or even years?

The purpose of this book is to present, discuss, and evaluate the empirical research evidence dealing with such issues.

Summary

Adult development and aging deals with the description, explanation, and modification of changes that occur during the adult life course. The developmental approach focuses on changes within the individual over time (intraindividual changes), and on the extent to which such changes occur at different rates among different individuals (interindividual differences). It is also important to identify major similarities between younger and older adults, so as not to exaggerate the negative effects of aging.

HUMAN AGING AND LIFE EXPECTANCY

Human aging is caused by processes within the individual that significantly decrease the probability of survival. Unlike illnesses and diseases, these changes are universal, inevitable, and irreversible. We all grow old, and none of us can become young again.

Life expectancy at birth has increased dramatically during the past century. In 1900, the average man and woman could expect to live about 46 and 49 years; today, the corresponding figures are approximately 70 and 77.5 years. Much of these gains are due to sharp reductions in the number of premature deaths, such as accidents and illnesses during infancy and childhood. That is, many more Americans are reaching old age than ever before. There have also been smaller but important increases in life expectancies at older ages, indicating that those who do survive until old age are likely to live a few years longer than did their counterparts of a century ago.

The percent of elderly Americans has increased markedly since 1940, a trend that is expected to continue for the next half century. In fact, the most rapidly growing segment of the American population is the "old-old" (age 75 or more). Such demographic changes have focused attention on many important problems and issues, and have caused a considerable growth of interest in the scientific study of adult development and aging.

CHAPTER 2

Research Methods and Issues

Many things that people once "know" to be true have proved to be wholly incorrect. To cite just two famous examples, we are now well aware that the earth is not flat and that it is not at the center of our universe. This enlightenment was made possible by scientific research, which is superior to subjective opinion in one important respect: it relies on hard data that can be verified and reproduced. When research study after study points to a particular conclusion, only an unusually stubborn individual would continue to argue otherwise.

During the past few decades, gerontologists and geriatricians have taken a closer look at some popular beliefs about aging—for example, that the majority of adults age 65 and older are physically and psychologically incapacitated, lonely, and poverty stricken. Researchers in various disciplines, including psychology, sociology, biology, and economics, have investigated such important issues by obtaining appropriate empirical data. Not infrequently, this research has shown that prevailing stereotypes about aging and the elderly have about as much validity as the flat-earth theory.

Although specific research methods vary from one discipline to another, there is a common underlying logic that binds them together. There are also common problems: tracing the course of important variables during adulthood, such as intelligence and personality, has proved to be far from an easy task. In this chapter, therefore, we will discuss some of the ways in which researchers gather and interpret information about adult development and aging. We will also examine some of the major methodological difficulties that pervade research in this area.

We realize that your interest in this subject may be more practical than theoretical, and that you may have no plans ever to design and conduct a research study. Even so, there is good reason to be concerned with methodological issues. The behavioral sciences are relatively young, and can boast of few (if any) flawless research methods. Therefore, the procedures selected by an investigator may to some extent bias the results in a particular direction. *What* we know about adult development and aging is often inextricably linked with *how* this information has been obtained, and we must consider both of these aspects in order to avoid serious misinterpretations.

Basic Principles

Statistical Inference

VARIABLES. Scientific research deals with relationships among **variables,** or characteristics that can take on different values. For example, an economist may be interested in the relationship between aging and level of income: does the financial state of most adults improve, decline, or remain about the same as they grow toward old age? Or a cognitive psychologist may hypothesize that aging is related to significant declines in intelligence, memory, or the ability to learn.

In the preceding examples, age, income, learning, memory, and intelligence are variables; there are at least some people who score at different levels. If, instead, every adult had precisely the same degree of intelligence or ability to remember, these phenomena would *not* be variables. They would be constants, and researchers would find them to be of much less interest—albeit considerably easier to describe, because knowing the score of one individual would tell you everyone else's score as well. Thus variation is the *raison d'être* of the research scientist.

POPULATIONS AND SAMPLES. Researchers in the behavioral sciences must contend with an extremely troublesome problem: they can never measure *all* of the cases in which they are interested. For example, a gerontologist cannot obtain data from all 30-year-olds and all 60-year-olds in the United States; a physiological psychologist cannot study the heart and lungs of all adults in the world; an experimental psychologist cannot observe the maze behavior of all rats. The behavioral scientist wants to know what is happening in a given **population**—a large group of people, animals, objects, or responses that are alike in at least one respect. Yet it would be much too time-consuming and expensive to measure such populations in their entirety. In fact, because the population of interest may well consist of millions of people (e.g., Americans over age 65, females,

males, blacks, whites), even measuring a substantial proportion of cases is out of the question. What to do?

One reasonable procedure is to measure a relatively small number of cases drawn from the population (that is, a **sample**). A sample of, say, 100 people can readily be interviewed, given a written questionnaire, or used as subjects in a laboratory experiment. However, conclusions that apply only to the 100 people who happen to be included in the sample are unlikely to be of much interest. To advance our knowledge to any significant degree, a researcher must be able to draw much more general conclusions, such as: "the friendships and social relationships of 60-year-olds in the United States tend to be no less satisfying than those of 30-year-olds." A finding like this is typically obtained from a research study that included 100 or 200 subjects, yet it is stated in terms of the entire populations from which the samples were drawn—that is, all 60-year-olds and all 30-year-olds in the United States.

How is this possible? There are various mathematical procedures for drawing inferences about what is happening in a population, based on what is observed in a sample from that population (**inferential statistics**). (See Figure 2.1.) We will not discuss such procedures here, because they are dealt with extensively in other texts (e.g., Welkowitz, Ewen, & Cohen, 1982). For our purposes, the important point is that there is *no* way to ensure that a sample is in fact representative of the population from which it came. No matter how carefully a researcher draws a sample, it is still possible that statistics computed from this sample (e.g., means, standard deviations, correlation coefficients) will differ to a substantial extent from the corresponding population values (parameters). The use of appropriate inferential statistics does make correct inferences about the population more likely, but not certain. Therefore, no single study ever proves or disproves a theory or hypothesis; more substantial evidence must be collected before definitive conclusions can be attempted. For this reason, we must expect to meet with some ambiguity and controversy when we review the findings of research on adult development and aging.

Common Research Designs

EXPERIMENTAL DESIGNS. In **experimental designs,** the experimenter directly manipulates one or more variables (**independent variables**) and observes the results on various other variables (**dependent variables**). For example, suppose that a gerontologist wishes to ascertain whether a certain training program will enable middle-aged Americans to learn difficult verbal material more quickly. One

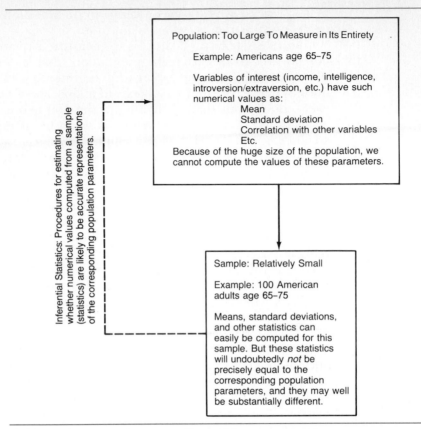

FIGURE 2.1   Populations and samples.

way to test this hypothesis is by obtaining two groups of Americans age 45–60, one of which receives the new training program (the **experimental group**). The second group does *not* undergo training; this **control group** is used as a baseline for evaluating the performance of the experimental group. To control for the effects of irrelevant variables (such as intelligence), the decision as to which subjects receive the training program is made **randomly** (e.g., by flipping a coin), so that each subject has an equal chance of winding up in the experimental group or the control group. Learning may be indexed by testing the ability of subjects to recognize or recall the material after a specified period of time. (See Figure 2.2.)

In this experiment, receiving or not receiving training is the independent variable, and amount learned is the dependent variable. If the experimental group performs significantly better on the tests of recognition and recall than does the control group, this would

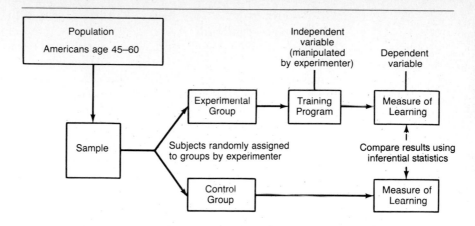

Note: While the control group does *not* receive the training program it would normally be given some unrelated activity that would take about the same amount of time. Otherwise the experimental group might perform better on the measure of learning solely because the experimenters spent more time with that group, causing a significant increase in motivation.

FIGURE 2.2   A simple experimental design.

support the hypothesis that the training program is beneficial. Because subjects were assigned randomly to treatments, it is unlikely that the observed differences between the two groups were due to some other reason—such as a disproportionate number of more intelligent people in the experimental group, or an unusually large number of adults with poor memories in the control group. Thus experimental designs typically permit cause-and-effect statements to be made, such as "this training program caused improved performance on a verbal learning task."

One important advantage of the experimental design is that it puts the researcher in control; he or she can test hypotheses by stipulating precisely what the different experimental conditions will be. But this is also a disadvantage, because the resulting experiment may well be artificial and unrealistic (Harre & Lamb, 1984, p. 154). For example, some subjects in the learning experiment previously described may not be motivated to perform well because they regard the task as irrelevant to their everyday lives. This issue will be discussed further in Chapter 5.

QUASIEXPERIMENTAL DESIGNS.   Although **quasiexperimental designs** also utilize independent and dependent variables, subjects are *not* assigned randomly to treatments. Suppose that a gerontologist wishes to test the hypothesis that repeated exposure to loud noise causes significant hearing losses. In theory, it might be desirable to assign subjects randomly to one of two groups: an experimental group that is subjected to very loud noise, and a control group that does not receive this treatment. If the experimental group suffers significantly greater auditory declines than does the control group, the hypothesis would be supported. In practice, however, we obviously cannot risk inflicting significant auditory damage on subjects in order to obtain information.

One alternative is to use a quasiexperimental design. Exposure to loud noise would remain the independent variable, while amount of hearing loss would be the dependent variable. However, preexisting groups would be used instead of randomization. That is, we might compare the auditory ability of adults from three different backgrounds: relatively noisy American cities, less noisy rural American environments, and even less noisy primitive cultures that have no access to radio or television. If those who live in quieter environments demonstrate significantly less hearing loss than those in noisier environments, this would provide some support for the hypothesis. (See Figure 2.3.)

Quasiexperimental designs have more drawbacks than experimental designs, because the failure to assign subjects randomly to groups makes it harder to rule out alternative explanations. Primitive cultures and large American cities differ in many ways other

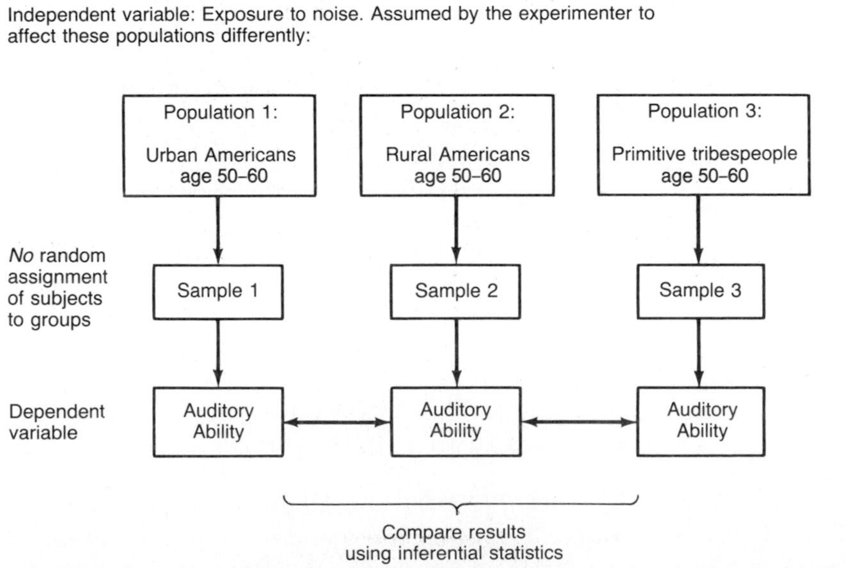

Independent variable: Exposure to noise. Assumed by the experimenter to affect these populations differently:

Population 1:	Population 2:	Population 3:
Urban Americans age 50–60	Rural Americans age 50–60	Primitive tribespeople age 50–60

No random assignment of subjects to groups

Sample 1	Sample 2	Sample 3

Dependent variable

Auditory Ability	Auditory Ability	Auditory Ability

Compare results using inferential statistics

FIGURE 2.3   A quasiexperimental design.

than noise level, and some of these differences could conceivably be responsible for any observed differences in hearing loss. However, quasiexperimental designs do enable researchers to gain useful information in situations where experimental designs are not feasible.

CORRELATIONAL DESIGNS. In **correlational designs,** subjects are not assigned to groups by the experimenter, nor are there specific independent and dependent variables. Instead, two or more variables are measured in order to ascertain the co-relationship between them.

To illustrate, suppose that a gerontologist wishes to determine the relationship between intelligence and age. One possible approach is to obtain a sample of adults of various ages, measure the age and intelligence of each subject, and compute the correlation coefficient between these two variables. (See Figure 2.4.) If the older subjects are much lower in intelligence than are the younger adults, a sub-

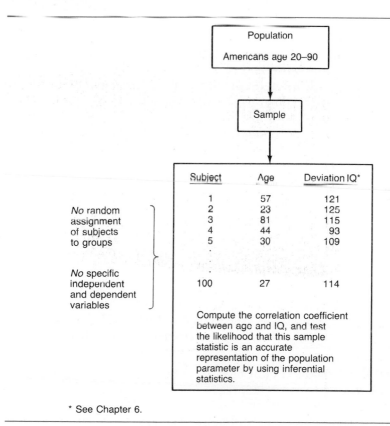

FIGURE 2.4   A correlational design.

stantial negative correlation will be obtained. If the older subjects are considerably higher in intelligence, a large positive correlation will be obtained. And if there is no consistent relationship, with some older subjects demonstrating higher intelligence and some having lower intelligence, the correlation will tend toward zero.

Correlational designs typically do *not* permit cause-and-effect statements to be made. There are three possible reasons for a high correlation between two variables (X and Y): X causes Y, Y causes X, or the co-relationship between X and Y is caused by some third variable. For example, a high positive correlation was once obtained between the number of storks in various European cities and the number of births in each city. That is, cities with more storks had more births, while cities with fewer storks had fewer births. Taken at face value, these data might seem to support the fable that babies are brought by storks. In actuality, this correlation was caused by a third variable: size of city. Storks like to nest in chimneys. Larger cities have more houses and thus more chimneys, providing more nesting places for storks. And larger cities also have more births, because there are more people. Conversely, smaller cities have fewer people, births, houses, chimneys, and storks. Although this example may well be apocryphal, it does illustrate the difficulty of ascertaining cause and effect when the correlational design is used.

Although correlational and experimental designs differ in many important respects, they are by no means wholly unrelated. In fact, it is desirable to convert significant results obtained from experimental designs into correlation coefficients. A discussion of such issues is beyond the scope of this book, however. (See Cohen, 1965; Welkowitz, Ewen, & Cohen, 1982, pp. 206–211.)

AFTERWORD: GERONTOLOGICAL RESEARCH AND THE MEASUREMENT OF CHANGE.   As we observed in Chapter 1, the study of adult development and aging involves the study of change over time. This poses another important methodological problem: How best to study change? Should we obtain a sample of, say, 20-year-olds, and continue to study them for many years? Or might we save considerable time and effort by obtaining samples of adults of various ages, and comparing their performance on various tasks? Issues like these are vital to research on adult development and aging; yet they are by no means easy to resolve, as we will see in the following section.

Developmental Research Methods

Researchers have devised various strategies for studying adult development and aging, each of which has its own distinct advantages and disadvantages.

Chapter Glossary: Research Methods and Issues

Aging effect	Occurs when behavior or personality is influenced in some way by growing older.
Cohort effect	Occurs when behavior or personality is influenced in some way by the generation in which one was born, and by the corresponding social and historical forces.
Confounding	Occurs when two (or more) sources of variation are closely interrelated (e.g., aging and cohort), and the research design cannot reveal which one is causing the observed changes in the dependent variable.
Control group	A group which does *not* receive the treatment whose effects are being investigated by the researcher; used as a baseline against which to evaluate the performance of the experimental group.
Correlational design	Research wherein two (or more) variables are measured in order to ascertain the co-relationship between them, without designating any independent or dependent variables or assigning subjects randomly to groups.
Cross-sectional research	Research wherein all measurements are performed at about the same point in time.
Dependent variable	A variable presumed to change as a result of changes in one or more independent variables.
Experimental design	Research wherein the experimenter directly manipulates one or more independent variables in order to determine the effects on one or more dependent variables, and assigns subjects (usually randomly) to groups.
Experimental group	The group that receives the treatment whose effects are being investigated by the researcher.
External validity	The extent to which research findings can be generalized from the specific sample(s) included in the study to the population(s) of interest.
Independent variable	A variable manipulated by the experimenter in order to ascertain its effects on some other (dependent) variable(s).
Inferential statistics	Mathematical procedures for drawing inferences about what is happening in a population, based on what is observed in a sample from that population.

Internal validity	The extent to which a study enables us to identify the relationships among variables, notably cause-and-effect relationships.
Longitudinal research	Research wherein subjects are observed over a period of time, often years.
Parameter	A numerical quantity which summarizes some characteristic of a population.
Population	*All* of the cases in which a researcher is interested; a (usually very large) group of people, animals, objects, or responses that are alike in at least one respect.
Quasiexperimental design	Research which resembles the experimental design in that independent and dependent variables are clearly specified, but differs in that subjects are *not* assigned randomly to experimental or control groups.
Random assignment of subjects to groups	Assigning subjects to experimental and control groups in such a way that each subject has an equal chance of winding up in either group.
Sample	Any subgroup of cases drawn from a clearly specified population. In a *random sample*, each element in the population has an equal chance of being included in the sample.
Selective attrition	Occurs when subjects who drop out during the course of a longitudinal study are *not* representative of the group as a whole. This results in a sample that is atypical in at least some respects, and may well bias measurements taken during the latter part of the study.
Sequential research	Research strategies designed to eliminate the confounding that occurs in cross-sectional research (between aging effects and cohort effects) and in longitudinal research (between aging effects and time of measurement effects).
Statistic	A numerical quantity that summarizes some characteristic of a sample.
Time of measurement effect	Occurs when behavior or personality is influenced in some way by the time periods in which these characteristics are measured.
Variable	Any characteristic that can take on different values.

Longitudinal Research

DEFINITION.   In a **longitudinal** study, the same subjects are observed over a period of time, often many years. (See Figure 2.5). In 1955, for example, gerontologists at Duke University obtained a sample of 270 subjects whose ages varied from 59 to 94. On eleven different occasions during the next 21 years, the researchers administered measures of physiological functioning, intelligence, personality, reaction time, vision, audition, and attitudes toward retirement and other issues to those who remained in the study (Siegler, 1983).

ADVANTAGES.   The great advantage of longitudinal research is that it provides direct information about intraindividual change. If we wish to test the hypothesis that intelligence, memory, or any other

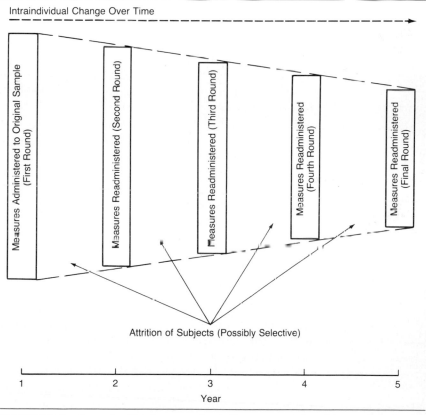

FIGURE 2.5   Longitudinal research: A five-year study with measurements obtained annually.

In a longitudinal study, measurements are obtained from the same subjects over a period of time, often years.   *Courtesy Marilyn McClenahan*

variable declines or increases during adulthood, the most obvious (and theoretically best) procedure is to study a sample of adults for a number of years and trace the course taken by this variable.

To illustrate, suppose that a sample of 100 30-year-olds is given a test of memory and obtains a mean score of 27.0. Thirty years later, all 100 subjects are rounded up and given the same test once more, and their mean score at age 60 is 18.0. If the difference between 27 and 18 is statistically significant (i.e., likely to be an accurate indication of what is happening in the corresponding populations), this finding would support the hypothesis that memory declines with increasing age. Because the same 100 subjects were studied over a period of 30 years, no critic could argue that the results were biased because the researcher inadvertently obtained a group of 60-year-olds with unusually poor memories (or an overly capable group of 30-year-olds).

DISADVANTAGES.   Considerable amounts of money and effort are required to study a sample of people for many years. Unfortunately, the resources of many researchers are so limited that longitudinal studies are simply out of the question.

Even when the longitudinal approach is feasible, the researcher will usually find that some subjects drop out before the study is completed. Some may move to far-away locations; others may die; still others may not be sufficiently motivated to continue participating. In the Duke study previously cited, only 44 of the original 270 subjects remained at the conclusion despite efforts like these:

The issue of sample maintenance is important in any longitudinal study. In the . . . Duke study, tremendous care and attention were given to developing relationships with the study participants so that their cooperation over the length of the study would be maximized. As an inducement to participation, the results of the physical examination were communicated to study participants and to their personal physicians shortly after completion of a given round of the study. . . . Special attention was paid to keeping in contact with subjects by sending birthday and Christmas cards and to continuing to stay in touch by mail, even if the subjects had moved away from the Durham area. (Siegler, 1983, pp. 141–142.)

If those who drop out are significantly different from those who remain, this **selective attrition** may well produce misleading results. That is, instead of being representative of the population from which the sample was drawn, the subjects who complete the study will be atypical in some important respects. This is by no means unlikely. For example, subjects with relatively little education may see less value in scientific research and be more likely to drop out. So too may those who are low in ability, and find the experimental task to be unpleasantly difficult. If so, measurements obtained toward the end of the longitudinal study will be based on a sample that is now unusually high in ability and educational level. If the variable being studied actually does decline with increasing age (e.g., intelligence during late adulthood), and if the sample becomes more and more capable as the study proceeds, these two effects will tend to cancel each other out. Thus the longitudinal study will *underestimate* the amount of intraindividual change over time. That is, the study will show *less* change (and perhaps considerably less) than is actually the case.

If, instead, the experimental task is a particularly easy one, subjects high in ability may become bored and be more likely to drop out. However, this form of selective attrition is not as common. Yet there are other reasons why a longitudinal study may *overestimate* the amount of intraindividual change, at least insofar as psychological variables are concerned. While such medical data as electrocardiograms and blood counts can be obtained rather accurately from the same subject at different times, measuring psychological change is a difficult and challenging task. What seems to be true change over time might actually represent nothing more than measurement error: psychological research instruments are far from perfect, and we cannot expect subjects to obtain precisely the same scores on two different occasions even if they have not changed at all. (See, for example, Fiske, 1974; Shanan & Jacobowitz, 1982.) Or one measurement period might bias the next one in the opposite direction

(underestimating intraindividual change) because the subjects remember their previous answers and repeat them.

Some critics argue that even when the longitudinal method does
detect significant intraindividual changes, it cannot guarantee that
these changes are due to aging. Suppose that the political attitudes
of a sample of 20-year-olds are measured in 1955 and again when
they reach middle age in 1985, and that the latter measurement
reveals a pronounced increase in liberalism. Taken at face value,
these data might seem to indicate that young adults will become
more liberal as they grow toward middle age. However, a more likely
explanation is that the results were due primarily to cultural influences. There were many changes in American society between 1955
and 1985, such as the increasing emphasis on the rights of women
and various minorities. Thus it may well be these trends, rather than
aging, that caused the increase in liberalism. If so, and if there are
no similar societal changes during the next 30 years, then we should
not expect today's young adults to become markedly more liberal by
the time they reach middle age. One way to deal with this problem
would have been by measuring the political attitudes of a sample of
young adults in 1985. If this group had proved to be about as liberal as the middle-aged group in the longitudinal study, this would
suggest that the results were indeed due to cultural influences rather
than to aging.

Other critics contend that if a longitudinal study continues for
many years, its procedures may become outmoded. Gerontologists
are not solely concerned with questions about aging; they also try to
improve their research methods. Thus a researcher who begins a
20-year study in 1975 may find that substantially improved designs
or instruments are available in 1985. There is no way for this researcher to go back in time, change the research design, and replace
the data obtained between 1975 and 1985. Yet by current standards, the data obtained with the old and inferior methods may be
too flawed to be useful. Although this criticism may be valid in some
instances, new and widely approved developmental research methods are usually not devised quickly enough (or often enough) to
vitiate most longitudinal studies.

However, it cannot be denied that longitudinal studies require
considerable patience. It can be quite frustrating to have to wait 10
or 20 years before the results can be published, nor does it do a
researcher's career much good to have a lengthy period without any
new publications. There may also be a fair amount of personnel
turnover during the life of a longitudinal study, and this may introduce another source of bias. Newer staff members may administer
or score subjective measures (e.g., the Rorschach) somewhat differ-

ently than did the original researchers, thereby producing score changes that have nothing to do with true intraindividual changes.

AFTERWORD.   In theory, longitudinal research is the most desirable way to study adult development and aging. This method enables the researcher to observe intraindividual change directly, and intraindividual change is what adult development is all about. (See, for example, Schaie, 1983). Research practice is another story, however. Of the disadvantages discussed previously, the most troublesome is the question of time and effort. A longitudinal study is a major undertaking, one that exceeds the resources of many researchers.

Are there any feasible alternatives? Some theorists contend that not all questions about adult development and aging require the longitudinal approach, or are important enough to justify it. According to this argument, valuable information can be obtained in some instances by using a more convenient research design—the cross-sectional study.

Cross-sectional Research

DEFINITION.   In a **cross-sectional** study, all measurements are performed at about the same point in time. (See Figure 2.6.) For example, a researcher may draw one sample of 20-year-olds and another sample of 60-year-olds and compare then on one or more variables, using any of the research designs discussed previously in this chapter (experimental, quasiexperimental, correlational).

ADVANTAGES.   Cross-sectional studies are much easier and less costly to carry out than are longitudinal studies. The process of gathering and analyzing the data typically takes a few months at most; years of observation are not required. There is no long wait for results to analyze and publish, nor is it likely that the research procedures will become outmoded during the course of the study.

It has been argued that cross-sectional research is appropriate when our objectives are limited to description. If we wish only to describe how today's 60-year-olds and 20-year-olds differ on certain variables, it is not unreasonable to draw a sample from each population and compare the resulting statistics.

DISADVANTAGES. Although the cross-sectional approach has achieved widespread popularity, it suffers from major methodological weaknesses. This method is not well suited for *explaining* age-

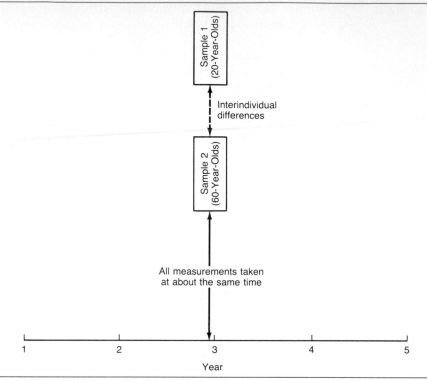

FIGURE 2.6   Cross-sectional research: A comparison of 20-year-olds and 60-year-olds.

related differences, primarily because it confounds the effects of aging and culture.

To illustrate, suppose that a researcher in the year 1980 who is interested in the area of personality draws one sample of 20-year-old United States citizens, and one sample of 60-year-old United States citizens. The researcher administers appropriate measures of personality to each group, and finds some statistically significant differences between the two samples. These results may have nothing at all to do with aging! The environmental and social influences during the 1920s and 1930s (when the 60-year-olds were children and adolescents) differed markedly from those in the 1960s and 1970s (when the 20-year-olds were children and adolescents). For example, each group experienced different educational practices and expectations; a college education was much less common 50 years ago. Each group encountered different levels of technology; television and jet planes did not exist 50 years ago. Social standards differed considerably, with the attitudes of the majority being considerably more conservative 50 years ago. And each group experienced different national and world events, such as the Depression and Prohibition versus the Vietnam War. Consequently, the personality differences discovered by this researcher might *not* be caused by growing from age 20 to age 60. They could easily result from the different influences on a child in the 1920s as opposed to a child in

The behavior and attitudes of teenagers are significantly influenced by the generation in which they grow up. Thus the group at the top, shown at their high school prom dinner in the 1950s, may have learned to be more conservative politically than are today's high school students, and they may retain these beliefs now that they have reached middle age. It can be difficult to distinguish such cohort effects from changes that are truly due to aging. *Elliott Erwin/Magnum; Ellis Herwig/Picture Cube*

the 1960s **(cohort effects).** That is, two different possibilities have been confounded in this study:

1. Personality may change as a result of growing from age 20 to age 60.

2. The personality of adults born in 1920 (the 1920 cohort) may differ from the personality of adults born in 1960 (the 1960 cohort) because they experienced different social and historical influences during childhood and adolescence.

More specifically, suppose the researcher finds that the 60-year-olds have more conservative attitudes about politics and sex than do the 20-year-olds. This does *not* necessarily mean that people typically become more conservative about these matters as they grow older. Because the 1920s were more conservative than the 1960s, it is much more likely that the 60-year-olds were also quite conservative as young adults, and stayed much the same thereafter.

Thus a result that appears to be due to aging in a cross-sectional study may be due instead to cohort effects. That is, we cannot determine whether any observed interindividual differences are due to intraindividual changes or to some wholly different reason. Because one primary goal of the developmental researcher is to study and explain intraindividual change, this is a serious disadvantage.

AFTERWORD.   Because cross-sectional studies are relatively easy to carry out, we will find numerous examples in the chapters that follow. But because such research confounds aging effects and cohort effects, the results must be interpreted with extreme caution. Admittedly, longitudinal studies are not exempt from cultural influences. But longitudinal research at least allows us to observe whether or not intraindividual change has occurred, whereas cross-sectional research does not. We must therefore conclude that in areas where appropriate longitudinal studies have been conducted, such research is more likely to provide us with accurate information about adult development and aging.

Sequential Research

RATIONALE.   As we have seen in the preceding pages, the scientific study of variables is seriously hindered when two or more sources of variation are confounded. The confounding of aging effects and cohort effects in cross-sectional research makes it extremely difficult to explain any differences that are obtained, however valuable the results may be for descriptive purposes.

There is a third source of confounded variation that we have not yet discussed: **time of measurement.** According to one famous (and possibly apocryphal) story, a social psychologist once hypothesized that the attitudes of young American adults toward foreigners become more tolerant with increasing age. This researcher obtained a sample of 20-year-old United States citizens, measured their attitudes toward citizens of various other countries, and repeated these measurements annually during the following ten years. In the last round of the study, a surprising development occurred: the subjects' attitudes toward the Japanese *declined* sharply. Before concluding that this change was due to aging, and that young adults in general become markedly more anti-Japanese on reaching age 30, we should note that this study began in the summer of 1933. The final measurements were obtained a few months after December 7, 1941, when the Japanese attacked Pearl Harbor; and it was this event, rather than aging, that produced the dramatic change in attitudes. Had the study ended just one year earlier, no such change would have occurred.

Thus there are three important sources of variation in studies of adult development and aging: aging, cohort, and time of measurement. To determine whether or not aging causes certain changes, researchers must somehow control for the effects of cohort and time of measurement. This is far from an easy task, however. Whereas cross-sectional studies confound aging effects and cohort effects, longitudinal studies confound aging effects and time of measurement effects. That is, because longitudinal research requires that subjects be measured at different times, any significant changes could be due either to aging or to the times at which the measurements were obtained. Even cross-sectional studies may be influenced to some extent by time of measurement effects, because the different samples may well be observed on different days.

In an attempt to resolve these problems, some theorists have created research designs that combine the cross-sectional and longitudinal methods. This approach, which strives to retain the advantages of each method while minimizing the disadvantages, is known as the **sequential research** strategy. (See, for example, Schaie, 1965; 1973; 1977; Schaie & Baltes, 1975). We hinted at just such a possibility in a previous example: when we studied the political attitudes of a sample of young adults as they grew to middle age between 1955 and 1985, obtaining a second sample of 20-year-olds in 1985 helped us to determine whether the observed increase in liberalism was due to aging or to cultural influences.

TYPES OF SEQUENTIAL RESEARCH.　There are three major sequential research designs. In any one type, two of the possible sources of variation (aging, cohort, time of measurement) are treated as independent variables, while the third source remains uncontrolled. Although it would be preferable to treat all three sources of variation as independent variables, this is impossible because they are *not* independent of one another: once the values of two of these sources are specified, the value of the remaining source is automatically determined.

To illustrate, suppose that we wish to study adults age 50 who are members of the 1910 cohort. The only possible way to do this would be to obtain the measurements in 1960. If we collect our measures at any other time, we will have subjects who are either the wrong age or members of the wrong cohort. In 1985, for example, the members of the 1910 cohort were 75 (not 50), while 50-year-olds were members of the 1935 cohort (not 1910).

The researchers must therefore decide which source of variation is least likely to bias the results of the study in question, and choose the sequential design which treats this source as the uncontrolled variable. If, say, time of measurement is regarded as the least likely source of bias, the researcher would select the sequential design which leaves this source uncontrolled and treats aging and cohort as independent variables. (The dependent variable is the one whose relationship to aging the researcher is trying to ascertain, such as attitudes, intelligence, or memory.) Thus the three types of sequential research are:

1. Treat age and cohort as independent variables; assume that time of measurement has no effect (*cohort-sequential strategy*).

2. Treat age and time of measurement as independent variables; assume that cohort has no effect (*time-sequential strategy*).

3. Treat cohort and time of measurement as independent variables; assume that aging has no effect (*cross-sequential strategy*).

An example of a *cohort-sequential* study is shown in Figure 2.7. The researcher has chosen to study the 1920 and 1930 cohorts, and to compare adults who are 40 and 50 years old. Thus age and cohort are the independent variables, because they are manipulated by the experimenter. Having made these decisions, there is no choice as to the time at which the measurements are taken. To study the 1920 cohort at age 40 and 50, the measurements must be made in 1960 and 1970; to study the 1930 cohort at age 40 and 50, the measurements must be made in 1970 and 1980. In this design, therefore, time of measurement is the uncontrolled variable.

A comparison of groups B and C alone (or groups D and E alone) would be a longitudinal study, because the same subjects are ob-

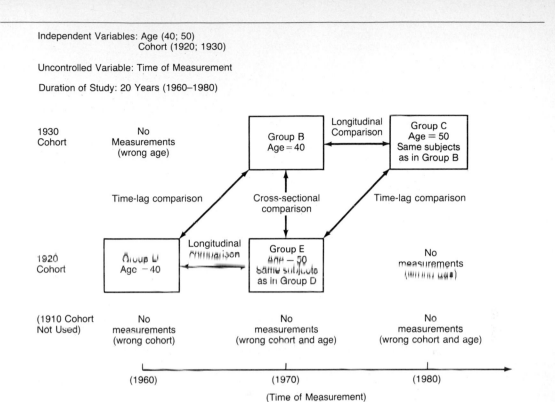

Independent Variables: Age (40; 50)
                       Cohort (1920; 1930)

Uncontrolled Variable: Time of Measurement

Duration of Study: 20 Years (1960–1980)

FIGURE 2.7   A cohort-sequential study.

served over time. Here, aging effects and time of measurement effects are confounded. A comparison of groups B and E alone would be a cross-sectional study (aging effects and cohort effects are confounded), because two different samples are compared at about the same point in time. And a comparison of groups B and D alone (or groups C and E alone) would involve the confounding of cohort effects and time of measurement effects, because different cohorts of the same age are measured at different times. (This is referred to as a time-lag comparison.) The cohort-sequential strategy strives for broader conclusions by including all of these groups in the statistical analysis. *If* it is correct to assume that time of measurement is not important, then this design makes it possible to compare the relative magnitude of aging effects and cohort effects.

  An example of a *cross-sequential* study is shown in Figure 2.8. The 1920 and 1930 cohorts have been selected for inclusion by the researcher, while the times of measurement have been designated as 1960 and 1970. Thus cohort and time of measurement are the in-

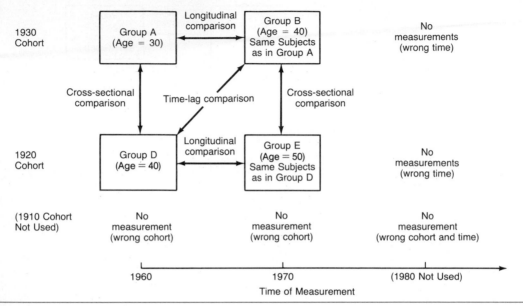

Independent Variables: Cohort (1920; 1930)
                              Time of Measurement (1960; 1970)

Uncontrolled Variable: Age

Duration of Study: 10 Years (1960–1970)

FIGURE 2.8   A cross-sequential study.

dependent variables. Having made these decisions, there is no choice as to the ages of the subjects in this study. When the 1920 cohort is measured in 1960, the members must be 40 years old; the 1930 cohort will be 30 years old in 1960; and so on. In this design, therefore, age is the uncontrolled variable.

Here, a comparison of groups A and D alone (or groups B and E alone) would be a cross-sectional study; a comparison of groups A and B alone (or groups D and E alone) would be a longitudinal study; and a comparison of groups B and D alone would be a time-lag study. In contrast, the cross-sequential strategy includes all of these groups in the statistical analysis. *If* it is correct to assume that aging effects are unimportant, then this design makes it possible to compare the relative magnitude of cohort effects and time of measurement effects.

The third type of sequential design, the *time-sequential* strategy, can be represented in a similar fashion. (See Figure 2.9.) Because the preceding discussion should serve as a sufficient introduction to

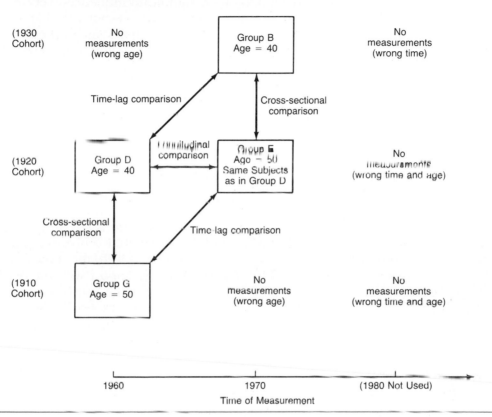

Independent Variables: Age (40; 50)
Time of Measurement (1960; 1970)

Uncontrolled Variable: Cohort

Duration of Study: 10 Years (1960–1970)

FIGURE 2.9   A time-sequential study.

sequential research, we will leave the details to the interested reader as an exercise.

EVALUATION.   Sequential research designs were devised because of dissatisfaction with the longitudinal and cross-sectional methods. When the underlying assumptions are justified, these strategies provide important information that cannot be obtained from the traditional methods. However, sequential designs also have serious drawbacks.

First of all, sequential designs cannot control for selective attrition. Such attrition is just as likely to occur in sequential research as in longitudinal research, and it is just as likely to create the kinds of problems discussed previously in this chapter.

Secondly, the assumptions that underly sequential research may well be questionable in many instances. Aging, cohort, and time of measurement are all potentially significant influences, yet we are required to assume that one of these sources is not a problem in each sequential design. This is particularly troublesome in the case of the cross-sequential strategy, where we must assume that aging itself is unimportant! Nor are matters much better with the time-sequential strategy, which assumes that cohort has little effect on the data. This may be a viable assumption in some instances; for example, declines in visual acuity are more likely to be caused by age-related physiological changes than by cultural influences. But it is highly questionable in many other cases, as we have seen throughout this chapter. Perhaps the assumption of the cohort-sequential strategy is most plausible, namely that time of measurement is relatively unimportant. Yet this source of bias can also be significant.

Finally, sequential designs can be extremely time consuming. The cohort-sequential study illustrated in Figure 2.7 requires some 20 years to complete (from 1960 to 1980). If we broaden the scope somewhat and include the 1940 cohort as well, the duration of the study increases to 30 years, because this cohort will not reach age 50 until 1990. Obviously, sequential research can be just as major an undertaking as longitudinal research—especially because one suggested solution to the problem of questionable assumptions is to carry out all three sequential strategies at once! As one critic has observed:

> Collectively, sequential designs appear to offer ingenious solutions to methodological problems in research on aging . . . However, completing an experimental aging study that adheres fully to the requirements of any one of these designs is not easy to accomplish. It requires the wisdom of a Solomon, the longevity of a Methuselah, the patience of a Job, and the backing of a Rockefeller. Moreover . . . the solutions arrived at through the use of a sequential design my be more illusory than real. (Kausler, 1982, p. 134.)

AFTERWORD. Sequential research is designed to separate sources of variation that are confounded in longitudinal and cross-sectional research. In theory, this approach should enable us to determine the extent to which any significant changes in the dependent variable are caused by aging effects, cohort effects, and/or time of measurement effects. As investigators become more familiar with these methods, and as further improvements are made, the quantity of sequential research may well increase. For the present, however, the aforementioned methodological problems and the considerable time and effort required by sequential designs have limited their use in developmental research.

The empirical evidence discussed in the following chapters will therefore be based primarily on cross-sectional and longitudinal research, with emphasis on the former. To interpret the results of this research correctly, you must ask yourself the following question: Could the findings be biased by confounded sources of variation? That is, in a cross-sectional study, are results attributed to aging more likely to be caused by cohort effects? In a longitudinal study, might results attributed to aging be biased by the times at which the measurements were taken? Until researchers develop more effective methods for answering such questions, common sense as well as statistical analyses must be used to interpret research results in adult development and aging.

Other Methodological Issues

Much more could be said about the methodological problems that confront developmental researchers. We will conclude our discussion by examining some of the factors that threaten the internal and external validity of a research study, and by taking a closer look at the meaning of chronological age.

Internal and External Validity

THREATS TO INTERNAL VALIDITY. In the preceding pages, we have seen that scientific research deals with the relationships among variables. These relationships may involve cause and effect, as when a gerontologist wishes to ascertain whether aging causes declines in intelligence or memory, or they may be correlational. The extent to which a research study correctly identifies such relationships is referred to as **internal validity.**

Among the most serious threats to the internal validity of a research study are confounding, selective attrition, and the effects of practice. If, say, aging effects and cohort effects are confounded, we cannot tell whether any observed changes in the dependent variable are caused by aging or by cultural influences. If the subjects who drop out during the course of a longitudinal study tend to be low in ability, leaving us with an unusually capable group during the later rounds of measurements, we may erroneously conclude that aging does not cause declines in the dependent variable. Or the earlier testings in a longitudinal study might bias subsequent ones: age-related declines in the dependent variable might be concealed because subjects benefit from the practice provided by the previous sessions, or because the procedures have become more familiar and less anxiety provoking. In each of these cases, the study is low in internal validity; it will *not* correctly identify cause-and-effect relationships among the variables of interest.

Various procedural factors may threaten the internal validity of a research study. Mechanical instruments may wear out over time, making it more (or less) difficult to obtain high scores during the latter part of a longitudinal study. Thus the researcher may attribute declining scores to aging when these changes are actually caused by switches that are harder to operate. Alternatively, there may be a significant amount of personnel turnover during the study. Score changes that seem to be age-related may occur because new, inexperienced staff members administer and evaluate the measures differently.

Comparing behaviors at different ages can also be a source of problems. Suppose that we accept "aggressiveness" as an important aspect of human behavior, and we wish to determine if this variable changes in any significant way during adulthood. We might find that a young adult is more likely to abuse someone physically, or to deliver a stinging insult. An older adult may, instead, prefer to spread unflattering rumors, or to engage in devious and subtle plots against another person. Should all of these behaviors be regarded as various forms of aggressiveness, or as something quite different? This is by no means an easy question to answer, but unless we can do so, we may well reach incorrect conclusions about the relationship between aging and aggressiveness.

THREATS TO EXTERNAL VALIDITY.   Earlier in this chapter, we observed that research scientists usually cannot study all of the cases in which they are interested. Instead, they must deal with relatively small samples from the specified population(s). **External validity** involves the extent to which the research findings can be generalized from the specific samples included in the study to the large populations in which the researcher is interested.

One particularly important threat to the external validity of a research study is the way in which the sample is obtained. To illustrate, let us suppose once again that we wish to measure the political attitudes of young adults as they grow to middle age. Because our goal is to draw conclusions about all young adults, it would be a poor idea to limit our sample to students at a particular university. College students differ in numerous respects from young adults in general, such as rating higher in intelligence and socioeconomic status. And students at any one university may well differ from those at other institutions, because they may have been subjected to higher or lower enrollment standards. Therefore, it is unlikely that the results obtained from this sample will apply to the population of young adults in general. We should, instead, draw a sample that includes young adults from all walks of life, including those who have never attended college. (It is perfectly legitimate to define the population of interest as all college students at a given university. In this case, we would be justified in obtaining a sample of only these students. But the results of such a study could safely be generalized *only* to the specified population, namely the young adults at this one university.)

Ideally, a researcher should obtain a **random sample** from the specified population. That is, each element of the population should have an equal chance of being included in the sample. This can be difficult to achieve in practice, however, and it is often necessary to settle for approximations of random samples.

Other significant threats to external validity involve the setting and measures used in the study. If the subjects must engage in laboratory tasks that seem artificial and unrelated to their everyday lives, their performance may suffer from a lack of motivation. Therefore, it may be incorrect to generalize the results of such studies to real-life situations, even if the sample was (more or less) randomly drawn from the specified population. For example, the ability to remember lists of unrelated words in the experimental laboratory may not be an accurate index of older adults' ability to remember what they read in the morning newspaper. (See Chapter 5.)

AFTERWORD.   The factors listed previously are not the only threats to the internal and external validity of a research study, but they are among the most important. A further discussion of such issues is beyond the scope of this book, and the interested reader is referred to Cook and Campbell (1979), Nesselroade and Labouvie (1985), and Schaie (1983).

The Meaning of Chronological Age

CHRONOLOGICAL AGE AND PHYSICAL, PSYCHOLOGICAL, AND SOCIAL MATURITY.   Even the apparently simple variable of chronological age has been a source of controversy. Some adults of a particular chronological age may devote considerable effort to remaining physically fit, with the result that they have the physiology of a much younger person. Conversely, a serious illness or unfavorable hereditary influences may cause a relatively young adult to look and feel much older. Nor does a person's level of psychological or social maturity necessarily correspond to his or her chronological age: some adults in their 40s and 50s are childishly dependent on their parents, while some young adults have the psychological maturity of a much older person.

In common with most gerontologists, we will refer to the approximate midpoint of the human life span as *middle age,* and to the latter portion as *old age.* We will also refer to adults who have reached old age as *elderly* or *the aged.* But because chronological age can differ considerably from physiological, psychological, and social age, terms like these are rough approximations at best. As is the case with any chronological age group, the elderly differ from one another in many important respects. Nor is there any sharp and universally recognized dividing line between old age and middle age, or between late middle age and early middle age, or between middle age and young adulthood. Such terms refer only to what is true on the average; the limitations of chronological age as a measure of adulthood make numerous exceptions inevitable.

The remaining chapters in this book are therefore organized by topic, rather than by periods related to chronological age. Also, many of the findings reviewed herein will be discussed in terms of general trends (e.g., how intelligence changes with increasing age).

CHRONOLOGICAL AGE AND CAUSATION.   It is also important to recognize that age itself actually does not "cause" anything. Time has no physical existence; it cannot impinge on our senses or alter our physiology. When we say that aging causes a decline in the efficiency of the cardiovascular system, we mean that this decline is caused by some factors yet to be determined that change with increasing age. That is, we are using age as a sort of proxy explanation until more specific information can be obtained. When researchers obtain the relevant data, we can make more definitive and useful statements, such as: older people have accumulated more damage due to smoking and cholesterol intake; smoking and high levels of cholesterol increase the probability of heart disease; thus quitting smoking and consuming less cholesterol will help to preserve cardiovascular health. In the meantime, it is useful to know that certain changes are age related, and that important aspects of human life differ significantly for young, middle-aged, and elderly adults.

AFTERWORD.   Because of the methodological difficulties discussed in this chapter, firm conclusions will not be available in some areas of interest. Nevertheless, important research has been and is currently being carried out. Quite a few common beliefs and stereotypes about adulthood have been shattered by appropriate empirical data, and significant discoveries have been made that are well worth your attention.

The social sciences are not exact sciences, and adult development and aging is no exception. If you are looking for a precise road map that will tell you exactly what to expect as you or your loved ones grow through adulthood, you are undoubtedly going to be disappointed. If instead you appreciate how difficult it is to understand and predict the behavior of those complicated organisms known as human beings, and if you are willing to be tolerant of the inevitable ambiguities and uncertainties that pervade this field, you will probably find the study of adult development and aging to be a rewarding one. Most of us will spend many years as an adult. The findings reviewed in this book represent the best scientific evidence as to what those years will be like.

Summary

Because scientific research relies on hard data that can be verified and reproduced, it has shattered many incorrect beliefs and stereotypes. However, even the best developmental research methods have significant weaknesses. What we know about adult development and aging is often inextricably linked with how this information has been obtained, and we must consider both of these aspects in order to avoid serious misinterpretations.

BASIC PRINCIPLES

Scientific research deals with the relationships among variables, or characteristics that can take on different values. Social scientists can never measure all of the cases in which they are interested; these populations are much too large. The researcher must instead deal with relatively small samples, and use appropriate statistical procedures to draw conclusions about what is happening in the corresponding populations.

Researchers in adult development and aging use three types of designs to study the relationships among variables. Experimental designs focus on cause-and-effect relationships: the researcher manipulates one or more independent variables and observes the effects on various dependent variables, while assigning subjects randomly to experimental or control groups. Quasiexperimental designs enable the researcher to study independent and dependent variables when subjects cannot be randomly assigned to groups, but make it more difficult to decide among possible causes. In correlational designs, two or more variables are measured in order to ascertain the co-relationship between them. There are no specific independent or dependent variables, subjects are not assigned randomly to groups by the experimenter, and cause-and-effect relationships are difficult to identify.

DEVELOPMENTAL RESEARCH METHODS

In a longitudinal study, the same subjects are observed over a period of time, often many years. In theory, longitudinal research is the most desirable way to study adult development and aging; it enables the researcher to observe intraindividual change directly. But this method requires considerable amounts of money and effort, and the results may be biased by such factors as selective attrition or practice effects. Thus many researchers have opted instead for cross-sectional studies that are much easier to carry out because subjects are observed at about the same point in time. However, the cross-sectional method suffers from a serious flaw: it confounds aging effects and cohort effects.

When sources of variation in a research study are confounded, the investigator cannot tell which one is responsible for changes in the dependent variable. In cross-sectional research, where aging effects and cohort effects are confounded, any observed changes in the dependent variable might be caused by either aging or the different social and historical influences experienced by each cohort. In longitudinal research, aging effects are confounded with time of measurement effects: any observed changes in the dependent variable might be caused by either aging, or extraneous events that occur during the study and affect all cohorts living through that period of history.

Sequential research strategies are designed to separate sources of variation that are confounded in longitudinal and cross-sectional research. However, these strategies also have serious drawbacks. They are vulnerable to selective attrition; the underlying assumptions may well be questionable in many instances; and they require considerable amounts of time, money, and effort.

OTHER METHODOLOGICAL ISSUES

Internal validity involves the extent to which a research study correctly identifies relationships among the variables of interest. Threats to the internal validity of a study include confounding, selective attrition, practice effects, and deficiencies in the apparatus or the ways in which instruments are administered and scored. External validity involves the extent to which the research findings can be generalized from the specific samples included in the study to the large populations in which the researcher is interested. Threats to the external validity of a study include poorly drawn samples, and settings and measures that are too artificial for the results to be generalized to real-life situations.

Chronological age is not necessarily related to an individual's physical, psychological, or social maturity. Terms like *middle age* and *old age* are, therefore, rough approximations at best, while age groups such as the elderly differ from one another in many important respects. Nor does age itself actually cause anything; time has no physical existence and cannot affect us directly. When we say that aging causes a particular change, we mean that this change is caused by some factors yet to be determined, and those factors change with increasing age. That is, age serves as a proxy explanation until more specific information can be obtained.

Because of the methodological difficulties discussed in this chapter, firm conclusions will not be available in some areas of interest. Nevertheless, important research has been and is currently being carried out. Most of us will spend many years as an adult. The findings reviewed in this book represent the best scientific evidence as to what those years will be like.

PART II

Physiological and Cognitive Development

CHAPTER 3

Physiological Aspects of Aging

Most of our physiological functions reach their maximum capacity prior to early adulthood, and then begin to wane. However, we tend not to notice the declines that occur during our twenties, thirties, and forties. These changes are very gradual, and they are likely to be compensated for by our increased experience and knowledge. Thus we may be more competent behind the wheel of an automobile at age 35 than at age 20 because we have learned to anticipate potential danger and to drive defensively, despite slight decrements in manual dexterity and perceptual response speed. Eventually, however, the physiological effects of aging become more pronounced. Are such declines likely to hinder us substantially later in life? Or do most adults find that their bodily processes sustain them fairly well as they grow toward old age?

In this chapter, we will begin to examine the empirical evidence dealing with this issue. First we will investigate the kinds of physiological changes that occur as we grow from young to old adulthood, or *how* we age. (Since this topic is too extensive to be treated in a single chapter, a discussion of sensation and perception, sexuality, and stress will be deferred until later in this book.) These changes do not occur according to a strict timetable. Some individuals may become prematurely gray haired during their late twenties or early thirties, while some may retain a youthful physique well past middle age. Adults age at different rates, and such groupings as "the middle-aged" and "the elderly" are actually rather heterogeneous with regard to their physical capacities, amount of energy, and degree of mobility and independence. (Recall our previous discussion of the limitations of chronological age as an index of adulthood.) We will therefore discuss general age-related trends, with the understanding that any specific adult may well differ significantly from this average picture.

51

A second important issue concerns *why* we age. Scientists have proposed various explanations for the unfailing tendency of human beings to grow older, and we will review the evidence regarding these theories of aging.

Although we characterized aging in Chapter 1 as universal and inevitable, not all adults are willing to "go gentle into that good night." Some prefer to rage against the dying of the light by seeking ways to ward off the specter of death, and to inhibit or even to reverse the physiological declines associated with aging. We will therefore conclude this chapter by reviewing such quests for the fountain of youth, which are as old as humanity itself. Included in our discussion will be a method for estimating, *very approximately,* your own probable life span.

Age-Related Physiological Changes

Prior to 1950, the only available data concerning aging and physiology were derived from cross-sectional comparisons between healthy young college students and ill, institutionalized elderly patients (Weg, 1983). Since these comparisons failed to control for health, they grossly exaggerated the negative effects of aging. More recent longitudinal studies have provided more accurate data about normal physiological changes during adulthood—i.e., those changes *not* associated with illness and injury. These researchers have found that our bodies possess an enormous reserve capacity: we can survive the loss of one lung, one kidney, more than half of the liver, and large amounts of the stomach and intestines, provided that we are not subjected to severe emotional or physiological stressors.

Because of this redundancy, many of our bodily processes decline very gradually even after middle age. To be sure, growing old does have disadvantages. But we can afford much of what we lose, and the age-related physiological declines that occur among healthy adults are not nearly as severe as is commonly believed.

Observable Characteristics

The process of aging leaves clearly visible traces. Although individual differences prevail, elderly adults do tend to look significantly different from the middle-aged, who typically appear different from young adults.

SKIN AND FACE.   The first facial indication of adult aging is the appearance of lines in the forehead, which usually occurs by age 30. Between ages 30 and 50, additional lines become evident elsewhere in the face. These include "crow's feet," caused by squinting; lines

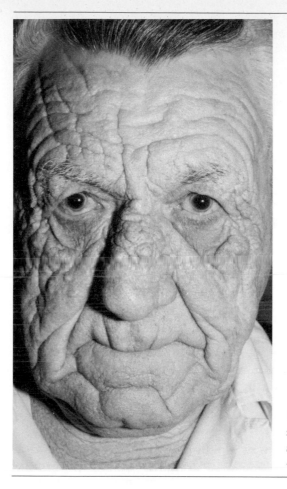

FIGURE 3.1 Typical effects of aging on the skin: Wrinkling, sagging, leathery appearance in sun exposed areas. Parker (1984, p. 494).

that link the nostrils to the sides of the mouth, which result from smiling; and furrowed brows, caused by frowning. Thus, during the first half of adulthood, repeated facial expressions produce some of the lines and wrinkles associated with aging. This implies that adults who frown less often, and those who avoid squinting by obtaining needed corrective lenses, will enjoy a smoother countenance.

After age 50, however, more extensive facial wrinkling is likely to occur. There is a significant decrease in collagen, the fiber that imbues the skin with resilience, and in the amount of water on the inside of the skin. This makes the skin stiffer and less elastic, resulting in more pronounced facial lines. These changes are hastened by frequent exposure to strong sunlight. The skin also becomes thinner and more spread out, somewhat like a piece of dough that has been stretched too far. This is evidenced in such ways as bags under the eyes and sagging skin on the cheeks. (See Figure 3.1.) Because of these changes, and an increase in capillary fragility, the skin of older adults is more vulnerable to bruising. By age 70, the skin has become rougher and has lost its uniformity of color, with a variety of shades clearly evident.

Our facial features also undergo changes during adulthood. By the time you reach old age, accumulations of cartilage will make your nose a half inch wider and another half inch longer. Your earlobes will become somewhat fatter, while your ears will grow about a quarter of an inch longer. The circumference of the head increases by a quarter of an inch every ten years, presumably because the skull thickens with increasing age. However, these changes are usually far less noticeable than are the age-related changes in the skin.

Since the trends discussed above are only average tendencies, how might you predict the rate at which your own skin and face will age? The aging of the skin is determined by hereditary influences, so you can obtain some valuable clues simply by observing your parents' features. In fact, except for such remedial actions as cosmetic surgery, about all you can do to preserve a more youthful skin is to avoid excessive exposure to the sun's ultraviolet rays. Furthermore, if you are female, the aging of your skin during the second half of adulthood will probably be more noticeable than if you are male (although dryness can be inhibited by using lotions and protective creams). One reason is that the production of skin oil (sebum) declines significantly after menopause in women, but remains virtually unchanged for men throughout adulthood.

HAIR.   Currently, scientific knowledge about age-related changes in the hair is not much greater than that possessed by the average hairdresser (Kligman, Grove, & Balin, 1985). Most adults over 40 experience some graying of scalp hair, which is caused by hereditary influences. Scalp hair also becomes thinner over the course of adulthood, especially after age 65. This thinning occurs in two ways: the rate of growth decreases, and individual strands of hair gradually decline in diameter. For example, in the case of 20-year-old men, the diameter of a single hair is 101 microns (millionths of a meter). For 70-year-old men, this diameter is only 80 microns. The density of scalp hair varies greatly from one adult to another, however, although blondes generally have more hairs than do brunettes.

Some men experience a loss of hair that begins at the temples, proceeds to the circle on the back of the head (the "monk's spot"), and continues until the entire top of the head is bare (**male pattern baldness**). This form of hair loss is due solely to hereditary influences, and cannot at present be prevented by scalp massages or other treatments. Other men retain most of their cranial hair throughout adulthood. Even in these cases, some hair loss usually occurs around the temples; but there are exceptions, as the case history of one noted American indicates:

A PRESIDENT'S UNUSUAL HAIRLINE

"It's a hairline you normally see only on a child or a eunuch," says Dr. Norman Orentreich, the inventor of the hair transplant. He is referring to President Ronald Reagan, who retained a straight line of hair above his forehead into his 70s. "He's not wearing a hairpiece," Orentreich says, "and he hasn't been castrated, so I'd have to assume that he happens to have some sort of rare hereditary variation [to account for the lack of hair loss around the temples]." Thus President Reagan's scalp is further proof of what gerontologists have come to realize during the past few decades, namely that individual variations in aging are enormous at every age and in every part of the body (Tierney, 1982, p. 45.)

Male pattern baldness also affects some 75 percent of all women, though rarely to the extent of becoming totally hairless. This pattern involves a thinning of the hair on the top and sides of the head, and can become so pronounced that some women in their seventies and eighties opt to wear wigs. Contrary to a common belief, however, childbirth does *not* cause scalp hair loss in women. (See Borst, 1982.)

In other areas of the body, an opposite trend is observed. As men grow older, hair becomes longer and more profuse in the ears, the nostrils, the eyebrows, and sometimes on the back. Most women past 65, especially those of Mediterranean origin, have an excessive growth of long, dark, and thick hair over the lip and chin. The reasons for such localized hirsutism are not yet known (Kligman et al., 1985).

HEIGHT.   A man's height decreases by about half an inch between ages 30 and 50, and by another three quarters of an inch between ages 50 and 70. This is due to the effects of gravity, which causes the muscles to weaken and the bones of the spine to deteriorate and become compressed.

The height loss for women is slightly greater, and may total as much as two inches between ages 25 and 75. One reason is a higher incidence of metabolic bone disease among women following menopause. Another important cause is a loss of bone calcium with increasing age, a decline that can be slowed by regular exercise and an appropriate diet.

WEIGHT.   As we grow from young adulthood to middle age, our weight tends to increase. (See Table 3.1.) Many of us become less

TABLE 3.1 Average Weight as a Function of Age, Sex, and Height

Men

Height		Age					
FEET	INCHES	18–24	25–34	35–44	45–54	55–64	65–74
5	2	*	*	*	*	*	148
5	3	*	151	*	151	*	146
5	4	146	151	158	165	154	147
5	5	138	155	156	161	163	155
5	6	154	160	165	166	163	160
5	7	157	168	173	172	168	167
5	8	155	166	177	170	170	169
5	9	166	176	172	178	175	172
5	10	165	185	184	183	184	181
5	11	176	178	188	187	187	188
6	0	175	190	195	193	184	183
6	1	186	195	210	196	189	*
6	2	191	191	*	*	*	*

Women

Height		Age					
FEET	INCHES	18–24	25–34	35–44	45–54	55–64	65–74
4	9	*	*	*	*	*	130
4	10	118	119	128	*	122	133
4	11	118	126	136	136	143	137
5	0	123	125	135	146	142	138
5	1	124	130	134	141	148	144
5	2	124	135	142	140	146	146
5	3	132	138	146	149	154	149
5	4	133	141	148	153	151	152
5	5	135	143	155	156	162	153
5	6	140	146	157	155	155	162
5	7	143	153	155	161	*	173
5	8	142	162	171	173	*	168
5	9	136	153	180	*	*	*

Note: Weights measured with no shoes and light outdoor clothing.

SOURCE: U.S. Department of Health, Education, and Welfare (1979). *Weight by Height and Age for Adults 18–74 Years: United States, 1971–74* (DHEW Publication No. (PHS) 79-1656). Hyattsville, MD.

active during this period, and there is a decrease in the rate at which the resting body converts food into energy (our **basal metabolism,** which slows down by about 3 percent every ten years). Because less metabolizing tissue is available after age 20, the number of calories required each day to maintain our present weight declines by about 10 percent every ten years.

If we were to reduce our food intake accordingly, our weight would remain about the same. But the typical pattern is to eat much the same amounts, or perhaps even more, as we grow from young adulthood to middle age. The result is an inability to burn up enough food; an accumulation of fat throughout the body; skin that becomes flabby in the waist and chest areas, which may increase in size by as much as five to six inches; and a gain in weight that may total 10 to 15 percent between age 20 and age 50. For obvious reasons, these changes are commonly referred to as "middle-age spread."

After middle age, however, our weight is likely to level off and begin a slow decline. During this period, we tend to lose more weight due to tissue and muscle deterioration than we gain in fat.

BREASTS.   Women's breasts sag with increasing age. The glandular tissues that produce firmness deteriorate over time, while the tissues that support the breast by connecting it with the underlying muscles become stretched. In general, small and broad-based breasts sag less than those that are large or narrow based.

These changes are determined in part by heredity, and partly by the woman's behavior. Chest muscle exercises are unlikely to lift a breast that is already sagging, but preventive measures can be helpful. These include wearing supportive brassieres before sagging becomes apparent, especially during pregnancy, breast-feeding, and vigorous exercise.

VOICE.   As we grow older, the vocal cords stiffen and vibrate at a higher frequency. By old age, therefore, the speaking voice increases in pitch by about two to three notes on the musical scale. The voice may also begin to quaver, presumably because there is some loss of control over the vocal cords.

AFTERWORD.   Most of the changes discussed above are so well known that they have become hallmarks of the aging process. These changes are primarily cosmetic; they have no direct effect on our vigor, daily functioning, or health. Nevertheless, their psychological effects can be considerable. Millions of middle-aged and elderly women (and some older men) suffer considerable damage to their self-esteem because of these changes, so much so that they spend substantial amounts of money on cosmetic products and/or surgery in an effort to appear younger. As Weg (1983, p. 251) observes, "Societal adoration of youth has placed a premium on looking young. . . . The young, unlined, and gently curvaceous body of the woman and the lithe but macho and powerful body of the man cannot be preserved forever. [Yet] . . . societal attitudes toward aging and the aged have helped to create the fearsome image of old age that can be likened to a punishment."

The desire to look young is understandable. Increasing age brings us closer to the specter of death (see Chapter 12), while youth is associated with vitality and the prospect of many years yet to live. Nevertheless, the preoccupation of our society with a young appearance seems to be excessive. Looking old is not an illness, nor is it necessarily indicative of any serious impairments in functioning. Rather, it is a normal consequence of the aging process.

Internal Changes

MUSCULATURE.   With increasing age, our muscle tissue slowly declines in strength, tone, and flexibility. Fiber is replaced by connective tissue, which causes the muscles to become stiffer and to heal more slowly after an injury. And muscle is gradually replaced by fat, leading to an overall softening of the body. Thus the typical 175-pound man possesses 70 pounds of muscle at age 30, when his strength is at its peak, but retains only about 60 pounds of muscle by old age.

One consequence of these changes is that strength decreases with increasing age, particularly after age 50. This has been observed in such areas as handgrip strength and knee extension strength, among others. To some extent, however, muscular decrements can be slowed by appropriate exercise. (See Buskirk, 1985; Shock, 1962; 1974; Smith, Bierman, & Robinson, 1978.)

THE HEART AND CARDIOVASCULAR SYSTEM.   The muscles of the heart also deteriorate as we grow older, so less blood is pumped with each heartbeat. In addition, the arteries become narrower and less flexible; accumulations of cholesterol collect on the artery walls, which are themselves growing thicker. The net effect is to clog the arteries, increasing the amount of resistance to the flow of blood from the heart. Thus the cardiovascular system of older adults operates less efficiently; the heart must work harder to accomplish less. (See Figure 3.2.)

The rate of the heartbeat at rest remains about the same throughout adulthood, but there is a significant decline in the maximum heartbeat during exercise. At age 30, for example, there may be as

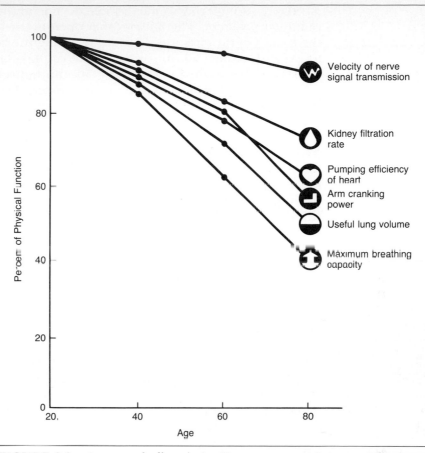

FIGURE 3.2 Average declines in bodily processes with increasing age. Dolnick (1982); Weg (1983, p. 253).

many as 200 heartbeats per minute of intense activity. This maximum declines to about 170 heartbeats at age 50, and to 150 heartbeats at age 70. It also takes longer for the older heart to return to the resting rate.

Regular and appropriate exercise, as prescribed by one's personal physician, is generally regarded as an effective way to improve cardiovascular health. Exercise lowers the rate of the heart at rest, increases the efficiency of the heart and blood vessels, lowers hypertension (high blood pressure), and reduces the amount of cholesterol in the blood. There is no evidence that exercise will prevent a heart attack, but it can make a satisfactory recovery more likely (Weg, 1983).

LUNGS.   Aging brings a measurable decline in the efficiency of the pulmonary system. The muscles that operate the lungs weaken and the tissues in the chest cage stiffen, reducing the ability of the lungs to expand. At age 30, for example, we can take a maximum of six quarts of air into the lungs. By age 50, this figure declines to about 4.5 quarts. And by age 70, the maximum possible air intake is only three quarts.

STAMINA.   Because of the aforementioned changes in the heart, lungs, and muscles, our stamina declines as we grow older. There is less oxygen available to us, and the heart disperses it more slowly through the bloodstream to the muscles. A healthy 70-year-old can still run a marathon with proper training, but it will take him or her at least an hour longer than it would at age 30.

One index of stamina is to determine how many pounds can be turned with a weighted crank in one minute, yet still have the heartbeat return to normal after two minutes of rest. Using this measure, our stamina decreases by about 15 percent between ages 30 and 50, and by another 15 percent between ages 50 and 70. (See, for example, Shock & Norris, 1970.)

Physiological changes in the heart, lungs, and muscles cause stamina to decline with increasing age. This gray-haired runner can complete a marathon if healthy and properly trained, but he will take at least an hour longer to do so than will a 30-year-old. *Bob Kalman/Image Works*

BONES AND JOINTS.   As we grow through adulthood, calcium losses cause the bones to become more brittle, less flexible, more vulnerable to injury, and slower to heal. Older adults may therefore be advised to increase their daily intake of calcium from the normal 800 mg to 1200–1500 mg (Guigoz & Munro, 1985). In addition, years of flexing wear down and loosen the cartilage around the joints. Thus our movements tend to be stiffer and slower after age 50, and we are more likely to experience some degree of pain in the joints (Hazzard & Bierman, 1978).

REFLEXES AND REACTION TIME.   Simple reflex time remains relatively constant during adulthood, as with the knee-jerk reflex (Hugin, Norris, & Shock, 1960). But aging produces a significant decrease in our ability to react quickly to stimuli (e.g., a novel sound), especially after age 70 (Shock, 1974; 1985). This is due primarily to changes in the brain, which takes longer to process information and to respond appropriately. Older adults therefore tend to perform more poorly on tasks that are highly speeded, an issue we will discuss further in Chapter 5.

DIGESTION.   The capacity to digest and absorb food does not decline appreciably with increasing age. When digestive problems do occur, they are usually attributable to other causes. Older adults are more likely to require laxatives and sedatives, and these drugs tend to reduce the efficiency of the digestive system. Or a loss of appetite may be caused by depression, a common form of adult psychopathology. (See Chapter 11.)

EXCRETION.   During the course of adulthood, each kidney loses approximately half of its nephrons (tubules). Because of this reduced reserve, the kidneys filter waste out of blood only half as fast at age 70 as at age 30. Another consequence is that stress is more likely to precipitate kidney failure in older adults.

The bladder loses some 50 percent of its capacity by old age, and it becomes less elastic. As a result, urinary elimination is more frequent, more urgent, and less complete among older adults. Constipation is more likely, however, due to slower peristalsis and increased absorption of water from the large intestine.

AFTERWORD: AGING AND VULNERABILITY TO DISEASE.   The physiological changes discussed above are part of the normal process of aging. Most of these changes are not troublesome in any practical sense. Some involve a certain amount of inconvenience or discomfort but are not incapacitating or fatal, such as stiffness in the joints or declines in muscle strength. Thus most older people accommodate well to these changes: approximately 87 percent of adults over age 65 are able to remain in their communities, suffer no significant limitations in their mobility, and demonstrate more than adequate coping behavior in meeting the challenges of everyday living (Brotman, 1980; Weg, 1981). Insofar as normal aging is concerned, then, there is no empirical support for the stereotype of the physiologically incapacitated and helpless older adult.

However, aging does have one ominous physiological aspect. Because of the reduced efficiency of most bodily systems, older adults are more vulnerable to disease than are young adults, and they are twice as likely to be physically disabled and to require hospitalization. Some age-related ailments can cause severe pain, such as arthritis. Others are fatal. Cardiovascular disease, cancer, and cerebrovascular accidents (strokes), the three leading causes of death in this country, have their greatest incidence among older persons. To more fully understand the nature of age-related physiological changes, therefore, we must now consider the relationship between aging and pathology.

Aging and Pathology

CHRONIC CONDITIONS.   **Chronic** conditions are characterized by a slow onset and a long duration. Although these disorders are rarely found among young adults, they account for the majority of disabilities after middle age. The most common are arthritis and hypertension.

Arthritis may take various forms: an inflammation of the joints (rheumatoid arthritis), degenerative joint disease (osteoarthritis), gout, connective tissue diseases, and others. The primary symptom, pain in the joints, can be intense—so much so that arthritis is currently the major cause of limited activity among older adults. However, the severity of this disease varies greatly from person to person; one adult with arthritis may suffer only from occasional flare-ups, whereas another may be housebound. As many as 80 percent of all recently retired persons experience some degree of arthritis (Kolodny & Klipper, 1978), while approximately 25 percent of adults age 45–64 and almost half of those 65 and older require treatment for this disorder. (See Figure 3.3.)

The etiology of arthritis is still unclear, nor are there any known cures. Various forms of treatment may help to alleviate pain and to maintain the mobility and strength of the afflicted joints, including anti-inflammatory drugs (e.g., aspirin; cortisone derivatives), mild exercise, heat, and cold. (See Howell et al., 1976; Smythe, 1975.)

Hypertension involves a consistent pattern of elevated blood pressure. Among the probable causes are excessive weight, stress,

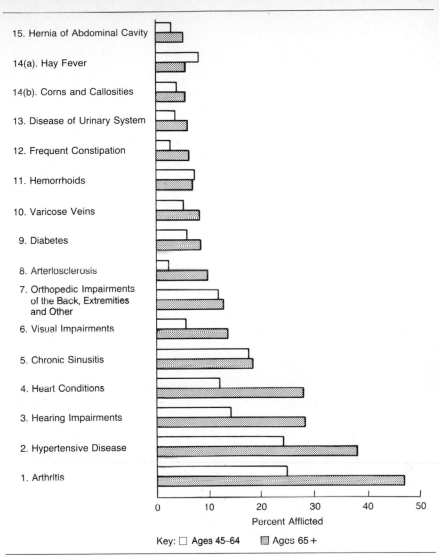

FIGURE 3.3   Most prevalent chronic conditions as a function of age (1981). United States Senate Special Committee on Aging (1983, p. 59).

and perhaps a high salt intake. In contrast to arthritis, hypertension does not produce noticeable pain. Yet it can have even more serious consequences, since it increases the likelihood of strokes and coronary heart disease (Castelli, 1978; Kannel & Sorlie, 1975; Robbins, 1978). Various prescription drugs are commonly used to control high blood pressure, while such therapeutic techniques as relaxation and meditation may also be helpful (Harvard Medical School News-letter, 1979).

ACCIDENTS.   From birth to age 44, you are more likely to die from an accident than from any other single cause. However, the odds against such an event are decidedly in your favor; the death rate due to accidents for this age group is only about 1 in 2,300.

Older adults have relatively low accident *rates*. For example, adults over age 65 suffer only about half as many accidents as do children age 6–16. But since the middle-aged and elderly have more brittle bones and less efficient bodily systems, the *consequences* of their accidents are more severe; healing is significantly slower, hospitalization is more often necessary, and death is more likely. Thus, for adults past age 75, the death rate due to accidents is approximately 1 in 600. (See, for example, Sterns, Barrett, & Alexander, 1985.)

MAJOR CAUSES OF DEATH.   The probability of dying from cardiovascular disease, cancer, or a stroke increases dramatically as we grow past middle age. Among adults age 25–44, only about 1 of every 4,000 suffers a fatal heart attack. This figure increases to approximately 1 in 300 for those age 45–64, while about 1 of every 25 adults past age 75 dies from heart disease. Similar age-related increases are found in the mortality rates for cancer and strokes. (See Table 3.2.) We will have more to say about death and dying in Chapter 12.

AFTERWORD: AGING, ACTUAL HEALTH, AND SELF-PERCEIVED HEALTH.   Whereas physical helplessness and dependency are *not*

TABLE 3.2   Leading causes of death in the United States as a function of age group (1978).

Cause	Death Rate at Age:			
	25–44	*45–64*	*65–74*	*75+*
Heart disease	1 in 4,000	1 in 300	1 in 80	1 in 25
Cancer	1 in 3,500	1 in 325	1 in 125	1 in 75
Cerebrovascular disease (strokes)	negligible	1 in 2,000	1 in 400	1 in 80
Accidents	1 in 2,300	1 in 2,300	1 in 1,600	1 in 600

Note: Rates are based on the total number of adults in each age group. For example, 1 of every 25 adults age 75 and older dies from heart disease.

SOURCE: Based on Sterns, Barrett, & Alexander (1985, pp. 706–707).

TABLE 3.3   Various health characteristics as a function of
age (1981).

Characteristic	Age			
	45–54	*55–64*	*65–74*	*75+*
Injuries per 100 persons per year	22	20	14	26
Days of restricted activity per person per year	24	31	35	48
Days of bed disability per person per year	8.5	9.5	11.5	18
Percent hospitalized at least once during the past year	10.9%	12.9%	16.6%	20.4%
Average number of days spent in hospital during past year	8.9	9.0	9.3	11.0

SOURCE: United States Senate Special Committee on Aging (1983, p. 69).

characteristic of old age, certain painful chronic disorders are more
likely (e.g., arthritis). As a result, adults past age 75 experience about
twice as many days per year of restricted activity and bed disability
as do those age 45–54. (See Table 3.3.) Also, the probability of suffering a fatal illness or accident is much greater after middle age.

Nevertheless, the majority of older Americans assess their health
favorably. As of 1981, some 75 percent of adults age 55–64 and 70
percent of those over 65 described their health as good or excellent
in comparison to others of their own age. These percentages are
only somewhat smaller than the corresponding figures for younger
adults: approximately 82 percent of the middle-aged (age 45–54)
and 92 percent of young adults (age 25–34) rates their health as
good or excellent (United States Senate Special Committee on Aging, 1983).

Personal health status is a function of both actual and self-perceived health. Adults who believe themselves to be physically healthy
are more likely to be active and independent, while those who regard themselves as in poor health tend to behave accordingly. To
be sure, the generally positive self-perceptions of older adults may
well be due in part to more pessimistic expectations. It is well known
that illness and disability are more common after middle age, so
older adults may regard some degree of pain and inconvenience as
normal for their age. Even so, we may conclude our discussion of
aging and pathology on an optimistic note: despite the greater likelihood of certain chronic disorders and potentially fatal illnesses, the
substantial majority of older adults do *not* regard themselves as in
poor health or as seriously disabled.

Chapter Glossary: Physiological Aspects of Aging

Antioxidants	Compounds that block much of the damage to bodily proteins caused by free radicals. Despite claims to the contrary, there is no convincing evidence that dietary supplements of antioxidants extend human life.
Arthritis	A disorder of the joints that is very common after middle age and may take various forms, such as inflammation or degeneration. The resulting pain may consist only of occasional flare-ups, or it may be so severe as to be debilitating.
Basal metabolism	The rate at which the resting body converts food into energy. Declines by about 3 percent for every ten years of life, so older adults need fewer calories per day to maintain their present weight.
Chronic disorder	A disorder characterized by a slow onset and a long duration.
Deoxyribonucleic acid (DNA)	A complicated molecule which controls the formation of proteins that cells require to maintain life.
Genetic cellular theories	Theories that attribute aging to an innate genetic program, much like a built-in biological clock.
Hypertension	A consistent pattern of elevated blood pressure that most often occurs after middle age. Causes include excessive weight, stress, and perhaps a high salt intake. Hypertension increases the likelihood of strokes and coronary heart disease.
Male pattern baldness	A loss of cranial hair with increasing age, which is caused by hereditary influences. Among men, the top of the head typically becomes entirely bare. Male pattern baldness also affects 75 percent of all women, though rarely to the extent of becoming totally hairless.
Nongenetic cellular theories (wear-and-tear theories)	Theories that attribute aging to progressive cell damage caused by the internal and external environment, rather than to an innate genetic program.
Physiological theories of aging	Theories that attribute aging to the failure of certain physiological systems to coordinate important bodily functions.
Ribonucleic acid (RNA)	A molecule that transfers genetic information from the DNA molecules to the location in the cell where proteins are assembled.

Theories of Aging

The physiological changes discussed in the preceding pages have been affecting humankind for thousands of years. Nevertheless, the underlying reasons for these changes remain a source of controversy; scientists still do not know *why* we age. Various biological theories of aging have been proposed, some of which appear to be quite promising. However, no one theory has as yet achieved general acceptance.

Genetic Cellular Theories

The maximum life span varies greatly among different species. As we observed in Chapter 1, the greatest recorded human age is 120 years. In contrast, the maximum life span for horses is 46 years; cats, 28 years; dogs, 20 years; black rats, 5 years; and the mayfly, only one day. (See Table 3.4; Comfort, 1964; Kirkwood, 1985.) Furthermore, humans with long-lived parents and grandparents live an average of six years longer than those whose parents die before the age of 50 (Dublin, Lotka, & Spiegelman, 1949). It has also been observed that human body cells grown in tissue cultures (in vitro) are able to divide only about 50 times, after which they age and die (Hayflick, 1965; 1973; 1980; 1986). The reproductive capacity of cells taken from old animals is even more limited; these cells can undergo only about half as many divisions as those obtained from young animals.

Findings such as these imply that cellular aging is caused by some process within the cell itself, rather than by the lack of environmental requirements. That is, some kind of clock mechanism exists in normal cells, and this mechanism controls the capacity of the cells to function and to replicate (Hayflick, 1986). Since there is a direct relationship between the life span of a species and the capacity of its cells to divide, this suggests in turn that age-related changes are programmed into the genes of each species. Thus, **genetic cellular theories** attribute aging to changes in two complicated kinds of molecules: **deoxyribonucleic acid (DNA),** which controls the formation of proteins required by the cell to maintain life (Watson, 1969); and **ribonucleic acid (RNA),** which transfers information from the DNA molecules to another location in the cell where the proteins are assembled.

DNA DAMAGE THEORIES.   Some genetic cellular theories posit that damage to the DNA molecules is responsible for human aging. This

Gerontologist Leonard Hayflick studies cells as they age *in vitro*. His findings suggest that cellular aging may be caused by a process within the cell
itself.   *Gerald Davis/Contact Stock Images*

damage may be caused by exposure to radiation, or it may consist
of harmful cellular mutations (e.g., Curtis, 1966; Szilard, 1959).

Although some early studies appeared to support DNA damage
theory, more recent research has unearthed some important contradictions. Mutations and radiation affect dividing cells, whereas the
physiological effects of aging are due primarily to cells that no longer
are able to divide. Mutations occur too slowly to account for the
pronounced physiological changes that occur with increasing age.
Furthermore, in marked contrast to aging, damage to the DNA
molecules is usually reversible because most cells contain appropriate repair mechanisms. (See Martin, 1980; Tice & Setlow, 1985;
Wheeler & Lett, 1974.) For these reasons, it is extremely doubtful
that damage to the DNA molecule itself plays much of a role in
aging (Shock, 1977).

TABLE 3.4 Maximum recorded life spans for various species.

Common Name	Maximum Life Span (Years)
Human	120
Galapagos tortoise	100+
Indian elephant	70
Eagle owl	68
Snapping turtle	58+
Chinese alligator	52
Horse	46
Golden eagle	46
Chimpanzee	44
Gorilla	39
Brown bear	36
Common toad	36
Domestic dove	30
Anaconda	29
Domestic cat	28
Swine	27
Porcupine	27
Domestic dog	20
Sheep	20
Gray squirrel	15
Vampire bat	13
Black rat	5
House mouse	3

SOURCE: Modified from Kirkwood (1985, p. 34).

ERROR THEORIES. An alternative model focuses on the transmission of genetic information from the DNA molecules to the place where proteins are assembled (ribosome). This transfer is accomplished with the aid of the RNA molecules. Errors are more likely insofar as the RNA molecules are concerned because these molecules are relatively unstable and are formed continuously, whereas DNA molecules are highly stable and are maintained throughout the life span of a cell. According to this model, errors in transmission produce a protein or enzyme which is *not* an exact copy of the original, and which therefore cannot carry out its function of maintaining life. As a result, the cells grow older and die, and so do we. (See Martin, 1977; Medvedev, 1964; Orgel, 1963; Reff, 1985.)

To date, error theorists have not been able to specify the precise nature of the hypothesized errors in transmission. In fact, the details of the transfer process itself have not yet been clearly identified. While the error hypothesis is a promising one, it remains a source of active controversy and research (Meier, 1984).

Nongenetic Cellular Theories

Some researchers argue that in vitro experiments with culture tissue are not applicable to aging as it occurs in living tissue (in vivo), and that the concept of an innate biological clock is therefore incorrect. Instead, these theorists contend that aging involves a gradual deterioration of bodily cells that is *not* internally programmed. Consider an automobile that ages over a period of years: the engine becomes less efficient, the battery dies, rust invades the exterior, and so on. These changes are more or less predictable but do not follow any specific timetable, internal or otherwise. Rather, wear and tear plays a major role: a car sheltered in a garage and rarely driven will last far longer than one driven 20,000 miles per year and parked in the street.

Unlike machines, the human body has mechanisms for self-repair. New cells are continually formed to replace old ones, while molecules may undergo replacement within a single cell. Nevertheless, various factors might conceivably cause cells to wear out faster than the repairs can take place. Thus **nongenetic cellular theories** assume that with the passage of time, changes occur in the cells which impair their effectiveness. That is, aging is due to progressive damage to the organism from its internal and external environment.

ACCUMULATION THEORIES.   According to some theorists, aging is caused by the accumulation of various harmful substances in the cells of the organism. All older cells contain a dark-colored, insoluble substance (lipofuscin), with the amount of this material increasing at a constant rate over time. (See Carpenter, 1965; Naeim & Walford, 1985; Strehler, 1964; 1978.) It is logical to assume that this "cellular garbage" interferes with cellular functioning, since it takes up space and serves no useful purpose, and that it might even ultimately result in the death of the cell. But while this hypothesis is a tenable one, there is as yet no conclusive evidence in its favor (Rowlatt & Franks, 1978).

CROSS-LINKAGE THEORIES.   A second possibility is that with the passage of time, harmful cross-linkages (bonds) develop between component parts of the same molecule or between two different molecules. Extracellular proteins (e.g., collagen) develop an increasing number of cross-linkages with increasing age, and collagen is related to the aging of the skin (as we have seen). This model posits that cross-linkages ultimately lead to severe oxygen deficiency, and to other biochemical failures (Verzar, 1963; Bjorksten, 1968). However, the available empirical evidence concerning cross-linkages and aging is also inconclusive (Harman, 1981; Schofield & Davies, 1978).

FREE RADICAL THEORY.   A third nongenetic cellular theory attributes aging to the operation of "free radicals," or unstable chemical compounds which tend to react quickly with other molecules in their vicinity. These reactions are assumed to affect the structure and function of bodily enzymes and proteins, notably those proteins that are essential to the life of the cell. (See Harman, 1968; 1981; Scoggins, 1981.) However, experimental tests of free radical theory have not led to any definitive conclusions (Shock, 1977; Meier, 1984).

Physiological Theories

A third group of theories attributes aging to the failure of certain physiological systems, and to the resulting inability of these systems to coordinate important bodily functions. According to this model, a particular organ or system of the body is primarily responsible for repairing cells that can no longer reproduce themselves. When such "hot spot" organs wear out, cells can no longer be replaced and the organism dies (Latham & Johnson, 1979).

IMMUNOLOGICAL THEORIES.   The immune system protects the body against invading microorganisms, and against atypical mutant cells which may form within the body (e.g., cancer). It does so in two ways: by generating antibodies that react with the proteins of foreign organisms, and by forming special cells that engulf and digest the foreign cells.

Aging has a pronounced negative effect on the capabilities of the immune system. The production of antibodies peaks during adolescence and declines thereafter (Makinodan, 1974), and the ability to recognize mutated cells also declines with increasing age. Thus the increase in cancer rates among older adults, discussed previously, may well be due to failures of the immune system. In fact, some theorists define aging as a disease of the immune system. For example, one interesting hypothesis relates aging to the development of antibodies which act against normal and necessary bodily cells. (See Goodwin, 1981; Harrison, 1985; Walford, 1969; 1974; Weksler, 1981.) Although there is as yet little evidence that malfunctions of the immune system cause aging, this hypothesis is a viable one that deserves more widespread experimental testing.

NEUROENDOCRINE THEORIES.   The neuroendocrine system is a complicated interactive system which includes a number of glands (e.g., pituitary, thyroid, pancreas, adrenal, ovaries, and testes) and the hypothalamus. Its function is to regulate various important bodily processes, such as metabolic rate, glucose and water level, and temperature.

The functioning of the endocrine system declines significantly with increasing age. For example, when blood sugar rises, the pancreas of older adults does not release sufficient insulin as quickly. (See Silverstone et al, 1957; Finch & Landfield, 1985.) This is one reason why diabetes is so prevalent among the middle-aged and elderly (Figure 3.3). However, whether aging is actually caused by endocrine changes is not yet known.

Afterword

Do we possess a built-in biological clock, which governs the rate of aging and perhaps even the time of our death? Or do our cells undergo a gradual breakdown over time that is *not* genetically programmed, with aging due primarily to cellular wear and tear? Or is aging caused by the failure of certain physiological coordinating systems, such as the immune or endocrine systems?

As the preceding survey indicates, we do not yet know the answers to these questions. The theories discussed above represent only a sampling of those that have received research attention during the last few decades. Conceivably, there may be some truth in all of them. Since each one of these theories focuses on a different aspect of the aging process, they are not necessarily incompatible. Or we might find that some of these theories ultimately make a significant contribution to our understanding of aging, while others fall by the wayside as further empirical evidence is collected. Research into the causes of aging is still at an early stage, hence the large number of competing theories. But interest in this area is flourishing, so we may reasonably expect more conclusive findings to emerge in the not too distant future.

Lengthening Life

The quest for perpetual youth is as old as recorded history. People of various eras have tried to reverse the process of aging with magic, potions, sorcery, rituals, unusual diets, vitamins, and chemicals of various kinds.

Many of these procedures appear ludicrous by modern standards.

Myths About Aging: Physiological Aspects

MYTH	*BEST AVAILABLE EVIDENCE*
Our physiological processes remain at a fairly constant level of efficiency until we approach old age, at which time they undergo a drastic decline.	Most of our bodily functions reach their maximum capacity prior to early adulthood, and begin a gradual decline thereafter.
Most adults proceed at much the same rate through a series of similar physiological stages.	Age-related physiological changes do *not* occur according to a strict timetable. Adults age at different rates, and such groupings as "the elderly" are more heterogeneous than is commonly believed.
Most adults past age 65 are so physiologically incapacitated that they must depend to a great extent on other people.	Helplessness and dependency are *not* characteristic of old age. Some 87 percent of adults over 65 are able to cope more than adequately with the demands of everyday living.
Taking large doses of antioxidants (or ginseng, or selenium, or pantothenic acid, or vitamin C) will extend the length of your life.	There are *no* drugs, pills, powders, vitamins, dietary supplements, or diets with proven antiaging capacities.

The ancient Babylonians and Australian aborigines sought to prolong life by administering semen potions, or aphrodisiacs made from tigers' testes, to the feeble or dying. When the biblical King David was old and ill, his doctors prescribed close contact with a young female virgin, trusting that this would enable him to absorb her youth. The Taoists of 300 B.C. believed that men could achieve greater longevity by failing to reach sexual climax, thereby preserving their life essence or semen. And the sixteenth-century explorer Ponce de Leon heard tales of a fountain in the Bahamas whose waters rejuvenated the aged, and set out to find it. Navigation techniques not being very advanced in those days, he never did locate the fountain of youth. Instead he accidentally discovered Florida, which ironically is now a major retirement area for the elderly. (See Segerberg, 1974; Trimmer, 1970.)

Despite centuries of efforts like these, there are as yet *no* scientifically accepted elixirs, drugs, or dietary supplements that will extend the length of human life. There *are* ways to improve your chances of staying healthy and living longer, but these methods involve the more difficult course of changing your behavior.

Modern Quests for the Fountain of Youth

People today are of course much more realistic about the possibility of lengthening human life—or are we? According to a recent investigation by the Select Committee on Aging of the House of Representatives, Americans spend more than *$2 billion per year* on unproven antiaging remedies (Meister, 1984). Some of these popular prescriptions are based on misrepresentations or overgeneralizations of gerontological research findings, while others are pure quackery:

ANTIAGING HEALTH FRAUDS

'Moon dust,' promoted as a cure for arthritis and other afflictions, cost $100 for three ounces—and turned out to be just plain sand. The 'miracle spike,' a tube containing about a penny's worth of barium chloride (a chemical used in rat poison), was supposed to be worn around the neck as a cure for cancer and diabetes. It cost $300. The 'Congo Kit,' billed as a cure for arthritis, was actually two hemp mittens.

These are just three of several hundred worthless, unproven, and sometimes harmful products uncovered by a House subcommittee during a four-year investigation of quackery completed [in 1984]. . . . "We found the inventiveness of the quacks to be as unlimited as their callousness and greed," said Rep. Claude Pepper (D-Fla.), chairman of the House Aging subcommittee on health and long-term care. "We found promoters who advised arthritics to bury themselves in the earth, sit in an abandoned mine, or stand naked under a 1,000-watt bulb during the full moon. These suffering souls have been wrapped in manure, soaked in mud, injected with snake venom, sprayed with WD-40, bathed in kerosene . . . [There is] a tremendous amount of money to be made in selling hope to the desperate." (Colburn, 1985, p. 1.)

Not all antiaging treatments are as bizarre as the examples cited above. In this section, we will discuss some of the more plausible approaches.

GEROVITAL.   One purported antiaging drug, Gerovital (GH3), has been in use for more than thirty years. Its main ingredient is procaine hydrochloride, best known to Americans as the local anesthetic Novocain. Thousands of people believe in Gerovital and buy it where they can—England, Mexico, Jamaica, and other islands of the Caribbean. (Nevada is the only American state that has approved the clinical use of Gerovital.) Yet there is no reliable empirical evidence that Gerovital has any antiaging properties, although it does appear to be useful as a mild antidepressant (Schneider & Reed, 1985; Weg, 1983).

ANTIOXIDANTS.   Some advertisements and popular best-sellers contend that life can be extended by taking large doses of **antioxidants,** compounds that block much of the damage to bodily proteins caused by free radicals. Although some laboratory experiments have obtained significant positive results with specially bred mice, there is as yet no convincing evidence that antioxidants will extend human life. As we have seen, free radical theory remains controversial. Even if this theory is correct, the body's need for antioxidants can be met simply by eating a variety of nutritious foods, and there is no indication that surplus amounts will do a better job of fighting free radicals. Some antioxidant supplements are actually useless because they are digested before body cells can use them (e.g., superoxide dismutase or SOD), while large doses of certain other antioxidants can be harmful (National Institute on Aging, 1984).

DNA AND RNA.   Some proponents of DNA damage theory argue that supplements containing DNA and RNA will slow aging, cure senility, and treat skin and hair changes. Here again, there is no scientific evidence to support these claims (National Institute on Aging, 1984). In fact, as we have seen, DNA damage is no longer regarded as a likely cause of aging.

OTHER DIETARY SUPPLEMENTS.   Various other dietary supplements have been promoted as antiaging remedies. These include selenium, ginseng, para aminobenzoic acid (PABA), pantothenic acid, and vitamins C and E.

Although selenium is an essential nutrient, there is no evidence that it reverses or retards the aging process, and excess amounts are toxic. Ginseng is notorious as an aphrodisiac and rejuvenator, yet there are no convincing empirical data to support these claims. Large doses of ginseng may well produce such side effects as nervousness, insomnia, gastrointestinal disorders, and elevated blood pressure. Huge doses of PABA do appear to darken gray hair, but also tend to cause nausea, vomiting, and blood disorders. Pantothenic acid is a component of Royal Jelly, the substance that turns female bees into long-lived fertile queens instead of short-lived sterile workers. This useful vitamin is present in so many foods that deficiencies are virtually impossible, making supplemental doses unnecessary. Nor is there scientific reason to believe that dietary supplements of vitamin C, or of any other vitamin, have any effects on the aging process.

RESTRICTED DIETS.   Yet another proposed method for extending life is to eat fewer calories while maintaining a nutritionally sound diet ("undernutrition without malnutrition"). Unlike other diets, this regimen is *not* discontinued when the dieter achieves the weight generally accepted as ideal, but is continued indefinitely.

Insofar as laboratory animals are concerned, the preponderance of research evidence does support this hypothesis. In some studies, rats and mice were fed a diet that was nutritionally adequate but severely restricted in calories. While the growth of these animals suffered considerably, they had much longer average and maximum life spans than did control animals who were allowed to eat all they wanted. Milder caloric restrictions, begun early in life, have been found to produce moderate life extension with only slight reductions in growth. At present, however, there is no evidence that restricted diets will inhibit aging in humans. In fact, it would seem that the heaviest and thinnest members of a given cohort have the shortest survival rates, while those slightly over their ideal body weight live the longest. (See Schneider & Reed, 1985.)

AFTERWORD.   The vast sums of money spent on purported antiaging remedies attest to the desperation with which some people regard the prospect of aging and death. At present, there are no liquids, pills, powders, or any other substances with proven antiaging capacities. There are some valid steps that can be taken to help ensure a longer life, however—as we will see in the following section.

Life-Lengthening Behaviors

Psychological and social factors are now almost universally recognized as important determinants of human longevity. These include stress, personality variables, marital status, social relationships, and such psychological disorders as depression. These issues will be discussed in the chapters dealing with stress, interpersonal relationships, and adult psychopathology. Insofar as physiological factors are concerned, empirical evidence indicates that your chances of remaining healthy and living longer depend to a considerable extent on your own behavior.

NOT SMOKING.   Smoking has been clearly related to oral and lung cancer, other pulmonary diseases, and cardiovascular disease. Conversely, ceasing or reducing the amount of smoking decreases the likelihood of premature death (e.g., Smith, Bierman, & Robinson, 1978). Thus: to live longer, don't smoke.

The research evidence is clear. If you want to live longer, *don't* follow this woman's example: Don't smoke. *Howard Dratch/Image Works*

DIET. Eating a balanced diet and maintaining a desirable weight will also increase your longevity. Obesity is related to diabetes, osteoarthritis, cardiovascular disease, and hypertension, while the effects of stress are greater among individuals who suffer from nutritional deficiencies. (See Weg, 1983.) Food and vitamins are *not* elixirs of youth, but appropriate nutrition will help to reduce the likelihood of harmful and fatal illnesses.

EXERCISE. Appropriate regular exercise helps to maintain cardiovascular health, strong muscles, and flexible joints, and to reduce hypertension and the amount of body fat. Conversely, the absence of even minimal exercise is related to reduced cardiovascular efficiency, a loss of bone calcium, and gastrointestinal problems.

Some skeptics contend that the beneficial effects of exercise are overrated. They point out that noted jogging authorities have suffered fatal heart attacks while engaging in their favorite sport (e.g., James Fixx). In laboratory studies with rats, however, both average and maximum life spans have increased significantly when exercise was begun early in life. (See Schneider & Reed, 1985.)

Conducting appropriately controlled research with human subjects is more difficult. Suppose that we compare one group of adults who exercise regularly with a second group of adults who do not exercise at all, and we find that the first group has a significantly longer life span. This does not necessarily mean that exercise improves longevity. Those adults who exercise frequently may have been healthier in the first place; they may have opted for more physical activity because they had an unusually high degree of vitality and energy. Similarly, those who avoid exercise may do so because they are less healthy and have less energy to expend.

In an attempt to resolve such problems, investigators at the Stanford University School of Medicine undertook what may well be the most comprehensive study ever to relate exercise and longevity. They traced the health and life styles of some 17,000 Harvard graduates, age 35–74, from the mid-1960s until 1978. The findings indicated that regular exercise lengthens human life by about one to two years on the average, although the amount of exercise required may well be considerable. For example, those ambitious enough to walk more than 35 miles per week reduced their risk of death by almost 50 percent. In contrast, the reduction in death rate was 11 percent for adults who walked 5–10 miles weekly, and only 4 percent for those who walked five miles or less. In general, the optimum expenditure of energy appeared to be about 3,500 calories per week, or the equivalent of six to eight hours of strenuous bicycling or singles tennis. Regimens that burned up more than 3,500 calories tended to cause injuries that negated most of the benefits derived from the exercise. (See Clark & Springen, 1986; Elmer-DeWitt, 1986.)

OTHER FACTORS.   Those who have regular health checkups tend to live longer; even serious illnesses can often be readily treated if caught in the early stages. The use of seat belts when riding in an automobile is also recommended by most authorities. Although there are occasional cases where seat belts have proved disadvantageous in an accident, the odds are much greater that they will help to avoid serious injury and even death. Alcoholic beverages should be used in moderation if at all, and never when driving. And sufficient time for sleep, rest, and relaxation is also conducive to longer life. (See National Institute on Aging, 1984).

AFTERWORD.   The recommendations listed above may seem trite or even sermonic. But they are effective, whereas the same cannot be said of the various antiaging remedies currently being sold on the open market. However, considerably more effort is required: rather than merely consuming some magical antiaging substance, you must engage in and/or change various important behaviors.

How long will *you* live? Even if we omit the possibility of accidents or other acts of God, there is no scientific way to answer this question with any great degree of accuracy. However, some of the more important physiological, psychological, and social contributors to longevity have been incorporated into the questionnaire shown in Table 3.5. By answering these questions, you can obtain a *very approximate* guide to your personal longevity. More importantly, this questionnaire will help to improve your understanding of the factors which play a significant role in lengthening human life.

Summary

AGE-RELATED PHYSIOLOGICAL CHANGES

Age-related physiological changes do not occur according to a strict timetable. Adults age at different rates, and such groupings as "the middle-aged" and "the elderly" are actually rather heterogeneous with regard to their physiological characteristics and capacities. Nevertheless, some important general trends can be identified.

The process of aging leaves clearly visible traces. Lines form in the forehead and elsewhere in the face. The skin becomes stiffer, less elastic, more spread out, and eventually loses its uniformity of color. Cranial hair becomes thinner and more gray or white. Height decreases by an inch or two, due primarily to years of coping with the effects of gravity. Weight increases from young adulthood to middle age, but tends to decline somewhat thereafter. Women's breasts sag. These changes are primarily cosmetic; they have no direct effect on our vigor, daily functioning, or health.

With increasing age, muscle tissue slowly declines in strength, tone, and flexibility. The cardiovascular, pulmonary, and excretory systems become less efficient. Our stamina decreases. The joints become more brittle and less flexible. Simple reflex time is relatively unaffected, but our ability to react quickly to stimuli declines significantly. These changes may cause some inconvenience or discomfort, but they are *not* incapacitating. The vast majority of older adults remain in their communities, suffer no significant limitations on their mobility, and cope more than adequately with the challenges of everyday living.

Aging does have one ominous physiological aspect: because of the reduced efficiency of most bodily systems, older adults are more vulnerable to chronic disorders, diseases, and fatal illnesses and ac-

TABLE 3.5   Estimating your personal longevity.

1. Basic Life Expectancy.
If you were born in 1970, your basic life expectancy is 67 years if you are male and 75 years if you are female. Write down your basic life expectancy in the space at the right. (If you were born considerably before or after 1970 and wish to enter a more precise estimate, consult Table 1.2, Chapter 1, under the heading "Life Expectancy at Birth.")   _____
   For each item that follows, decide how it applies to you and add or subtract the appropriate number of years from your basic life expectancy.

2. Current Longevity.
   A. If you are now in your fifties or sixties, add 10 years, since you have already proven yourself to be quite durable.   _____
   B. If you are now over age 60 and active, add another two years.   _____

3. Family History.
   A. If two or more of your grandparents lived to age 80 or beyond, add five years.   _____
   B. If any parent, grandparent, sister, or brother died of a heart attack or stroke before age 50, subtract four years. If instead any one of these relatives died from these diseases prior to age 60, subtract only two years.   _____
   C. Subtract three years for each case of diabetes, thyroid disorders, breast cancer, cancer of the digestive system, asthma, or chronic bronchitis among your parents or grandparents.   _____

4. Marital Status.
   A. If you are married, add four years.   _____
   B. If you are over 25 and not married, subtract one year for every unwedded decade.   _____

5. Economic Status.
   A. Subtract two years if your family income is over $40,000 per year.   _____
   B. Subtract three years if you have been poor for the greater part of your life.   _____

6. Physique.
   A. Subtract one year for every ten pounds you are overweight.   _____
   B. For each inch that your waist measurement exceeds your chest measurement, deduct two years.   _____

C. If you are over 40 and *not* overweight, add three years.   _____

7. **Exercise.**
   A. If your exercise is regular and moderate (e.g., jogging three times a week), add three years. But if your exercise is regular and vigorous (e.g., long-distance running three times a week), add five years instead of three years.   _____
   B. If your job is sedentary, subtract three years. But if it is active, add three years.   _____

8. **Alcohol.**
   A. If you are a light drinker (one to three drinks a day), add two years. If instead you are a teetotaler, subtract one year. And if instead you are a heavy drinker (more than four drinks per day), subtract seven-and-a-half years.   _____

9. **Smoking.**
   A. If you smoke cigarettes: less than one pack per day, subtract two years; one to two packs per day, subtract four years; two or more packs per day, subtract eight years.   _____
   B. Subtract two years if you regularly smoke a pipe or cigars.   _____

10. **Disposition.**
    A. Add two years if you are a reasoned, practical person.
    B. Subtract two years if you are aggressive, intense, and competitive.   _____
    C. Add three years if you are basically happy and content with life. If instead you are often unhappy, worried, and plagued by feelings of guilt, subtract three years.   _____

11. **Education.**
    A. If you failed to complete high school, subtract two years. If instead you had four additional years of school after high school, add one year.   _____
    B. For a fifth year of school after high school, add two more years.   _____

12. **Environment.**
    A. If you have lived most of your life in a rural environment, add four years. But if you have lived most of your life in an urban environment, subtract two years.   _____

13. **Sleep.**
  A. If you typically sleep more than nine hours per
     night, subtract five years.   _____

14. **Temperature.**
  A. If the thermostat in your home is set no higher
     than 68°F, add two years.   _____

15. **Health Care.**
  A. If you have regular medical and dental checkups,
     add three years.   _____
  B. If you are frequently ill, subtract two years.   _____

The final figure entered above is the estimate of your personal longevity. Please note that this is only a rough approximation. Although this
questionnaire is based on factors known to be correlated with longevity,
these correlations are far from perfect, and the number of years lived
by any one individual may differ significantly from the estimated longevity.

SOURCE: Schulz (1978, pp. 97–98).

cidents. The most common chronic disorder is arthritis, which may
take various forms. The primary symptom, pain in the joints, varies
from mild to debilitating. A second major chronic disorder, hypertension, involves a consistent pattern of elevated blood pressure.
Hypertension increases the likelihood of strokes and coronary heart
disease. Older adults have relatively low accident rates, but the consequences of their accidents tend to be more severe. The probability
of dying from cardiovascular disease, cancer, or a stroke increases
dramatically after middle age. Despite these age-related problems,
the majority of older Americans assess their health favorably.

THEORIES OF AGING

Although age-related physiological changes have been affecting humankind for thousands of years, scientists still do not know *why* we
age. Various biological theories of aging have been proposed, no
one of which has as yet achieved general acceptance.

Genetic cellular theories posit that age-related changes are programmed into the genetic structure of each species, much like a
built-in biological clock. Some researchers contend that aging is caused
by damage to DNA molecules, which control the formation of essential bodily proteins. Other theories focus on errors in the transmission of genetic information from the DNA molecules to the place
where proteins are assembled, which is accomplished with the aid
of RNA molecules.

Nongenetic cellular theorists reject the concept of an innate biological clock. Instead, they contend that aging is due to progressive cell damage from the internal and external environment (wear and tear). Such damage has been attributed to the accumulation of waste materials within the cells, to the formation of harmful cross-linkages between parts of the same molecule or between two different molecules, and to the operation of protein-destroying chemical compounds (free radicals).

According to a third group of theories, aging is caused by the failure of certain physiological systems to coordinate important bodily functions. Some researchers define aging as a disease of the immune system, which protects the body against harmful microorganisms and mutant cells. Other theorists relate aging to changes in the endocrine system.

At present, the available empirical evidence does not strongly support any of the aforementioned theories of aging. Research into the causes of aging is still at an early stage, but the great interest in this area suggests that more conclusive findings may well emerge in the not too distant future.

LENGTHENING LIFE

The quest for perpetual youth is as old as recorded history. People in ancient times tried to reverse or retard the aging process by resorting to magic, rituals, and potions; today, billions of dollars are spent on unproven antiaging treatments and dietary supplements. Despite centuries of effort (and some claims to the contrary), there are as yet *no* scientifically accepted drugs, liquids, pills, powders, chemicals, or vitamins that will extend human life. Empirical evidence does indicate that you can stay healthy and live longer by not smoking, eating a balanced diet and maintaining a desirable weight, obtaining appropriate regular exercise, having regular health checkups, using seat belts when riding in an automobile, using alcoholic beverages in moderation if at all (and never when driving), and allowing sufficient time for sleep, rest, and relaxation.

CHAPTER 4

Sensation and Perception

This chapter deals with the ways in which we take in, organize, and experience the world around us, and with important age-related changes in these processes. One stereotype associated with old age is that of sensory deterioration; stage and screen comedians commonly portray the elderly as myopic and hard of hearing. Yet if our sensory and perceptual abilities do decline markedly as we grow through adulthood, this is surely no laughing matter. All information about our environment, and many pleasurable (and painful) experiences, come to us through our senses: perceiving and avoiding various obstacles while walking or driving, reading an interesting book, watching a favorite television program, observing if the weather is fair or foul, listening to some good music, engaging in friendly conversation, enjoying a tempting meal, or caressing a loved one, to cite just a few examples. We are so used to relying on our sight, hearing, and other senses that we typically take them for granted. Yet our physical capacities do tend to decline as we grow older, as we observed in the preceding chapter.

We must therefore ask: how do our sensory and perceptual abilities change with increasing age? Should you expect to suffer serious sensory losses on reaching old age, or only minor impairments that will have little effect on your daily functioning? Are some kinds of tasks more seriously affected by sensory losses than others, so that older adults should be advised to avoid certain activities or jobs? This chapter will concentrate primarily on vision and audition, the two most widely researched senses. We will also discuss smell, taste, touch, and kinesthesis (the sense of position and movement, which can be a serious problem for some elderly individuals).

Vision

Declines in visual ability may well have important practical consequences for older adults. Gradually changing vision may be the reason for gradually decreasing mobility and independence, increased isolation, the occurrence of frightening visual impressions, and significant reductions in income (Yurick et al., 1984). As with other aspects of aging, however, the magnitude of age-related visual changes varies considerably from one individual to another.

The Anatomy of the Visual System

THE LENS. Most visual sensations originate in some external object, which emits or (more often) reflects certain amounts and wavelengths of light. The **lens** of the eye bends the light rays which pass through it in order to project a suitably sharp, inverted image on the retina (discussed below). The eye is able to focus on different objects because a set of muscles makes appropriate changes in the shape of the lens: it is flattened when the object is at a distance and thickened when the object is closer. These adjustments are known as **accommodation.** (See Figure 4.1.)

Interestingly, recent research suggests that the lens continues to grow and develop throughout the adult life span. New fibers continually cover older ones, similar to the growth rings found in tree trunks. Thus the lens contains cells derived from all age periods (Ohrloff & Hockwin, 1983; Tripathi & Tripathi, 1983).

THE IRIS. The **iris,** a muscle which surrounds the pupillary opening, controls the amount of light that enters the eye. It contracts when there is a significant increase in light and dilates when the illumination decreases, with the pupil changing size accordingly (the **pupillary reflex**).

THE RETINA. The **retina** serves a particularly important function: it transforms the incoming light energy into nerve impulses that can be communicated to the brain.

There are two kinds of photoreceptor cells in the retina, cones and rods. (See Figure 4.2.) **Cones** are most plentiful in the **fovea,** a small circular region located at the center of the retina, and more sparse toward the periphery. The cones make daytime vision possible, since they respond to high levels of illumination, and they are

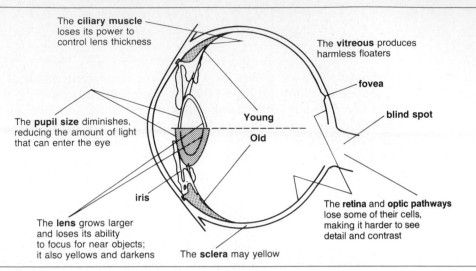

The **ciliary muscle** loses its power to control lens thickness

The **vitreous** produces harmless floaters

fovea

blind spot

Young

Old

The **pupil size** diminishes, reducing the amount of light that can enter the eye

iris

The **lens** grows larger and loses its ability to focus for near objects; it also yellows and darkens

The **sclera** may yellow

The **retina** and **optic pathways** lose some of their cells, making it harder to see detail and contrast

FIGURE 4.1   Anatomy of the eye: Major structures and anatomical differences between young and old. Modified from Weale (1985, p. 31).

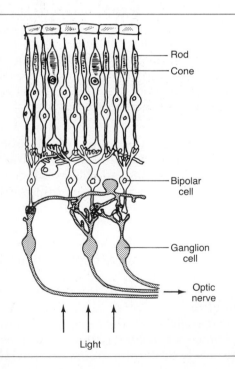

Rod

Cone

Bipolar cell

Ganglion cell

Optic nerve

Light

FIGURE 4.2   Anatomy of the eye: Cones and rods. Gleitman (1983, p. 123); Coren, et al. (1978).

also responsible for all sensations of color. **Rods** are completely absent from the fovea, and are more plentiful in the periphery of the retina. The rods make night vision possible, since they operate at low levels of illumination. However, they convey only colorless sensations. When your eyes take some time to adjust to a dark room after having been exposed to bright light, the size of your pupils increases and you shift from cone vision to rod vision, a process known as **dark adaptation.** We need both kinds of receptors because the range of light to which we are exposed is enormous: the brilliant midday sun is *one hundred billion* times brighter than our absolute threshold, or the dimmest stimulus which the eye is capable of detecting. In all, the eye contains some six million cones and 120 million rods.

THE OPTIC NERVE AND BLIND SPOT.   The cones and rods report to the brain indirectly, through two intermediaries: bipolar cells and ganglion cells. The ganglion cells extend throughout the retina at one end, and converge into a bundle of fibers at the other. This bundle leaves the eyeball as the **optic nerve.** The point where the optic nerve intersects the retina is known as the **blind spot,** since it contains no receptors of any kind and cannot produce any visual sensations at all.

VISUAL ACUITY.   Our visual system enables us to distinguish one object from another, an ability known as **visual acuity.** In daylight, visual acuity is greatest in the fovea, where the cones are most densely bunched. Therefore, to see a particular object most clearly, you must move your eyes so that the object's image falls on both foveas. At night, however, you cannot see a faint star by looking at it directly. Rods are responsible for night vision, and there are none in the fovea. Under these conditions, you must look off at an angle and let the image of the star fall on the periphery of the retina—as experienced sailors know well.

Age-Related Changes in the Visual System

Long before old age, our eyes begin to undergo significant changes. For example, the pupillary reflex responds more slowly after age 50, and the pupils do not dilate as completely. The lens becomes larger, more yellow, and less flexible after age 40. And the cornea, the transparent covering of the iris, decreases in luster by age 40 and increases in curvature and thickness past age 50 (Hunt & Hertzog, 1981). Some of these anatomical changes have important functional consequences.

DARK ADAPTATION.   As we grow older, our eyes adapt to the dark less rapidly and less effectively. (See Figure 4.3; *lower* threshold intensities indicate a *better* ability to see in the dark.) Middle-aged and elderly adults have considerably more difficulty dealing with sudden and pronounced decreases in illumination, as when going from bright sunlight into a darkened movie theater. When designing environments for older adults, therefore, it is important to avoid abrupt transitions in light intensity, shadows, and glare (as might result from shiny floors or the chrome on wheelchairs).

In general, the middle-aged and elderly need a higher level of illumination in order to perceive visual stimuli as well as young adults. Thus older adults are less efficient at tasks that must be performed under low illumination, such as detecting dimly lit signals or patrolling dark areas at night.

ACCOMMODATION.   The process of accommodation also deteriorates with increasing age, particularly between ages 40 and 55 (e.g., Bruckner, 1967). This reduced ability to focus on nearby objects *(presbyopia)* may well necessitate corrective measures, such as reading glasses or bifocals. Tasks like driving an automobile will also be more difficult, since we must often shift our focus back and forth from points far down the road to the gauges directly in front of us.

VISUAL ACUITY.   Our ability to identify stationary objects **(static visual acuity)** shows a decided drop with age; the percentage of adults with 20/20 vision declines markedly after age 45. (See Figure 4.4.) Our ability to identify moving objects **(dynamic visual acuity)** also decreases appreciably as we grow older, though not necessarily at the same rate as static visual acuity (Burg, 1966; Heron & Chown, 1967). In one study, a group of young adults (mean age 33 years) and a group of elderly adults (mean age 66 years) were asked to identify a small road sign while in a moving automobile at night. Although the two groups were matched on static visual acuity, they performed very differently: the younger adults were able to read the sign at distances some 25 percent greater than the elderly subjects (Sivak, Olson, & Pastalan, 1981). This implies that older drivers will react more slowly to road warning signs and to other external stimuli because this task depends on dynamic visual acuity, an ability which has declined. The frequency of driving accidents has also been shown to be positively correlated with dynamic visual acuity, especially for older subjects (Hills, 1980). These findings suggest that the common eye chart is *not* sufficient to predict the performance of middle-aged and elderly adults on tasks like driving an automobile, since it measures only static visual acuity.

In some instances, degenerative changes in the retina may cause

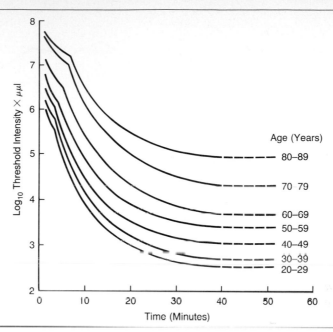

FIGURE 4.3   Dark adaptation as a function of age and time in the dark. Hunt & Hertzog (1981); McFarland et al. (1960).

such severe difficulties that large-print books, magnifiers, and other visual aids are needed. However, these changes normally do not occur until extreme old age (Welford, 1980).

COLOR SENSITIVITY.   The yellowing of the lens after age 40 affects our ability to see certain colors, notably those at the blue-green end of the spectrum. The effect is somewhat like viewing the world through yellow sunglasses: older adults can discern yellows, oranges, and reds more easily than violets, blues, and greens. This is not a serious defect, but it can cause problems under some conditions (e.g., a tennis court illuminated at night with bluish light, or a white soup bowl on a white place mat). For this reason, the color controls on television sets in homes for the elderly must often be set at atypical values in order to make the hues appear more realistic.

THE QUALITY OF VISUAL INFORMATION PROCESSING.   The elderly have somewhat more difficulty recognizing shapes, numbers, letters, and words (Szafran, 1968). The differences between younger and older adults are rather small, however, indicating that age is a relatively minor factor insofar as these visual abilities are concerned.

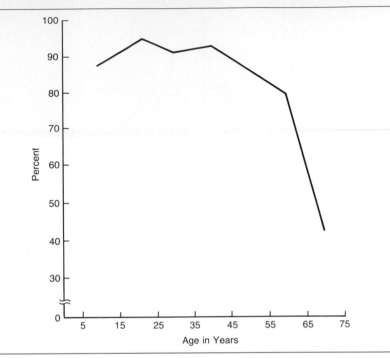

FIGURE 4.4   Percentage of population with 20/20 vision as a function of age. Hunt & Hertzog (1981); Deparmtent of Health, Education, and Welfare (1977).

THE SPEED OF VISUAL INFORMATION PROCESSING.   Numerous studies indicate that we process visual information more slowly as we grow older. In studies of critical flicker frequency, for example, subjects are typically shown a rapidly flashing light. Older adults require a significantly longer interval between the flashes in order to perceive that the light is not on continuously, indicating that the sensitivity of the visual system declines with age. A related experimental procedure is to show subjects a stimulus object, followed shortly thereafter by a masking stimulus which blocks it from view. Here again, the elderly require a significantly longer exposure time in order to identify the original stimulus (Hunt & Hertzog, 1981; Kline & Szafran, 1975; Walsh, 1976).

Some studies require the subject to locate a target object in a field of distracting stimuli as quickly as possible, a task that depends on both sensory processes and decision-making ability. (See Figure 4.5.) Adults age 60 and older perform such visual scanning tasks significantly more slowly than do young adults (e.g., Rabbitt, 1965; 1968; 1977; 1979). This is especially true if the subject must concentrate

Z	N	O	R	E	X	V
L	A	I	Q	B	D	W
S	M	K	E	O	P	Y
E	L	A	X	R	V	Q
N	A	W	O	M	D	C
V	L	O	A	Y	K	J
B	Q	N	S	H	R	U

Task: To mark each horizontal line that contains a "Q" under severe time pressure (e.g., there are 500 lines in all and a one-minute time limit).

FIGURE 4.5   Sample visual scanning task.

on other tasks simultaneously, as when the driver of an automobile must pick out the relevant information from a lengthy road sign while continuing to guide the car. However, there appears to be relatively little decline in visual scanning ability between ages 20 and 50. Thus, if an employer is seeking someone to proofread a manuscript in a brightly lit room, there would be little reason (insofar as

As we grow older, it becomes more difficult to process visual information quickly. This is especially true when we must concentrate on two or more tasks simultaneously, such as trying to glean information from a lengthy road sign while maintaining a safe distance from the car in front.   *Raymond Depardon/Magnum*

this visual ability is concerned) to prefer a 20-year-old to a 40-year-old.

Alternatively, subjects may be asked to detect a target letter flashed on a display screen. Here again, elderly adults perform more poorly if the letter may appear anywhere on the screen, forcing them to divide their attention. But if the target letter always appears at the center of the screen, allowing subjects to focus their attention on a single spot, no significant age differences in performance are obtained. (See Plude & Hoyer, 1985; 1986.)

AFTERWORD.   As we grow older, changes in the eye reduce the quality or intensity of the light that enters the retina. These changes imply that older people are in effect operating under poorer lighting conditions than are young adults, a decline that can be mitigated but not eliminated by increased illumination (Kline & Schieber, 1985; Welford, 1980).

Although the visual system changes considerably during adulthood, our eyes remain our most reliable sense. The deterioration that occurs is not drastic enough to incapacitate older adults, but it can make some visual tasks considerably more difficult. For example, if rapidly moving targets must be detected under conditions of low illumination, young adults will perform this task far better than the middle-aged or elderly. If instead the task requires rapid identification of single, motionless stimuli, young adults may be somewhat superior. But if the task is one of visual scanning, young adults will have little or no advantage over the middle-aged, although the elderly will be at a disadvantage. Thus the negative effects of aging on your visual system tend to be greater for tasks that are more complicated. However, appropriate training can improve the visual performance of older adults on some complicated tasks (Bell & Sekuler, 1986).

Disorders of the Auditory System

COMMON EYE COMPLAINTS.   As we observed in the preceding section, there is a gradual decline in our ability to focus on nearby objects after age 40. Presbyopia cannot be prevented, but it is easily compensated for with eyeglasses or contact lenses.

In bright light, you may observe tiny spots or flecks floating across your field of vision. These "floaters" are normal and usually harmless, although a sudden change in the type or number of spots may indicate a significant problem.

Sometimes the tear glands produce too few tears, resulting in itching and burning sensations or even reduced vision. Such dry eyes can be safely and effectively treated with prescription eyedrops ("artificial tears"). Conversely, excessive tears may result from an increased sensitivity to light, wind, or temperature, or from an eye infection or blocked tear duct. These problems are also readily treated and corrected (National Institute on Aging, 1983a).

MAJOR EYE DISEASES.   Cloudy or opaque areas may develop in part or all of the lens, inhibiting the passage of light and causing a significant decline in vision. (See Figure 4.6.) These **cataracts** usually form gradually, without pain, redness of the eye, or excessive tears; they are most common after age 60. Some recent research evidence suggests that cataract formation may be linked to enzyme modifications, or to changes in the characteristics of lens protein (Hoenders & Bloemendal, 1983; Lerman, 1983; Ohrloff & Hockwin, 1983). Some cataracts remain small enough to be safely ignored. Those large to cause significant problems can be surgically removed, a safe procedure that is almost always successful.

Glaucoma occurs when the fluid pressure in the eye becomes excessive, causing internal damage and gradually destroying one's vision. If glaucoma is detected in its early stages, however, it can usually be controlled well enough to prevent blindness. Common methods for this purpose include prescription eyedrops, oral medication, laser treatments, or perhaps surgery. As with cataracts, the initial stages of glaucoma seldom involve any pain or discomfort, so routine eye examinations of adults over 35 typically include a test for eye pressure (National Institute on Aging, 1983a).

Most serious of all are the **retinal disorders,** which are the leading causes of blindness in the United States. In **senile macular degeneration,** a specialized part of the retina that is responsible for sharp central and reading vision (the macula) loses its ability to function effectively. Warning signs include blurred vision when reading, a dark spot in the center of one's field of vision, and distortion when viewing vertical lines. If detected early enough, senile macular degeneration may be amenable to laser treatments. **Diabetic retinopathy** occurs when small blood vessels that normally nourish the retina fail to function properly. As the name implies, this disease is one of the possible complications resulting from diabetes. The early stages of diabetic retinopathy are denoted by distorted vision, the later stages by serious visual losses. **Retinal detachment,** a separation between the inner and outer layers of the retina, has a more favorable prognosis: detached retinas can usually be surgically reattached well enough to restore good, or at least partial, vision. This is probably the best known of the retinal disorders,

NORMAL VISION—A person with normal vision or vision corrected to 20/20 with glasses sees this street scene. The area of the photographs is the field of vision for the right eye.

CATARACT—An opacity of the lens results in diminished acuity but does not affect the field of vision. There is no scotoma, but the person's vision is hazy overall, particularly in glaring light.

With cataracts, print appears hazy or lacking in contrast.

MACULAR DEGENERATION—The deterioration of the macula, the central area of the retina, is the most prevalent eye disease. This picture shows the area of a decreased central vision called a central scotoma. The peripheral or side vision remains unaffected so mobility need not be impaired.

With macular degeneration, print appears distorted and segments of words may be missing.

GLAUCOMA—Chronic elevated eye pressure in susceptible individuals may cause optic nerve atrophy and loss of peripheral vision. Early detection and close medical monitoring can help reduce complications.

In advanced glaucoma, print may appear faded and words may be difficult to read.

FIGURE 4.6 Effects of some major visual disorders. Courtesy of Lighthouse Low Vision Service, copyright 1985, The New York Association for the Blind.

Most adults maintain good eyesight into their eighties and beyond, although corrective lenses may well be necessary.   *Dan Chidester/Image Works*

due to media coverage of cases involving famous athletes (e.g., champion boxer Sugar Ray Leonard).

AFTERWORD.   It is desirable to have a complete eye examination every two to three years, to permit the early detection of diseases like cataracts and glaucoma. This is especially true for those who have diabetes, or a family history of eye disease. However, visual disorders are by no means inevitable with increasing age. Most of us maintain good eyesight into our eighties and beyond, albeit with the aid of corrective lenses in many cases. Furthermore, we also have the option of adapting the environment in ways that will maximize the visual competence of older adults.

Audition

The Anatomy of the Auditory System

THE EARDRUM.   Auditory sensations are caused by physical movements in the external world, which disturb the surrounding air particles. These particles push other air particles in front of them, ultimately creating a chain reaction of sound waves that travel in all directions—much like the ripples that spread when a stone is thrown

Chapter Glossary: Sensation and Perception

Accommodation	The process whereby the eye focuses on objects at different distances. The lens is flattened when viewing an object that is far away, and thickened when an object is closer.
Auditory nerve	The bundle of cells which exits the cochlea and communicates sound impulses to the brain.
Basilar membrane	A membrane which bisects most of the cochlea, lengthwise. Responsible for most (but not all) sensations of pitch.
Blind spot	The point where the optic nerve intersects the retina. Contains no visual receptors, and cannot produce any sensations.
Cataracts	Cloudy or opaque areas which may form in part or all of the lens, inhibiting the passage of light and causing a significant decline in vision. A disorder which can usually be safely resolved through surgery.
Central auditory impairment	An inability to understand language, even though sound detection is not affected. An incurable but rare disorder that results from damage to nerve centers within the brain, as from a stroke or head injury.
Cochlea	A coiled tube in the inner ear, which contains the basilar membrane and auditory hair cells.
Conductive hearing loss	A decline in the ability to perceive external sounds and speech, caused by blockage in the outer and middle ear. Readily amenable to treatment in most instances.
Cones	Photoreceptor cells in the retina that respond to high levels of illumination and are responsible for daytime vision and sensations of color. Most plentiful in the fovea.
Dark adaptation	The process of shifting from cone to rod vision, which enables us to see in a dark room after having been exposed to bright light. Becomes less rapid and less effective as we grow older.
Decibel	A unit for measuring the relative intensities of sound.
Diabetic retinopathy	*See* retinal disorders.
Dynamic visual acuity	The ability to identify a moving object, or features thereof, by sight.

Eardrum	A taut membrane which vibrates in response to sound waves entering the outer ear.
Fovea	A small circular region located at the center of the retina.
Frequency	A variable related to the wavelength of a sound, which we perceive as pitch.
Glaucoma	A disease that occurs when the fluid pressure in the eye becomes excessive, causing internal damage and gradually destroying one's vision.
Gustation	The sense of taste.
Hair cells (of the ear)	The auditory receptors, located in the cochlea.
Hertz	A unit for measuring the frequency of a sound.
Intensity	A variable related to the energy or amplitude of a sound, which we perceive as loudness.
Iris	A muscle which surrounds the pupillary opening, and controls the amount of light entering the eye.
Kinesthesis	The sense of balance, which arises from sensations of movement or strain in the muscles, tendons, and joints.
Lens	Part of the eye which bends the light rays passing through it, in order to produce a sharply focused image on the retina.
Loudness	The quantity of sound that is perceived by an individual.
Olfaction	The sense of smell.
Optic nerve	The bundle of cells which exits the retina and communicates visual impulses to the brain.
Ossicles	Three small bones which communicate incoming sound vibrations from the eardrum to the oval window.
Oval window	A membrane which separates the middle ear from the inner ear, and communicates sound vibrations from the third ossicle to the fluid in the cochlea.
Pitch	The quality of a sound that is perceived by an individual, as with different notes on the musical scale.
Presbycusis	A progressive loss of hearing in both ears for high-frequency tones; often involves difficulty in understanding speech. Onset is gradual, and becomes pronounced after age 50.

Presbyopia	A gradual decline in our ability to focus on nearby objects; normally occurs after age 40.
Pupillary reflex	An automatic contraction (dilation) of the pupil of the eye when there is a significant increase (decrease) in illumination.
Retina	Part of the eye that transforms incoming light energy into impulses that can be communicated to the brain. Includes the cones, rods, and fovea.
Retinal detachment	*See* retinal disorders.
Retinal disorders	The most common causes of blindness in the United States. Varieties include senile macular degeneration, wherein a specialized part of the retina that is responsible for sharp central and reading vision loses its ability to function effectively; diabetic retinopathy, which occurs when small blood vessels that normally nourish the retina fail to function properly; and retinal detachment, a separation between the inner and outer layers of the retina.
Rods	Photoreceptor cells in the retina that respond to low levels of illumination, and are responsible for night vision. Most plentiful in the periphery of the retina, and completely absent from the fovea.
Senile macular degeneration	*See* retinal disorders.
Somesthesis	Sensations that arise from stimulation of the skin, viscera, and kinesthetic receptors.
Static visual acuity	The ability to identify a stationary object, or features thereof, by sight. Usually refers to situations where the observer is also stationary.
Visual acuity	The ability to distinguish one object from another by sight.

into a lake. Some of these sound waves are collected by the outer ear and funneled toward a taut membrane, the **eardrum,** which responds by vibrating. (See Figure 4.7.)

THE OSSICLES AND OVAL WINDOW.   The eardrum transmits its vibrations across an air-filled cavity, the middle ear, by way of a mechanical bridge. This connecting link consists of three small bones (**ossicles**), which respond to the vibrations of the eardrum by mov-

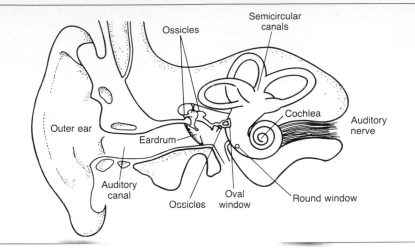

FIGURE 4.7   Anatomy of the ear: Major structures. Gleitman (1983, p. 119); Lindsay & Norman (1977).

ing in sequence. The third ossicle imparts the initial vibratory pattern to a membrane which separates the middle ear from the inner ear (the **oval window**).

THE COCHLEA AND AUDITORY NERVE.   The movement of the oval window creates waves in the fluid which fills the **cochlea,** a coiled tube in the inner ear. The pressure resulting from these waves causes deformations in the **basilar membrane,** which bisects the cochlea throughout most of its length. (See Figure 4.8.)

The anatomical structures described thus far are merely accessories, which conduct and amplify the sound waves so that they can affect the true auditory receptors—**hair cells** lodged near the basilar membrane. The deformations of this membrane stimulate the hair cells by bending them, whereupon the cells communicate appropriate sound impulses to the brain via the **auditory nerve.** Thus our sense of hearing depends on mechanical pressures within the ear, yet it is capable of detecting stimuli that are far away. As a result, the auditory sense has been likened to feeling at a distance (Gleitman, 1983).

LOUDNESS AND PITCH.   The brain transforms physical sensations of sound into two psychological dimensions, **loudness** and **pitch.** Sounds are louder when the original movements in the environment are more intense, increasing the height (amplitude) of the resulting sound waves. Higher pitches are heard when the frequency

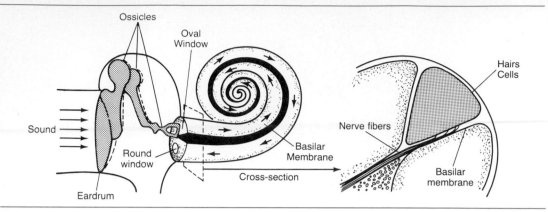

FIGURE 4.8   Anatomy of the ear: The middle ear and cochlea. Gleitman
(1983, p. 120); Lindsay & Norman (1977); Coren et al. (1978).

of the sound waves is greater (i.e., when there are more waves per
second). At higher frequencies, the sensation of pitch is determined
by the place on the basilar membrane where the peak deformation
occurs: the closer this maximum point is to one end of the membrane, the higher (lower) the pitch that we experience. At low frequencies, however, deformation is equal throughout the basilar
membrane. Here, pitch is determined instead by the firing frequency of the auditory nerve. Finally, for moderate frequencies, pitch
is probably related to both the place and firing frequency mechanisms.

The intensity of a sound, which we perceive as loudness, is measured in **decibels.** Zero decibels corresponds to our threshold of
hearing; a whisper is about 20 decibels; normal conversation is approximately 60 decibels; shouting is about 100 decibels; and the
loudest rock band on record registered some 160 decibels (which is
about 20 decibels *higher* than the threshold of pain!). The frequency
of a sound, which we perceive as pitch, is usually measured in **hertz**
(or kilohertz, where one kHz = 1,000 hertz). The piano ranges from
27.5 hertz at its lowest note through 261.6 hertz (middle C) to 4,180
hertz at its highest note. Young adults can hear tones from 20 to
20,000 hertz, with the greatest sensitivity occurring at the middle of
this region.

Age-Related Changes in the Auditory System

SENSITIVITY TO TONES AND PITCH.   Most often, methods for
measuring our hearing use pure tones as the test stimuli. Losses in

our ability to detect these tones begin to occur by about age 40, although pronounced changes are not evident until some time later. For example, the typical 30-year-old male can detect a 6 kHz tone (6,000 hertz) at a volume of about 4 decibels, which is softer than the rustling of leaves. Yet the same tone must be presented to the average 65-year-old man at approximately 40 decibels, the level of normal conversation, in order to be heard. (Average tone sensitivities for men in Western industrial society, as a function of age, are shown in Figure 4.9.) The greatest declines occur at frequencies above 2.5 kHz, due primarily to atrophy and degeneration of the hair cells and supporting mechanisms in the cochlea. To the extent that a job requires the detection and/or discrimination of middle- to high-frequency tones, many middle-aged and elderly adults may well be at a significant disadvantage. Older adults may also have more difficulty understanding words that are shouted, since this often increases the pitch of the voice as well as the loudness.

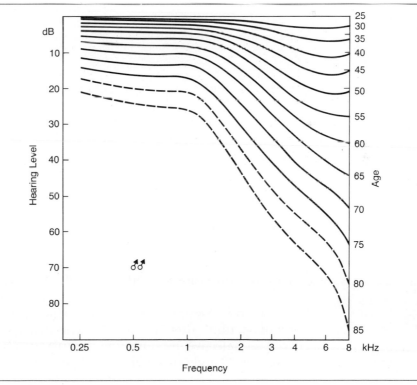

FIGURE 4.9   Ability to detect pure tones as a function of age and frequency (data for men only). Hunt & Hertzog (1981).

The ability to detect middle to high frequency tones declines with increasing age. But it is still possible to perform competently on many auditory tasks, as in the case of this elderly music teacher.   *Alan Carey/Image Works*

SPEECH PERCEPTION.   Our ability to perceive and understand speech also declines with increasing age, although the magnitude of this loss depends to a considerable extent on prevailing listening conditions. In one study (Bergman, 1976), speech perception was studied under three markedly different conditions:

- *Normal speech:* No background noise or interference.

- *Selective listening:* Trying to understand one person's speech with competing voices in the background.

- *Interrupted speech:* Trying to understand speech that is interrupted electronically several times per second, as might happen if a radio program were afflicted with intermittent static.

As shown in Figure 4.10, little decline was found in normal speech perception until after age 60. A somewhat greater decrement occurred in selective listening, amounting to about 10 percent between ages 20 and 50 and almost 20 percent by age 70. The greatest impairment was found in our ability to perceive interrupted speech: this loss was approximately 35 percent between ages 20 and 50, and

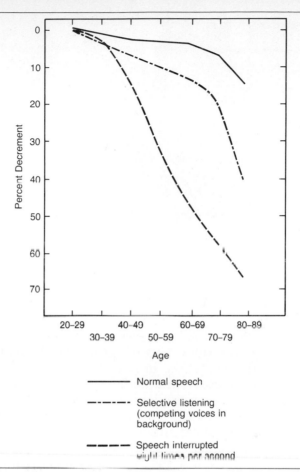

FIGURE 4.10   Ability to perceive speech under different listening conditions: Percent decrement from age 20 years. Bergman, et al. (1976).

reached 60 percent by age 70. These decrements are generally attributed to an increase in the time required by the auditory cortex to process the incoming information, and to changes in the peripheral nervous system. Such findings indicate the importance of securing good listening conditions, and improving the acoustic properties of buildings, where older adults are concerned. It may also be helpful to maximize visual communication cues, as by seating nursing home residents face to face in dining rooms and lounges so they can observe one another's lip movements and facial expressions.

Since the ability to perceive and understand speech differs from

Not all declines in auditory ability are due to increasing age. Some are caused by environmental events in our noise-ridden, industrialized society. *Joel Gordon*

the ability to perceive pure tones, standard audiological evaluations now include tests of speech discrimination as well as tone discrimination. Where indicated by the subjects' symptoms, tests of more complex central auditory functions are also conducted. In view of these complications, hearing tests should be performed by a qualified audiologist, rather than by a hearing aid dealer or lay person. The trained audiologist is also able to assess the extent to which an individual is handicapped by the degree of hearing loss indicated by the test scores. This assessment requires an understanding of the subject's living and working environment.

AFTERWORD: AGING VERSUS ENVIRONMENT.   Compared to vision, our hearing suffers considerably more of a decline as we grow older. However, not all changes in the auditory system are due to increasing age. Certain environmental events can produce marked impairments in hearing, notably the exposure to intense high-frequency noise for a long period of time.

For example, significant noise-related hearing losses and even deafness are common among rock musicians (Kryter, 1970). When a large sample of Wisconsin residents was compared with members of a less technological (and less noisy) culture, Sudanese tribesmen, the latter showed much smaller losses in hearing with increasing age (Bergman, 1980). Cordless telephones, which have the ringer in the earpiece, and personal stereos, which deliver intense sound more

directly to the eardrum through earphones, are currently being
evaluated as potentially serious sources of hearing loss. In fact, it
appears that the United States population as a whole is becoming
increasingly hard of hearing: from 1940 to 1980, the incidence rate
of deafness increased from under 200 per 10,000 to approximately
300 per 10,000 (Hunt & Hertzog, 1981).

If we were to consider only our own culture, we might erroneously conclude that substantial declines in hearing with increasing
age are an inescapable part of the human condition. In actuality,
however, both aging and our environment contribute to the hearing
losses commonly found among middle-aged and elderly Americans.
The atrophy of our auditory system is one price that we pay for
living in a noise-ridden, industrialized society. To be sure, our society does pay some attention to preventing such losses; employees
who operate noisy machinery, and adults who practice with hand-
guns or rifles at firing ranges, may well be required to wear industrial earmuffs or earplugs. Yet given the prevalence of noise that
we encounter, it is by no means unlikely that tomorrow's adult
Americans will also experience significant hearing troubles, perhaps
even more than we do today.

Disorders of the Auditory System

PRESBYCUSIS.   Some 13 percent of Americans over the age of 65
show advanced signs of **presbycusis.** This disorder involves a progressive loss of hearing in both ears for high-frequency tones, which
is often accompanied by severe difficulty in understanding speech
(Matlin, 1984). Presbycusis results from the deterioration of mechanisms in the inner ear; this may be caused by aging, long-term
exposure to loud noises, certain drugs, an improper diet, or genetic
factors. The onset of this disorder is gradual, and it typically becomes pronounced after age 50.

Hearing aids alone are unlikely to resolve this problem. They serve
to amplify sounds in the external world, yet speech will remain distorted because of the inner ear degeneration. Speech reading, in-
formational counseling, and hearing aid orientation are important
aspects of comprehensive aural rehabilitation with patients suffering from presbycusis (Garstecki, 1981).

CONDUCTIVE HEARING LOSS.   **Conductive hearing loss** occurs
when sound waves are unable to travel properly through the outer
and middle ear. This disorder is caused by impediments in the ear,

such as dense wax, excessive fluid, an abnormal bone growth, or an infection. Sufferers experience external sounds and other people's voices as muffled, while their own voices appear louder than normal. This disorder is less common than presbycusis, and can usually be resolved through flushing of the ear, medication, or surgery.

CENTRAL AUDITORY IMPAIRMENT.   Those who suffer from **central auditory impairment** have great difficulty understanding language. However, the ability to detect external sounds is not affected. This rare disorder is caused by damage to the nerve centers within the brain, which typically results from an extended illness with a high fever, lengthy exposure to loud noises, the use of certain drugs, head injuries, vascular problems, or tumors. Unlike presbycusis, central auditory impairment may occur at any age; it may also interact with presbycusis in older adults. There is no cure for central auditory impairment, although rehabilitation by an audiologist or speech-language pathologist may be helpful in some instances (National Institute on Aging, 1983b).

AFTERWORD.   It has been estimated that 30 percent of all adults between the ages of 65 and 74, and 50 percent of those between 75 and 79, suffer some degree of hearing loss. In the United States alone, the total amounts to more than 10 million older people (National Institute on Aging, 1983b). In fact, hearing impairments rank second only to arthritis among the leading health problems of senior adults (Harris, 1978).

Hearing disorders have significant practical consequences: failing to understand what other people are saying, which may significantly affect relationships with family and friends; letting a ringing telephone or doorbell go unanswered and missing an important caller; being unable to enjoy movies, plays, concerts, and television programs without closed captions; having to give up driving an automobile because the warning signal of an ambulance or fire engine cannot be heard. In addition, stimuli such as the plumbing sounds from another room or the wind rustling in the trees provide an important auditory background that helps us to keep in touch with our surroundings. When hearing-impaired persons cannot detect these background stimuli, they may well become afraid to venture out into all but the most familiar environments. As a result, hearing losses have caused elderly people to be incorrectly diagnosed as confused, unresponsive, uncooperative, or even pathologically depressed, thereby denying them help that would have been readily available. Hearing impairments may even lead to true depression, with sufferers becoming so frustrated at their inability to communicate with other people (or so suspicious because others always seem to mumble incoherently) that they withdraw from social interactions.

Despite these serious consequences, all too many adults steadfastly refuse to admit that they have a hearing problem. Whether this defensive behavior is due to fear, vanity, or misinformation, it is clearly unwise. Most hearing impairments are amenable to treatment, at least to some extent; so the best course is to face the issue squarely, and seek appropriate medical assistance. The most common method for improving the hearing of elderly patients is through the amplification provided by an appropriate hearing aid (Rappaport, 1984). Hearing aids may take various forms, such as an instrument that hooks behind the ear, an amplifier built into the temple of a pair of eyeglasses, a device worn inside the ear, or a larger receiver carried in a shirt pocket. (See Figure 4.11.) One or two hearing aids may be worn, depending on the extent and nature of the hearing loss. Hearing aids do not restore hearing to normal, and the quality of sound obtained through a hearing aid is much different from what the healthy individual hears without one. So older adults may well show some resistance to such aids or have difficulty in adjusting to them. It may therefore be desirable to have the patient's spouse, or other close relative or friend, participate in the sessions with the audiologist and provide encouragement and support. Nevertheless, the benefits provided by the hearing aid are likely to be well worth the initial difficulties. Hearing is the sense most affected by aging, so it is important to be aware of the need for possible corrective action as one grows past middle age.

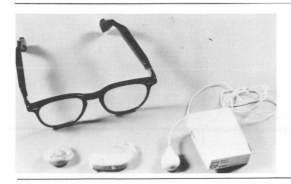

FIGURE 4.11   Typical hearing aids. Rappaport (1984, p. 116).

Taste and Smell

Our senses of taste and smell are closely interrelated. For example, both of these senses play an essential role in determining the desirability of various foods. It is therefore difficult to study these senses separately, although some researchers have sought to do so. Partly for this reason, and partly because few older adults express serious complaints about impaired taste and/or smell, there is relatively little age-related data to draw upon in this area.

Taste (Gustation)

TASTE SENSITIVITY AND AGING.   Sensory researchers have identified four primary qualities of taste: sweet, bitter, sour, and salty. Taste sensitivity experiments typically present the subject with a solution based on one primary quality (e.g., a sucrose solution in the case of sweetness), and a separate quantity of water. The keener the subject's sensitivity to, say, sweetness, the smaller the concentration of sucrose that can be differentiated from plain water.

Several studies suggest that adults past age 50 have more difficulty detecting all four primary taste sensations (e.g., Byrd & Gertman, 1959; Cooper, Bilash, & Zubek, 1959; Schiffman, 1977). In general, however, the data are equivocal: different research methods (such as stimulating the tongue with a weak galvanic current), or even the same methods used by different investigators, have at times produced conflicting results (Engen, 1977). This may be due in part to bias caused by factors related to age, such as poor health, which affect the taste sensitivity of older adults. Some recent findings suggest that while older adults may have a higher threshold for detecting taste sensations, they are just as good as young adults at discriminating among different sensations that are above threshold (Bartoshuk et al., 1986).

TASTE PREFERENCES AND AGING.   Our senses of taste and smell discriminate more effectively among different substances (qualitatively) than among different concentrations of the same substance (quantitatively). Nevertheless, even less research has been conducted on age-related taste preferences than on sensitivity. In one study, such different foods as corned beef and apples were liquefied in a blender to remove all textural cues; the results suggested that older adults dislike bitter stimuli more than younger subjects do (Engen, 1977).

Smell (Olfaction)

OLFACTORY SENSITIVITY AND AGING.   Several studies have found that our ability to detect various odors declines with age (e.g., Kimbrell & Furchgott, 1963; Rous, 1969; Schiffman & Pasternak, 1979). In one recent study, 1,955 volunteers ranging in age from 5 to 99 were tested with 40 chemically simulated scents that included cinnamon, cherry, pizza, gasoline, tobacco, mint, soap, grass, lemon, motor oil, and root beer. The results suggested that olfactory ability is usually at its best between the ages of 20 and 40, begins to diminish slightly by age 50 and 50, and declines rapidly after age 70. Among subjects aged 65–80, some 60 percent suffered severe losses in olfactory sensitivity, while about 25 percent lost all ability to smell. For those over 80, the proportion with severe olfactory losses was 80 percent, while nearly half could not smell anything (Doty, cited by Rensberger, 1984). Another study, based on two small samples of adults, age 18–26 and 66–93, found that the older group required a stimulus twice as strong in order to detect the smell of menthol (Murphy, 1983). Furthermore, it has been argued that age-related declines in olfactory sensitivity are related to declines in gustatory sensitivity. Murphy (1985) compared the ability of young adult women (mean age 19 years) and elderly women (mean age 71 years) to identify blended foods. When the subjects were allowed to use all of their senses, the younger group performed significantly better. But when the subjects were prevented from using their sense of smell by having their nostrils pinched closed, the performance of the younger group fell to the same level as that of the older group. The older subjects also had more difficulty with the cognitive aspects of this task, such as finding ways to name and recall these unusual odorless food stimuli (a topic that will be discussed in the next chapter).

However, other findings suggest that odor sensitivity remains quite stable as we grow older (Rovee, Cohen, & Shlapack, 1975). As with taste, poor health may be most responsible for losses in olfactory sensitivity. Thus some reviewers have concluded that once confounding variables associated with age are eliminated, the sense of smell appears to be unaffected by age per se (Matlin, 1984).

OLFACTORY PREFERENCES AND AGING.   Although the elderly appear to have different odor preferences than children, these differences are seen at about age 30 and cannot be attributed to aging (Engen, 1977). Here again, those elderly adults who report little difference among pleasant and unpleasant stimuli are likely to do so because of poor health rather than aging per se.

Myths About Aging: Sensation and Perception

MYTH	*BEST AVAILABLE EVIDENCE*
The majority of elderly adults suffer such serious visual deterioration that they require major visual aids, such as large-print books and magnifiers.	Most of us maintain good eyesight into our eighties and beyond. (Eyeglasses or contact lenses may well be necessary, however, since the percent of adults with 20/20 vision does decline markedly after age 45.) Large-print books and magnifiers are normally not necessary until extreme old age.
The effects of aging are much the same for all visual tasks.	Some visual abilities decline significantly more with increasing age than do others. Tasks that involve perceiving objects that are dimly lit, moving, or masked by other stimuli become considerably more difficult after middle age, while locating a target object in a field of distracting stimuli becomes more difficult after about age 60. In general, the effects of aging are more pronounced on visual tasks that are more complicated.
The majority of elderly adults suffer such serious auditory deterioration that they have considerable difficulty perceiving speech and loud sounds.	Hearing is the sense most affected by aging, and there is some indication that the population of the United States is becoming increasingly hard of hearing. But serious hearing impairments are the exception rather than the rule, especially among those who obtain regular hearing checkups after middle age.
Those hearing losses that do occur among elderly Americans are due exclusively to aging.	The hearing losses suffered by Americans are caused in part by environmental conditions and events, notably the long-term exposure to such intense noise as rock music and loud industrial machinery. Thus some less-technological cultures show considerably smaller losses in hearing with increasing age.

AFTERWORD. Given the paucity of research in this area, and the various conflicting results, it is difficult to make any definitive statements about the relationship between aging, taste, and smell. If recent findings concerning olfactory losses are replicated by future research, and if it is also shown that these losses are *not* due to poor health or other confounding factors, more pessimistic conclusions about this sense may then be justified.

Somesthesis: The Skin and Kinesthetic Senses

The Skin Senses

Data concerning the skin senses are also sparse, often dated, and frequently contradictory. Furthermore, any decrements in somesthetic sensitivity among the elderly may well be due to the more frequent occurrence of disease and injury, rather than to aging per se.

TOUCH. The importance of our sense of touch is easily taken for granted. Nevertheless, this sense is involved in many important behaviors: judging the smoothness of a piece of wood or the closeness of a shave, identifying a switch on the automobile console without taking one's eyes off the road, caressing a loved one. There is some indication that a small percentage of the aged experience a decline in touch sensitivity. Yet it has also been suggested that tactile sensitivity increases with age, because the skin of elderly adults deforms more easily and exposes more touch spots to external stimuli. (See, for example, Jalavisto, Orma, & Tawast, 1951; Zwislocki, 1960.)

VIBRATION. Changes in vibratory sensitivity are helpful in diagnosing and assessing disorders of the nervous system. It appears that some older adults are significantly less sensitive than young adults to vibratory stimuli, particularly in the lower extremities (Goff et al., 1965; Perret & Regli, 1970). However, such decrements have not been shown to have any notable practical consequences for those individuals who do experience them.

TEMPERATURE. The temperature sensitivities and preferences of older adults do not appear to differ in any significant way from those of younger subjects (Rohles, 1969). But the ability to cope with cold temperatures and maintain bodily warmth, and the ability to cope with hot environments, decline with increasing age (Finch, 1977; Krag & Kountz, 1950). This may explain in part why mortality rates increase among the elderly when there are sudden and extreme changes in ambient temperature.

Seasonal variation in mortality has been shown to occur in all American states, even those with temperate climates. (See Table 4.1.) This suggests that factors other than the acute effect of low absolute temperature contribute to these variations, such as abrupt temperature changes. The magnitude of the seasonal effect on mortality is large: during the coldest month of 1979 (January), there were approximately 20,000 more deaths from all causes and 12,000 more deaths from heart disease than for the warmest month (August). (See Anderson & Rochard, 1979; Collins et al., 1977.)

PAIN.   Given the increased likelihood of pathology among the elderly, any age-related changes in pain sensitivity would have important practical consequences. Perhaps for this reason, pain is the skin sense most often subjected to age-related studies. Unfortunately, these data are highly contradictory: many studies report a marked decline in pain sensitivity with increasing age, numerous others find no such decrements (e.g., Harkins et al., 1986), and a few even report increased pain sensitivity among older adults (Kenshalo, 1977).

This issue may perhaps be resolved in part by examining sensitivity to different types of pain as a function of age. For example, it may be that older adults experience reduced pain sensitivity to superficial somatic pain, but show increased sensitivity and decreased tolerance to deep somatic pain (Newton, 1984).

Kinesthesis

One important and distressing problem faced by the elderly is their susceptibility to falls, and the sometimes fatal complications that result. Such falls may be caused by dizziness, by muscular weakness, or by decreased input from the **kinesthetic** receptors that detect movements or strain in the muscles, tendons, and joints. Once again, however, the evidence is equivocal: there are studies which report little or no decline in kinesthetic sensitivity with advanced age, and others that find some deterioration (Kenshalo, 1977).

Afterword

Here again, the available data are too equivocal to permit any definitive conclusions. Some older adults may experience some declines in somesthetic sensitivity, but the great majority probably need not be concerned about the possibility of serious deterioration.

TABLE 4.1 Average number of deaths per day, by age and month, in the United States (1979).

Age[1]	Total	January	February	March	April	May	June	July	August	September	October	November	December
All ages[1]	5,251	5,576	5,465	5,286	5,270	5,201	5,091	5,030	4,840	5,007	5,254	5,335	5,573
Under 45 years	603	576	580	590	588	610	625	634	614	619	602	599	603
45–64 years	1,159	1,237	1,211	1,173	1,173	1,156	1,134	1,123	1,105	1,093	1,153	1,158	1,196
65–74 years	1,233	1,304	1,290	1,249	1,245	1,224	1,192	1,178	1,164	1,165	1,233	1,252	1,302
75 years and over	2,254	2,457	2,382	2,273	2,262	2,209	2,138	2,093	2,056	2,128	2,265	2,324	2,472

[1] Includes figures for age not stated.
SOURCE: Feinleib (1984).

It is not clear whether our sense of position and movement declines with increasing age. But older adults are more susceptible to falls, and to the sometimes fatal complications that may result.   *Raymond Depardon/Magnum*

In comparison with vision and audition, little is known about the relationship between aging and our other senses. Whether this gap in our knowledge exists because the issue is relatively unimportant (i.e., these other senses change very little as we grow older), or because researchers have found these questions to be too difficult or too uninteresting to investigate, is a question that is as yet unanswered.

Summary

VISION

The lens bends the light rays passing through it in order to project a suitably sharp image on the retina, while the iris controls the amount of light that enters the eye. The retina transforms light energy into nerve impulses with the aid of two kinds of photoreceptor cells: cones are responsible for day vision and sensations of color, while rods are responsible for night vision. The shift from cone to rod vision is known as dark adaptation.

As we grow older, dark adaptation becomes less rapid and less effective. It becomes increasingly more difficult to focus on nearby objects, and to shift back and forth rapidly between far and near objects. The ability to identify both stationary and moving objects declines, with some older individuals experiencing greater losses in dynamic visual acuity. It becomes more difficult to discern colors at the blue-green end of the spectrum, and visual information processing takes place more slowly. These changes are not debilitating, but they do make certain tasks considerably more difficult to perform.

Common eye complaints include presbyopia, floaters, dry eyes, and excessive tearing. These problems are usually readily amenable to treatment. Major eye diseases include cataracts, glaucoma, and the retinal disorders, the last of these representing the leading causes of blindness in the United States. Although eye ailments are common enough to warrant complete examinations every few years, most older adults maintain good eyesight into their eighties and beyond, albeit with the aid of corrective lenses in many instances.

AUDITION

External sound waves are collected by the outer ear and funneled toward the eardrum, which responds by vibrating. These vibrations are then transmitted via the ossicles, oval window, cochlear fluid, and basilar membrane to the auditory receptors, the cochlear hair cells. The brain transforms physical sensations of sound into two psychological dimensions. The intensity of a sound, which we perceive as loudness, is measured in decibels. The frequency of a sound, which we perceive as pitch, is measured in hertz or kilohertz.

Losses in our ability to detect pure tones begin by about age 40, but do not become pronounced until some time later. The greatest declines occur at frequencies above 2.5 kHz. Declines in our ability to understand speech normally do not become pronounced until after age 50; the extent of these losses depends in large part on prevailing listening conditions. Hearing tests include tests of tone discrimination and speech discrimination, and should be conducted by a trained audiologist. Auditory losses may result from aging, from such environmental conditions as prolonged exposure to intense noise, and from various ear diseases.

Major auditory disorders include presbycusis, conductive hearing loss, and central auditory impairment. Audition is the sense most affected by aging: about 30 percent of all adults between ages 65 and 74, and 50 percent of those between 75 and 79, suffer some degree of hearing loss. Yet all too many older adults refuse to admit that they have a hearing problem, with the result that some have been incorrectly diagnosed as unresponsive, uncooperative, or even pathologically depressed.

TASTE AND SMELL

Several studies suggest that adults past age 50 have more difficulty detecting all of the four primary taste sensations, but the data in this area are equivocal. Very few studies have dealt with age-related taste preferences; one experiment suggests that older adults dislike bitter stimuli more than do younger subjects.

Data concerning age-related changes in olfactory sensitivity are also contradictory. One recent large-scale study reported substantial losses in sensitivity after age 70; an earlier study found that this ability remains stable as we grow older. Changes in odor preference are unlikely to occur after age 30. For both taste and smell, losses in sensitivity most often result from poor health rather than from aging per se.

SOMESTHESIS: THE SKIN AND KINESTHETIC SENSES

Data concerning the skin senses are also sparse, often dated, and frequently equivocal. Some declines with increasing age have been observed in touch and vibratory sensitivity, and in the ability to cope with cold temperatures. Some studies report a marked decline in pain sensitivity with increasing age; others do not. Here again, decrements in sensitivity are probably due more to the increased likelihood of disease and injury at older ages than to aging per se.

One important problem faced by the elderly is their susceptibility to potentially fatal falls. There is some indication that this may be due in part to decreased input from the various kinesthetic receptors.

As compared to vision and audition, little is known about the relationship between aging and our other senses. However, the growing research interest in these topics suggests that important new information may well become available in the not-too-distant future.

CHAPTER 5

Learning and Memory

No one has ever seen memories, yet they pervade our everyday life. Memory makes it possible for you to recall your loved one's names and faces, what foods you like and where to obtain them, where you can safely sleep at night, how to do your job or perform your favorite sport, whether or not you liked last night's date or last month's vacation, previous events in the novel that you have not yet finished reading—and even your own identity, which depends on a continuous sense of self that links your past with your present. Without this invaluable ability, you would be forced to live from one disconnected moment to the next, trying to discover over and over again the information that would enable you to survive.

The ability to learn is also vital to our existence. Learning enables you to outgrow the dependency of infancy and childhood, and become a self-sufficient adult. Because you are able to learn, you can develop new skills and hobbies. You can profit from your painful or disappointing mistakes by switching to behaviors that are more rewarding. You can have a child and care for it properly, even though you have never done so before. You can move to a new city and become able to negotiate unfamiliar terrain without getting lost. You can acquire new friends, or pursue a new romance. Without the ability to learn, these activities would be impossible. Your knowledge would forever be frozen at a constant level; you would be unable to recognize potential new friends the next time you saw them, or to become familiar with street names and directions in your new home city. In fact, you would be unable to cope with *any* situation that you did not already know how to handle.

Because learning and memory are so essential to survival, many older adults are even more fearful about the prospect of declines in these abilities than they are about the possibility of sensory and physical impairments. In the preceding two chapters, we have seen that many of our physiological mechanisms do decline to varying degrees with increasing age; these include physical strength and endurance, circulation, respiration, excretion, audition, and vision. Memory and learning also depend to a considerable extent on physiological processes. Therefore, we must ask: what changes occur in these important cognitive functions as we grow older?

This is not an easy question to answer. One problem is methodological: suppose that we try to determine the relationship between aging, learning, and memory by comparing the performance of younger and older adults on a variety of cognitive tasks (the cross-sectional method). There are various reasons why older adults might perform more poorly, other than declines in the ability to learn and remember. For example, middle-aged and elderly adults may be less motivated to do well on apparently meaningless laboratory tasks. Their educational level may well be lower than that of young adults. Their health may be significantly poorer. Or they may have had fewer recent opportunities to practice their cognitive skills because they have long since left school, or have retired from their jobs. That is, inferior performance by older adults could be due largely to cohort effects, rather than to aging. If instead we try to minimize cohort effects by conducting a lengthy longitudinal study, our results may prove to be obsolete when the study is completed some 10 or 15 years later; the field of learning and memory is currently undergoing continuous and extensive changes (Hartley, Harker, & Walsh, 1980). For these reasons, obtaining accurate age-related data in the experimental laboratory can be a highly challenging task.

Another problem faced by researchers in this area involves the conceptual distinction between learning and memory, which is far from clearcut. You cannot remember something unless your previously acquired at least some knowledge of it, a phenomenon that sounds very much like learning. Conversely, one common test of whether or not you have learned something is your ability to remember it at a later date. Thus experimental studies which purportedly deal with memory must of necessity also involve learning, and vice versa.

Furthermore, learning and memory are more complicated constructs than might be apparent. Some years ago, for example, Tulving (1972; 1983) posited two distinct kinds of memory: **episodic memory** records experiences in terms of time and place, while **semantic memory** involves our storehouse of general knowledge about the meanings of words, numbers, symbols, and their interrelationships. If you recall that you ate a hamburger and french fries for lunch yesterday, and where this meal took place, you are relying on your episodic memory. That is, you are remembering the time and

place of a specific personal event, without making any effort to analyze or understand it. Your memory of what hamburgers and french
fries are, where they come from, and how to calculate the bill is
quite a different matter. You may readily recall that hamburgers
are a form of meat obtained from livestock, and that french fries
are made from a vegetable taken from the earth (potatoes), but it is
very unlikely that you remember precisely when and where you first
acquired this knowledge. These understandings are aspects of semantic memory, which is concerned with abstract and conceptual
relationships. Semantic memories tend to last much longer than episodic memories; you will probably always remember that potatoes
grow in the ground and only become french fries later on, yet you
may find it difficult or impossible to recall specific episodes from
five years ago when you ate french fries. One reason for this is that
understanding a concept often requires activating a larger network
of facts and their relations than does merely noting when and where
an event takes place. (Some important episodic memories may be
long lasting, however, such as the date and place of one's marriage.)

Nor does this appear to be the whole story. More recently, Tulving (1985) concluded that the nature of memory is still more complicated: there is a third form, which he calls **procedural memory.**
This type of memory enables us to retain learned connections between stimuli and responses, and to deal adaptively with our environment, without necessarily recalling specific information from the
past. An experienced baseball shortstop can field a ground ball and
quickly throw it to the right base because he has done so many times
before; he does not need to recall previous episodes involving
grounders or understand the reasons for his play in order to follow
the correct procedure. (In fact, if he tries to do so, he will undoubtedly take too long to make the play and the batter will be safe.)
Procedural memory is evidenced only by making the correct overt
response, whereas information from episodic and semantic memory
can be consciously considered, elaborated upon, and used purpo-
sively. While not all theorists agree with this tripartite conception of
memory, it does illustrate the complexities that we will encounter
when we try to ascertain the relationships among aging, memory,
and learning. As we will see, aging may well have quite different
relationships to some kinds of memory and learning than to others.

To date, the two most influential models for studying learning
and memory have been associationism and information processing.
These theories have determined the kinds of research questions that
have been asked in these areas, and the methods used to answer
them. We will therefore begin this chapter by reviewing some of the
major adult developmental findings in the realm of associationism.

Whereas few modern psychologists would characterize themselves as associationists, these data are important because they provided the point of departure for more recent theories. Next we will investigate the currently more popular information-processing model. Our discussion will also touch on important practical issues, such as studies of everyday memory and methods for helping adults to improve their memory and ability to learn.

Associationist Approaches to Learning and Memory

As the name implies, **associationism** attributes all learning and memory to the association of stimuli and responses (S–R) that occur closely together in time. According to this model, learning consists of the formation and strengthening of these S–R bonds. Memory is evidenced when a stimulus is presented, and a response which has been previously associated with this stimulus (i.e., learned) is emitted. And forgetting results when the bond between a stimulus and a response grows weak or disappears.

To illustrate, consider Pavlov's famous experiment on classical conditioning. A dog was presented with a light (or tone); this was immediately followed by food, which caused the dog to salivate. After numerous repetitions of this procedure, the dog regularly salivated

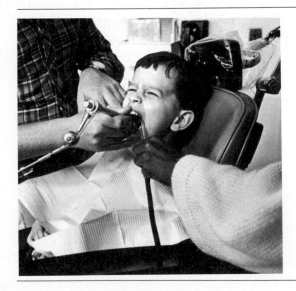

Some fears are due to classical conditioning, for example when the stimulus of the dentist's chair has been repeatedly associated with the pain and discomfort of having one's teeth drilled. *Joel Gordon*

to the light alone. Because the light stimulus and the salivation response repeatedly occurred within a second or so of each other, a
new S–R bond was formed between these elements. Similarly, some
people fear the dentist's chair because of classical conditioning; this
stimulus has repeatedly been associated with the pain and discomfort of having their teeth drilled. That is, an S–R bond has been
formed between the dentist's chair and pain.

Since associationism defines learning and memory in terms of single S–R bonds, how can it explain more complicated forms of behavior? Simple S–R elements may be combined into a lengthy chain,
wherein responses also serve as stimuli. Furthermore, associated
stimuli and responses may be covert as well as overt. For example,
suppose that you are trying to answer an essay question on an examination. Your first response to this stimulus is to write down a
word or sentence, which is possible because you have previously
learned to associate certain aspects of this essay question with other
information. This response then serves as a stimulus that elicits a
subsequent response, such as writing down a second sentence (or
perhaps deciding to erase what you have written and substitute a
better alternative). Here again, you will be able to do this if you
previously formed a strong S–R bond between these ideas. If not,
the first sentence that you wrote down will not elicit any response,
and you will unhappily conclude that you have forgotten the material (or that you failed to learn it well enough). Alternatively, the
first sentence may be associated with information that you decide
not to include in your answer because it is not relevant. But this
information may be associated with yet another idea, which you do
regard as suitable. This chain would then take the form S–r–s–R,
where the small r and s represent the association that occurs only as
a covert thought. Thus the simple building blocks formed by S–R
bonds can be combined into highly complicated patterns.

Various forms of learning and memory have been explained in
associationist terms. There is relatively little age-related research
concerning classical conditioning, however, and the data that do exist tend to be dated and of little current relevance. The same is true
of the second major type of conditioning, Skinnerian operant conditioning. We will therefore limit our survey of associationism to
two areas that are of greater gerontological importance: motor skill
learning and verbal learning.

Motor Skill Learning and Memory

DEFINITION.   **Motor skill learning** refers to any task wherein the
subject must learn a sequence of bodily movements. Some motor

skill tasks are fairly simple, such as unlocking a door or operating the ignition of an automobile. Often, however, the learner must associate various bodily responses with the perception of rapidly changing environmental stimuli. For example, driving an automobile in traffic requires you to make frequent changes in the pressure you exert on the gas pedal and brake, and in the position of the steering wheel, in response to what you observe in front of and around you. Motor learning is also exemplified by buttoning your shirt, pouring juice into a glass without spilling any, hitting a baseball, brushing your teeth, playing a guitar, racking up a high score in a video game, typing, and countless other everyday activities. Associationists contend that motor skill learning involves a chain of S–R bonds, but that the stimuli are often internal: the kinesthetic cues produced by your response at one stage of the sequence trigger the subsequent response.

MOTOR SKILL LEARNING AND AGING.   Many motor skills are acquired in childhood, adolescence, or early adulthood, and are practiced so often that they become effortless and do not require conscious attention. These skills therefore tend to persist until very late in life.

For example, pilots between the ages of 40 and 60 have as few or fewer accidents than younger pilots (Birren, 1964). Similarly, industrial workers age 65 and over have fewer disabling accidents than employees age 25–34 (McFarland & Doherty, 1959; Sterns, Barrett, & Alexander, 1985). The one notable exception concerns speeded responses: older adults are more likely to incur accidents caused by the failure to act quickly enough, such as being hit by a moving object because they cannot get out of the way in time. But when response speed is not a factor, the accident rate tends to decrease with increasing age (King, 1955).

To be sure, there are some atypical and extremely complicated motor skills that do decline to some extent with increasing age. Thus it is not unusual for professional athletes and practitioners of certain arts to retire by middle age because they can no longer perform effectively. But even here, there are many well-known examples of individuals who continued to perform well at a relatively advanced age: cellist Pablo Casals, pianist Arthur Rubinstein, and golfer Sam Snead, to name just a few. While there have been relatively few age-related studies of motor skill learning during the past decade, serious concern about the deterioration of previously learned motor skills with increasing age does not appear to be warranted. (See Welford, 1984.)

While it is reassuring to find that our basic motor skills are not greatly affected by aging, we must also ask how difficult it is for older adults to acquire new motor skills. Some elderly individuals will be faced with such tasks as learning to operate a wheelchair, while some may wish to take up golf or other sports during retirement. Although research interest in this area has also waned in recent years, it does seem that older adults have greater difficulty learning new motor skills, especially if cognition is required between the visual input and the bodily response.

In one study, subjects of various ages were required to make a series of key-pressing responses. On each trial, the subject had to choose one of twelve keys, depending on which one of twelve signal lights was turned on. In the simpler condition, the position of the correct key matched the position of the light. Here, the effect of age on performance was minimal. But when the difficulty of the task was increased, as by requiring the subject to press the key on the far left when the fifth light from the left was turned on, subjects age 55–72 fared considerably worse than those age 15–54 (Kay, 1954; 1955). Associating a sign or signal with a key immediately next to it is a common experience, as with the call button next to each name on the intercom of an apartment building, and older adults may find it more difficult to overcome their more extensive prior experience when old habits happen to give the wrong answer. Whatever the reason, the capacity to develop new and fairly complicated motor skills declines considerably by old age.

Verbal Learning and Memory

A great deal of research on adult learning and memory has focused on verbal stimuli and responses, an area first investigated by Hermann Ebbinghaus in the 1870s. Basing his ideas directly on associationism, Ebbinghaus concluded that memory consists of S–R bonds between various ideas or events. He believed that using prose or poetry to test these associations would present formidable problems, since different excerpts might well differ considerably in difficulty. Therefore, Ebbinghaus developed his own stimuli: nonsense syllables consisting of consonant/vowel/consonant combinations, such as SEB, WUC, and LUP. (See Walsh, 1983). In more recent verbal learning research, single words are also often used as stimuli.

SERIAL AND PAIRED-ASSOCIATE LEARNING: DEFINITIONS.   In **serial learning,** the subject is required to learn a list of words or nonsense syllables in the exact order in which they appear. In some studies, the subject is asked to reproduce the entire list from memory. More often, however, the subject must anticipate the item that follows a preceding one. That is, items on the list are presented one at a time, and the subject must quickly state the item that will appear next. Typically, items at the beginning of the list are easiest to recall; this is known as the **primacy effect.** Most difficult of all to remember are items in the middle of the list. Items at the end of the list are recalled more often than those in the middle (albeit not as readily as items at the beginning), a phenomenon referred to as the **recency effect.**

In **paired-associate learning,** on the other hand, pairs of items are used (e.g., SEB—GIF, WUC—ZEH, LUP—DOF). During the "study phase," the subject is shown each of the S–R pairs; the time permitted to examine each pair is referred to as the **inspection interval.** This is followed by the "test phase": the left-hand member of each pair is presented by itself, and the subject must reply with the right-hand member before it is revealed by the experimenter a few seconds later. The time allowed the subject to respond to each item is known as the **anticipation interval.** Alternatively, the experiment may dispense with the study phase and include only the test phase; the subject will undoubtedly make no correct responses on the first trial, but is likely to demonstrate at least some learning thereafter. In either case, the order of the pairs is usually changed on subsequent trials, but the specific items in each pair remain the same. (See Figure 5.1.)

For both serial and paired-associate learning, the difficulty of the task may be measured in two ways: the number of *trials* needed to learn the entire list without error, or the number of *errors* that are made until the list is learned perfectly. Memory may be indexed by the number of trials required on the following day to return to the previous level of accuracy.

Both of these forms of learning have various real-life analogues. Memorizing a list of instructions in the correct order, or the sequence of stations you pass through when taking the commuter train home from work, are examples of serial learning. Associating an English word with the corresponding word in a foreign language, or memorizing the names of certain cities and the nickname of the National Football League team that plays in each one, involve paired associate learning.

VERBAL LEARNING AND AGING: I. STIMULUS RATE.   Most studies of verbal learning and aging have been cross-sectional, and are subject to the limitations of this type of research. Since learning and memory are unobservable processes, these abilities can only be inferred from **performance** on various tasks; and task performance may be influenced by cohort effects, individual differences, and other variables, as well as by genuine age-related changes in ability.

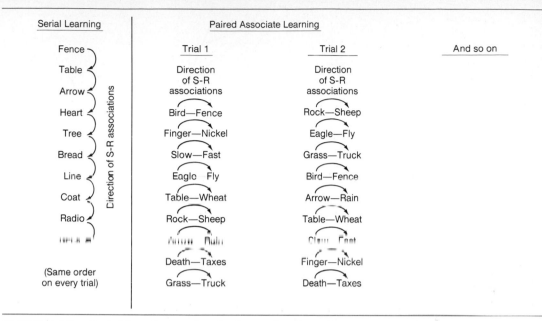

FIGURE 5.1   Serial learning and paired associate learning compared.

Nevertheless, some fairly clear and important trends have emerged from this body of research.

First of all, older adults consistently perform more poorly on both serial and paired-associate learning tasks than do young adults (e.g., Arenberg, 1967; Arenberg & Robertson-Tchabo, 1977; Bromley, 1958; Canestrari, 1963; 1966; 1968; Eisdorfer, Axelrod, & Wilkie, 1963; Eisdorfer & Service, 1967; Zaretsky & Halberstam, 1968a; 1968b). To illustrate, findings from six paired-associate studies are summarized in Figure 5.2. While there are some discrepancies insofar as specific patterns are concerned, all of these studies indicate a significant decline in performance with increasing age, sometimes beginning as early as age 30 or 40. Because such declines have been observed so frequently in empirical research, it has been widely concluded that they cannot be due solely to cohort effects or other forms of bias. Our capacity to learn and remember must decrease as we grow older, at least to some extent.

Why might this be true? One possible answer involves the ability of older adults to cope with speeded tasks: it has been found that the faster the rate at which the stimulus items are presented, the greater are the age-related differences in performance. In one study (Canestrari, 1963), a sample of young adults (age 17–35) and a sam-

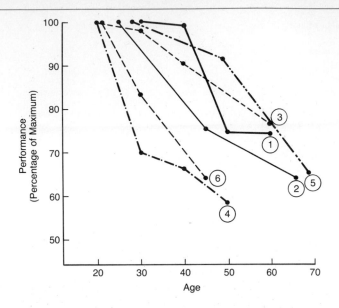

Note. Performance scores are expressed as a percentage of the maximum score across all ages. The circled numbers refer to different experiments: (1) Canestrari, 1968; (2) Gladis & Braun, 1958; (3) Hulicka, 1966; (4) Monge, 1971; (5) Smith, 1975; (6) Thorndike et al., 1928.

FIGURE 5.2 The relationship between age and performance on paired associate learning tasks. Salthouse (1982, p. 126).

ple of adults nearing old age (age 60–69) were required to learn three tasks. Each task was presented at a different pace:

- *Fast pace:* Inspection and anticipation intervals of 1.5 seconds.

- *Slow pace:* Inspection and anticipation intervals of 3.0 seconds.

- *Self-paced:* Unlimited inspection and anticipation intervals. Subjects could take all the time they needed to examine each pair during the study phase, and to respond to each item during the test phase.

Although the younger group performed better under all three conditions, the most striking age differences occurred at the fast pace. (See Figure 5.3A.) When stimuli were presented every 1.5 seconds, the older group made many more errors of omission. Their performance suffered not because they usually gave wrong words as answers, but because they often failed to provide any response at all. Conversely, older adults fared better in the self-paced condition because they took significantly more time than did the younger group,

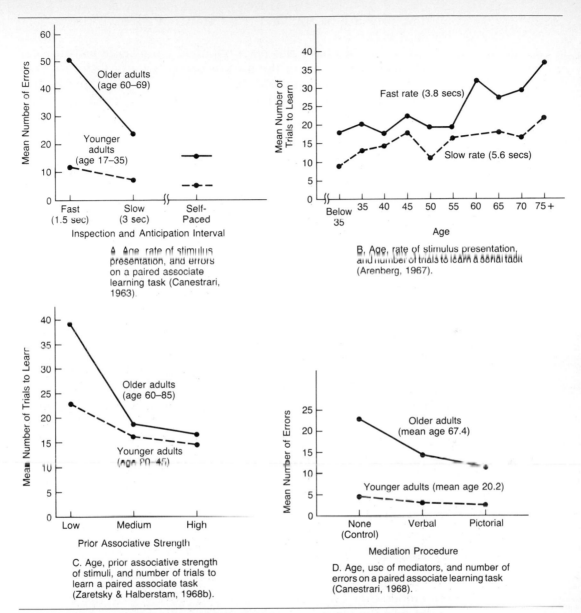

FIGURE 5.3 Aging and verbal learning: Some typical research findings. Kausler (1982, pp. 378, 381, 385, 387).

especially during the test phase. Subsequent research has confirmed that longer anticipation intervals reduce age differences in performance on paired-associate tasks, although middle-aged and elderly subjects rarely perform as well as young adults even when there is no time pressure of any kind (e.g., Monge & Hultsch, 1971; Salt-house, 1982).

Similar findings have also been obtained from serial learning experiments. When items in the list are presented at a faster rate, all subjects perform more poorly. But the adverse effects are greater for older adults, especially those past middle age (Arenberg, 1967; see Figure 5.3B).

These data suggest that older adults perform more poorly on learning and memory tasks because they cannot respond as quickly. We will return to this hypothesis later in this chapter, when we discuss research based on the more recent information-processing approach to learning and memory.

VERBAL LEARNING AND AGING: II. MEDIATORS. Paired-associate studies have shown that the relationships among aging, learning, and memory also depends on how often the items in each pair have been associated in the past. Older adults perform much more poorly than young adults when the paired items are low in prior associative strength, such as *finger—nickel;* but they are at less of a disadvantage if each pair consists of commonly associated items, such as *slow—fast* or *eagle—fly* (Canestrari, 1966; Kausler & Lair, 1966; Zaretsky & Halberstam, 1968a; 1968b). In one study, older adults (age 60–85) averaged approximately 40 trials to learn the task when the prior associative strength of the paired items was low, while younger adults (age 20–45) required only about 23 trials. But when the prior associative strength of the paired items was high, the superiority of the younger group dropped to approximately three trials. (See Figure 5.3C.)

Findings like these led verbal learning researchers to posit the importance of **mediators,** or intervening links between the stimulus and response that can serve as an effective aid to learning and memory. For example, the *finger—nickel* association might be more easily acquired and recalled by using the verbal mediator "five," since there are five fingers on each hand and a nickel is worth five cents. Thus, if the subject silently says "five" when presented with this pair during the study phase, this mediator may make it easier to remember that the correct response is "nickel." Or the mediator might take the form of a pictorial image, with the subject visualizing a finger holding a nickel (Paivio, 1971). Apparently, older adults do not use mediators as often or as well as do younger adults (Canestrari, 1968; Hulicka & Grossman, 1967; Poon, Walsh-Sweeney, & Fozard, 1980). This makes little difference when the prior associative strength of the paired items is so high that mediators are not needed (e.g., *slow—fast*), but places older adults at a significant disadvantage when the paired items are so dissimilar that a mediator would be helpful.

If older adults are provided with specific training in the use of mediators, such as mnemonic devices, there is some improvement in their performance on paired associate tasks. This is especially true when pictorial mediators are used. (See Figure 5.3D.) But even with this assistance, older adults are still unable to match the performance of young adults. Similar findings have also emerged from serial learning research (Bugelski, Kidd, & Segmen, 1968; Miller, Galanter, & Pribram, 1960). For example, if the list to be learned consists of ten items, subjects may first be asked to learn a series of rhymes involving the numbers one through ten (e.g., "one is a bun," "two is a shoe," "three is a tree"). Then, when the serial list is presented, the learner is advised to form a distinctive image of the first word interacting with a bun. For example, if this word is *car*, the subject might envision a sandwich consisting of a bun piled high with lettuce, tomato, and a Chevrolet. Similarly, each of the other nine rhymes helps the subject to form a pictorial image that will make it easier to recall the corresponding item on the list. Or subjects may be asked to imagine a trip through a familiar environment, such as their own home, and to key an image of each word on the list to a distinctive location. Thus *car* (the first word on the list) might be visualized in the hallway, *horse* (the second word on the list) in the living room, and so forth. Once this has been done, the subject recalls the list by mentally traveling the route once again in the same order and naming the object found at each location. Both of these methods have been found to promote rapid serial learning in young adults. Their effectiveness with middle-aged and elderly subjects is less certain; some promising results have been obtained, while other studies have reported negative findings. (See, for example, Bower, 1970; Mason & Smith, 1977; Smith, 1975.)

These results suggest that there may be a genuine loss in mediational ability with increasing age, possibly due to physiological deterioration in the central nervous system, and that this loss is in part responsible for the inferior performance of older adults on learning and memory tasks. It is possible, however, that the poorer mediational ability of older adults may be due partly or largely to disuse. The use of mediators may be most common fairly early in life, as when college students use this technique to increase the amount of material that can be recalled on an examination. If so, younger generations may perform better on paired associate and serial tasks because they have had more recent practice with the use of mediators. Whatever the reason, this issue has also exerted a strong influence on more recent learning and memory research—as we will see later in this chapter.

AFTERWORD.   Although the findings of verbal learning studies have stimulated a great deal of modern research, the traditional associa-

Chapter Glossary: Learning and Memory

Acquisition	The initial process in the act of remembering, wherein new information first enters memory (is learned) and is encoded in some form (e.g., phonemically).
Anticipation interval	The time allowed the subject to respond to each item during the test phase of a paired-associate learning task.
Associationism	A philosophy that attributes all learning and memory to the association of stimuli and responses that occur closely together in time (S–R bonds).
Attentional deficit hypothesis	Posits that our capacity to pay attention to stimuli, or the speed with which we can switch the focus of our attention, declines with increasing age. As a result, older adults must expend more effort to process information more deeply.
Cued-recall task	An experimental procedure wherein subjects must learn lists of items (e.g., common words) and are given clues that will help them retrieve the information from memory, such as the first letter(s), a rhyme, a synonym, or a general description of the correct answer.
Decay	The erosion of a memory trace due to as yet unidentified physiological processes, resulting in forgetting of the information.
Depth-of-processing model	Posits that there is only one kind of memory structure, and that the duration of memory traces depends on whether we merely pay attention to superficial aspects of the information or understand its meaning. The latter form of processing is deeper and produces more durable memory traces.
Digit-span test	An experimental procedure wherein the subject is read a sequence of digits, which must immediately be repeated back in the same order. (In a more difficult modification of this task, the digits must be repeated back in reverse order.)
Echoic memory	The auditory form of sensory memory.
Ecological validity	The extent to which experimental tasks resemble activities that are common in everyday life.
Encoding	The process of converting sensory information into a form that is more readily remembered. This can be accomplished by converting the sensory data into words, imagery, or an abstract representation.

Episodic memory	In Tulving's theory, a form of memory that records the time and place of specific personal events.
Free-recall task	An experimental procedure wherein the subject is presented with a series of items, usually common words, which are to be recalled in any order.
Iconic memory	The visual form of sensory memory.
Information-processing model	A conception of human learning and memory that is based on the principles underlying modern electronic computers (i.e., the ways in which computers perceive, acquire, store, transform, retrieve, and use considerable amounts of information). *See* process theory; structural theory.
Inspection interval	The time allowed the subject to examine each stimulus pair during the study phase of a paired-associate learning task.
Interference	Forgetting due to prior or subsequent learning.
Mediator	A verbal or pictorial link between a stimulus and a response. The use of mediators can significantly improve performance on learning and memory tasks.
Motor-skill learning	A form of learning that involves bodily movements, such as unlocking a door or buttoning a shirt.
Paired-associate learning	A form of learning wherein pairs of items are used (e.g., common words, nonsense syllables), and subjects must reply with the second member of each pair when presented with the first member.
Performance	How well or how poorly a subject does on an experimental task; the visible evidence as to whether or not learning or remembering has occurred. Typical indicators are speed of response and error rates.
Phonemic	Pertaining to the sound structure of a word.
Primacy effect	In serial learning, the tendency to recall the items at the beginning of the list most easily.
Primary memory (short-term memory)	In structural theory, the separate and distinct memory system that has a very small capacity and retains information for from one or two seconds to about half a minute.
Procedural memory	In Tulving's theory, stored knowledge of how to act that enables us to engage in skilled activities.
Process theory	A theory that emphasizes the mental activities which we perform in order to learn or remember information.

Recall	Producing a response by searching one's memory for the correct answer, as on an essay examination. One form of retrieval.
Recency effect	(1) In serial learning, the tendency to recall the last few items more easily than items in the middle of the list, albeit not as easily as items at the beginning. (2) In free-recall tasks, the tendency to recall the last few items most easily.
Recognition	Identification of an item or event as familiar or previously experienced; multiple-choice examinations test the accuracy of recognition. One form of retrieval.
Retention	The second process in the act of remembering, wherein information is stored for later use. Some theorists prefer to characterize this stage in terms of encoding (q.v.).
Retrieval	The third process in the act of remembering, wherein certain information is distinguished from everything else in memory and is brought back to awareness for current use. Material may be retrieved through recognition or recall.
Secondary memory (long-term memory)	(1) In structural theory, the separate and distinct memory system that has an enormous capacity and retains information for from one or two minutes to many years. (2) Memories that last for from one or two minutes to many years, but whose duration is best explained in terms of process theory.
Semantic	Pertaining to the meaning of a word.
Semantic memory	In Tulving's theory, a form of memory that consists of general knowledge, meanings, and abstract relationships.
Sensory memory	A form of memory that holds incoming visual or auditory information for from one quarter of a second to a few seconds after the stimulus is withdrawn.
Serial learning	A form of learning wherein the subject must repeat back a list of items (common words, nonsense syllables) in the exact order in which they were presented.
Structural theory	A theory that focuses on separate and distinct memory systems which store information in the human brain.
Study phase	The period during which subjects in an experiment practice and try to learn the material in question.
Test phase	The period during which subjects in an experiment are examined for their ability to remember the material in question.

tionist approach to the study of learning and memory has fallen into disfavor. As we observed at the outset of this chapter, psychologists now believe that there are several distinct kinds of memory. Serial and paired-associate tasks have little to do with the role of knowledge, or with the understanding of concepts and abstract relationships. Thus the associationist assumption that these tasks tap *the* ability to learn and remember is now regarded as a serious oversimplification.

A related criticism involves the relevance of serial and paired-associate tasks to real-life learning and memory. It has been argued that even if there is a true age-related decline in our ability to recall lists of unrelated items, this decrement may have little or no bearing on our ability to perform such everyday functions as gleaning new information from the daily newspaper or remembering the events in a novel that we began a few nights ago. That is, serial and paired-associate tasks may be low in **ecological validity.** these findings may not apply very well to the behavior of men and women in their natural environments.

Nonsense syllables and unrelated single words may even be perceived as so irrelevant by older adults that they strongly object to the experiment, and do not care how well (or how poorly) they perform. For example, Hulicka (1976) tried to administer a paired associate task to subjects age 65–80, using two letters as stimuli and single words as responses (e.g., *TL–insane*). This experiment suffered an extremely high dropout rate, with many of these elderly subjects refusing to make the effort to learn "such nonsense." But they carried out the task willingly when it was made more meaningful, as by using occupation names as stimuli and personal surnames as responses (e.g., *lawyer–Johnson*). The poorer performance of older adults when meaningless stimuli are used is a common research finding, although there are exceptions (e.g., Hanley-Dunn & McIntosh, 1984). For these reasons, some researchers have sought to measure the relationships among aging, learning, and memory by using more meaningful material, such as coherent sentences and paragraphs. This significant methodological change has also been accompanied by efforts to develop theoretical models that are more appropriate to this form of research.

Because of criticisms like these, most modern theorists have rejected the associationist account of learning and memory in favor of alternative conceptions. The most notable of these is the information-processing approach, which is based on the principles that underlie modern electronic computers.

Information-Processing Approaches to Learning and Memory

Introduction

The **information-processing model** distinguishes between two major aspects of learning and memory; *structure* and *process*. **Structural theories** focus on the ways in which information is organized in the human brain, or how our memory banks are constructed. **Process theories** emphasize the mental activities that we perform when we try to put information into memory (learn), or make use of it at some later date (remember).

STRUCTURAL THEORIES.   In an effort to understand how human memory is structured, some psychologists have tried to glean important clues from the design of electronic computers. Like human beings, computers can store remarkable amounts of information for long periods of time. To this end, computers possess several different kinds of memory. There is an input or peripheral buffer memory, which stores incoming information until enough data has been read into the computer for the analysis to begin. A working memory holds the information being actively analyzed by the computer. And the core memory stores large amounts of inactive information for later use. Accordingly, one prominent theory posits that there are three distinct types of human memory-storage structures:

1. Sensory Memory: The very brief persistence of a visual, auditory, or other form of sensation after the stimulus is withdrawn. Sensory memories last for perhaps a fraction of a second after the presentation of a stimulus, and are a nearly exact replica of that stimulus. However, if the information is not converted to some more durable form, it will be quickly lost (Bourne, Dominowski, & Loftus, 1979).

2. Primary Memory (also referred to as "short-term memory"): Memories that last from one or two seconds up to about half a minute. When someone talks to you, you can understand the meaning of each sentence because the initial words are still fresh in your mind when the end of the sentence is reached, even though you may well forget the entire conversation shortly thereafter. Or you may be introduced to someone at a party and retain this name long enough to say it while shaking hands, but be unable to recall it half an hour later. Or you may look up a number in the telephone directory and remember it long enough to dial it accurately, get a busy signal, and then have to look up the same number again because you can no longer recall it (and have neglected to write it down).

These common experiences suggest that the ability to remember information for very short periods of time is distinctly different from the capacity for longer-term memories. In this structural theory, therefore, primary memory is conceptualized as a temporary and limited-capacity storage system. It holds relatively little information at any one point in time, and the information which it contains decays very rapidly. What can be done to prevent this material from being lost completely? If the information in primary memory is rehearsed or elaborated upon, as by repeating it several times, it will enter secondary memory (see below). The process of rehearsal and elaboration that enables information to proceed from primary memory to secondary memory is called **encoding.** (See Smith & Fullerton, 1981; Poon, 1985.) As we will see later in this chapter, old persons exhibit substantial encoding deficits when compared to younger persons.

3. Secondary Memory (also referred to as "long-term memory"): Memories that last from one or two minutes to many years. You have a great many of these memories at your disposal: your name, birth date, and other biographical data; similar information about your loved ones; various facts and abstract relationships that enable you to perform well on a job or in school; geographical data about the city, state, and country in which you live; recollections of experiences that you have had in the recent and distant past; information concerning your hobbies, such as what happened in a novel you began last night or yesterday's baseball scores; and much more.

Since secondary memory covers such a wide range of briefer and longer-lasting information, why do you need a sensory and a primary memory at all? Without sensory memories, brief though they are, you would lose track of incoming information too quickly for any of it ever to be remembered. Sensory memories occur automatically, without any effort on your part, and they preserve information in your nervous system just long enough for it to undergo further processing. If you pay attention to this information, it is read out from sensory memory and enters the next stage in the processing system—primary memory.

Primary memory plays an important role in the control and assimilation of information. If you tried to store all of the immense amount of data that reaches you through your senses, you would be inundated with so much data that you could not function at all.

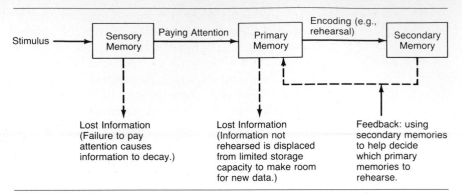

FIGURE 5.4   A structural model of learning and memory.

That is, too much information that arrives too rapidly will overload your cognitive system beyond its limits. For example, you would undoubtedly find it impossible to understand what a friend is saying while simultaneously trying to read a book and note the baseball scores being announced on a radio sportscast. Primary memory narrows down the information at your disposal to manageable limits because its storage capacity is very small (as we will see later in this chapter). Older data are frequently expelled to make room for new data, thereby making it easier for you to decide which information is important enough to be committed to secondary memory.

To illustrate, suppose that you are introduced to a group of twelve strangers at a party. Your primary memory will probably not be able to store all of these names at once. Instead, you may recall only four or five names. Faced with this more manageable input, you might then choose to focus on one name belonging to an attractive member of the opposite sex and repeat this name to yourself several times, with this rehearsal making it more likely that the name will enter your secondary memory (and that you will recall it later on). And this choice may be influenced by some useful feedback from your secondary memory, as when you recall some prior experiences with attractive members of the opposite sex that proved to be very pleasant.

This structural model is summarized in Figure 5.4. It assumes that human memory consists of three fixed structures, each of which represents one stage in the processing of the information that reaches us through our senses. Each form of memory has a particular function, and a typical length of time during which information is stored therein. (See Table 5.1.) One appealing aspect of this model is that it emphasizes a well-known and important aspect of human learning and memory, namely that some memories last considerably longer

TABLE 5.1   A comparison of sensory memory, primary memory, and secondary memory.

Characteristic	Sensory Memory	Primary Memory	Secondary Memory
How information is entered	Without effort	Paying attention	Encoding (e.g., rehearsal)
How information is maintained	Not possible	Continued attention	Continued rehearsal, organization of the information
Form of information	Literal copy of input	Acoustic, visual, or semantic codes	Abstract symbols and their relationships (e.g., meanings)
Capacity	Large	Small (3–7 items)	Enormous
Duration of information	About one quarter second (iconic memory); one-quarter to five or six seconds (echoic memory)	From one or two seconds to about half a minute	From one or two minutes to many years
Function	To preserve information until it can be consciously processed	To maintain active control of cognitive activity	To store information for later use
How information is forgotten	Decay	Decay and interference	Decay, interference, poor retrieval strategies
Computer analog	Input (buffer) memory	Working memory registers	Core memory; peripheral storage (e.g., disks, tapes)

than others. It has proved to be very influential in learning and memory research, especially during the 1950s and 1960s.

More recently, however, this model has been found to have some significant flaws. (See, for example, Craik & Lockhart, 1972; Schneider & Shiffrin, 1977). Although this is a structural theory, it also defines how information proceeds from one memory structure to another. That is, you presumably must pay attention to the information in sensory memory for it to proceed to primary memory, and you must rehearse the information in primary memory for it to enter secondary memory. This is a question of process, not structure. As researchers explored such issues further, many came to believe that the three structures are not nearly as functionally separate as this model implies. Instead, they concluded that process is more important than structure. That is, longer-lasting information is *not* shifted from one memory structure to another. It endures in memory because the individual has processed it more deeply, as by understanding its meaning rather than merely repeating it over and over. To these psychologists, then, learning and memory are better conceptualized in terms of process theories.

PROCESS THEORIES.   The act of remembering depends on three basic processes. First of all, to remember anything, you must first have learned it. For example, suppose you take an examination in French and are asked to translate the word *heureux.* Unless you previously learned that this word means "happy," you cannot possibly remember the answer during the test. This initial process is known as **acquisition.**

The second process is that of **retention,** wherein the information is filed away for future use. Your French test may occur days or weeks after the acquisition period, so you must retain the meaning of *heureux* until it is time to demonstrate your knowledge.

The third process, **retrieval,** concerns your efforts to dredge up a particular memory from all the others that you have acquired. You may be unable to translate *heureux* during the examination, yet you spontaneously remember the answer a few hours later without consulting your French text. This information must have been stored in your memory at exam time, since you did no subsequent studying of any kind. You acquired and retained it, but were unable to retrieve it.

Previously stored material can be retrieved in two ways. In **recall** tasks, you must produce the correct answer by searching your memory for the correct word or words (as in our example). In **recognition** tasks, you are shown various possible answers and must choose the correct one. Recall is considered to be a more demanding test of retrieval than is recognition, as you undoubtedly know from your experience with essay versus multiple-choice examinations.

Notice once again the intimate relationships between learning and memory. If you cannot remember important information during an examination, the problem might be one of retrieval: you learned the material but could not remember it during the examination, possibly because you were anxious or fatigued or because the answers you needed became confused with other information. However, the problem might instead be one of acquisition: you never really learned the material. You may not have studied very effectively; perhaps you merely read through the assigned chapters once, or you stared at the text while allowing your attention to wander to other matters. Conversely, if your studying was thorough enough so that you clearly understood what you read (as, for example, if you rewrote it in your own words), you are much more likely to remember this information during the examination. According to this theory, then, memory depends in part on how deeply you process the material in question. Understanding its meaning will produce much longer-lasting memories than just paying attention to it or rehearsing it repeatedly.

To illustrate, one sample of subjects was asked to participate in an experiment that was described as an investigation of perception and reaction time. Words printed in all upper-case or all lower-case letters were presented very briefly via a tachistoscope, one at a time (e.g., *friend, CRATE, table*), and the subjects were required to answer yes or no questions about each word as quickly as possible. At the shallowest level of processing, subjects were asked to indicate whether the physical structure of a word was lower-case type or upper-case type; this required only a brief scanning of the stimulus. To obtain a deeper level of processing, subjects were questioned about the sound of a word (e.g., "Does the word rhyme with *blend*?"). The deepest level of processing was induced by having subjects answer questions about the semantic features of a word (e.g., "Does the word fit this sentence: 'He met a ____ in the street'?"). Afterwards, to their complete surprise, subjects were tested for their ability to recognize the words used in the experiment. The results indicated that deeper levels of processing produced more durable memory traces: the semantic questions led to significantly better recognition than the phonemic questions, which in turn led to significantly better recognition than did the questions dealing only with the physical structure of the words (Craik & Tulving, 1975; see Figure 5.5). Thus, as we noted at the outset of this chapter, information processed in terms of many meaningful relationships (e.g., semantic memories) tends to last longer than information processed less thoroughly (e.g., episodic memories).

Although process theories are currently more popular than structural theories, useful age-related data have been derived from both structurally oriented and process-oriented research. We will therefore devote some attention to both models in the pages that follow.

Structural Considerations: I. Sensory Memory

By temporarily preserving the physical characteristics of a stimulus, even for a fraction of a second, **sensory memory** retains information just long enough for you to process it. The capacity of the sensory memory storage systems is relatively large; you take in much more information with a single glance than you can possibly use.

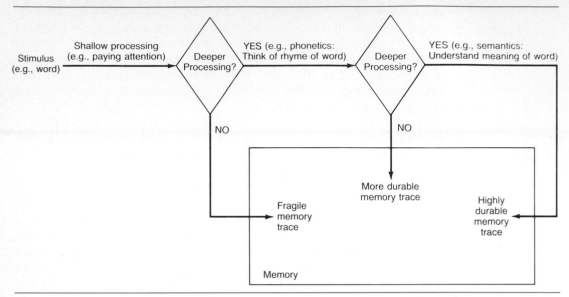

FIGURE 5.5   A depth-of-processing model of learning and memory.

But sensory memories rarely interfere with one another because their duration is so brief, so it is rather easy to distinguish among them.

DEFINITIONS: ICONIC AND ECHOIC MEMORY.   **Iconic memory** is a type of sensory memory that is based on the visual system (Neisser, 1967). It is the peripheral information store that maintains a faithful representation of a visual stimulus for less than one second after this stimulus is removed. In one noted study, three-by-four arrays of letters were presented to subjects via tachistoscope for 50 milliseconds (Sperling, 1960):

$$
\begin{array}{cccc}
L & V & R & D \\
Z & P & S & Q \\
M & X & T & F
\end{array}
$$

Immediately after each array was withdrawn from view, subjects were asked to name all twelve letters (the method of "whole report"). This typically proved to be impossible, and subjects averaged only about four to five correct letters per array. Yet many subjects also reported that they actually saw more letters, but could no longer remember them an instant later when asked what they had seen. This suggested a most interesting possibility: a visual mental picture (*icon*) of the entire array was formed in the subject's memory, but it faded away so rapidly that only four or five letters could be recalled.

To test this hypothesis, a modified version of this experimental procedure was used. Subjects were now asked to name only one row of letters, with this row not specified until a fraction of a second after the array disappeared (the method of "partial report"). A high-frequency tone was used to request the top row, a middle-frequency tone specified the second row, and a low-frequency tone designated the bottom row. Under these conditions, the performance of the subjects was nearly perfect. But when there was so much as a one-second delay between the removal of the array and the designation of the row to be recalled, performance dropped to the usual level of about 40 percent correct (Sperling, 1960). These results clearly indicated that the entire icon must be available for an instant in sensory memory, enabling subjects to scan it and recall the designated row of letters. Subsequent research has estimated the duration of iconic memory to be approximately one quarter of a second (e.g., Averbach & Coriell, 1961; Haber & Nathanson, 1968; Haber & Standing, 1969; 1970; McCloskey & Watkins, 1978).

A second important type of sensory memory is based on the auditory system. **Echoic memory** is the peripheral information store that maintains a faithful representation of an auditory stimulus for a very brief period after this stimulus is removed (Neisser, 1967; Rumelhart, 1977). The auditory analog of Sperling's procedure utilizes a cleverly designed set of stereophonic earphones: subjects simultaneously hear one list of letters (or numbers) in the left ear, a different list in the right ear, and a third list that appears to be coming from the middle of the head because it is presented binaurally. Typically, each list is three items long. When the whole report method is used, subjects are asked to name all nine items. If instead the partial report method is used, subjects are informed visually whether to report the list from the left ear, the right ear, or the middle. Here again, the partial-report method produces significantly better performance than does the whole-report method, indicating that a substantial number of these auditory items are briefly retained in echoic memory (Darwin, Turvey, & Crowder, 1972).

Echoic memories last somewhat longer than iconic memories. Their duration in the preceding experiment was approximately two seconds, while other estimates have varied from one quarter of a second to as much as five or six seconds (e.g., Crowder & Morton, 1969; Crowder & Prussin, 1971; Crowder & Raeburn, 1970; Massaro, 1972; Routh & Mayes, 1974).

SENSORY MEMORY AND AGING.   Insofar as iconic memory is concerned, adults over age 60 do tend to have considerable difficulty with Sperling's partial-report task. However, this is *not* due to decrements in sensory memory. The rapid shifting of attention becomes more difficult with increasing age (Chapter 4), and older adults apparently cannot focus their attention on the designated row fast enough to retrieve it before the iconic memory trace fades (Walsh & Passe, 1980). Also, the elderly deal with this task inefficiently; they focus too strongly on the top row of letters in the array (Salthouse, 1976). Since sensory memory occurs automatically, without any effort on our part, these task difficulties are irrelevant to the question at hand. They represent methodological sources of bias, which make it virtually impossible for Sperling's task to reveal the true relationship between aging and iconic memory.

In order to obtain valid age-related data in this area, researchers have had to devise tasks that make fewer demands on the subjects' attention and response strategies. One good alternative is to briefly expose two successive stimuli, with the interval between them varying from a small fraction of a second to one or two seconds. The goal is to determine the largest interstimulus interval for which the two stimuli are perceived as connected, rather than as separate and distinct. This provides an indication as to the maximum duration of the iconic memory trace, or how long it can last and obtrude on the second stimulus. For example, suppose that both the first and the second stimulus consist of a series of meaningless dots. When the two stimuli are superimposed, however, they form a recognizable nonsense syllable such as *VOH*. (See Figure 5.6.) If these stimuli are presented a half second apart, and if the subject correctly reports the nonsense syllable, the iconic memory trace of the first stimulus must have persisted for half a second (Eriksen & Collins, 1967). And if the iconic memory trace lasts significantly longer for younger adults than for older adults, we may reasonably conclude that this form of memory does decline with increasing age. In general, however, research in this area has found that iconic memory is largely unaffected by aging. (See, for example, Amberson et al., 1979; Kline & Baffa, 1976; Kline & Orme-Rogers, 1978; Kline & Schieber, 1981; Walsh & Thompson, 1978).

As compared with iconic memory, the methodological problems involved in testing the relationship between aging and echoic memory are even more formidable. Since older adults more often suffer from significant hearing impairments than from visual disorders (Chapter 4), it can be difficult to distinguish between age-related declines in echoic memory and decrements caused by poor health. However, the available evidence suggests that echoic memory is also largely unaffected by aging (e.g., Arenberg, 1968; 1976; Crowder, 1980; Parkinson & Perey, 1980).

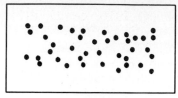

First Stimulus

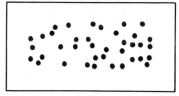

Second Stimulus

First and Second
Stimuli Superimposed

FIGURE 5.6   An experimental method for determining the duration of iconic memory. Eriksen & Collins (1967).

As we observed previously in this chapter, older adults have greater difficulty with highly speeded learning and memory tasks. However, it has been shown that older adults do *not* suffer any significant slowing of iconic or echoic memory (Cerella, 1985).

In sum: there appears to be no significant relationship between aging and the capacities of iconic and echoic memory. (There is virtually no age-related research dealing with any other form of sensory memory.) If there is any truth to the common belief that our ability to learn and remember declines significantly with increasing age, the reasons must lie elsewhere.

Structural Considerations: II. Primary Memory

DEFINITION.   The function of **primary memory** is to hold a sufficiently small amount of information for conscious processing. Therefore, the storage capacity of this "working memory" is extremely limited; it has been estimated at only about three to seven unrelated letters, digits, or words (Baddeley, 1970; Craik, 1971; Crannell & Parrish, 1957; Miller, 1956; Murdock, 1967; Watkins, 1974). Primary memories are also of very brief duration, lasting from one or two seconds up to about half a minute. You typically encounter a great deal of information while driving to school or work, reading the daily newspaper, or simply observing the environment, yet you forget much of this information a few moments later.

Because of these characteristics, primary memory is able to regulate the cognitive system and keep it from being overloaded with so much information that it cannot function. Thus primary memory is somewhat like the loading platform of a warehouse: items must first pass through this register before they can enter secondary memory, only a limited number of items are handled at any one time, and old items are quickly cleared away so that new items can be processed.

PRIMARY MEMORY AND AGING.   There are several different ways in which primary memory might be adversely affected by aging. We will consider each of these in turn.

Does the storage capacity of primary memory decrease with increasing age? Conceivably, middle-aged and elderly adults might be able to store even less information in primary memory than do young adults. One experimental procedure commonly used to test this hypothesis is the **digit-span test:** the subject is read a sequence of digits, which must immediately be repeated back in the same order. The stimuli may vary from as few as two or three digits to as many as twelve or more, and the number of digits that the subject can reliably report reflects the storage capacity or his or her primary memory. Various studies have found that age differences in performance on this task are small or nonexistent, indicating that primary memory capacity remains stable as we grow older (e.g., Botwinick & Storandt, 1974; Bromley, 1958; Craik, 1968a; Drachman & Leavitt, 1972; Talland, 1965; 1968).

Corroborating evidence comes from a second methodological approach, the **free-recall task.** The subject is presented with a series of items (usually common English words, sometimes nonsense syllables), which are to be recalled in *any* order. Enough items are presented so that the subject cannot remember all of them. This task produces a somewhat different form of recency effect than is the case with serial learning: the last few items in the list are recalled first. This is attributable chiefly to primary memory, although the very last item may be recalled from sensory memory. Therefore, if older adults have significantly more difficulty recalling the last few items than do young adults, this would suggest that the storage capacity of primary memory declines with increasing age. However, this does not appear to be the case. Older adults perform as well as young adults in this regard, indicating once again that age differences in the storage capacity of primary memory are minimal (Craik, 1968b; Raymond, 1971; see also Craik, 1977).

Does the duration of primary memories decrease with increasing age? As a second possibility, older adults may forget the information in primary memory more quickly than do young adults. This issue has been widely researched, using a simple but ingenious procedure. Subjects are given one nonsense syllable to remember for from 1 to 18 seconds. To prevent them from rehearsing the syllable during this interval (which would enable it to enter secondary memory), they are then immediately presented with a 3-digit number, and they must count backwards by threes from this number until the time comes to recall the syllable (e.g., 346, 343, 340, 337, and so on). As the retention interval increases from 1 to 18 seconds, performance declines sharply, indicating once again the brief duration of primary memories (Brown, 1958; Peterson & Peterson, 1959). However, various studies have shown that performance on this task is *not* greatly affected by aging. That is, older adults are able to retain information in primary memory for about as long as do young adults (e.g., Elias & Hirasuna, 1976; Keevil-Rogers & Schnore, 1969; Kriauciunas, 1968; Mistler-Lachman, 1977; Schonfield, 1969; Puglisi, 1980).

Are age differences in performance significantly greater on more difficult primary memory tasks? Tasks that involve primary memory can be made considerably more difficult by requiring cognitive activity between the stimulus and the response. For example, suppose that the digit-span test is modified so that the subject must repeat the stimulus digits in reverse order: if the stimulus is 5 3 8 4 7, the correct response is 7 4 8 3 5. In marked contrast to the results obtained with the standard digit-span test, performance on this task does decline significantly with increasing age (Botwinick & Storandt, 1974).

A second possible way to increase the difficulty of primary memory tasks is by emphasizing response speed, rather than accuracy. (Recall that verbal learning research found age differences in performance to be significantly greater on highly speeded tasks.) In one study, subjects age 19–21, 33–43, and 58–85 were shown a set of 1, 3, 5, or 7 digits. Immediately thereafter, a single digit was presented, and subjects were asked to decide as quickly as possible whether this test item was or was not included in the original set. The larger the number of items in the set, the slower were the responses of all subjects, and the greater was the disadvantage of the two older groups. (See Figure 5.7.) This suggests that older adults search primary memory for specific information more slowly than

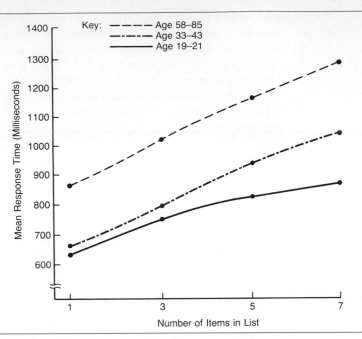

FIGURE 5.7   Aging and performance on a speeded primary memory task. Anders, Fozard, & Lillyquist (1972).

do young adults. However, the oldest group performed most poorly even when there was only one item in the original set and virtually no searching was required. Thus other factors must also influence the performance of middle-aged and elderly subjects on this task, such as how quickly the test digit is perceived and encoded (Anders, Fozard, & Lillyquist, 1972; see also Sternberg, 1966; 1969).

In sum: the first two lines of research discussed above clearly indicate that primary memory is largely unaffected by aging. To be sure, this conclusion appears to be most justified insofar as relatively undemanding tasks are concerned. Significant age differences may well be obtained on primary memory tasks that require cognitive activity (such as reorganizing the stimuli before reporting them), or are highly speeded. Nevertheless, we may reasonably conclude that if aging does have a pronounced effect on learning and memory, this must be due chiefly to the remaining component in the structural model—secondary memory.

Structure and Process: Secondary Memory

CONCEPTUAL ISSUES. **Secondary memory** stores information in terms of abstract symbols and their relationships, and is capable of retaining data for from one or two minutes to a great many years. The capacity of secondary memory is enormous; it includes the information that enables you to speak, read, recall your name and age, learn a part in a play, remember what you had for dinner or saw on television last night, and much more. Some indication as to the capacity of secondary memory can be gleaned from the fact that the average college student possesses a reading vocabulary of approximately 50,000 words, as well as large amounts of other information. (See Craik & Lockhart, 1972; Gleitman, 1983.)

When older adults complain of marked deterioration in their ability to recall important information, they are typically referring to secondary memory. For example:

A 73-YEAR-OLD FORMER INTERIOR DECORATOR

Mrs. W. is a physically healthy, articulate, and intelligent woman. During the past few years, however, her memory has become a serious problem. The Seattle Center Coliseum is a famous building in her home city, and she has visited it in the past, yet she can no longer recall its name. Instead, she must refer to it in such roundabout terms as "that great big thing were everyone goes to watch things." Similarly, Poland and Russia are "that place and the other, larger one to the east of it." At first, her memory lapses were small; but now she even has trouble remembering the names of furniture or colors, information that she used to work with every day. "It gets worse every year, every month," she says. "If it continues to do that, I wonder when I won't be able to remember anything." (King, 1982.)

A NOTED MUSICIAN

Composer Aaron Copland encountered considerable difficulty while writing his autobiography at an advanced age. "I have no trouble remembering everything that happened 40 to 50 years ago—dates, places, faces, and music," Copland claimed. "But I'm going to be 90 my next birthday, November 14, and I find I can't remember what happened yesterday." Copland's problems with secondary memory are clearly indicated by the fact that he actually would be only 80 years old on his next birthday. (Kausler, 1982, p. 397.)

Are these examples unusual and extreme, suggesting the early stages of a dementia, or do they indicate what will befall most of us in old age? Before we can investigate this important issue, we must first mention a troublesome conceptual problem: insofar as secondary memory is concerned, the distinction between structure and process has become blurred.

As we have seen, structural theory explains longer-lasting memories in terms of *where* they are stored (that is, in secondary memory). In contrast, process theory explains longer-lasting memories in terms of *how* you deal with the information (you process it more deeply, as by understanding its meaning). Nevertheless, various psychologists have hypothesized that older adults perform more poorly on tasks that involve secondary memory (a structural concept) because they do not encode or retrieve the information as well as do young adults (process concepts). Other psychologists have argued that age-related differences in secondary memory are due to the speed with which the information is processed. Therefore, the following discussion will perforce include both structural and process concepts.

SECONDARY MEMORY AND AGING: I. ACQUISITION, RETENTION, AND RETRIEVAL.   One of the clearest findings in the field of aging and memory is that the secondary memory of older adults is inferior to that of young adults (Hartley, Harker, & Walsh, 1980; Walsh, 1983). In an effort to explain these age-related declines, some researchers turned their attention to the basic processes of acquisition, retention, and retrieval. Retention was soon eliminated as a potential cause (Craik, 1977; Hultsch & Craig, 1976), so research in this area focused on the two remaining alternatives: the observed age-related declines in performance may occur because the information is not stored or encoded in secondary memory (problems of acquisition), or because the information exists in secondary memory but is not accessible at the time when it is supposed to be recalled (problems of retrieval).

To study acquisition, experimental tasks were chosen that presumably minimized the importance of retrieval. Some of these tasks involved recognition, a relatively easy test of retrieval. Another common procedure is the **cued-recall task:** subjects must learn a list of words, but they are helped to retrieve the correct answers by being given such clues as the first letter, a rhyme, or a synonym of each word. Presumably, if older adults perform significantly more poorly on these tasks than do young adults, this would suggest that the observed age-related declines in secondary memory are due primarily to problems of acquisition. When researchers wished instead to study retrieval, the more demanding free-recall task was often used. Poorer performance by older adults on this task would presumably imply that age-related declines in secondary memory are due primarily to retrieval problems. Various studies using these procedures found that both acquisition and retrieval are adversely affected by aging (e.g., Botwinick & Storandt, 1974; Craik, 1968b; 1977; Drachman & Leavitt, 1972; Erber, 1974; Hultsch, 1975; Laurence, 1967a; 1967b; Smith, 1977; 1980).

The basic assumption underlying this body of research is that acquisition and retrieval can be studied independently. Unfortunately, this assumption now appears to be untenable (Hartley, Harker, &

Myths About Aging: Learning and Memory

MYTH

Most old persons suffer from severe memory impairments, and cannot remember such basic information as the names of their loved ones and where they live.

BEST AVAILABLE EVIDENCE

Secondary memory does decline significantly with increasing age, but usually not to this extent. Memory impairments of this magnitude typically result from severe illnesses, such as Alzheimer's disease or other dementias (Chapter 11). Memory declines in healthy middle-aged and elderly adults are likely to take the form of absentmindedness, such as forgetting what one said an hour ago and repeating it to the same listener or deciding to do something ten minutes from now and then forgetting to do so.

Most middle-aged and elderly adults conform to the maxim, "you can't teach an old dog new tricks."

This is true only for certain kinds of tasks. Older adults perform more poorly on tasks that involve learning new motor skills, the cognitive reorganization of material between the stimulus and the response, dividing attention among several tasks simultaneously, and highly speeded tasks. On many other kinds of tasks, middle-aged and elderly adults are capable of significant amounts of learning.

Walsh, 1980). As we observed previously in this chapter, acquisition and retrieval are very closely related: you cannot remember something (retain and retrieve it from memory) unless you have first learned (acquired) it, although more thorough acquisition makes retrieval easier. Furthermore, there is some indication that older adults acquire information in different ways than do young adults (as we will see). For these reasons, it is extremely difficult to hold retrieval constant and study acquisition alone, or to hold acquisition constant and study retrieval alone. This means that despite the research efforts described above, we cannot determine whether the common age-related declines in secondary memory are due more to problems of acquisition or to problems of retrieval. Therefore, let us turn to research strategies that seek to explain these declines in other terms.

SECONDARY MEMORY AND AGING: II. ORGANIZATION STRATE-GIES. One good way to improve the acquisition and retrieval of secondary memories is by organizing the information. To remember some 15 items on a shopping list, for example, you might sort them into such categories as meats, vegetables, desserts, and beverages. (See Figure 5.8.) If, instead, the items to be remembered do not have any obvious common features, they can be organized by using verbal or pictorial mediators (as we observed in our discussion of verbal learning). Conceivably, then, older adults may perform more poorly on secondary memory tasks because they do not organize the information as effectively as do young adults.

To test this hypothesis, Hultsch (1971) asked adults age 20–29,

A. *Unorganized Material*

Verbal Information: a Shopping List			*Numerical Information: Scores on a 10-Point Quiz*					
Pound cake	Potatoes	Cola	5	9	7	10	6	5
Broccoli	Lamb	Corn	8	4	7	2	8	8
Steak	Pudding	Chicken	10	7	8	5	7	9
Juice	Hamburger	Bacon	6	10	7	5	10	7
Peas	Milk	Pie						

B. *Organized Material*

Meat	*Vegetables*		*Score*	*Frequency*
Steak	Potatoes		10	4
Hamburger	Broccoli		9	2
Chicken	Peas		8	4
Lamb	Corn		7	6
Bacon			6	2
			5	4
			4	1
			3	0
Desserts	*Beverages*		2	1
Pound cake	Cola		1	0
Pudding	Milk		0	0
Pie	Juice			

Note: When presented with stimuli like these for a fixed period of time, most people will learn and recall more when the information is organized.

FIGURE 5.8 Effective organization as an aid to learning and memory.

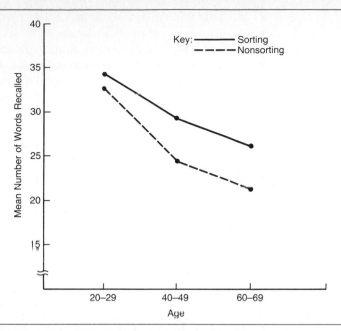

FIGURE 5.9   The effect of improved organization (sorting) on the recall of words as a funciton of age. Hultsch (1971).

40–49, and 60–69 to sort a list of words into categories and then recall the words. Control groups matched on age inspected the words for the same number of trials, but did not perform the sorting task. The results showed that sorting significantly improved the performance of the two oldest groups, albeit not to the level achieved by the youngest subjects. (See Figure 5.9.) Apparently, older subjects who were not instructed to organize the material by sorting it into categories tended not to do so on their own. (See also Hultsch, 1974; Mandler, 1967.)

Corroborating evidence has been obtained from the free-recall task. Subjects in one study were given various lists of words to learn, some of which were much more similar than others (e.g., *horse— monkey—elephant* versus *cow—table—necklace*). Age differences in performance proved to be significantly smaller on lists that contained conceptually related words, suggesting once again that older adults do not spontaneously organize unrelated items (Laurence, 1967b).

Although there are some exceptions to these findings (e.g., Laurence, 1966), we may conclude that the failure to use effective organization strategies is partly responsible for the poorer performance of older adults on secondary memory tasks. This accords well with the verbal learning studies discussed previously, which showed that older adults do not use mediators as often or as well as do young adults. One possible reason is that organization requires considerably more mental effort at more advanced ages, a hypothesis that will be examined further in the following sections.

SECONDARY MEMORY AND AGING: III. DEPTH OF PROCESSING.   Another way to produce longer-lasting memory traces is by processing the information more deeply. As illustrated in Figure 5.5, understanding the meaning of a word (semantics) represents a deeper level of processing than does knowing the sound of the word (phonemics), while phonemic encoding requires a deeper level of processing than does merely observing the physical characteristics of the word. This suggests a third possible reason for the observed age differences in performance on secondary memory tasks: older adults either cannot or do not choose to process information as deeply as do young adults.

This hypothesis has been supported by various empirical data. In one study, four groups of younger and older adults were given lists of unrelated nouns. One group was asked to count the number of letters in each word, while a second group was instructed to make up a rhyme for each word (shallow processing). A third group generated appropriate adjectives for each word, and a fourth group formed a mental image of each word and rated it for vividness (deep processing). Afterwards, all subjects were given an unexpected free-recall test of the list of nouns. For those subjects who performed the shallow-processing tasks (letter counting and rhyming), there were no significant age differences on the free-recall test. But for subjects who carried out the tasks requiring deeper processing (generating adjectives and forming images), young adults recalled significantly more of the nouns than did older adults. That is, the older subjects were less proficient at building strong memory traces through deeper processing (Eysenck, 1974).

Further evidence for the importance of depth of processing comes from a study by Craik and Simon (1980). Younger and older adults were presented with lists of sentences that contained key words to be recalled later on, such as "the highlight of the circus was the clumsy *bear*" or "the lock was opened with the bent *pin*." Then, during a cued-recall test, subjects were given either the specific adjective used in each sentence ("clumsy," "bent") or a general description of the correct answer ("wild animal," "fastener"). The adjective cues proved to be a more effective aid to retrieval for the younger subjects, while the general descriptions led to better recall for the older adults. This implies that the younger adults processed the information more deeply; they remembered "clumsy" and "bent" because they encoded the context in which the key words appeared. Conversely, the older adults did not pay attention to the context and encoded only the key words, just as though only these words had been presented. Because of this shallower processing, their retention was relatively poor, and they needed a broader clue in order to recall the information. This study also found that on cued-recall tasks, phonemic cues (the first two letters of the word to be recalled) were more helpful to older adults than were semantic cues (synonyms). This indicates once again that older adults typically encode information at relatively shallow, phonemic levels.

Why do older adults fail to process information as deeply as do young adults? According to the **attentional deficit hypothesis,** our capacity to pay attention to stimuli declines considerably by old age. Older adults must therefore expend more mental effort to process information more deeply, with the result that they are less likely to do so (Craik, 1977; Craik & Byrd, 1982; Craik & Simon, 1980; Rabinowitz, Craik, & Ackerman, 1982). For example, if subjects must perform two or more tasks simultaneously, the need to divide attention in this way proves to be much more demanding for older than for younger adults. (See Guttentag, 1985.) This age-related decline in the total attentional capacity that is available for information processing may be due to biological changes. Or younger adults may profit from more recent opportunities to practice similar mental tasks, as on school examinations.

Although the attentional deficit hypothesis has merit, there is an important exception: greater skill may compensate for increased age. Deep processing need not always require greater effort, as when repeated practice enables some of these responses to become nearly automatic (Bransford et al., 1980). Whatever the underlying reasons may be, shallower processing is one major reason for the poorer performance of older adults on secondary memory tasks.

SECONDARY MEMORY AND AGING: IV. SPEED OF PROCESSING.   As might be expected in an area as complicated as learning and memory, not all psychologists agree with the depth-of-processing model. In our survey of research on verbal learning and primary memory, we observed that older adults have considerably more difficulty with speeded tasks. According to some psychologists, structural changes in the nervous system have much the same effect on secondary memory. These theorists argue that differences in processing strategies are relatively unimportant. Rather, older adults perform more poorly on secondary memory tasks because they cannot process the information as quickly, both during acquisition and retrieval (Birren, 1974; Salthouse, 1980; Waugh & Barr, 1980).

Various studies indicate that this theory exaggerates the importance of speed of processing. Older adults do not necessarily fare better when stimuli to be retained in secondary memory are presented at slower rates of speed, implying that a lack of sufficient encoding time is *not* a sufficient explanation for age-related differences in performance (Craik & Rabinowitz, 1985). Nor are the responses of older adults on free-recall or cued-recall tasks necessarily slower than those of young adults (Macht & Buschke, 1984). While our cognitive processes undoubtedly do operate more slowly as we grow older, such changes represent only one of the factors responsible for age-related decrements in performance on secondary memory tasks.

AFTERWORD.   Insofar as secondary memory is concerned, older adults do not acquire or retrieve information as well as do young adults. They do not organize information as effectively. They do not process information as deeply. And the speed at which they process information may well be slower.

Since the evidence reviewed in the preceding pages was primarily cross-sectional in nature, these findings may have been partly influenced by cohort effects. Nevertheless, it is reasonable to expect some troublesome impairments in secondary memory as you grow toward old age. You are also likely to encounter such lapses in your dealings with older adults. (Memory impairments may also result from various illnesses, such as Alzheimer's disease, strokes, and alcohol or drug abuse. Such issues are discussed in Chapter 11.)

To what extent do such impairments affect the everyday lives of older adults? This is not an easy question to answer, as we will see in the following section.

The Issue of Ecological Validity

As was the case with verbal learning research, the information-processing studies discussed above have been criticized on the grounds of low ecological validity. These studies typically used such tasks as remembering lists of unrelated single words, which is not a common activity in everyday life. Conceivably, the skills tapped by these tasks may differ significantly from the ability to recall the contents of a novel, the names of important people and places, or other meaningful material. (See, for example, Neisser, 1978; 1982.) Therefore, some researchers have used experimental tasks that are more similar to everyday activities in order to study the relationship between aging, learning, and memory.

CONNECTED DISCOURSE: SENTENCES AND PARAGRAPHS.   To improve the ecological validity of information-processing research, some investigators have replaced the usual lists of unrelated words with meaningful sentences or paragraphs. When long passages are used, exact reproduction is not required; subjects are allowed to paraphrase, or to recall the basic ideas in their own words. For example, if a paragraph includes the statement "no casualties were reported," full credit is given if the subject recalls that "there were no casualties." If artificial laboratory tasks do exaggerate the relationship between aging and learning and memory, age differences in performance should be considerably smaller when these more meaningful stimuli are used.

Insofar as learning is concerned, one study presented younger and older adults with 215-word and 957-word passages. The older subjects had significantly greater difficulty understanding this material, as measured by multiple-choice recognition tests (Taub, 1976). It is not clear whether these age-related differences in comprehension are limited to adults who are average in verbal ability (Taub, 1979), or whether they also occur among highly educated and verbally superior adults (Finkle & Walsh, 1979). In general, however, the ability to comprehend meaningful discourse does appear to decline with increasing age.

Evidence concerning the recall of meaningful sentences and paragraphs is more equivocal. Some researchers have compared the ability of younger and older adults to recall normal sentences, foolish near-sentences (e.g., "The Declaration of Independence sang overnight while the cereal jumped by the river"), and random groupings of words. Not surprisingly, the younger subjects performed significantly better on this secondary memory task. But age differences were *greatest* when the normal sentences were used, despite the better ecological validity (Botwinick & Storandt, 1974; Craik & Masani, 1967). However, if subjects are asked to recall the major idea(s) in a sentence rather than the exact words, age differences in performance appear to be reduced (Till & Walsh, 1980; Walsh & Baldwin, 1977; Walsh, Baldwin, & Finkle, 1980).

When memory is tested with longer passages (e.g., 60–300 words), some findings indicate that older adults perform more poorly than young adults on both free-recall and recognition tasks (Cohen, 1979; Gordon & Clark, 1974; Taub & Kline, 1978). Yet other studies have found no significant performance differences among young, middle-aged, and elderly adults on such tasks as free recall, giving a one-sentence summary of the passage, and completing a partly filled-in outline (Meyer et al., 1979a; 1979b). Although some studies of secondary memory do suggest that older adults are at less of a disadvantage when connected discourse is to be recalled, the empirical data in this area appear to be too inconsistent for any definitive conclusions to be drawn.

SPATIAL MEMORY.   Most adults readily learn and remember how to proceed from one place to another without getting lost, as when going from home to the supermarket, to school, or to work. This task may appear to be a simple one, yet it actually involves a complicated set of behaviors: we must know where we wish to go, how best to reach our destination, and where to make various changes in direction while en route. Since spatial learning is considerably more involved than recalling single words, and since older adults typically perform much more poorly on more difficult tasks, it is likely that our ability to negotiate our environment declines appreciably with increasing age.

To test this hypothesis, young and elderly adults were asked to recall as many buildings as they could in their local downtown area. All subjects were also required to locate familiar buildings on a grid. On both tasks, the elderly subjects demonstrated significantly less knowledge about their geographical environment than did young adults (Evans et al., 1984). As with verbal stimuli, older adults appear to organize this information less effectively, making retrieval more difficult. Other studies have also found significant age differences in spatial memory, using such tasks as placing drawings of buildings in the proper position on a maplike display and finding one's way in an unfamiliar building (Ohta & Kirasic, 1983; Perlmutter et al., 1981).

Declines in spatial memory pose a particular problem for the institutionalized elderly. One study focused on residents of a nursing home who ranged in age from 72 to 93 years, were ambulatory, had adequate vision, and were cognitively alert. Most of these subjects had difficulty identifying the location of various places in the nursing home, with this problem more common among the older residents. By comparison, a small group of college undergraduates who spent a mere 40 minutes touring the nursing home achieved consistently better identification scores than did the elderly adults who had been living there for some time (Weber, Brown, & Weldon, 1978). This implies that such institutions must do more to help residents learn and become comfortable with their environment, as by providing distinctive furnishings or other cues in different areas.

MEMORY FOR EVERYDAY TASKS.   Other researchers have sought to resolve the problem of ecological validity by designing experimental tasks that resemble common daily activities, such as keeping appointments. To illustrate, ten young adults (age 22–37) and ten older adults (age 65–75) were instructed to telephone the experimenter once a day at a fixed time of their own choice. They were told that if they called more than five minutes late, they would be considered to have missed the appointment. A telephone answering service recorded the day, time, and caller. This proved to be one of the few studies wherein the performance of the older adults was clearly superior: the young subjects much more often called late, or forgot their appointments entirely. Even when random and irregular calling times were substituted, making the task more difficult, the older adults still remembered significantly more appointments than did the young adults (Moscovitch, cited by Harris & Morris, 1984). The older subjects were apparently more motivated to perform well on this task, so they made greater use of such external aids as writing down the appointment times on a sheet of paper and keeping it in plain sight.

AFTERWORD: IMPROVING LEARNING AND MEMORY.   Taken as a whole, the research findings discussed above suggest that the case of Mrs. W. is an extreme one; most elderly adults need not expect to undergo this degree of memory deterioration. Nevertheless, we are likely to encounter at least some troublesome impairments in learning and memory as we grow toward old age. What can be done

Research evidence clearly indicates that the secondary memory of older adults is inferior to that of younger adults. One good way to combat the effects of such declines, and to deal more effectively with daily activities, is by using such external aids as memoranda and shopping lists.   *Pamela Price/Picture Cube*

to help older adults cope with these decrements, and to deal more effectively with their daily activities?

One possibility is to provide formal training in the use of organization strategies, such as categorization and mediators. (See, for example, Poon, Walsh-Sweeney, & Fozard, 1980.) Such training does tend to improve the performance of older adults on learning and secondary memory tasks, albeit not to the level achieved by young adults. But if the attentional deficit hypothesis is correct, and the mental energy that powers our cognitive activity declines with increasing age (as physical energy certainly does), older adults may find it too difficult to deal with secondary memory tasks that require sustained amounts of attention.

A better approach may be to encourage the use of external aids, as proved so helpful in the Moscovitch telephone appointment study. B. F. Skinner, the noted behaviorist, offers some useful recommendations in this regard:

> *IMPROVING MEMORY THROUGH INTELLECTUAL*
> *SELF-MANAGEMENT: B. F. SKINNER'S ADVICE.*
>
> [Suppose that] ten minutes before you leave your house for the day, you hear a weather report: it will probably rain before you return. It occurs to you to take an umbrella . . . but you are not yet able to execute [this behavior]. You can solve that kind of problem by executing as much of the behavior as possible when it occurs to you. Hang the umbrella on the doorknob, or put it through the handle of your briefcase, or in some other way start the process of taking it with you.
>
> Here is a similar intellectual problem: in the middle of the night it occurs to you that you can clarify a passage in the paper you are writing by making a certain change. At your desk the next day you forget to make the change. Again, the solution is to make the change when it occurs to you, using, say, a notepad or tape recorder kept beside your bed. The problem in old age is not so much how to have ideas as how to have them when you can use them. A written or dictated record, consulted from time to time, has the same effect as the umbrella hung on the doorknob. . . . In place of memories, memoranda. (Skinner, 1983, p. 240; see also Skinner & Vaughan, 1983.)

Skinner also offers useful strategies for dealing with potentially awkward social situations. If he is with his wife and cannot recall the name of an acquaintance, and there is some chance that she could have met this person, he simply says to her: "Of course, you remember . . . ?" By prearrangement, before it becomes apparent that he has forgotten the name, the wife interrupts with "Yes, of course. How are you?" The acquaintance may not recall ever having met the Skinners, but will hopefully be too unsure of his or her memory to raise any questions. When speaking, elderly adults should use simple sentences, so that they don't forget key ideas in the course of a lengthy digression. Or if older adults are having a conversation and fear that they will forget a clever idea by the time their turn to speak arrives (and they are too polite to interrupt!), they can keep repeating this material silently to themselves until the other person has finished talking.

Skinner himself has put his own advice to good use, drawing on strategies like these to continue writings scholarly works at the age of 80. Thus the memory decrements that do occur with increasing age need not always have a detrimental effect on overt behavior—provided, of course, that one is sufficiently determined and resourceful.

Summary

Learning and memory are closely interrelated. You cannot remember something unless you previously acquired some knowledge of it, and one common test of whether or not you have learned something is your ability to remember it at a later date. Also, learning and memory are complicated and unobservable processes. We must draw inferences about them based on the performance of subjects on experimental tasks, which we can observe directly.

ASSOCIATIONIST APPROACHES TO LEARNING AND MEMORY

Associationism attributes all learning and memory to the association of stimuli and responses that occur closely together in time. Although this conception was most popular a few decades ago, it has provided an important point of departure for more modern theories.

Motor skill learning refers to any task wherein the subject must learn a sequence of bodily movements. Many motor skills persist until very late in life because they are acquired during childhood, adolescence, or early adulthood, and are practiced so often that they become nearly automatic. The primary exception occurs with tasks that require speeded responses, on which older adults perform more poorly. The capacity to develop new motor skills does decline with increasing age, especially with regard to complicated tasks.

A great deal of associationist research on learning and memory has focused on verbal stimuli and responses. In serial learning, the subject is required to learn a list of words or nonsense syllables in the exact order in which they are presented. In paired-associate learning, pairs of words or nonsense syllables are used, and the subject must learn to reply with the second member of the pair when presented with the first member. On both kinds of tasks, older adults consistently perform more poorly than do young adults. Possible reasons are that older adults cannot respond as quickly, and that there is a significant loss in the ability to rehearse or organize the information (and to resort to other mnemonic strategies) with increasing age.

More recently, associationist theory has been criticized on several grounds. Serial and paired-associate tasks would seem to ignore certain important aspects of learning and memory, such as semantic memory. These tasks also appear to be low in ecological validity. Modern theorists have therefore sought to develop alternative conceptions of learning and memory, the most notable of which is the information-processing approach.

INFORMATION-PROCESSING APPROACHES TO LEARNING AND MEMORY

The information-processing model is based on the principles that underlie modern electronic computers. Although this analogy is only a rough one, it serves to emphasize the importance of encoding, storing, and retrieving information for the purposes of solving problems, taking action, and acquiring new information. Structural information-processing theories focus on the ways in which information is stored and organized in the human brain, while process theories emphasize the mental activities that we perform when we try to learn or remember information.

The most prominent structural theory posits that there are three distinct types of memory storage systems: sensory memory, primary memory, and secondary memory. Information must first pass through sensory memory in order to reach primary memory, and must pass through primary memory in order to enter secondary memory. Sensory memory very briefly preserves the physical characteristics of a stimulus, so that we have just enough time to select information by paying attention to it. This form of memory is relatively unaffected by aging. Primary memory holds a sufficiently small amount of information for conscious processing, and retains this material for at most half a minute. This form of memory is also largely unaffected by aging. Secondary memory stores information in terms of abstract symbols, has an enormous capacity, and is capable of retaining data for many years. Performance on secondary memory tasks does decline significantly with increasing age.

According to process theory, there is only one kind of memory storage system, and the duration of memory traces depends on how deeply or thoroughly we process the information. The act of remembering depends on three basic processes: acquisition, retention, and retrieval. There is relatively little relationship between aging and retention. Insofar as secondary memory is concerned, older adults do not acquire or retrieve this information as well as do young adults. It is very difficult to study acquisition and retrieval independently of each other, however, so researchers have been unable to determine which of these processes is more affected by aging. Information-processing research has confirmed that older adults perform more poorly on secondary memory tasks because they do not organize the material as effectively as do young adults, as by using categories or mediators. Older adults also do not process information as deeply as do young adults, which results in less durable memory traces. Our capacity to pay attention to stimuli may decline with increasing age, with the result that older adults must expend more mental effort to process information more deeply. The poorer performance of older adults on secondary memory tasks may also be due in part to the slowing of our cognitive processes as we grow older, although this is at most only one of the factors responsible for the observed age differences.

In an effort to improve the ecological validity of laboratory research, some investigators have instead used experimental tasks that are more similar to everyday activities. The ability to comprehend meaningful discourse, such as sentences and paragraphs, does appear to decline as we grow older. Evidence concerning the recall of this material is more equivocal; some studies have obtained significant age differences, while others have not. Significant age-related decrements have been found in spatial learning and memory, which has important implications for the well-being of the institutionalized aged.

Taken as a whole, the research reviewed in this chapter indicates that there is a significant decline in secondary memory with increasing age. However, these decrements need not always have a detrimental effect on overt behavior. Training in the use of organizational categories and mediators may help older adults to improve their performance on learning and memory tasks, while intellectual self-management and the use of external aids can enable older adults to deal effectively with their daily activities.

CHAPTER 6

Intelligence and Creativity

Among the most admired of human characteristics are intelligence and creativity. More intelligent people can perform important mental behaviors more easily, and are more likely to succeed in school or in various professions. Creative individuals have made monumental contributions to virtually every area of human endeavor, including music, art, literature, the physical and social sciences, inventions, and recreation. Accordingly, the relationship between these variables and aging is of considerable importance. Will your capacity for intelligent thought decline markedly as you grow older? Should you expect to lose much of your capacity for original, creative work as you grow past middle age? Such issues have a significant bearing on the satisfactions you are likely to experience later in life.

The relationship between aging and intelligence has been widely investigated by social scientists. Much of the early psychological research on aging dealt with the performance of subjects on various intelligence tests. Whereas these cross-sectional studies indicated a pronounced decline in test scores with increasing age, more recent longitudinal research has cast considerable doubt on this pessimistic conclusion. There is less empirical evidence dealing with aging and creativity, but some important discoveries have been made in this area as well.

In this chapter, we will examine gerontological data dealing with intelligence and creativity. First, however, we must survey the efforts that have been made to define these important but complicated variables.

The Meaning of Intelligence

The Problem of Defining Intelligence

What is **intelligence?** The general meaning of this concept is well known: It refers to the range of behavior from dull to bright, slow-witted to quick-witted, stupid to clever. High intelligence presumably makes it easier to use words and numbers correctly, to remember substantial amounts of information, and to reason out the solutions to problems of various kinds.

Nevertheless, it is extremely difficult to state an exact definition of intelligence. Are there several primarily separate forms of intelligence (e.g., verbal, numerical, spatial), so that an individual may be considerably brighter in some areas and duller in others? Or is intelligence a general phenomenon that has a similar effect on all mental activity? Although the very first model of intelligence adopted the latter hypothesis (Spearman, 1904), most modern psychologists prefer the former approach. Yet they disagree as to whether intelligence consists of two or three distinct abilities, half a dozen, or perhaps even as many as 150. (See, for example, Anastasi, 1976; Guilford, 1984.)

The concept of intelligence is also subject to cultural issues. People who come from different countries, societies, ethnic groups, and/or socioeconomic groups are likely to undergo markedly different experiences and training during their formative years. Thus the meaning of intelligence may well vary from culture to culture.

Furthermore, it is not always easy to distinguish between intelligence and related variables. Consider, for example, the stereotype of the aged guru, who passes on priceless secrets about life to those who seek such knowledge. This individual would generally be regarded as unusually wise, rather than intelligent. Yet there is very little research evidence dealing with wisdom, and virtually none concerning wisdom and aging. (See Clayton & Birren, 1980.) Or consider a musical genius like Beethoven, who was unquestionably creative. Is it reasonable to regard him as unintelligent, simply because he may not have scored particularly high in verbal and mathematical ability?

For these reasons, we will not attempt to formulate a word-for-word definition of intelligence. Instead, we will explicate the meaning of this concept by discussing several different approaches to its measurement.

Conceptualizing Intelligence: The Psychometric Approach

HISTORICAL BACKGROUND.   Prior to the twentieth century, the nature of intelligence was very poorly understood. In these unenlightened times, intelligence was measured with such physiologically oriented tests as muscular strength, sensitivity to pain, visual and auditory acuity, and reaction time.

The pioneering step in defining intelligence as we know it today was taken by a French psychologist, Alfred Binet. By 1900, most industrialized nations had established compulsory elementary education. This new requirement presented a formidable problem: some children might well be mentally retarded, and in need of special education classes. Others might only appear to be backward because they came from an intellectually impoverished home, and would be quite able to cope with regular classes. How, then, could truly dull children be identified? To deal with this problem, the French minister of public instruction appointed a special committee, of which Binet was a member. Their solution, achieved in 1905, ushered in the **psychometric approach** to intelligence: they decided to develop an objective diagnostic instrument to assess each child's intellectual capacity.

Binet and his collaborator, Theodore Simon, assumed that intelligence is a general aptitude that relates to many kinds of mental functioning (Binet & Simon, 1905). Their landmark test included cognitive tasks that varied widely in content and difficulty: copying a drawing, repeated back a string of digits, recognizing coins and making change, explaining why certain statements are absurd. Binet also assumed, correctly, that intelligence increases with age until maturity. Therefore, in the 1908 revision of his test, he arranged the items according to age level. First, the difficulty of each item was determined by administering the test to some 300 normal children between the ages of 3 and 13 years. Then, items passed by 80 percent to 90 percent of children of a specific age (e.g., 7 years) were grouped at that age level. This made it possible to express a child's cognitive ability in terms of **mental age (MA).** For example, suppose that a child passes all items through the six-year level, half of those at the seven-year level, and no others. This child's mental age is equal to 6 years plus an additional half year, or 6.5 years.

THE INTELLIGENCE QUOTIENT (IQ).   If a 5-year-old child has a mental age of 6.5, and a 9-year-old has a mental age of 8.0, which one is more intelligent? Although the former child has a lower MA, this child's performance is well above the level expected from his or her chronological age (CA). Conversely, the latter child is performing at a level below the average of his or her age group. To make such comparisons easier, a German psychologist, William Stern, proposed the use of the **intelligence quotient (IQ)** in 1912:

$$IQ = \frac{MA}{CA} \times 100$$

In the preceding example, the first child has an IQ of $(6.5/5) \times 100 = 130$, indicating superior intelligence. The IQ of the second child is $(8.0/9) \times 100 = 89$, which is below average. An average IQ occurs when MA = CA, and is equal to 100.

PROBLEMS IN THE MEASUREMENT OF ADULT INTELLI- GENCE. The well-known intelligence quotient, which was devised for use with children, is badly flawed as an index of adult intelligence. Intelligence does not grow forever, any more than height does, while our chronological age consistently increases. If this intelligence quotient were to be used with adults, it would seem as though we all become shockingly dim-witted as we grow toward old age. To illustrate, if your MA is 18.0 years and your CA is 12 years, your IQ is an impressive 150. There may be some decline in your intelligence with increasing age (an issue to be discussed later in this chapter), yet you will surely remain quite bright throughout your life. But if your MA remains at about 18 years by the time your CA reaches 54 years (which is by no means unlikely), your IQ would be 33, a value that indicates severe mental retardation! Obviously, this is an absurdity.

One possible alternative is to use mental age as the index of adult intelligence. In the preceding example, your MA remains at about 18 years, which does give a more accurate picture. This procedure is suitable for some kinds of research; but it provides no indication of whether your intelligence is above or below average, let alone how far above or below. Thus a popular alternative is to compare an individual's test score to the average score obtained by a sample of adults of the same age, using such statistical procedures as means, standard deviations, standard scores, and percentile ranks.[1] For example, if your score on an intelligence test is one standard deviation above (below) the mean of your age group, this will place you in the top (bottom) 16 percent of that group. A score that is two standard deviations above or below average represents the top or bottom 2 percent. Since the standard deviation on some prominent intelligence tests is approximately 15, these scores are sometimes translated into **deviation IQs:** 115 represents one 15-point standard de-

---

[1] For a discussion of these and other basic statistics, see Welkowitz, Ewen, and Cohen (1982).

viation above the average of 100 (and therefore places you in the top 16 percent of your age group), 130 represents two standard deviations above average, 90 represents two thirds of a standard deviation below average, and so on. Note that although the popular concept of IQ is retained, mental age plays no part at all in these calculations; all that is involved is the comparison of a subject's test score to the mean score of his or her age group.

Another serious problem with tests like Binet's is that they equate intelligence with educational aptitude. Since the original purpose of these tests was to predict the academic success of children, the test constructors defined high intelligence in terms of the capacity to do well on classroom tasks. If those who obtained higher test scores received higher grades in school, and those who scored lower received lower grades, the test was assumed to be a valid measure of intelligence. Insofar as adults are concerned, however, this rationale may well be inappropriate. Most middle-aged and elderly adults have long since left school, and have little need for purely academic talents. Also, one's success or failure in life cannot be evaluated in terms of such simple criteria as letter grades. As an alternative, some attempts have been made to devise tests of adult intelligence that are based on real-life situations (e.g., Demming & Pressey, 1957; Gardner & Monge, 1977; Schaie, 1978; Scheidt & Schaie, 1978). The items on these tests may deal with such issues as where to look in the yellow pages of the telephone directory if you want to buy an Airedale, the title of a person who baptizes a baby, how best to drive a car in rush-hour traffic, and a knowledge of the major diseases that afflict the elderly—quite a different matter from such common intelligence test items as repeating back a string of digits, explaining the meaning of the word "tantamount," or identifying the author of *Huckleberry Finn*. There is some indication that older adults may be at less of a disadvantage when these innovative tests are used, but this issue is still essentially unresolved. This research area is still in its infancy, and it is plagued with criterion problems: it is difficult to find an external standard that can be used to validate the test and show that high scores do signify high intelligence, now that school grades are not relevant.

In sum: the psychometric approach has contributed substantially to our understanding of intelligence. But some significant problems do arise when this approach is used to measure the intelligence of adults, especially older adults. Therefore, we may well ask: what alternatives to the psychometric approach currently exist?

Conceptualizing Intelligence: Other Approaches

THE PIAGETIAN APPROACH.   Jean Piaget, the noted Swiss child psychologist, devoted considerable attention to the development of human intellectual processes. Rather than dealing with the usual verbal and mathematical abilities, Piagetian theory is concerned with various innovative concepts. For example, "object permanence" involves the child's awareness of the identity and continuing existence of objects when they are seen from different angles, or are out of sight. "Conservation" concerns the child's ability to recognize that an attribute of an object remains constant even though its perceptual appearance changes, as when the same quantity of liquid is poured into differently shaped containers.

The Piagetian approach is an influential one in developmental psychology. But this theory deals primarily with childhood (especially early childhood), as does virtually all of the related empirical research. Since the relevance of this approach to adult aging and development is yet to be demonstrated, it will not be discussed further. (See Anastasi, 1976, pp. 77, 276; Ginsburg & Opper, 1969.)

THE INFORMATION-PROCESSING APPROACH.   Some investigators have tried to link individual differences in intellectual ability with such cognitive processes as learning, memory, and attention, as measured by the kinds of laboratory tasks discussed in the preceding chapter. These theorists argue that the hard-to-define concept of intelligence is best explained in terms of differences on these more fundamental, better-understood variables. Thus people who are "more intelligent" may actually be better learners, may acquire new information and retrieve data from memory more efficiently, or may be better able to pay attention to the task at hand. (See, for example, Hunt, 1978; 1980.)

Some studies do suggest that scores on intelligence tests are positively correlated with performance on certain laboratory tasks, including serial learning and free recall. But considerably more research is needed in order to evaluate the merits of the information-processing approach to intelligence.

AFTERWORD.   Although the psychometric approach to intelligence suffers from various conceptual and methodological problems, it has produced most of the available gerontological research evidence. Therefore, our investigation of the relationship between aging and intelligence will perforce be couched primarily in terms of test scores.

Intelligence and Aging

WAIS Studies

THE WECHSLER ADULT INTELLIGENCE SCALE.   The intelligence test most often used with adults is the **Wechsler Adult Intelligence Scale,** or **WAIS** (Wechsler, 1958). Like most modern psychologists,

Wechsler conceptualized intelligence as consisting of a number of different abilities. He was particularly concerned with Binet's emphasis on verbal skills: one can presumably be intelligent, yet not overly proficient in the English language. Wechsler sought to remedy this defect by devising an intelligence test that consisted of two types of scales, **verbal** and **performance.** Each of these includes a number of subtests, as summarized below and shown in Figures 6.1 and 6.2.

VERBAL SCALES

1. *Information:* 29 questions covering a wide variety of information that is readily available to adults in our culture, but excluding specialized or academic knowledge.

2. *Comprehension:* 14 items dealing with the necessity for certain actions or rules, the meanings of proverbs, and so on.

3. *Arithmetic:* 14 problems involving elementary school arithmetic, to be solved without using paper and pencil.

Information
1. Who wrote *Huckleberry Finn?*
2. Where is Finland?
3. At what temperature does paper burn?
4. What is entomology?

Arithmetic
1. How many 22 cent stamps can you buy for two dollars?
2. If two oranges cost 37 cents, what will a dozen oranges cost?
3. How many hours will it take a cyclist to travel 60 miles at a rate of 12 miles per hour?

Digit Span
1. Repeat these numbers in the same order:
   7–1–6–2–2–8–3.
2. Repeat these numbers backwards:
   9–4–1–5.

Comprehension
1. Why should we obey traffic laws and speed limits?
2. Why are antitrust laws necessary?
3. Why should we lock the doors and take the keys when leaving a parked car?
4. What does this saying mean: "Kill two birds with one stone."

Similarities
1. In what way are a hammer and a screwdriver alike?
2. In what way are a dog and a plant alike?
3. In what way are coal and gasoline alike?

Vocabulary
1. What does "careful" mean?
2. What does "tantamount" mean?

FIGURE 6.1　Test items similar to WAIS verbal subtests. Modified from Gleitman (1983, p. 393).

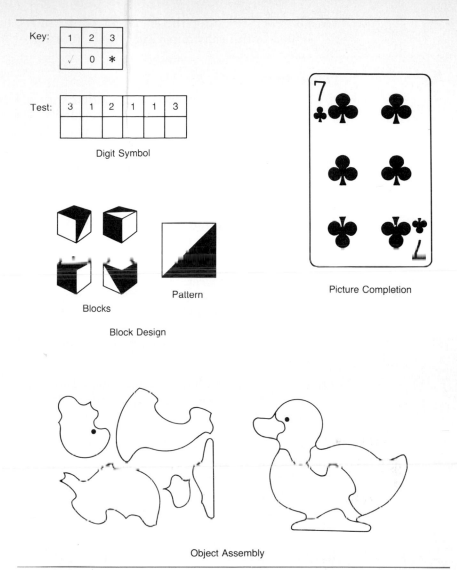

Digit Symbol

Block Design

Blocks

Pattern

Picture Completion

Object Assembly

FIGURE 6.2   Test items similar to WAIS performance subtests. Modified from Gleitman (1983, p. 393).

4. *Similarities:* 13 items involving the way in which two things are alike.

5. *Digit Span:* Repeating back sequences of from three to nine digits in the order presented, and repeating back sequences of from two to eight digits backwards (as discussed in the preceding chapter).

6. *Vocabulary:* Stating the meaning of 40 unrelated words, presented both orally and visually and in order of increasing difficulty.

PERFORMANCE SCALES

7. *Digit Symbol:* The subject is provided with a key that contains nine symbols paired with the nine digits. Using this key, the subject has 1½ minutes to fill in as many symbols as possible on the answer sheet.

8. *Picture Completion:* Identifying the missing component in a common picture. There are 21 pictures, which vary in difficulty.

9. *Block Design:* The subject is given a set of identical one-inch blocks whose sides are red, white, or half red and half white, and must assemble them so that the pattern on top matches a specified design.

10. *Picture Arrangement.* A set of cards, each of which contains a picture, must be rearranged in the proper sequence so as to tell a story (as though a comic strip in the daily newspaper were cut into separate panels and presented out of order, but without any dialogue). There are eight such items, which vary in difficulty.

11. *Object Assembly:* Four rather simple jigsaw-type puzzles, wherein pieces must be put together to form a flat picture of a familiar object.

Notice that the verbal subtests focus on the subject's store of knowledge in various areas: general facts (historical, literary, biological), how to deal competently with one's environment, arithmetical operations, the meanings of words. Only the arithmetic test has a time limit. In contrast, the performance subtests deal with primarily unfamiliar material and place a heavy emphasis on response speed. All of these subtests are timed, and bonus points are awarded for unusually fast solutions. Scores on the WAIS may be expressed simply in terms of points (raw scores), which is usually best insofar as aging research is concerned, or converted into deviation IQs.

THE CLASSIC AGING PATTERN.   When the relationship between aging and WAIS scores is investigated with cross-sectional studies, a fairly consistent pattern emerges. Both verbal and performance scores peak at a relatively early age (verbal scores by the mid-twenties, performance scores by the late teens), and then decline steadily with increasing age. These decrements are typically small on the verbal scales and much more pronounced on the performance scales, a phenomenon known as the **classic aging pattern.** (See Figure 6.3.)

In the WAIS Block Design Performance Scale, the subject is asked to assemble the blocks so that the pattern on top matches the design on the printed card. This subtest is timed; bonus points are awarded if the solution is reached with extraordinary speed. *Sepp Seitz/Woodfin Camp*

Among the verbal scales, the similarities and digit span subtests suffer the greatest declines with increasing age, while the remaining four subtests show little change. Conversely, substantial decrements are found on all of the performance scales. (See, for example, Botwinick, 1967; 1977; Doppelt & Wallace, 1955; Jones, 1959.) For this reason, IQ scores on the WAIS are age graded: the same score yields a higher IQ at an older age. For example, suppose that a 22-year-old achieves a performance score of 60 points. This individual's peer group has a fairly high mean, so the score of 60 translates into a deviation IQ of only about 112. But if a 71-year-old obtains a score of 60, this is equivalent to a deviation IQ of 140, since this older adult belongs to an age group with a much lower mean.

How much reliance can be placed on these findings? Cross-sectional studies are likely to *overstate* the extent of age-related declines in WAIS scores, since they do not control for cohort effects. Older adults may well be at a disadvantage on the WAIS because education and test taking were not stressed as much during their youth. They may obtain lower scores because they have considerably greater test anxiety, or because they are less familiar with the required facts and skills, rather than because their intelligence is lower. Accordingly, many modern researchers prefer to investigate the relation-

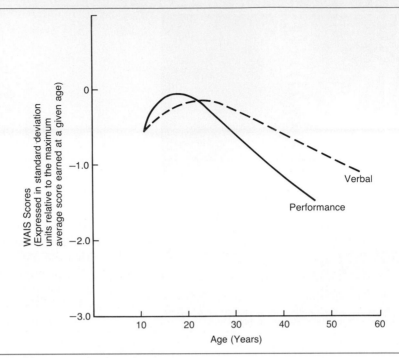

FIGURE 6.3   WAIS classic aging pattern. Jones (1959); Kausler (1982, p. 574).

ship between aging and intelligence by using longitudinal studies. But while this approach has definite advantages, it is no panacea, for it is likely to *understate* the extent of age-related declines in WAIS scores. Less capable subjects tend to drop out over the course of a longitudinal study, which inflates the group mean in later years (the phenomenon of selective attrition, discussed in Chapter 2). Thus it is hardly surprising that the declines in WAIS scores reported by these studies tend to be small, and often negligible. Some longitudinal studies even report modest increases in WAIS scores with increasing age, at least on the verbal scales. (See, for example, Siegler & Botwinick, 1979.)

Partly because there is no ideal research method, the field of aging and intelligence is rife with controversy and debate. Among those taking an optimistic view are Baltes and Schaie (1974; 1976; Schaie & Baltes, 1977), who conclude that the assumption of a universal decline in intelligence with increasing age is a myth. These researchers attribute much of the declines found in intelligence test scores to cohort differences, rather than to aging. They argue that these declines occur in varying degrees for different individuals, and for different areas of intellectual ability. And they stress the difficulties in using educationally designed intelligence tests with older adults, as noted previously in this chapter. According to Baltes and Schaie, those losses in test performance that do occur with increasing age are relatively plastic, and can be largely reversed through appropriate training (a conception known as **plasticity theory**).

In contrast, some theorists emphatically reject such optimism (Horn & Donaldson, 1976; 1977). They contend that virtually all of the research on aging and intelligence shows significant declines in test scores, and that any exceptions are due to methodological and procedural errors. Thus Horn and Donaldson attribute these declines to aging, not cohort, and do not regard them as reversible through training. Some interesting (albeit anecdotal) support for the more pessimistic position is also found in the following case history:

> REMINISCENCES OF A PROMINENT PSYCHOLOGIST
>
> D. O. Hebb, a noted psychologist in the field of learning and perception, retired in 1977. Hebb found that on reaching his 60s and 70s, he retained his addiction to difficult crossword puzzles, which draw primarily on previously acquired information [*crystallized intelligence,* discussed later]. But he gradually lost interest in solving mathematical brain teasers, which require the juggling of new ideas [*fluid intelligence*]. As Hebb put it: "I'm not quite senile, not yet. I can still keep up appearances, and there are points on which I can still outtalk younger colleagues. But—between you and me, privately—the picture is one of a slow, inevitable loss of cognitive capacity." (Hebb, 1978, p. 23.)

It is difficult to arrive at definitive answers when even the experts disagree. However, researchers have produced a substantial amount of empirical data dealing with aging and intelligence. Let us see whether an examination of this evidence points the way toward any general conclusions.

Fluid and Crystallized Intelligence

DEFINITION.   Intelligence is often conceptualized in terms of a number of specific intellectual abilities: verbal, numerical, reasoning, spatial relations, memory, and so forth. In contrast, one influential theory argues that psychological knowledge has not yet advanced far enough for us to identify the precise mental abilities that comprise intelligence (Cattell, 1940; 1963; Horn, 1970; 1978). Instead, this approach distinguishes between two general kinds of intelligence. **Fluid intelligence** involves the capacity to use unique kinds of thinking in order to solve unfamiliar problems, rather than merely

Chapter Glossary: Intelligence and Creativity

Classic aging pattern	The occurrence of pronounced declines on WAIS performance subtests, and smaller declines on the verbal subtests, with increasing age.
Convergent thinking	Solving a problem by narrowing down many possibilities and arriving at the one correct answer.
Creativity	A solution to a problem of significance to society that is original, unusual, ingenious, and relevant.
Crystallized intelligence	The capacity to use knowledge acquired through education or acculturation.
Deviation IQ	An index of intelligence obtained by statistically comparing a subject's test score to the mean score of his or her age group. Does *not* involve mental age.
Divergent thinking	Solving a problem by producing many different and unusual answers.
Extraneous variable	A variable which is at least partly responsible for lower intelligence test scores or fewer creative contributions with increasing age, but which does *not* involve a change in the capacity for intelligent or creative behavior.
Fluid intelligence	The capacity to use unique kinds of thinking in order to solve unfamiliar problems, rather than merely drawing on previously acquired information.
Intelligence	A concept that refers to the range of behavior from dull to bright, slow-witted to quick-witted, and so on. There is no one universally accepted definition of intelligence, nor is there agreement as to the number of specific abilities that are involved.
Intelligence quotient (IQ)	An index of intelligence obtained by dividing an individual's mental age by his or her chronological age, and multiplying the result by 100. Not appropriate for use with adults.
Mental age	An index that expresses one's intellectual ability in terms of the age of those who readily achieve the same level of performance on an appropriate intelligence test.
Performance scales (performance subtests)	Five subtests of the Wechsler Adult Intelligence Scale that do not require the use of words, and are highly speeded: digit symbol, picture completion, block design, picture arrangement, and object assembly.

Plasticity theory	Posits that those declines in intelligence test scores that do occur with increasing age can be largely reversed through appropriate training.
Psychometric approach to intelligence	Defining intelligence in terms of the psychological tests used to measure it, and the resulting test scores.
Terminal drop	A sudden and severe drop in WAIS scores that indicates the existence of physical illness, and serves as a warning of imminent death.
Verbal scales (verbal subtests)	Six subtests of the Wechsler Adult Intelligence Scale that require the use of words, and are for the most part not highly speeded: information, comprehension, arithmetic, similarities, digit span, and vocabulary.
Wechsler Adult Intelligence Scale (WAIS)	The most commonly used measure of adult intelligence, which consists of six verbal scales (which require the use of words) and five performance scales (which do not).

drawing on previously acquired information. For example, one aspect of fluid intelligence is measured with items like these:

In each of the following problems, there are four four-letter combinations. Three of the combinations in each group are alike in some way. Which combination does *not* belong in each group?[2]

1. VWXY   JKLM   PRTU   BCDE
2. HDOR   GDOR   LDOR   FDOR
3. MRCW   OUIE   XLVQ   TODI

Notice that the abilities tapped by this test are relatively unaffected by prior education and classroom learning. In contrast, **crystallized intelligence** involves the knowledge that has been acquired through education and acculturation. It is typically measured by using tests of vocabulary, information, and mechanical knowledge, all of which draw on one's acquired store of information. Thus crystallized intelligence is determined largely by personal experiences and intentional learning, while fluid intelligence is determined primarily by heredity and incidental learning. Both kinds of intelligence do involve some similar processes, however, such as perceiving rela-

[2] Answers: 1. PRTU (letters not in sequence); 2. LDOR (should be FDOR to continue the reverse sequence H–G–?–E followed by DOR); 3. TODI (not either all consonants or all vowels). Since these are hypothetical items only, other answers may be possible.

tionships among objects, abstract reasoning, concept formation, and problem solving. Also, it is quite possible for a single test to tap both fluid and crystallized intelligence. An example is the verbal analogies test (e.g., TOE is to FOOT as FINGER is to ?), which draws on both acquired knowledge about the meanings of words and an inherent ability to perceive semantic relationships.

RELATIONSHIP TO THE CLASSIC AGING PATTERN.   How does this theory relate to the WAIS? The WAIS verbal scales are concerned primarily with acquired information, which is the hallmark of crystallized intelligence. Conversely, the performance scales would seem to deal mainly with fluid intelligence. If we assume that the two types of intelligence become more and more independent of one another as we grow older, then the WAIS verbal and performance scores should indeed demonstrate different aging patterns.

Is this assumption a plausible one? Crystallized intelligence reflects our accumulated store of knowledge, which is likely to remain relatively stable or even increase as we grow older. That is, we should acquire enough new knowledge to equal or exceed that which we forget, especially since we inhibit forgetting in many areas by refining and applying what we know. Conversely, fluid intelligence is a more innate capacity. It does involve incidental learning, but also requires the use of an efficient brain and nervous system. Since our physiological capacities are known to degenerate with increasing age, a corresponding decline in fluid intelligence is to be expected (Horn & Donaldson, 1980).

This rationale leads to the conclusion that crystallized intelligence should remain stable or even increase with increasing age, at least through about age 70, while fluid intelligence should decline during adulthood. (See Figure 6.4.) And this is essentially what occurs in the classic aging pattern: WAIS verbal scores (which reflect crystallized intelligence) show much smaller declines than do performance scores (which reflect fluid intelligence). This also implies that declines in fluid intelligence may be compensated for by gains in crystallized intelligence, resulting in little if any loss in functioning. Some evidence does indicate that fluid intelligence declines and crystallized intelligence increases as we grow older, although some of these data are based on specially designed tests of fluid intelligence rather than on the WAIS. (See, for example, Cunningham et al., 1975; Hayslip & Sterns, 1979; Horn & Cattell, 1967; Kausler & Puckett, 1980.)

Some WAIS studies have found that for adults aged 70 and older, score declines are of about equal magnitude on both the verbal and performance scales, and are much greater than for younger subjects (e.g., Eisdorfer & Wilkie, 1973). Why might the classic aging pattern

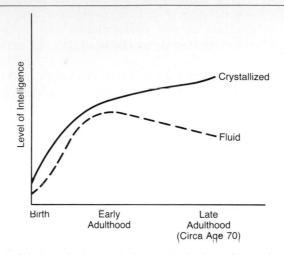

Note. This figure illustrates only the *hypothesized* age changes for fluid and crystallized intelligence, in accordance with the text discussion. Some research evidence does support this hypothesis, but considerably more is needed before definitive conclusions can be drawn.

FIGURE 6.4   Hypothesized age changes for fluid intelligence and crystallized intelligence. Kausler (1982, p. 586).

not apply to the very old? Conceivably, those over 70 are more affected by retirement and declining health, and are therefore more likely to become socially isolated. (See Chapter 8.) As a result, their opportunities to acquire new information are more limited; they forget more than they learn; and their store of information decreases, resulting in a marked decline in crystallized intelligence. There is some indication that both fluid and crystallized intelligence do follow a similar pattern of deterioration in very late adulthood, reversing the earlier trend shown in Figure 6.4 (e.g., Baltes et al., 1980). However, considerably more research is needed to evaluate this hypothesis.

As might be expected in the controversial realm of intelligence, not all psychologists agree with the fluid-crystallized distinction. In fact, one noted critic has even characterized these concepts as "fanciful" (Guilford, 1980). Nevertheless, this conception does offer an interesting theoretical explanation for the pattern that is so often observed when WAIS scores are related to aging.

The Influence of Extraneous Variables

In the preceding pages, we have been careful to state that *WAIS scores* change with increasing age. However, these score changes may not necessarily reflect an equal change in *intelligence*. The observed declines in test performance may instead be exaggerated (or, less often, deflated) by the operation of certain **extraneous variables.**

EDUCATION AND TEST ANXIETY.   As we observed earlier in this chapter, tests like the Binet and WAIS equate intelligence with educational success. Formal schooling is much more widespread today than it was fifty years ago. Therefore, older adults tend to have fewer years of education than do younger adults. Since many of the WAIS verbal scales emphasize material taught in the classroom, the aged are likely to be less familiar with the required information. And since less schooling also implies less experience with examinations, older adults tend to be more anxious about taking an intelligence test. They are also less efficient at devising appropriate test-taking strategies, such as guessing freely when there is no penalty for doing so. Furthermore, many elderly individuals have heard a great deal about declines in intelligence with increasing age. Thus they are likely to be concerned about the possibility of becoming senile, and to fear that their scores on the WAIS will reveal this. Accordingly, even well-educated older adults may well experience debilitating test anxiety. Some even refuse to take the test at all (Whitbourne, 1976; see also Birren & Morrison, 1961).

The evidence in this area provides support for those who attribute age-related declines in WAIS scores to cohort effects, rather than to aging. To a significant extent, older adults obtain lower test scores because they have had less formal education and/or are higher in text anxiety, rather than because their intelligence is lower. Thus the declines in test scores obtained by the early cross-sectional studies, which are particularly vulnerable to cohort effects, would seem to exaggerate the declines in intelligence that occur with increasing age.

CAUTIOUSNESS.   Some theorists have suggested that older adults are overly cautious, and that this is the primary reason for their failure to guess on an intelligence test even when it is to their advantage to do so. (There is no penalty for guessing on the WAIS.) However, the preponderance of research evidence does *not* support the hypothesis that cautiousness increases as we grow older. (See Chapter 7.) Therefore, this inefficient test-taking behavior of the elderly appears to be due more to anxiety, which may lead to excessive cautiousness in this particular situation.

HEALTH.   Most of us find it harder to perform well on cognitive tasks when we are ill. Since the elderly are more prone to disease and injury than are younger adults, some of the age-related declines in WAIS scores might reasonably be attributed to poor health. However, the research evidence in this area is equivocal.

One study found that for subjects aged 65–91 years, even mild illnesses were associated with lower scores on most WAIS scales, especially the performance scales (Botwinick & Birren, 1963). For another sample with a mean age of about 76 years, hearing losses were significantly related to lower WAIS scores, notably on the information and vocabulary subtests (Granick, Kleben, & Weiss, 1976). Conversely, other investigators obtained no significant differences in WAIS scores between healthy adults and those suffering from heart disease (Thompson, Eisdorfer, & Estes, 1970). Another study found that while hypertensives did not perform as well on the WAIS as did normotensives, the differences were small and clinically insignificant (Schultz et al., 1986). Mild elevations in blood pressure have even been related to modest *increases* in WAIS and other intelligence test scores over a ten-year period, although subjects with very high blood pressure did tend to obtain lower scores (Eisdorfer, 1977; Hertzog et al., 1978; Wilkie & Eisdorfer, 1973).

While it is logical to assume that poor health adversely affects the test performance of the elderly, there appear to be some definite exceptions to this rule. Conceivably, the extent to which an adult's functioning is impaired may be more relevant than merely having an illness: a hearing loss that makes it difficult to understand the examiner's questions may well be more disadvantageous than a heart disease that is in remission and does not greatly affect one's daily activities.

It has also been suggested that a significant decline in cognitive functioning occurs a few years prior to death, which is reflected by a sharp drop in intelligence test scores (Kleemeier, 1962). This **terminal drop hypothesis** has been supported by a number of studies (e.g., Baltes & Labouvie, 1973; Riegel & Riegel, 1972; Riegel, Riegel, & Meyer, 1967; Steuer et al., 1981). However, several studies have either failed to obtain any evidence in favor of terminal drop, or have found the relationship between WAIS scores and death to be statistically significant but of little practice importance (Botwinick et al., 1978; Palmore & Cleveland, 1976). There is also some disagreement as to whether the sum of all verbal and performance scores should be used to predict terminal drop (Reimanis & Green, 1971), or only the scores on certain subtests (Jarvik & Falek, 1963). These controversies have been attributed in part to sampling and statistical errors, such as studies which did not begin to take measurements far enough in advance of the subjects' deaths (Siegler, 1975).

One interesting new approach to the study of terminal drop has been developed by Suedfeld and Piedrahita (1984). They analyzed published letters written by 18 eminent individuals, all deceased, during the last ten years of their lives. Each letter was scored for the degree of cognitive complexity reflected therein. Some of the noted personages whose writings were included in this study died from prolonged illnesses (e.g., Lewis Carroll, Sigmund Freud, Aldous Huxley, Franz Kafka, D. H. Lawrence, Napoleon I, Queen Victoria), while others died quite suddenly (Louis Brandeis, Robert Browning, Gustave Flaubert, Franz Liszt, Walter Raleigh). The results obtained from both groups supported the terminal drop hypothesis, albeit in somewhat different ways: the sudden-death group suffered a drastic decline in the cognitive complexity of their writings during their last year of life, while the protracted-illness group showed a substantial decline in cognitive complexity during the five years prior to their deaths. While the available evidence in this area is not unequivocal, it appears that a substantial drop in intelligence test scores and/or in the cognitive complexity of one's writings may indeed forecast the occurrence of death within a few years.

FATIGUE.   There is some indication that older adults fare more poorly on long intelligence tests because they become tired more quickly (Furry & Baltes, 1973). Thus shorter test segments and more frequent rest pauses may be necessary with the elderly, as is the case with interviews (Chapter 11).

RESPONSE SPEED.   As we have seen, you must respond quickly on some WAIS subtests in order to obtain a high score. Since older adults perform more poorly on speeded tasks, some critics contend that they face an unfair disadvantage on these subtests. But other theorists argue that response speed reflects the functioning of the central nervous system, is related to cognitive ability, and should be an aspect of tests given to the aged.

Various studies have shown that if the digit symbol and picture arrangement subtests are administered without any time limits at all, the typically large age-related declines on these subtests do *not* disappear, although they are reduced. (See, for example, Doppelt & Wallace, 1955; Klodin, 1975; Storandt, 1976; 1977.) Whether response speed should be regarded as an extraneous variable is open to question, but it is only partly responsible for poorer test performance among the elderly.

AFTERWORD.   Of the extraneous variables discussed above, the most influential are educational level and test anxiety. Health, fatigue, and (perhaps) response speed are also significant, although the evidence concerning these variables is not as clear cut.

Psychological testing is not an exact science. No test is perfectly reliable or valid: the best test usually will not produce identical scores for the same person on two different occasions, even if there has been no change at all during this time, nor will it measure a concept like intelligence without tapping at least some undesired attributes as well. We can indeed glean useful and important information about intelligence at various ages from score changes on well-constructed tests. But we must remember that these score changes are also influenced by the operation of various extraneous variables, so they do not necessarily reflect an equal degree of change in intellectual ability.

Other Findings and Issues

LONGITUDINAL STUDIES USING OTHER INTELLIGENCE TESTS. Although the WAIS is the most popular test of adult intelligence, it is by no means the only one. As noted previously in this chapter, some studies of aging and intelligence have utilized specially designed tests of fluid intelligence. Other studies have focused on such measures of intelligence as the Army Alpha, a verbal test first used during World War I for the screening and placement of new recruits. Still other studies have used the test of Primary Mental Abilities (Thurstone, 1938; Thurstone & Thurstone, 1941), which includes subtests dealing with verbal comprehension, numerical ability, word fluency (e.g., naming as many words as possible beginning with the letter *T*), spatial relations, memory, perceptual speed, and general reasoning ability.

As was the case with the WAIS, these longitudinal studies report smaller score declines with increasing age than do cross-sectional studies. In some of these studies, those decrements that were found did not begin until after age 50. (See, for example, Owens, 1966; Schaie & Labouvie-Vief, 1974.) We may conclude that insofar as longitudinal research is concerned, the results obtained from other intelligence tests do not contradict those derived from the WAIS.

INITIAL LEVEL OF ABILITY.   Some theorists have suggested that if you achieve a superior score on an intelligence test as a young adult, you will suffer less of a decrement later in life than will those whose scores are average or below. However, the research evidence concerning this hypothesis is equivocal. Some studies report that an individual's initial level of ability is not significantly related to subsequent changes in test scores (e.g., Eichorn, 1973; Eisdorfer, 1962; Troll, Saltz, & Dunin-Markiewitz, 1966). Other studies have found that young adults with higher test scores do show smaller declines with increasing age (Bayley & Oden, 1955; Blum & Jarvik, 1974; Riegel, Riegel, & Meyer, 1967; Siegler & Botwinick, 1979). Still other findings suggest that it is the less capable subjects who experience smaller decrements as they grow older (Baltes et al., 1972). In view of these contradictions, any conclusions in this area must await the results of future research. It does appear that those young adults who are high in intelligence are likely to remain so throughout their lives, although their margin of superiority in some intellectual areas may grow smaller relative to other adults of the same age.

EVIDENCE CONCERNING PLASTICITY THEORY.   If age-related declines in test scores can be reversed by appropriate training, such findings would support those theorists who take an optimistic view of aging and intelligence. Some efforts have been made to devise and evaluate training methods for improving the test scores of the elderly. But these interventions have achieved only modest success, and have not eliminated score differences between older and younger adults. For example, one study found that training improved the test performance of elderly subjects with regard to one form of fluid intelligence, but not numerous others (Plemons, Willis, & Baltes, 1978).

Afterword

In the preceding pages, we have reviewed a considerable amount of evidence dealing with aging and intelligence. Although controversy and debate abound in this area, some general conclusions do appear to be warranted by the available empirical data.

First, cross-sectional studies present an overly pessimistic picture of the extent to which intelligence declines with increasing age. These studies are particularly vulnerable to cohort effects, and to the operation of various extraneous variables.

Longitudinal studies do tend to underestimate the extent of age-related declines in intelligence. Such studies are vulnerable to selective attrition, to the operation of extraneous variables, and to other problems inherent in the measurement of change. (See Chapter 2.) However, longitudinal studies do appear to present a more accurate picture of the relationship between aging and intelligence. Thus Botwinick (1977) has concluded that many intellectual functions do not begin to decline until about age 50 or 60, especially those involving verbal ability, and that these declines tend to be small. There are important exceptions, however, notably with regard to perceptual integration and response speed. Declines in these abilities begin at an earlier age, and are more substantial.

Intelligence is not a unidimensional concept. It includes a variety

Myths About Aging: Intelligence and Creativity

MYTH	BEST AVAILABLE EVIDENCE
There is a universal decline in intelligence with increasing age. Thus you are very likely to suffer serious and widespread deterioration in intellectual ability during your old age.	Some intellectual abilities do show significant decrements as we grow older, especially after middle age. But the declines in other abilities are small, and do not appear to have much effect on one's daily functioning. Age-related changes in intelligence test scores may not accurately reflect true changes in intelligence because of cohort effects, extraneous variables, selective attrition, and/or other methodological problems. The majority of elderly adults do *not* suffer extreme deterioration in intelligence, although some losses may be expected in such areas as perceptual integration, response speed, and certain aspects of memory.
There is a universal decline in creativity after middle age. If you have not made any creative contributions by about age 40, you probably never will.	Some studies do suggest that creativity peaks by about age 35, and declines steadily thereafter. However, age-related changes in the number of creative contributions may not accurately reflect true changes in creativity because of the operation of various extraneous variables. There are numerous, and striking, examples of creativity by middle-aged and elderly individuals.

of intellectual abilities, many of which appear to remain more or less stable with increasing age. You may well notice declines in certain abilities as you grow past middle age, such as memory (Chapter 5), response speed, and perceptual integration. You may also find that some of these declines become more pronounced when you reach old age. But so long as you are fortunate enough to avoid a serious organic brain disorder (Chapter 11), any grave concern about the possibility of widespread deteriorations in intelligence during your life span does *not* appear to be warranted.

The Meaning of Creativity

Creativity may be defined as the solution to a problem of significance to society that is original, unusual, ingenious, and relevant. Examples may be found in virtually every area of human endeavor: a Beethoven developing a new form of symphony, a medical researcher who discovers a badly needed vaccine, a writer who produces a dramatically important work of fiction or nonfiction, an inventor who devises an innovative and effective industrial machine or home appliance, and so forth. Creativity is *not* the same as intelligence, nor can it be measured with the kinds of tests discussed previously in this chapter (e.g., Thurstone, 1951).

Convergent and Divergent Thinking

We typically conceptualize the solution to a problem in terms of a single correct answer. Examples of such **convergent thinking** include deducing the identity of the murderer in a mystery story, determining the answer to a problem in elementary algebra, deciding on the correct bid in a game of bridge, or answering a multiple-choice examination question correctly. In each of these cases, various clues and data are presented, and the respondent must narrow down the many possibilities to one and only one answer.

Although convergent thinking is very common in our society, it is by no means the only type of problem solving. In fact, creativity is more closely related to the ability to produce many different and unusual answers to a problem (**divergent thinking**). Suppose that you are asked to list twenty different uses for a newspaper, other than the obvious one of reading it. Some answers are very common and would not be regarded as creative, such as using the newspaper to start a charcoal fire or to line a garbage pail. To qualify as original, a response must be one that is practical but given by few people, such as using the newspaper to cut out words for a kidnaper's ransom note. The more original answers that one can produce, the more creative the individual.

Convergent thinking often leads in a smooth and uninterrupted fashion to the correct answer. In contrast, creativity typically occurs in unanticipated bursts of illumination. The creative individual usually does spend a considerable amount of time totally immersed in the problem, but this frequently fails to produce the desired result. The individual then puts the problem aside for awhile, often with some discouragement, only to find that the needed creative thoughts arrive suddenly and spontaneously during this rest period. Most often, crucial creative insights do not occur at the composer's piano, scientist's laboratory, or writer's desk. Instead they may take place while one is enjoying a peaceful walk in the woods, a ride in a carriage, a warm bath (as in the famous case of Archimedes' "Eureka, I have found it!"), or even a night's sleep (with the solution appearing in the form of a dream). Paradoxically, then, *not* thinking consciously about a problem (at least for awhile) may be the best way to arrive at a creative solution.

Measures of Creativity

No one measure of creativity has achieved the widespread acceptance and popularity accorded to the WAIS. As a further illustration of the difference between creativity and intelligence, consider these tests of divergent thinking devised by Guilford (1967):

- *Word Fluency:* Write as many words as possible containing a specified letter. The letter may appear anywhere in the word.

- *Expressional Fluency:* Write a meaningful four-word sentence, where each word must begin with a specified letter (e.g., W_____ A_____ M_____ S_____).

- *Alternate Uses:* List as many uses as possible for a specified object (e.g., a newspaper), other than the most obvious one.

- *Ideational Fluency:* Given a specified category (e.g, "things that will burn"), name as many things as possible that belong in that category.

- *Plot Titles:* Given a one-paragraph description of a short story plot, write a brief, interesting, and relevant title for that story.

- *Consequences:* Given a hypothetical event (e.g., people no longer need or want sleep), list as many consequences of this event as possible (e.g., no more alarm clocks).

- *Making Objects:* Using only a given set of figures (e.g., circle, triangle), draw a specified object (e.g., a face, a lamp).

- *Match Problems:* Given a set of matchsticks that form a pattern (e.g., two rows of three square boxes), remove a certain number of matchsticks so as to produce a specified result (e.g., remove three matchsticks to reduce the number of boxes from six to four).

Nevertheless, intellectual ability is by no means wholly unrelated to creativity. For example, after numerous possible solutions have been produced by divergent thinking, it is still necessary to use your cognitive capacities to evaluate these alternatives and decide on the best one. Also, to make a creative contribution in fields like music, literature, medicine, and science, you must first be able to understand and deal with the basic concepts and principles of these disciplines. But it is quite possible to be creative without having the ability to obtain high scores on intelligence tests, or to do very well on intelligence tests yet not be particularly creative.

Creativity and Aging

Research Findings

To date, gerontologists have been considerably less interested in creativity than in intelligence. Some studies of divergent thinking do indicate that older adults produce fewer unusual responses than young adults on laboratory tasks, although little decline is evident in the capacity for common and uncreative answers (Bromley, 1956; 1957; Renner et al., 1978). Other researchers have sought to identify highly creative contributions in such fields as chemistry, physics, painting, mathematics, philosophy, inventing, and psychology, and then to determine the ages of the contributors at the time these works were produced. Some of these studies have been criticized on methodological grounds: if fewer people live to be 70 years old than to be 40, there will perforce be fewer creative contributions by people over 70 than by young adults (e.g., Dennis, 1956a; 1956b; 1958; 1966). Yet even when this potential source of bias is taken into account, there appears to be a significant decline in the number of creative contributions with increasing age. Various studies suggest that the quantity of such contributions peaks during the thirties and declines sharply thereafter, as shown in Figure 6.5. (See, for example, Alexander, 1945; Lehman, 1942; 1953; 1956; 1958; 1960; Lehman & Gamertsfelder, 1942; Lyons, 1968; Zusne, 1976.)

Nevertheless, this rule is characterized by many famous exceptions. For example, painter Claude Monet began his "Water Lily" series at age 73. Benjamin Franklin invented the bifocal lens at age 78. Sophocles wrote *Oedipus Rex* at age 75. George Bernard Shaw wrote his first play at age 48. And Bach and Beethoven produced some of their most creative works toward the latter part of their lives (Denny, 1984). In our review of empirical data concerning aging and intelligence, we found methodological problems capable of producing an overly pessimistic picture. Might this also be true in the case of creativity?

Some studies suggest that creativity declines after age 40, but there are many famous exceptions. For example, painter Claude Monet did not begin his noted *Water Lily* series until age seventy-three. *The Bettman Archive*

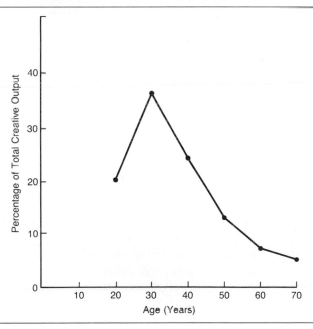

FIGURE 6.5 The relationship between aging and creative contributions in many academic disciplines. Lehman (1953); Botwinick (1967).

The Influence of Extraneous Variables

A change in the *number of creative contributions* with increasing age may not necessarily reflect an equal change in the *capacity for creativity*. The observed declines in creative performance may instead be exaggerated (or, less often, deflated) by the operation of certain extraneous variables.

PROMOTIONS.   As creative people grow older, they are more likely to be promoted to positions that remove them from active participation in their disciplines. For example, a creative college chemist or psychologist may become a department head or dean, and be required to devote most of the work day to administrative matters. Thus the reduced creative output of older adults may well be due in part to significant changes in the nature of their jobs, rather than to any loss in creative capacity.

LACK OF REINFORCEMENT.   Not infrequently, a contribution is not recognized as creative until long after it first appears. A typical example concerns the Nobel Prize, which is often awarded decades after the occurrence of the research which it commemorates. As behaviorist psychologists have clearly shown, delaying a reward until long after the behavior in question is a poor way to maintain that behavior. Consequently, creative performance may decline with increasing age simply because it is not adequately reinforced.

ENVIRONMENTAL INFLUENCES.   Some older adults may live in environments that promote convergent thinking, and discourage divergent thinking. Thus an institution for the aged may emphasize the necessity of doing things in one and only one way, rather than encouraging new (and perhaps superior) responses. This suggests that age-related declines in creativity may be partly due to the failure to request or expect such behavior.

PERSONALITY CHARACTERISTICS.   Creativity has been related to such personality characteristics as flexibility and tolerance of ambiguity. If these characteristics are negatively affected by aging, a corresponding decline in creativity may be expected. This extraneous variable is probably not an overly influential one, however, since the available research evidence indicates that personality tends to remain relatively stable during adulthood. (See Chapter 7.)

Afterword

Although various studies have found significant declines in creative output with increasing age, the true relationship between aging and creativity is still uncertain. There are numerous examples of highly creative works by older adults. Also, declines in creative performance may well be due to the operation of various extraneous variables, rather than to true losses in creative capacity.

As is the case with intelligence, some degree of optimism appears to be in order. Although you are likely to produce a greater number of creative contributions during the first half of your life, exceptions to this rule are far from uncommon. Nor does it necessarily follow that your capacity for creative work will deteriorate markedly after middle age. However, considerably more research is needed before firm conclusions can be drawn in this area.

Summary

THE MEANING OF INTELLIGENCE

Intelligence refers to the range of behavior from dull to bright, slow-witted to quick-witted, stupid to clever. High intelligence presumably makes it easier to use words and numbers correctly, to remember substantial amounts of information, and to reason out the solution to problems of various kinds. Intelligence is not a unitary concept; it includes a number of specific intellectual abilities. However, it is extremely difficult to state an exact definition of intelligence.

The psychometric approach, which was originated at the beginning of the twentieth century by Alfred Binet, involves the use of formal psychological tests to define and measure intelligence. The well-known intelligence quotient is unsuitable for use with adults, so deviation IQs or similar measures are commonly used in aging research. A major problem with tests like Binet's is that they equate intelligence with educational aptitude. Insofar as adults are concerned, this rationale may well be inappropriate: most older adults have long since left school, and their success or failure in life cannot be evaluated in terms of such simple criteria as letter grades. Unfortunately, this difficulty is not easily resolved.

Some of the theoretical alternatives to the psychometric approach include the Piagetian approach, and the information-processing approach. However, virtually all of the available empirical evidence concerning aging and intelligence has been provided by the psychometric approach.

INTELLIGENCE AND AGING

The intelligence test most often used with adults is the Wechsler Adult Intelligence Scale (WAIS), which consists of six verbal scales and five performance scales. Numerous studies have found that both verbal and performance scores peak by about age 18–25, and then decline steadily with increasing age. These decrements are typically small on the verbal scales and much more pronounced on the performance scales, a phenomenon known as the classic aging pattern. For this reason, deviation IQ scores on the WAIS are age graded: the same score yields a higher IQ at an older age.

There is no ideal research method for studying intelligence and aging. Cross-sectional studies are likely to overstate the extent of age-related declines in WAIS scores, since they do not control for cohort effects. Longitudinal studies are likely to understate the extent of age-related declines in WAIS scores, since they are vulnerable to selective attrition and other methodological problems concerning the measurement of change. In view of these uncertainties, it is hardly surprising that some noted researchers disagree strongly as to the relationship between aging and intelligence. Some theorists optimistically conclude that the assumption of a universal decline in intelligence with increasing age is a myth, and that those losses in test scores that do occur can be largely reversed through appropriate training. Others argue that virtually all of the research on aging and intelligence shows some significant declines, and attribute exceptions primarily to methodological and procedural errors.

One theory distinguishes between two general kinds of intelligence. Fluid intelligence involves the capacity to use unique kinds of thinking in order to solve unfamiliar problems, and is believed to decline with increasing age. Crystallized intelligence involves the knowledge that has been acquired through education and acculturation, and presumably remains stable up to about age 70. These age trends are similar to the WAIS classic aging pattern, since the verbal subtests deal primarily with crystallized intelligence and the performance subtests emphasize fluid intelligence.

Changes in test scores may not necessarily reflect an equal change in intelligence. The observed declines in test performance may instead be influenced by the operation of various extraneous variables, including amount of education, test anxiety, health, fatigue, and (perhaps) response speed. Insofar as health is concerned, a sharp drop in intelligence test scores may well forecast the occurrence of death within a few years (terminal drop).

Longitudinal studies using other intelligence tests have not markedly contradicted the results obtained from the WAIS. Researchers have also sought to determine the relationship between initial level of ability and subsequent changes in intelligence test scores with increasing age, and whether or not age-related declines in test scores can be reversed by appropriate training. However, the available evidence in these areas is equivocal.

The early cross-sectional studies dealing with aging and intelligence presented an overly pessimistic picture of age-related declines in intelligence. It appears that many intellectual functions do not begin to decline until about age 50 or 60, especially those involving verbal ability, and that these declines tend to be small. There are important exceptions, however, notably with regard to perceptual integration, response speed, and certain aspects of memory. While losses in some intellectual abilities are to be expected with increasing age, grave concern about the possibility of widespread deterioration does not appear to be warranted.

THE MEANING OF CREATIVITY

Creativity may be defined as the solution to a problem of significance to society that is original, unusual, ingenious, and relevant. It pertains to virtually all areas of human endeavor.

Creativity is more closely associated with the ability to produce many different and unusual answers to a problem (divergent thinking), rather than the ability to find the one right answer to a problem (convergent thinking). Creativity is not the same as intelligence, and cannot be measured with intelligence tests. There are some commonly used measures of divergent thinking, which include such subtests as word fluency, alternate uses, consequences, and match problems.

CREATIVITY AND AGING

Various studies suggest that the quantity of creative contributions peaks by age 30–40, and declines sharply thereafter. However, this rule is characterized by numerous famous exceptions. Also, observed changes in creative performance may be influenced by such extraneous variables as promotions, lack of reinforcement, and environmental influences.

All in all, the relationship between aging and creativity is still uncertain. Various factors may increase the likelihood of creative output during the first half of life, but this does not necessarily imply that serious losses in creative capacity occur with increasing age. Considerably more research is needed in this area before definitive conclusions can be drawn.

PART III

Personality and Social Development

CHAPTER 7

Personality and Aging

What happens to the personality of an adult as he or she grows older?

If you speculate about this issue for a few moments, you will probably conclude that there are a variety of possible (and interesting) answers. First of all, the personalities of most adults may *change* in certain ways. The precise nature of these changes may be a controversial issue: some adults might learn from their experiences, alter their patterns of behavior appropriately, and cope more and more effectively with the demands of living as they grow older. Some adults might become enmeshed in self-defeating behavior patterns, and deal less and less effectively with their environment and problems. Or the personality development of some adults might be only partially constructive, and fall somewhere between these two extremes. Thus we might find that personality often follows the old maxim of "two steps forward and one step backward," with a given adult showing positive growth at some times and negative changes on other occasions. But whatever the specific details might be, one important possibility to be considered is that the adult personality does change significantly with increasing age.

Alternatively, personality may be largely determined by an early age and remain *stable* throughout adulthood. The precise age at which personality development ceases may be a controversial issue: perhaps as early as age five or six years (as in Sigmund Freud's theory), perhaps during adolescence. Nevertheless, if this hypothesis is correct, we would expect to find that the personality of each and every adult shows little or no change over the years—not to mention extremely short textbook chapters on the subject of personality and aging.

While the issue of stability versus change is of primary impor-

tance, we could list many more possible relationships between age
and personality. For example, the adult personality might change if
sufficiently strong stimulation is experienced (i.e., strong enough to
affect an older and less impressionable individual), but not otherwise. If the change hypothesis is supported, we might find that most
adults follow much the same pattern or stages of personality development. Or we might discover that the personalities of different
adults develop in quite different ways, depending on each individual's previous life history and current situation.

The preceding speculations are intended to suggest the potentially intriguing and important nature of this area. However, psychology strives to be the science of human behavior; and a science
relies on empirical data, rather than on speculation or anecdotal
information. Thus our goal in this chapter (as elsewhere in this book)
is to seek out scientifically acceptable evidence.

Substantive and Methodological Issues

On the surface, our initial question about personality and aging might
seem to be a readily answerable one. However, appearances are often
deceptive. The study of personality and aging is fraught with difficulties, and some reviewers have even concluded that the attempt
to apply the scientific method to this area has been an abject failure.
These critics argue that the fledgling field of personality is still in a
"prescientific" state—one wherein psychologists cannot empirically
demonstrate any satisfactory and convincing answers, even in areas
where the answers would seem to be obvious from experience or
common sense. (See, for example, Fiske, 1974; 1978; Neugarten,
1977, pp. 626–629.) Before we survey those findings that do exist,
therefore, let us first consider some of the problems that plague
those who seek to investigate this challenging area.

Methodological Issues

As we observed in Chapter 2, various methodological problems and
issues must be faced by those who wish to conduct research on adult
development and aging. These include the limitations of cross-sectional studies; the common inability to conduct longitudinal studies
(which also have their limitations); the problem of determining which
effects are truly due to aging, as opposed to cohort or to major life
experiences; the weaknesses of chronological age as a measure of
aging; trying to understand the meaning of different behaviors at
different ages; and procedural and mathematical difficulties that
hinder the accurate measurement of psychological change. (You may

This husband and wife posed for these two photographs in 1944 and 1984. Although they have aged physically, their personalities probably have not changed nearly as much. *Courtesy of Evelyn, Bill, and Eric Seidman* (left) *and Wayne Sorce* (right)

wish to review our earlier discussion of these issues before proceeding further.)

LABORATORY RESEARCH, CLINICAL INSIGHT, AND FIELD STUDIES. Insofar as personality is concerned, yet another important methodological controversy must be considered: how should this variable be studied?

Some psychologists insist that a science must generate formal and objective predictions, ones that can be tested under the controlled conditions of the research laboratory. By these lights, concepts that are difficult to evaluate empirically (such as the Freudian id, ego, and superego), or hypotheses and theories that do not stimulate a considerable amount of research, are regarded as inferior and unscientific.

Other psychologists regard the research laboratory as inevitably artificial and unrealistic, a place where objectivity is gained by studying only small and trivial aspects of human behavior. Instead, they prefer to derive their information about personality from observations of patients in psychotherapy. They point out that psychopathology differs from normality in degree, rather than in kind, so the more extreme behaviors of, say, the neurotic will reveal universal principles that would be much harder to detect in relatively well-adjusted people. And they argue that the intense misery of psychopathology may well be the only motive that will make a person submit to sufficiently prolonged study by a psychologist, and reveal important but deeply personal issues.

If laboratory research methods in psychology were as effective as those of other sciences, such an approach might well be superior. Clinical observation is subjective and uncontrolled, and the power of suggestion may influence the patient's behavior in ways that support the therapist's theories. Or the therapist may more readily perceive evidence that supports his or her conception of personality, and disregard contradictory data. Therefore, the prospect of objective validation through laboratory research is highly appealing. Unfortunately, psychology is a much younger science than physics or chemistry, its subject matter is quite different, and its techniques are less well refined. Practical and financial limitations often require the use of small and/or atypical samples, such as college students, laboratory animals, or volunteers. Experimental procedures are often too insensitive to measure the deeper aspects of personality with any accuracy, or even to ensure that the effects intended by the experimenter are created within the minds of the subjects. And human beings differ rather significantly from chemical elements, or inert physical objects. For these reasons, the insights available from experiences of real importance to people (such as psychotherapy) are extremely valuable—even essential—to those who wish to unravel the mysteries of the human personality. (See, for example, Burton, 1974; Ewen, 1984; 1985; Neugarten, 1977; Oppenheimer, 1956; Sechrest, 1976; Wachtel, 1980.)

A third method for studying personality involves the administration of questionnaires to adults in various locales (e.g., institutions for the aged; their homes). Such field surveys tend to be less artificial than laboratory research, but are also less amenable to experimental controls. Thus they possess some of the strengths and weaknesses of both of the approaches discussed above.

In sum, there is some merit to all three procedures for studying the human personality. We will therefore consider all of these sources in our quest for scientifically acceptable evidence concerning personality and aging.

The Meaning of Personality

The study of personality and aging is hindered not only by the methodological difficulties discussed above, but by basic substantive issues as well. Perhaps the most serious of these concerns the term *personality:* you will not find any unanimity among psychologists as to the meaning of personality (let alone any one accepted definition), nor any firm consensus regarding those aspects of human behavior to which it refers.

To be sure, psychologists do tend to agree on certain general considerations. **Personality** is most often conceptualized as the organized, distinctive pattern of behavior that characterizes a particular individual. Typically, then, the concept of personality is a comprehensive one: it includes the individual's physical, mental, emotional, and social characteristics. It also incorporates such specific areas as motivation, normality and psychopathology, interpersonal behaviors, thoughts, dreams, defensive behaviors and mechanisms, beliefs, and values, among others. In addition, personality is generally considered to be relatively stable and enduring. It may change over a long period of time (e.g., the many years that constitute adulthood), and a person may well behave differently in different situations. But personality involves long-lasting and important characteristics of an individual, ones that continue to exert a strong influence on behavior. Some aspects of personality are unobservable, such as thoughts, memories, and dreams, while others are observable (overt actions, "body language"). And virtually all theories agree that at least some vital aspects of personality are concealed from oneself *(unconscious)*, though the extent and importance of such unconscious materials and processes vary from theory to theory. (See, for example, Darley et al., 1981, p. 397; Ewen, 1985.)

Because personality encompasses so much of our behavior, its study is extremely important. Yet because it is difficult to measure unobservable and unconscious processes with any accuracy, the study of personality is also highly challenging. Furthermore, from a historical perspective, it is only quite recently that personality has become a widely used concept in describing and understanding human behavior. Thus it should not be surprising that the field of personality is rife with controversy and disagreement. When we examine the evidence concerning personality and aging, therefore, we will of necessity acknowledge these important substantive issues by discussing separately some of the different approaches to (and conceptions of) personality.

Adulthood and Personality Development

Stage Theories

Some investigators have opted for a comprehensive, and ambitious, strategy. They have divided most or all of adulthood into a series of stages, ones that are supposedly experienced by most or all adults.

STAGES BASED ON LIFE SITUATIONS.　Several theorists have defined adult stages in terms of situations or events that are expected to occur during specified periods in one's life.

Levinson (1978; Levinson et al., 1974) posits 6 stages which focus primarily on early and middle adulthood. He based his conclusions on interviews with forty men from 4 occupational groups, including blue-collar and white-collar workers, business executives, and academicians. Therefore, these stages apply to men only. They are:

1. *Age 20–24: Leaving the Family.* This is a transitional period from adolescence to early adulthood. During this time, the young man moves out of his family's home and establishes psychological distance from them.

2. *Early Twenties to Late Twenties: Entering the Adult World.* This is a time of exploration, with the young man trying out various occupational and interpersonal adult roles.

3. *Early Thirties to Early Forties: Settling Down.* During this period, the man deepens his commitment to his chosen occupational and social roles.

4. *Age 35–39: Becoming One's Own Man.* This is the high point of early adulthood, a time when the man's adult roles become well established.

5. *Early Forties: The Midlife Transition.* The man now begins to experience a feeling of bodily decline, and a clear recognition of his own mortality.

6. *Middle Forties: Restabilization and the Beginning of Middle Adulthood.* Some men make new creative strides during this period, while others lose their vitality.

The simplicity of Levinson's model makes it appealing to non-professional readers, and some popular books and articles have been based on it (e.g. Gail Sheehy's *Passages,* 1976). A somewhat different set of situational stages, derived from clinical observation, has been suggested by Gould (1972):

1. Age 16–18. This is a time of conflict between autonomy (wishing to get away from one's parents) and dependency (wishing to remain protected and guided by them).

2. Age 18–22. The young adult now feels more autonomous and somewhat removed from the family, but worries about being recaptured and made dependent by them. The peer group is used as an ally to help cut family ties.

3. Age 22–28. This is a time of autonomy, feeling separate from one's family, and concentrating on building one's own life. Peers are still important, but self-reliance is even more so.

4. Age 29–34. The adult now questions his or her life choices and grows tired of fulfilling these roles, but continues to do so.

5. Age 35–43. Time appears to be growing short for shaping the behaviors of one's adolescent children, or for succeeding in life. The adult's parents renew previous requests for help with their problems and conflicts, possibly in an indirect way.

6. Age 43–53. This is a time of bitterness, and feeling that the course of one's life can no longer be changed. Also typical of this period are blaming one's parents for a lack of fulfillment in life, finding fault with one's children, and seeking sympathy from one's spouse.

7. Age 53–60. Feelings during this period are more positive than during one's forties. Relationships with oneself, spouse, parents, children, and friends become warmer and more satisfying.

A third set of stages is based partly on situations, and partly on human physiology. Bühler (1968; see also Kimmel, 1980, pp. 8–12) observed that there appear to be five major biological phases during one's life. She and her students examined some 400 autobiographies collected during the 1930s in Vienna, and proposed five life stages to correspond to these biological phases:

Age	Biological Phase	Stage of Life
0–15	Progressive growth.	Remaining at home; goals in life are not yet chosen.
15–25	Continued growth, combined with the ability to reproduce sexually.	Experimenting with self-chosen life goals, including various temporary professional and social roles.
25–45	Stability.	Specific life goals are chosen, and a sense of direction is firmly established. Vitality is high.
45–65	Loss of sexual reproductive ability.	Abandonment of some activities, due to a loss of physical ability. Considerable interest in assessing one's success or failure in achieving the self-determined life goals.
65 on	Biological decline.	Feelings of fulfillment or failure in life. Speculations about death. Often, a preoccupation with religious questions. Previous activities continue, possibly combined with new short-term goals that are intended to satisfy immediate life needs.

STAGES DEVISED BY NOTED PERSONALITY THEORISTS.   In contrast to the situational approaches discussed above, personality theorists have tended to produce more complicated and psychodynamically oriented models of human behavior.

Sigmund Freud's clinical observations led him to conclude that personality is firmly established by about age five to six years, so his well-known psychosexual stages (e.g., oral, anal, phallic) end well before adulthood. This is currently regarded as one of Freud's significant errors, for most modern psychologists have concluded that personality continues to develop through older childhood and adolescence. But Freud is also widely praised for calling our attention to infancy and childhood, which are indeed the most important periods for personality development. Also, as we will see later in this chapter, his hypothesis that personality does not change during adulthood remains a highly tenable one. (See, for example, Freud, 1905/1965a; 1933/1965b; 1916–1917/1966. For a discussion of

Freudian, Eriksonian, and other theories of personality, see Ewen, 1985.)

Erik Erikson, a clinician trained in psychoanalysis by Freud's daughter, Anna, has sought to remedy some of the major deficiencies of Freudian theory while retaining its strengths. Most importantly for our purposes, Erikson posits a series of eight stages that extend from infancy through old age. Just as the development of our physical organs unfolds according to a predetermined genetic schedule, all eight Eriksonian stages are present in some elementary form at birth and unfold according to an innate plan. However, the course of healthy personality development can easily be disrupted. Every Eriksonian stage is characterized by a specific psychosocial problem or "crisis" (in the medical sense of a crucial turning point for better or worse, rather than in the political sense of imminent catastrophe). Each crisis is brought on by the growing person's internal psychological maturity, and by the resulting greater demands made by the parents and society, and each one must be resolved during the appropriate stage for personality development to proceed successfully. Furthermore, the outcome of any stage need not be permanent. A severe later crisis may well revive earlier ones and nullify prior accomplishments, while subsequent favorable conditions may facilitate the resolution of previous failures. (See, for example, Erikson, 1963; 1968.) Only the last three of Erikson's stages deal with adulthood:

Stage 6: Young Adulthood. The crisis of this stage is intimacy versus isolation. To resolve it successfully, the young adult must learn to sacrifice some of his or her own wishes in order to form close relationships with other people.

Stage 7: Adulthood. The crisis of this stage is generativity versus stagnation. Successful resolution is denoted by an interest in procreation and the next generation, and a widening interest in and concern for other people.

Stage 8: Maturity. The crisis of this stage is ego integrity versus despair. Successful resolution is indicated by feelings of satisfaction and affirmation about the life one has lived, and relatively little fear of death.

One of the few other personality theorists who has devised formal developmental stages is Harry Stack Sullivan, a noted American psychiatrist who rejected both Freud's and Erikson's versions of psychoanalysis. Sullivan posits seven specific epochs through which personality may develop, six of which occur prior to adulthood. One

Chapter Glossary: Personality and Aging

Cognitive theory	An approach to the study of personality that stresses mental phenomena, such as perceptions and expectations.
Coping styles	The ways in which individuals adapt to and deal with the changing circumstances of life.
External locus of control	A consistent belief that obtaining rewards and avoiding punishments depend primarily on mere chance and the actions of other people.
Extraversion	A trait characterized by outgoingness, venturing forth with careless confidence into the unknown, and being particularly influenced by other people and events in the external world.
Field dependence	A tendency to rely primarily on external stimuli when making perceptual judgments, and thus to be more easily distracted by irrelevant stimuli in the environment.
Field independence	A tendency to rely primarily on internal stimuli when making perceptual judgments.
Internal locus of control	A consistent belief that obtaining rewards and avoiding punishments depend primarily on one's own actions and behaviors.
Introversion	A trait characterized by shyness, inscrutability, and a keen interest in the inner world of one's own psyche.
Personality	The organized, distinctive pattern of behavior that characterizes a particular individual. Includes the individual's physical, mental, emotional, and social characteristics.
Rigidity	A trait characterized by an inability to shift from one form of behavior to another, even though such a shift might well be advantageous to the individual.
Stage	A period in one's life, usually consisting of several years, during which most or all people of the same age supposedly encounter much the same experiences and problems.
Trait	A specific aspect of personality that initiates and guides consistent forms of behavior, such as shyness, friendliness, ambitiousness, cleanliness, and literally thousands of others.
Type	A pattern of personality and behavior that supposedly applies to numerous individuals.

reason why Sullivan has little to say about adulthood is that he defines it psychologically, rather than chronologically, and he doubts that very many people in our society will ever attain this degree of maturity. "I believe that for the great majority of our people, preadolescence [the psychological stage which normally corresponds to a chronological age of about 8½ to 10 years] is the nearest that they come . . . that from then on, the stresses of life distort them to inferior caricatures of what they might have been" (Sullivan, 1947/1953, p. 56; see also Sullivan, 1953/1968).

Carl Jung, the Swiss psychiatrist who once was a psychoanalyst but who split with Freud in order to devise his own theory of personality, does not posit a formal series of developmental stages. However, Jung does draw a sharp distinction between youth and middle age. During adolescence and early adulthood, the individual is most concerned with materialism and sexuality. But the period from about age 35 to 40 serves as the gateway to the latter half of life, which is a time of considerable importance. "A human being would certainly not grow to be seventy or eighty years old if this longevity had no meaning for the species. The afternoon of human life must also have a significance of its own, and cannot be merely a pitiful appendage to life's morning" (Jung, 1930–1931/1971, p. 17; see also Jung, 1933; 1917–1928/1972). According to Jung, middle age is highlighted by a shift to more spiritual and cultural values; by drastic reversals in one's strongest convictions and emotions, often leading to changes of profession, religion, and/or spouse; and perhaps by at last becoming one's own self and realizing one's true potentials, though this ideal is rarely if ever achieved to the fullest.

EVALUATION OF STAGE THEORIES.   Stage theories have a certain appeal: they cover a broad range of people and ages, and they are simple enough for the general public to comprehend and use as a developmental yardstick. They are also attractive because they propose that individuals continue to grow and develop throughout their lives, thereby providing hope for those whose current lives are far from satisfactory. Unfortunately, the stage approach suffers from serious flaws, and it has proved to be of little value in understanding adult personality development.

For example, both Levinson's and Gould's models include a stage that represents a midlife crisis. (For Levinson, it is the early 40s; for Gould, age 43–53.) But when Costa and McCrae (1978) examined this empirically, using self-reports, they found no evidence for a general crisis at midlife. Instead they discovered that those who suffer such personal crises tend to experience them across the whole range of adulthood, and tend to be more neurotic. This implies that the midlife crisis may well occur less frequently, or not at all, in relatively normal people. (Recall that both Levinson and Gould based their conclusions on relatively small, select samples.)

Even the sample used in Costa and McCrae's longitudinal study can be criticized as being unrepresentative, since it consisted of volunteers. Accordingly, Farrell and Rosenberg (1981) undertook a major midlife study to address this issue. They obtained a sample of 500 men, ranging in age from 25 to 30 and from 38 to 48. A battery of measures was administered to both groups, including one instrument specifically designed to assess the existence of a midlife crisis. No significant age differences were obtained on the midlife-crisis scale. Currently, few (if any) psychologists who study adult personality development accept the idea of universal, unidirectional stages. (See, for example, Shanan & Jacobowitz, 1982, pp. 151–152, 155–156; Thomae, 1980, pp. 285–286.)

Conceptually, the stage approach is a dubious one. As we have noted, adults of the same chronological age may well differ significantly from one another with regard to their physiological, psychological, and/or social development. Even though the stage theorists undoubtedly intend their age ranges as general guidelines, rather than as inflexible boundaries, it still seems highly unlikely that all (or even many) adults will encounter the same stage at similar ages. Even when specific ages are not emphasized (as in Erikson's theory), differences among adults are probably too great for a stage model to have widespread applicability. (The belief that adults become increasingly more alike as they grow older is one of the many myths about aging; see, for example, Kausler, 1982, p. 2.) The problem of obtaining adequate and representative samples has also been a particularly difficult one for the stage theorists, since they are attempting to draw conclusions about such a wide range of ages and behaviors. Thus it is hardly surprising (though it is disappointing) that the various stage theorists have produced highly inconsistent and contradictory models, so much so that even one who is sympathetic to this approach cannot know what to believe.

Some of the specific ideas proposed by the stage theorists may ultimately prove to be worthwhile. For now, however, we can only conclude that we must look elsewhere for scientifically acceptable answers to our questions about personality and aging.

Trait Theories

A popular conceptual alternative is to define personality in terms of **traits,** or specific components that initiate and guide consistent forms of behavior. (See, for example, Allport, 1937; 1955; 1961.) To illustrate, a person with the trait of "friendliness" will usually be motivated to seek out other people, start a conversation, and express an interest in their activities. Conversely, an individual with the trait of "shyness" will tend to avoid others, show little concern for them, and remain silent. Other traits include ambitiousness, cleanliness, enthusiasm, punctuality, talkativeness, dominance, submissiveness, generosity, penuriousness, and so forth (with emphasis on the "and so forth," since Allport estimates that there are some 4,000–5,000 traits!).

As is often the case with psychological theory, the exact nature of traits is a matter of some controversy. Allport concludes that every adult personality is unique, and is composed of numerous "personal traits" that differ (often in rather subtle ways) from those of anyone else. But since a particular culture does tend to evoke roughly similar modes of adjustment, he concedes that there are some general aspects of personality ("common traits") which can be used to compare most adults. Other trait theorists contend instead that there is some degree of genuine, fundamental commonality among adults.

In this section, we will examine the evidence concerning aging and some particularly important traits.

LOCUS OF CONTROL.   This trait was first conceptualized by Rotter (1966). Locus of control refers to a consistent belief about obtaining rewards and avoiding punishments: some people believe that this depends primarily on their own actions and behaviors (**internal locus of control**), while others expect their good and bad experiences to be caused largely by mere chance and the actions of other people (**external locus of control**). Like virtually all traits, locus of control is a continuous variable; an individual may fall anywhere along the scale from strongly internal to strongly external. More internally oriented adults are likely to try and run their own lives in their own way, while those who are more externally oriented tend to see little point in such efforts.

The available evidence strongly indicates that for both younger and older adults, internals are superior to externals in psychological adjustment. In particular, internals are more likely to cope well with personal crises, to be satisfied with their lives, and to enjoy a positive self-concept (e.g., Kuypers, 1972; Lefcourt, 1976; Palmore & Luikart, 1972; Reid et al., 1977; Wolf & Kurtz, 1975).

One possible exception to this general rule concerns internals who have been institutionalized, and live in an environment that features high constraints and firm rules imposed by others (e.g., a nursing home). Will these internals also demonstrate superior adjustment, or will they become frustrated and disappointed because they can not control their own destinies in such a setting? Much of the evidence bearing on this issue is mixed, with some findings favoring internals (Reid et al., 1977), some favoring externals (Felton & Kahana, 1974), and some indicating no relationship between locus of control and adjustment (Wolk, 1976). Schulz (1976) sought to cast some further light on the question of institutionalization by dividing residents of a church-affiliated home into four groups. One group was able to control the time and duration of visits from other people over a two-month period (high internal control); a second group knew when visits would take place but could not control the time and duration; and a third group was unable to control any aspects of the visits (low internal control, or high external control). The fourth group received no visits at all. Members of the first two groups showed significant (and comparable) improvements in psychological well-being, activity levels, and health status. The third and fourth groups did not, supporting the superiority of internality.

Though locus of control is clearly an important aspect of the adult personality, our fundamental question remains: does this trait change as one grows older? Some cross-sectional and longitudinal studies suggest that adults become more external over the years (e.g., Bradley & Webb, 1976; Lachman, 1983; Siegler & Gatz, 1985). Yet one four-year cross-sequential study found that the elderly are more internal than the middle-aged (Lachman, 1985), whereas some cross-sectional research indicates that older adults are more internal than young adults (e.g., Gatz & Siegler, 1981; Staats, 1974). And still other studies report more complicated relationships between aging and locus of control, such as an increase in internality from age 15 to 39 and a decrease after age 60 (Lao, 1974) or greater externality for college students and adults over 70 (Ryckman & Malikioski, 1975).

One possible explanation for these conflicting results is that locus of control appears to involve a number of different dimensions (Levenson, 1974; Paulhus, 1983). Older adults may be more external than college students insofar as intelligence and health are concerned, since these variables are known to decline in late adulthood. But older adults may be more internal with regard to social competence, since they have had more experience dealing with people. Although the latter hypothesis is yet to be tested, some recent evidence does support the former (Lachman, 1986). This implies that measuring locus of control with a unidimensional instrument, such as Rotter's, may well be an oversimplification.

Taken as a whole, the available research evidence does *not* indicate that middle-aged and elderly adults are considerably more external than are young adults. This casts considerable doubt on the common belief that the elderly perceive themselves as powerless and dependent on others.

EXTRAVERSION–INTROVERSION.   This well-known and important trait was originated by Jung (1921/1976); some subsequent concep-

Myths About Aging: Personality Development

MYTH	BEST AVAILABLE EVIDENCE
During adulthood, your personality will develop through a series of specific stages that is much the same for all individuals.	There is no single set of stages that accurately describes the course of adult personality development. In fact, it appears that most aspects of personality remain fairly stable throughout adulthood.
During your forties (or thereabouts), you will experience a "midlife crisis"—a time of considerable psychological turmoil, worry, and despair.	Most adults do not experience an unusually severe crisis at midlife. Those who do tend to have suffered similar crises throughout their adulthood
The elderly are much more likely to view themselves as powerless pawns, influenced primarily by external events which they cannot control.	Young adults who are characterized by an internal locus of control tend to remain so through old age.
As you grow to old age, you will become more and more rigid, crochety, and unyielding.	Growing older does *not* necessarily make one more rigid and inflexible. Those born many years ago are likely to be more rigid than those born more recently, because the prevailing standards of yesteryear were more conservative.
As you grow to old age, you will become much less active.	An individual's level of activity tends to remain fairly stable throughout adult hood.

tual modifications have been suggested by Eysenck (e.g., 1967; Eysenck & Eysenck, 1969). People who are primarily **extraverted** are consistently outgoing, venture forth with careless confidence into the unknown, and are particularly influenced by other people and by events in the external world. Conversely, those who are more **introverted** are shy, inscrutable, and keenly interested in the inner world of their own psyche. According to Jung, we inherit a predisposition to be more introverted or more extraverted, but both tendencies are present in every personality. Consequently, even extraverts (introverts) must allow free expression to their introverted (extraverted) aspects in order to be psychologically healthy.

During the past two decades, there has been a sharp controversy concerning the course of this trait during adulthood. Some investigators contend that adults become more introverted as they grow older (e.g., Botwinick, 1973; Neugarten, 1977, pp. 636–637; Neugarten & Associates, 1964). Others regard this as yet another of the many myths about aging, and argue instead that introversion–extraversion tends to remain relatively stable during adulthood (e.g., Costa & McCrae, 1976; 1978; 1980; Kausler, 1982, p. 602; Shanan & Jacobowitz, 1982, pp. 151–152). The studies reporting stability may perhaps be somewhat more compelling, since they are more recent and make greater use of longitudinal designs, but it is difficult at present to reach any firm conclusions about the course of extraversion–introversion during adulthood.

ACTIVITY.   Another common conception about the elderly is that they are markedly less active than younger people. Here, the evidence is fairly clear: studies of subjects varying from the lower middle class to the college educated, using methods as varied as responses to questionnaires and direct observations of overt behavior, indicate that activity level tends to remain stable during adulthood.

Research indicates that personality traits, such as activity level, tend to remain stable during adulthood. Chances are that these runners will continue to lead active lives as they grow older.   *Sarah Putnam/Picture Cube*

(See, for example, Heyman & Gianturco, 1973; Nystrom, 1974; Palmore, 1970; Stone & Norris, 1966; Thomae, 1976; 1980, p. 287.)

Activity is a rather complicated trait that is influenced by various factors—physiological, psychological, and cultural. For example, some adults may be physically unable to engage in strenuous activity; some adults may not want to, for various personal reasons; and some cultures or subcultures may stress the desirability of more or less active pursuits, such as physical fitness or watching television. Based on the available data, however, the stereotype of the less-active elderly person must be rejected as incorrect.

RIGIDITY.   This trait involves an inability to shift from one form of behavior to another, even though such a shift might well be advantageous to the individual. Such self-defeating inflexibility is commonly believed to be more characteristic of older people. At first glance, the evidence appears ambiguous: some studies do seem to support this view (Heglin, 1956; Schaie, 1958), while others report no appreciable change in rigidity during adulthood (Angleitner, 1976; Schaie & Parham, 1976; 1977). But when some possible confounding factors are carefully examined, a more consistent picture begins to emerge.

Some aspects of intelligence are known to decline somewhat as an adult grows older (Chapter 6), and the correlation between intelligence and rigidity is moderately high. Thus it has been suggested that older people may behave less flexibly because of this decrease, rather than because of any increase in rigidity. However, the evidence dealing with this issue is ambiguous (e.g., Chown, 1961; Schaie, 1958).

More importantly, there would seem to be various forms of rigidity. Researchers have found it necessary to distinguish among four varieties: (1) rigidity in solving specific problems, as in mathematics; (2) rigidity in dealing with familiar but constantly changing situations; (3) rigidity in coping with unfamiliar surroundings; and (4) rigidity in one's attitudes toward other people and objects. An adult who behaves rigidly in some of these ways may well act more flexibly in others, hence studies which treat rigidity as a simple unidimensional variable are likely to produce misleading results. (See Chown, 1961; Riegel, 1959; Riegel & Riegel, 1960; Schaie, 1958.)

Most importantly, the apparent increased rigidity of the elderly has been shown to be due primarily to cohort effects, rather than to aging (Schaie, Labouvie, & Buech, 1973; Schaie & Labouvie-Vief, 1974). That is, members of earlier generations are typically more rigid than those born later. This is not overly surprising, since there are various social-historical factors that might well cause later cohorts to be more flexible: increasingly liberal standards of acceptable behavior and an increasing number of people attending college, to name just two. But whatever the reason, the most convincing evidence is once again on the side of trait stability: merely growing to an older age does *not* necessarily make an adult more rigid and inflexible.

CAUTIOUSNESS.   Yet another belief about the elderly is that they are considerably more cautious than younger adults, and less likely to make risky decisions. Here, unfortunately, the available data are confusing and contradictory. Some studies do appear to support this stereotype, but the accuracy of these findings is highly questionable because of serious methodological flaws: questionnaires tainted by low reliability and a poor response format, or improperly designed laboratory experiments. For example, one sample of subjects was invited to choose among a series of tasks that varied from a high probability of achieving a small reward (more cautious) to a low probability of achieving a large payoff (more risky). However, the average expected payoffs were approximately equal for all of the possible task choices. That is, the amount the subject might reasonably expect to win by the end of the experiment was about the same regardless of which tasks were chosen. Thus there was no incentive for subjects to select the more risky alternatives, making it impossible to draw any firm conclusions about the effects of aging on cautiousness. (See Kausler, 1982, pp. 612–616; Okun, 1976; Okun, Stock, & Ceurvorst, 1980.)

Other researchers have found that when the total reward is in fact commensurate with the degree of risk, there is no significant difference in cautiousness between younger and older adults (Birkhill & Schaie, 1975; Okun & Elias, 1977). To date, however, studies of aging and cautiousness have not controlled for possible cohort effects; virtually all have used the cross-sectional design. Furthermore, cautiousness (like rigidity) appears to be a multidimensional trait, and this additional complication has also by and large been ignored. (See Okun & Elias, 1977; Okun, Siegler, & George, 1978.) Therefore, any generalizations about aging and cautiousness must be held in abeyance until more suitable data have been obtained.

FIELD INDEPENDENCE–FIELD DEPENDENCE.   This trait, first conceptualized by Witkin and his associates (1962), refers to the way in which a person perceives the external world. When making perceptual judgments, those who are **field independent** rely largely on internal stimuli, while **field-dependent** people rely primarily on external stimuli. Therefore, field-dependent individuals are more likely to be distracted by irrelevant stimuli in the environment.

To clarify the nature of field independence–field dependence, let us consider one common way of measuring this trait. The subject is placed in a dark room, and is able to see only a lighted square that contains a lighted rod.

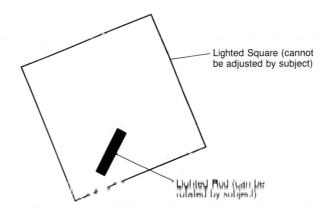

The subject's task is to adjust the rod so that it is horizontal (or, on some trials, vertical) with respect to the floor of the room. Since the square background is tilted, the subject must ignore this distraction and rely on internal judgments in order to succeed. The better one is able to do this, the more field independent one is.

Virtually all of the studies on aging and field independence–field dependence have used the cross-sectional design, which does not control for possible cohort effects. However, it has been suggested that this normally important source of bias can be safely ignored in this one instance: any changes in field independence–field dependence during adulthood would seem to be due primarily to variations in the individual's perceptual system, rather than to any social-historical factors (Lee & Pollack, 1978). If this argument is correct, the available (cross-sectional) evidence does indicate that adults become more field-dependent as they grow older (e.g., Eisner, 1972; Kogan, 1973; Lee & Pollack, 1978; Markus, 1971; Panek et al., 1978).

One important practical application of this trait deserves mention. It has been shown that irrespective of age, field-dependent drivers tend to have more automobile accidents than those who are field independent (Mihal & Barrett, 1976). Thus greater field dependency among the aged may well be at least partly responsible for their above-average frequency of driving accidents.

TRAITS DEFINED BY PERSONALITY INVENTORIES.   In the preceding sections, we have endeavored to suggest the basic nature of gerontological trait research. Before we leave this area, however, there is one additional topic that merits discussion: the measurement of traits (and other aspects of personality) by means of standardized inventories.

Some measures of personality consist of written, multiple-choice or true-false questionnaires. The one most often used with older adults is the Minnesota Multiphasic Personality Inventory (MMPI), which contains 550 items and is intended primarily for the diagnosis and measurement of psychopathology. Also quite popular, but designed to tap more normal characteristics, is the Sixteen Personality Factor Questionnaire (Cattell, Eber, & Tatsuoka, 1970). The 16 PF yields scores on sixteen traits, such as reserved versus outgoing, humble versus assertive, serious versus happy-go-lucky, and shy versus venturesome.

Other measures of personality are less structured, and serve as a sort of screen on which the subject can project important unconscious (and conscious) feelings, beliefs, and motives. Perhaps the best known of these projective techniques is the Rorschach, wherein subjects are asked to describe what they see in a series of inkblots (Rorschach, 1921/1942). Another prominent projective device, the Thematic Apperception Test (TAT), uses pictures of people in rather ambiguous situations. For each picture, the subject is asked to make up a story that tells what led up to the events shown, what is happening at the moment, and what the outcome will be (Murray et al., 1938).

Here again, gerontological researchers must contend with significant methodological problems. First of all, it is considerably more difficult to administer measures of personality to the elderly than to younger adults. A long questionnaire (such as the MMPI) may represent a formidable obstacle to an elderly person, who is likely to respond rather slowly. Motor impairments may make it difficult for some elderly subjects to handle questionnaire booklets, and to cope with computer-scored answer forms. Other aged individuals may be troubled by visual deficiencies, which prevent them from perceiving Rorschach inkblots and TAT pictures accurately. On both questionnaires and projective techniques, some older adults may be unable to give appropriate answers because of impairments in memory and/or abstract thinking. And since the elderly grew up in an era when psychology was far less popular than it is now, they may well regard measures of personality as meaningless and refuse to take them seriously. Secondly, analyzing the results obtained from personality measures is not an easy task. Just as it can be difficult to separate aging effects from cohort effects, some measures of personality (e.g., the Rorschach) are affected by such potentially confounding variables as cognitive ability and socioeconomic status. (See Lawton, Whelihan, & Belsky, 1980.)

As a result, the evidence dealing with aging and measures of personality is quite limited. Studies using the 16 PF indicate that the elderly are more reserved, serious, conscientious, shy, socially aware, self-reproaching, conservative, and self-reliant than younger adults, but lower in intelligence. However, these findings may well be due to cohort effects rather than to aging (except for intelligence, some aspects of which decline somewhat with increasing age). With regard to the MMPI, older adults tend to score higher (i.e., more pathological) on hypochondria and depression, but lower on psychotically oriented scales like schizophrenia and paranoia. There is also some evidence in support of the stability hypothesis: One longitudinal study of physically and emotionally healthy men reported considerable stability in MMPI scores over a 30-year period (Leon et al., 1979). Data concerning the Rorschach and TAT are less common, although the latter does appear to be more useful with elderly subjects.

One interesting new psychometric approach is that of McCrae and Costa (1984), who have devised a measure of personality based on the mathematical procedure of factor analysis. Their "NEO Inventory" taps three major traits, each of which includes six subordinate traits. Thus "Neuroticism" involves an unusual proneness to anxiety and tenseness, anger and irritability, depression, and fears of shame and ridicule; a lack of self-control; and an inability to deal adequately with stress. "Extraversion" is denoted by warmth and friendliness, a desire to be with other people, assertiveness, keeping busy and behaving energetically, seeking excitement and taking risks, and frequent positive emotions (e.g., happiness). "Openness to Experience" is characterized by a willingness to experience one's own feelings strongly, and without defensive distortions; a vivid imagination and a tendency to develop elaborate daydreams; a sensitivity to art and beauty; a willingness to try something new, such as an unusual meal or a visit to a foreign country; actively seeking out new ideas; and an open-mindedness to values which differ from one's own.

Although Costa and McCrae are well respected in the field of gerontological research, their tripartite trait model is as yet too new for any definitive evaluations to be made. In fact, considerably more data—and perhaps new measures specifically designed for use with older adults—are needed before extensive conclusions can be drawn about aging and traits defined by personality inventories.

EVALUATION OF TRAIT THEORIES. The most serious criticism of trait theories concerns the issue of circularity. For example, if we characterize people who avoid others and tend to remain silent as "shy," can we then turn the same definition around and conclude that these individuals engage in these behaviors *because* they are shy?

Clearly, we cannot; such circular reasoning would explain nothing at all about the causes of shyness. This lack of explanatory power is particularly evident in a statement made by Allport himself: "[A man] likes blue because he likes blue" (Evans, 1970, p. 37). As B. F. Skinner, the noted behaviorist, has observed:

> [The trait theorist begins] by observing a preoccupation with a mirror which recalls the legend of Narcissus, [invents] the adjective "narcissistic" and then the noun "narcissism," and finally [asserts] that the thing presumably referred to by the noun is the cause of [this] behavior. . . . But at no point in such a series [does the theorist] make contact with any event outside the behavior itself which justifies the claim of a causal connection. (Skinner, 1953/1965, p. 202.)

It has also been argued that human behavior is not consistent enough to be analyzed in terms of traits alone. These critics contend that people may well be shy (or aggressive, or serious, or whatever) on some occasions but not others, and that psychologists must therefore concentrate on the complicated interactions between traits and specific situations. In addition, the occurrence or nonoccurrence of a given trait may well be influenced by the individual's chronological age, biological age, sex, mental health, and physical health, and by prevailing social conditions. "Any prediction of the behavior of the aged based entirely on expected correlations between age and trait scores must fail if the interaction of [these] other variables cannot be calculated" (Thomae, 1980, p. 293; see also Diener, Larsen, & Emmons, 1984; Mischel, 1968; 1973; 1977). Even Allport himself expressed a similar concern (1968, p. 63).

Trait theory also has staunch advocates, however, and has stimulated a considerable amount of research. (See, for example, Bem & Allen, 1974; Costa & McCrae, 1976; 1978; 1980; McCrae & Costa, 1984; Wiggins, 1974.) Furthermore, as we have seen, gerontological trait research has added significantly to our knowledge. Stereotypes of the elderly as more rigid and inflexible, more likely to view themselves as powerless pawns, and less active than younger adults have been shattered by appropriate hard data. The popular beliefs that older adults are more introverted and more cautious have also been strongly challenged, though here the evidence is more equivocal. The advantages of an internal locus of control, and the potential drawbacks of field dependency (as when driving an automobile), represent useful and important findings. The bulk of the evidence suggests that traits tend to remain rather stable during adulthood, supporting the belief of most psychologists that personality is determined relatively early in one's life. And some researchers even claim that trait theory can provide valid explanations of human behavior if appropriate statistical procedures are used, such as factor analysis (e.g., Cattell, 1965; 1973; 1979; 1980).

Perhaps this controversy can be at least partially resolved as follows: trait theory does appear to be seriously lacking in *explanatory* power; it does *not* tell us *why* people behave as they do. And it may indeed be an oversimplification to study traits without taking situational and other factors into account, although this interaction model has not as yet been applied to the study of aging. However, basic trait theory has provided some useful *descriptions* of human behavior. While description is neither as profound nor as scientifically satisfying as explanation, it is a necessary first step; and in this respect, at least, trait theory seems to be worthwhile.

Cognitive Theories

As we observed earlier in this chapter, the most common definition of personality includes and individual's physical, mental, emotional, and social characteristics. There are some theorists who contend that the mental aspects are most important, however, and that personality should be studied primarily in terms of cognitions.

For example, George Kelly (1955) concludes that our everyday behaviors closely resemble those of the research scientist. That is, each of us creates our own hypotheses and experimental tests for dealing with the world in which we live, and it is these self-created concepts ("personal constructs") that determine our behaviors. To illustrate, suppose that you become ill. If you construe your malady as "cancer" (or, more generally, as "life threatening"), you will undoubtedly be quite anxious and fearful. You may actually have only a cold, which is not at all life threatening, but this is immaterial. It is your interpretation of the situation that is responsible for your fearful behaviors, and objective reality is unimportant—at least until you decide to test your hypothesis by conducting an appropriate experimental test, such as asking a trusted doctor for an honest opinion. (See also Dollard & Miller, 1950, pp. 97–124.)

One of the few cognitive theorists who has devoted much attention to adulthood and aging is Hans Thomae (1970; 1980). For example, Thomae concludes that an adult's subjective health is strongly influenced by cognitions and perceptions. Thus an elderly person with a malignant disease may refuse to perceive the gravity of the situation, and behave calmly and efficiently, until the doctor recommends surgery. Then, even though there has been no real change in the patient's physical condition, the altered perceptions triggered by this new event may well lead to fear and despair.

In general, many adults expect their physical health to decline as they approach old age. When they do become ill, they conceptualize this as normal for their age. Thus they may well face ill health with relative equanimity, and self-reports of their health may be similar to those of younger adults who are not ill. Some data do show that the very old are much less likely than young or middle-aged adults to become depressed when they are ill, even though their illnesses may be more severe. (See Blazer & Williams, 1980; Brody & Kleban, 1983; Thomae, 1980, pp. 295–299.)

Thomae has also applied his cognitive theory to perceptions of other aspects of one's life, including economic status, housing, and expected future events. His approach may well be a useful one; but it is also relatively new, so this is yet another area where further research is needed.

Type Theories

One of the strong historical traditions in gerontological research has been to examine the ways in which we cope with the changing circumstances of life, and to describe these behaviors in terms of personality types (Breytspraak, 1984). This theory posits that early in our lives, we develop patterns of behavior for coping with the challenges that we confront. Over time, these **coping styles** evolve into specific personality **types,** which may then be used to predict the ways in which we will deal with new situations. This implies that it is more important to know how an individual has dealt with challenges in the past, than to know the specific situation that currently confronts someone.

In one early study, Reichard, Livson, and Petersen (1962) obtained a sample of 87 men aged 55 to 84. These researchers focused their attention on possible personality differences among those men who adjusted successfully, or unsuccessfully, to aging and retirement. They identified five personality types that seemed to summarize the coping styles of these men:

1. The Mature Type. These men evaluated themselves realistically, and were relatively self-accepting and free of conflict. They found considerable satisfaction in their activities and personal relationships, took their old age for granted, and felt that their lives had been rewarding. Thus they made the best of their current situation.

2. The Rocking-Chair Type. These men were generally passive, happy to be free of responsibility, and willing to leave everything to other people.

3. The Armored Type. These men maintained complicated systems of defenses against perceiving their own passivity and helplessness, presumably to protect themselves from the fear of growing old. They also tried to support these defenses by keeping active.

4. The Angry Type. These men adjusted poorly to retirement. They were bitter because they felt that they had failed to achieve their goals, and aggressive in that they blamed others for these disappointments.

5. The Self-Hating Type. These men also adjusted poorly to retirement, and felt that they had failed in life. However, they turned their anger inward and blamed themselves.

Similar data have been reported by Neugarten and her associates (Neugarten, Crotty, & Tobin, 1964; Neugarten, Havighurst, & Tobin, 1968). They identified four distinct personality types: integrated, armored-defended, passive-dependent, and unintegrated. No significant relationship was found between these types and age, however, indicating once again that there are no sharp discontinuities in personality throughout adulthood.

EVALUATION OF TYPE THEORIES.   Although type theories are appealingly simple, they also have their drawbacks. In particular, some critics contend that personality is far too complicated to be described in terms of types. That is, there are so many respects by which a person could be categorized (e.g., liberal, narcissistic, introverted, authoritarian, and so forth) that any individual would have to be located in literally hundreds of types. "Typologies are convenient and seductive, but none has ever been invented to account for the total individual" (Allport, 1961, p. 17; see also Adler, 1927/1957; 1929/1969). Even Carl Jung, whose theory of personality includes some important typologies, has warned that human nature cannot be classified into a small number of categories.

The use of types may well be helpful in certain instances, since some individuals undoubtedly do behave in similar ways on some occasions. Nevertheless, it is important to recognize that typologies may well oversimplify the nature of the human personality.

Sex-Related Theories

A few studies suggest that during the latter part of life, the personalities of men and women change in contrasting ways: men become less aggressive and domineering by about middle age, while women grow more assertive and dominant from middle to old age. (See, for example, Gutmann, 1975; Lowenthal et al., 1975; Neugarten, 1977, p. 636; Neugarten & Gutmann, 1958.)

These findings may indicate that older men and women are more free to depart from traditional sex roles. For example, elderly women may feel that they can be less nurturant and more dominant now that they no longer have children to raise. Elderly men may see less need to be aggressive, since they are no longer caught up in the competitive struggle to bring home a sufficient income.

However, it has also been suggested that these results are due to a methodological artifact: better-educated subjects are less likely to drop out of longitudinal studies. Since those with more education also tend to be less influenced by traditional sex roles, the more recent data in such studies are biased in favor of male-female similarity, and the whole study thus gives the misleading impression that the sample has changed over time in this direction (Urberg & Labouvie-Vief, 1976; see also Reedy, 1983, pp. 123–124).

Furthermore, studies which do show decreases in masculinity among men indicate that these changes are very small. Given the rate of decrease observed in one study, it would take older men 136 years to reach the same level of femininity as the average college woman! (See Douglas & Arenberg, 1978; McCrae & Costa, 1984.)

Still other (cross-sectional) studies report instead that middle-aged men and women tend to be similar on a variety of personality traits (e.g., Ryff & Baltes, 1976). All in all, then, the evidence concerning sex-related personality reversals during the latter part of adulthood must be regarded as equivocal at best.

Afterword

Many adults erroneously believe that their personalities change, usually for the better, as they grow older (Woodruff & Birren, 1972). Nevertheless, the evidence reviewed in this chapter indicates that personality tends to remain stable during adulthood. This does *not* mean that our survey of this area has been a waste of time, however, or that the personality of a given adult cannot be changed.

First of all, the data we have examined deal with the normal course of aging. If an adult is sufficiently motivated to undertake appropriate special efforts, such as formal psychotherapy, significant personality change is indeed possible.

Secondly, numerous important discoveries have been made during the past decade or two. As we have seen, various stereotypes of the aged have been shattered by empirical data. We are warned not to expect an easy solution to our problems through miraculous personality transformations during adulthood, but encouraged not to fear traumatic midlife crises or marked deteriorations in personality. Furthermore, while our personalities may remain stable during adulthood, the world around us does not. Thus we have learned to be less concerned with the ways in which life experiences change the adult personality, and more interested in how the adult personality influences our attempts to deal with a complicated and changing environment.

Finally, while we have stressed the importance of various methodological problems, this by no means implies a bleak outlook for future research in this area. There is renewed interest in the scientific study of personality and aging, and increased sophistication in the design of more recent research. Therefore, the next decade may well provide us with even more valuable insights concerning personality and adulthood.

Summary

SUBSTANTIVE AND METHODOLOGICAL ISSUES

The study of personality and aging is complicated by methodological problems. Some of these were discussed in Chapter 2: The considerable time, effort, and money required to conduct longitudinal studies, and their vulnerability to selective attrition; the inability of cross-sectional research to distinguish between aging effects and cohort effects; the weakness of chronological age as a measure of aging; the problem of understanding the meaning of different behaviors at different ages. Also, the three most common ways to study personality—laboratory research, clinical insight, and field surveys—all have significant strengths and weaknesses.

With regard to substantive issues, there is no unanimity among psychologists as to the meaning of personality. However, personality is most often conceptualized as the organized, distinctive pattern of behavior that characterizes a particular individual. This comprehensive definition includes an individual's physical, mental, emotional, and social characteristics. Personality is extremely important because it encompasses, and influences, so much of our behavior. Yet its study is also highly challenging, because a significant portion of personality involves processes that are unobservable or even unconscious.

ADULTHOOD AND PERSONALITY DEVELOPMENT

Some investigators have chosen to divide most or all of adulthood into a series of stages, which are supposedly experienced by most or all adults. Stage theories are appealing because they are simple and straightforward, cover a broad range of people and ages, and propose that we continue to grow and develop throughout our lives.

However, they have proved to be of relatively little value in understanding adult personality development. It is doubtful whether most
adults are sufficiently alike to pass through the same stages at all,
let alone at similar ages.

A popular conceptual alternative is to define personality in terms
of traits, or specific components that initiate and guide consistent
forms of behavior. Most traits tend to remain stable during adulthood, although field dependency does appear to increase with increasing age. In particular, the evidence refutes the common beliefs
that the elderly are more similar to one another, more likely to perceive themselves as powerless pawns, more rigid and inflexible, and
less active than younger adults. It is also questionable whether older
adults are more introverted and more cautious, though here the
data are more equivocal. Some investigators have sought to measure
the traits of older adults with standardized personality inventories,
but more research is needed in this area before extensive conclusions can be drawn. Trait theory has been criticized for circular definitions that lack explanatory power, and for presenting an unrealistically consistent picture of human behavior. But this approach has
devoted advocates as well, and has provided useful and important
descriptive information.

Some theorists contend that personality should be studied primarily in terms of cognitions. They argue that an individual's behaviors are determined by perceptions and interpretations of events
in the environment, rather than by objective reality. As yet, however, there are relatively few applications of this theory to the area
of adulthood and aging.

Yet another possible approach is to discuss the adult personality
in terms of types, or patterns of personality and behavior that supposedly apply to numerous individuals. Thus it has been suggested
that we develop coping styles early in life, which later evolve into
specific personality types. For example, the mature type deals positively and constructively with old age and retirement, while other
types react with varying kinds of defenses and hostility. While the
use of typologies may be helpful in certain instances, they may also
represent an oversimplification of the human personality.

A few studies suggest that during the latter part of life, the personalities of men and women change in contrasting ways. However,
the evidence concerning such sex-related personality reversals is
equivocal at best.

Although the evidence indicates that personality tends to remain
stable during adulthood, those who are sufficiently motivated to
undertake appropriate special efforts (such as formal psychotherapy) may indeed experience significant personality change. While
research findings warn us not to expect an easy solution to our

problems through miraculous personality transformations during adulthood, they encourage us not to fear traumatic midlife crises or marked deteriorations in personality. We have learned to be less concerned with the ways in which life experiences change the adult personality, and more interested in how the adult personality influences our attempts to deal with the world around us.

CHAPTER 8

Relationships and Interpersonal Behavior

Interpersonal relationships are vital to our existence. Most of us choose to spend at least some time with interesting acquaintances, with warm and supportive close friends, and with loved ones who occupy a unique and special place in our lives. Also, sooner or later, many adults opt for that singular and intimate form of relationship known as marriage.

In our quest to understand the course of adult development, therefore, we must deal with yet another crucial question: does aging affect interpersonal behavior? For example, do adults tend to have more, fewer, or about the same number of friends as they grow toward old age? Does the frequency and enjoyment of sexual behavior decline markedly after middle age? Are marriage and relationships with one's children significantly more or less satisfying for the elderly? More generally, is old age a time of marked social isolation? To be sure, various stereotypes suggest that older is *not* better. Examples include elderly parents who supposedly lament that their children no longer visit them, and aged individuals who presumably live alone and ignored in impoverished circumstances. As noted throughout this book, however, such stereotypes often prove to be mere myths when held up to the light of empirical evidence. Therefore, let us once again reserve judgment until we have examined appropriate research data.

In this chapter, we will investigate the course of interpersonal relationships during adulthood. First, we will present a conceptual system for organizing and examining these relationships. We will then discuss the characteristics of adult friendships, and the nature and dynamics of such intimate relationships as love, marriage, parenting, and grandparenting. We will conclude with a survey and critical evaluation of currently popular psychological theories about the interpersonal behavior of the elderly.

Classifying Major Life Events: Temporal and Statistical Normativity

Definitions

Most of us experience many major life events between birth and death, such as going to college, choosing a job, getting married, and having children. Furthermore, many of these events are commonly expected to occur at fairly specific ages. In one early study, for example, a sample of middle-class and middle-aged adults concluded that men and women should complete their education and get married in their early twenties, and should become grandparents by age 45–50 (Neugarten et al., 1968; see Table 8.1).

Of course, not all adults adhere to such social norms: some marry considerably later in life, some devote more years to their education, and so on. Thus one useful way to classify the many life events that we experience is according to the age at which they occur. More specifically, an event is **temporally normative** if it occurs at an age that is typical for most people in that culture. Examples include Americans who become widowed or suffer a stroke at age 65–70, or who get married for the first time at age 25. Conversely, an event is **temporally non-normative** if it occurs at an atypical age. In our society, becoming widowed or suffering a stroke at age 35, or getting married for the first time at age 45, are temporally *non-normative* life events.

A second good way to classify life events is according to their frequency, regardless of age. Thus an event is **statistically normative** if it happens to the majority of individuals in a given culture. Most people in this country experience marriage and retirement at some point in their lives, so these life events are statistically normative. In contrast, few Americans of any age suffer from strokes or spinal cord injuries, or are lucky enough to win a state lottery. Therefore, these life events are **statistically non-normative.**

If we combine these dimensions, the result may be depicted as a two-by-two table. (See Table 8.2.) Note that whether an event is *temporally* normative or non-normative depends solely on the *age* at which it occurs. Conversely, whether an event is *statistically* normative or non-normative depends solely on *how many people in that culture* ex-

TABLE 8.1   Attitudes of a middle-class, middle-aged sample toward various age-related characteristics (1965).

Characteristic	Age Range Designated as Appropriate or Expected	Percent of Sample Agreeing	
		Men (N=50)	Women (N=43)
Best age for a man to marry	20–25	80	90
Best age for a woman to marry	19–24	85	90
When most people should become grandparents	45–50	84	79
Best age for most people to finish school and go to work	20–22	86	82
When most men should be settled on a career	24–26	74	64
When most men hold their top jobs	45–50	71	58
When most people should be ready to retire	60–65	83	86
A young man	18–22	84	83
A middle-aged man	40–50	86	75
An old man	65–75	75	57
A young woman	18–24	89	88
A middle-aged woman	40–50	87	77
An old woman	60–75	83	87
When a man has the most responsibilities	35–50	79	75
When a woman has the most responsibilities	25–40	93	91
When a man accomplishes the most	40–50	82	71
When a woman accomplishes the most	30–45	94	92

SOURCE: Neugarten et al. (1968).

perience that event at some point in their lives. (See Schulz & Rau, 1985.)

Implications

Virtually all of us experience some life events from each of the four cells in Table 8.2. By definition, however, most of us spend most of

TABLE 8.2   Classifying major life events according to temporal and statistical normativity.

	Temporally Normative	*Temporally Non-normative*
Statistically Normative	Getting married for the first time at age 25 Becoming widowed at age 65 Retiring at age 65 Having first child during late twenties	Getting married for the first time at age 45 Becoming widowed at age 35 Retiring at age 40 Having first child at age 45
Statistically Non-normative	Suffering stroke at age 65 Spinal cord injury at age 10–20	Suffering stroke at age 35 Spinal cord injury at age 55 Winning state lottery (any age)

SOURCE: Schulz & Rau (1985, modified).

our time dealing with statistically and temporally normative events. Since these events are the most common, they are also the ones for which friends, loved ones, and society are best prepared to offer any necessary assistance. For example, experienced college counselors and professors are likely to understand and help resolve the scholastic and emotional problems of the 20-year-old student, while widowhood support groups are generally effective for those over 60.

What of those relatively few adults who experience an unusually large number of non-normative life events? Since these events are by definition rare and unpredictable (albeit perhaps more interesting), friends, relatives, and society are less likely to know how to provide appropriate help. Thus a woman who is widowed at age 25 may have no friends who can give her appropriate emotional support, since they are all too young to have undergone a similar experience. A 45-year-old man who enters college for the first time may prove to be somewhat of a puzzle to his counselor and professors. An adult who marries and has children late in life may have some difficulty dealing with teachers and other parents, who do not expect a 6-year-old child to have a 50-year-old father and a 40-year-old mother. Or a person who suffers a spinal cord injury at any age may find that this rare event leaves friends feeling helpless and confused, and unable to respond effectively. In fact, adults who must

An older adult is likely to find college work more stressful than his younger classmates because this life event is temporally non-normative.   *Eli Heller/Stock, Boston*

deal with many non-normative life events (and the corresponding stress) may well be more likely to suffer physical illness, psychopathology, or even premature death.

A further discussion of stress and non-normative life events will be deferred until Chapter 10. The remainder of this chapter will concentrate on those life events that are statistically normative, including marriage and parenting.

Adult Friendships

Some social scientists prefer to explain the behavior of friends, lovers, spouses, and families in roughly similar terms. But while friendships may vary from casual to loving, even the best and closest of these would seem to differ in many significant respects from an intimate relationship with one special person. In accordance with those theorists who support the latter view, we will treat friendship and marriage in separate sections.

The Purposes of Adult Friendships

Why do adults have friends? What sorts of people are we likely to choose as our friends? The answers to these questions are by no means simple ones, since friendships can serve various important purposes.

INTERPERSONAL SIMILARITY.   The popular notion that opposites attract one another may hold true in rare instances, but is *not* generally supported by empirical evidence. Instead, we are usually attracted to those who have similar beliefs, values, and personalities (Griffitt, 1974; Kandel, 1978; Levinger, Senn, & Jorgensen, 1970; Lowenthal et al., 1975). People who resemble ourselves may be easier to communicate with and relate to, since they tend to perceive events in similar ways. Or it may be reassuring to see our own characteristics and opinions reflected, and thereby implicitly endorsed, by someone else.

PSYCHOLOGICAL SUPPORT.   Not all studies support the importance of interpersonal similarity. Some findings suggest that while we may at first be drawn to those who resemble ourselves, long-term friendships actually depend far more on psychological support: a good friend is one who makes you feel good (Bailey, Finney, & Heim, 1975; see also Troll & Smith, 1976). Thus mutual trust, and feeling comfortable with one another, may ultimately prove to be more important determinants of friendship than similarity. As we have seen, however, even close friends may find it difficult to offer effective psychological support in the case of non-normative life events.

SELF-DISCLOSURE.   One vital aspect of a close and trusting friendship is **self-disclosure,** or revealing information about ourselves that we would normally keep secret. Most of us seem to need at least one confidant with whom we can safely share our innermost thoughts and feelings, especially those which seem particularly vulnerable to criticism by other people (e.g., Candy, 1977; Lowenthal & Haven, 1968). The loss of this important confidant may even lead to depression, while maintaining this relationship makes it easier to survive other crises and personal disasters.

PHYSICAL ATTRACTIVENESS.   To many psychologists, an individual's inner personality is much more important than mere physical characteristics. Yet even in our psychologically enlightened era, physical attractiveness remains an attribute of prime importance. It is a major determinant of success in our society (Berscheid & Walster, 1974), and it significantly affects most people's perception of the ideal friend (Dion, Berscheid, & Walster, 1972; Walster et al., 1966). A man who is seen with a good-looking friend, especially a female, is likely to enjoy increased stature in the eyes of his friends and associates (Sigall & Landy, 1973). Apparently, then, many of us still assume that what is beautiful is good and worthwhile.

However, those of us who are less than beautiful need not despair. Research has shown that for both same-sex and cross-sex friendships, people tend to choose those who are approximately similar in physical attractiveness (e.g., Cash & Derlega, 1978; Murstein & Christy, 1976; Shanteau & Nagy, 1979). That is, most adults normally do *not* pursue friendships with the most physically attractive candidates. Instead, we select those similar enough to ourselves so that our overtures are less likely to be rejected.

INTELLIGENCE AND COMPETENCE.   We tend to prefer friendships with people who are intelligent and competent, perhaps because such individuals are more likely to provide us with effective support and assistance. In fact, in the long run, intelligence may be an even more important component of personal attractiveness than physical characteristics (Gross & Crofton, 1977; Solomon & Saxe, 1977).

OTHER FACTORS.   We tend to value friends who are psychologically and emotionally stimulating, and who introduce us to enjoyable new experiences. We are also likely to choose friends who are usually pleasant and agreeable; who clearly like and approve of us; and who live close to us, making them more accessible on those occasions when we need a friend (Backman & Secord, 1959; Kaplan & Anderson, 1973; Kipnis, 1957; McCormick, 1982).

Less is known about the choice of cross-sex versus same-sex friendships. Traditionally, cross-sex friendships have been viewed with marked suspicion: Can they really remain platonic, or must a sexual element inevitably intrude? At present, there is relatively little research dealing with this issue. Married couples appear to resolve this problem by associating primarily with other couples, with the presence of the other spouse presumably allaying any fears of infidelity (Hess, 1972).

Friendships and Aging

Most of the available information about friendships and aging has been obtained from cross-sectional studies. Therefore, these data must be interpreted with caution.

NUMBER OF FRIENDSHIPS.   The number of friends that one has, especially close friends, appears to remain relatively stable throughout the adult life span (e.g., Antonucci, 1984; Babchuck, 1978–79; Lowenthal et al., 1975). One of the rare longitudinal studies in this area, which focused on a sample of men from age 50 to age 64, also found no significant decline in the number of friendships during these years (Costa, Zonderman, & McCrae, 1983). However, there is some indication that casual friendships may become less common with increasing age. We also appear to change our best friends frequently during young adulthood, but only rarely after middle age. (See Fischer, 1982; Fischer et al., 1977; Stueve & Gerson, 1977). These findings suggest that as we grow through adulthood, we do *not* suffer an increasing shortage of good friends; but we do sift through our various interpersonal relationships, and retain those which we value the most.

PURPOSES AND BENEFITS. Some data indicate that adults past middle age interact with their friends less often, while increasing the amount of time spent with relatives (Stueve & Fischer, 1978). Yet other studies report that for adults age 55 and over, the frequency of contact with close friends is significantly related to satisfaction with life in general, whereas the frequency of contact with family members is not (e.g., Arling, 1976; Blau, 1981; Graney, 1975; Larson, 1978; Palmore, 1981; Spakes, 1979; Wood & Robertson, 1980).

Why should close friendships be so beneficial for older adults? The answer is far from clear, since little research attention has been devoted to the relationship between aging and the various reasons for having friends. However, psychological support appears to be particularly important. Adults of all ages who receive such support from their friends consistently cope better with such adverse life events as physical disabilities, losing a job, and widowhood. Asking a close friend for help may be easier than calling on one's adult children because the latter appears to involve a greater loss of independence (Lee, 1985). Furthermore, the amount of psychological support that is provided by close friends does not appear to decline appreciably with increasing age, at least insofar as normative life events are concerned. (See Antonucci, 1984; Cobb & Kasl, 1977; Kasl & Berkman, 1981; Lopata, 1973; Schulz & Decker, 1983.) There is even some indication that close friends can give effective support in the case of some non-normative life events, such as rape and cancer (Burgess & Holmstrum, 1978; Vachon et al., 1977). One possible explanation is that while these specific events are rare ones, they are not wholly dissimilar from illnesses or injuries in general, which most friends have at least some experience in dealing with.

Some studies also suggest that adults of all ages who have more friends and social contacts enjoy lower mortality rates and better mental health (Berkman & Syme, 1979; Hirsch, 1981; House, Robbins, & Metzner, 1982; McKinlay, 1981; Mitchell & Trickett, 1980). Similar findings have also been obtained for older white males with numerous social ties (Blazer, 1982; Schoenbach et al., 1986). Overall, the evidence seems very strong that having friends and social relationships is important for physical and mental health, even though a few investigators have obtained no significant relationship between the number of friends and psychological well-being (Lieberman, 1982; Schaefer et al., 1981).

AFTERWORD.   All in all, research evidence provides little support for the stereotype of the friendless and lonely older adult. While this unfortunate picture is undoubtedly accurate in some instances, it represents the exception rather than the rule. To be sure, the number of casual friends that one has may well decrease to some extent with increasing age. But most adults do not suffer any appreciable decline in the number of close friends as they grow through adulthood, or in the amount of psychological support that is received from these friends. Let us now see whether similar optimistic conclusions can be drawn concerning the more intimate forms of interpersonal relationships.

Love, Marriage, and Divorce

Love is probably the ultimate form of interpersonal relationship. Yet throughout most of recorded history, the meaning of love has been shrouded in mystery. Until recently, most social scientists regarded love as too intangible, complicated, and unscientific (and much too personal and controversial) to study empirically (Berscheid & Walster, 1978; Wrightsman & Deaux, 1981). The subject of love is no longer shackled with these taboos and doubts, and researchers have begun to take a serious interest in this most important phenomenon.

Conceptions of Love

As might be expected of an area that has only recently been subjected to empirical research, there is as yet no single definition of love that is widely accepted by social scientists.

PASSIONATE AND COMPANIONATE LOVE.   According to Walster and Walster (1978), there are two kinds of love. **Passionate love** is characterized by total absorption in another person, intense physiological arousal, and moments of ecstasy and complete fulfillment. In contrast, **companionate love** is highlighted by affection for those who are closely involved in our lives. Companionate love tends to be more common than passionate love, and more typical of long-term relationships.

D-LOVE AND B-LOVE.   Abraham Maslow, a noted personality theorist, has posited a different dichotomy of love. **D-love** ("deficiency love") takes the form of a selfish need to receive love from other people, and is often accompanied by anxious and manipulative efforts to win the loved one's affection. Nevertheless, D-love is by no means wholly undesirable. This need must be satisfied in order for us to develop unselfish **B-love** ("being love"), which is non-possessive, giving, honest, and richer and more enjoyable than D-love. That is, if we do not receive sufficient love at some periods in our lives, we will be unable to give genuine love to other people (Maslow, 1968, 1970).

THE ART OF LOVING.   Other personality theorists regard love as a phenomenon that transcends mere one-to-one relationships. To Erich Fromm, the "art of loving" involves four main aspects: a genuine caring for and giving to other people, an accurate knowledge of their true feelings and wishes, a respect for their right to develop in their own way, and a sense of responsibility toward all humanity:

> Love is not primarily a relationship to a specific person; it is . . . an *orientation* of *character* which determines the relatedness of a person to the world as a whole . . . If I truly love one person I love all persons, I love the world, I love life. (Fromm, 1956/1974, pp. 38–39.)

According to Fromm, everyone has the capacity for genuine love. However, fulfilling this potential is very difficult. We all begin life as wholly self-centered (narcissistic) infants, and pathogenic experiences in later life can all too easily cause us to revert to this immature state. For example, authoritarian parents who use the child to fulfill their own frustrated ambition for social or professional success, or parents who are overly pessimistic, joyless, narcissistic, or physically abusive, may well cause the child's healthy ability to love to be replaced by narcissistic tendencies (Fromm, 1941; 1947; 1956).

PSYCHOMETRIC CONCEPTIONS.   How can we determine empirically if someone is in love with a given person? Simply asking this individual if he or she is in love, and receiving a yes or no answer, would seem to be a rather inaccurate and unscientific approach. A more detailed alternative has been developed by Rubin (1970), who constructed two nine-item scales. One of these is designed to measure romantic love, the other to tap how much the other person is liked:

Sample Love-Scale Items	*Sample Liking-Scale Items*
"I would forgive _____ for practically anything."	"I think that _____ is unusually well adjusted."
"If I could never be with _____, I would feel miserable."	"_____ is the sort of person who I myself would like to be."
"I feel that I can confide in _____ about virtually everything."	"Most people would react very favorably to _____ after a brief acquaintance."

Subjects are asked to indicate the extent of their agreement with each item, using a scale ranging from 1 (most negative) to 9 (most positive). In one study, 158 college couples who were dating but not engaged were asked to complete these scales twice: once with respect to their dating partner, and once with respect to a close friend of the same sex. The results indicated that there is a conceptual distinction between romantic love and liking. The data also revealed significant differences in the nature of the relationships formed by men and women. To be sure, men and women loved their dating partners and liked their same-sex friends about equally. But women liked their love partners more than men did, and loved their same-sex friends more than men did. That is, women tended to include more liking in their love relationships and more loving in their liking (friendly) relationships (Rubin, 1970; see also Bloom, 1972).

Love and Marriage

THE DEVELOPMENT OF LOVE. Many relationships that end in marriage proceed through a fairly standard sequence: casual dating, more frequent dating, going steady, informal engagement (being "engaged to be engaged"), and—ultimately—formal engagement. As the relationship progresses, the initial, idealized image of the loved one yields to a more realistic appraisal of the other's strengths and weaknesses (Pollis, 1969). Apparently, "love is blind" only at the outset.

In any loving relationship, different factors tend to be important during different stages. The early attraction is typically based on relatively superficial aspects, such as physical attractiveness. In later stages, however, we are more likely to value opportunities for self-disclosure, similar beliefs, and similar levels of emotional maturity. Thus self-disclosure is usually limited for some time, with few deeply personal matters being shared with one's partner. Only gradually do we become willing to confide our innermost thoughts and feelings to the one we love (Adams, 1979; Altman & Taylor, 1973; Levinger, 1974; 1978).

There also appears to be an inverse relationship between attraction and attachment. Attraction is high during the early stages, due to novelty and intrigue; but attachment is low, since there has not yet been sufficient time to develop firm emotional bonds. If the relationship should end at this time, the couple will normally experience only temporary unhappiness and disappointment. As the relationship continues, the novelty and corresponding attraction decreases, while the attachment becomes much more powerful. Thus a breakup during this later period can cause emotional pain that is never completely overcome.

ENDURING LOVE: MARRIAGES THAT LAST.   Why do some loving relationships survive for many years? A recent study focused on 351 couples who remained married for 15 years or more, 300 of whom reported that they were happily married. The most frequently cited reason for the enduring relationship was: "My spouse is my best friend" (Lauer & Lauer, 1985; see Table 8.3). Liking one's spouse

TABLE 8.3   Why marriages endure: Reasons most often given by a sample of 351 couples married for at least 15 years, in order of frequency.

Men	Women
1. "My spouse is my best friend."	1. "My spouse is my best friend."
2. "I like my spouse as a person."	2. "I like my spouse as a person."
3. "Marriage is a long-term commitment."	3. "Marriage is a long-term commitment."
4. "Marriage is sacred."	4. "Marriage is sacred."
5. "We agree on aims and goals."	5. "We agree on aims and goals."
6. "My spouse has grown more interesting."	6. "My spouse has grown more interesting."
7. "I want the relationship to succeed."	7. "I want the relationship to succeed."
8. "An enduring marriage is important to social stability."	8. "We laugh together."
9. "We laugh together."	9. "We agree on a philosophy of life."
10. "I am proud of my spouse's achievements."	10. "We agree on how and how often to show affection."

SOURCE: Lauer & Lauer (1985, abridged).

as a person, meaningful communication and self-disclosure, open-ness, trustworthiness, caring, and giving were considerably more important to a lasting marriage than passionate love. Other factors that were typical of lengthy marriages included recognizing and accepting the spouse's faults, believing that marriage is a long-term commitment, and avoiding displays of intensely expressed anger. The following quotes were typical:

A MAN MARRIED FOR 24 YEARS:

"[My wife] isn't perfect. But I don't worry about her weak points, which are very few. Her strong points overcome them too much." (p. 24)

A MAN MARRIED FOR 20 YEARS:

"Commitment means a willingness to be unhappy for awhile. I wouldn't go on for years and years being wretched in my marriage. But you can't avoid troubled times. You're not going to be happy with each other all the time. That's when commitment is really important." (p. 25)

A MAN MARRIED FOR 36 YEARS:

"Discuss your problems in a normal voice. If a voice is raised, stop. Return after a short period of time. Start again. After a period of time both parties will be able to deal with their problems and not say things that they will be sorry about later." (p. 26)

Virtually all of these couples preferred relatively placid and peaceful interactions; in fact, only one couple reported that they typically yelled at each other. Interestingly, sex was far down the list of reasons for a happy marriage. Although sexual relations were by no means unimportant to these couples, fewer than 10 percent stated that sex was one of the primary factors in keeping the marriage together. However, the men and women in this study did place considerable emphasis on sexual fidelity. One wife who had been married for 27 years stated that while she could resolve almost any problem with her husband given enough time, infidelity "would probably not be something I could forget and forgive." (p. 26)

Paradoxically, then, a relationship that may have originated primarily because of passionate love may well have to develop strong elements of friendship and companionate love in order to endure. As these investigators concluded, "The redemption of difficult people through selfless devotion may make good fiction, but the happily married people in our sample expressed no such sense of mission. Rather, they said, they are grateful to have married someone who is basically appealing and likable" (Lauer & Lauer, 1985, p. 24; see also Feldman, 1964).

ROLE FACTORS IN MARRIAGE.   In 1983, a *Newsweek* cover story emphasized the increasing prevalence of "househusbands." According to empirical research during the late 1970s, however, the demise of the traditional housewife role has been greatly exaggerated. Many couples do tend to share household duties while they are childless. But this egalitarianism usually does not continue after the first child is born, even if both spouses are working. Instead, the need to earn more money and the generally higher income potential for men drives the husband to concentrate on his career, leaving the wife to assume primary responsibility for the home and family. As a result, couples with children are likely to adopt traditional roles: the wife does most of the housework, prepares the meals, and takes care of the children; while the husband may make minor house repairs, shovel snow, mow the lawn, and take out the garbage (Campbell, Converse, & Rodgers, 1976; Hoffman & Manis, 1978; Pleck, 1977). Conversely, shared duties and role equality are most often found in childless marriages.

Divorce

DEMOGRAPHICS.   The preceding sections have focused on the more pleasant aspects of marital relationships: being attracted to another person, learning to share our innermost feelings, liking as well as loving one's spouse. However, marriage is not without a certain degree of risk. Each year, the blissful expectations of more than one million American couples are shattered by divorce. The divorce rate in this country has increased consistently during the past three decades and doubled between 1968 and 1978, with the result that the average duration of a marriage in the United States is currently 9.4 years. In fact, divorce has become statistically normative (more or less); it terminates one of every two marriages (Glick, 1979; Lauer & Lauer, 1985).

Divorce is most common among adults aged 30–45, and among black females. (See Figure 8.1.) Youthful marriages, where both the man and woman are below age 21, are significantly more likely to end in divorce than marriages after the age of 30. Nevertheless, the elderly are far from immune. Among Americans age 65 and older, more than half a million are divorced, and approximately 10,000 new cases are registered each year. As we will see in Chapter 10, divorce among the elderly may well be even more stressful and pathogenic than widowhood.

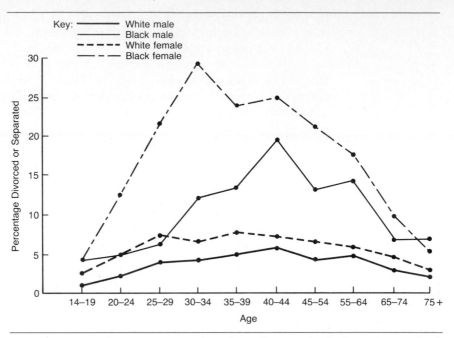

FIGURE 8.1   Divorce rate as a function of age and ethnic group. United States Department of Commerce, Bureau of the Census (1976).

CAUSES OF DIVORCE.   In marked contrast to couples with happy marriages, who tend to regard one another as best friends, those headed for divorce are likely to have arguments that become increasingly severe. Instead of one spouse backing off when the other is upset and initiating peace-making overtures, anger and rejection are met with greater anger and rejection, causing the conflict to escalate and increasing the likelihood of leaving permanent emotional scars. (See Raush et al., 1974.) Other common causes of divorce include drunkenness, desertion, brutality, and adultery (Bennett, 1984). The personality of each spouse is also an important consideration, for those with a strong commitment to maintaining the marriage are more likely to do so even in the face of serious obstacles (as we have seen).

The increasing divorce rate in this country may also be due in part to the easing of divorce laws and the establishment of "no-fault" divorces, where incompatibility and breakdown of the relationship are accepted as sufficient grounds. Also, since women have made greater inroads into the workplace during the last half century (Chapter 9), their financial status has improved. Thus not as many women must remain mired in an unhappy marriage in order to survive economically. For these reasons, the increased divorce rate in this country is not entirely negative; it may well indicate that more people can now extricate themselves from relationships that have become unbearable.

STAGES OF DIVORCE.   Divorced people tend to proceed through several behavioral stages, much like a rite of passage (Chiriboga, 1979). At first they prefer to nurse their psychological wounds in isolation, so they segregate themselves from other people. Next they experience a period with no clear social identity; they are no longer married, but not yet truly single. During the first few months after the divorce is granted, many men who were fed and cared for by their wives must now learn to prepare their own meals and keep the house clean. Conversely, many women must learn those tasks which were formerly performed by their husbands, such as having the car repaired or balancing the checkbook. The ex-spouses spend much of this time in dealings with one another, often arguing bitterly over financial matters. However, not all of these interactions are negative. One study found that some 12 percent of divorced couples had sexual relations with one another during the first two months following the divorce, and most stated that they would turn first to their ex-spouses if they needed help handling a crisis (Hetherington, Cox, & Cox, 1976). Ultimately, divorced individuals do begin to seek out other people and reestablish themselves socially.

THE EFFECTS OF DIVORCE.   Divorce is usually a traumatic experience. There is some indication that when one spouse favors and initiates the divorce, that individual is more likely to establish a satisfactory life in the future, while the other spouse tends to suffer long-lasting emotional scars. On the whole, however, divorce would seem to affect women more deeply than men. Only 14 percent of divorced American women are awarded alimony, and fewer than half of these receive it regularly; while 44 percent are awarded child support, with fewer than half receiving it regularly (Lake, 1976). Thus, despite the improving financial status of women in this country, numerous divorcees must either find ways to support themselves (and their children, if any) or else accept a markedly reduced standard of living. Older women are likely to have particular difficulty in this regard because their generation was not as tolerant of women in the workplace, making it less likely that they ever developed any income-producing skills. In contrast, divorced men are usually employed, so they can continue to derive income and satisfaction from their work.

Furthermore, establishing a satisfying heterosexual relationship may well be particularly difficult for divorced older women. There are

Divorce is likely to cause serious financial difficulties for women, especially those with children. Fewer than half of the women who are awarded alimony or child support actually receive it on a regular basis.   *Michael Weisbrot*

more single women than single men, so divorced women are less often asked by friends to serve as blind dates or unattached party guests. The woman is most likely to gain custody of the children, and to become anxious about their reactions and possible jealousy to any dates and sexual relationships that she may have. Thus it is hardly surprising that divorced women (and single men) show the most symptoms of stress in our society (Douvan, 1979).

The effect of divorce on children varies with their age, and with the parents' ability to cope with the resulting problems. Young children tend to blame themselves for the divorce, to worry about being abandoned, and to have fantasies that their parents will reconcile. Adolescents are likely to experience initial anger and turmoil, but are generally better able to cope with the divorce. There is also some evidence that after a divorce, parents are less affectionate with their children, adolescent girls become more promiscuous, and boys are more feminized. (See Anthony, 1974; Hetherington, 1972; Hetherington, Cox, & Cox, 1977; Hetherington & Duer, 1972; Kelly & Wallerstein, 1976; Wallerstein & Kelly, 1974; 1975; 1976.) However, children in single-parent families appear to function better than children in families with two parents where there is frequent conflict (Rutter, 1979).

Divorce can also be a shattering experience for the husband as well. It has been argued that divorce laws and decrees are often unfair not only to women, but to men as well. Some fathers report that their efforts to gain joint custody of the children involved years of expensive legal wrangling, and caused so much hard feeling that the relationship with the children was seriously impaired. Others contend that they are denied proper visitation by their ex-wives, presumably due to the latter's anger and bitterness. As one fathers'-rights activist put it, "I've seen some men sobbing away, so overcome by the system. . . . The system is so stacked against men that they don't fight" (Leo, 1986).

Nevertheless, if a marriage is truly unbearable and if the couple's religious and personal beliefs permit, the least of evils may well be to end it and give each spouse the opportunity to find happiness elsewhere. In any case, it appears that divorce will remain a common phenomenon for the foreseeable future.

AFTERWORD: INTIMATE RELATIONSHIPS AND AGING.   Empirical data indicate that it is disadvantageous to marry too early; youthful marriages are more likely to end in divorce. Also, divorces are most common between the ages of 30 and 45. For the most part, however, it is difficult to draw any age-related conclusions with regard to marriage and divorce. Some adults find marriage to be an increasing source of love and fulfillment as they grow older, while others experience increasing conflicts that make continuation of the marriage virtually impossible. Some useful clues as to why marriages endure or fail have been unearthed by social scientists; but these factors involve the personality, motivation, and interpersonal behavior of the spouses, rather than age per se.

The relationship between love and aging is also far from clear, partly because adults pursue many diverse courses insofar as intimate relationships are concerned. Some marry young, some do so later in life. Some marry once, for better or worse, while some marry numerous times. Some eschew marriage altogether and remain single throughout their lives, possibly engaging in a number of loving relationships along the way. And some find fulfillment from homosexual relationships, rather than heterosexual ones. We can only conclude that the love which adults derive from intimate relationships does not necessarily decline in quantity or quality with increasing age, at least until old age makes the death of the loved one more likely. The negative relationship between age and the capacity for sexual expressions of love has also been exaggerated, as we will see in the following section.

Chapter Glossary: Interpersonal Relations

Activity theory	Posits a positive correlation between the social activity of the elderly and their satisfaction with life. That is, reduced social activity is assumed to be dissatisfying to the aged.
B-love	In Maslow's theory, love that is unselfish, nonpossessive, giving, honest, and richer and more enjoyable than D-love.
Companionate love	A form of love highlighted by affection for those who are closely involved in our lives. More common, and more typical of long-term relationships, than is passionate love.
Control	The ability to regulate or influence the outcomes that befall us through the behaviors that we choose.
Control theories	Posit that the well-being and interpersonal behaviors of adults are strongly influenced by the amount of control that they have over their environment. Examples include locus of control theory (discussed in the preceding chapter), learned helplessness theory, and self-efficacy theory.
D-love	In Maslow's theory, the selfish need to receive love and affection from others. A prerequisite to the emergence of B-love.
Disengagement theory	Posits a process of mutual withdrawal between the aged and society. This decreased interpersonal activity is assumed to be satisfying to the aged, helpful to society, universal, and inevitable.
Exchange theory	Posits that we interact with other people to the extent that the rewards we receive, both material and non-material, exceed the costs we incur.
Learned helplessness theory	Posits that if we are exposed to numerous life events which we cannot control, we will develop an expectation that future events will also be uncontrollable, which is likely to lead to self-dissatisfaction and depression.
Passionate love	A form of love characterized by total absorption in another person, intense physiological arousal, and moments of ecstasy and complete fulfillment.
Self-disclosure	Revealing information about oneself that one would normally keep secret. An important aspect of both close friendships and loving relationships.

Self-efficacy theory	Posits that we undertake tasks which we judge ourselves as capable of performing, but avoid activities which appear to exceed our abilities.
Social comparison theory	Posits that we all possess a basic drive to evaluate our abilities and opinions. If we cannot obtain appropriate objective data, we perform these self-evaluations by comparing ourselves with other people.
Statistically non-normative life event	A major event in one's life that happens to few other people in that culture. In this country, examples include suffering a stroke or winning a state lottery.
Statistically normative life event	A major event in one's life that also happens to the majority of people in that culture. In this country, examples include getting married or retiring from work.
Temporally non-normative life event	A major event in one's life that occurs at an age which is atypical for people in that culture. In this country, examples include getting married for the first time at age 45 or becoming a widow at age 25.
Temporally normative life event	A major event in one's life that occurs at an age which is typical for people in that culture. In this country, examples include getting married for the first time in one's twenties or becoming a widow at age 65.

Sexuality and Aging

Heterosexual Relationships

RESEARCH PROBLEMS AND PREVAILING STEREOTYPES.   As was the case with love, human sexuality has only recently been subjected to much empirical research. This is also an extremely personal and sensitive area, and it is one that poses significant conceptual and methodological problems. For example, should researchers define heterosexuality solely in terms of intercourse? If so, should sexual behavior be measured in terms of frequency (number of coital acts per week or month), percentages (how many adults of a given age still participate in sexual intercourse), or level of intensity (degree of physical arousal and excitement)? Or perhaps a sound definition of human heterosexual behavior should also include less overt behaviors, such as thoughts, fantasies, wishes, and affectionate touching. But is behavior that does not end in orgasm truly sexual? When does friendly caressing turn into sexual foreplay? To complicate matters further, it has been argued that we engage in sex for many reasons. The most obvious motive is lust, and the need to satisfy biological and reproductive drives. But sex may also be used to obtain affection and intimacy, to exert power over another person, to escape boredom, to make up with a loved one after a fight, to gratify feelings of pride and self-esteem, and to confirm one's masculinity or femininity (Neubeck, 1972).

Until recently, very little was known about the relationship between sexuality and aging. And since no one knew much about the sexual desires and behaviors of the middle-aged and elderly, it was widely assumed that there was nothing to know—that is, that older adults did not and should not have any interest in sex. In one early study that used a sentence completion task, a sample of college students most often stated that "sex for most old people is negligible, unimportant, and past" (Golde & Kogan, 1959). More recently, the majority of a sample of 646 college students concluded that their parents had sexual intercourse no more than once a month, while some 25 percent of this sample believed that their parents had abandoned sex completely (Pocs et al., 1977). These views are so incorrect as to be ludicrous, yet they are by no means limited to laymen. When middle-aged and elderly patients complain of sexual difficulties or disinterest, some physicians respond with supposedly humorous statements like "Well, what can you expect at your age?" or "Maybe you've had as much [sex] as you're going to get!" (Labby, 1984). This smug and insensitive attitude is likely to feed the patient's loss of sexual self-confidence, thereby creating a self-fulfilling prophecy: sex in later adulthood becomes impossible because the individual believes that it is abnormal and impossible. All too many older adults accept this erroneous stereotype, abandon any efforts to engage in sex, and miss out on some of the major interpersonal satisfactions and rewards that their lives still have to offer.

During the last few decades, however, we have become increasingly aware that there is indeed sexual life after middle age. To be sure, some adults have ambivalent feelings about sex and welcome advancing age as an excuse to abandon it. More often, however, the fear of losing the capacity to obtain sexual pleasure and intimacy is a very powerful one. As an anonymous sage once observed, "Sex doesn't make you live longer, it only makes you want to!" (Labby, 1984, p. 183). Thus, insofar as many middle-aged and older adults are concerned, it is fortunate that empirical data about sexuality and aging have begun to allay such fears.

Young Adulthood.   Most researchers define heterosexual behavior as that which results in or is intended to result in orgasm, notably coitus. Using this definition, young men tend to be more sexually active than young women. Some 44 percent of men and 30 percent of women report having had sexual intercourse by age 16, with these figures increasing to 95 percent for men and 81 percent for women by age 24. Similarly, the median age for the first act of coitus has been estimated as 18 for men and 20 for women. (See Hunt, 1974; Sorensen, 1973; Wilson, 1975.)

There is some indication that the frequency of sexual behavior has increased during the past few decades, especially among younger adults and young women. (See Figure 8.2.) This increase is a cohort effect. Social standards have changed considerably during the last half century; sexual behavior is now more accepted (and expected). As a result, younger generations are undoubtedly more willing to report (or even to exaggerate) their sexual activity. As psychologist Rollo May has observed, "[Whereas] the Victorian nice man or woman was guilty if he or she did experience sex, now we are guilty if we *don't*" (1969, p. 40). Conversely, couples who grew up during the more conservative 1940s are more likely to favor modesty, and to understate the extent of their sexual behavior. It has also become more acceptable for women to state openly that they have sexual desires and interests, due in part to the efforts of female advocacy groups.

Figure 8.2 also indicates that the frequency of sexual behavior among married couples does decrease from young adulthood to

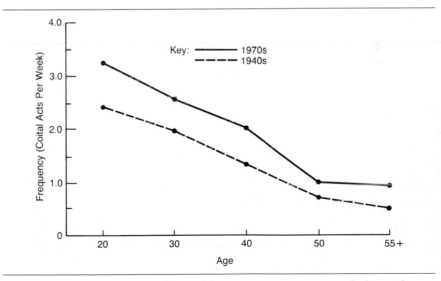

FIGURE 8.2   Frequency of sexual intercourse among married couples, 1940s and 1970s. Mussen, Conger, Kagan, & Geiwitz (1979).

middle age. This is due in part to environmental constraints: many couples have children during this period, and the rigors of night feedings or the presence of an active child or teenager may well make some reduction in sexual activity more convenient. Aging is also partly responsible for this decrease, particularly insofar as men are concerned.

MALE SEXUALITY AND AGING.   Numerous studies have found that male sexual activity declines with increasing age. The peak of male potency occurs during the late teens, although the first substantial drop in interest and desire is usually not experienced until about age 50 (Pfeiffer, Verwoerdt, & Davis, 1972). A second significant drop in the number of men who remain sexually active has been reported to occur at about age 70–80. However, there is some disagreement as to the extent of this decline. In various studies, some of which were longitudinal, the percent of men who remain sexually active at older ages has been estimated as follows:

At age 60: 53–60 percent*; 95 percent
At age 70: 45 percent*; 70 percent*; 70 percent
At age 78: 25 percent*
(*= longitudinal study)

TABLE 8.4   Frequency of sexual intercourse reported by men and women in a medical group insurance plan.

Group	*Percent Reporting Intercourse*					*Percent Still Sexually Active*
	Not at All	*Once a Month*	*Once a Week*	*2–3 Times a Week*	*More than 2–3 Times a Week*	
MEN, AGE						
46–50	00	05	62	26	07	100
51–55	05	29	49	17	00	95
56–60	07	38	44	11	00	93
61–65	20	43	30	07	00	80
66–70	24	48	26	02	00	76
WOMEN, AGE						
46–50	14	26	39	21	00	86
51–55	20	41	32	05	02	80
56–60	42	27	25	04	02	58
61–65	61	29	05	05	00	39
66–70	73	16	11	00	00	27

NOTE: For men, N=261; for women, N=231. There were at least 41 subjects in each subgroup.
SOURCE: Pfeiffer, Verwoerdt, & Davis (1972).

(See Hegeler, 1976; Kinsey, Pomeroy, & Martin, 1948; Pfeiffer, 1974; Pfeiffer, Verwoerdt, & Wang, 1968; 1969; Verwoerdt, Pfeiffer, & Wang, 1969.)

The results of a cross-sectional study of men age 45–69, all of whom were members of a medical group insurance plan, are shown in Table 8.4. While older men were less sexually active, 76 percent of the oldest group continued to have sexual intercourse one or more times per month (Pfeiffer, Verwoerdt, & Davis, 1974). Some more recent studies suggest that levels of male sexual activity after middle age remain even more stable (George & Weiler, 1981). It has also been estimated that 60 percent of married couples where both spouses are between ages 60–70 have intercourse at least occasionally (Busse & Blazer, 1980), as do 25 percent–30 percent of couples past age 75 (McCary, 1978). Few researchers have focused on men over 80, but some instances of sexual intercourse by men age 80 or even older have been reported (Leaf, 1973).

These data point to two significant conclusions. As age increases, fewer men are sexually active, and those who are active are less so than younger men. Nevertheless, a substantial number of men continue to engage in sex throughout much or even all of their adult lives. Although aging does appear to be partly responsible for declines in sexual capacity and interest among men, an important question remains: Why are some older men still sexually active, while others are not?

FACTORS AFFECTING MALE SEXUAL ACTIVITY.   As a man grows older, several physiological changes begin to occur in response to overt sexual stimulation. It takes two to three times longer to achieve full penile erection, and direct physical stimulation by the partner may well be necessary. Ejaculation is significantly less forceful. The volume of seminal fluid decreases. And more time is required following orgasm before another erection is possible (Burt & Meeks, 1985; Masters & Johnson, 1966; 1970). If the woman fails to understand the nature of these changes, the couple's sex life may be adversely affected. For example, instead of attributing the man's desire to have sex without ejaculation to the effects of aging, the woman may erroneously conclude that he does not find her attractive or that he is having an affair with someone else. On purely physiological grounds, however, there is no reason why these changes should have a profound effect on the man's sexual activity. Nor is there any scientific support to date for the idea of a male menopause (Kolodny, Masters, & Johnson, 1979).

More importantly, men who have had more sexual experiences early in life tend to remain more sexually active during middle and old age. This has been referred to as the "use it or lose it" syndrome (Solnick & Corby, 1983; see also Pfeiffer & Davis, 1972). As Masters and Johnson put it: "The most important factor in the maintenance of effective sexuality for the aging male is consistency of active sexual expression. . . . For the male geriatric sample . . . those men currently interested in relatively high levels of sexual expression report similar activity levels from their formative years. It does not appear to matter what manner of sexual expression has been employed, as long as high levels of activity were maintained" (1966, pp. 262–263). Conversely, extended periods of abstinence pose a serious risk to the sexual functioning of the older male. Therefore, if the man's partner becomes unavailable (as through hospitalization), masturbation may be a valuable way of maintaining sexual capacity and interest.

A second determinant of sexual activity among older men is physical health. Men who are (or who believe they are) in poor health are significantly less likely to engage in sexual intercourse (Pfeiffer & Davis, 1972). Sex is unappealing when one does not feel well, and ill health is more common at older ages. However, the general belief that intercourse is likely to precipitate fatal heart attacks in older men is *not* supported by empirical data. Although sexual activity is somewhat stressful, deaths during intercourse are rare and account for only 1 percent of sudden coronary fatalities. It has also been argued that some seven out of ten such deaths occur during extramarital affairs, and are due largely to the accompanying guilt and anxiety (Butler & Lewis, 1976). And other investigators have concluded that the oxygen cost during sexual intercourse is no greater than when climbing a flight of stairs, walking briskly, or performing ordinary tasks (Hellerstein & Friedman, 1970). Even adults who have had heart attacks can usually resume sexual activity upon recovery, possibly with the aid of nitroglycerin (or other coronary dilator) ten minutes prior to intercourse if angina is unusually likely (Labby, 1984).

Thirdly, the sexual desires of older men may be inhibited by negative attitudes. As we observed at the outset of this section, all too many men accept the stereotype of the sexless older adult and erroneously conclude that they can no longer function effectively in this area. One or two failures to sustain an erection may therefore lead to a vicious circle: the resulting performance anxiety makes it progressively more difficult to enjoy sex, and the ensuing failures produce still more performance anxiety. Other attitudes which may lead to a decline in sexual activity include possible monotony resulting from many years of sex with the same partner, and worries about work and career problems (Masters & Johnson, 1970).

In sum: men are more likely to remain interested in sex through middle and old age if they enjoyed sex more often during young adulthood (or even if they merely had sexual experiences more often), if they are in good health, and if they believe that they can indeed maintain effective sexual behavior as they grow older.

FEMALE SEXUALITY AND AGING. In marked contrast to men, women reach their sexual peak in their mid-thirties and suffer relatively little loss in capacity thereafter. To be sure, middle age does bring some physiological changes: lubrication of the vagina decreases, the vaginal walls lose elasticity, more precoital stimulation may be required, orgasmic experiences may be somewhat slowed, and menstrual periods eventually cease (Burt & Meeks, 1985). However, there is no evidence that these changes cause any significant decline in female sexual capacity. For example, while menopause may inhibit sexual desire if the woman (erroneously) believes that it must, the resulting freedom from the possibility of unwanted pregnancy may produce a reduction in anxiety and greater sexual satisfaction. Also, while the duration and intensity of orgasmic episodes may be reduced, the subjective levels of sensual pleasure appear to continue unabated. As Kinsey et al. (1953) put it, "[There is] no evidence that the female ages in her sexual capacities," while Masters and Johnson (1966) concluded that "there is no time limit drawn by the advancing years to female sexuality." Orgasmic response has been observed in women age 70–80 and older (Kleegman, 1959; Solnick & Corby, 1983).

Nevertheless, the number of women who remain sexually active and the frequency of these activities decrease substantially with increasing age. In the study reported in Table 8.4, for example, the percent of women who engaged in sexual intercourse declined from 86 percent at age 46–50 to 27 percent at age 66–70. And fewer women than men in each age group remained sexually active, with the greatest differences occurring in the oldest groups. Similarly, other studies have found that only 20–40 percent of 60-year-old women and 15–30 percent of 70-year-old women engage in sex (Newman & Nichols, 1960; Verwoerdt, Pfeiffer, & Wang, 1969). Thus, while the sexual *capacity* of women declines relatively little with increasing age, their sexual *activity* decreases markedly and is significantly lower than that of men of similar ages. How can this apparent paradox be explained?

FACTORS AFFECTING FEMALE SEXUAL ACTIVITY. Numerous studies have found that female sexual activity depends to a large extent on the presence of a socially acceptable and sexually capable partner, such as a healthy spouse. Thus marital status is an important predictor of sexual activity among older women, but not among men (e.g., Kinsey et al., 1953; Pfeiffer & Davis, 1972; Pfeiffer, Verwoerdt, & Davis, 1972; Pfeiffer, Verwoerdt, & Wang, 1968; 1969).

American women marry men who average four years older, and who are therefore likely to become ill and/or lose interest in sex before the woman does (Newman & Nichols, 1960). Furthermore, women in our society live an average of seven years more than men, so there are many more widows than widowers (Brotman, 1971). For these reasons, middle-aged and elderly women are much more likely to be without an appropriate sexual partner than are older men. In fact, some 53 percent of women past age 65 are widows, while there are approximately 30 single men for every 100 single women over 65. Thus the woman's superior sexual capacity at older ages proves to be a dubious benefit, since her sexual activity is likely to be limited by the declining health or death of her (usually older) male partner. According to Kinsey et al. (1953), "[The decrease in sexual activity among women is] controlled by the male's desires, and it is primarily his age rather than the female's loss of interest or capacity which is reflected in this decline."

Women who enjoy sex more during young adulthood, and those who experience more coital orgasms, are more likely to remain sexually active in later life (Christenson & Gagnon, 1965; Pfeiffer & Davis, 1972). However, mere frequency of intercourse during early adulthood is not significantly related to female sexual interest and activity after middle age. Also, in contrast to men, physical health appears to have little influence on the sexual functioning of older women (Solnick & Corby, 1983).

PROBLEMS OF THE INSTITUTIONALIZED ELDERLY.   Negative stereotypes and the loss of sexual interest are particularly common among institutionalized men and women. In one nursing home, 49 percent of the residents agreed that "sex over 65 is ridiculous" (Kahana, 1976). Although this decline in sexual activity is due to ill health in some instances, it is furthered by the attitudes and actions of many nursing home personnel. Few institutions provide sufficient privacy for sexual intercourse, while many ignore the desires of nonmarried residents by segregating men and women and/or ridiculing any expressions of sexual interest (Solnick & Corby, 1983; see also Burnside, 1975; Schlessinger & Miller, 1973). Conversely, ending the isolation of male and female residents tends to produce better social adjustment, a richer social life, reduced anxiety, and at least some increases in pleasurable sexual activity (Silverstone & Wynter, 1975; Wasow, 1977). At present, however, the sexual rights of the institutionalized elderly remains an essentially unresolved issue.

AFTERWORD.   Elsewhere in this chapter (and in this book), we have had to conclude that the relationship between aging and important

All too many men and women in nursing homes are denied this couple's opportunity for love and affection because of the misguided belief that the aged should not be interested in intimacy.   *Frank Siteman/Picture Cube*

aspects of human behavior is ambiguous. Here, the evidence is considerably more clear cut. Male sexual capacity and interest decline to some extent with increasing age, especially after about age 70, but this decrement is not nearly as great as has been widely believed. The sexual capacity of women decreases relatively little as they grow through adulthood, but the frequency of their sexual activity declines even more than that of men. Women tend to marry men who are older, and who are therefore likely to become ill and/or die before the woman does. So women are much more often without a socially acceptable and sexually capable partner.

Nevertheless, many men and women remain sexually active throughout much or all of adulthood. According to Comfort (1974, p. 442), "Most people can and should expect to have sex long after they no longer wish to ride a bicycle." The findings discussed above have led to profound changes in our conception of sexual behavior among older adults. Even more importantly, these discoveries should enable many older adults to liberate themselves from the shackles of negative stereotypes and self-defeating doubts, and to enjoy the pleasures of this most intimate form of interpersonal relationship.

Homosexual Relationships

Less is known about the relationship between aging and homosexual activity, possibly because homosexuality has long been regarded as a form of mental illness. In 1973, however, the American Psychiatric Association removed homosexuality from the official list of mental disorders (DSM-II; see Chapter 11). Currently, homosexuality is considered a mental disorder only if the individual is distressed about his or her homosexuality and would prefer to be more heterosexual (American Psychiatric Association, 1979).

Whatever the reasons, the status of this area resembles that of research on heterosexuality and aging some 50 years ago. According to one common stereotype, homosexual males supposedly find aging to be particularly stressful, lonely, and depressing:

THE MYTH OF THE AGING MALE HOMOSEXUAL.

One popular myth about the older male homosexual is that he "no longer goes to bars, having lost his physical attractiveness and his sexual appeal to the young men he craves. He is over-sexed, but his sex life is very unsatisfactory. He has been unable to form a lasting relationship with a sexual partner, and he is seldom sexually active any more. When he does have sex, it is usually in a 'tearoom' (public toilet). He has disengaged from the gay world and his acquaintances in it. He is retreating further and further into the 'closet' . . . He is labeled an 'old queen,' as he has become quite effeminate." (Kelly, 1977, p. 329.)

There are few empirical studies dealing with such issues, however, and the minimal data that do exist offer little support for the prevailing stereotypes. Older homosexual males tend to report that they are still sexually active, and that their sexual relationships are quite satisfactory (Kelly, 1977; Kimmel, 1977). While some of these subjects stated that sex became less important as they grew older, others indicated that their sex lives were now more satisfying than in young adulthood. Virtually all preferred sexual contacts with men of similar ages, rather than with young men. There was also some indication that aging was not overly depressing for these homosexual men because they had previously learned how to cope with living alone, and because they had developed a network of friends on whom to rely for social and sexual companionship.

Data concerning homosexual women are even more sparse, although one study suggests that gay females tend to discontinue sexual activity at an early age (Christenson & Johnson, 1973). If homosexuality continues to be regarded with increasing tolerance, future research may well shed more light on the relationship between this form of interpersonal behavior and aging.

Myths About Aging: Interpersonal Relations

MYTH

Middle-aged and elderly adults have significantly fewer friends than do young adults.

Few middle-aged adults, and virtually no elderly adults, have any interest in sex.

Sexual intercourse should be avoided by men past middle age, because it is very likely to precipitate a fatal heart attack.

A century ago, elderly parents and their children lived together more often because families were more caring. The modern family is much more isolated, both geographically and emotionally.

Most parents aged 65 and older are neglected by their adult children who never visit them, or who callously place them in nursing homes at the slightest provocation.

BEST AVAILABLE EVIDENCE

The number of casual friendships does decline to some extent with increasing age. But older adults have as many close friends as do young adults, and these relationships contribute significantly to their overall life satisfaction.

Many adults remain sexually active throughout much or all of adulthood. The sexual capacity of men does decline with increasing age, but not as much as has been widely believed. There is no evidence that aging has any important negative effects on the sexual capacity of women.

Deaths during sexual intercourse are very rare. Such deaths account for no more than 1 percent of all sudden coronary fatalities, and it has been alleged that the majority occur during extramarital affairs and are due in large part to anxiety and guilt.

There has been no significant change in the mutual caring shown by the American family. A century ago, elderly parents did live with their children more often, but this was due primarily to financial necessity; there was no social security system or variety of private pension plans. Today, more elderly parents live alone because they want to and can afford to do so, but most live no more than a half hour away from at least one adult child.

Approximately 80 percent of parents over age 65 see at least one of their adult children every one to two weeks. Most families place elderly parents in nursing homes only as a last resort, and with the utmost reluctance.

Intergenerational Relationships

Parents and Adult Children

As we observed in Chapter 1, more people are living to an older age than ever before. Many of these aging individuals are parents; some 81 percent of middle-aged and elderly adults have living children (Atchley & Miller, 1980). Since it is statistically normative to have children prior to age 35, most of the children of older Americans are also adults. During the past few decades, therefore, the relationship between parents who are past middle age and their adult children has become increasingly important.

There are two major issues for us to explore in this area. First, are adult children likely to ignore their aging parents in order to put their own interests and children first? That is, does parenthood become significantly less satisfying as one grows past middle age? Secondly, ill health is more common at older ages. Elderly parents may therefore become partly or wholly dependent on their adult children because of health problems, ranging from gradually increasing arthritic disability or a sudden fall that fractures a hip to the ravages of Alzheimer's disease (Chapter 11). How well do these intergenerational relationships cope with the demands posed by an elderly parent who requires considerable care?

FREQUENCY OF CONTACT. According to popular belief, elderly parents are grossly neglected by their children—or, even worse, are callously placed in nursing homes at the slightest provocation and promptly forgotten. This notion is supported by two of the most pervasive cultural myths in this country, which live on even though they are fallacious. The first of these myths holds that at some unspecified point in the past (perhaps circa 1900), the American family was far more devoted to one another than is the case today:

> *THE MYTH OF THE CLASSICAL DEVOTED FAMILY.*
>
> This myth portrays the family of some 100 years ago as "a pretty picture of life down on grandma's farm. There are lots of happy children, and many kinfolk live together in a large rambling house. Everyone works hard . . . All boys and girls marry, and marry young. Young people, especially girls, are likely to be virginal at marriage and faithful afterward. Though the parents do not arrange their children's marriages, the elders do have the right to reject a suitor and have a strong hand in the final decision. After marriage, the couple lives harmoniously, either near the boy's parents or with them, for the couple is slated to inherit the farm." (Goode, 1963, p. 6.)

The second, related myth is that the modern American family has become isolated, and that today's children take much worse care of their parents than was the case in the "good old days":

THE MYTH OF THE MODERN ISOLATED NUCLEAR FAMILY.

According to this myth, today's family has "fewer children, and they are economic liabilities rather than assets. They leave the nest at a relatively early age, marry without parental approval or guidance, receive training (at parental expense of course) for occupational advantage in a direction that takes them away from their parents. Contact is limited to occasional letters and obligatory telephone calls on holidays; exceptions to these patterns occur only when the children need money. As the parents experience the inevitable decrements of advancing age, such as widowhood and failing health with the attendant economic exigencies, the children are concerned but not motivated to do anything about it because they are too wrapped up in their own problems; too busy with their own careers, children, and mortgages to spare the time or resources their parents need. . . . [This implies that] if middle-aged children paid more attention to their elderly parents, the parents would be less lonely, better adjusted, happier, and more satisfied with their lives." (Lee, 1985, pp. 22, 26).

These myths have been soundly contradicted by empirical data. It is true that since 1900, the proportion of adults past age 65 who live with their children has declined from about 60 percent to approximately 10 percent (Smith, 1979; White House Conference on Aging, 1981). And many more elderly adults now live alone, especially women (Kobrin, 1976; Michael, Fuchs, & Scott, 1980; Soldo, Sharma, & Campbell, 1984). However, this does *not* mean that modern elderly parents are more often neglected by their children. The financial status of the aged has improved dramatically during the last fifty years (Chapter 9), so today's older adults can better afford to maintain their independence and live by themselves. Although it was much more common for parents to live with their children circa 1900, there is no evidence that they *wanted* to; they may well have had little choice in an era that had no social security system or private pension plans (Lee, 1985). Supporting this position is the fact that parents who currently live with their children tend to have extremely low incomes, indicating that they have chosen this course primarily because they cannot afford anything else (Lawton, 1980; Soldo, 1979).

Even though fewer parents now live *with* their children, the number who reside *near* at least one adult child has increased. As of 1975, more than half of all older Americans with children lived within ten minutes' distance of at least one child, while some 75 percent were no more than a half hour away (Shanas, 1979). Thus the frequency of contact between today's older parents and their adult children is quite high. In one study of subjects in the United States, Britain, and Denmark, over 80 percent of all elderly parents saw at least one of their adult children during the preceding week (Shanas et al., 1968). More recent findings are similar: Some 55 percent of older parents saw one adult child within the previous 24 hours, while approximately 80 percent did so during the past one to two weeks (Harris & Associates, 1975; 1981; Shanas, 1979).

Even when elderly parents become seriously ill, their children maintain frequent contact. About twice as many aged parents are cared for by relatives as are placed in nursing homes and other institutions (Shanas, 1979). Most residents of nursing homes either have no close relatives to call upon because they never married or outlived their children, or are so ill that they cannot be cared for at home. Rather than relegating their elderly parents to nursing homes at the slightest excuse, today's adult children typically regard institutionalization with the utmost reluctance and take this step only as a last resort.

QUALITY OF CONTACT.   Frequent contact does not in and of itself ensure a rewarding interpersonal relationship. However, research data have also shown that most older parents and adult children have highly positive feelings for one another. In fact, many of these parents feel close enough to their children to use them as confidants (e.g., Atchley & Miller, 1980; Harris & Associates, 1975). These relationships are also motivated by a sense of duty, and are likely to involve the provision of mutual aid. This may take the form of housework, advice, moral support, baby sitting, or financial assistance, with the last two of these more often provided by the parents. Thus it appears that many elderly parents continue to provide for their children whatever they can, for as long as they can (normally, at least through age 75). In turn, adult children support their parents when the latter's health or financial condition deteriorates.

CARING FOR AN ELDERLY PARENT.   It is becoming increasingly likely that adult children will have to care for an elderly, infirm parent. The "old-old" (age 85 or more) are the most rapidly growing segment of the American population (Brody et al., 1983), and the lingering geriatric and terminal illnesses are now the rule rather than the exception (Chapters 11 and 12). To be sure, a lucky few have parents who retain much of their health and independence even in old age:

AN AUTONOMOUS ELDERLY COUPLE.
Mr. R., age 98, is troubled by arthritis and some hearing loss, but he still cooks for himself in his New Jersey home. His wife, age 96, can

no longer see well and has grown forgetful, but she still does her own shopping. Their 69-year-old married daughter lives a half mile away, and finds it a simple matter to care for her parents. "There are just some little things to worry about," she says, "like whether he locked the back door at night, or has he checked the windows in case of a storm." (Gelman et al., 1985.)

More often, however, caring for an elderly parent is far more difficult. The demands made on adult children in such situations can be extremely severe, as the following case histories indicate (Gelman et al., 1985):

INTERGENERATIONAL CONFLICT.

Mr. J.'s ailing mother stayed at his home for two months. She had a falling out with his wife during this time, and also expressed displeasure with him. Even though he is 60 years old, "to her I'm still a child," he says. "Of course I try to resist that, but she doesn't think I have sense enough to turn out the lights. She thinks I'm irresponsible. When I go to light the stove, she gives me hell until I've properly disposed of the match."

A BLIND, PARALYZED WIDOW.

Mrs. L., a 79-year-old widow, is blind and paralyzed on one side of her body. Her two adult daughters have to put her to bed and get her up each day, dress her, move her to the dining room, and feed her. On weekends they take her to a park to sit in the sun, or to visit their married sister. The daughters have no time for any private life; neither has married.

A PARTLY PARALYZED, INCONTINENT MAN.

Mr. B. is 85 years old, partly paralyzed, and incontinent. His 60-year-old son hired a home attendant to care for his father, but the attendant found the task far too rigorous and quit in a week. Reluctantly, the son decided on a nursing home. "I had to either make that decision or keep changing his diapers myself," he says. He visits his father two to three times a week, but comes away depressed. "It would be good if Dad died," he says bluntly. "I don't see anything in him that shows me that he's comfortable."

How well does the modern family respond to such challenges? Numerous studies show that today's adult children are expending considerable effort, and are incurring substantial costs, to help their elderly parents in time of need. For example, 87 percent of one sample of 700 elderly persons received at least half of the help they needed from their children or other relatives (Morris & Sherwood, 1984; see also Cicirelli, 1981; Moon, 1983; Schulz, Tompkins, & Wood, in press; Shanas, 1980; Stoller, 1983; Stoller & Earl, 1983). In fact, the care provided by children (and other kin) have helped to prevent or at least postpone the institutionalization of many elderly parents (e.g., Branch & Jette, 1983; Brody, 1978; 1981; Cantor, 1980).

Nevertheless, such kin networks are not without serious problems. Caring for an ill elderly parent can be so demanding that even the most loving, considerate child suffers considerable resentment and guilt (e.g., Cantor, 1983). Young parents who have only recently begun to recover from the financial and emotional strain of rearing their own child, or who must still contend with these burdens, may well find it difficult to cope with a parent who is now almost as helpless as an infant. Furthermore, seeing one's formerly authoritative and powerful parent become childishly dependent can prove to be psychologically disturbing. Those children who live far from their parents may be spared this daily anguish, but they must contend with the tactical problems of trying to help from a distance and with the guilt evoked by not being present. As a result, caregivers are three to four times more likely than their elderly parents to report symptoms of depression and anger (Gelman et al., 1985). Women are particularly vulnerable in this regard, since it is the daughter who most often assumes primary responsibility for the elderly parent. If she is also working and a mother, she may well find that this trio of responsibilities leaves her with so little time for leisure and recreation that her health and well-being decline.

Secondly, elderly parents may be less willing to receive help from their children than the children are to provide it. Independence and autonomy are highly valued in our society, and the elderly are no exception. In one study, for example, the majority of elderly adults differed significantly from young adults by stating that they would rather pay a professional for assistance than ask a family member (Brody et al., 1983). Elderly parents know that their adult children have their own lives to live, and that caring for an invalid is demanding and disruptive. Therefore, they may regard it as demeaning and distasteful to become dependent on their children. Those who take this course may well do so because they have (or believe that they have) no other choice, and at considerable cost to their self-esteem and desire for independence (Lee, 1985). Also, because of the well-known "generation gap," parents may find it less pleasant to live with their children because they have much more in common with people of their own age.

These problems are likely to become even more severe in the not-too-distant future. It has been estimated that by the year 2040, the number of Americans over age 85 will increase from the present 2.2 million to nearly 13 million, while the number over 65 will grow from 26 million to 66.6 million. (See Chapter 1.) In about 50 years, then, we may find a large number of old-old adults being cared for by old relatives, which may well be too great a strain for all concerned.

AFTERWORD.   Since family caregivers are likely to need help coping with ill parents, and since elderly parents are likely to fare better psychologically if they are not forced to depend on their adult children, formal support groups would seem to be eminently desirable. Virtually every part of this country does have an agency on aging, which provides basic information and assistance with regard to home health services and other problems. But once a family member assumes in-home responsibility for an elderly parent, the United States government takes a hands-off approach. Medicare does *not* provide for respite care, where a qualified professional fills in for the family caregiver for a few days. Nor does Medicare cover chronic long-term nursing home care, which currently costs about $18,000 per year. Caring for the ill elderly is at present a prominent issue among this country's health policy planners, so some form of federal assistance may perhaps be forthcoming in the foreseeable future.

Empirical data clearly show that today's adult children are doing an outstanding job of caring for their elderly parents. But demographic data indicate that this problem may soon become so widespread as to make outside support essential. As Gelman et al. (1985, p. 68) put it: "If a society can be judged by the way it treats its elderly, then we are not without honor—so far. But as we all grow older, that honor will demand an even higher price."

Grandparenting

The increasing human life span has also produced more modern families that span three, or even four, generations. Becoming a grandparent is now more common in middle age than in old age, and may even occur as early as age 40 (Butler & Lewis, 1976; Kivnick, 1982). As a result, today's children and young adults are likely to have at least some contact with one or more grandparents.

Grandparents are often pictured as having warm and close relationships with their grandchildren, partly because they can enjoy the pleasures of these interactions without having to shoulder parental responsibilities. We have all heard stories of grandfathers who go fishing with their grandsons on a regular basis, grandmothers who spend part of each day teaching their granddaughters to sew or bake cookies, and grandchildren who tenderly care for an aging or ill grandparent. Although some researchers have focused on issues like these, there are very few empirical data dealing with grandparenting.

FREQUENCY OF CONTACT. There is no indication that modern grandparents are being neglected by their grandchildren. Approximately three out of every four Americans over age 65 have living grandchildren. About 75 percent of these elderly adults see their grandchildren at least once every week or two, while some 50 percent do so every few days (Harris & Associates, 1975).

While grandparent–grandchild interactions are frequent, they are usually peripheral in the lives of both parties. As with elderly parents and adult children, grandparents most often live apart from their grandchildren (Atchley, 1977). Thus interactions between grandparents and grandchildren typically take the form of special events, such as an outing or a telephone call, rather than occurring routinely within the household. "The rocking-chair grandparent is no longer an appropriate image; neither is the child carer, cookie baker, or fishing companion" (Troll, 1980, p. 476; see also Hagestad, 1985).

QUALITY OF CONTACT. Some researchers have sought to determine the typical ways in which grandparents behave toward their grandchildren. In one classic study (Neugarten & Weinstein, 1964), interviews of 70 middle-class sets of grandparents revealed five specific styles of behavior:

1. Formal: Maintaining a clear distinction between parent and grandparent. Although these grandparents were interested in their grandchildren, they limited their assistance to occasional gifts or babysitting. This style was more common among grandparents past age 65.

2. Fun-seeker: Enjoying mutually pleasurable activities with the grandchildren; being informal and playful.

3. Surrogate Parent: Assuming the mother's parental responsibilities because she worked outside the home, or was otherwise unable to care for her children. This style was determined by necessity rather than by choice; grandparents preferred not to become surrogate parents unless there there was no good alternative. The surrogate parent was almost always the grandmother, rather than the grandfather.

4. Reservoir of Family Wisdom: Assuming an authoritarian position and dispensing information, advice, and resources to the grandchildren. A relatively rare style that was more often adopted by grandfathers than by grandmothers.

Grandparenthood provides a rewarding opportunity to indulge one's grandchildren without the responsibilities that burden a parent. *Susan Lapides/Design Conceptions*

5. Distant Figure: Maintaining little contact with the grandchildren, except for such occasions as birthdays or holidays.

More recently, Kivnick (1982) investigated the ways in which being a grandparent are meaningful and rewarding. Some 286 grandparents completed a lengthy questionnaire, and the responses were subjected to the mathematical procedure of factor analysis. The results indicated that grandparenthood is rewarding for several reasons. There is the opportunity to *spoil and indulge* one's grandchildren, since grandparents are usually not burdened by the same responsibilities as parents. Grandparenthood provides a form of *immortality through clan,* since the grandparent leaves behind not only children but also grandchildren. Grandparents enjoy receiving the grandchild's respect as a wise, helpful *valued elder.* Grandparenthood also facilitates a *reinvolvement with one's personal past,* as by recalling relationships with one's own grandparents. However, grandparenthood is more central in the lives of some grandparents than others.

Other researchers have focused on the ways in which grandparents and grandchildren seek to influence one another's attitudes and styles of life. Many grandparents pass along recommended religious, social, and vocational values to their grandchildren (Cherlin & Furstenberg, 1985; Troll & Bengtson, 1979). This may be done through such methods as storytelling, giving friendly advice during an outing or visit, or working together on special projects. In turn, grandchildren may introduce their grandparents to such recent cultural innovations as new toys and games or styles of dress, thereby helping the grandparents to reduce their feelings of alienation from an ever-changing world. However, there is usually an unspoken agreement to protect the relationship by avoiding topics likely to cause conflict. For example, during the 1960s, grandparents and radical student grandchildren were unlikely to discuss such volatile issues as hair length and clothing preferences. These mutually avoided, sensitive areas have been referred to as "demilitarized zones" (Hagestad, 1978).

Despite efforts like these, social scientists have been unable to agree upon standard styles of grandparenting. One possible reason is that grandparents may vary in age from 40 to 100 or more, while grandchildren may vary from newborn infants to age 60 or older. There may well be little common ground between the way a 50-year-old adult treats a 2-year-old child and the behavior of an 80-year-old adult toward a 16-year-old adolescent, even though both cases involve interactions between a grandparent and a grandchild. For example, some data indicate that grandparents age 50–70 show more positive emotions about their grandchildren than do grandparents in their 40s and 80s (Troll, 1980). Thus grandparent—grandchild interactions may well be too idiosyncratic to be described in terms of generally applicable styles. (See Bengtson & Robertson, 1985).

LEGAL RESPONSIBILITIES AND RIGHTS OF GRANDPARENTS.   As we observed earlier in this chapter, divorce has become very common in this country. This can pose considerable problems for grandparents, who may become caught in the middle of the marital conflict. The legal responsibility of grandparents is extensive, for they can be sued for grandchild support in many states. Yet their legal rights are very few; grandparents have virtually no standing insofar as visitation or adoption of their grandchildren is concerned (Wilson & DeShane, 1982). Since parents tend to function as gatekeepers by limiting or encouraging grandparent–grandchild interactions, a bitter ex-wife or ex-husband can and may prevent grandparents from ever seeing a cherished grandchild.

Theories of Interpersonal Behavior

In the preceding pages, we have concentrated primarily on the *what* and the *how* of adult interpersonal relationships: what happens to the number of friendships with increasing age, how grandparents behave toward their grandchildren, whether older parents and their adult children interact frequently, and so on. In addition, social scientists are keenly interested in explaining *why* adults behave as they do toward other people.

For example, we have seen that elderly parents tend to be considerably more reluctant to seek help from their adult children than the children are to provide it. Why should this be so? The fear of disrupting the children's lives is a sensible explanation, but a very specific one. A more general theoretical argument might be that people are uncomfortable with relationships wherein power is markedly unequal. Few individuals enjoy receiving a great deal from a loved one or close friend, yet being unable to give anything in return. According to this theory, then, adults who are unable to maintain a fairly equal amount of give-and-take in an interpersonal relationship will dislike this relationship and tend to avoid it. (See Lee, 1985). Theories like this one have the potential advantage of explaining a wide range of adult interpersonal behavior, rather than dealing only with a specific example.

During the past three decades, social scientists have proposed several such theories to explain the interpersonal behavior of older adults. Devising a useful theory is not an easy task, and no one of these theories is as yet regarded as clearly superior to all of the others.

Control Theories

CONCEPTIONS OF CONTROL.   To many noted theorists, the need to master and control our environment is a fundamental aspect of human nature. For example, Alfred Adler (e.g., 1927) concluded that the primary goal underlying all human behavior is that of striving for superiority. Everyone begins life as a weak and helpless child, and we all possess the innate drive to overcome this inferiority by mastering our formidable environment. Erich Fromm (e.g., 1947) argued that we have an inherent need to transcend our childhood helplessness by exerting a significant effect on our environment, as through creativity and love. Erik Erikson (1963) also theorized that human beings have a fundamental need to master the environment, an achievement that affords pleasures over and above those obtained by satisfying our biological needs. And numerous other social scientists agree that control over our environment is greatly preferred to a lack of control, and that the ability or inability to exert this control has a profound effect on the physical and psychological well-being of adults of all ages (e.g., Baron & Rodin, 1978; Glass & Singer, 1972; Rodin, Timko, & Anderson, 1985; Wortman & Brehm, 1975).

In general, **control** is defined as the ability to regulate or influence the outcomes that befall us through the behaviors that we choose. However, the specific way in which control is conceptualized varies from one theory to another. One example, **locus of control theory,** was discussed in the preceding chapter: people who are high in internal control believe that they can obtain rewards and avoid punishments primarily through their own efforts, while people who are high in external control expect their good and bad experiences to be caused largely by mere chance and the actions of other people (Rotter, 1966). **Learned helplessness theory** asserts that if we are exposed to numerous life events which are beyond our control, we will develop an expectation that future events will also be uncontrollable. Ultimately, this sense of helplessness may lead to serious self-dissatisfaction and even depression (Seligman, 1975). According to this theory, the most serious psychological damage occurs when we blame ourselves for the disasters in our lives. If a man attributes the death of his beloved wife to his own negligence or lack of care, he will suffer greater and longer-lasting depression than will a man who believes that his wife died because of a random event that he could neither predict nor control. **Self-efficacy theory** defines control in terms of the perceived ability to carry out a task. It states that we undertake tasks which we judge ourselves as capable of performing, but avoid activities which appear to exceed our abilities (Bandura, 1977; 1981). People who perceive themselves as high in self-efficacy are more likely to persist in the face of obstacles or negative experiences, while those who are low in perceived self-efficacy tend to view their problems as overly difficult and to quit in the face of adversity.

CONTROL AND AGING.   As adults grow past middle age and move into their sixties, seventies, and eighties, their physical, psychological, and economic resources are likely to decrease. Such declines limit their ability to control the environment and achieve desired goals, which may lead to feelings of helplessness and depression and to a decrease in social activity. Conversely, affording the aged more control over their surroundings is likely to produce a marked increase in well-being and interpersonal behavior. For example, as we observed in Chapter 7, residents of a church-affiliated home who had some control over visits that they received were significantly higher in physical and psychological health than were residents who had no control over such visits (Schultz, 1976). In a related study, one group of residents of a nursing home heard a talk which encouraged them to take more responsibility for their daily activities. A second group listened to a communication that stressed the staff's responsibility to control residents' behavior. The former group became more active, and reported feeling significantly happier (Langer & Rodin, 1976; see also Reid, 1977; Reid, Haas, & Hawkins, 1977; Reid & Ziegler, 1980; Rodin, 1983; in press, a; in press, b; Rodin & Langer, 1977; 1980; Schulz, 1980; Schulz & Brenner, 1977; Schulz & Hanusa, 1978; 1979; 1980).

In sum: numerous studies have shown that control of the environment is a major determinant of well-being throughout the adult life course. The amount of research dealing with control and the elderly is increasing rapidly, so we may expect still more important contributions to be forthcoming in this area.

Exchange Theory

DEFINITION.   Our relationships with other people may bring us various material and non-material rewards. For example, we may receive compliments which increase our self-esteem, entertainment, attention and affection, a valued gift, or compliance with our needs and wishes. We may also incur various costs, such as having to endure boredom or irritation, suffering anxiety (as on a first date), spending money, or investing time (which might otherwise be devoted to useful solitary activities). That is, interpersonal relationships can be viewed as processes wherein the people involved see to maximize the rewards and minimize the costs.

According to **exchange theory,** interpersonal interactions will be initiated and continued so long as they are sufficiently rewarding for both parties—that is, if the rewards exceed the costs (Dowd, 1975). At any given moment in an interpersonal relationship, the rewards enjoyed by each party are unlikely to be precisely equal. However, the person who is currently gaining more from the relationship is obligated to try and restore a more equal balance in the future. If instead one individual is consistently unable to provide sufficient rewards, the other is likely to terminate the relationship because the costs are too great. An interpersonal relationship involves give-and-take, and it will not survive if one individual gives or receives too little (that is, if the relationship is imbalanced).

EXCHANGE THEORY AND AGING.   Since the elderly tend to have less power and resources than younger adults, their interpersonal relationships are particularly likely to be imbalanced. The only apparent recourse is to use compliance as a reward, and to yield consistently to the wishes of the other person. This ultimately results in a serious loss of self-respect, however, whereupon the elderly are likely to withdraw from social activity. According to exchange theory, then, the aged presumably engage in fewer interpersonal relationships because of their inability to reward other people and maintain balanced interactions.

CONCEPTUAL DIFFICULTIES.   There are several conceptual difficulties with the exchange approach. First of all, intrinsic, self-determined rewards can compensate for the absence of any specific returns from another person. Some individuals continue to interact with the elderly on the grounds of duty, charity, or a genuine interest in the aged, even though they obtain no extrinsic rewards at all. This implies that interactions which are imbalanced in terms of extrinsic rewards may continue to exist, rather than terminating as exchange theory predicts. (See Schulz & Manson, 1984).

In addition, the effective reward and cost value of any interpersonal interaction is deceptively difficult to calculate. Our satisfaction with an interaction depends to a great extent on how the associated rewards and costs compare to our prior expectations, rather than on their absolute value. If, for example, we receive moderate rewards from an interpersonal interaction, we will tend to be happy if we expected very little but rather unhappy if we expected a great deal, even though the amount of the reward is the same in both cases.

Exchange theory has raised some interesting issues. However, these conceptual difficulties indicate that it cannot be accepted as a definitive explanation of the interpersonal behavior of the aged.

Reference Group Theory and Social Comparison Theory

DEFINITION.   According to reference group theory, we use important other people as a frame of reference to evaluate our behavior, attitudes, values, and beliefs (e.g., Blau, 1981; Merton, 1957). In particular, **social comparison theory** states that we all possess a basic drive to evaluate our abilities and opinions (Festinger, 1954). When possible, we base these self-assessments on appropriate objective evidence: a college student may conclude that he is poor in mathematics or art because he consistently obtains low grades in these subjects, or an athlete may decide to try out for the Olympics because she has won ten consecutive matches in the hundred-yard dash. However, many important questions lack objective answers (e.g., "How happy am I, and how good is my life?" or "Am I doing as well professionally, financially, or socially as I should be?"). In the absence of clear objective standards, we perform our self-evaluations by comparing ourselves with other people. If we rate ourselves favorably compared to others, we will tend to feel satisfied and content. But if we conclude that others are much better off, we are likely to become unhappy and depressed.

SOCIAL COMPARISON THEORY AND AGING.   The reference group that we use for our self-evaluations is likely to vary depending on the specific attribute that we are evaluating; it may even be a group from our past, rather than the present. In order to apply social comparison theory to the elderly, therefore, we must first ask: with whom do they typically compare themselves? If the institutionalized aged base their self-evaluations primarily on other elderly residents, who are more or less equal in most important respects, dissatisfaction is unlikely. But if the elderly usually compare themselves to younger people, or to their own status of years ago, they will probably be unhappy. The many real declines that they have experienced, as in living conditions, financial status, physical capacities, and daily routine, will make their present circumstances seem considerably inferior (Schulz, 1982; Schulz & Manson, 1984).

Only indirect evidence is available concerning this issue. Numerous studies indicate that both the institutionalized and the noninstitutionalized aged do *not* differ significantly from younger adults in morale, well-being, and level of depression (Larson, 1978; Zemore & Eames, 1979). We may therefore infer that negative social comparisons are not a serious problem for the aged. They apparently adjust their expectations to realistic levels, rather than dwelling on people who are more fortunate or on their own past.

Disengagement and Activity Theories

DEFINITION.   According to **disengagement theory,** there is a process of mutual withdrawal between the aged and society (Cumming & Henry, 1961). Elderly individuals withdraw from society because they realize that their capacities have diminished, and they wish to protect themselves as much as possible from failure and rejection. Society withdraws from the elderly because it needs to replace them with younger, more capable persons in order to remain vibrant and viable. This mutual disengagement takes the form of a decrease in the number and diversity of contacts between the aged and society, and is assumed to be universal, inevitable, and mutually satisfying.

Almost from its inception, disengagement theory sparked a controversy that has persisted for more than a decade. The major opposition has come from proponents of **activity theory,** which posits that the social activity of the elderly is positively correlated with their satisfaction with life (Lemon, Bengtson, & Peterson, 1972). Activity theory does agree with disengagement theory in one respect: as we grow older, our social activity is assumed to decrease. But activity theory states that this decrease is *dissatisfying*, and that those older adults who are exceptions to this rule are happier. In contrast, disengagement theory predicts that reduced social activity is *satisfying* to the aged.

CONCEPTUAL DIFFICULTIES. Choosing between these diametrically opposed theories would seem to be an easy task, but this is not the case. Both views are supported by a sizable amount of research evidence, and the same data has at different times been interpreted as favorable to both theories. Since one test of a good theory is that it can be effectively disconfirmed (and discarded), and since this does not appear to be true for activity theory and disengagement theory, we may reasonably conclude that both of these theories are at least somewhat flawed (Hochschild, 1976; Schulz & Manson, 1984). It has been argued that both theories are not stated precisely enough for them to be convincingly disconfirmed even if they are incorrect, and that they fail to take into account the complicated nature of the interactions between the elderly and society. While disengagement theory and activity theory have stimulated some important research, neither one appears valid enough to fully explain the interpersonal behavior of the elderly.

Afterword

Since theories are by definition unproved speculations about reality, they often appear to be frustratingly inaccurate. However, they serve an important purpose. Established facts are often lacking in scientific work, and a theory offers guidelines that will serve us in the absence of more precise information. Although some of the theories discussed above appear to be marred by conceptual flaws, all have points of interest and importance. In particular, enabling the elderly (and younger adults as well) to exert more control over their environment is likely to produce a pronounced increase in well-being. Furthermore, these theories tend to be more complicated than our overview might indicate. Therefore, the interested reader is encouraged to obtain more information by consulting the original sources cited in the preceding pages.

Summary

CLASSIFYING MAJOR LIFE EVENTS.

Most of us experience many major life events between birth and death. One useful way to classify these events is according to the age at which they occur: an event is temporally normative if it occurs at an age that is typical for most people in that culture, and temporally non-normative if it occurs at an atypical age. A second good way to classify life events is according to their frequency, regardless of age: an event is statistically normative if it happens to the majority of individuals in a given culture, and statistically non-normative if it is experienced by relatively few people. Non-normative events are likely to be quite stressful, and adults who must deal with many such events are more vulnerable to physical and psychological illnesses or even premature death.

ADULT FRIENDSHIPS.

Friendships can serve a variety of important purposes. They provide opportunities for self-disclosure, and furnish us with psychological support. We also tend to choose friends who have similar beliefs and personalities; who are physically attractive, intelligent and competent, pleasant and agreeable, and emotionally stimulating; who like and approve of us; and who live close to us.

Although casual friendships tend to become less frequent with increasing age, the number of close friends that one has remains relatively stable throughout the adult life span. Apparently, as we grow older, we sift through our interpersonal relationships and retain those which we value the most. Close friendships contribute significantly to the well-being and overall life satisfaction of older adults. Because of the well-known "generation gap," the elderly are likely to have more in common with people of similar ages than with their children. Also, asking a close friend for help would seem to involve less loss of independence than calling on one's adult children.

LOVE, MARRIAGE, AND DIVORCE.

Various conceptions of love have been proposed by social scientists. These include such distinctions as passionate love versus companionate love, D-love versus B-love, and narcissism versus genuine love. Efforts have also been made to measure love psychometrically, using written questionnaires.

Many relationships that end in marriage proceed through a fairly standard sequence that begins with casual dating, and ends with formal engagement. In any loving relationship, different factors tend to be important during different stages. It also appears that there is an inverse relationship between attraction and attachment, with many long-term loving relationships becoming more placid over the years. Among couples married for many years, the most commonly cited reason for the enduring relationship is: "my spouse is my best friend." Other factors typical of lengthy marriages include meaningful communication and self-disclosure, openness, trustworthiness, caring, believing that marriage is a long-term commitment, and avoiding displays of intensely expressed anger. Families with children tend to follow traditional marital roles, with the wife doing the housework, while role equality is most often found in childless marriages.

Marriage also entails some risk, however; approximately one of every two marriages ends in divorce. Divorce is most common among adults aged 30–45, black females, and those who married prior to age 21. Yet more than half a million Americans aged 65 or more are divorced, with many new cases registered each year. Common causes of divorce include drunkenness, desertion, brutality, adultery, and increasingly bitter arguments. Divorced people tend to proceed through several behavioral stages, ranging from isolation to reestablishing social contact. Divorce is typically a traumatic experience for all concerned, most notably women and the spouse who did not initiate the divorce. But it may be argued that if a marriage is truly unbearable, the least of evils may well be to end it and give each spouse the opportunity to find happiness elsewhere.

SEXUALITY AND AGING.

Until recently, very little was known about the relationship between sexuality and aging. As a result, it was widely assumed that there was nothing to know—that is, that older adults had no interest in sex. During the past few decades, however, we have become increasingly aware that there is indeed sexual life after middle age.

Insofar as young adults are concerned, men tend to be more sexually active than women. There is some indication that the frequency of sexual behavior has increased during the last few decades, especially among younger adults and young women, although these data are to some extent inflated by cohort effects. The frequency of sexual behavior among married couples does tend to decrease from young adulthood to middle age, but this is due largely to such environmental constraints as the presence of young children.

Male sexual capacity has been found to decline with increasing age, but not nearly as much as had been widely believed. There is likely to be a significant drop in sexual ability and interest at about age 50, and again at about age 70–80. As age increases, fewer men are sexually active, and those who are active are less so than younger men. Nevertheless, a substantial number of men continue to engage in sex throughout much or even all of their adult lives. Men are more likely to remain interested in sex through middle and old age if they engaged in sex more often during young adulthood, if they are in good health, and if they believe that they can maintain effective sexual behavior as they grow older.

There is no evidence that aging causes any significant declines in female sexual capacity. However, sexual activity among women does decrease markedly with increasing age. Since women tend to marry men who are older, and since men tend to die at a younger age, women are more likely to be without a socially acceptable and sexually capable partner. Women who enjoy sex more during young adulthood are more likely to remain sexually active in later life, provided that an appropriate partner is available.

At present, the sexual rights of the institutionalized elderly remains an essentially unresolved issue. Nor is much known about the relationship between aging and homosexual behavior.

INTERGENERATIONAL RELATIONSHIPS.

Contrary to popular belief, modern American families are no less caring than were families of some 100 years ago. It is true that since 1900, the number of elderly parents who live with their children has declined markedly. But the financial status of the aged has improved dramatically during the past fifty years, so today's older adults can better afford to maintain their independence and live by themselves. In fact, the number of older parents who reside near at least one adult child has increased over the years. Thus today's adult children see their elderly parents often, and expend considerable effort and money to help their parents in time of need. Children typically regard the institutionalization of an aged parent as a last resort, and the caregiving that they provide has helped to prevent or at least postpone it in many instances.

Nevertheless, the demands of caring for an ill parent can cause even the most loving and dedicated child to become resentful and guilty. There is also some indication that elderly parents may be less willing to receive help from their children than the children are to give it, primarily because this loss of independence is demeaning. Since the number of old-old and old adults is expected to increase dramatically during the next fifty years, the problem of caring for the ill elderly is likely to become particularly acute in the not-too-distant future.

There is no indication that grandparents are being neglected by their grandchildren; contact is frequent, albeit typically peripheral in the lives of both. Although some researchers have tried to establish the ways in which grandparents behave toward their grandchildren, it appears that such interactions are too idiosyncratic to be described in terms of generally applicable styles. Divorce may pose a problem to grandparents, since their legal responsibilities are great while their rights are very few.

THEORIES OF INTERPERSONAL BEHAVIOR.

Social scientists are also interested in explaining why adults behave as they do toward other people, and various theories have been devised for this purpose. Control theories hold that the need to master our environment is a fundamental aspect of human nature. Among the more popular control theories are locus of control theory, learned helplessness theory, and self-efficacy theory. Numerous studies have shown that control over the environment is a major determinant of well-being throughout the adult life course, and that providing the elderly with greater control leads to significant improvements in physical and psychological health.

Exchange theory views interpersonal relationships as processes wherein the people involved seek to maximize their rewards and minimize their costs. This theory posits that the elderly engage in fewer interpersonal relationships because they are unable to reward other people and maintain balanced interactions. However, this theory suffers from important conceptual difficulties.

Social comparison theory states that we all possess a basic drive to evaluate our abilities and opinions, and that we often perform these self-assessments by comparing ourselves with other people. However, negative social comparisons do not appear to be a serious problem for the aged.

Disengagement theory posits a process of mutual and satisfying withdrawal between the aged and society. In contrast, activity theory holds that any substantial decrease in interpersonal activity among the elderly is dissatisfying to them. Although both of these theories have stimulated important research, neither one appears valid enough to stand alone as an explanation of adult interpersonal behavior.

Because theories are by definition unproved speculations about reality, they often appear to be frustratingly inaccurate. But established facts are often lacking in scientific work, and theories offer guidelines that will serve us in the absence of more precise information. All of these theories have points of interest and importance, and have made at least some contribution to our understanding of aging and interpersonal behavior.

CHAPTER 9

Work and Retirement

In this chapter, we turn to yet another integral aspect of human existence. For most people, work provides the income necessary to support themselves and their families. Yet while economic considerations are often of greatest importance, people work for many reasons. Work may be interesting for its own sake: a writer, a carpenter, or a mechanic may derive considerable satisfaction from creating an innovative book, a well-crafted piece of furniture, or a finely tuned automobile engine. Work also contributes to an individual's self-esteem and sense of identity, or to the lack thereof. Society expects men in particular to hold a job, and it accords greater respect to some forms of work than to others (e.g., physicians and judges versus janitors and garbage collectors). In fact, when a person is asked "Who are you?," occupation is one of the most frequently given answers. Work also offers important social rewards and punishments, since it typically involves contacts with coworkers, supervisors, subordinates, and clients. Thus you are likely to spend a substantial part of your life at work, and in preparation for it. Most people also expect that they will someday retire from the world of work, an event that usually represents a significant change in their style of living.

The effects of work are by no means limited to the job environment. Low-level and low-income jobs may compel the employee to live in meager surroundings and to subsist on the bare necessities of life, as well as providing a boring and tedious work day. Conversely, higher-level positions tend to provide a better standard of living and more interesting work. However, a high-level job may have an adverse effect on the employee's family relationships because it is so stressful and time consuming. In one study (Evans & Bartolomé, 1980), some 40 percent of the wives of mangers re-

273

ported that their husbands' stress at work spilled over into their home lives:

THE RELATIONSHIP BETWEEN THE QUALITY OF WORK LIFE AND THE QUALITY OF NONWORK LIFE.

"What annoys me is when he comes home tense and exhausted," observed the wife of one manager who was in her early thirties and had been married for eleven years. "He flops into a chair and turns on the TV. Or else he worries and it drives me up the wall. If he's happy, that's OK. But three years ago he had a very tough job. He was always at the office, even weekends. We had no holidays at all and he was always tense at home—when he was home, that is. . . . I think he should get out of the commercial U.S.A.-type rat race." Another manager had been dissatisfied with his job for many years. His fifty-year-old wife commented: "I think that his work has an enormous effect on our family life, but he doesn't. We've often had violent arguments about it. He considers himself as one of those men who doesn't rant and rave and destroy his family, even when he is having problems at his work. And there I agree. . . . Instead, he closes up like a shell. Total closure. . . . He just doesn't exist. He's completely absent. It's quite clear that you can't reproach him for being disagreeable or aggressive, but it's just as bad in its way. . . . It's a big burden for a wife to bear."

If the employee's job satisfaction is high, there may instead be a positive spillover into the home and family life. According to one wife, "[My husband] really enjoys his work. . . . It's so much easier to live with someone who is happy." However, an intense interest in the job may provoke marital strife because the employee spends too little time with the spouse. "My wife feels that I should work less hard, travel less, and be content with a smaller salary," said one manager. "Sure, we don't need the money that much, but that isn't the point. What she doesn't realize is that I work for the satisfaction that it gives me. If I didn't work as hard, I'd be much less satisfied. I'd be miserable when I'm at home, and things would be even worse than now."

Thus work affects the quality of our lives in two main ways: directly **(intrinsically)**, through our satisfaction and dissatisfaction with the events that take place on the job; and indirectly **(extrinsically)**, through its influence on such nonwork areas as home and family life (Kahn, 1981; Rice, 1984). Intrinsically, work may be engrossing and self-fulfilling or tedious and unpleasant. Extrinsically, work may or may not serve as the means to such important ends as housing, food, clothing, educating one's children, and recreation. Some individuals value the intrinsic aspects of work more highly, while some are more concerned with the extrinsic aspect. But in either case, work has a pronounced effect on our overall well-being and satisfaction with life in general. (See Figure 9.1.)

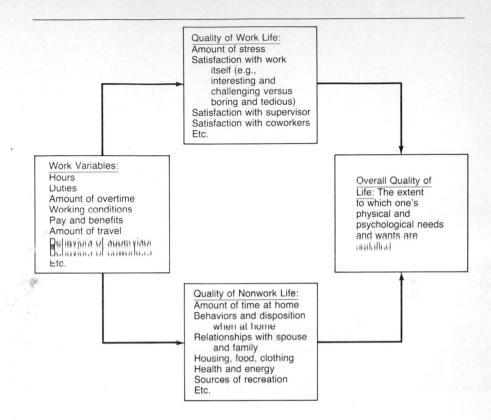

Note. Any single work variable may affect only the quality of work life or both the quality of work and nonwork life. Also, any single work variable may have effects that are positive, or negative, or both. For example, more overtime may lead to better housing (through greater income), but also to less time at home and poorer health. A change to more challenging and interesting duties may improve both the quality of work and nonwork life (because the employee is happier), or it may improve the quality of work life but have an adverse effect on the quality of nonwork life (because the employee neglects the family to spend more time at work, resulting in more marital strife).

FIGURE 9.1   Relationships among work variables, quality of life at work, quality of life away from work, and overall quality of life. Modified from Rice (1984).

The relationship between work and aging is of considerable importance, and there are various interesting and provocative issues for us to explore in this area. With so many more of us living to old age than ever before, there may well be more middle-aged and older adults who wish to work. Are these older adults poorer employment risks? That is, are they more likely to perform at unacceptable levels, to develop negative attitudes that will interfere with organizational goals, or to become injured or ill? Or are older adults generally as competent as younger employees, but more likely to be the targets of unfair stereotypes and prejudicial treatment? Are more women of various ages seeking employment instead of or in addition to motherhood, and how does this affect their satisfaction with their adult years? Since work is so important to us, is retirement likely to be a painful experience? Are retirees prone to major psychological and physical trauma, or even death, because they are no longer needed at work? Does retirement typically involve such a severe drop in income that the retiree's standard of living declines substantially? Should retirees expect an increase in marital difficulties, now that they must spend day and night with their spouses? As these questions indicate, an understanding of adult development and aging cannot be divorced from the world of work and retirement.

Our discussion will focus on two major areas. First we will consider work and its relationship to age and gender. We will then turn to a discussion of retirement, its dynamics, and its likely effects on retirees and their families.

Work and Adult Development

Work and Aging

JOB PERFORMANCE.   As we observed in Chapter 4, some sensory and physiological capacities decline significantly with increasing age. For jobs which require these abilities, corresponding age-related decrements in performance may also be expected. To illustrate, airline pilots who reach age 60 are legally prohibited from flying commercial airplanes because of declines in sensory and processing abilities.

Aging appears to have little detrimental effect in some professional and artistic fields, and may even be related to improved performance. Artists and musicians often do their best work late in life; Dali, Monet, Picasso, and Artur Rubinstein made outstanding creative contributions during their sixties, seventies, and eighties. Conversely, deteriorating physical skills force most professional athletes to retire by age 35 or 40. The most productive years for mathematicians occur during their twenties and thirties, and their performance declines markedly with each decade. Therefore, even the greatest mathematicians must spend most of their lives burdened with the knowledge that they have passed their prime. Age-related decrements in job performance are also found in other physical sciences. When Nobel laureate I. I. Rabi was asked about the age at which physicists tend to run down, he replied:

It very much depends on the individual. . . . I've seen people run down at thirty, at forty, at fifty. I think it must be basically neurological or physiological. The mind ceases to operate with the same richness and association. The information retrieval part sort of goes, along with the interconnections. I know that when I was in my late teens and early twenties, the world was just a Roman candle—rockets all the time. . . . You lose that sort of thing as time goes on. . . . Physics is an otherworld thing; it requires a taste for things unseen, even unheard of . . . These faculties die off somehow when you grow up. . . . Profound curiosity happens when children are young. . . . Once you are sophisticated, you know too much—far too much. (Gardner, 1983, p. 154).

The research evidence in this area is equivocal, which may well be due in part to the limited information provided by chronological age (Chapter 9). Some studies of workers at various jobs locally find significant declines in performance with increasing age, while numerous others do not. For example, one study of 1,572 design and development engineers from age 21 to 60 and above found that rated job performance was highest for those in their thirties, and declined for each successive five-year age group. But educational experience and job complexity were more closely related to performance rating than was age, and a significant number of engineers continued to be highly rated throughout their careers (Graves, Dalton, & Thompson, 1980; see also Atchley, 1985; Doering, Rhodes, & Schuster, 1983). The most justified conclusion appears to be that age often bears little or no relationship to job performance, but that some exceptions may be expected in certain jobs and professions. Nor does there seem to be much truth to the old maxim that "you can't teach an old dog new tricks." Rather, the greater experience of older workers often makes it easier for them to adapt to the requirements of related job situations.

JOB SATISFACTION.   Throughout much of history, work was regarded as a necessary evil: arduous and demanding, valued for the extrinsic benefits that it provided, and rarely (if ever) gratifying for its own sake. To cite one famous example, a major attraction of the biblical Garden of Eden was the lack of any need to work; while Adam was punished for eating the forbidden fruit by being told by God, "In the sweat of thy face shalt thou eat bread" (Holt, 1982).

This gloomy conception of work has changed considerably during the last half century, facilitated in part by the discoveries of industrial social psychology. Research has shown that if an organization takes the trouble to make the workplace more conducive to the needs and wants of its employees, it may well reap such benefits as reduced absenteeism and turnover—and perhaps improved production as well, although the relationship between job satisfaction and productivity has proved to be considerably more complicated than might be expected. (See, for example, McGregor, 1960; Vroom, 1964.) Also, as our society has become more concerned with humanitarian issues and the rights of the individual, we have become less willing to accept the belief that an activity which occupies so much of our time and energy should cause extensive dissatisfaction. Although there are more than a few employers who still retain the traditional concept of work, the importance of intrinsic job variables has achieved widespread acceptance (as we have seen). Thus the concept of **job satisfaction** currently encompasses such aspects as the work itself (e.g., interesting versus boring), opportunities for autonomy and control (such as the freedom to decide how to do your work), chances for advancement, and relationships with the supervisor and coworkers, as well as such traditional aspects as pay, fringe benefits, working conditions, and job security (e.g., Kahn, 1981; Smith, Kendall, & Hulin, 1969).

The importance of some of these work variables appears to vary from early to late adulthood. One study found that young adults were more concerned with such intrinsic factors as chances for advancement, recognition and approval, and enjoyment of their work. Older employees tended to be more concerned with pay, working conditions, and company policy regarding such issues as coffee breaks and absenteeism (Rosenfeld & Owens, 1965). In another study dealing with engineers aged 20–69, younger adults once again proved to be more interested in opportunities for promotion and for professional and personal development, while older workers were less willing to move to a new city. However, such aspects of the job as pay increases, feeling a sense of accomplishment, working on challenging projects, and having good relations with one's supervisor were important to young and old workers alike (Breaugh & DiMarco, 1979). Although the findings in this area are somewhat equivocal, we may conclude that opportunities for promotion and developing one's skills are more important to young adults than to middle-aged and older workers.

In general, however, the relationship between aging and job satisfaction is far from clear. Some theorists have suggested that this relationship is U-shaped: satisfaction is initially high for the new employee because of a honeymoon effect, declines as time goes by and reality sets in, and then increases because the worker forms more accurate expectations of the rewards that can be derived from the job (e.g., Morse, 1953). Other investigators have reported a more or less linear relationship between age and job satisfaction, with older employees tending to be more satisfied (Hulin & Smith, 1965). While the data are too equivocal to permit any firm conclusions, there is

certainly no convincing evidence that older workers tend to be less
satisfied with their jobs than younger adults, or that they are more
likely to develop morale problems (Doering, Rhodes, & Schuster,
1983). If anything, the reverse appears more likely to be true: very
dissatisfied younger adults may well quit and find jobs more to their
liking before they reach more advanced ages, while middle-aged and
older workers are likely to have so much difficulty finding new jobs
that they learn to be satisfied with what they have.

HEALTH AND ABSENTEEISM.   Older workers are less likely than
young adults to be injured on the job. But when they do sustain an
injury, they are more likely to be disabled and to require more time
to recover (Doering, Rhodes, & Schuster, 1983). Older workers are
also less likely to be absent than younger workers, but there is an
important exception to this trend: those who suffer from chronic ill
health have higher rates of absenteeism because they require more
time to convalesce. These findings imply that rather than rejecting
older job applicants out of hand, organizations can obtain valuable
employees by ascertaining the health of these applicants relative to
the requirements of the job (Quirk & Skinner, 1973).

PROBLEMS OF THE OLDER WORKER.   The United States Department of Labor defines a "mature" worker as one at or past the age
of 40. In many respects, these older workers face significantly greater
problems than do young adults.
  Older employees are less likely to lose their jobs than are younger
workers, due in part to their seniority. However, they find it much
more difficult to obtain a job if they do become unemployed. To be
sure, the Age Discrimination in Employment Act of 1967 prohibited
the denial of employment to applicants over 40 because of their age.
And many older adults are as competent, have as positive attitudes,
and are less likely to be injured or absent than are young employees. Nevertheless, severe **age discrimination** still exists in the world
of work. Between 1979 and 1983, the number of age discrimination
complaints increased by some 300 percent, and more than $24.6
million was awarded by the courts to over 5,000 individuals because
of violations of the ADEA (Atchley, 1985). Furthermore, there is
good reason to believe that these figures seriously understate the
actual extent of job-related age discrimination. Many people undoubtedly fail to file for damages because they are unaware of the
protection offered by the ADEA, because they erroneously believe
that it is extremely difficult to file a complaint, or because they despair of ever proving that their rejections were due to age. Case
histories like this following are far from uncommon:

A 59-YEAR-OLD MASTER PRINTER.
In December of 1956, a large printing company that published several popular magazines ceased operations and closed its plant. Seniority thus offered no protection to Mr. H., a master printer with 42 years of experience. Mr. H. had very strong ties to his present community; he had been born there, many of his relatives and all of his friends lived there, and he was active in his church and in local politics. To remain there, he was willing to change professions and to accept significantly less money than he had made as a printer. Jobs were available in local manufacturing companies, and his skills would have made it easy for him to adapt to their machinery. Nevertheless, he could not secure employment. Understandably bitter, he reluctantly opted for early retirement at age 62. (Atchley, 1985, pp. 189–190.)

Such age discrimination appears to be due in part to negative stereotypes about older workers. In one study, a sample of 42 business students was asked how they would deal with various job problems:

- A recently hired shipping room employee who seemed unresponsive to customer calls for service.

- Whether to terminate or retain a computer programmer whose skills had become obsolete.

- Whether to transfer an employee to a higher-paying but more demanding job.

- Whether to hire someone for a position that required not only knowledge of the field, but also the capacity to make quick judgments.

- Whether to honor a request from a production staff employee to attend a conference dealing with new theories and research relevant to production systems.

- Whether to promote an employee to a marketing job that required fresh solutions to challenging problems, and a high degree of creative and innovative behavior.

When the employees in these situations were described as "older," they were more likely to be fired or turned down for the job or promotion than when they were characterized as "younger." Since the work-related qualifications of these hypothetical employees were otherwise identical, the adverse treatment could only have been due to age. (See Rosen & Jerdee, 1976a; 1976b.) Although this study dealt only with students, research evidence also indicates that managers unfairly stereotype older workers as resistant to change, uncreative, slow to make decisions, and untrainable.

Age discrimination is also caused by the nature of organizational fringe benefits. Pensions for older workers are more costly to employers, since contributions must be spread over a shorter period. Health insurance costs are also considerably higher for those aged 45 to 65 than for young adults. (See Taggart, 1973; Zillmer, 1982.) Employers may therefore reject older applicants or try to phase out older workers so as not to incur these greater expenses, even though the ADEA prohibits justifying such decisions on the grounds of high pension costs.

In sum: despite legal safeguards, age discrimination is still a problem in the world of work. All too many older workers are unfairly denied the opportunity to earn needed income, fulfill their potentials, satisfy their need for self respect, and enjoy the other rewards that the workplace has to offer. And all too many short-sighted organizations fail to improve their production and profits because they refuse to employ these potentially competent, valuable workers.

MIDLIFE CAREER CHANGES.   If changing jobs is so difficult for those over 40, midlife career changes would seem to pose even greater problems. Some popular periodicals and scientific researchers do conclude that midlife career changes are becoming increasingly common (e.g., Sarason, 1977; Siegler & Edelman, 1977). However, there is little statistical evidence to support this conclusion (Atchley, 1985).

According to one study, which focused on men in their thirties and forties, midlife career changes are most often due to three factors: failing to realize one's potential in the first career, finding a new career that is potentially more satisfying, or changing one's life goals due to such events as divorce, widowhood, or sudden unemployment (Clopton, 1973). But another study of managerial and professional men aged 34 to 54 indicated that such career changes are more often due to external causes, such as losing one's old job, rather than to the employee's wishes and intentions. Some 34 percent of this sample changed careers solely because of external circumstances, while another 26 per cent experienced external pressures and also wanted to change careers. Only 17 percent changed their careers just because they wanted to (Thomas, 1977). Given the prevalence of age discrimination in the workplace, it would seem that midlife career changes may not be as feasible as some theorists believe.

AFTERWORD.   The study of work and aging is more problematical than might be apparent. Job satisfaction is a multidimensional variable, and there is some indication that aging is more closely related to some facets than to others (e.g., the importance of chances for advancement). Job productivity is also a multidimensional variable: the quality of an individual's work is not necessarily related to the quantity that he or she produces, while many jobs lack any obvious or easily obtainable quantitative measure of performance (e.g., teaching, clinical psychology, politics). In fact, the problem of determining satisfactory criteria of job performance has often proved to be a major stumbling block in industrial psychology research. When we also recall the limitations of chronological age as an index of human capacities, it is hardly surprising that relatively few clear relationships between aging and work variables have emerged from the research literature. Instead, such variables as job level and job complexity appear to be more important than age per se. Older workers are likely to be more experienced, to have reached higher-level positions, and to have more challenging and demanding jobs, and it is these aspects which are more closely related to their job performance and satisfaction.

Insofar as age discrimination at work is concerned, more definitive conclusions are justified. It is eminently fair to exclude older workers from jobs which they can no longer perform adequately because of physiological or physical deterioration. Some would also argue that providing more jobs for older workers would reduce the number of openings available to young adults, who are more likely to need the income from work to support their families. Our economic society is a complicated one, and justifiable to attempts to reduce unfairness to one group may inadvertently cause other groups to suffer. Nevertheless, adults in their forties and early fifties still have much of their work lives ahead of them. Many of these individuals have a strong desire to work, and are as or more competent than young adults. To discriminate against these employees solely because of age is not only illegal and harmful to the individual, but is also likely to cost the organization valuable and productive workers.

Gender Differences

DEMOGRAPHY.   The **labor force** consists of all people who are employed plus those who are unemployed but are looking for work. Since our society has long regarded men as the primary breadwinners, and women as the primary child rearers, it is not surprising to find considerably more men in the labor force. In 1980, for example, the labor force included almost 90 percent of men between the ages of 20 and 24, and from 90 percent to 95 percent of men between 25 and 54. The corresponding figures for women ranged from 65 percent to 70 percent. (See Figure 9.2.)

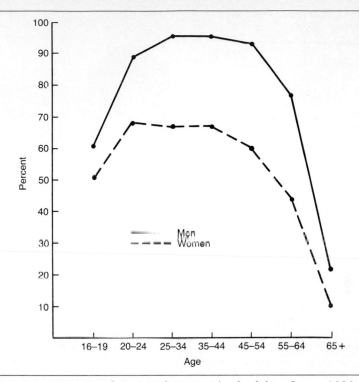

FIGURE 9.2   Percent of men and women in the labor force, 1980.
United States Bureau of the Census (1981).

As with men, women work for many reasons. Historically, the most
important of these is economic: many women must work to support
themselves (and perhaps their children as well), including the divorced (Chapter 8) and the poor. Since non-whites are more likely
to be economically disadvantaged than are whites, the work force
has traditionally included many more non-white women than white
women, although these rates have tended to converge during the
last three decades (United States Senate Special Committee on Aging, 1986).

More recently, the increasing emphasis on individual rights has
been reflected in pressures for more equal job opportunities for
women. Our society has to some extent relinquished the stereotype
that except in cases of dire financial need, the woman's place is in
the home. Women have felt increasingly free to join the work force
in order to express their independence, to provide a second income
that will enable their families to enjoy some of the more expensive
pleasures in life, or to fulfill their potentials and need for achievement. Thus there has been an increase in the percent of working
women during the last half century, although this trend has leveled

Women have made considerable gains in some occupations once dominated by men and have achieved some important positions. But they have
not done nearly as well in other areas and may well be paid less than men
for the same type of work.   *MacDonald/Picture Cube*

off to some extent in recent years. Whereas only 25 percent of those
at work in 1940 were women, this figure increased to 33 percent by
1958, to 41 percent by 1978, and to 44 percent by 1984. Women
have made considerable gains in some occupations once dominated
by men: between 1972 and 1981, the proportion of accountants who
were women rose from 22 percent to 38 percent, women economists
from 12 percent to 25 percent, and women bartenders from 28 percent to 48 percent (Samuelson, 1985). However, women have not
done nearly as well with regard to managerial and administrative
positions. (See Table 9.1.) Also, women working full time in 1983
earned only 64 percent of what men did, a figure that has remained
fairly steady for decades.

THE COMPARABLE WORTH CONTROVERSY.   To some theorists, the
lower pay typically received by women is a clear sign of **sex discrimination.** They argue that employers are paying men significantly more
for much the same work, and/or are denying women access to higher-
level and more lucrative positions. It has therefore been suggested
that the demands and difficulty of various jobs be rated numerically, so that pay can be determined solely according to this criterion
and men and women will receive comparable pay for comparable
work.

TABLE 9.1   Jobs held by men and women during 1958, 1968, and 1978 (in percents).

Year	All Jobs		Managerial and Administrative Jobs		Clerical Jobs	
	Men	Women	Men	Women	Men	Women
1958	67.3	32.7	13.6	5.0	6.9	30.1
1968	63.4	36.6	13.6	4.5	7.1	33.8
1978	58.8	41.2	14.0	6.1	6.2	34.6

SOURCE·   United States Bureau of the Census, Social Indicators III (1980).

Other theorists have taken strong exception to this proposal. They point out that women are much more likely than men to discontinue their work in order to bear and raise children, which has a negative effect on their seniority and chances for advancement. Statistical data indicate that women as a group have fewer years of experience and less seniority than do men (Samuelson, 1985). Also, if the mother chooses to return to work after the child is born, she may prefer a lower-level and less demanding job so that she can spend more time at home. These critics generally agree that there is sex discrimination in the workplace, but they contend that the best way to alleviate this problem is by allowing pay to fluctuate freely in accordance with the supply and demand for the jobs in question.

This issue is likely to remain a controversial one. Given the difficulty of evaluating the demands made by different jobs, as well as the opposition to such programs, it seems unlikely that an effective system for determining comparable worth will be forthcoming in the near future.

CAREER AND/OR MOTHERHOOD.   As Figure 9.2 indicates, the majority of young women seek some form of employment. More than 50 percent of women aged 16 to 19, and approximately 70 percent of women aged 20 to 24, belonged to the labor force in 1980. Some of these women opt for full-time careers, while some leave the labor force permanently in order to raise a family. Various studies have shown that women who elect to work full time are no less (or more) satisfied with their adult years than are those who opt for motherhood (e.g., Baruch & Barnett, 1980; Blood & Wolfe, 1960; Wright, 1978). As Carl Jung, the noted psychiatrist, once observed: "The shoe that fits one person pinches another; there is no universal recipe for living" (1931, p. 41).

Still other women choose to combine work and family roles, either for financial reasons or because they enjoy their jobs and do not wish to abandon them. Research evidence indicates that married women who work enjoy better mental health than those who do not, but they also experience greater interrole conflicts than do male workers. This is apparently due to the fact that the woman's multiple roles tend to be salient simultaneously, whereas the man's multiple roles are more likely to operate sequentially. That is, the woman's family responsibilities normally continue throughout the day, so she is more likely to encounter situations where she must be at work yet take care of home and children at the same time. Conversely, the man can more often concentrate solely on work during the day and pursue family activities during the evening. (As we observed in the preceding chapter, the role of the "househusband" has been greatly exaggerated. After the first child is born, the husband typically seeks to earn more income, while the wife assumes primary responsibility for family matters.) Thus married women who work perceive the home as more of a burden and are more likely to cite scheduling conflicts as a source of problems, while working men more often view their home environment as a support system (Hall, 1975; Kessler & McCrae, 1981; Sekaran, 1983; Staines & Pleck, 1983; Welch & Broth, 1977). The working married woman is particularly likely to experience interrole conflicts if she has young children, if her decision to work is not supported by her husband, if she works for many hours during the week, and if she has a higher level of career aspiration (Gore & Mangione, 1983; Holahan & Gilbert, 1979a; 1979b).

AFTERWORD.   The stereotype that the woman's place is in the home has been shattered by empirical data: women who choose to work are no less satisfied with their adult lives than are women who opt to raise a family, nor is there any indication that they are in general less competent employees than are men. However, women who elect to combine work and family roles may find it difficult to meet their obligations in both areas. Although sex discrimination is still a significant problem in the workplace, the influence of women at work has increased considerably during the past four decades—and is likely to continue to do so in the future.

Retirement

Leaving the world of full-time work involves financial, psychological, and physical changes. For most people, retirement brings a reduction in annual income. Work can no longer be used to gratify

Chapter Glossary: Work and Retirement

Age discrimination

Denying an individual a job, a promotion, more pay, or other desired work benefit solely because of his or her chronological age. Although illegal, age discrimination is still a significant problem in the world of work.

Early retirement

Leaving the world of full-time work prior to the age mandated by the company or by law (e.g., 65 or 70). Usually requires the individual to accept lower retirement benefits.

Extrinsic benefits of work

The extent to which the income and other benefits obtained from work gratify such nonwork needs and wants as food, housing, clothing, and recreation.

Intrinsic benefits of work

The extent to which work is gratifying and enjoyable for its own sake.

Job satisfaction

The extent to which one likes or dislikes various aspects of the work situation. These include pay and fringe benefits, the work itself (e.g., whether it is interesting or boring), the supervisor, the coworkers, chances for advancement, opportunities for autonomy and control over one's work, job security, and working conditions.

Phases of retirement

Distinct emotional and psychological periods that are presumably encountered during retirement, such as the honeymoon period, rest and relaxation, disenchantment, reorientation, the daily routine, and termination. Some retirees may omit some of these phases, or may encounter them in a different order.

Retired person

An individual who is *not* working full time *and* who receives at least some income from a pension earned through prior employment.

Retirement

Leaving the world of full-time work and beginning to collect one's pension or related benefits.

Sex discrimination

Denying an individual a job, a promotion, more pay, or other desired work benefit solely because of his or her gender; most often used to refer to the unfair treatment of women at work. Although illegal, sex discrimination is still a significant problem in the world of work.

Work force

All those adults who are currently employed, plus all those who are currently seeking employment.

the retiree's self-esteem and need for achievement. The opportunity for meaningful and enjoyable social interactions with coworkers, supervisors, and subordinates is no longer available. And instead of spending some eight hours per day in the work environment, the retiree must now either remain at home or find other activities to fill the day.

Thus it is not uncommon to hear about people who retire and then die unexpectedly within weeks or even days, presumably because they cannot cope with this major life change. Less extreme but equally prevalent are anecdotes about retirees who require psychiatric help because they feel useless and depressed, or because they cannot tolerate having to spend both day and night with their spouses. Nevertheless, these stories do not necessarily indicate that retirement causes ill health. Retirement may instead *result from* an existing physical or mental disorder. Most people do not retire until age 60 or later, and health tends to decline toward the end of the adult life span. If some adults choose to retire because poor health makes it too difficult for them to function at work, and if their disorders become considerably more serious or even terminal in subsequent months, it is clearly erroneous to conclude that an otherwise healthy individual was made ill by retirement. (Compare with the discussion of stressful life events in Chapter 10.) Also, as we have seen, work may be valued more for its extrinsic than its intrinsic aspects; it may be boring and stressful rather than interesting and enjoyable, yet serve as an essential source of income. For some, or even many jobs, then, retirement may represent more of a relief than a deprivation. In this section, we will seek to determine whether the supposedly adverse effects of retirement are supported by research evidence, or whether these beliefs are merely more of the myths that pervade the field of adult development and aging.

Introduction

DEFINITION.   **Retirement** can be defined in various ways. Some theorists regard any person who performs no gainful employment during a given year as retired. Others apply this definition only to those who are currently receiving retirement pension benefits. And still others consider anyone who is not employed full time, year round, as retired.

For purposes of the present discussion, a retired person is one who is *not* employed at a *full-time* paying job *and* who receives at least some income from a pension due to prior employment. Thus retirement is an *earned* reward, one that results from having previously been a member of the labor force. Also, retirement does not necessarily mean a total separation from the world of work. Some retirees opt for part-time jobs or choose to do some work on a self-employed basis, as we will see later in this chapter.

DEMOGRAPHIC CONSIDERATIONS: MANDATORY VERSUS VOLUNTARY RETIREMENT.   The proportion of older people who retire has increased dramatically since the turn of the century. In 1900, approximately 60 percent of men over 65 were actively employed. By 1982, however, this figure dropped to 18 percent (Gottschalk, 1983; Schulz & Manson, 1984).

Some might attribute this decline primarily to mandatory retirement policies, which require an employee to retire at a specific age (e.g., 65 or 70). However, the empirical evidence indicates otherwise. In 1970 the Age Discrimination in Employment Act was amended to prohibit mandatory retirement before age 70 in most sectors of the economy. Surprisingly, however, this did *not* produce a substantial increase in the number of older workers. In fact, between 1970 and 1983, the percent of men aged 65 to 69 in the labor force decreased from 39 percent to 25.5 percent. A decline also occurred for men 60 to 64 years old, from 73 percent to 57 percent. (See Table 9.2.) Thus, even though adults are now able to work for more years than ever before, more and more are opting for **early retirement.** Only about 4 percent to 7 percent of those who retire are compelled to do so against their will because of age (Parnes & Nestel, 1981; Reno, 1971; 1972; Schulz, 1974).

Apparently, then, mandatory retirement does *not* force many well-

TABLE 9.2   Percent of middle-aged and older men and women in the labor force, 1970 and 1983.

	Men		Women	
Age	*1970*	*1983*	*1970*	*1983*
40–44	94.6	95.0	52.1	68.3
45–49	93.5	93.5	53.0	65.3
50–54	91.4	88.7	52.0	58.3
55–59	86.8	81.0	47.4	48.0
60–64	73.0	56.8	36.1	33.6
65–69	39.0	25.5	17.2	13.9
70+	18.2	12.3	8.1	4.5

SOURCE: Atchley (1985, p. 177).

qualified and willing employees to leave work prematurely. We must therefore look elsewhere to ascertain the reasons for the increasing popularity of early retirement.

The Pre-Retirement Years

ATTITUDES TOWARD RETIREMENT.   Almost all working adults expect to retire someday, usually before age 65. The majority of young and middle-aged workers probably do not think about retirement to any great extent. However, most employees past age 45 who do speculate about retirement view it as positive and desirable (e.g., Fialka, 1983; Goudy, 1981; Prentis, 1980).

Some cross-sectional studies suggest that there is a significant negative relationship between age and attitudes to retirement. However, this finding is due to cohort effects rather than to aging: more recent generations are more accepting of retirement. In 1951, for example, the majority of steelworkers believed that retirement was justified only if an employee was physically unable to continue working. But by 1960, the same majority concluded that retirement is a benefit which they deserve for having worked for so many years (Ash, 1966). Of considerably more importance than age is the worker's financial status: the higher the income that one expects to receive during retirement, the more favorable are the attitudes toward this life event.

How prevalent are optimistic views of retirement? Approximately 67 percent of employed adults do *not* anticipate financial problems during retirement, even though they also expect retirement to reduce their incomes by up to 50 percent from preretirement levels (Atchley, 1985). Few employees take concrete action to ensure that their retirement income will be adequate; only about 4 percent to 8 percent of men aged 60 and older participate in formal retirement preparation programs (Beck, 1984; Harris & Associates, 1975; 1981). However, there is no indication that this lack of formal preretirement planning has any substantial impact on post-retirement well-being.

FACTORS AFFECTING THE DECISION TO RETIRE.   Since mandatory retirement policies affect only a very small number of employees, the decision to retire must most often be due to other reasons. These include the employee's job level and job satisfaction, age discrimination and employer pressures to retire, actual and self-perceived health, the expectation of a more enjoyable life, and the influence of one's family, friends, and coworkers.

Those who hold higher-level jobs tend to regard retirement more favorably because of their sound financial position, but are also more likely to postpone retiring because they find their work to be too enjoyable. As Dr. Charles B. Huggins, 81-year-old Nobel Prize-winner in physiology and medicine, put it: "Why should I retire as long as I love my work and can still do it well? I'm not a furniture mover, you know. . . . Research has always been my pleasure as well as my job. There is nothing that matches the thrill of discovery" (Klein, 1983). Employees with low-level jobs are also likely to put off retirement, but for reasons that are primarily financial. These workers favor retirement in theory, since their jobs are typically dull and routine, but they often cannot afford it because of their low income and poor pension plans. Consequently, middle-level employees are the ones most likely to choose early retirement. They tend to have adequate retirement programs, and don't enjoy their jobs enough to want to continue working past the minimum retirement age. (See, for example, Atchley & Robinson, 1982; Streib & Schneider, 1971.) A common expectation of these workers is that life will be more satisfying if they retire.

Age discrimination is also a factor in the decision to retire early, as we have seen. Employers may well refuse to hire qualified job applicants who are past middle age; or they may find various ways to let older workers know that their continued presence on the job is no longer desired, as by transferring them to less attractive positions or treating them with less respect and consideration. As a result, older employees and job applicants may reluctantly decide that early retirement is their only feasible option.

Since older workers do suffer declines in certain physical and physiological capacities, and since they are more likely to become disabled when they do sustain injuries on or off the job, some may be compelled to retire because they find that the job has become too demanding. Most men who opt for early retirement under Social Security cite health as their reason for doing so (Reno, 1971). However, this finding probably cannot be accepted at face value: to some employees, health is undoubtedly a more socially acceptable reason for retiring early than admitting that they just don't want to work anymore (T. H. Schulz, 1976.) For those who reach the normal retirement age of 65 or 70, health issues appear to have little effect on the decision to retire (Palmore, George, & Fillenbaum, 1982).

Family and peer pressures may also influence the decision to retire. Some spouses and children may want the employee to retire at an earlier age, while others may not. An adult who lives in a leisure community populated primarily by retirees may experience peer pressure to conform, while another employee who lives among full-time workers may face precisely the opposite pressures (Atchley, 1976).

AFTERWORD.   Some workers do choose early retirement because they sincerely believe that their health is inadequate, or because of employer, family, or peer pressures. Some are forced to retire because they have reached a specific age. We do not mean to minimize the plight of those who find their work to be psychologically or financially rewarding, yet who are compelled against their wishes to retire. Nevertheless, research evidence clearly indicates that retirement is most often a welcome, desired event. The majority of employees retire voluntarily because they expect to enjoy life more as a result, and because they anticipate few financial problems. In fact, more and more adults are choosing early retirement for these reasons. Let us now ascertain whether these positive expectations are likely to be realized.

Retirement and its Effects

PHASES OF RETIREMENT.   Some theorists have suggested that retirees tend to proceed through a series of distinct psychological and emotional stages (Atchley, 1976; 1982; 1985). Retirement may well begin with a euphoric and busy *honeymoon* phase, during which the individual eagerly tries to do many of the things that were ruled out by full-time work (such as extended travel). This intense activity may be followed by a period of letdown or *disenchantment*, especially if the individual's prior expectations of retirement were unrealistically positive.

> *DISENCHANTED WITH RETIREMENT.*
> Mr. A., a 64-year-old former data technician for the U.S. Postal Service, found that retirement was not the paradise he had expected. "I spent the first eight months [of retirement] fixing up my lawn and house," he observed. "Then I ran out of things to do." Similarly, Mr. D., a 68-year-old retiree, found that "three years of loafing were all I could take." (Long, 1983.)

These retirees must now take stock of themselves and their life situation, adjust to the realities of retirement, and seek out appropriate new activities. If this *reorientation* phase is successful, the retiree then settles into a predictable and generally satisfying *retirement routine*. Such retirees accept the limitations brought on by advanced age, keep busy to at least some extent, are self-sufficient, and manage their own affairs. Very few choose to isolate themselves from other people; most want to retain at least some social contacts, especially with their families (Chapter 8). But there are retirees who cannot resolve the reorientation phase successfully, and who remain in a state of disenchantment even after some years have passed.

Finally, some elderly adults become so ill that they can no longer function independently; they are more properly described as sick or disabled rather than retired (the *termination* phase). A few may instead terminate retirement by returning to full-time work.

The phases described above are not intended to represent an inevitable sequence. Some retirees may not experience some phases, or may encounter them in a different order. For example, death may claim a retiree before the termination phase is reached. Some retirees may not have enough money for the activities involved in a honeymoon period, and may therefore omit this phase. Several cross-sectional studies suggest that many retirees proceed directly from the honeymoon phase to the retirement routine, without suffering a period of disenchantment (e.g., Atchley, 1976; 1982). Other retirees may prefer to indulge in a period of *rest and relaxation* either immediately after retirement, or following the honeymoon period. This inactivity typically gives way to boredom and restlessness, however, whereupon the retiree enters the reorientation phase and must face the challenge of establishing a satisfactory daily routine.

Research evidence concerning this phase model is sparse and somewhat equivocal. Some tentative findings indicate that enthusiasm does tend to be high immediately after retirement, and that some degree of emotional letdown or reassessment is likely during the second or third year of retirement (Adams & Lefebvre, 1981; Ekerdt, Bossé, & Levkoff, 1985; Haynes, McMichael, & Tyroler, 1978). Other studies have failed to find any evidence of a honeymoon effect (Beck, 1982). Perhaps the most important inference to be drawn from the phase model is that some retirees ultimately experience strong and prolonged feelings of disenchantment, while many others do not. That is, some adults find it considerably easier to adjust to retirement than do others. Why is this so? How do successful retirees make this period more satisfying and rewarding? The answer appears to involve several important aspects of the individual's life style prior to retirement: financial status, degree of social and recreational activity, and health.

FINANCIAL EFFECTS.   Some early cross-sectional studies have suggested that retirement produces a substantial drop in income, so much so that the retiree's standard of living and satisfaction with life are adversely affected. However, this conclusion has now been shown to be inaccurate. One longitudinal, multivariate, and large-sample study analyzed data obtained from six extensive research programs, which spanned from 2 to 10 years and comprised a total of more than 23,000 men and women aged 45 to 70 and older. The results indicated that financial differences between retirees and those who are still working are due in large part to differences in the amount of preretirement income, rather than to retirement per se. Early retirement does have more of an adverse financial effect than later retirement, since the individual must usually accept a smaller income in order to begin to collecting benefits sooner. But when preretirement level of income is statistically controlled, most of the purported negative financial consequences of retirement turn out to be small or insignificant (Palmore, Fillenbaum, & George, 1984). Although there is a drop in income at retirement, the typical retired household is no more likely than the employed household to feel economically strapped or to draw upon savings (McConnel & Deljavan, 1983). As Sylvester J. Scheiber, the research director of the Employee Benefit Research Institute in Washington, D.C., has observed: "The idea that the word 'aged' is synonymous with 'poor' is a myth" (Gottschalk, 1983).

A similar conclusion has been reached by the President's Council of Economic Advisers, which recently reported that the financial status of retirees has improved markedly during the last thirty years. Most elderly people today live in homes that are paid for, with enough money to enjoy their leisure years (DeMott, 1985). In fact, due in part to the automatic cost-of-living increases in Social Security payments that began in 1974, America's senior citizens have received *greater* percentage increases in their average annual incomes during the past decade than did those below age 65.

FINANCES AND RETIREMENT: A TYPICAL EXAMPLE.
"I hear all these retired folks complaining that they don't have this and they don't have that," says Mr. H., a 74-year-old retired shipping clerk. "I'm not pinched. . . . My house is paid for. My car is paid for. Both my sons are grown up. I don't need many new clothes. Every time I go out and eat somewhere, I get a senior citizen's discount. This is the happiest period of my life. These are my golden years." (Gottschalk, 1983.)

The picture is by no means entirely bright, however. Those with lower-level jobs and poor fringe benefits may well find themselves in serious financial difficulty during retirement. This is particularly true for those who are low in education and/or have been the object of prejudice in the workplace, such as blacks and women:

AN ECONOMICALLY DISADVANTAGED RETIREE.
Mrs. B. is a black 72-year-old widow who lives in a senior citizen's housing project in Washington, D.C. She once worked as a janitor, a job that provided minimal retirement benefits. Now she barely scrapes by on her annual Social Security income of $3,800, plus $800 from her late husband's veteran's pension. "It's just terrible," she says. "So-

cial Security payments are so low that they don't even want you to have enough money to eat or to buy medicine. . . . Social Security benefits may go up $15, but the cost of everything I need has already gone up $15 or $20." (Gottschalk, 1983.)

Here again, however, preretirement characteristics rather than retirement per se were primarily responsible for Mrs. B.'s financial difficulties. In fact, many low-level and minority group employees earn so little income that retirement has virtually no financial effect; their pay is essentially replaced by food stamps and other age-related income supports. As the authors of one longitudinal study concluded, "the presence of these supports, and the finding that retirement had no adverse effects on the [incomes of black men], forcibly indicates how low their work-related income must have been" (Fillenbaum, George, & Palmore, 1983).

In sum: while the aged were indeed an economically disadvantaged group some thirty years ago, this is no longer true. For this reason, some observers have become critical of Social Security. As *Time* magazine recently reported: "Providing decent living standards for the elderly puts a great burden on younger people. Today's workers are paying for benefits to retirees that far exceed contributions the retirees made during their working years. An individual who goes on Social Security [in 1985] has put about $50,124 into the system during his lifetime. If he gets the average 1985 payment of $594 a month, it will take seven years to recoup that" (DeMott, 1985).

However, there is another side to the story. Even as recently as 1984, older Americans had a lower economic status than other adults in our society. (See Figure 9.3.) Furthermore, the economic status of the elderly is far more varied than that of any other age group. While some older adults have substantial financial resources, a surprising number have practically none. Thus comparisons of average figures may well be misleading, with the high values for some retirees obscuring the fact that quite a few elderly adults are below or just barely above the poverty level (United States Senate Special Committee on Aging, 1986). Thus there is a significant number of elderly individuals who suffer serious financial problems during retirement.

Whether or not the younger generation is supporting the elderly to an unfair extent is a highly controversial issue. (See Figure 9.4.) The economic status of the aged is likely to remain a source of keen political debate. However, the stereotype of the elderly retiree who lives from hand to mouth on a meager fixed income, resides in a drab and dingy apartment, and struggles desperately to secure the bare necessities of life must be emphatically rejected in light of the available research evidence.

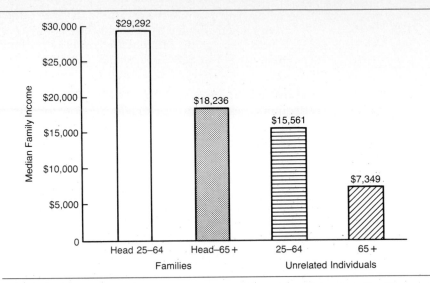

FIGURE 9.3   Median family income as a function of age for families and for unrelated individuals (1984). (Source: United States Senate Special Committee on Aging (1986, p. 41).

ACTIVITY VERSUS BOREDOM.   Here again, the general picture is an optimistic one: the majority find retirement to be a busy and satisfying period. In particular, those individuals who developed satisfying hobbies and recreational activities prior to retirement are most likely to enjoy their years away from full-time work. However, those who had few avocations during their working years may well find that retirement is disenchanting and depressing. Thus a county coordinator of adult and community education in Florida observes: "Our biggest battle is loneliness. A lot of people dream about paradise. They sell their homes and move here. After the drapes are up and the carpets are down, paradise can turn into a living hell if they don't find something to do" (Long, 1983).

Those retirees who do become bored and disenchanted may seek to resolve their problems by joining a senior center and developing new interests. Or part-time work may prove to be an effective and rewarding way to keep busy. One Florida retirement community is filled with elderly gas station attendants, grocery store baggers, retail clerks, and owners of small businesses. Most of these older adults are paid at or near the federal minimum of $3.35 per hour, yet they value this opportunity to be active.

We may conclude that there is a close relationship between an individual's preretirement and retirement life styles. Those who begin retirement with many avocational (or vocational) activities that

THE WAR BETWEEN THE GENERATIONS

BY JOSEPH A. KING

Not long ago, while waiting on line at our local movie theater, I tuned in to the conversations of the people around me. Ahead were two couples—in their late 60s, I think—chatting about their grandchildren, tax-free municipal bonds and, at one point, the expensive Gucci bag one of the ladies was clutching. Behind me several students who attend the college I had taught at for 21 years talked about the horrendous cost of textbooks, the fare increase on the Bay Area Rapid Transit and their inability to find a decent one-bedroom apartment for less than $500 a month.

The ticket office opened. The two elderly couples—who, I gathered from my eavesdropping, lived in the luxury retirement community of Rossmoor in Walnut Creek—stepped up and paid $2.50 a ticket: half price. Having just turned 60, I qualified for the discount, too. The youngsters behind me paid the full $5.

This minor incident got me to thinking about the old and the young in America and about some inequities in our system. I am a recently retired person and, though not yet 65, I already receive substantial discounts at restaurants and theaters. In a few years I will get a double exemption on my income tax and a 90 percent discount on our public-transit system. My income from pension and investment is several times above the poverty level and growing. My mortgage payment is $128 per month, a trifle, on a 30-year note, at 6 percent with 10 years to go. My four children have completed college, are out on their own, and my disposable income now far exceeds what it was when my wife, Betty, and I were raising them. The government, the capitalist establishment and the Good Lord have been magnificent to us.

King taught English at Diablo Valley College in Pleasant Hill, Calif., for 21 years. He retired last May.

I do not think that Betty and I, or the well-to-do couples who preceded us into the movie theater on discounted tickets, are an insignificant segment of that class of people deceptively and plaintively labeled "senior citizens" in political debate. History has never been kinder to us. We have lots of money. In 1984 the poverty rate of those 65 and over was 12.4 percent and lower than the national average of 14.4 percent. We have lots of votes. Few politicians dare irritate us; aspiring young ones pander to us. We are a formidable political lobby.

Nasty backlash: We also have one of the most effective public advocates on our side—the venerable Claude Pepper, Democrat of Florida. A liberal of the old New Deal school who has served 38 years in the Senate and the House of Representatives, always as a spokesman for the underdog, Claude Pepper has been a hero of mine for a long, long time. I deplored his loss of a Senate seat after a Red-baiting campaign during the McCarthy era. I cheered his resurrection as a member of the House. But now his activities worry me. With triple-focus glasses, two hearing aids, a pacemaker in his chest and a plastic valve in his heart, he is promoting a bill that prohibits mandatory retirement at 70. At 85 the chairman of the powerful Rules Committee, member of the Select Committee on Aging, fiercely defends federal supports for senior citizens even as young heads of households with mortgage payments of $1,000 per month try their damnedest to get a solid footing in the work force and to raise their families. Even as college students with marginal incomes pay increased transit fares for the privilege of sitting next to Rossmoor residents in Guccis who pay 10 cents on the dollar. Even as a fifth of all American children live in households below the poverty line.

What really worries me is the distinct possibility, indeed the inevitability, of a nasty backlash by the young against the old. This backlash awaits only the emergence of ambitious politicians willing to set one generation against another. I fear they will find a field ready for demagogues to conquer—troops of young people who have much justice on their side. For the liberal assumption that most old folks are poor and needy has become only a half-truth.

Legal responsibility: Those who wage war against the heartless oppressors of the aged will remind us, for sure, that there is a large number of really poor seniors who exist on pitifully small pensions, social security and supplemental-security-income allowances. Yes, their number is great, but I also know that many are also beneficiaries of outside resources, especially in the form of unreported help from their children. They have no legal responsibility to support their parents, yet many children do so generously if surreptitiously, so that seniors can have it both ways: aid from the state and gifts.

The larger picture is not one of the young voluntarily helping the old, but of the transfer of income to the elderly. The fact is that 12 percent of the population, those 65 and over, receives 50 percent of all government expenditures for social services. We seniors end up with the cash, the disposable income, while our progeny are taxed and shortchanged. This is certainly a turnabout, something rather new, I think, in a society which believes that each generation should do better than the one before.

I'm uncomfortable about accepting all the perks that come to me, stashing increasing amounts of disposable income in banks and investments, cheering for Claude Pepper and deciding in kingly fashion just how much largesse should be bestowed on children working hard to pay $500 per month for one-bedroom apartments. No, I won't be able to vote for the Party of the Young. I have interests to defend. Yet I wonder if we are being well served by Claude Pepper and other advocates of the status quo. Would not more help be available for the real poor—old and young— if so many perks and exemptions did not go to the affluent?

Senior Benefits

Bravo! It is a pleasure indeed to find a senior citizen like Joseph King who demonstrates some empathy for those of us who have not yet reached retirement age (MY TURN, April 14). We do not share the perks of the elderly and are compelled to struggle with a system that places a heavy burden on middle-income working families.

CAROL WELLS
Carson City, Nev.

Joe King is still living in his ivory tower. Senior citizens from an affluent retirement community in California are not typical of the entire country, and he is naive to think he'll be able to exist comfortably for another 25 years with inflation. Wait until he's assessed $3,000 per month for a good nursing home.

HARRIETTE WETSEL
Akron, Ohio

While the aged are the primary beneficiaries of social security and Medicare, these social-insurance programs are intergenerational and *all* Americans benefit from their success. They help young and old, rich and poor alike. Thus, social security helps relieve children of the financial burden of caring for aging parents while providing parent independence and dignity in their retirement years; it also provides children with benefits when they survive the death of a contributing parent. Finally, because such support programs bind families together when health or economic security are threatened, if there is a backlash it will be one of young and old against Reagonomics, not young and old against each other as King fears.

CLAUDE PEPPER, *Chairman*
House Select Committee on Aging
Washington, D.C.

As I wax creative with rice and vegetables for my family of four the night before payday, it irks me to think that the FICA deduction from tomorrow's check might be going to a couple living in a $500,000 house a mile away. I'd begrudge my loss of that money less if I knew it was going to one of the thousands of single mothers living below the poverty level.

CATHARINE BEECHER
Phoenix, Ariz.

I have no pension. As a registered nurse, I came out of the war with battle stars and a husband who divorced me when I was 57. King lives in another world, cushioned and protected. I resent his generalizations about the affluent elderly.

DOROTHEA M. FASSETT
Southgate, Mich.

As a product of the Depression, I saved all my life for an independent retirement. I worked 41 years and when I retired, 18 years ago, I thought I'd saved enough to maintain my standard of living. Not so! My dollars are now worth around 30 cents and my standard of living has been going steadily downward.

FRED D. CROWTHER
Oxford, Md.

Has King seriously considered the plight of those older people for whom an occasional movie at discount prices is probably the only affordable diversion? For most of them, a movie at regular prices would be unthinkable, let alone a concert or a show. A discount might make it possible to buy that can opener so

badly needed for arthritic hands, or to take that bus trip, or to buy necessary medication.

MARIANNE BRACHMAN
Waterbury, Conn.

King's statistics are deceiving. Most retired people live on fixed incomes that shrink when prices rise and interest rates drop. Furthermore, they spend a disproportionate share of their income on rapidly rising medical costs and supplemental health insurance.

JULES BRANDELL
Shorewood, Wis.

As a comfortable young retiree, Joe King fails to realize that poverty is prevalent among the very old. His life expectancy is another 20 years and he'd do well to stop flaunting his affluence and put some of his income back into his savings pool.

RICHARD L. MELA
Essex, Conn.

Most senior benefits are derived from paid-in social-security taxes deposited over a very long period of time. The return of these funds that the government is paying out with one hand is being taxed back with the other. As for "perks," King's choice of the word is unfortunate. What perk does a low subway fare provide? The incentive to become old?

GILBERT KIVENSON
Canoga Park, Calif.

FIGURE 9.4   The financial status of the retired: Conflicting opinions. *Newsweek* (April 14, 1986, p. 8; May 5, 1986, pp. 11–12, 14).

they want to pursue are likely to find this time of life to be full and rewarding. Conversely, those with few hobbies and non-job social activities during their working years may well find that they have far too much time on their hands during retirement. (Compare with the discussion of the stability of personality during adulthood in Chapter 7, and the social life styles of the elderly in Chapter 8.)

HEALTH.   Early cross-sectional studies also suggested that health is likely to be adversely affected by retirement. Here again, however,

Those who develop satisfying hobbies prior to retirement are more likely to enjoy their years away from work, as with this retiree's interest in Bonsai gardening. *John Maher/Stock, Boston*

these findings have been largely contradicted by more recent longitudinal studies. As discussed previously, poor health after retirement may well be caused by deteriorating health before retirement. Some workers exaggerate their health problems in order to have a more socially acceptable reason for seeking early retirement. And declines in health may be due simply to advancing age, rather than to retirement; ill health is one of the stressful life events that we are more likely to encounter as we grow older (Chapter 10). In actuality, retired people are no more likely to be sick than are people of the same age who are still working (Streib & Schneider, 1971; see also Ekerdt, Baden, Bossé, & Dibbs, 1983; Haynes, McMichael, & Tyroler, 1978).

There are individuals who do retire in reasonably good health, only to deteriorate thereafter. Yet such cases tend to be balanced by those wherein there is an *improvement* in health after retirement because the individual is no longer subjected to stressful, unhealthy, or dangerous working conditions. In fact, in one longitudinal study, some 38 percent of a sample of 263 men claimed that retirement

Myths About Aging: Work and Retirement

MYTH	*BEST AVAILABLE EVIDENCE*
Most middle-aged and older adults are poor employment risks. Compared to young adults, they do inferior work, have poorer attitudes because they are more set in their ways ("you can't teach an old dog new tricks"), and more often become injured or ill.	There are some jobs where age-related decrements in performance are found, such as those requiring certain perceptual and memory tasks (Chapters 4 and 5). In general, however, there is no indication that older workers perform more poorly on most jobs, or that they are more likely to suffer from low morale. Older workers are *less* likely than young adults to be injured on the job, although they are more likely to become disabled and to take longer to recover when an injury or illness does occur.
A woman's primary role is to have children, so those who choose instead to pursue full-time careers will find their adult lives to be significantly less fulfilling.	Women who pursue full-time careers are no less (or more) happy with their adult years than are those who opt for motherhood.
Since work is so important to us, retirement is likely to cause severe psychological trauma or even an early death.	Most people adjust reasonably well to retirement, and do *not* experience serious psychological or physical trauma because they have left the world of full-time work.
Mandatory retirement policies cause widespread dissatisfaction, since many adults would work past age 65 or 70 if allowed to do so.	Very few workers are adversely affected by mandatory retirement policies. Most employees retire voluntarily, and more and more are opting for early retirement.
Most elderly retirees live in near-poverty, reside in drab apartments, and have great difficulty acquiring even the bare necessities of living.	While there are important exceptions, the majority of retirees live in homes that are paid for and have enough money to enjoy themselves during retirement.

Because retirement causes husband and wife to spend so much more time together, it produces a substantial increase in marital strife.	There is no indication that retirement causes signficantly more marital problems for most retired couples.
Most retirees relocate to such places as Florida and Arizona.	Only a small percentage of retirees change their residences because of retirement.

had a positive effect on their health (Ekerdt, Bossé, & LoCastro, 1983; see also Minkler, 1981; Palmore, Fillenbaum, & George, 1984).

All in all, the evidence does *not* indicate that retirement exerts a significant negative effect on the physical and mental health of the retiree. In particular, there is no justification whatsoever for the sterotype of retirees who suffer severe psychological breakdowns, or even an early death, because they are no longer needed at a full-time job.

MARITAL DIFFICULTIES.   Another myth about retirement is expressed in the saying, "I married you for better or for worse, but not for lunch." That is, the extensive contact between husband and wife during retirement is believed by some to bring a substantial increase in marital tension and strife. For example, the director of a Florida mental health clinic concluded that marriages sometimes develop strains under the pressure of the enforced togetherness that retirement brings. "For the first time in their lives," he noted, they have to eyeball each other 24 hours a day" (Long, 1983).

In many instances, however, the relationship between husband and wife improves after retirement. The spouses are now able to enjoy mutual recreational activities, and they have time for caring and communication that may not have existed during the working years. This appears to be more true for middle-class and upper-middle-class couples, where the wife is likely to welcome her husband's retirement and increased involvement in household tasks. But in working-class marriages, the wife is more likely to expect and to value exclusive control over the household. When her husband uses some of the extensive free time created by retirement to participate in household chores, she may well become irritated because her domain has been invaded (Kerckhoff, 1966). Alternatively, preretirement factors may play a significant role. An increase in marital strife may occur after retirement only because the marriage was an unhappy one to begin with, and neither spouse enjoys the idea of having to spend more time with the other. In sum: there is no strong evidence that retirement has an adverse effect on the marriages of most elderly couples.

CHANGES IN RESIDENCE.   Another common belief is that most adults change their residence soon after retirement. In actuality, migration rates decline substantially from age 25 onward and rise only slightly at retirement (Wiseman, 1978). Retirement meccas such as those in Florida and Arizona would seem to command a disproportionate amount of media attention, perhaps because of their extremely high densities of older adults. Yet only a very small proportion of retirees move to such communities; the overwhelming majority do *not* relocate (Atchley, 1985).

Afterword

Some studies purport to show that retirement has a severe adverse effect on income, physical and mental health, life satisfaction, self-esteem, and marital harmony. However, these studies all too often overlook the possibility that the people in question had such problems even before they retired. More carefully controlled longitudinal studies indicate that the effects of retirement are considerably more positive. Retirement does bring a drop in income, but this often involves little or no change in the retiree's standard of living. Although there are exceptions, retirement does *not* in general cause ill physical or psychological health, feelings of uselessness and depression, dissatisfaction with life in general, declines in self-esteem or increased marital strife. Some jobs are not intrinsically satisfying, and some employees do not mind retirement because they value the extrinsic aspects of work more highly. Or some employees who do enjoy the intrinsic aspects of their jobs may decide that 40 years of work is quite enough, and that it is time for a new life style. While there are those who continue to work into their seventies and beyond, retirement has become a respected and desirable life event in our society. The majority of adults welcome it as an earned reward for their many years of work, and retire voluntarily in order to pursue other activities.

The plight of those individuals who do suffer severe financial and emotional problems during retirement is a painful one, and their problems should not be underestimated. Future research in this area may profitably focus on identifying and assisting those who are likely to experience such difficulties. But the empirical evidence clearly indicates that the lot of most retirees has improved dramatically during the last three decades; few lead impoverished lives, either financially or socially. Retirement is most often a positive and welcome event, one that opens the way to a rewarding and busy twilight of the human life span.

Summary

WORK AND ADULT DEVELOPMENT

For most of us, work provides the income necessary to support ourselves and our families. Work may also be interesting for its own sake, contribute to our self-esteem and sense of identity, and provide important social rewards and punishments. Thus work exerts a significant effect on the quality of our lives and overall well-being in two major way: intrinsically and extrinsically.

Aging appears to have little detrimental effect on job performance in some professional and artistic fields. For example, artists and musicians often do their best work late in life. Conversely, the most productive years for mathematicians and professional athletes occur during their twenties and thirties. However, the research evidence in this area is equivocal. The most justified conclusion appears to be that age often bears little or no relationship to job performance, but that some exceptions may be expected in certain jobs and professions.

There is some indication that young adults are more concerned with chances for advancement, and for professional and personal development, than are middle-aged and older workers. In general, however, the relationship between aging and job satisfaction is far from clear. While the data are too equivocal to permit any firm conclusions, there is no convincing evidence that older workers tend to be less satisfied with their jobs than young adults.

Older workers are less likely than young adults to be injured on the job, or to be absent. But when they do sustain an injury, they are more likely to be disabled and to require more time to recover.

Even though many older adults are as competent and as satisfied as young employees, and even though federal legislation prohibits the denial of employment to those over 40 because of their age, severe age discrimination still exists in the workplace. This is due in part to negative sterotypes about older workers, who are more likely to be incorrectly perceived as resistant to change, slow to make decisions, and untrainable. Also, pensions and other fringe benefits for older workers are more costly to the employer.

Some theorists have argued that midlife career changes are becoming increasingly common, but there is little statistical evidence to support this conclusion. When such career changes do occur, they are most often caused by such external pressures as losing one's old job.

The study of work and aging is more problematical than might be expected. Job satisfaction and productivity are multidimensional variables, and chronological age provides only limited information about human capacities. Such age-related variables as job level and job complexity appear to be more closely related to job satisfaction and performance than age per se. To discriminate against employees over 40 solely because of age is not only illegal and harmful to the individual, but is also likely to cost the organization valuable and productive workers.

There are significantly more men than women in the labor force, but the percent of women has increased substantially during the last half century. Women have made considerable inroads into some occupations once dominated by men. They have not done nearly as well with regard to managerial and administrative positions, and their income has remained at only about 64 percent of what men receive.

Some theorists have argued that the difficulty of various jobs should be rated numerically, so that men and women can be assured of comparable pay for comparable work. Other theorists point out that while there is still sex discrimination in the workplace, women have hurt their own chances for advancement and higher pay by willingly discontinuing their work in order to bear and raise children. They conclude that the fairest course is to allow pay to fluctuate freely in accordance with supply and demand. Given the difficulty of evaluating the demands made by different jobs, it appears unlikely that an effective system for determining comparable worth will be forthcoming in the near future.

Women who elect to pursue full-time careers are no less (or more) satisfied with their adult years than are women who opt for motherhood and raising a family. Married women who work enjoy better mental health than those who do not, but are also more likely to experience interrole conflicts. In the majority of couples, women still have primary responsibility for family matters, so those who elect to combine work and family roles may find it difficult to meet their obligations in both areas. While sex discrimination remains a significant problem in the world of work, the influence of women has increased considerably during the past four decades and is likely to continue to do so in the future.

RETIREMENT

A retired person is one who is not employed at a full-time paying job *and* who receives at least some income from a pension earned through prior employment. The proportion of older people who retire has increased dramatically since the turn of the century. While it is often assumed that mandatory retirement policies compel many people to leave work sooner than they would like, this belief is not supported by the empirical evidence. In fact, more and more people are opting for early retirement.

Most employees past age 45 who speculate about retirement view it as positive and desirable, and regard it as a reward which they deserve for having worked for so many years. Nor do most adults anticipate financial problems during retirement. Those who hold higher-level positions tend to regard retirement more favorably because their financial position is sound, but are also more likely to postpone retiring because they find their work to be too enjoyable. Employees with low-level jobs are likely to favor retirement in theory, since their jobs tend to be dull and routine, but they often cannot afford to retire early because of their low income and poor pension plans. Thus middle-level employees are the ones most likely to opt for early retirement, since they tend to have adequate retirement programs but don't enjoy their jobs enough to want to continue past working age. A common expectation of these workers is that life will be more satisfying if they retire. Age discrimination, family and peer pressures, and health are also factors in the decision to retire early. However, the importance of health may well be exaggerated: to many employees, health is undoubtedly a more socially acceptable reason for retiring early than admitting that they just don't want to work anymore.

Some theorists have suggested that retirees tend to proceed through a series of distinct psychological and emotional stages, such as a honeymoon effect, disenchantment, rest and relaxation, reorientation, the retirement routine, and termination. However, the research evidence concerning this model is sparse and somewhat equivocal. Perhaps the most important conclusion is that some retirees ultimately experience strong and prolonged feelings of disenchantment, while many others do not. This appears to depend in large part on the individual's life style prior to retirement. Those who tended to have adequate finances, numerous satisfying hobbies and recreational activities, good health, and happy marriages prior to retiring are likely to find it considerably easier to adjust to retirement and to enjoy these years. Those with poor finances, few avocations, ill health, and unhappy marriages before retiring may well find that retirement is disenchanting and depressing.

In general, the majority of elderly adults find retirement to be a satisfying and busy period. The financial status of retirees has improved markedly during the last thirty years, and the sterotype of the elderly retiree who lives from hand to mouth on a meager income and who resides in a drab and dingy apartment must be rejected in the light of the available research evidence. Many retirees find that leaving the world of full-time work gives them time to pursue desired activities that was not previously available, although some find it necessary to accept low-level part-time jobs in order to keep busy. There is no indication that retirement per se exerts a significant negative effect on the physical and mental health of the retiree, or that it has an adverse effect on the marriages of most couples.

The plight of those who do suffer serve financial and emotional problems during retirement should not be underestimated. But retirement is most often a positive and welcome event, one that opens the way to a rewarding and busy twilight of the human life span.

PART IV

Crises and Problems

CHAPTER 10

Stress and Coping

A capable college student becomes so tense during an important examination that she cannot recall even the simplest facts, and turns in a blank paper. A college football team needs to win its final game to earn a bowl invitation, trails by two points late in the game, and fights its way down to the opponent's goal line, only to have its normally reliable field goal specialist kick the ball so low that the defense blocks it easily. An employee who must deal every day with irascible customers and a demanding supervisor, but who cannot find another job or afford to quit, develops intense stomach pains.

Stories about the adverse effects of stress on human beings are virtually a daily occurrence in the news media. We hear about major traumatic events that result in serious physical or mental disorders; we read about certain types of work that are considered so stressful as to cause physical illnesses; we find that some athlete's performance was subpar because he or she experienced too much stress. However, stress need not always be disadvantageous. A student who is too nonchalant about a forthcoming exam may fail to prepare adequately, and receive a poor grade. Or a top-rated football team may be so relaxed for a game with an inferior opponent that they suffer an ignominious defeat. While too much stress may well be injurious, too little may result in lackluster and inferior performance.

Nevertheless, the debilitating effects of excessive stress are of primary concern in today's society. There exist across the land numerous programs designed to teach people how to cope with stress. Many self-help books claim that heart attacks, depression, anxiety, hypertension, and other health problems can be avoided by changing our life styles in ways that will reduce stress. And a thriving pharmaceutical industry dispenses vast quantities of anti-anxiety medications, such as Valium and Librium. Thus stress is widely regarded as a major disrupting force in the lives of individuals of all ages, and concern with this problem appears to have reached epidemic proportions.

What might this imply about the course of adult development? Conceivably, life may become more stressful with increasing age. Adults must typically contend with such new and demanding situations as work, marriage, raising children, divorce, the death of a loved one, and, eventually, retirement and old age. However, the opposite hypothesis is also a reasonable one. That is, we may well become more sure of ourselves as we grow older, and more established in work and family roles. The security provided by this firmer foundation in life, and increased maturity, may render us less vulnerable to those sources of stress that we encounter.

In this chapter, then, we will examine empirical data dealing with stress and coping during adulthood. We will begin with a brief historical tour of the development of scientific interest in stress research, which will illustrate the diverse approaches used by various theorists. We will then define the concept of stress by presenting and discussing a general theoretical model. We will conclude by examining the relationship between aging and stress, with emphasis on those sources of stress typically encountered during the adult life course and ways of coping with them.

The Scientific Study of Stress

Historical Background

FIGHT OR FLIGHT.   The scientific study of stress is a relatively recent phenomenon. Early in the twentieth century, Walter Cannon observed that animals must respond quickly to life-threatening challenges in the environment in order to survive. Depending on the specific circumstances, the appropriate reaction might be to fight (as when faced with an opponent of lesser stature) or to flee (if menaced by a vastly superior enemy). Accordingly, Cannon characterized the standard response to danger as the **fight-or-flight** reaction. He showed that it is associated with the activation of specific aspects of the central nervous system, which result in increased cardiac output, heart rate, and arterial pressure (Cannon, 1929). Thus Cannon was among the first to investigate the effects of threatening external stimuli on an organism's behavior.

THE GENERAL ADAPTATION SYNDROME.   Undoubtedly the most prominent researcher in the field of stress and coping is Hans Selye.

He dates the origin of the concept of stress to an experience he had in 1936, as a student of medicine at the University of Prague. Selye attended an introductory lecture on diagnosis presented by a famous hematologist, von Jaksch, who questioned five patients suffering from unrelated maladies. Without using any complicated instruments or chemical examinations, von Jaksch correctly diagnosed each of the patients. While Selye was impressed by this demonstration, he was also puzzled by the fact that von Jaksch

> [had not] said a word about all those signs and symptoms of disease which were perfectly obvious even to me, without previous knowledge of practical medicine . . . All five patients, whatever their disease (one suffered from cancer of the stomach, another from tuberculosis, yet another from intense burns) had something in common: *they all looked and felt sick.* This may seem ridiculously childish and self-evident, but it was because I wondered about the obvious that the concept of *stress* was born (Selye, 1983, p. 3)

Later, while attempting to discover a new sex hormone, Selye observed that laboratory rats given multiple doses of a crude ovarian extract developed such symptoms as gastric ulcers and enlargement of the adrenal gland. On investigating further, he found that crude extracts from other organs, extreme cold or heat, pain, and infectious agents all produced similar results. He therefore concluded that organisms exposed to a noxious stimulus of any kind exhibit the same pattern of responses. To Selye, this **General Adaptation Syndrome** consists of three stages:

1. The Alarm Reaction. When an organism is confronted with a stressful situation, the immediate reaction is alarm. This represents a general call to arms of the body's defenses, and is accompanied by such typical symptoms of injury as excessively rapid heartbeat (tachycardia), loss of muscle tone, decreased temperature, and decreased blood pressure.

2. The Stage of Resistance. During this stage, the body tries to limit the effects of the stressful situation. The symptoms evidenced during the first stage diminish or disappear, and the organism is prepared for either fight or flight.

3. The Stage of Exhaustion. If the choice between fight or flight proves to be unsuccessful in reducing stress, the organism loses its ability to adapt to the situation and enters the stage of exhaustion. This can result in tissue breakdown, or even in death.

Each of these stages is accompanied by specific physiological changes. During the alarm reaction, for example, the cells of the adrenal cortex discharge secretory granules into the bloodstream. Conversely, during the stage of resistance, the cortex becomes rich in secretory granules. According to Selye, if these physiological changes do not occur, the organism is not experiencing stress.

In his later work, Selye (e.g., 1974) made two important additional contributions. He pointed out that not all stress is bad; in fact, too little stress can also have negative effects. Thus the moderate stress that may help a student or athlete to perform well must be distinguished from excessive stress, which is damaging because the organism cannot cope with the situation and enters the stage of exhaustion.

Selye also observed that stressful situations affect different individuals differently, depending on their biological makeup, age, training, dietary deficiencies, and other factors. For example, some athletes seem unusually able to rise to the occasion and perform well when the game hangs in the balance, while others are more likely to "choke" under pressure and commit grave errors. Or a job that drives one employee to stomach ulcers may be handled with relative calm by another worker.

Although Selye's work represents a landmark in the study of stress, it does suffer from some significant shortcomings. (See, for example, Elliott & Eisdorfer, 1982; Stotland, 1984.) One of these concerns his definition of stress, which suffers from circularity: a stressful event is defined as whatever evokes the General Adaptation Syndrome, and the occurrence of this syndrome is what tells us that an event is stressful. In fact, arriving at an acceptable definition of stress is far from an easy task—as we will see in the following section.

The Problem of Defining Stress

As was the case with *intelligence* (Chapter 6) and *personality* (Chapter 7), there is no single definition of **stress** that is widely accepted by researchers in this field.

STIMULUS DEFINITIONS.   One possible way to define stress is in terms of the external situation: a difficult and all-important examination, a demanding supervisor, and so forth. Thus Cannon focused on those dangerous stimuli that disrupt the organism's normal internal processes, while Selye's early research defined stress in terms of the noxious stimulus that evokes the General Adaptation Syndrome.

Although this approach is appealingly simple, it fails to recognize the importance of the organism's behavior. A demanding supervisor may be regarded as a mere annoyance by one employee, yet be perceived by a second worker as exerting enormous pressure. A forthcoming examination may cause one student considerable anxiety, while another student reacts with relative calm. Some people exhibit marked signs of stress when they travel by plane, while others do not. In each of these examples, the stimulus object or situation is the same, yet it is considerably more stressful for some individuals than for others. Therefore, some theorists prefer to conceptualize stress in markedly different ways.

RESPONSE DEFINITIONS.   A second approach is to label the potentially stressful stimulus or situation as the **stressor**, and to define stress in terms of the organism's **responses.** Thus Selye ultimately concluded that stress exists if and only if the General Adaptation Syndrome occurs, together with the expected physiological changes (which are supposedly the same for any and all noxious stimuli).

However, this approach has also been criticized as inadequate. There is some evidence that different stressful situations, such as public speaking and physical exercise, produce at least some bodily changes that are markedly different (Mason, 1974). It has also been suggested that an event can be stressful even if no physiological changes are immediately apparent. Furthermore, Selye's conception overlooks the importance of the individual's cognitions: how we interpret a given situation may have much more to do with the degree of stress that we experience than does objective reality. Some data indicate that if a stressor is not viewed as noxious or alarming, it produces physical responses that are negligible or even opposite to those predicted by Selye (Mason, 1971; see also the discussion of cognitive theories of personality in Chapter 7).

MORE COMPREHENSIVE DEFINITIONS.   In an effort to resolve the difficulties described above, some investigators have opted for a more comprehensive approach. They define stress in terms of the entire complex of stressors, responses (including physiological changes, cognitions, expectations, and perceptions), and related intervening variables or **mediators.** (See, for example, Lazarus, 1966; 1971.)

As an illustration, suppose that you hear footsteps approaching from behind. This stimulus may or may not be a stressor, depending in part on your cognitions and expectations: do you think that this is a mugger coming to attack you, or a friend or spouse planning to surprise you with a warm welcome? The degree of stress also depends on such mediators as the location and time of day: are you safely in your home with only your spouse present, or anxiously hurrying down a dark and deserted street at 3 A.M.?

As a second example, consider the stimulus of a failing grade on a college midterm examination. This event will be more stressful if the student appraises it as a disaster that cannot be overcome, but less stressful if it is perceived as only a minor setback or as a challenge to do better in the future. Mediators that may increase the degree of stress include pressure from one's family to achieve straight *A*'s, having goals that require an unusually high grade-point average (e.g., wishing to apply to medical school), or needing a passing grade in this course to avoid flunking out of school.

AFTERWORD.   Each of the approaches discussed above has been praised by some theorists, and criticized by others. However, the inclusion of cognitions and mediators in the definition of stress would seem to have distinct advantages. In particular, this helps us to understand why different individuals react differently to the same stressor. Therefore, we will focus on the comprehensive definition in the pages that follow.

A General Model of Stress

The relationships among the various components of stress are shown in Figure 10.1. Notice that with one exception, these relationships are bidirectional. For example, some stimuli may cause such responses as fight or flight, while some responses (e.g., cognitions) help to determine whether or not a stimulus is stressful. A stressor may ultimately lead to physical (or psychological) debilities, while a heart or stomach that has been weakened by stress can make one more vulnerable to subsequent external pressures. Thus stress operates in a circular and dynamic fashion, with each of the components continuously modifying and being modified by the other elements. (See Elliott & Eisdorfer, 1982.) For purposes of discussion, however, it is necessary to treat these components one at a time.

STRESSORS.   Some stimuli are much more likely to act as stressors than others. Few people would experience stress from a peaceful walk alongside a serene lake, with the sun shining and cool breezes blowing. Conversely, more than a few would find the following to be stressful:

External Pressures and Overstimulation. If you are required to achieve a level of performance that is very difficult for you, or to behave in ways that run counter to your strongest convictions, you

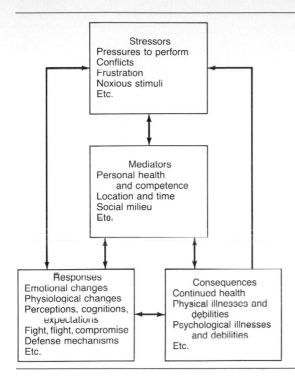

FIGURE 10.1 A general model of stress. Modified from Elliott & Eisdorfer (1982, p. 19).

may well experience considerable stress. This is particularly true if the pressures continue for a substantial period of time. Common examples include an unusually demanding job, college course, parent, or Army drill sergeant. However, such pressures are not always from without. Some people create considerable stress for themselves by establishing goals which they think are reasonable, but which are actually far too demanding and perfectionistic.

Boredom and Understimulation. External pressures are among the best-known sources of stress. Yet while we all welcome some opportunity to relax and take life easy, having nothing to do for too long can also be stressful. Some people enjoy facing a challenge, improving their skills, and achieving difficult goals, and cannot tolerate a succession of tasks that are too easy. Others welcome the excitement of risky vocations or avocations, such as tightrope walkers, test pilots, parachute jumpers, hang-gliders, automobile racers, and those who like to take rides on roller coasters. Thus stress and frustration can be caused by external demands and pressures that are too low, as well as those that are too high.

The loss of a loved one is a major source of stress; such statistically non-normative events as the death of a son in the military are even more so. *Mike Douglas/Image Works*

Conflicts. Stress may result from having to make difficult and painful decisions, wherein each alternative has serious drawbacks as well as advantages. For example, young men during the 1960s who opposed the Vietnam War had to choose between two very unpalatable alternatives. They could submit to the draft, and possibly risk their lives in what they regarded as a bad cause, in order to remain in good social standing; or they could avoid combat by going to prison. (Some sought to escape from this "avoidance-avoidance conflict" by emigrating to other countries, thereby incurring the pain of leaving their homes and loved ones.) Or a conflict may arise because the same object or goal has both positive and negative qualities (an "approach-avoidance conflict"). Thus a shy person may want to approach an attractive stranger and ask for a date, yet also fear the possibility of rejection and ridicule. A military commander may have to send men on a mission that is extremely important, but also likely to result in a very high casualty rate. Or a hungry laboratory rat may have to run through an electrified grid, and receive a moderately painful shock, in order to reach a food reward. Since either approaching or avoiding the goal is both desirable and undesirable, some discomfort is inevitable. The greater the strength of the conflicting alternatives, the greater the stress that is likely to result.

Frustration and Disappointment. Stress may also occur when our needs and wishes are frustrated, either by obstacles in the external world or by our own limitations. Examples include being turned down for a job or promotion because another applicant is superior, or because one lacks the necessary skills; losing a loved one, or a valued possession; extended periods of hunger, which are far from uncommon in various parts of the world; and a laboratory rat deprived of food, or of maternal attention. The greater the disappointment, or the longer the period of deprivation, the more stress one is likely to experience.

Noxious Stimuli. Stress can also be caused by exposure to such noxious stimuli as cold, heat, pain, and infectious agents. Alternatively, a noxious stimulus may be psychological rather than physical. For example, in marked contrast to tightrope walkers and test pilots, some people break out in a cold sweat when standing on a balcony that is only a few stories high. The more intense the stimulus, the greater the probable stress.

"A Martyrdom of Pinpricks." Numerous minor stressors that occur during the same period of time may have a cumulative effect, and produce considerable stress. An individual who accidentally rips a button off a shirt while hurrying to dress for work in the morning, finds an unexpected small dent in the family car, gets caught in moderate rush-hour traffic, and discovers that the coffee machine is out of order on arriving at work may react to this series of relatively trivial aggravations by becoming extremely upset. If, instead, one must deal with several major stressors at about the same time, such as losing one's job, the death of a loved one, and a serious illness, the effects may well be devastating.

Some of the more common stressors are summarized in Table 10.1. Once again, it is important to remember that these stimuli are only *potential* sources of stress. Their effect on a given individual depends in part on the other components of the model: responses, consequences, and mediators.

RESPONSES.   The importance of such responses as fight or flight, cognitions and expectations, and physiological changes was discussed previously in this chapter. For example, you will probably experience less stress if:

• You believe that you can handle a given situation without much difficulty.

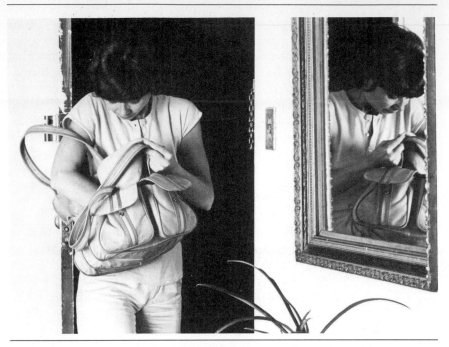

Major disasters are not the only causes of stress. Numerous minor stressors that occur during the same period of time, such as losing one's keys, may have a cumulative effect that results in considerable stress.   *Joel Gordon*

- You appraise the situation as a challenge that will enable you to improve your skills or gain desired rewards, or as a welcome source of excitement, rather than as a threat of harm or loss.

- You are able to attack and overcome your opposition.

- You can escape from a threatening or unpleasant stimulus.

There is a third alternative to the fight-or-flight dichotomy posited by Cannon, namely compromise or surrender. Rather than attacking or fleeing, you might agree that the best course is to obey the dictates of someone else. If you can do so without sacrificing important needs, or your self-esteem, you may well achieve a relatively stress-free solution.

Unfortunately, many stressful situations cannot be resolved so easily. Suppose once again that an employee who has an unpleasant job cannot afford to quit, dare not risk being fired by fighting with the boss, but also cannot surrender to demands that seem excessive

TABLE 10.1 Stressors commonly used in animal and human research.

Animal Research	Human Research	
	Experimental Stimuli	Natural Events
Approach-approach conflicts (having to choose between two positive objects)	Approach-approach conflicts	Bereavement
	Approach-avoidance conflicts	Changes in status (e.g., job, salary, marriage)
Approach-avoidance conflicts (being presented with an object that has both positive and negative qualities)	Avoidance-avoidance conflicts	Conflicts
	Electric shock	Daily "hassles"
	Loss of prestige	Frustration
Avoidance-avoidance conflicts (having to choose between two negative objects)	Noise	Migration
	Overstimulation	Physical illness (including surgery and hospitalization)
Competition	Sleep deprivation	Pressure to perform or achieve
Electric shock	Threatening, unpleasant films	Retirement
Exposure to cold	Uncontrollable situations	Social isolation
Exposure to heat	Understimulation	Threats to self-esteem
Exposure to novel stimuli		Traumatic experiences
Food deprivation		
Handling		
Immersion in ice water		
Immobilization		
Maternal deprivation		
Prolonged forced swimming		
Sensory deprivation		
Sleep deprivation		
Social crowding		
Social isolation		

SOURCE: Modified from Elliott & Eisdorfer (1982, pp. 14, 16).

and unfair. As has been shown by Freud and others, we may well try to make such bad situations more tolerable by unconsciously or (less often) consciously adopting various psychological **defense mechanisms.** Thus we may refuse to admit even to ourselves that a situation is far too stressful ("denial of reality"), and blindly continue on a course that is damaging to our health. Or we may direct our anger at a safer target, such as a spouse or family pet, instead of the boss ("displacement"). There are many such defense mechanisms, all of which provide a temporary measure of emotional relief. (See Table 10.2; Ewen, 1985, pp. 26–32.)

Though we all use defense mechanisms from time to time, they may well make matters worse in the long run. Since they conceal the truth from oneself, they preclude an effective solution to the problem; and since their operation is usually unconscious, the user cannot readily discard them in favor of a better course of action. Thus, while our thoughts and expectations may make a situation more stressful, it is also possible to encounter stress without being consciously aware of it. That is, we may flee from stress psychologically as well as physically.

CONSEQUENCES.   The responses evoked by stressors may have various long-term **consequences.** These include physical disorders, such as stomach ulcers, colitis, or headaches; psychological disorders, such as frequent anxiety or depression; or perhaps continued good health, if the level of stress is neither too high nor too low.

As elsewhere in this model, the relationship between responses and consequences is bidirectional. That is, consequences can also make certain responses more or less likely. Thus a physical or psychological debility may lead to more pronounced physiological changes when under stress, or to the greater use of defense mechanisms.

It is not always easy to distinguish between responses and consequences. The latter tend to occur some time after the stressor, whereas responses are more immediate. Also, consequences are more clearly identifiable as good or bad. Fight, flight, compromise, and even the defense mechanisms are not necessarily desirable or undesirable in and of themselves. Rather, it is the consequences of these responses that we typically assess as positive or negative. For example, fighting or confrontation may rectify a major social injustice, or injure an innocent party or destroy a marriage. Running away may save the life of someone threatened by a wild animal in a forest, or cost the lives of one's fellow soldiers in battle. Expecting to do well on a task may lead to better performance, or to overconfidence and failure. Compromise and surrender may enable one to profit from the superior plans and ideas of someone else, or lead to staggering violations of moral and ethical behavior. Thus the German soldiers who helped run concentration camps during World War II typically sought to excuse their heinous deeds, and reduce stress, by arguing that they were "only following orders."

TABLE 10.2 Some common defense mechanisms.

Defense Mechanism	Definition	Example
Denial of reality	Refusing to believe, or even to perceive, some threat in the external world.	A person receives criticism that is clearly justified, but believes that it is wholly erroneous and due to prejudice.
Displacement	Transferring feelings or behaviors, usually unconsciously, from one object to another that is less threatening.	A person angry with the boss remains quiet at work, and then releases this anger by shouting at his or her spouse.
Fantasy	Gratifying unfulfilled needs by imagining situations in which they are satisfied.	A poor child pretends to be an All-American football player.
Identification	Reducing painful feelings of self hate by becoming like illustrious objects or people.	A socially unpopular or lonely person dresses like a famous rock music star.
Intellectualization	Unconsciously separating threatening emotions from the associated thoughts or events.	A patient in psychotherapy discusses his or her painful problems in a dry voice, devoid of feeling.
Overcompensation	Unconsciously attempting to make up for a deficiency in one area by excelling in another, and carrying this to damaging extremes.	A person who is very short, or who suffers from extreme self-hate, becomes a warmonger or dictator.
Projection	Unconsciously attributing one's own threatening impulses, emotions, or beliefs to other people or things.	A person who is murderously angry, but who finds this too threatening to accept consciously, believes that others are out to get him or her.
Rationalization	Using and believing superficially plausible explanations in order to justify illicit behavior, and reduce feelings of guilt.	People who cheat on their tax returns or school examinations justify themselves by arguing that "everyone does it."
Reaction formation	Unconsciously adopting the opposite of one's true	A person who has homosexual desires, but

(Continued)

TABLE 10.2   Some common defense mechanisms.

Defense Mechanism	Definition	Example
	(but highly threatening) beliefs, emotions, and impulses.	who finds this too threatening to face consciously, becomes an outspoken crusader against homosexuality.
Regression	Unconsciously adopting behaviors typical of an earlier, and safer, time in one's life.	An adult faced with a traumatic life event, such as a painful divorce, becomes childishly dependent on his or her parents.
Repression	Unconsciously eliminating threatening material from one's mind, and being unable to recall it on demand.	Despite intense effort, an adult cannot remember the strong anger felt toward his or her parents during childhood.

MEDIATORS.   As noted previously, mediators help us to understand why the same stressor has different effects on different people. Common mediators include one's personal competence, physical health, and ability to ward off illnesses and external threats; the physical setting, such as location and time of day; and the social milieu, as with the support or lack of support provided by one's immediate family.

AN ILLUSTRATIVE EXAMPLE: ENVIRONMENTAL DEMANDS AND PERSONAL COMPETENCE.   As a further illustration of the general model, let us consider once again the potentially stressful effects of external pressures.

Some environments are more demanding than others, and are more likely to evoke symptoms of stress. The relationship between this potential stressor and an individual's responses is mediated by **personal competence:** some people are considerably more capable than others, and are better able to deal with more extreme levels of pressure. Furthermore, people tend to be more competent in some respects than in others. Thus an athlete who can make quick and highly skilled physical movements, but who is not overly high in verbal or mathematical ability, may experience more stress during a classroom examination than on the football field. Personal competence is a multidimensional variable; it includes biological health, ego strength, cognitive skills, and sensorimotor functioning. To determine the likelihood that a given situation will be stressful, we must therefore consider the types of skills that are required and the individual's competence in these areas.

One interesting theoretical model that deals with these relationships is depicted in Figure 10.2. Consider first the individual whose life situation corresponds to Position Number 1 (high personal competence and moderate environmental stress). Suppose that this individual is a middle-aged man, who lives in an area with a high crime rate. He is physically agile, however, and his self-confidence is very high. Because of these competencies, his response to his demanding environment is markedly positive: he goes about his business despite the risks, and actually enjoys his self-image as a courageous individual who will not be cowed by the young toughs in his neighborhood (Lawton, 1980).

Person Number 2 is much less competent than Individual Number 1. Yet both are equally free of emotional strain, and both per-

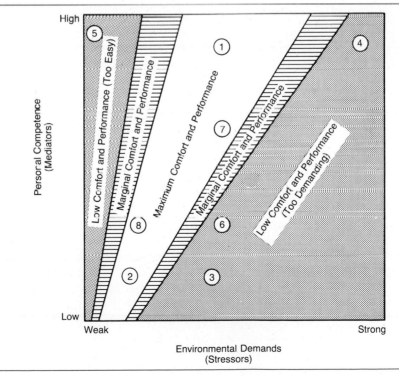

FIGURE 10.2 Environmental demands, personal competence, and stress. Modified from Lawton (1980, p. 12).

form up to the limit of their respective capabilities, because they are both well suited to their environments. That is, much fewer demands are made on Person Number 2. Placing the second individual in the environment of the first one would produce considerable stress, emotional disturbances, and a breakdown in performance (Position Number 3).

No matter how high your personal competence may be, there is always the possibility of encountering so much stress that your behavior will deteriorate markedly; everyone has a breaking point. Person Number 4 is extremely competent, but is under so much pressure that she responds as adversely as Individual Number 3. Person Number 5 illustrates a point made previously in this chapter, namely that experiencing too little pressure for too long can also be stressful. The area of this section is considerably smaller than that of the section at the extreme right, however, indicating that people are more likely to suffer from too many environmental demands than from too few. For both persons Number 4 and Number 5, some of the possible consequences of experiencing so much stress include depression, social withdrawal, and/or the loss of self-respect and self-confidence.

How does this model concern aging? Suppose that as Individual Number 1 grows toward old age, his personal competence decreases to Position Number 6. (Research evidence indicates that this is more likely to be the exception than the rule, but is true for some elderly adults. See, for example, Lawton, 1980.) His environment has not changed, but he no longer has sufficient competence to deal with it effectively, so he is likely to show symptoms of stress. He might therefore undergo training designed to improve his personal competence, possibly increasing it to a level that will once again make the environmental demands tolerable (Position Number 7). If his decline in competence is irreversible, or if he does not wish to undergo such training, he could instead move to a less stressful environment (Position Number 8). Other common ways of achieving a temporary reduction in environmental demands are simply sitting back and relaxing for awhile, or taking a much-needed vacation.

Although the model depicted in Figure 10.2 is logically appealing, further research is needed to evaluate its practical and predictive utility. After you develop ulcers, colitis, or a severe depression, it is easy to argue that your personal competence was poorly matched to the demands of your environment. But it is very difficult to predict in advance whether a given level of environmental demands, together with a particular level of personal competence, will or will not prove to be stressful. Nevertheless, the model does help to clarify the relationships between stress, environmental demands, and personal competence. It also illustrates once again that stress must

Chapter Glossary: Stress and Coping

Consequences	Effects of stressors that are further removed in time than responses, and are more clearly identifiable as good or bad.
Coping with stress	Using thoughts (conscious or unconscious), and/or actions, in order to eliminate or at least reduce the demands made by a stressor.
Defense mechanism	A method for reducing anxiety, and restoring a measure of self-esteem, that is usually (but not always) unconscious. Thus we may flee from stress psychologically (i.e., by concealing the truth from ourselves) as well as physically
Emotion-focused coping	Coping with stress by trying to achieve an emotional acceptance of the existing situation.
Fight-or-flight reaction	The tendency to resolve a stressful situation by either attacking or escaping. (In actuality, there is also a third alternative: compromise or surrender.)
General Adaptation Syndrome	According to Selye, a pattern of responses which occurs whenever an organism faces a threatening or noxious stimulus. Consists of three stages: the alarm reaction, the stage of resistance, and the stage of exhaustion.
Mediators	Variables which affect the relationships among stressors, responses, and consequences.
Personal competence	A multidimensional variable that includes such characteristics as biological health, ego strength, cognitive skills, and sensorimotor abilities.
Problem-focused coping	Coping with stress by taking action intended to resolve, or at least modify, the existing situation.
Responses	More immediate reactions to stressors, which are not in and of themselves desirable or undesirable. Includes fight, flight, or compromise; cognitions, expectations, and perceptions; physiological changes; and the defense mechanisms.
Stress	A complicated phenomenon involving the interrelationships among stressors, responses, consequences, and mediators. Typically, there is some threat or demand that affects one's inner stability.
Stressor	A stimulus that is likely to impose some demands, or some degree of threat, on an individual.

| Type A individual | A person characterized by intense ambition, competitiveness, aggressiveness, and perfectionism. Such individuals are more likely to suffer heart diseases and an early death. |
| Type B individual | A person who is relatively easygoing, rarely impatient, and not overly competitive or preoccupied with achievement. Type *B* individuals may be just as serious and successful as Type *A* individuals, but are less prone to heart disease. |

be understood in terms of stressors, responses, mediators, and consequences.

AFTERWORD.   In the preceding pages, we have seen that stress is not a simple phenomenon. Stressors may cause certain kinds of responses, or responses may cause certain stimuli to be more or less stressful. A response may lead to desirable or undesirable consequences, or a particular consequence may make certain responses more or less likely. Some people find a given stimulus to be quite stressful, while others do not. And some mediators affect the relationships among the other components of the model. Thus it is virtually impossible to make simple statements that are also accurate, like "situation *X* is always stressful" or "stressor *A* invariably leads to response *B*."

We cannot expect any one research study to deal with all (or even most) of this ever-changing, interrelated system. Of necessity, stress researchers typically simplify matters by studying one aspect of the model at a time. With this caveat in mind, let us now proceed to examine the evidence concerning the relationship between stress and aging.

Stress and Aging

The Effects of Major Life Events

METHODOLOGICAL ISSUES.   To reduce the study of stress to manageable proportions, some researchers prefer to focus on the effects of major life events. It is reasonable to hypothesize that events like marriage and divorce are at least somewhat stressful, even though different individuals may well respond in different ways, and that some of these events are more stressful than others. Accordingly, some investigators have sought to quantify the amount of stress caused by various life events (Holmes & Holmes, 1970; Holmes &

Rahe, 1967; Rahe & Arthur, 1978). The most stressful of all events, the death of a spouse, is arbitrarily assigned a rating of 100. The degree of stress associated with other events is then estimated relative to this standard, based on responses obtained from test populations. For example, divorce is accorded an intensity rating of 73; marriage, 50; and trouble with one's boss, 23. (See Table 10.3.) If you have been exposed in recent months to events that sum to 300 or more, it is estimated that the probability of your developing a major illness within the next two years is as high as .80.

The numerical scale shown in Table 10.3 is commonly cited in textbooks and articles. Yet it is controversial, and has been strongly attacked on methodological grounds. This scale implies that stressful life events, notably those with high intensity ratings, *cause* such undesirable consequences as major illnesses. However, some of these life events may well *result from* existing disorders. (Recall once again that in the general model of stress, the relationships between potential stressors, responses, consequences, and mediators are primarily bidirectional.) Having sexual difficulties or more arguments with one's spouse, or being fired at work, could be due to an underlying psy-

Even joyful events, such as marriage, may be significant sources of stress. Some investigators regard marriage as more stressful than being fired from a job, although this is a complicated issue that also depends on such personal factors as age and competence. *Hazel Hankin*

TABLE 10.3   Stressful life events: The social readjustment rating scale.

Life Event	Scale of Impact	Life Event	Scale of Impact
Death of spouse	100	Trouble with in-laws	29
Divorce	73	Outstanding personal achievement	28
Marital separation	65		
Jail term	63	Wife begins or stops work	26
Death of close family member	63	Beginning or ending school	26
Personal injury or illness	53	Change in living conditions	25
Marriage	50		
Fired at work	47	Revision of personal habits	24
Marital reconciliation	45	Trouble with boss	23
Retirement	45		
Change in health of family member	44	Change in work hours or conditions	20
Pregnancy	40	Change in residence	20
Sex difficulties	39	Change in schools	20
Gain of new family member	39	Change in recreation	19
Business readjustment	39	Change in church activities	19
Change in financial state	38	Change in social activities	18
Death of close friend	37	Small mortgage or loan	17
Change to different line of work	36	Change in sleeping habits	16
Change in number of arguments with spouse	35	Change in number of family get-togethers	15
High mortgage	31	Change in eating habits	15
Foreclosure of mortgage or loan	30	Vacation	13
		Christmas	12
Change in responsibilities at work	29	Minor violations of the law	11
Son or daughter leaving home	29		

SOURCE: Holmes and Rahe (1967).

chological or physical illness. If this disorder then becomes more evident in subsequent months, it is clearly erroneous to conclude that an otherwise healthy individual was laid low by stress. (See Elliott & Eisdorfer, 1982; Siegler, 1980.)

This scale also focuses on those events that require us to make significant readjustments in our lives: learning to live without a spouse, moving to a new location or a new school, changing jobs, and so on. Yet stress can be caused by chronic conditions that do not necessitate personal change. For example, an employee may face a consistent overload or underload at work. No daily or monthly readjustment is involved, since the situation remains essentially the same, yet considerable stress may result. Or apparently minor daily hassles can accumulate to produce serious effects, as we have seen. These important sources of stress are not tapped by the readjustment scale.

Furthermore, this scale contains an overabundance of events that are more likely to befall young adults. The elderly are much less likely to get married or divorced, take out a mortgage, change their schools, be confined to jail, or switch to a different line of work, to cite just a few examples. Suppose, then, that gerontological studies based on this scale find that these life events occur much less frequently with increasing age. While this might conceivably mean that the elderly lead relatively stress-free lives, it more probably reflects the youth-oriented emphasis of this particular set of events (Goldberg & Comstock, 1980; Kasl, 1983; Rabkin & Struening, 1976). Some researchers have sought to remedy this problem by developing a geriatrically oriented scale of recent life events (Kiyak, Liang, & Kahana, 1976), but this measure has not become popular among gerontologists.

Finally, such numerical scales of stress may well sacrifice too much accuracy in order to gain simplicity. For example, the degree of stress caused by trouble with your boss is influenced by various mediators. If your skills are in great demand, and you have many possible job opportunities, this life event will probably be much less stressful than if you cannot afford to quit or be fired. Or pregnancy, and the gain of a new family member, may be much more stressful to an unmarried teenager than to a happily married 30-year-old woman. Therefore, expecting these potential stressors to have intensities of 23 and 39 in all instances may well be a serious oversimplification.

One possible alternative is to collapse the various life events into four major categories: changes in personal relationships, changes in financial resources, changes in environment and location, and changes in health. Then, separate scores may be obtained for each category (Wilson & Schulz, 1983; see also Schulz, 1985). Conceivably, we might find that changes within each category are more extreme for the elderly. For example, a relationship change for a young adult might involve breaking up with a boy- or girlfriend, whereas an aged individual might more often have to face the death of a loved one. Or we might hypothesize that the elderly are more likely to experience threats from several categories, such as suffering financial losses and having to relocate to a nursing home.

Another intriguing alternative is to focus on those irritating and frustrating daily hassles that we all must contend with. (Recall our previous discussion of "a martyrdom of pinpricks.") A scale to measure this stressor has been developed by Richard Lazarus and his associates (Delongis et al., 1982). They found that daily hassles predicted the outbreak of psychosomatic diseases significantly better than did life events scores, possibly because they occurred closer in time to these consequences.

Despite the controversy that surrounds the use of numerical scales, both life events and daily hassles can be useful tools for assessing stress. Consider, for example, the death of a spouse from cancer or an automobile accident. Here, it is not very likely that some response or consequence of the surviving spouse caused this unfortunate event. Rather, it is more logical to assume that the stressful event caused various undesirable consequences. We may therefore ask: does the likelihood that we will encounter stressful life events and daily hassles change markedly as we grow older?

LIFE EVENTS AND AGING.   Growing old is widely believed to be quite stressful. Events such as retirement, widowhood, having all of one's children leave home, and failing health are more likely to occur during the second half of life. On the other hand, numerous other stressful life events are more likely to befall young adults (as we have seen). If the elderly expect certain events to be a natural aspect of old age (e.g., ill health), they may well suffer relatively little stress. Also, as we grow older, increased experience in living may make it easier to deal with stress.

What has empirical research evidence to say about this issue? In one study, young newlyweds showed *more* emotional stress than adults aged 50 and 60 (Lowenthal et al., 1975). Another study reported a relatively low incidence of stressful life events for 375 subjects, whose ages ranged from 45 to 70: in an eight-year period, 80 percent had not retired, 75 percent had no major illnesses, 94 percent had not been widowed, and 85 percent did not experience the last child leaving home (Palmore et al., 1979; see also Shanan & Jacobowitz, 1982). No comparison data were obtained from young adults, however.

Various research findings have associated changes in residence with negative consequences among the aged. In one study, patients were matched on such factors as age, sex, race, health, length of hospitalization, and ability to ambulate. Those transferred from one California institution to another had a significantly higher death rate than a control group that was not relocated (Killian, 1970). When patients who relocated from their homes to an institution were compared with patients transferred from another institution, the former group lived for an average of about one month less, presumably because they experienced a more severe environmental change (Schulz & Aderman, 1974; see also Horowitz & Schulz, 1984; Schulz, 1978). Here again, however, a life event like relocation may instead be caused by an existing physical or psychological illness—hence the need to control for level of health when trying to ascertain the effects of stress.

The relationship between expectations and stressfulness is supported once again by the research evidence in this area. As we observed in Chapter 8, life events are more likely to be stressful if they are temporally non-normative (i.e., if they occur at an atypical age). Not surprisingly, mortality rates for the widowed are significantly higher than for married controls matched on age and sex. However, there is a markedly lower rate of illnesses and death when widowhood occurs at older ages. This event is more easily anticipated when one is old, and may therefore be less stressful. An elderly widow is also more likely to have at least some friends who are widows, and who are willing and able to provide needed emotional support. Conversely, young widows tend to find themselves in so atypical a position that their friends do not know how to provide effective help. (See Kraus & Lilienfeld, 1959; McNeil, 1973; Morgan, 1976; Stroebe et al., 1982.)

In contrast to widowhood, divorce is *less* common among the elderly. Therefore, when the aged do have to go through a divorce, they typically experience more extreme suffering and illnesses than do young adults (Chiriboga, 1982). In fact, one extensive study of the widowed found that older men suffered much more following a divorce or separation than did those who lost a spouse through death (Hyman, 1983). Thus the stressfulness of a life event is significantly influenced by its temporal normativity.

Age-related differences have also been observed with regard to daily hassles. Middle-aged men tend to worry more about economic problems, such as rising prices and taxes, while young adults express more concern with social and academic difficulties (Delongis et al., 1982).

In sum: certain stressful life events are more likely to occur at different ages. (See Table 10.4.) Also, a life event is likely to cause considerably more stress if it occurs at an atypical age. Thus the relationship between aging and stress is not a simple one. Potential stressors like widowhood, ill health, and having to care for a disabled relative are *more intense* when they occur at younger ages, but are *more common* at older ages. Conversely, such potential stressors as divorce and one's first job are *more common* at younger ages and *more intense* at older ages.

TABLE 10.4   Aging and the likelihood of specific stressful
life events.

Some Events More Likely to Occur During the First Half of Life	*Some Events More Likely to Occur During the Second Half of Life*
Beginning or ending school	Having to care for a disabled relative
Beginning to work (first job)	Ill health
Divorce	Last child leaving home
Jail term	Relocation to a nursing home
Marriage	Retirement
Pregnancy	Widowhood and the death of friends
Taking out a mortgage	

POSITIVE LIFE EVENTS AND STRESS.   Stress is not due only to negative life events, like widowhood and divorce. As indicated in Table 10.3, such happy occasions as marriage, pregnancy, and a good new job are also common sources of stress. This has been attributed to the resulting dramatic changes in one's self-image and style of living:

STRESSED BY SUCCESS.

Mrs. J. was most embarrassed to be seeking the help of her university counselor. In the past few months, everything in her life had gone beautifully. She had just finished her doctoral dissertation, which her advisor regarded as outstanding. She had received an award as the best teacher-scholar at her university, and had lined up a publisher for the book she was writing. Though jobs were scarce, she had secured a position at an excellent Eastern university. Yet she felt very strange, like everything was unreal. She questioned whether she deserved this success, and wondered if she would wake up one day to find that it had all disappeared.

The counselor helped Mrs. J. to understand the reasons for her stress. Because of her new job, she would soon be moving to a new area, thereby losing the respect and support she received in her present community. Her previous self-image as "just a nice, average person" had been greatly exceeded by her successes, and it was frightening to abandon this old, comfortable, and predictable view of herself. Her success also meant a change in the relationship with her husband: previously she had moved because of his job changes, but now he was going to have to move because of hers. When she realized that her grief and anxiety about losing her familiar roles was natural and understandable, she was able to face her new situation with considerable pleasure. (Schneider, 1984. See also Berglas, 1986.)

Stress and Longevity

Is stress significantly linked with a shorter life span? If so, the aged may represent a relatively select and stress-resistant group. That is, suppose that those adults who do experience considerable stress are more likely to die at a fairly young age. Studies of the elderly will therefore fail to reveal an abnormal number of negative consequences, because many of the adults who would show such symptoms have been weeded out by death.

This important issue has been investigated by medical, psychological, and sociological researchers. A significant relationship has been found between stress and heart disease, with sudden cardiac death often preceded by several months of increased stress. There is some indication that such potential stressors as rejection by a loved one, a setback or continued emotional strain at work, or a loss of prestige increase the likelihood of coronary diseases. (See, for example, Jenkins, 1971; Russek, 1962; 1965; Sales, 1969; House, 1975.) As noted above, relocation has been linked with higher death rates among the elderly. Also, stressful life events have been related to the occurrence of suicide attempts (Dohrenwend & Dohrenwend, 1974).

As is now well known, individual behavioral styles mediate the levels of stress that we experience. The so-called **Type A individual** is characterized by intense ambition, competitiveness, aggressiveness, restlessness, and perfectionism. These are the people who make business calls while waiting in the dentist's office, rather than waste a single moment of time; frequently battle against self-imposed deadlines; are perceived by their spouses as driving themselves much too hard; prefer respect to affection; and treat life as a deadly serious game which they are out to win. The **Type B individual** may be equally serious, and just as successful. But these people are more easygoing, are seldom impatient, do not feel compelled by time pressures, and are less competitive and preoccupied with achievement. Although type theories may well oversimplify the nature of human beings (Chapter 7), this distinction appears to be a useful one: the incidence of coronary heart disease has been found to be two to three times greater among Type A individuals, and as much as six times greater for Type A men between the ages of 39 and 49 (Friedman & Rosenberg, 1959; 1974; Jenkins, 1974; 1975; Suinn, 1977). Thus the characteristics of Type A individuals apparently make them more vulnerable to potential stressors, and more likely to suffer such negative consequences as heart disease and an early death.

We may conclude that stress is associated with decreased life expectancy, particularly for middle-aged men who fit the Type A description. Therefore, the selective attrition caused by death may be

Myths About Aging: Stress and Coping

MYTH	BEST AVAILABLE EVIDENCE
Stress is always disadvantageous and debilitating, and should be avoided whenever possible.	Extreme stress can have debilitating effects. But too little stress can inhibit your motivation, and lead to lackluster and inferior performance. Some people enjoy facing a challenge, improving their skills, and achieving difficult goals; while others willingly seek out risky and stressful vocations or avocations. Stress may also facilitate personal growth and development, as when one learns to deal with disappointment and frustration.
The intensity of a stressor can be assessed by assigning it a single score that applies in all instances. For example, the death of a spouse is always more stressful than divorce.	A life event is likely to be more stressful if it is temporally non-normative. For example, the elderly are likely to find divorce even more painful than widowhood. Thus the intensity of a given stressor may well vary as a function of the age at which it occurs.
You will experience much more stress during the second half of your life than during the first half.	There is some truth to this idea, since some extremely stressful life events are more likely to occur during old age (e.g., widowhood, terminal illnesses). But the relationship between aging and stress is more complicated than this. Some traumatic life events are more common at older ages, but are more intense when they occur at younger ages. Other potential stressors are more common at younger ages and more intense at older ages.
As you grow older, your ability to cope with those stressful life events that you do face decreases markedly.	If your health, economic resources, and social resources decline as you grow toward old age, your ability to cope with stress may be compromised. But if these capacities remain more or less intact, there is no reason to expect your ability to cope with stressful life events to decline with increasing age.

another reason why the consequences of stress have not been found to be more severe among the aged.

Coping with Stress

Coping with stress refers to a particular class of responses: those thoughts (conscious and unconscious), and/or actions, which we use to eliminate or alleviate the demands made by a stressor.

AGING AND COPING ABILITY.   Does our ability to cope with stress decline as we grow older? If so, we should expect to find that negative consequences often occur for the first time at relatively advanced ages. However, this does not appear to be the case. For relatively normal older adults (i.e., those who do not have a history of serious physical or psychological disorders), stressful but temporally normative life events have *not* been found to cause significant personality changes or increases in maladjustment (Chiriboga, 1981; Costa & McCrae, 1980; Maas & Kuypers, 1974; Palmore et al., 1979). For those older adults who suffer from ill health, or from a significant decline in economic and social resources, the ability to cope with stress may be compromised. But there is no indication that more normal elderly individuals suffer any appreciable decrement in their ability to cope with stress.

AGING AND COPING PROCESSES.   When you are faced with a stressful life event, one possible course is to take action designed to resolve the troublesome situation **(problem-focused coping).** For example, if you discover that you have the symptoms of a potentially serious illness, you might seek out expert medical advice. If instead you must contend with a demanding parent or boss, you might choose among such task-oriented tactics as fight, flight, or compromise. That is, you may regard the stressful situation as a problem that can be solved by appropriate action.

Alternatively, you might try to achieve an emotional acceptance of the existing situation **(emotion-focused coping).** Faced with the possibility of a major illness, you might concentrate on maintaining a positive and optimistic attitude. Or you might prefer to put this issue out of your mind, perhaps with the aid of one or more defense mechanisms. The differences between the problem-focused and emotion-focused methods for coping with stress are further illustrated by the following self-report items and statements (Folkman & Lazarus, 1980; Schmitz-Scherzer & Thomae, 1983):

Problem-focused Coping	*Emotion-focused Coping*
"I got the person responsible to change his or her mind."	"I looked for the 'silver lining.'"
"I made a plan of action and followed it."	"I accepted sympathy and understanding from another person."
"I stood my ground and fought for what I wanted."	"I tried to forget the whole thing."
	"Well, maybe I am not too well off, but what can you expect for someone my age."
	"Even if I am bad off, there are many whose health is worse."

Is there a relationship between aging and the choice of coping procedure? Unfortunately, the data in this area are both sparse and somewhat equivocal. One study found that both problem-focused and emotion-focused coping were used in virtually all stressful situations, regardless of the age of the individual (Folkman & Lazarus, 1980). This may have been due in part to the restricted age range of the sample used in this study, which varied from 45 to 64 years. Had young and/or very old adults been included, age effects might well have been obtained. A tendency was found for older adults to encounter a greater number of stressful events that involved health issues, and fewer events that concerned their families or work. This suggests that emotion-focused coping may be more common among the elderly, since they are more likely to be faced with life events that cannot be successfully resolved by the problem-solving approach (e.g., incurable injuries or illnesses).

Evidence bearing on this hypothesis has been reported by Schmitz-Scherzer and Thomae (1983). They conducted a longitudinal study of some 222 German men and women, primarily from West Germany. The older cohort was born between 1890 and 1895, while the younger cohort was born between 1900 and 1905. The subjects were assessed on six separate occasions between 1965 and 1977, so the ages at the times of assessment varied from 60 to over 80. Among other measures, subjects were asked the extent to which they perceived various problem areas to be stressful. Over the 12-year period, health problems became considerably more prominent with increasing age; while family, economic, and housing problems either remained at about the same level or declined markedly. (See Figure 10.3.) The younger adults in this study were also more likely to use problem-focused coping (finding the best doctor or treatment; getting the most out of their health insurance), while the older adults relied more on emotion-focused coping (learning to accept their disabilities; revising their expectations of life accordingly).

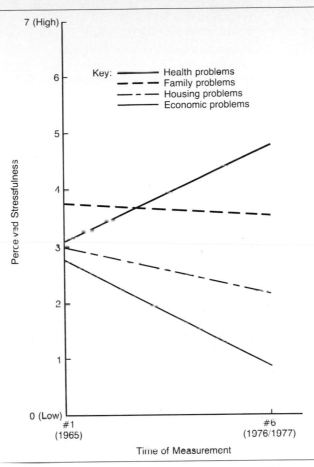

FIGURE 10.3   Stress caused by various problem areas for a sample of German adults. Modified from Schmitz-Scherzer & Thomae (1983, p. 211).

   In sum: both problem-focused and emotion-focused coping are commonly used to deal with stress. Emotion-focused coping may perhaps be more prevalent among the elderly, and this may well be an adaptive solution in view of the kinds of stressors that they most often face.

DEVELOPING COPING SKILLS THROUGH PSYCHOTHERAPY. Some adults may be too overwhelmed by anxiety, or too lacking in essential skills, to make effective use of either problem-focused or emotion-focused coping. For example, consider once again the student who becomes so anxious during an examination that she forgets even the simplest information. Or a man may become unreasonably angry about minor annoyances, thereby adding to the problem instead of resolving it.

Difficulties like these are often amenable to formal psychotherapy. The following case history illustrates how behavior therapy can help clients improve their ability to cope with stress:

> *TEST ANXIETY AND SYSTEMATIC DESENSITIZATION.*
>
> Miss C., a 24-year-old art student, repeatedly failed her examinations because of marked anxiety. To improve her ability to cope with this stressor, she sought help from a behavior therapist.
>
> Miss C. was first taught techniques of deep muscular relaxation, which involved successively tensing and relaxing the various muscles of her body in a sequence predetermined by the therapist. She was then asked to construct an "anxiety hierarchy," in which the feared stimuli are listed in order of the amount of anxiety evoked. Thus she specified the most anxiety-provoking item as going to the university on the day of the examination, the next most feared item as beginning to answer the exam questions, the third most feared item as the moment just before the doors to the examination room opened, and so on down to a fourteenth and least anxiety-provoking stimulus (learning that the exam was scheduled for a date one month in the future).
>
> Miss C. was then asked to imagine the bottom (fourteenth) stimulus in the hierarchy, while practicing the techniques of deep relaxation. After this had been well learned, she practiced relaxing while imagining stimulus Number 13, and gradually proceeded up the hierarchy until she could relax while imagining the topmost situation. This required some thirty therapy sessions, and proved effective when tested in the arena of real life: four months later, she passed her examinations without anxiety. (Wolpe, 1973, pp. 115–116.)

(For a formal definition and discussion of this and other methods of psychotherapy, see Chapter 11.)

Afterword

Stress is a significant problem in our society. It is experienced by adults of all ages, and it is associated with higher illness and mortality rates, especially among middle-aged "Type A" men.

The relationship between aging and stress is a complicated one, and involves various important issues. What potential stressors are most likely to be salient during young adulthood, middle age, and old age? What mediators cause different people to respond to stressors in different ways? How do adults of different ages cope with stress? How can we best deal with potential stressors, so as to minimize the probability of negative consequences? What methods of psychotherapy should be used to help adults improve their coping skills? As we have seen throughout this chapter, gerontological researchers and social scientists have discovered many important answers to these questions. Given the current interest in the scientific study of stress, we may expect further valuable findings to be forthcoming within the next decade.

Summary

THE SCIENTIFIC STUDY OF STRESS.

Walter Cannon was among the first to investigate the effects of threatening external stimuli on an organism's behavior. He characterized the standard response to danger as the fight-or-flight reaction. Modern investigators have added a third alternative to Cannon's dichotomy, namely compromise or surrender.

Undoubtedly the most prominent name in the field of stress research is that of Hans Selye. He concluded that organisms exposed to a noxious stimuli of any kind exhibit a three-stage pattern of responses, which he called the General Adaptation Syndrome. He also argued that stress occurs if and only if each stage is accompanied by specific physiological changes, a contention that has been challenged by modern researchers. Selye pointed out that too little stress can also have negative effects, and that individual differences play an important role in the response to stressful situations.

Selye's definition of stress suffers from circularity: a stressful event is whatever evokes the General Adaptation Syndrome, and the occurrence of this syndrome is what tells us that an event is stressful. However, it is not easy to arrive at an acceptable definition of stress. Some theorists have defined stress solely in terms of the external situation, or solely in terms of the organism's responses, but these approaches overlook important considerations. Accordingly, some investigators prefer to define stress in terms of the entire complex of stressors, responses, mediators, and consequences. This approach more readily enables us to understand why different individuals react differently to the same stressor. It also emphasizes that the relationships among the various components of stress are primarily bidirectional: stress operates in a circular and dynamic fashion, with each of the components continuously modifying and being modified by the other elements.

Among the more common stressors are external pressures and overstimulation, boredom and understimulation, conflicts, frustration and disappointment, and noxious physical and psychological stimuli. Important responses include physiological changes, emotional changes, expectations, cognitions, perceptions, fight, flight, compromise, and the psychological defense mechanisms. The possible negative consequences of stress include such physical and psychological disorders as anxiety, depression, stomach ulcers, colitis, headaches, and coronary diseases. Or, if the level of stress is neither too high nor too low, good health and performance may result. Common mediators include personal competence, physical and psychological health, the physical setting, and the social milieu. For example, personal competence mediates the relationship between the stressfulness of one's environment, responses, and consequences.

Stress is not a simple phenomenon. It is virtually impossible to make simple statements that are also accurate, like "situation X is always stressful" or "stressor A invariably leads to response B." Of necessity, therefore, stress researchers typically simplify matters by studying one aspect of this phenomenon at a time.

STRESS AND AGING.

It is reasonable to hypothesize that certain life events are stressful to varying degrees, even though different individuals may well respond in different ways. Some investigators have sought to quantify the amount of stress caused by various life events, but such scales have been strongly attacked on methodological grounds. The relationship between aging and stress is complicated, and is affected by the temporal normativity of the life event. Some stressful events are more common at advanced ages but more intense when they occur at younger ages, while others are more common at younger ages and more intense at older ages.

Stress is associated with coronary and other diseases, and with a decreased life expectancy. The likelihood of suffering a stress-related illness that leads to death is greater for middle-aged men who fit the Type A description. Thus the selective attrition caused by death may be another reason why the consequences of stress have not been found to be more severe among the aged.

For those adults whose health, economic resources, and social resources remain reasonably intact, there is no indication that the ability to cope with stress declines with increasing age. Both problem-focused coping and emotion-focused coping are typically used in stressful situations. Some studies suggest that the elderly rely more on emotion-focused coping, however, perhaps because they must more often contend with situations that are not amenable to the problem-focused approach (e.g., incurable illnesses or injuries). Some adults may be too overwhelmed by anxiety, or too lacking in essential skills, to make effective use of either problem-focused or emotion-focused coping. Often, formal psychotherapy can help these individuals improve their ability to cope with stress.

Gerontological researchers have investigated various important issues: determining those stressors most likely to be salient at different ages, identifying important mediators, ascertaining how adults of different ages cope with stress, and using various psychotherapeutic methods to help adults improve their coping skills. The scientific study of stress has produced much valuable information in these areas, and is likely to continue to do so in the foreseeable future.

CHAPTER 11

Adult Psychopathology

During the past decade, mental health researchers have reported some disturbing findings. Some 15 percent of all Americans are believed to suffer from various forms of psychopathology, ranging from mild to severe. It is also estimated that an additional 10 percent have experienced some of the symptoms typical of emotional disorders, such as depression and anxiety. When we transform these percentages into head counts, the implication is staggering: more than 30 million people in the United States have mental problems that are serious enough to require professional help, while an additional 20 million are troubled to some extent by psychological disturbances. In fact, mental/emotional illnesses incapacitate more people than *all* other health problems combined. (See Coleman et al., 1980, pp. 3–4; Kiesler, 1983.)

Because psychopathology often originates during childhood, many noted psychologists and psychiatrists have concentrated their professional attention on the early years of life. Currently, however, social scientists are taking a greater interest in adult psychopathology. With so many more of us living into our sixties, seventies, and beyond, two issues have become increasingly important. First of all, what happens to those individuals who do develop mental health problems early in life? Are these disorders likely to be resolved at some point during adulthood, perhaps with the aid of formal psychotherapy? Or, since personality tends to remain stable during adulthood (Chapter 7), should we expect such difficulties to persist into old age? Secondly, are there neuroses or psychoses whose onset typically occurs at an advanced age? For example, if you are a young adult with no prior history of mental disorder, are you likely to suffer so much organic brain deterioration on reaching old age that you can hardly function? Or will you tend to retain your psychological health and vigor?

There has also been a growth of interest in the treatment of adult psychopathology. Whereas some mental health professionals still contend that anyone past the age of 40 or 50 cannot be helped by psychotherapy, numerous others are actively working with the aged. It has also been shown that some illnesses which are amenable to treatment, such as depression, have been mistaken for similar but incurable diseases like Alzheimer's (Wolinsky, 1983). Important discoveries like this, and the resulting improvements in diagnostic techniques, are making it possible to alleviate the anguish of many more elderly patients.

In this chapter, then, we will examine the empirical evidence dealing with adult psychopathology and psychotherapy. We will focus on the most important varieties of adult psychopathology, the continued frequency with which they occur at various ages, and appropriate methods of treatment.

Varieties of Adult Psychopathology

The Problem of Classification: DSM-II, DSM-III, and DSM-III-R

Classification is an important aspect of every science, including psychology. Before we can arrive at meaningful explanations of human behavior, we must first organize what would otherwise be an overwhelming amount of data into a convenient framework.

One popular system for classifying the various forms of psychopathology is **DSM-II,** the 1968 version of the *Diagnostic and Statistical Manual of Mental Disorders* prepared by the American Psychiatric Association. DSM-II is a revision of a system first used by the United States Army during World War II, and includes many terms which have become familiar to the general public (e.g., "obsessive-compulsive neurosis," "anxiety neurosis," "paranoid schizophrenia"). These categories do conveniently summarize important symptoms and patterns of behavior, and facilitate better communication among those interested in psychopathology. Unfortunately, DSM-II has proved to suffer from several significant defects.

Most importantly, all too many patients have symptoms which do *not* fall within one specific DSM-II classification. The typical case history spans several categories, such as "considerably obsessive-compulsive with some paranoid behaviors and fairly high anxiety." Furthermore, psychologists and psychiatrists have generally been unable to match particular forms of treatment with specific DSM-II disorders. If this classification system were truly accurate, we might well expect certain therapeutic techniques to be useful with obses-sive-compulsive neurosis, other procedures to be more effective with anxiety neurosis, and so on. Instead, most psychotherapists of a given persuasion (e.g., Freudian, Adlerian, Rogerian, behaviorist) use that basic approach to treat a wide variety of disorders.

In an attempt to resolve these difficulties, the third and fourth versions of the *Diagnostic and Statistical Manual* were published in 1979 and 1987 respectively. **DSM-III** and **DSM-III-R** are designed to be atheoretical (that is, useful to clinicians of varying orienta-tions), and to specify more precisely the criteria that should be used to classify an individual within a given category. The popular term *neurosis* has been entirely omitted, on the grounds that it has been used in so many different ways as to have lost its meaning. (Not all psychologists and psychiatrists agree with this decision, however, and "neurosis" continues to enjoy widespread usage.) DSM-III and DSM-III-R also differ from DSM-II by evaluating people on five dimensions or axes, including specific maladapative or psychiatric symptoms (Axis I), any long-standing personality or developmental problems (Axis II), and any medical or physical disorders that may also be present (Axis III).

A synopsis of Axis I is presented in Table 11.1. Note, for exam-ple, the obsessive-compulsive disorder, which is characterized by persistent thoughts and/or actions which one cannot seem to stop. To illustrate, an individual may be obsessed with thoughts of harm-ing a loved one, or feel compelled to check the alarm clock 15 or 20 times upon retiring at night to be sure that it is set properly. This category was treated as separate and distinct from anxiety neu-rosis in DSM-II, but it is now classified as one of the anxiety disor-ders. Thus DSM-III-R more clearly indicates that obsessions, com-pulsions, and anxiety typically occur together. Notice also that some disorders have known physical causes, while others are primarily psychological in origin.

DSM-III-R includes 16 major categories in all, and each of these contains anywhere from 4 to 40 or more subcategories. Just as DSM-II proved to be fallible, we may reasonably expect that new discov-eries will someday cause DSM-III-R to become outdated; even these new categories are not etched in stone. A full discussion of DSM-III-R is beyond the scope of the present book, however, and the interested reader is referred to one of the major textbooks on ab-normal psychology (e.g., the most recent edition of Coleman et al. or Davison & Neale).

The Problem of Assessment

Even with the more precise criteria provided by DSM-III-R, it is no simple task to decide which classification applies to a given adult.

TABLE 11.1 A synopsis of DSM-III-R.

1. Organic Mental Disorders: Disorders that have a known physical cause, such as an injury to or pathology of the brain.

A. Dementias Arising in the Senium and Presenium. Degenerative change in brain tissue occurring before age 65 (presenile) or after age 65 (senile).

a. Primary Degenerative Dementia of the Alzheimer Type. Involves a multifaceted loss of intellectual abilities, such as memory, judgment, abstract thought, and changes in personality and behavior. Generally progressive, with onset either before (presenile) or after (senile) age 65.

b. Multi-infarct Dementia. Stepwise deterioration in intellectual functioning which occurs when localized areas of brain tissue are destroyed because of an inadequate supply of blood.

B. Psychoactive Substance-Induced Organic Mental Disorders. Organic brain damage caused by the use of a specific substance, such as alcohol or drugs.

2. Schizophrenia: Characterized by a gross distortion of reality; disorganization and fragmentation of thought, perception, and emotion.

3. Delusional (Paranoid) Disorders: Characterized by delusions of persecution and/or grandeur, jealousy, rigidity.

4. Mood Disorders: Characterized by disturbances of emotion and mood. Includes bipolar disorder (in DSM-II, manic-depressive disorder), major depression.

5. Anxiety Disorders: Characterized by unusually high anxiety and efforts to defend against it. Includes phobic disorder (in DSM-II, phobic neurosis), anxiety states (in DSM-II, anxiety neurosis), obsessive-compulsive disorder (in DSM-II, obsessive-compulsive neurosis).

6. Dissociative Disorders: Characterized by escaping from one's own personality and identity. (In DSM-II, hysterical neurosis, dissociative type.) Includes psychogenic amnesia, multiple personality.

7. Somatoform Disorders: Characterized by complaints of bodily symptoms for which there are no physical causes. Includes conversion disorder (in DSM-II, hysterical neurosis, conversion type), hypochondriasis (in DSM-II, hypochondriacal neurosis).

8. Psychosexual Disorders: Characterized by problems associated with sexual behavior, such as failure to attain an erection (male erectile disorder), inhibited orgasm, vaginismus, or premature ejaculation.

9. Psychoactive Substance Use Disorders: Disorders caused by the abuse of or addiction to a specific substance, such as alcohol, tobacco, or drugs (including barbiturates, cocaine, amphetamines, hallucinogens, and others).

10. Disorders Usually First Evident in Infancy, Childhood, and Adolescence: The lengthy category includes such disorders as mental retardation, anorexia nervosa, bulimia, attention disorders, and conduct disorders.

Note: For purposes of convenience, this table presents primarily the major categories of Axis I delineated by DSM-III-R. Catetories not relevant to the present chapter have been deemphasized, and many subcategories have been omitted.

SOURCE: *Diagnostic and statistical manual of mental disorders (Third Edition, Revised).* Washington, D.C.: American Psychiatric Association, 1987.

To answer this important question, clinicians typically rely on such formal **assessment** procedures as interviews and psychometric tests.

INTERVIEWS.   You have undoubtedly encountered the interview at some point in your life, as, for example, when you applied for a job or admission to college. The clinical interviewer pays close attention not only to *what* is said, but also to *how* the respondent answers. In particular, the emotions that accompany the interviewee's statements often provide the clinician with valuable clues regarding any mental disorders that may be present.

The specific information elicited during a clinical interview depends largely on the theoretical orientation of the interviewer. To cite just two examples: Freudian psychoanalysts believe that personality development is virtually complete by about age five to six years, so they devote many of their questions to the patient's childhood. In contrast, behavior therapists prefer to focus their inquiries on the client's current behaviors and problems. Clinical interviews also vary in the degree to which they are structured. Most therapists prefer to operate from vague outlines and compose specific questions as the interview proceeds, while some are more comfortable with a structured format that lists all of the questions to be asked.

Whatever one's theoretical orientation, interviewing patients requires considerable skill and sensitivity. Psychological assessment procedures may be particularly frightening to older people, who are more likely to regard any illnesses they may have as incurable. Thus the interviewer must avoid such behaviors as irritability, impatience, and boredom, which are likely to increase the patient's fears and feelings of rejection. (See Gurland, 1982.) The interviewer must also be alert to such potentially important factors as the patient's cultural background, educational level (which is likely to be lower among the elderly), cohort, and language ability. In addition, the clinical interview is most likely to be effective with an elderly patient if:

- It is part of a more general interview, one that includes physical as well as mental issues.

- Any tests of intellectual capacity are scattered throughout the interview, rather than massed.

- The pace is unhurried, even if the patient takes considerable time to respond.

- The patient is allowed to talk spontaneously about his or her problems at both the opening and close of the interview.

- It ends with a clear statement of the next step in the assessment (or treatment) process.

- It is searching and comprehensive, and does *not* shy away from such potentially sensitive areas as suicidal feelings, sexual problems, and feelings about growing old and dying.

- The patient leaves with reduced anxiety, and the feeling that the session has been completed successfully. Any distressing or emotionally laden topics should *not* be raised near the end of the interview.

- Its length is limited to the patient's attention span, and physical and psychological tolerance (e.g., how easily the patient becomes fatigued).

- The interviewer is sensitive to such problems as hearing and vision impairments, speaks slowly and clearly and in a low-pitched voice (without shouting), allows the patient to see the interviewer's lips move, brings up important points more than once, and uses a quiet room with no echo.

PSYCHOMETRIC INSTRUMENTS. Such well-known measures of personality as the MMPI, Rorschach, and TAT were discussed in Chapter 7. There are also numerous psychometric instruments that can be used to assess specific conditions, such as organic brain syndromes, depression, cognitive impairment, somatic disturbances, social maladjustment, and so on. For ease of reference, and to avoid unnecessary repetition, we will discuss some of these instruments when we examine the corresponding disorders.

Afterword

When DSM-III-R is used in combination with appropriate assessment procedures, it is possible to arrive at very detailed diagnoses. However, this is far from a universal practice. A quite different picture is evident from actual doctors' notes, concerning those elderly patients in long-term care institutions who suffer primarily from physical problems. These patients are frequently diagnosed in such simple terms as "depressed" or "senile," with no indication as to the procedure used to arrive at this conclusion. More often than not, it would seem that these diagnoses were made casually, during the course of a physical examination. Thus the problems of classification and assessment are compounded by the common failure to use the best available procedures.

Adult Epidemiology

Introduction

Now that we have established *what* the various kinds of psychopathology are, we must ascertain *how often* and *where* these disorders occur. The greater the frequency of a particular illness, the more urgently we need to diagnose and treat it correctly. The study of the distribution of illnesses in time and place, and of the factors which influence this distribution, is known as **epidemiology.**

METHODS OF STUDY.   One way to obtain epidemiological data is by examining hospital records or **case registers,** and counting up how often each disorder occurs. Unfortunately, this straightforward procedure may well produce misleading results. Many individuals who suffer from certain disorders, such as depression, never go to a hospital or visit a psychotherapist. Using this method, therefore, numerous cases of pathology will remain undetected.

Instead, the epidemiologist may resort to a potentially more accurate method: assessing the mental health of every person in a specified geographical area, either directly or indirectly. However, such **field surveys** are expensive and difficult to conduct. They are most feasible in geographically isolated communities (e.g., islands such as Iceland), where the number of people to be assessed is relatively small and there is little movement of the population to other areas. To date, the majority of field surveys have been conducted in northern Europe and Japan (Kay & Bergmann, 1982).

INCIDENCE AND PREVALENCE RATES.   Whatever the method, the results of epidemiological studies are typically expressed in two different ways. **Incidence rates** refer to the number of *new* cases of disease that occur within a specified period of time among a specified population. This includes those who contract the given illness for the first time, and those who suffer a recurrent episode after having experienced a period of health:

$$\text{Incidence Rate} = \frac{\text{Number of New Cases}}{\text{Population at Risk}}$$

The denominator of this fraction, the **population at risk,** consists of all adults in the specified geographical area who might conceivably contract this illness. (Appropriate census or other demographical data may be used to determine this figure.) For example, suppose that 50 new cases of depression occur each day among those age 65 and over in Baltimore, Maryland. Since there are approximately 100,000 people aged 65 and above in Baltimore, the daily incidence rate would be 50/100,000 or .0005 (or .05 percent). Alternatively, incidence rates may be based on a monthly or yearly period.

In contrast, **prevalence rates** refer to the *total number* of people in a given community who suffer from the illness in question:

$$\text{Prevalence Rate} = \frac{\text{Total Number of Cases}}{\text{Population at Risk}}$$

This figure may be based on a single point in time ("point prevalence"), or a specified period of time ("period prevalence"). Thus a 7 percent point prevalence rate of depression among adults in Baltimore would mean that at the specified point in time, 7 percent of the adults in this city were found to suffer from depression. Prevalence rates may instead be reported as rates per thousand; in the preceding example, this would be expressed as 70 per 1,000.

When the frequency of an illness changes markedly at different ages, or when we are primarily interested in the relationship between aging and psychopathology, epidemiological results are best reported in terms of age-specific incidence and prevalence rates. To illustrate, we might find that the incidence rate for depression in Baltimore is 35 per 1,000 for people aged 60-69, but only 10 per 1,000 for those aged 50-59. Or we might discover that the incidence rate for this disorder remains much the same throughout adulthood.

AFTERWORD.   Age-specific incidence and prevalence rates will help us to answer the questions we posed at the outset of this chapter. If a mental disorder which originates in childhood or adolescence does tend to persist into old age, we will find high prevalence rates and low incidence rates among the elderly. If instead a disorder typically occurs for the first time at an advanced age, the incidence rates will be markedly higher at older ages.

Age-specific incidence and prevalence rates are readily available for most major mental disorders. Before we turn to these findings, however, a note of caution must be sounded. As mentioned above, such different sources as field surveys and case registers may well yield significantly different figures for the same disorder. There is also some question as to the reliability of psychiatric diagnosis with elderly patients, even when attempts are made to be detailed and precise (e.g., Klerman, 1983). Various investigators have used different methods of diagnosis and assessment, making it difficult to compare the results of different studies. Thus the data to be discussed in the following sections should be taken as a general indication of the extent of these disorders, rather than as a mathematically exact determination.

Organic Brain Syndromes

Organic brain disorders can be divided into two major categories: acute and chronic. Both are characterized by disorientation, and by an impaired capacity to remember recent events and learn new information. **Acute Organic Brain Syndrome** is reversible, however, and its onset is usually sudden. In contrast, **Chronic Organic Brain Syndrome** has a relatively slow onset and is *not* reversible.

ACUTE ORGANIC BRAIN SYNDROME (AOBS).   The disorientation of the AOBS patient is often greatest during the evening, when daylight begins to fail (the "sundown syndrome"). The level of confusion varies markedly from day to day, however, or even during the course of a single day. The patient's mood is unstable, and may change suddenly from a dreamy state to fear, anger, excitement, suspicion, or perplexity. People are misidentified, and their actions are often misunderstood. Delusions may also occur, as with the belief that some external force is trying to take away the patient's mind. There are various causes of AOBS:

- Brain tumors.

- The overuse of drugs and alcohol.

- The misuse of prescription drugs.

- Hypoglycemia, a diabetic condition caused by an improper ratio of caloric intake to insulin dosage.

- Congestive heart failure, especially among individuals whose cognitive functioning is already marginal or deteriorated.

- Infections.

- Metabolic and nutritional disorders, such as an underactive thyroid gland, pernicious anemia, serious vitamin B deficiencies, and hormonal imbalances.

- Severe pain, chronic discomfort, or extreme stress.

AOBS typically lasts for only a short time, and it is difficult to distinguish from other disorders. Therefore, incidence and prevalence rates have not been calculated for the general population.

Chapter Glossary: Adult Psychopathology

Antidepressants	Drugs which relieve depression by producing an elevation in mood.
Anxiety	An extremely unpleasant emotion, similar to intense nervousness.
Assessment	Determining which form(s) of psychopathology afflict a given individual.
Behavior therapy	A form of psychotherapy which is designed to change pathological behaviors and alleviate troublesome symptoms, and is based on the principles and procedures of experimental psychology.
Case register method	Determining how often various forms of psychopathology occur by examining hospital or therapist records, and tallying the frequency of each disorder.
Chemotherapy	The use of appropriate drugs to treat psychopathology. The most popular method of somatic therapy.
Depression	An emotional state characterized by frequent and powerful feelings of dejection, worthlessness, and hopelessness.
DSM-II	The 1968 version of the *Diagnostic and Statistical Manual of Mental Disorders*, prepared by the American Psychiatric Association. Until recently, the most widely accepted method for classifying the various forms of psychopathology.
DSM-III and DSM-III-R	The 1979 and 1987 revisions designed to replace DSM-II, which classify the various forms of psychopathology according to five axes and eliminate the term "neurosis."
Electroconvulsive therapy (ECT)	A form of somatic therapy wherein electric shocks are administered to one or both hemispheres of the brain.
Epidemiology	The study of the distribution of illnesses in time and place, and of the factors which influence this distribution.
Field survey	Determining how often various forms of psychopathology occur by assessing the mental health of every person in a specified geographical area, either directly or indirectly.
Functional disorder	A disorder which cannot be attributed primarily to physical causes.
Group therapy	A form of psychotherapy wherein a number of patients, usually from five to ten, meet with one or two therapists.

	May be insight therapy, behavior therapy, or some combination thereof.
Incidence rate	The number of new cases of a particular disorder that occur during a specified period.
Individual therapy	A form of psychotherapy wherein one patient meets privately with one therapist. May be insight therapy, behavior therapy, or some combination thereof.
Insight therapy	Psychotherapy designed to help patients obtain an intellectual and emotional understanding of the causes and dynamics of their disorders.
Major tranquilizers (antipsychotic drugs)	Drugs used to make psychotic patients more manageable, and to improve their contact with reality.
Minor tranquilizers	Drugs used primarily to reduce anxiety in neurotic patients.
Neurosis	A form of psychopathology characterized by anxiety and efforts to defend against it. Hospitalization is usually not necessary.
Organic brain syndromes	Mental disorders caused by physical damage to the brain. *Acute organic brain syndrome* has a sudden onset, and is reversible. *Chronic organic brain syndrome,* which includes the senile and presenile dementias, has a relatively slow onset and is not reversible.
Population at risk	All people in a specified geographical area who might conceivably contract the disorder under study.
Prevalence rate	The total number of people in a given community who suffer from a particular disorder, either at a single point in time or during a specified period of time.
Psychosis	A severe functional disorder characterized by gross breakdowns in personality and distortion of reality (e.g., schizophrenia). Usually requires hospitalization.
Psychosurgery	A form of somatic therapy, now almost obsolete, wherein areas of the brain are surgically destroyed.
Psychotherapy	A general term that may refer to any established psychological method for treating mental disorders.
Somatic therapy	The use of physical methods to alter a patient's physiological and psychological state. Varieties include electroconvulsive therapy, psychosurgery, and chemotherapy.
Stimulants	Drugs that tend to increase feelings of alertness and reduce fatigue.

Clinical experience does indicate that the prevalence rate for older adults admitted to medical wards is about 15 percent, and that the frequency of these symptoms increases markedly after age 60 (Kay & Bergmann, 1982).

CHRONIC ORGANIC BRAIN SYNDROME (COBS). This is the disorder causing the most concern among the aged in North America and Europe. Included in this category are such degenerative brain diseases as Senile Dementia, Presenile Dementia, Alzheimer's disease, and Multi-infarct Dementia. (See Table 11.1.)

Both **Senile Dementia** and **Presenile Dementia** are typified by a gradual and progressive inability to deal with the common activities of everyday life, failures in memory and intellectual functioning, and a disorganization of personality. The primary difference between the two is in the time of onset: Presenile Dementias occur prior to age 65, with deterioration sometimes beginning as early as age 40–50, while Senile Dementias occur at age 70 or later.

Considerable attention is currently being devoted to **Alzheimer's disease,** which has been singled out as a "disease of catastrophic proportions" by the United States Department of Health and Human Services. This disorder has the distinction of being recognized as both a Presenile and a Senile Dementia, though it is not yet clear whether the early form and the late form differ only in time of onset or in more significant ways as well. Alzheimer's disease is one of the most common forms of dementia; it strikes an estimated 5 percent of all Americans and non-Americans over the age of 65, and 20 percent of all adults over 80 (Brody, 1982; Butler, Besdine, & Brody, 1980).

The causes of Alzheimer's disease are not yet known. Some researchers believe that the cholinergic system of the brain may be responsible, since the brains of Alzheimer's victims exhibit a significant decrease in an enzyme called choline acetyltransferase (Davics & Maloney, 1976; Perry et al., 1977; Perry et al., 1978). Other researchers contend that the brains of Alzheimer's victims possess considerably more trace metals, such as aluminum, though here the evidence is equivocal (e.g., Crapper, Kirshnan, & Quittkat, 1976; McDermott et al., 1977). A third area of investigation concerns the possibility of genetic determinants. The risk of Senile Dementia, Down's syndrome, leukemia, and Hodgkin's disease has been found to be significantly higher among relatives of patients suffering from Alzheimer's disease than in the general population (Heston & Mastri, 1977; Larson, Sjogren, & Jacobson, 1963). Finally, a fourth suspected cause of Alzheimer's disease is slow-acting viral agents (Goudsmit et al., 1980).

Whatever the causes, Alzheimer's disease is associated with various physiological changes in the brain. These include a loss of

Rita Hayworth was one noted victim of Alzheimer's disease, currently regarded as a disease of catastrophic proportions by the United States Department of Health and Human Services.   *UPI/Bettmann Newsphotos*

neurons, widened fissures, narrower and flatter ridges, senile plaques scattered throughout the cortex, and the replacement of normal nerve cells in the basal ganglia with tangled threadlike structures. The onset of Alzheimer's disease is deceptively mild, and its course is one of steady deterioration. In the early stages, memory impairment may be the sole observable symptom. There may also be subtle personality changes, including apathy, lack of spontaneity, and withdrawal from social interactions. In subsequent stages, cognitive and personality changes become more apparent. In the final stages, patients may be completely mute and inattentive, and totally incapable of caring for themselves. The ravages of Alzheimer's disease are graphically illustrated by these case histories:

CASE 1. A FORMER WRITER.
He had been a successful writer for more than 40 years, celebrated for his ability to remember the details of a complex and important

story virtually without using notes. But soon after his retirement at age 68, he began to experience difficulty in finding the right words to express himself, and he frequently appeared to lose the thread of his thoughts. Within months, he couldn't remember his schedule for the day. In a few years, he could not remember if he had just eaten.

It became necessary to give the man sedatives and sleeping pills, otherwise he would wander around the entire night. When not sedated, he became irritable and sometimes violent. Eventually, he had to be placed in a nursing home, where he continued to decline until he was unable to perform even the simplest functions for himself. He could not remember the names of those close to him. (Fischman, 1984, p. 27.)

CASE 2. A 46-YEAR-OLD SUPERVISOR.

She immediately forgets the plot of the last television show she watched, and she has trouble reading newspaper articles because she loses the gist of the story after two or three sentences. She has long since forgotten the names and phone numbers of relatives, and no longer cooks or drives because she can't remember how. "Can you imagine the embarrassment of an educated woman not knowing who the president is, or having to ask where the bathroom is in your own house?" she asks in frustration. (Clark et al., 1984, p. 60.)

CASE 3. A HARVARD GRADUATE.

This 57-year-old man was diagnosed as having Alzheimer's disease three years ago. Now he stays home, while his wife holds down a part-time job. She must leave handwritten notes around the house so that he will remember to turn off the gas, or not go out until she comes back. He often speaks in cryptic, broken sentences. He sometimes can't remember the names of his stepchildren, or even his wife. One night he brought her a can of beer, and she reminded him that she prefers it in a glass. He went back and forth to the kitchen four or five times, always forgetting to bring the glass. She yelled at him, then felt guilty. Yet despite the stress, she clings to every moment because she knows her time with him is limited. (Clark et al., 1984, pp. 58–59.)

Alzheimer's disease is incurable. When its onset takes place after the age of 65, death typically occurs some five years later, though some sufferers linger much longer. Clark et al. (1984) suggest that Alzheimer's may well be the cruelest of all diseases because it kills its victims twice: first there is the living death of being unable to remember the simplest fact, or perform the simplest daily function; then the body gradually sinks into coma and death.

A second common form of dementia is **Multi-infarct Dementia.**

TABLE 11.2   A comparison of Alzheimer's Disease and
Multi-infarct Dementia.

Characteristic	Alzheimer's Disease	Multi-infarct Dementia
Age of onset	60s–70s	40s–50s
Sex most affected	Probably females	Males
Course of disease	Progressive	Stepwise
Physical impairments	Few, appear late in life	Frequent

It is important to distinguish between this disorder and Alzheimer's
disease in order to provide appropriate treatment, although this is
difficult to do without special training and the use of sophisticated
equipment. Multi-infarct Dementia has an abrupt onset, progresses
in stages, and is more prevalent among males. It is caused by an
inadequate flow of blood to the brain, which results in the destruction of localized areas of brain tissue ("infarcts"). The symptoms of
Multi-infarct Dementia include impairments in memory and judgment, abstract thinking, and impulse control. There may also be a
significant change in personality, depending on the location of the
infarcts. Multi-infarct Dementia follows a stepwise course, with clearly
differentiated levels of severity at different times, whereas the development of Alzheimer's disease is more gradual and progressive.
Also, physical impairments are more common with Multi-infarct
Dementia. (See Table 11.2.)

The prevalence and incidence rates of COBS, moderate and severe forms, are shown in Tables 11.3 and 11.4. Note that these rates

TABLE 11.3   Prevalence rates (in percents) of Chronic Organic
Brain Syndrome (moderate and severe forms) by sex.

Age	Males (N = 1008)	Females (N = 1259)	Both Sexes (N = 2267)
65	3.9	0.5	2.1
70	4.1	2.7	3.3
75	8.0	7.9	8.0
80	13.2	20.9	17.7
All ages	6.2	6.3	6.3

Note: The above data were obtained by pooling the results of studies conducted in Japan, Sweden, and the United Kingdom.
SOURCE: Kay & Bergmann (1982, p. 43).

increase dramatically with increasing age. To be sure, studies based on different countries and methods may well yield appreciably different results. Yet we may conclude that COBS is a disorder most likely to occur during old age and (to a lesser extent) middle age, rather than one that originates early in life and persists throughout adulthood.

ASSESSING ORGANIC BRAIN SYNDROMES.   As we have seen, one of the hallmarks of organic brain disorders is some degree of cognitive impairment. Thus one widely used test for initially assessing this condition, the Mental Status Questionnaire (Kahn et al., 1960), consists of ten straightforward items:

1. What is the name of this place?
2. Where is it located (address)?
3. What is today's date?
4. What is the month now?
5. What is the year?
6. How old are you now?
7. When were you born (month)?
8. When were you born (year)?
9. Who is the President of the United States?
10. Who was the President before him?

TABLE 11.4   Annual incidence rates per 1,000 of Chronic Organic Brain Syndrome: Results of three studies.

| Country | Method | Duration | N & Sex | Average Annual Incidence Per 1,000 For Ages: | | |
				60–69	70–79	80+
Iceland	Case register	2 years	22,206 M	0.8	2.6	9.4
			25,130 F	0.7	2.8	8.3
United Kingdom	Case register	5 years	9,228 M	1.1	2.4	6.9
			15,581 F	0.8	2.8	6.7
Sweden	Field survey	3 years	2,071 M	0.3	4.8	8.6
			2,127 F	1.2	3.6	13.7

SOURCE: Kay & Bergmann (1982, p. 45).

Cognitive impairment may also result from physical health problems, such as chronic infections, thyroid malfunction, malnutrition, or the misuse of medications. To distinguish this from the organic brain syndromes, multiple tests may well be necessary. These may include more sensitive cognitive batteries, a CAT Scan, an EEG, blood tests, urinalyses, and/or an evaluation of the patient's diet and medication. Or, since organic brain syndromes frequently affect the patient's ability to function alone, it may be useful to administer a measure of dependence. The instrument most commonly used for this purpose is the Index of Activities of Daily Living (Katz et al., 1963), which measures the degree of assistance needed in such areas as bathing, dressing, continence and elimination, and feeding. Thus patients suffering from dementia may confuse the hot and cold taps in the shower and suffer a painful burn, don winter clothing in the middle of summer, or forget where to relieve themselves when the need for elimination arises.

AFTERWORD.   Organic brain syndromes are more likely to occur at more advanced ages, and are particularly troublesome because of their severity and frequency. The positive side of the story is that the odds are against your ever contracting an organic brain disorder, even if you live into your eighties. The negative side is that a substantial number of adults suffer from this devastating, demeaning illness. Hopefully, the increased amount of research currently being devoted to this area will produce some significant results in the not-too-distant future.

Schizophrenia

Of those mental disorders that *cannot* be attributed primarily to physical causes (**functional** disorders), **schizophrenia** is probably the most severe. This psychosis is characterized by a gross distortion of reality, and by disorganization and fragmentation of thought, perception, and emotion. The speech of schizophrenics is often broken and incomprehensible to other people, or even to the patients themselves. Hallucinations are common. And the level of fear is very high, especially about being deluged by external stimuli which the patient cannot screen out. One of the best-known varieties, paranoid schizophrenia, is also typified by absurd and illogical delusions of persecution and/or grandeur: the sufferer feels taken advantage of and plotted against by various mythical enemies, and may conclude that he or she is some noted personage such as Christ. (See, for example, Arieti, 1974.)

Schizophrenia typically originates in childhood, although the symptoms may not become clearly evident until a later age. It is

TABLE 11.5   A general comparison of prevalence and incidence rates for various disorders.

Disorder	Prevalence Rate, All Adults	Prevalence Rate, Ages 60 and Older	Change in Incidence Rate with Increasing Age
Chronic Organic Brain Syndrome	Low to moderate	Moderate to high, depending on age	Increases
Schizophrenia	Low to moderate	Low	Decreases
Neurosis	High	Moderate	Decreases
Depression	Low to moderate (severe forms); very high (mild and moderate forms)	High	Little change through age 75
Alcoholism	Moderate	Moderate, but decreases with increasing age	Insufficient data

generally believed that the period of risk for an initial outbreak of schizophrenia ceases at about age 45. However, case register data indicate that it is possible for this illness to first become apparent as late as age 70. The frequency of schizophrenia among the elderly is often underestimated, since it is all too easy to mistakenly diagnose this psychosis as an organic brain syndrome. The true prevalence rate is probably in the area of 3 to 5 per 1,000 at risk, or 0.5 percent. Thus schizophrenia is much less common among older adults than are the organic brain syndromes, and the probability that you will contract this disorder for the first time as you grow older is considerably smaller. (See Table 11.5.)

Neurosis

The disorders classified under the heading of **neurosis** by DSM-II are less severe than the organic brain syndromes and psychoses, but are far more common among the population as a whole. The primary symptom of neurosis is intense and painful anxiety: the sufferer often feels nervous and afraid for no apparent reason. Other symptoms may include obsessions and compulsions, or thoughts and actions that the individual cannot seem to stop repeating over and over; phobias, or anxiety caused by a specific object or situation that is actually not dangerous; depression; hypochondria, or an exaggerated preoccupation with one's health and excessive anxiety about the possibility of becoming ill; and dissociative disorders, as when one escapes from one's own personality through psychogenic amnesia.

Neurosis most often originates in childhood, and (to a lesser extent) adolescence. (See, for example, Adler, 1927/1957; 1929/1969; Freud, 1933/1965b; 1916–1917/1966; Horney, 1945; 1950; Rogers, 1961; Sullivan, 1953/1968.) Perhaps for this reason, this disorder has proved to be of relatively little interest to those who wish to focus on the problems of the middle-aged and elderly; it has not received much attention from geriatricians. The prevalence rate of neurosis among the elderly is probably about 4 percent to 9 percent, while the incidence rate decreases with increasing age (Kay & Bergmann, 1982). As with schizophrenia, then, you are less likely to contract a neurosis for the first time as you grow older.

Depression

DEFINITION.   Most of us experience periods of **depression** from time to time, but this is not necessarily indicative of psychopathology. Clinical depression is characterized by negative changes in mood that are powerful and pervasive: the sufferer experiences unusually strong and frequent feelings of dejection, worthlessness, gloom and dismay about the past, and hopelessness about the future, and often apprehension as well. For example:

CASE 4. A 64-YEAR-OLD RETIRED TRAVEL AGENT.

Mrs. H. and her husband have two sons who live in another section of the country; she hears from them only when they need financial assistance. She has led a pleasant and even exciting life, including extensive travel and active participation in community affairs. She believes that she has been a failure in life, however, and that she has not treated her husband or her sons properly. She has also become obsessed with the idea that if she were to kill herself, this drastic act would enable her family to draw closer together. Her physical health is excellent, and she is not subjected to unusual life stresses; yet she has a strong tendency for negative thinking about herself. (Gallagher & Thompson, 1983, pp. 27–28.)

CASE 5. A 73-YEAR-OLD WIDOWER.

Three years ago neighbors found Mr. B., a widower for 10 years, collapsed in his apartment. He was unkempt, unshaven, confused, and disoriented as to place and time. His only response to questions was, "I just want to die." The little food in his apartment apparently had not been touched for days. There was no evidence of alcohol or drug use, but lab tests did reveal a kidney infection and dehydration. He refused to eat, and complained that he was miserable. He viewed treatment as worthless because it was "only" extending his life. His speech and thinking were markedly slowed, his emotions were dulled, and he saw no hope for the future. (Gallagher & Thompson, 1983, p. 25.)

We will see how a psychotherapist treated each of these cases later in this chapter. Somatic symptoms and physiological changes are also common aspects of depression, while distorted perceptions and thoughts may occur in some instances.

It is not easy to distinguish depression from the dementias. Approximately 50 percent of all depressed patients demonstrate some degree of cognitive impairment, with some 15 percent exhibiting severe, dementia-like symptoms. Conversely, about 25 percent of all patients suffering from dementia are also depressed. One way to differentiate true dementia from the dementia syndrome caused by depression is that the latter is reversible, whereas the former is not. (See Boller et al., 1984.) Some theorists also distinguish between depression and related functional disorders, such as the demoralization that results from membership in a low status group or from the loss of health and power. In contrast to depression, demoralization is *not* accompanied either by physiological symptoms or by perceptual and thought distortions (Gurland, 1982; Gurland & Toner, 1982).

INCIDENCE AND PREVALENCE RATES.   Among the elderly, depression is the most common functional disorder. The probable prevalence rate of depression is 12 percent to 15 percent, with 2 percent to 4 percent of these patients suffering from such extreme forms as bipolar (manic-depressive) disorder. (See, for example, Blazer & Williams, 1980; Gurland et al., 1983.) Depression tends to be more frequent among males older than 75, which corresponds closely to changes in suicide rates. (See Chapter 12.)

For adults of all ages, those who are seriously ill tend to be more depressed. This is due primarily to being helpless and highly dependent on other people, however, rather than to being ill per se. Cancer patients capable of normal activity have been found to be significantly less depressed than bedridden diabetics, even though the former illness is at least as severe. Some data also indicate that when the level of physical disability is statistically controlled, the relationship between illness and depression disappears. (See, for example, Cassileth et al., 1984; Gurland et al., 1983; Larson, 1978; Linn et al., 1980.) Furthermore, the relationship between physical disability and depression appears to be more prominent among the middle-aged than the elderly. One reason for this (as we observed in Chapter 7) is that the elderly are more likely to conceptualize ill health as normal for their age, so they tend to face their illnesses with relative calm and equanimity.

ASSESSING DEPRESSION.   There is no one universally accepted way to assess depression. The prevalence rates for this disorder vary according to the procedures and diagnostic criteria that are used, and the population being studied.

One of the most widely used instruments for assessing depression is the Beck Depression Inventory (Beck et al., 1965), which asks subjects to rate the presence or absence of various symptoms on a four-point scale of intensity. Prevalence rates based on such symptom checklists tend to be higher than rates ascertained from diagnostic interviews. Also quite popular, especially for use with the elderly, is the brief and self-administered Zung Self-Rating Depression Scale (Zung, 1965; 1967). Six items from this scale discriminate particularly well between depressed and nondepressed aged individuals (Okimoto et al., 1982):

1. I am more irritable than usual.

2. My life is pretty full.

3. I'd do better if I felt better.

4. I feel downhearted, blue, and sad.

5. I feel that others would be better off if I were dead.

6. I don't have much to look forward to.

However, Zung's scale has also been criticized on several grounds. It contains a preponderance of somatic items, as compared to those which tap psychological distress. Also, some items are worded positively while others are worded negatively, which may well be confusing to older adults. (See Gallagher & Thompson, 1983.) A relatively new instrument which may prove useful with the elderly is the Geriatric Depression Scale (Yesavage et al., in press), which contains 30 yes/no items concerning how the subject felt during the past week.

AFTERWORD.   Although depression is the most common functional disorder among the aged, this does *not* mean that you are likely to become more depressed as you grow older. Depression ranks so high because the frequency of other functional disorders declines with increasing age. In fact, the incidence rates for all functional disorders other than depression and dementia appear to be lowest after age 65. (See, for example, Gurland, 1976; Gurland & Toner, 1982; Kay & Bergmann, 1982; Smyer & Gatz, 1983.) Thus the normal course of aging is not necessarily (or even usually) accompanied by increases in depression, save perhaps for men past the age of 75.

Alcoholism

It is difficult to draw firm conclusions about the prevalence and incidence of alcoholism. Here again, there are a variety of formal definitions and diagnostic criteria. Also, in contrast to depression, there is not much epidemiological data dealing with alcoholism. However, it is estimated that alcoholism afflicts some 2 percent to 10 percent of the elderly. This disorder is more frequent among widowers, people who are experiencing legal difficulties, and those who never married.

Of those alcoholics who undergo formal treatment, approximately 10 percent are 60 years old or more. The prevalence of alcoholism decreases with increasing age, however, especially in the case of heavy drinkers. This is due in part to the death of many alcoholics at a young age, as from cancer, cardiovascular diseases, accidents, or suicide. It is also partly due to a high rate of spontaneous remission (cures that occur without any formal treatment), with an estimated one third of all alcoholics permanently terminating their problem drinking at some point in their lives. (See Atkinson & Schuckit, 1981.) As these findings indicate, a decrease in prevalence rates is not always desirable: it may be caused by a substantial number of cures, but it may also result from a significant number of fatalities.

Afterword

Some of the major findings reviewed above are summarized in Table 11.5. The disorder most clearly associated with increasing age is chronic organic brain syndrome. The prevalence of depression is also relatively high among the elderly, primarily because the incidence of all other functional disorders decreases with increasing age. Thus epidemiology, prevalence rates, and incidence rates have proved to be extremely helpful in focusing our attention on the disorders of greatest importance, although (as always) more data are needed regarding some illnesses before definitive conclusions can be drawn.

The Treatment of Adult Psychopathology

At present, there are numerous methods for treating the many forms of psychopathology. There are also various professions that provide formal or informal psychotherapy, including psychology, psychiatry, psychoanalysis, behavior therapy, social work, peer and pastoral counseling, and nursing (to name just a few).

For our purposes, psychotherapeutic procedures may be classified

Myths About Aging: Adult Psychopathology

MYTH	BEST AVAILABLE EVIDENCE
If you live into your eighties or beyond, you are very likely to suffer such severe mental deterioration that you become mindless or "senile."	Dementias do afflict a significant proportion of the elderly, and are more likely to occur with increasing age. But even if you live to be 80 or older, the chances of your contracting a dementia are considerably less than 50-50.
Since depression is the most common form of functional psychopathology among the elderly, you are likely to become more depressed as you grow toward old age.	Depression ranks so high because the frequency of all other functional disorders decreases with increasing age, not because its frequency increases markedly. Thus you are *not* particularly likely to become more depressed as you grow older.
Middle-aged and elderly adults are not amenable to treatment by insight and behavior therapy.	It is harder to change older individuals, who are more set in their ways, and some psychotherapists do prefer to exclude middle-aged and elderly patients. Nevertheless, successful insight and behavior therapy has been and is being done with the middle-aged and elderly.

into four major categories: somatic therapy, insight therapy, behavior therapy, and group therapy. Each of these includes a large number of subcategories, giving the clinician an almost endless menu of techniques from which to choose. To keep our discussion within reasonable bounds, we will focus primarily on those methods used to treat the more prevalent varieties of adult psychopathology.

Somatic Therapy

Somatic therapies utilize physical methods to alter a patient's physiological and psychological state. There are three types of somatic therapy: electroconvulsive therapy, psychosurgery, and chemotherapy (the most common).

ELECTROCONVULSIVE THERAPY (ECT). The use of **electroconvulsive therapy** (or "shock therapy") has declined in recent years. This is due partly to advances in chemotherapy, and perhaps also

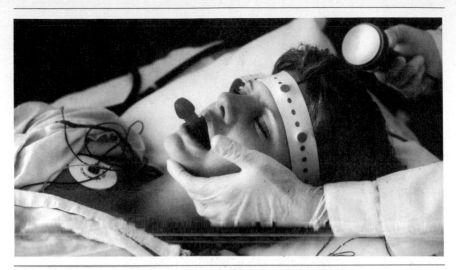

Although controversial, electroconvulsive shock therapy may be the treatment of choice in some instances. *Will McIntyre/Photo Researchers*

to negative media coverage about the side effects of ECT. Yet ECT can be a valuable method for treating severe depression in adults, particularly those between the ages of 40 and 60. (There is little research evidence concerning patients over 60.) It has been argued that ECT is at least as effective as antidepressant medication, and that its side effects are usually *not* severe: the most common of these, impaired memory, is presumably resolved within a few weeks. There is also a fairly recent modification of ECT wherein electric current is administered to only one side of the brain, rather than to both cerebral hemispheres. This method appears to lessen any distressing side effects, without decreasing therapeutic effectiveness.

To be sure, ECT has undoubtedly led to severe brain damage in some instances. All too often, any apparent improvements brought on by ECT have ended in relapses. Some psychologists argue that the memory impairments associated with ECT can last for months, or even longer. And even when ECT does produce seemingly miraculous cures, the reasons for such successes are by no means clear. (See Coleman et al., 1980, pp. 618–620.) Yet when the patient is deeply depressed or suicidal, medical complications make the use of appropriate drugs too risky, and/or other methods have proved ineffective, ECT may in fact be the treatment of choice.

PSYCHOSURGERY. During the 1940s and 1950s, **psychosurgery** was widely used to treat schizophrenia and severe depression. The best-known technique, prefrontal lobotomy, involved severing the nerve fibers which connect the deeper centers of the brain with the frontal lobes. Today, however, psychosurgery has been largely (and justifiably) discontinued. Its side effects are serious and irreversible, a classic case of a "cure" that is worse that the disease. For example, prefrontal lobotomy results in permanent brain damage and impairments of necessary, normal functions. Also, the increased availability of antipsychotic drugs has provided clinicians with a less harmful and more effective alternative.

Psychosurgery may still be used in rare cases where all other methods have failed, or to alleviate uncontrollable violent seizures and intense pain in terminal patients. Even here, however, lobotomy has been replaced by modern methods which limit the destruction of brain cells to a very minute area.

CHEMOTHERAPY.   Among the somatic therapies, chemotherapy (pharmacotherapy, drug therapy) has become the treatment of choice, particularly for elderly patients suffering from depression (Gallagher & Thompson, 1983). Chemotherapy is widely used throughout the United States and Canada, and has made it possible to discharge many mental patients who would otherwise have had to remain hospitalized. The drugs used to treat mental disorders fall into four categories: minor tranquilizers, major tranquilizers, stimulants, and antidepressants. All of these drugs have the potential for both good and evil: they effectively provide symptomatic relief, but may also become addictive.

Minor tranquilizers are the drugs most often used in chemotherapy—so often, in fact, that they have become part of the American culture. (See Chapter 10.) Included in this category are such well-known trade names as Miltown, Librium, and Valium. Minor tranquilizers are typically used to reduce minor to moderate levels of neurotic anxiety, and with outpatients who suffer from psychosomatic disorders that involve tension.

Major tranquilizers are used primarily to make schizophrenic patients more manageable, and to improve their contact with reality. These tranquilizers are therefore often referred to as **antipsychotic drugs;** common trade names include Thorazine, Stelazine, and Haldol. By 1970, more than 85 percent of all patients in state mental hospitals were receiving some form of major tranquilizer (Davison & Neale, 1978). The major tranquilizers have enabled some schizophrenics to be released from mental hospitals, but these drugs are far from a cure-all. Some have unpleasant side effects, such as dryness of the mouth, blurred vision, grogginess, constipation, and an inability to prevent the mouth muscles from making sucking and lip-smacking movements. The unfortunate result is that many patients simply stop taking this medication, and must therefore be readmitted to the hospital. Even those who continue to take the antipsychotic drugs may achieve only a marginal adjustment to the community. In spite of these difficulties, the major tranquilizers represent the best method currently available for the treatment of schizophrenia.

Stimulants, such as Dexedrine and Ritalin, are most often used with elderly patients for two reasons: to overcome the fatigue and cognitive impairments associated with dementia, and to treat mild cases of depression. (See Raskin, 1981.) However, the evidence regarding the effectiveness of such stimulants with the elderly is mixed. Some critics have even concluded that stimulants do *not* alleviate most of the cognitive impairments that afflict the elderly (Salzman, 1981). These drugs appear to be less useful with patients who are older, or who have suffered from their symptoms for a longer period of time. Stimulants may also increase the risk of serious heart and central nervous system disorders, especially when used in combination with certain other drugs (e.g., antidepressants). Currently, then, the use of stimulants with aged patients is a controversial issue.

Antidepressant drugs consist of two major types: tricyclics (e.g., Norpramin, Elavil), and monoamine oxidase inhibitors or MAOs (e.g., Nardil, Marsalid). The effectiveness of MAOs for treating depression is controversial, and their side effects can be severe. MAOs may cause damage to the liver, brain, and cardiovascular system, and they may even interact with other drugs or certain common foods to produce death. Thus noninstitutionalized patients who suffer from memory impairments should normally avoid MAOs, as they may well forget what foods they are prohibited from eating. However, there is some indication that MAOs may be useful with apathetic and fatigued elderly patients. Tricyclics have been demonstrated to be generally effective in cases of depression, and are usually preferred to MAOs for all age groups. The side effects of tricyclics include dryness of the mouth, blurred vision, dizziness, constipation, and palpitations. Improvement typically begins to appear after about one to two weeks of treatment, and peaks during the fourth to sixth week. There are some elderly patients who show a heightened sensitivity to tricyclics, however, regarding both therapeutic effectiveness and the adverse side effects.

With increasing age, the capacity to absorb, process, and excrete antidepressants (and other drugs) undergoes significant changes. To reduce the likelihood of unwelcome side effects, the preferred course with elderly patients is to begin treatment with dosages that are quite low and increase the levels very gradually.

Chemotherapists seeking to alleviate the symptoms of dementia have also experimented with numerous other drugs, including vasodilators and hormones. (See Yesavage & King, 1981.) At present, however, the effectiveness of these purported mental stimulants must generally be regarded as unproven.

EVALUATION.   Chemotherapy is the most popular and most effective form of somatic therapy. However, it does involve the possibility of addiction and adverse side effects. It is all too possible for both patients and mental health professionals to lean too heavily on the use of medication, rather than trying to attack and resolve the underlying problem in more demanding ways (e.g., psychotherapy). Yet chemotherapy has helped individuals suffering from relatively mild disorders to cope more effectively with the problems of living, and it has enabled severely ill patients to establish contact with reality and to regain some degree of normal functioning. In this area, then, there are no easy answers. But significant progress has been made compared to a mere half century ago, when psychosurgery was all too often the treatment of choice.

Insight Therapy

DEFINITION.   **Insight therapy** differs from somatic therapy in virtually every respect. The basic assumption underlying insight therapy is that in many instances, people behave in self-defeating and pathological ways because they are not aware of their true motives, beliefs, and feelings. Thus the primary goal is to help patients understand the causes and dynamics of their disorders, both intellectually and emotionally. And insight therapy uses verbal communication, rather than physical methods.

Many insight therapists concentrate on the childhood causes of the patient's problems, and on bringing important unconscious material to consciousness. However, some prefer to emphasize the present and more conscious aspects of behavior. Ideally, the insights provided by this form of therapy enable patients to make appropriate changes in their behavior, and ultimately lead to constructive personality change as well.

VARIETIES OF INSIGHT THERAPY.   There are numerous kinds of insight therapy: Freudian psychoanalysis, ego analysis, Jungian therapy, Adlerian therapy, Rogerian client-centered therapy, existential analysis, Gestalt therapy, rational-emotive therapy, and transactional analysis, to name just a few. (See, for example, Corsini, 1984.) These popular approaches are widely used with adults through middle age, and even with adolescents and children, but are rarely employed with elderly patients.

One reason for this is Freud's belief that patients over age 45 are too inflexible to profit from insight therapy, a view by no means limited to psychoanalysts (Gotestam, 1982). Also, many of the disorders which are of particular interest to geriatricians are not amenable to this form of treatment. "Mere words" can be quite effective in alleviating the miseries of neurosis, but are of little value when the patient suffers from organic brain damage. If memory disturbances prevent the aged from remembering important details of the past, or (in more extreme cases) what the therapist said a few days ago, it will be difficult or impossible for them to generate and maintain any meaningful insights. However, the failure to use insight therapy with elderly patients may also be due in part to bias. When the aged and younger adults suffer from similar symptoms, some therapists may be all too prone to judge the former as having an organic disorder.

Nevertheless, successful insight therapy is being performed with the aged. For example:

THE TREATMENT OF MRS. H. (CASE NUMBER 4).
Because of Mrs. H.'s strong tendency to think negatively about herself, cognitive therapy was selected as the treatment of choice. This approach stresses the role played by distorted, negative thoughts in producing negative mood swings and depression.

Mrs. H. was asked to keep a daily record of her negative thoughts, and to bring this to each therapy session for discussion. For example, she became unreasonably angry when her husband forgot to pick up some clothes from the cleaners, and grew intensely sad at night when she thought about her sons. Her view of life reflected an "all-or-none" philosophy: "either I'm a great success and completely happy, or a total failure and miserably unhappy." And she dwelt on the past in such terms as "if only I had . . ." and "I can't be happy unless things are the way they used to be."

With the aid of the therapist, Mrs. H. soon realized that such thoughts served to fuel her depression. She learned to recognize them as distorted and fallacious, and to reassess her situation from a more realistic perspective. Thus she learned that she could find new sources of happiness to replace the pleasures which she had enjoyed in the past, but which were no longer possible: "things change in life all the time, and this can open new paths to satisfaction." She also traced the roots of her negative thinking to her guilt about having been a working mother long before this was socially acceptable, and to the corresponding belief that she had seriously neglected her husband and children in order to pursue her own career. By learning to monitor her thoughts, and to replace her overly negative cognitions with more realistic appraisals, Mrs. H. was able to achieve a marked decrease in depression. (Gallagher & Thompson, 1983, pp. 27–29.)

EVALUATION.   Evaluating the effectiveness of insight therapy in general is a controversial issue, and establishing the relative merits of specific approaches is even more so. Some critics claim that the cures supposedly achieved by insight therapy are actually due to a placebo effect, or would have occurred spontaneously even if the patients had not undergone therapy. Conversely, many mental health professionals argue that insight therapy is demonstrably successful in many instances. The latter view is probably closer to the truth, and is supported by evidence that is more convincing. (See, for example, Bergin & Strupp, 1970; Bergin & Suinn, 1975; Fisher & Greenberg, 1977; Smith et al., 1980; Strupp & Bergin, 1969.) But it is virtually impossible to determine any numerical success rates for insight therapy, or to draw firm conclusions about which of the various approaches yields better results with adult patients.

It is even more difficult to evaluate the merits of insight therapy with the aged. There are many studies dealing with the effectiveness of this form of therapy, but very few of these concern the elderly. Thus one critic has observed that after 40 years of treating the aged with psychodynamic psychotherapy, only two experimental studies support claims of its efficacy, and both of these suffer from serious methodological flaws (Gotestam, 1982, p. 788). We can only conclude that successful insight therapy with elderly patients appears to be possible, at least in some instances, but that this form of treatment is much more often reserved for those who have not yet passed middle age.

Behavior Therapy

DEFINITION.   Conceptually, **behavior therapy** falls somewhere between insight therapy and somatic therapy. The goal of this form of therapy is to change pathological behaviors and alleviate troublesome symptoms, using the principles and procedures devised by experimental psychologists in their study of normal behavior.

Behavior therapy is less concerned with promoting understanding on the part of the client, and with the issue of childhood causes, than is insight therapy. The behavior therapist is fully responsible for the success or failure of treatment, whereas some failures of insight therapy are attributed largely or entirely to the patient's resistances (i.e., unconscious attempts to defeat the purpose of therapy, avoid necessary but threatening personal change, and remain ill). Finally, the procedures of behavior therapy differ considerably from those of insight (or somatic) therapy.

VARIETIES OF BEHAVIOR THERAPY.   The behavior therapist can draw upon a wide variety of psychological techniques. Some of these include:

Assertive Training. Clients who are overly inhibited (or overly aggressive) in certain situations are helped to reduce their anxiety, and gain reinforcements, by expressing their feelings in an honest and socially appropriate way. This is accomplished by having the client role-play his or her typical behavior in such situations, and then adopt changes suggested (or actually enacted) by the therapist.

Aversion Therapy. An aversive stimulus, such as a safe but painful electric shock to the finger, is used to reduce the probability of undesirable behaviors (e.g., taking a drink by an alcoholic). Aversion therapy is relatively controversial, since it involves some discomfort for the client.

Implosive Therapy. A phobic client is engulfed with massive doses of the anxiety-provoking stimulus in a safe setting. Since the client cannot avoid the feared stimuli, he or she learns that they are actually not dangerous.

Modeling. This is a method for increasing the probability of desirable behaviors. The client observes one or more people demonstrating these behaviors, either live or on film, and is then rewarded for imitating them.

Reciprocal Inhibition. A positive stimulus is used to evoke responses that will inhibit the anxiety caused by a phobic stimulus. The anxiety-provoking stimulus is first presented at a considerable distance, while the positive stimulus (e.g., candy) is given to the client. Since it is difficult to feel happy and afraid at the same time, the strong pleasure evoked by the positive stimulus inhibits the weak anxiety caused by the distant aversive stimulus. The procedure is repeated with the anxiety provoking stimulus gradually brought closer and closer, enabling the client to learn that it is actually not dangerous.

Systematic Desensitization. Phobic anxiety is reduced by having the client list the feared stimuli in hierarchical order, and then imagine being in these situations while practicing previously taught techniques of muscular relaxation. In some instances, the client may be asked to use the relaxation techniques while actually in the anxiety-provoking situation.

Token Economy. The probability of desirable behaviors is increased by following them with conditioned positive reinforcers, such as plastic tokens, which can later be exchanged for primary rewards of the client's own choice. (See, for example, Gambrill, 1977; Rimm & Masters, 1979.)

As an illustration, consider the token economy. This approach was initially evaluated in institutional settings with geriatric, psychotic patients. These elderly adults first learned that a sufficient number of tokens could be exchanged for various primary rewards, such as a private room or increased opportunities to watch television. They were then systematically reinforced with tokens for such desired behaviors as making their beds, combing their hair, brushing their teeth, and proceeding in an orderly manner from their rooms to the dining room. Although the token economy did not cure the patients' psychoses, it did result in marked improvements: the frequency of the desired behaviors increased dramatically when the tokens were used, and then decreased again when (as a check on the results) the tokens were eliminated. (See, for example, Ayllon & Azrin, 1968; Kazdin, 1977.)

As a second example, let us return to one of the cases discussed previously:

> *THE TREATMENT OF MR. B. (CASE NUMBER 5).*
>
> Mr. B. first received a series of 10 ECT treatments over a six-week period, and was released from the hospital as markedly improved. He functioned reasonably well for about eight weeks, when he again began to experience severe mood shifts.
>
> Unlike Mrs. H., Mr. B. had few negative thoughts about himself. He was intensely lonely, however, and had had no meaningful interpersonal relationships since the death of his wife ten years ago. He also found few activities to be pleasant, and many to be unpleasant. Accordingly, behavior therapy was selected as the treatment of choice.
>
> Relaxation training helped to decrease the aversiveness of Mr. B.'s interpersonal encounters, while role-playing and other techniques enabled him to improve his communication skills and develop more positive interactions with other people. He was encouraged to leave his apartment to have lunch, and then visit the park or his neighbors, so as to use his newly developed skills. Eventually he started to take the initiative to plan social activities, such as attending the local senior center and joining a card club. By the end of therapy, Mr. B. had significantly increased his social relationships. His depression was markedly reduced, and remained so during a one-year follow-up period. (Gallagher & Thompson, 1983, pp. 25–26.)

EVALUATION. Although behavior therapy was originally introduced as a simpler and less expensive substitute for insight therapy, both approaches are currently regarded as useful and valuable in their own right. In fact, the rationale for behavior therapy has become so broad that some procedures have been classified under both headings. In cognitive restructuring, for example, psychopathology is attributed to the irrational beliefs with which clients indoctrinate themselves. The therapist therefore strives to help clients replace irrational beliefs like "I am a worthless person because I made a mistake," with rational ones like "It's disappointing that I made a mistake, but it's not a catastrophe; I'll do better next time." The treatment of Mrs. H., discussed previously, is a case in point: some psychologists include such cognitive restructuring among the techniques of behavior therapy (e.g. Gambrill, 1977). If behavior therapy also includes methods specifically designed to promote insight and understanding, and to change unobservable thoughts as well as overt actions, the distinction between this form of therapy and insight therapy blurs considerably.

Problems of definition notwithstanding, behavior therapy is being applied with increasing frequency to the problems that afflict the elderly. Because behavior therapy emphasizes experimental methods, its effectiveness is supported by considerable research evidence; unfortunately, few of these studies deal with aging. As we have seen, however, the token economy has demonstrated its usefulness with elderly patients. There is also some indication that other methods may be successful with the aged, including assertive training and relaxation training. Behavior therapy is less expensive than insight therapy, and less time consuming. Insight therapy may well last for years, whereas clients like Mrs. H. and Mr. B. were treated in a matter of months. In fact, some procedures of behavior therapy are so simple that they can be self-applied.

Like insight therapy, behavior therapy is of proven value with adults not yet past middle age. It also appears reasonable to conclude that with a variety of elderly clients, some form of behavior therapy may well be one treatment of choice.

Group Therapy

Psychotherapy often takes the form of individual therapy, where one patient meets privately with one therapist. Many varieties of insight and behavior therapy are also amenable to **group therapy,** wherein a number of patients (usually from five to ten) meet together with one or two therapists.

Group therapy has several important advantages. It enables the sufferer to interact with and learn from other patients, rather than just the therapist. A patient who feels "crazy" or hopeless may derive considerable comfort from learning that other people have similar problems and experiences. Also, while those who suffer from psychological disorders are likely to have difficulty understanding themselves, they may well be able to make insightful and important comments about other members of the group. The presence of several patients makes it possible to conduct valuable exercises, which cannot be used in individual therapy. For example, an apprehensive patient may be taught to trust other people by being gently lifted off the ground and rocked back and forth by them. Becoming part of a cohesive group can increase the sufferer's motivation to work at the difficult task of personal change. (See Yalom, 1970.) And group therapy is less expensive than individual therapy, since several patients share the cost of each session.

The primary disadvantage of group therapy is its lack of confidentiality. The therapist may instruct the group members not to reveal sensitive material to outsiders, but cannot prevent them from doing so. Also, if the therapist is not sufficiently skilled or careful, inappropriate input from other patients may promote undesirable goals and beliefs rather than constructive ones.

The use of group therapy among the institutionalized aged is increasing, and the results appear to be quite promising (Hartford, 1982; Sherwood & Mor, 1982). For example, in one small but well-controlled study (Wolk & Goldfarb, 1967), group therapy proved to be significantly helpful in overcoming depression and improving interpersonal relations. It also produced positive change among long-term, chronic patients who were diagnosed as having organic brain syndromes. This latter result suggested an important and hopeful conclusion: the monotony of hospital life may lead to apathetic and unresponsive behavior which is mistakenly attributed to an organic disorder, but is actually reversible.

Other studies have reported favorable results for group therapy with elderly outpatients, consciousness-raising therapy groups with noninstitutionalized widows of all ages, and behavior group therapy (Barrett, 1978; Gallagher, 1979; Hartford, 1982). Many forms of group therapy have been used with the elderly, including music therapy (playing an instrument, singing, listening to recordings, writing songs), art therapy, drama therapy (acting, reading plays, writing plays, role-playing life situations), dance and movement therapy, and creative writing therapy. These approaches have led to such positive outcomes as improved self-confidence and self-worth, and an increased ability to cope with crises and personal losses (Hartford, 1982). Providing therapy in the context of a "Coping with Depression" class has also been demonstrated to be effective (Thompson et al., 1983). In sum, the available evidence strongly suggests that group therapy is yet another useful approach for treating adults of all ages.

Afterword

The treatment of adult psychopathology is not without serious problems. Some disorders are incurable, some useful methods have adverse side effects, there may well be some bias against using certain forms of psychotherapy with the elderly (e.g., insight therapy), and some aged individuals may not be able to afford therapy even when it is available.

Nevertheless, there is a markedly positive side to the story. The quality of differential diagnosis is improving, when one wishes to take the necessary time and effort, and an increasing number of therapeutic procedures are being brought to bear on various geriatric disorders. Psychotherapy has long demonstrated its value for those not yet past middle age. Because of the efforts discussed in this chapter, many of the problems that afflict the elderly are also being alleviated; and the latter part of life is, for an increasing number of people, a meaningful and fulfilling period.

Summary

VARIETIES OF ADULT PSYCHOPATHOLOGY

Before we can arrive at meaningful explanations of human behavior, we must first organize what would otherwise be an overwhelming amount of data into a convenient framework. The system currently used to classify the various forms of psychopathology is DSM-III-R, prepared by the American Psychiatric Association. However, terminology from the previous system, DSM-II, is still widely used as well.

Mental health professionals use interviews and psychometric tests to decide which DSM-III-R classification applies to a given adult. Interviewing elderly patients requires considerable skill, and various important guidelines must be followed for the interview to be effective. There are many psychometric instruments which can be used to assess specific conditions.

DSM-III-R and the various assessment procedures make possible very detailed diagnoses. Yet elderly patients are all too often classified as "senile" or "depressed," with no indication as to the procedure used to arrive at this conclusion.

ADULT EPIDEMIOLOGY

The greater the frequency of a particular disorder, the more urgently we need to diagnose and treat it correctly. Field surveys and the case register method are commonly used to obtain epidemiological data, which are typically expressed in terms of incidence rates and prevalence rates.

Organic brain syndromes are caused by physical damage to the brain, and are more likely to occur with increasing age. Acute organic brain syndrome has a more favorable prognosis, but is difficult to distinguish from other disorders. Chronic organic brain syndrome, which includes the senile and presenile dementias, has a less favorable prognosis; this is the disorder causing the most concern among the aged in North America and Europe. Of particular concern is Alzheimer's disease, a terminal and devastating disorder which afflicts some 20 percent of all adults over 80. The causes of this disease are still unknown.

Functional disorders are those which cannot be attributed primarily to physical causes. Schizophrenia is not as prevalent among the elderly as the organic brain syndromes. Neurosis is more common than the organic disorders and psychoses among the population as a whole, but is of lesser interest to geriatricians because it usually originates during childhood and (to a lesser extent) adolescense. Depression is the functional disorder that is most common among the elderly. However, the normal course of adult development is not necessarily (or even usually) accompanied by increases in depression. Rather, the incidence rates for all other functional disorders decrease with increasing age.

The prevalence rates for alcoholism decrease with increasing age. This is partly because many alcoholics die at a young age, and partly due to spontaneous remission.

THE TREATMENT OF ADULT PSYCHOPATHOLOGY

There are many professions that seek to treat adult psychopathology, many forms of therapy, and many specific therapeutic procedures.

Somatic therapy utilizes physical methods to alter a patient's physiological and psychological state. Electroconvulsive therapy, wherein electric currents are administered to one or both hemispheres of the brain, may occasionally be of value in treating geriatric disorders. Psychosurgery, wherein areas of the brain are surgically destroyed, has deservedly become almost obsolete. Chemotherapy, or drug therapy, is currently the most popular method of somatic therapy. Drugs used in chemotherapy include minor tranquilizers (to treat neurosis), major tranquilizers (to treat psychoses, such as schizophrenia), stimulants (of uncertain value with the elderly), and antidepressants (which produce elevations in mood). Although many of these drugs have unpleasant side effects, they may well be the best available procedures for treating certain disorders.

The basic assumption underlying insight therapy is that in many instances, people behave in self-defeating and pathological ways because they are not aware of their true motives, beliefs, and feelings. Thus insight therapy is designed to help patients obtain an intellectual and emotional understanding of the causes and dynamics of their disorders, using verbal communication rather than physical methods. Although successful insight therapy has been performed with the elderly, this approach is most often reserved for those who are not yet past middle age.

The goal of behavior therapy is to change pathological behaviors, and alleviate troublesome symptoms, by drawing on the principles and procedures of experimental psychology. Specific procedures include assertive training, aversion therapy, implosive therapy, modeling, reciprocal inhibition, systematic desensitization, the token economy, and (perhaps) cognitive restructuring. Behavior therapy is being increasingly applied to the problems that afflict the elderly, and the results appear to be quite promising. Like insight therapy, behavior therapy is of proven value with those not yet past middle age.

In group therapy, a number of patients (usually from five to ten) meet together with one or two therapists. Among the procedures used in group therapy are insight therapy, behavior therapy, music therapy, art therapy, drama therapy, dance and movement therapy, and creative writing therapy. As with behavior therapy, group therapy appears to be useful with adults of all ages.

The treatment of adult psychopathology is not without serious problems. Some disorders are incurable, some useful methods have adverse side effects, there may well be some bias against using certain forms of psychotherapy with the elderly, and some aged individuals may not be able to afford therapy even when it is available. Nevertheless, the efforts of mental health professionals are helping to alleviate many of the problems that afflict older adults, and to make the latter part of life a meaningful and fulfilling period for an increasing number of people.

CHAPTER 12

Death and Dying

In Chapter 1, we observed that many more of us are living to old age than ever before. There has also been a significant change in our manner of dying: illnesses which are of long duration (**chronic**) have replaced those which are brief and severe (**acute**) as the major causes of death. This means that dying will be a fairly drawn-out process for many of us. Furthermore, this process is likely to place considerable demands on those family members and friends who are with us during this difficult time. As a result, death and dying has become an important aspect of adult development and aging.

Partly for this reason, recent years have seen a remarkable crescendo of discussion about death and dying. Library shelves are now filled with volumes concerning the philosophical, religious, sociological, anthropological, psychological, and medical views of death. It is not unusual for more than 700 books to be published on these topics in a single year. Entire journals are now devoted to the inspection, dissection, and analysis of every imaginable aspect of death and dying. It has even been suggested that death has become chic in the American culture (Rosenbaum, 1982).

This fascination with death is hardly new. Noted philosophers from Epicurus to Bertrand Russell, playwrights, poets, novelists, and many others have written incisively about death for more than two thousand years. During the past two decades, however, our quest for knowledge has taken a significant turn: for the first time, investigators in a variety of disciplines have sought to collect systematic empirical data about death and dying. Much of this data-gathering has been stimulated and carried out by psychologists; but sociologists, anthropologists, and physicians have participated as well. This area is also prone to methodological problems, and some researchers have drawn intriguing but overly speculative conclusions that go far beyond the actual evidence. Yet we can now answer some important questions about death and dying, and make educated guesses in various areas where firm conclusions are not yet possible.

This chapter will address four major issues. First we will examine the demography of death, including leading causes and mortality rates. Next we will survey the evidence dealing with the fear of death, which some psychologists and philosophers believe to be a major determinant of human behavior. Our third topic concerns the experiences of the terminally ill, and the effects on their families and friends. For example, do all of the dying proceed through a series of similar psychological stages? Or are their experiences with the specter of death primarily different? Part four deals with the grief and bereavement that result from the death of someone close to us, and how there intense and painful feelings may be alleviated.

The Demography of Death

Although the course of human history has been highlighted by astonishing scientific advances, methods for preventing death exist only in the realm of science fiction. In 1982, for example, the number of deaths in the United States totaled approximately 2 million (National Center for Health Statistics, 1983). However, important changes have occurred in the most common causes and places of death.

Causes of Death

In the preceding chapter, we observed that classification is an important aspect of any science. This also applies to the study of mortality rates: causes of death are classified according to formal criteria established by the World Health Organization, aided by such standardized instruments as the death certificate. This useful form records such information as immediate and other causes of death; whether death was due to an accident, suicide, or homicide; the time and place of death; and biographical data, such as the deceased's name, sex, age, birthplace, and immediate family. (See Figure 12.1.)

LEADING CAUSES OF DEATH.   As noted at the outset of this chapter, deaths in our society are more often due to chronic than to acute illnesses. In 1982, fifteen leading causes accounted for 89 percent of all deaths in the United States. (See Table 12.1.) Deaths from communicable diseases, such as tuberculosis, influenza, and pneumonia, have decreased markedly since 1900. Conversely, people today are more likely to die from such degenerative diseases as heart

TYPE/PRINT IN PERMANENT BLACK INK

FOR INSTRUCTIONS SEE OTHER SIDE AND HANDBOOK

U.S. STANDARD CERTIFICATE OF DEATH

LOCAL FILE NUMBER   STATE FILE NUMBER

DECEDENT

1. DECEDENT'S NAME (First, Middle, Last) | 2. SEX | 3. DATE OF DEATH (Month, Day, Year)

4. SOCIAL SECURITY NUMBER | 5a. AGE—Last Birthday (Years) | 5b. UNDER 1 YEAR (Months / Days) | 5c. UNDER 1 DAY (Hours / Minutes) | 6. DATE OF BIRTH (Month, Day, Year) | 7. BIRTHPLACE (City and State or Foreign Country)

8. WAS DECEDENT EVER IN U.S. ARMED FORCES? (Yes or no) | 9a. PLACE OF DEATH (Check only one; see instructions on other side)
HOSPITAL: ☐ Inpatient ☐ ER/Outpatient ☐ DOA OTHER: ☐ Nursing Home ☐ Residence ☐ Other (Specify)

9b. FACILITY NAME (If not institution, give street and number) | 9c. CITY, TOWN, OR LOCATION OF DEATH | 9d. COUNTY OF DEATH

10. MARITAL STATUS—Married, Never Married, Widowed, Divorced (Specify) | 11. SURVIVING SPOUSE (If wife, give maiden name) | 12a. DECEDENT'S USUAL OCCUPATION (Give kind of work done during most of working life. Do not use retired.) | 12b. KIND OF BUSINESS/INDUSTRY

13a. RESIDENCE—STATE | 13b. COUNTY | 13c. CITY, TOWN, OR LOCATION | 13d. STREET AND NUMBER

13e. INSIDE CITY LIMITS? (Yes or no) | 13f. ZIP CODE | 14. WAS DECEDENT OF HISPANIC ORIGIN? (Specify No or Yes—If yes, specify Cuban, Mexican, Puerto Rican, etc.) ☐ No ☐ Yes Specify: | 15. RACE—American Indian, Black, White, etc. (Specify) | 16. DECEDENT'S EDUCATION (Specify only highest grade completed) Elementary/Secondary (0-12) College (1-4 or 5+)

PARENTS

17. FATHER'S NAME (First, Middle, Last) | 18. MOTHER'S NAME (First, Middle, Maiden Surname)

INFORMANT

19a. INFORMANT'S NAME (Type/Print) | 19b. MAILING ADDRESS (Street and Number or Rural Route Number, City or Town, State, Zip Code)

DISPOSITION

20a. METHOD OF DISPOSITION ☐ Burial ☐ Cremation ☐ Removal from State ☐ Donation ☐ Other (Specify) _____ | 20b. PLACE OF DISPOSITION (Name of cemetery, crematory, or other place) | 20c. LOCATION—City or Town, State

21a. SIGNATURE OF FUNERAL SERVICE LICENSEE OR PERSON ACTING AS SUCH ► | 21b. LICENSE NUMBER (of Licensee) | 22. NAME AND ADDRESS OF FACILITY

PRONOUNCING PHYSICIAN ONLY

ITEMS 24-26 MUST BE COMPLETED BY PERSON WHO PRONOUNCES DEATH

Complete items 23a-c only when certifying physician is not available at time of death to certify cause of death. | 23a. To the best of my knowledge, death occurred at the time, date, and place stated. Signature and Title ► | 23b. LICENSE NUMBER | 23c. DATE SIGNED (Month, Day, Year)

24. TIME OF DEATH ___ M | 25. DATE PRONOUNCED DEAD (Month, Day, Year) | 26. WAS CASE REFERRED TO MEDICAL EXAMINER/CORONER? (Yes or no)

CAUSE OF DEATH

27. PART I. Enter the diseases, injuries, or complications that caused the death. Do not enter the mode of dying, such as cardiac or respiratory arrest, shock, or heart failure. List only one cause on each line. | Approximate Interval Between Onset and Death

IMMEDIATE CAUSE (Final disease or condition resulting in death) ► a. _____ DUE TO (OR AS A CONSEQUENCE OF):

Sequentially list conditions, if any, leading to immediate cause. Enter UNDERLYING CAUSE (Disease or injury that initiated events resulting in death) LAST b. _____ DUE TO (OR AS A CONSEQUENCE OF):

c. _____ DUE TO (OR AS A CONSEQUENCE OF):

d.

PART II. Other significant conditions contributing to death but not resulting in the underlying cause given in Part I. | 28a. WAS AN AUTOPSY PERFORMED? (Yes or no) | 28b. WERE AUTOPSY FINDINGS AVAILABLE PRIOR TO COMPLETION OF CAUSE OF DEATH? (Yes or no)

29. MANNER OF DEATH ☐ Natural ☐ Pending Investigation ☐ Accident ☐ Could not be Determined ☐ Suicide ☐ Homicide | 30a. DATE OF INJURY (Month, Day, Year) | 30b. TIME OF INJURY ___ M | 30c. INJURY AT WORK? (Yes or no) | 30d. DESCRIBE HOW INJURY OCCURRED

30e. PLACE OF INJURY—At home, farm, street, factory, office building, etc. (Specify) | 30f. LOCATION (Street and Number or Rural Route Number, City or Town, State)

CERTIFIER

31a. CERTIFIER (Check only one)

☐ CERTIFYING PHYSICIAN (Physician certifying cause of death when another physician has pronounced death and completed Item 23) To the best of my knowledge, death occurred due to the cause(s) and manner as stated.

☐ PRONOUNCING AND CERTIFYING PHYSICIAN (Physician both pronouncing death and certifying to cause of death) To the best of my knowledge, death occurred at the time, date, and place, and due to the cause(s) and manner as stated.

☐ MEDICAL EXAMINER/CORONER On the basis of examination and/or investigation, in my opinion, death occurred at the time, date, and place, and due to the cause(s) and manner as stated.

31b. SIGNATURE AND TITLE OF CERTIFIER | 31c. LICENSE NUMBER | 31d. DATE SIGNED (Month, Day, Year)

32. NAME AND ADDRESS OF PERSON WHO COMPLETED CAUSE OF DEATH (ITEM 27) (Type/Print)

REGISTRAR

33. REGISTRAR'S SIGNATURE ► | 34. DATE FILED (Month, Day, Year)

PHS-T-003 REV. 1/89

Left margin: NAME OF DECEDENT: For use by physician or institution — SEE INSTRUCTIONS ON OTHER SIDE — SEE DEFINITION ON OTHER SIDE — SEE INSTRUCTIONS ON OTHER SIDE — SEE DEFINITION ON OTHER SIDE — DEPARTMENT OF HEALTH AND HUMAN SERVICES — PUBLIC HEALTH SERVICE — NATIONAL CENTER FOR HEALTH STATISTICS – 1989 REVISION

FIGURE 12.1 A typical death certificate. Courtesy Indiana State Board of Health.

TABLE 12.1   Mortality rates for the United States, 1982.

Rank	Cause of Death	Percent of Total Deaths
1	Heart diseases	38.2
2	Malignant neoplasms (including tumors, cancers)	21.9
3	Cerebrovascular diseases (including strokes)	8.0
4	Accidents (motor vehicles, 2.3; all others, 2.5)	4.8
5	Chronic obstructive pulmonary diseases	3.0
6	Pneumonia and influenza	2.5
7	Diabetes mellitus	1.7
8	Suicide	1.4
9	Chronic liver disease and cirrhosis	1.4
10	Atherosclerosis	1.3
11	Homicide and legal intervention	1.1
12	Certain conditions originating in the perinatal period	1.0
13	Nephritis and nephrosis	0.9
14	Congenital anomalies	0.7
15	Septicemia	0.6
—	All other causes	11.3

SOURCE: National Center for Health Statistics (1983, p. 5).

ailments, cancer, and strokes. However, there has been a decline in heart diseases and strokes since 1950. (See Figure 12.2.)

THE DEMOGRAPHICS OF SUICIDE.   Suicide is of some interest to geriatricians because of its relationship to depression, one of the most common adult disorders (Chapter 11), and because suicide rates vary considerably as a function of age (as well as race and sex). Suicide is most common among white males, especially those over 65. This is the group that most often achieves the dominant positions in our society, and suffers the greatest losses in status and financial rewards with retirement and old age. For white females and non-whites, on the other hand, suicide rates generally peak during early and middle adulthood and then decline during old age. (See Figure 12.3.)

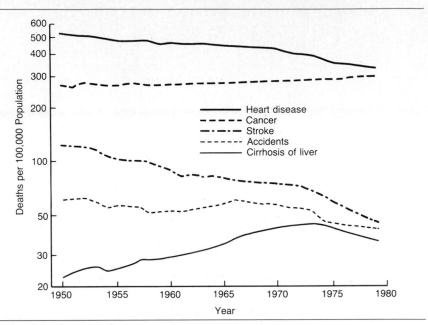

FIGURE 12.2 Death rates for persons 45–64 years of age in the United States, 1950–1979. National Center for Health Statistics (1982).

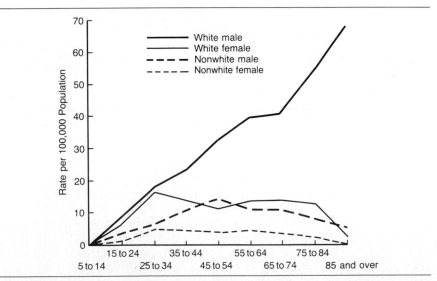

FIGURE 12.3 Suicide rates by age and ethnic group. National Center for Health Statistics (1967).

TABLE 12.2   Percent of deaths in and out of institutions in the United States, 1949 and 1958.

| | Percent of Deaths | | |
Location	*1949*	*1958*	*1979**
Not in an Institution	50.5	39.1	15
In an Institution	49.5	60.9	85
General hospitals	(39.5)	(46.6)	
Convalescent and nursing homes, homes for the aged, etc.	(1.6)	(6.0)	
Nervous and mental hospitals	(3.2)	(3.5)	
Chronic disease and other special hospitals	(0.9)	(1.5)	
Tuberculosis hospitals	(0.9)	(0.6)	
Maternity hospitals	(0.2)	(0.1)	
Other	(3.2)	(2.6)	

*Cancer deaths only.
SOURCE: Adapted from Lerner (1976, p. 140); Mor & Hiris (1983).

Places of Death

Relatively little research attention has been paid to the locations where Americans are most likely to die, even though this information can readily be obtained from death certificates. From 1949 to 1979, deaths were much more common in institutional settings. (See Table 12.2.) However, recent data obtained from studies examining the impact of hospice programs suggest a reversal of this trend (Mor & Hiris, 1983; Morris et al., 1984). These researchers report that when patients are given a choice, they prefer to die at home. Furthermore, dying at home may occur in as many as 50 percent of the cases if the patient is enrolled in a hospice program. This is possible because many of the health and social services typically delivered in an institutional setting are provided in the patient's home.

Regardless of whether one dies at home or in an institution, various medical personnel will play an important role in the process of dying. Many terminal patients come to rely on these professionals not only for medical care, but also for social and emotional support. This is likely to cause problems for both the staff and the patient, as we will see in a subsequent section.

The Fear of Death

Some theorists believe that the **fear of death (death anxiety),** conscious and unconscious, is the prime mover for all human behavior.[1] In his Pulitzer Prize-winning book, *The Denial of Death,* Ernest Becker (1973) argues that:

> *Of all things that move man, one of the principal ones is his terror of death.* . . . The idea of death, the fear of it, haunts the human animal like nothing else; it is a mainspring of human activity—activity designed largely to avoid the fatality of death, to overcome it by denying in some way that it is the final destiny for man.

The overriding importance of death anxiety as a motivator is characteristic of the school known as existential psychology, typified by Rollo May:

> To grasp what it means to exist, one needs to grasp the fact that he might not exist, that he treads at every moment on the sharp edge of possible annihilation and can never escape the fact that death will arrive at some unknown moment in the future. . . . Without this awareness of nonbeing . . . existence is vapid [and] unreal. . . . [But] with the confrontation of nonbeing, existence takes on vitality and immediacy, and the individual experiences a heightened consciousness of himself, his world, and others around him. . . . [Thus] the confronting of death gives the most positive reality to life itself. (May, 1958/1967, pp. 47–49.)

As these experts suggest, the fear of death can be both a destructive and a creative force. This universal fear may lead to neurosis, or even to psychosis; but it is also responsible for the pleasures of existence, and for many of humanity's most outstanding achievements. Because of death anxiety, some people are motivated to transcend their physical mortality through their productions: artists and writers may hope that their works will live forever, scientists may seek major discoveries that will have lasting benefits for all of humankind, politicians may strive to have their accomplishments permanently recorded on the pages of history, and so on. Or, for many people, having children may be a form of immortality.

---

[1] Some writers use the term *fear* when the cause is known and readily available to consciousness, and reserve the term *anxiety* for causes that are vague or unconscious. Others use the two terms more or less interchangeably, as will we in this book.

Although existentialist theory is important and provocative, it is by no means universally accepted. Others have argued that most of us experience little anxiety over the prospect of dying because it looms far in the future (e.g., Schulz, 1978). In fact, many different conceptions of death have been proposed by philosophers, religious leaders, psychologists, and others, some of which date back to ancient Greece. Nevertheless, there does appear to be general agreement on at least one point: death is an experience that few people eagerly seek out. We may therefore ask: what is it about death that makes it so undesirable to most of us?

Reasons for Fearing Death

There are two general reasons why death is markedly unattractive: it involves physical suffering and psychological suffering. These two categories are not mutually exclusive; neither one exists in isolation, and each can intensify the other.

THE FEAR OF PHYSICAL SUFFERING.   As noted previously, deaths from chronic degenerative diseases (e.g., cancer) have increased markedly since 1900. We are all aware that patients with terminal cancer may experience months or even years of pain, undergo forms of therapy that have distressing side effects, or suffer the removal of limbs or breasts. To many people, the possibility of such extreme pain and deterioration is frightening indeed.

THE FEAR OF NONBEING.   Human beings are the only creatures on earth who must live with the constant awareness that they will someday cease to exist. As we have seen, this knowledge of our ultimate nonbeing can arouse intense anxiety.

THE FEAR OF COWARDICE AND HUMILIATION.   We may also fear that we will become cowards in the face of death, either because of the accompanying physical pain or because we dread the thought of not existing. Thus the aforementioned sources of death anxiety may well create the "fear of fear itself."

THE FEAR OF FAILING TO ACHIEVE IMPORTANT GOALS.   Some people define the length of their lives in terms of accomplishments, rather than years. If a university professor were asked how long he or she wanted to live, the reply might well be: "Long enough to write two more books." Or an elderly person may express the desire to survive until an important birthday or anniversary, or an offspring's wedding. We may therefore fear death because it will deprive us of cherished goals and experiences.

Chapter Glossary: Death and Dying

Acute illness

A disorder that has a relatively sudden onset, and is of brief duration. Acute illnesses are more likely to end in a recovery than are chronic illnesses.

Bereavement

A state of desolation caused by the death of a loved one. Similar to *grief*.

Chronic illness

A disorder that has a slow onset, and is of long duration. Chronic illnesses, such as cancer, have replaced acute illnesses as the major causes of death in the United States.

Death anxiety

A synonym for the fear of death.

Direct measure

A measure of death anxiety that taps only the conscious and public level. Typically takes the form of written questionnaires.

Fear of death

Tension and uneasiness caused by the knowledge that our lives will someday end. A multidimensional variable, usually assumed to be partly or primarily unconscious.

Hospice approach

A relatively new method of caring for terminal patients, which is designed to meet such important needs as the alleviation of pain and the desire for attention and love.

Indirect measure

A measure designed to tap the less-conscious aspects of death anxiety. Typically involves relatively complicated experimental procedures.

Kübler-Ross stage theory

Posits five emotional and psychological stages through which all dying patients presumably proceed: denial, anger, bargaining, depression, and acceptance. *Not* supported by the preponderance of research evidence.

Paraprofessional therapy (for the bereaved)

Therapy conducted by people who are *not* trained health-care professionals, but who have lost a spouse and gone through the bereavement process themselves.

Professional therapy

Therapy conducted by someone formally trained in a health-care discipline, such as medicine, psychology, psychiatry, or social work.

Terminal illness

An illness from which there is no reasonable hope of ever recovering, although there may be periods of remission and apparent health.

Terminal phase of life   The last decline in health that ends in death, from which there is no major remission. A time of steady and rapid deterioration, especially of the central nervous system.

THE FEAR OF THE IMPACT OF DEATH ON ONE'S SURVIVORS.   Yet another source of death anxiety is the probable impact on one's survivors. Where finances permit, life insurance and trust funds can help parents alleviate the economic impact on their children. But finding some way to relieve the psychological and emotional impact is quite another matter.

THE FEAR OF PUNISHMENT.   Some religions preach that transgressors are doomed to dire fates, such as consignment to Hell. Believers may therefore become profoundly afraid of what they will experience after they die. However, it is also possible that religion will have precisely the opposite effect. That is, those who believe in more supportive religions may find that their faith significantly reduces their fear of death.

THE FEAR OF THE DEATH OF OTHERS.   Death anxiety is not limited to our own demise. We may also fear losing someone close to us, and having to experience their physical and psychological suffering. Each of the fears already listed can also be experienced vicariously, in relation to the death of a loved one.

In theory, then, there are numerous reasons why the fear of death might dominate our lives. But does it? To answer this important question, let us now turn to an examination of the relevant research evidence.

Research on Death Anxiety

CONCEPTUAL AND METHODOLOGICAL ISSUES.   Most often, death anxiety has been assessed by written questionnaires. A typical example of these **direct measures** is Templer's (1970) Death Anxiety Scale, which consists of fifteen true-false items:

1. I am very much afraid to die.
2. The thought of death seldom enters my mind.

3. It doesn't make me nervous when people talk about death.

4. I dread to think about having to have an operation.

5. I am not at all afraid to die.

6. I am not particularly afraid of getting cancer.

7. The thought of death never bothers me.

8. I am often distressed by the way time flies so very rapidly.

9. I fear dying a painful death.

10. The subject of life after death troubles me greatly.

11. I am really scared of having a heart attack.

12. I often think about how short life really is.

13. I shudder when I hear people talking about a World War III.

14. The sight of a dead body is horrifying to me.

15. I feel that the future holds nothing for me to fear.

The responses to these items are mathematically combined into a single death-anxiety score. Various comparable questionnaires have been devised by other researchers (e.g., Boyar, 1964; Collett & Lester, 1969; Lester, 1967; Sarnoff & Corwin, 1959; Tolor & Reznikoff, 1967).

How psychometrically sound are these instruments? On the positive side, there is some support for their validity. For example, psychiatric patients who were rated high in anxiety by a clinician scored significantly higher on Templer's scale than did a control group. Subjects who viewed a movie depicting gruesome automobile accidents showed significantly greater death anxiety on Boyar's scale than did subjects who watched an innocuous movie. Intercorrelations between various death anxiety questionnaires have been found to vary from +.41 to +.72, indicating a fairly high degree of agreement (Durlak, 1972; Handal et al., 1984–85).

Unfortunately, these questionnaires suffer from some serious conceptual flaws. First of all, they assess only the *public and conscious* aspects of death anxiety. Our *conscious but private* feelings may well be quite different, but too sensitive and intimate to share with other people. If subjects believe that such fears are a sign of serious personal weakness, or that these fears are no one else's business, they may deliberately falsify their answers in order to appear more courageous. Some studies do indicate that when subjects are identified by name, they report less fear of death than when the questionnaires are administered anonymously (Jones & Sigall, 1971; Schulz, Aderman, & Manko, 1976).

Furthermore, the fear of death is typically assumed to be partly or primarily *unconscious.* Since this repressed aspect is hidden even from ourselves, it cannot be assessed by instruments which depend entirely on conscious self-reports, even if subjects are trying their best to be honest and accurate. For this reason, attempts have been made to tap the less-conscious aspects of death anxiety by using various **indirect measures.** Some of these include:

- *The Word Association Test:* The experimenter states a single word, and the subject must reply with the first word that comes to mind (Jung, 1905; 1910). Subjects with greater death anxiety will presumably respond more slowly to death-related words (e.g., *cemetery),* or will give more unusual responses, than is the case with neutral words.

- *The Color Word Interference Test:* The subject is asked to state the color in which a word is printed, while disregarding its meaning. Here again, subjects with greater death anxiety will presumably respond more slowly to death-related words than to equally common but more neutral words.

- *The Death Anxiety Slideshow Measure:* Subjects are shown a series of slides. Some are death oriented, such as a slide of the word *graveyard* followed by a picture of a graveyard; while others are neutral, as with the word *greenness* followed by a picture of a backyard lawn scene. During this presentation, a physiological measure of anxiety is obtained by monitoring the subjects' heart rates. Subjects who fear death more will presumably show more pronounced changes in heart rate to the death-oriented slides than to the neutral ones.

In theory, if much of our death anxiety is beyond our awareness, we should show considerably more fear on these indirect measures than on direct questionnaires. Some studies do find this to be the case, indicating that a significant part of death anxiety is unconscious (e.g., Feifel, 1974; Feifel & Branscomb, 1973; Feifel, Freilich, & Hermann, 1973; Feifel & Nagy, 1980). However, the evidence in this area is equivocal. Other investigators have reached precisely the opposite conclusion: they report that subjects obtain similar scores on direct and indirect measures, which implies that we do *not* repress our fear of death (e.g., Littlefield & Fleming, 1984–85). It has also been argued that the indirect measures of death anxiety are of questionable validity. One study found little or no relationship among these measures, indicating that they do *not* assess the same concept (Handal et al., 1984–85).

To some extent, these conflicting findings reflect the difficulty of studying unconscious processes in the research laboratory. Psychology is still a young science, and current research methods may well be too insensitive to measure the deepest aspects of our personalities with any accuracy. (See Chapter 7.) In any case, the available evidence neither confirms nor refutes the hypothesis that death anxiety is at least partly unconscious. Until and unless researchers are able to unearth more definitive data, this hypothesis must remain tenable but controversial.

Another problem with most direct questionnaires is that they treat death anxiety as a unidimensional concept. That is, they yield only a single score for each subject. Although this assumption is appealingly simple, it is almost certainly erroneous. We have seen that death anxiety has aspects that are conscious and public, conscious and private, and (very possibly) unconscious. We have also noted various reasons why we may fear death, and it is quite possible to suffer from some of these anxieties but not from others. Thus an unmarried person may fear the physical suffering associated with dying, but have no survivors to worry about. A devoted parent may be extremely concerned with the impact of his or her death on the children, but much less anxious about the possibility of physical pain. Or dedicated scientists and artists may fear the interruption of their work far more than any other aspect of dying.

Here, the empirical data are more clearcut. Even Templer's straightforward scale has been found to include several distinct factors: the fear of the unknown aspects of death, the fear of suffering, the fear of loneliness at the time of death, and the fear of personal extinction (Conte et al., 1982). There is one questionnaire which does distinguish among four sources of death anxiety, though all are public and conscious: death of self, death of others, dying of self, and dying of others (Collett & Lester, 1969). These investigators obtained low intercorrelations among the four subscales, indicating once again that death anxiety is multidimensional. And still other researchers have drawn a similar conclusion (e.g., Florian & Har-Even, 1983–84; Kastenbaum & Costa, 1977; Littlefield & Fleming, 1984–85).

How many dimensions does this variable have? As yet, the answer is far from certain. If we consider the conscious and unconscious aspects of death anxiety together with the various reasons for fearing death, numerous possible varieties may be identified. In Table 12.3, for example, cell number 1 refers to the death-related fears of physical suffering that you are willing to reveal publicly. Cell number 2 concerns the physical fears that you are aware of, but

TABLE 12.3 The multidimensional nature of death anxiety: 21 possible varieties.

Reasons for Fearing One's Own Death	Psychological Level		
	Public and Conscious	Private and Conscious	Unconscious
Physical suffering (and bodily deterioration)	1	2	3
Nonbeing	4	5	6
Cowardice and humiliation	7	8	9
Interruption of goals	10	11	12
Impact on survivors: psychological and emotional suffering	13	14	15
Impact on survivors: economic hardship	16	17	18
Punishment	19	20	21

Note: These varieties are purely hypothetical, and are presented only for purposes of discussion and illustration; they have *not* been confirmed by empirical research. Also, all of the fears listed above can be experienced vicariously, in relation to the death of a loved one.

may not wish to share with other people. Cell number 3 deals with those physical fears that you will not admit even to yourself. Cells number 4 through number 6 involve your fears of nonbeing, so prominent in existential theory; and so on. All of the varieties listed in Table 12.3 may not be important, or even truly different from one another. But it does seem clear that death anxiety is far too complicated a concept to be summarized by a single score, or perhaps even by just two or three scores.

In sum: research on death anxiety has all too often relied on simple unidimensional scores, based solely on the public and conscious level. It is only recently that investigators have begun to tap the true richness and complexity of this variable, including its multidimensionality and possible unconscious aspects.

SUBSTANTIVE FINDINGS. Death anxiety has been studied in relation to various aspects of adult behavior. As might be expected from the preceding discussion, relatively few clear and consistent patterns have emerged from the available data. In this section, we will explore some of the more interesting questions posed by researchers in this area.

Does our fear of death become stronger as we grow older? More recent studies have *not* found pronounced increases in death anxiety during the first half of adulthood, at least at a conscious level. In fact, some studies of young adults have yielded small but statistically significant negative correlations between age and direct measures of death anxiety. This weak, inverse relationship has been observed for junior college students (mean age 27 years), and for members of such death-related professions as funeral personnel and firemen. However, the same studies also obtained mostly nonsignificant correlations when indirect measures were used to assess death anxiety, and for subjects in such professions as secretarial work and teaching (Handal et al., 1984–85; Lattaner & Hayslip, 1984–85). Similar nonsignificant results were reported in an earlier large-scale study, wherein the Death Anxiety Scale was administered to more than 2,000 subjects of various ages (Templer, Ruff, & Franks, 1971).

The relationship between aging and the fear of death does appear to be moderated by physical health. Adults who suffer from serious illnesses, especially acute disorders, tend to show greater death anxiety than do healthy adults (Viney, 1984–85). These patients are likely to express considerable concern with such fears as physical suffering, nonbeing, and cowardice and humiliation (e.g., "I worry about whether I'll have the strength to die with dignity"). Since ill health is more likely to occur at advanced ages, a corresponding age-related increase in death anxiety may be expected. However, the failure to verbalize such fears does *not* necessarily mean that death anxiety is absent. As we have seen, our conscious and private feelings may differ from those that are conscious and public. Furthermore, the tendency to repress our death anxiety may well increase as we pass middle age and death becomes a more immediate threat. It has been found that adults past the age of 50 are more likely to deny their fears of death, yet their unconscious death anxiety is just as high as that of younger adults (Corey, 1961; Feifel & Branscomb, 1973). As was the case with young adults, however, the evidence does *not* indicate that healthy men and women become more afraid of death (at least at a conscious level) as they grow from middle to old age.

Are such personal characteristics as sex and religious beliefs related to death anxiety? As noted previously in this chapter, it is conceivable that religious beliefs might either intensify or alleviate the fear of death. More recent studies of young adults indicate that both of these possibilities do occur in at least some instances (DaSilva & Schork, 1984–85; Florian & Har-Even, 1983–84), while some earlier studies have found that religious beliefs more often operate in a positive direction. That is, those who are strongly religious and believe in an afterlife are less afraid of death than people who are not as religious (Jeffers, Nichols, & Eisdorfer, 1961; see also Osarchuk & Tatz, 1973).

The evidence concerning gender and death anxiety is also inconsistent. Some researchers have found that females show higher anxiety on direct measures, and are less likely to repress their fears of death. If this pattern were a reliable one, it could be argued that men are more reluctant to admit their death anxiety because they regard such fears as unmasculine. However, various other studies have not obtained significant differences in death anxiety between the sexes. (See, for example, DaSilva & Schork, 1984–85; Lester, 1984–85; Pollak, 1979–80.) All too many researchers in this area have based their conclusions solely on unidimensional death anxiety scores, so further research of a multidimensional nature is needed before firm conclusions can be drawn.

Is death anxiety higher among the mentally ill? The data in this area are also equivocal, and consist primarily of unidimensional studies. Some of these suggest that the mentally ill score unusually high on direct questionnaires, while others report no significant differences between psychiatric patients and more normal subjects (Templer, 1971; Templer & Ruff, 1971; Feifel & Hermann, 1973). However, those who actually attempt suicide appear to have less conscious fear of death than does the general population (Lester, 1967; Tarter, Templer, & Perley, 1974).

Does death anxiety influence the likelihood of participating in life-threatening activities? People who are high in death anxiety might seem less likely to engage in risky, life-threatening professions and avocations. To test this hypothesis, Feifel and Nagy (1980) obtained samples of such risk-takers as alcoholics, drug addicts, and inmates serving prison sentences for committing violent crimes. Also included were a sample of deputy sheriffs, who engage in life-threatening behaviors that are socially acceptable; and a control group of federal government employees, who were not involved in such risky behaviors. The results did *not* support the hypothesis; the various risk-taking groups were not significantly lower (or higher) in conscious or unconscious death anxiety than the control group.

Do dreams provide any evidence about unconscious fears of death? Most psychologists agree that dreams provide important clues about our unconscious wishes, feelings, beliefs, and motives, although dream interpretation can be a difficult and controversial affair. (See, for example, Foulkes, 1966; Freud, 1900/1965a; Fromm, 1951; Hall, 1966; Jung, 1964.) In one study, subjects who scored either high or low on direct measures of death anxiety had a significantly higher proportion of death-related dreams than did subjects with moderate scores (Handal & Rychlak, 1971). This curvilinear relationship suggests once again that some people who have relatively little death anxiety at the conscious level, public and private, may well be considerably more afraid at an unconscious level.

AFTERWORD. The evidence reviewed fails to support the existentialist belief as to the overwhelming importance of death anxiety.

However, it could be argued that the negative findings are due partly or largely to methodological difficulties. While hypotheses involving the unconscious aspects of death anxiety remain controversial, a number of studies do suggest that a significant part of these fears is indeed beyond our awareness. More data, and more valid indirect measures, are needed in order to determine the extent to which death anxiety influences human behavior.

Based on the available evidence, there is no reason to expect that you will become increasingly preoccupied with the prospect of your own death as you grow through adulthood. However, serious physical illnesses represent an important exception. When such disorders make the prospect of death more imminent and real, anxiety is likely to increase markedly; and these fears may take various forms, since death anxiety is not unidimensional. As a result, helping terminally ill patients to deal with their anxieties is far from an easy task—as we will see in the following pages.

The Process of Dying: The Terminal Stages of Life

A **terminal illness** is one from which the patient has no reasonable hope of ever recovering, although there may be periods of remission and apparent health. Terminality has been defined in various ways; according to the United States Department of Health and Human Services, an illness is terminal if a physician certifies that the individual has a life expectancy of six months or less (Schulz & Schlarb, in press).

The **terminal phase of life** is the last decline in health that ends in death, from which there is *no* major remission. This phase is a time of steady and rapid deterioration, especially of the central nervous system, and it may well be evidenced by sudden sharp declines in scores on mental and psychomotor tests. (Recall the discussion of terminal drop in Chapter 6.)

Interest in these terminal stages of life is currently at an all-time high, and for good reason. As we observed at the outset of this chapter, deaths in our society are much more often due to prolonged chronic diseases than to quickly terminating acute illnesses. This is particularly true for the aged, among whom 80 percent of all deaths occur. Therefore, virtually all of us will eventually have to deal with the *process* of dying—as a patient, as a concerned family member or friend, or perhaps in some professional capacity. Yet there is at present relatively little empirical information about such important issues as the typical duration of terminal illnesses; the magnitude of the accompanying disabilities, physical pain, and psychological distress; coping strategies used by terminal patients; or

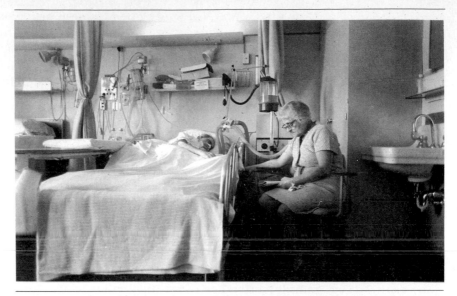

Deaths in the United States are much more often caused by prolonged chronic diseases than by quickly terminating acute illnesses. This slow process of dying causes considerable difficulties for the loved ones of the terminally ill patient. *Michael Weisbrot*

even the number of patients who are aware that their illnesses are terminal.

The Medical Staff and the Dying

For health-care professionals, the terminal prognosis implies a dramatic shift in treatment strategy. That is, instead of doing everything possible to bring about a recovery, the medical staff must concentrate instead on managing the patient's last days. This can cause significant social, emotional, and psychological problems for all concerned.

ATTITUDES AND BEHAVIORS OF PHYSICIANS AND NURSES. Numerous studies indicate that physicians and nurses have difficulty dealing with terminal illnesses. To cope with this stressful situation, they may well resort to such psychological defense mechanisms as denial of reality and intellectualization (Chapter 10). Thus physicians and nurses may avoid the patient who is in the process of dying, or even fail to make eye contact during those meetings that do take place. They may seek to have minimal contact with the patient's family. Or they may refer to the patient in distant and unemotional terms, as by using bed location or type of illness rather than the patient's name. (See, for example, Buckingham et al., 1976; Kastenbaum & Aisenberg, 1971; Kübler-Ross, 1969; Marie, 1978; Pearlman et al., 1969.) Physicians react more defensively to certain aspects of terminal care than do nurses, possibly because they are more responsible for the patient's treatment. For example, physicians tend to argue that patients should not participate in decisions about their treatment plans, should not be encouraged to talk about their terminality, and should not be cared for by family members as well as the medical staff. In contrast, nurses are more concerned with comforting terminal patients and caring for their emotional needs. Further evidence of this difference is provided by nursing journals, which typically concentrate on appropriate emotional responses to the terminal patient. Conversely, nonpsychiatric medical publications on death deal almost exclusively with technical treatment issues. (See Barton, Crowder, & Flexner, 1979–80; Campbell, Abernethy, & Waterhouse, 1983–84; Hatfield et al., 1983–84.)

The defensive behaviors of physicians and nurses have been attributed partly to personality factors, and partly to the training which they receive. Medical students are taught to focus on saving lives, rather than to help those who cannot be cured (Lief & Fox, 1963). Student nurses learn to avoid mistakes by concentrating on daily routines, which are designed for nonterminal patients (Quint, 1967). On a personal level, defeat is distasteful to most people, and is likely to be especially painful when it involves such traumatic outcomes as the death of one's patient. Because of their concern and desire to help, physicians and nurses may identify with the patient's fears and death and become anxious themselves. Some investigators also contend that physicians are unusually high in death anxiety, choose this profession as a way of defending against these fears (consciously or unconsciously), and prefer to avoid those emotionally threatening cases where death is inevitable (e.g., Feifel et al., 1967; Feifel & Heller, 1960; Wahl, 1962). Or the medical staff may feel guilty because they cannot effect a cure, an emotion that has been compared to the guilt that often results from remaining alive when a loved one dies. Since feelings of anxiety and guilt tend to be regarded as unprofessional, they are likely targets for such defense mechanisms as repression, denial of reality, and intellectualization (Campbell, 1980; Cassem & Hackett, 1975).

Such defensive behaviors may enable physicians and nurses to avoid excessive stress, and to perform more efficiently under admittedly difficult conditions. However, these behaviors may also have unfortunate consequences. In particular, terminal patients are likely to receive less contact and emotional support from the medical staff than they would like. Also, the aforementioned differences in outlook may cause physicians, nurses, and other members of the health-care team to clash over how best to care for the dying patient. However, there is some indication that matters may be improving. Physicians who took a course in medical school on dealing with the terminally ill reported better rapport with such patients, and less personal discomfort, than physicians who did not take such a course (Dickinson & Pearson, 1980). It has also been reported that those physicians with a higher probability of encountering terminally ill patients are more likely to respond openly, and to spend more time talking with them (Rea, Greenspoon, & Spilka, 1975; Dickinson & Pearson, 1979). Hopefully, therefore, health-care professionals are learning to deal more effectively with the process of dying.

INFORMING THE PATIENT. Should physicians tell patients that an illness is terminal? Most people do want to be told, although there are always important exceptions that must be recognized (Blumenfeld, Levy, & Kaufman, 1978–79). Thus some practitioners have argued that it is best to be truthful, but gentle, so that patients can be helped to reach a calm acceptance of death. (See, for example, Hoerr, 1963; Kübler-Ross, 1969; Lasagna, 1969; Lirette et al., 1969; Noyes, 1971; Wahl, 1969.)

Nevertheless, it appears that the majority of physicians prefer *not* to inform patients that their condition is terminal (Caldwell & Mishara, 1972; Hatfield et al., 1983–84). This is usually justified on emotional grounds: telling the patient has been likened to the cruelest thing in the world, or to a torture worse than a Nazi concentration camp. As a result, many terminal patients appear to remain unaware of their condition to the end. In some notable instances, however, researchers have focused on the responses of patients who were told that their days were numbered.

Stages of Dying: Kübler-Ross's Theory

According to some theorists, all dying patients proceed through much the same series of emotional stages. One noted example is Elisabeth Kübler-Ross's pioneering work, *On Death and Dying* (1969), which conceptualizes dying as a five-stage process. (See also Kübler-Ross, 1975.)

THE FIVE STAGES. On learning of the terminal prognosis, the patient's initial reaction is shock and numbness. This is gradually replaced by the first distinct stage in the dying process, *denial*. During this stage, patients steadfastly refuse to believe that they are doomed. For example, they may argue that their X-rays or laboratory reports have been confused with someone else's. According to

Kübler-Ross, this stage serves an adaptive purpose by acting as a buffer: it allows patients time to collect themselves after the terrible and unexpected news, and to mobilize other defenses that are not as radical.

Denial is followed by *anger*. The patient is irate because cherished activities and plans have been interrupted, and is jealous of those who can look forward to years of life. This anger is readily vented on anyone who comes in contact with the patient, and often on God as well. This stage can therefore be a particularly difficult one for the patient's family, friends, and medical staff.

The third stage, *bargaining,* is relatively brief. The patient now decides that an agreement can be made which will postpone the inevitable, as by promising good behavior or obedience to God. If the patient does survive until the date specified in this mythical agreement, the bargaining process is likely to begin all over again. For example, Kübler-Ross tells of a patient who asked for just enough time to attend her eldest son's wedding. She left the hospital on the day of the wedding, returned the next day, and immediately began bargaining for enough time to attend her second son's wedding.

The fourth stage, *depression,* is typically brought on by an anticipated or actual turn for the worse. Markedly intensified symptoms, serious bodily deterioration, or the surgical removal of a breast or limb often results in severe depression.

If patients are given enough time and emotional support to work through this anguish, they reach the final stage of the dying process: *acceptance.* This is a time of relative calm, with patients no longer depressed or angry about their impending death.

EVALUATION.   Kübler-Ross's work has been sharply criticized on methodological grounds. (See, for example, Kalish, 1981; Schulz, 1978; Schulz & Aderman, 1974; Shneidman, 1973.) Her conclusions were based on subjective clinical observations of 200 patients, and there is no clear statement of the assessment procedures which she used to identify and discriminate among the various stages. This makes it extremely difficult for other health-care professionals to determine the stage that a given patient is in, which tends to vitiate the predictive and practical value of her theory.

The reasoning which underlies some of Kübler-Ross's proposed stages has also been questioned. It has been argued that depression, which she associates with increasingly severe symptoms, is actually a side effect of the drugs used to alleviate the resulting pain (Schulz, 1978). Alternatively, the depression of terminal patients has been attributed to their declining ability to interpret and deal with events in the environment (Lieberman, 1965).

When researchers have used more objective methods of measurement, the results have generally failed to support Kübler-Ross's model. For example, on learning that their illnesses were terminal, patients in two studies adopted a pattern of behavior that remained basically unchanged until death. Some continued to pursue their usual daily life activities, while others withdrew from social relationships. None went through a succession of different periods or stages (Kastenbaum & Weisman, 1972; Weisman & Kastenbaum, 1968). Furthermore, many terminal patients claim to be unaware of the severity of their illnesses even at the end (Achte & Vauhkonen, 1971; Hinton, 1963). This suggests that denial often persists throughout the terminal phase of life, rather than subsiding at a relatively early stage.

As we observed in Chapter 7, clinical observation has advantages as well as drawbacks. Psychological research is far from an exact science, and clinical insights (such as Kübler-Ross's) can provide important and useful information. But here again, it appears that human behavior is too complicated to be described in terms of universally applicable stages. In particular, Kübler-Ross's five-stage theory is *not* supported by the preponderance of research evidence.

Needs Evoked by the Terminal Phase of Life

The terminal phase of life is more accurately characterized by the needs which it evokes among dying patients, and among their families and friends. These needs can be subsumed under two main headings: physical and socioemotional. The former category involves the alleviation of physical pain, which is likely to be intense in terminal illnesses. The socioemotional category includes the need to preserve a sense of dignity and self-worth, the need to receive emotional and social support, and the need for economic and legal assistance. We will discuss each of these in turn.

THE NEED TO ALLEVIATE PAIN.   For most terminal patients, the single most important need is to alleviate the pain that accompanies their illness. The two most common and effective palliatives for this pain are drug therapy and surgical procedures. Unfortunately, the patient must endure some adverse side effects in either case. Drugs result in altered states of consciousness, while surgery may significantly decrease the patient's mobility.

Drug therapy is the more popular of the two methods, partly because addiction is not a serious consideration when the patient's death is imminent. (See, for example, Neale, 1971; Kavanaugh, 1974.) It can be controversial, however. Some theorists contend that if a terminal patient's agony can only be relieved by using such controlled substances as marijuana or heroin, it is only right and humane to do so, even if this should require a change in existing laws. Others argue that illicit drugs must not be used even with the terminally ill. In some cases, the use of hard liquor or morphine may be a viable alternative.

DIGNITY AND SELF-WORTH.   The dignity and self-respect of terminal patients can be greatly enhanced by allowing them to help plan their own treatment (Benoliel, 1979; Saunders, 1975; Schulz, 1976; see also the discussion of internal locus of control in Chapter 7). Dying patients need to participate in the decisions that will affect the remainder of their lives, rather than passively submitting to plans contrived solely by the medical staff. This does require that patients be fully informed about their condition, and about possible methods of treatment. It therefore appears best to abandon the all-too-common policy of benign neglect, and tell dying patients that their prognosis is terminal. While the possibility of significant exceptions must be recognized, the advantage of being a legitimate participant in the treatment process would seem to outweigh the short-term trauma caused by the terrible news. It also appears desirable to involve the patient's family in the treatment process, so that they too can exert some control over the course of events (Davidson, 1978; Kaylor, 1979; Rose, 1976). As we have seen, however, not all physicians are willing to include patients and their families in such decisions.

Terminal patients can also be helped to preserve a sense of dignity in other ways. Intake procedures should be unhurried and humane, rather than rushed and/or bureaucratic. The medical staff should communicate with patients and their families as intellectual equals, and use clear language rather than hiding behind vague and confusing generalities (Dowsett, 1972; Kalish, 1981; Liegner, 1975; Simpson, 1976; Vanderpool, 1978).

EMOTIONAL, SOCIAL, AND SPIRITUAL SUPPORT.   Because of the traumatic nature of terminal illnesses, most patients need considerable caring and emotional support from the medical staff. The family is also likely to need counseling, both before and after the patient's death, to help them deal with their feelings of grief and loss. Dying patients and their families should be allowed to interact with one another in privacy, and as often as they may wish. If psychological defenses prevent them from communicating openly and effectively with one another, appropriate professional assistance should be provided. It is also important to honor the beliefs and personal preferences of patients from different religious, ethnic, and social backgrounds (Benoliel, 1979; Hampe, 1975; Jaffee, 1979; Mount, 1976).

ECONOMIC AND LEGAL CONCERNS.   The emotional trauma of the terminal stages of life can easily obscure important economic and legal details. If prolonged hospitalization is necessary, the escalating costs of medical care are likely to pose a particularly serious problem. Thus the family of the dying patient may well need help determining whether their insurance coverage is adequate, including Medicare, Medicaid, and/or policies from commercial companies. If it is not, other possible sources of financial aid should be brought to their attention, such as the United Way and other charitable institutions.

If terminal patients have not previously prepared their wills and planned their estates, they should be encouraged and assisted to do so as soon as possible. The family may also need help with various legal details, such as filling out estate tax forms and other documents after the patient's death.

MEETING PHYSICAL AND SOCIOEMOTIONAL NEEDS: THE HOSPICE APPROACH.   Meeting the needs discussed above may well exceed the capacities of standard health-care institutions, even where inpatients are concerned. When we also consider the plight of those terminal patients who are not sufficiently disabled to require hospitalization, and who therefore do not receive at least some support each day from health-care professionals, the problem becomes acute indeed.

Fortunately, there is one relatively new and effective solution: the **hospice approach** (Cohen, 1979; Comptroller General, 1979; Franklin, 1984; Holden, 1976; Vandenbos, DeLeon, & Pallak, 1982; Wilson, Ajemian, & Mount, 1978). The primary goal of the hospice is to help terminally ill patients continue their lives with as little distruption in normal activities as possible, while remaining primarily in the home environment. An interdisciplinary team consisting of a physician, nurse, social worker, and counselor strives to keep the patient alert, involved with family and friends, and as free from pain as possible, with the aid of anti-pain drugs and a warm emotional atmosphere. Thus the team spends considerable time talking with and listening to patients, comforting and reassuring them, holding hands, and so forth. In addition, the family is an important part of the treatment plan. They are encouraged to help care for the patient, as by preparing special meals. This active involvement with the patient, together with the bereavement counseling that is

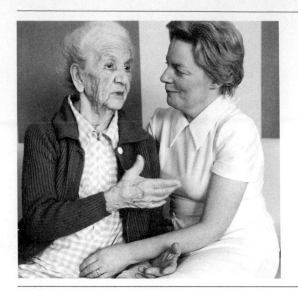

One particularly important goal of the hospice is to meet the emotional needs of the terminally ill.   *Leslie Starobin/Picture Cube*

provided after the patient's death, may well reduce the feelings of guilt that typically follow the loss of a loved one.

A recent National Hospice Study has shed some light on the psychological state of the terminally ill (Greer & Mor, 1983). In particular, this large-scale study (N = 1,745) reveals what terminal patients consider to be important some 2–8 weeks prior to their deaths. During this difficult time, supportive friends were most often mentioned as a source of strength, followed by religion and being needed by someone else. When these patients were asked what they wanted during the last three days of their lives, the most common responses were having certain people present, being physically able to do things, and feeling at peace. The results also indicated that patients tended to vacillate between such contrary feelings as calm and frightened or content and hopeless, rather than remaining consistently depressed. These findings were derived from measures which tapped only the public and conscious level, so it is conceivable that more negative emotions might have been detected had deeper levels been assessed. But these results may also reflect the benefits of providing sufficient care for both terminal patients and their families, as illustrated by the following case history:

A DISFIGURED 53-YEAR-OLD TERMINAL PATIENT.
Mr. G. suffered from a particularly unsightly and painful cancer, which was eroding the lower part of his face. He therefore became increasingly depressed, and wished he could die and "get it over with." He and his wife were very close, however, having been married for only

Myths About Aging: Death and Dying

MYTH

You will become more afraid of death as you grow toward old age, and your death becomes more imminent.

It is kinder for physicians not to tell elderly patients that they have a terminal illness.

People who engage in risky, life-threatening vocations or avocations have significantly less fear of death than those who do not.

Among those adults whose spouses die, elderly widows and widowers are much more likely to die themselves a short time later.

BEST AVAILABLE EVIDENCE

Serious physical illnesses are related to an increase in death anxiety, and are more likely to occur at advanced ages. But the evidence does *not* indicate that healthy men and women become more afraid of death as they grow from adulthood to old age, at least at a conscious level.

Most people of all ages want to know if they have a terminal illness. Although there are exceptions, the advantages of being a legitimate participant in the treatment process are likely to outweigh ther short-term trauma caused by learning the truth.

There appear to be no significant differences in death anxiety between those who defy death and those who do not.

Young adults who lose a spouse to death appear to be at higher risk than older widows and widowers.

---

six years. Mrs. G. was well aware of her husband's wish for death, but could not accept the thought that she would soon be without him. Her fears, although understandable, added to Mr. G.'s depression and lack of courage.

Drug therapy was used to alleviate Mr. G.'s pain and make his life less intolerable, while those medical staff who were not horrified by his appearance provided close emotional support that helped him to relax. His wife was also given similar support, and began to face up to the situation. Two weeks later, Mr. G.'s general condition was much worse, but both he and his wife were calm and had enjoyed Christmas together. When he then developed pneumonia, his wife agreed that it would be wrong to prolong his life with antibiotics and added, "I'm ready for him to go now." He died, peacefully, the following day. (Parkes, 1981a.)

The hospice approach is becoming increasingly popular in this country. The first American hospice began providing home services in 1974, based on models in London and Montreal (Liss-Levinson, 1982). By early 1983, the Joint Commission for the Accreditation of Hospitals estimated that there were more than 1,100 hospices in the United States (Federal Register, 1983). To be sure, we still have much to learn about this last, difficult phase of human life. But the increasing prevalence of the hospice approach augurs well for the future treatment of the terminally ill—and for the care of those who love them.

Grief and Bereavement

The shattering impact of a terminal illness does not end with the patient's death. The family and friends of the deceased must contend with painful feelings of grief and bereavement, which may last for months or even years.

Anticipated versus Unanticipated Deaths

When a loved one's death is expected, the psychological consequences are usually less severe than when death occurs suddenly and unpredictably. To illustrate, Parkes (1975) compared two groups of widows and widowers below the age of 45. One group suffered sudden bereavement, with the terminal phase lasting from one day to two weeks, while the second group had more time to anticipate the impending death of their spouses. The former group had much more difficulty coping with their loss. They reported significantly more depression, anxiety, and loneliness, both initially and some two to four years later. Denial was also more common in this group, as with the belief that they would one day wake up to find that their spouse had not died. Members of the sudden bereavement group were also less likely to go out with friends and relatives, or to remarry. Others research findings confirm that women whose husbands die unexpectedly are less likely to remarry than those who lose a spouse after a long terminal illness, and that sudden death is more likely to evoke various kinds of disbelief. During the funeral services, for example, such denial may take the form of insisting on a closed casket, a private service, or no service at all. (See Glick et al., 1974; Nichols, 1981.)

Why do anticipated and unanticipated deaths have such different effects on the survivors? The answer involves two important psychological variables: guilt, and perceived control of the environment.

PERCEIVED CONTROL OF THE ENVIRONMENT.   The cause of anticipated deaths is usually clear and understandable, such as a specific disease with a predictable course. As a result, the survivor can take some action to reduce the probability of ever having to face a similar tragedy. For example, a widower whose wife died of lung cancer may seek out women who are nonsmokers. But when death results from sudden and unexpected causes, such as an accident or murder, the survivors tend to remain fearful because they perceive themselves as having no control over the possibility of a recurrence. Thus a widow whose husband was shot to death in the street at night may well be afraid to go out in the evening, or a widower whose wife was killed in a driving accident may refuse to enter an automobile. For these sufferers, death is a constant presence that could strike again as unpredictably as before.

GUILT AND COMMUNICATION.   When death is caused by a fairly lengthy terminal illness, family and friends have time to prepare for the inevitable while the patient is still alive. They can share their loved one's innermost feelings, perform acts of caring and concern, and expiate some of their guilt prior to the moment of death. (The hospice approach involves the family in the treatment process for just these reasons, as we have seen.) No loving relationship is completely without ambivalence, as Freud has shown; novelists may argue that love means never having to say you're sorry, but most real-life human beings need and want to make some important apologies before a loved one dies. Though a prolonged terminal illness is difficult for all concerned, it does allow time for the initial shock to diminish and for the anticipation of loss. In turn, this anticipatory grief can provide the impetus for meaningful communication with the terminal patient.

While anticipatory grief does help the family to begin the painful process of adapting to life without the loved one, there are limits to what it can accomplish. Plans can easily be confused with wishes, and those who prepare too soon and too actively for the death of a loved one may begin to believe that they want that death to occur (Parkes, 1981a). Nor are prolonged terminal illnesses free from moments of acute grief or denial, as when the family first learns the terrible news. But a sudden death tends to be even more traumatic, since it allows no time at all for anticipatory grief. In such instances, the bereaved can only agonize at length about all the things they wanted to tell and do for the deceased, but never did—and, now, never will. Thus unanticipated deaths are more likely to evoke grief that is intense and prolonged, or even pathological.

Normal versus Pathological Grief

Pathological (morbid) grief differs from normal grief in duration and intensity, rather than in kind. Acute grief normally lasts for some two weeks to two months after the death of the loved one, and healthy mourning may take from nine months to two years (Arkin, 1981; Margolis et al., 1981, p. xi). Conversely, acute grief would be regarded as pathological if it continued for many months or years after the funeral. There is no strict timetable for grieving, however, and some bereaved individuals may require more time for the healthy venting of painful emotions than others (Joyce, 1984).

NORMAL GRIEF.   A certain amount of grief is beneficial and adaptive. It helps bereaved individuals to detach themselves emotionally from the deceased (Freud, 1917/1963), and to reconcile an internal world filled with memories of the loved one with an external world where that person no longer exists (Parkes, 1972; 1981b). Thus the process of grieving is a process of learning: the bereaved individual gradually and painfully adopts a new view of the world, one where the loved one is permanently absent.

Normal grieving typically proceeds through several phases. The initial phase begins at the time of death and continues for several weeks thereafter, and is characterized by feelings of confusion, shock, and denial. Thus one widow observed that "all during my husband's funeral, I kept wishing the entire process would be over so that he and I could resume our normal life," while her daughter refused to attend the funeral so that she could think of her father as still being alive (Vachon, 1981). Emotional numbness may also serve as a barrier against overwhelming pain and suffering:

> *A 27-YEAR-OLD WIDOW.*
>
> Mrs. O. viewed her husband's body shortly after his death from cancer. "I, I didn't want to believe it, and yet I saw it right there, so it was as though I were torn between what I wanted to believe and what was really there. . . . The following few hours was just, I don't know, it was not me or something, I couldn't . . . I just didn't do anything, just, just blank. They gave me his watch and I held it in my hand . . . didn't feel anything, just complete blank." (Parkes, 1981b.)

Responses like these normally give way to an all-encompassing sorrow, which is expressed through periods of crying and weeping that may last for days or weeks. The bereaved individual may try to cope by keeping busy with time-consuming activities, or may resort to tranquilizers or sleeping pills. Anger, displacement, and projection are common, as by blaming a faultless medical staff or God for the loved one's death. Fears of a nervous breakdown and/or some suicidal wishes are also not unusual during this time:

> *THE CASE OF MRS. O. (CONTINUED):*
> Three weeks after her husband's death, Mrs. O's grief was still at its peak, and she was missing him very strongly. "All of a sudden I miss him, then it hurts. . . . I try to keep my hands very busy, but I haven't been able to do any reading or anything because my mind just wanders away. . . . I have really simple goals, to make him happy . . . and all of a sudden I felt nothing more to do, feel so lost that I don't know. . . . I tried so hard to have dreams so I can see him, but all I end up is dreaming that I couldn't find him . . . it's especially hard to realize that he's not there anymore. . . . I wish I [was] not so young so I can join him sooner."

About one month after the funeral, the bereaved individual begins to confront the reality of daily living without the loved one. This intermediate phase may continue for up to one year, and is characterized by various forms of behavior. The mourner may engage in obsessional reviews of scenes associated with the loved one's death, and express such self-reproaches as "if only I had made him wear his seat belt" or "I should have forced her to go to the doctor sooner." This verbalization of guilt feelings is primarily beneficial, because it allows mourners to expiate their real or imagined transgressions and more readily accept their loss. (See Arkin, 1981; Glick et al., 1974.) The bereaved individual may also express concern as to the meaning of death, and wonder why this tragic event had to happen. Some mourners gain relief by attributing the death to the will of God, while others are never able to find an answer that satisfies them. Or the bereaved may engage in activities that were formerly shared with the loved one, such as watching television during the evening or going to a favorite restaurant, and experience the illusion that the deceased is present. In fact, the mourner may even call out to the deceased and expect a response. (This phenomenon is most common in the case of unanticipated deaths.) The hallucinations that may occur during bereavement are often therapeutic, and usually do not indicate the existence of a severe emotional disturbance (Vachon, 1981).

Ideally, the mourner ultimately realizes that life with the loved one cannot be restored. But since the mourner has not yet been able to replace the old pattern of living with a satisfactory alternative, apathy and depression are common. Life is lived from day to day, without much of a plan for the future:

THE CASE OF MRS. O. (CONCLUDED):

One year after her husband's death, Mrs. O. observed, "I'm still rather confused . . . What action should I take for my future life, and what do I want? I keep on asking myself and I haven't really come up with anything." Mrs. O. kept herself busy in an effort to avoid depression, but was well aware that such activity was futile. She also expressed difficulty adjusting to her new role as an unmarried person. "I'm not exactly married and not exactly single. . . . I'm not waiting to die. I feel I have to live my life." But she had little idea how to achieve this goal. "I feel I'm very depressed, you know."

The final phase of normal bereavement is that of recovery. This phase is often triggered by a conscious decision not to dwell on the past any longer; life must proceed. The first steps in this direction may be small, with relatively minor aspects of life beginning to be enjoyed once again. But eventually a new direction emerges, and periods of depression and pining for the loved one become less frequent. The mourner is now more socially aggressive, and actively seeks out new friends and pastimes. (This may not be an easy task, however. Widows and widowers are all too often treated as stigmatized persons, not unlike the handicapped.) The bereaved individual also derives considerable comfort from his or her ability to survive the devastating event, and often develops valued new skills as well. Examples include widows who now learn for the first time to balance a checkbook, make minor house repairs, or maintain the automobile. Thus, like a phoenix rising from the ashes, many mourners do emerge from the bereavement process as more capable, self-confident, and emotionally secure people.

PATHOLOGICAL GRIEF.   Bereavement does not always proceed so favorably. One warning sign that grief may become pathological is a period of apparent calm, well-being, and zeal immediately following the loved one's death. This "calm before the storm" is typically followed by an abrupt and striking change in behavior: irritability or even intense hostility toward relatives and friends, and listlessness so pronounced that the individual does virtually nothing unless compelled by someone else. Because the normal grief responses have been denied expression, these bereaved individuals are also more likely to incur such psychosomatic disorders as ulcerative colitis, rheumatoid arthritis, and asthma.

Other forms of pathology which more often occur after bereavement include severe depression, anxiety states, suicide, insomnia, and an extreme degree of identification with the deceased. For example, one woman whose husband was rendered speechless by a stroke became unable to speak for ten days following his death

(Parkes, 1972). Or pathological grief may result in self-destructive behavior, such as giving away all of one's possessions, taking foolish economic risks, or shattering one's professional reputation by behaving stupidly and incompetently (Lindermann, 1944).

The long-term prognosis for those suffering from pathological grief is unfavorable. Such individuals are not only more vulnerable to various physical and psychological disorders; they are also more likely to die themselves.

Mortality and the Widowed: The Consequences of Pathological Grief

A death in the family significantly increases the mortality rates for close relatives, especially the surviving spouse. Compared to the general population, widows and widowers are at least twice as likely to die from a great variety of diseases (Hyman, 1969; Mathison, 1970; Parkes, 1964; Stroebe et al., 1982). Various theories have been proposed to explain this phenomenon, one of which appears to have particular merit.

THE SELECTION HYPOTHESIS.   Some researchers contend that the higher mortality rates for the widowed are nothing more than statistical artifacts. They argue that widows and widowers who are in good health tend to remarry fairly quickly, within six months after the funeral. Having reestablished a more or less normal life, these individuals can no longer be regarded as bereaved. Thus only the emotionally and physically ill remain single long enough to be included in research studies on bereavement, and their mortality rate is higher simply because of their various ailments—not because they have been widowed. However, the selection hypothesis has been soundly contradicted by empirical data. Various studies have shown that most widowed individuals do *not* remarry soon after the funeral; they wait considerably longer, or even forever (e.g., Cox & Ford, 1970; Ekblom, 1963; Kraus & Lilienfeld, 1959; Young, Bernard, & Wallis, 1970). Therefore, the relationship between mortality and widowhood cannot be dismissed as a mere statistical artifact.

THE HOMOGAMY HYPOTHESIS.   Suppose that healthy individuals prefer to marry those who are also healthy, leaving the physically and psychologically ill to marry each other. If this is the case, and one spouse dies shortly after the other, the second death could easily be due to poor health rather than grief.

Evidence concerning this hypothesis is both sparse and conflicting. One study did discover a tendency for spouses to die from similar causes (Parkes, Benjamin, & Fitzgerald, 1969), but an earlier study based on a very large sample (N = 2,572) found that husbands and wives usually do not die from the same diseases (Ciocco, 1940). Homogamy may make some small contribution to the higher mortality rates of the widowed, but it does not appear to be a major factor.

THE COMMON UNFAVORABLE ENVIRONMENT HYPOTHESIS. Two people who live together are exposed to much the same environmental conditions. If some habitats are more dangerous or prone to disease than others, spouses who reside in these areas may be more likely to die at about the same time simply because of their unfavorable environment.

This hypothesis implies that husbands and wives should tend to die from similar causes, which is not supported by the research evidence noted above. It cannot be ruled out completely, if only because infectious diseases may be communicated from one spouse to another in some instances, but it also would seem to be a minor factor at best.

THE DESOLATION HYPOTHESIS. The adverse effects of widowhood are most probably due to the loss of the will to live, which has also been referred to as the "giving-up complex" and the "broken heart syndrome" (Kalish, 1981). This state of hopelessness has been attributed to the mourner's inability to prevent the death of the loved one, and to the sense of helplessness which results from this perceived lack of control over the environment. (This is especially true when the death is unanticipated, as we have seen.) It may also be due to the disruption of customary daily activities, which also evokes a sense of helplessness, and to the loss of social, emotional, and economic support from the loved one (Stroebe et al., 1982).

One consequence of desolation and grief is a lowered resistance to disease. Fredrick (1971; 1981) has hypothesized that the prolonged stress caused by bereavement overstimulates the pituitary gland, leading to an excessive production of adrenocorticotropic hormones (ACTH) and corticosteroids. This in turn overly suppresses the inflammatory response, which is essential for the adequate functioning of the immunity mechanism. As a result, the mourner is more susceptible to bacterial, fungal, and viral infection. In addition, desolation is likely to evoke self-destructive behavior. The widowed may contribute to their own ill health by failing to get sufficient rest, by forgetting or refusing to take necessary medication, or by ignoring serious medical problems (Clayton, 1973; Morgan, 1976; Parkes, 1964; Yamamoto, 1970). These detrimental behaviors are not always due to grief and hopelessness, however. The widow or widower may become lax about such matters because the deceased used to provide the needed encouragement (or nagging!), but can no longer do so. Nevertheless, the higher mortality rates for the widowed appear to be best explained by the desolation hypothesis.

AFTERWORD.   Although mortality *rates* are significantly higher for the widowed, the actual *number* who meet with an early death is fairly small. The picture is by no means wholly bleak, for the majority of widows and widowers do recover from their grief and return to a normal life.

However, it is important to identify those high-risk individuals who are unusually likely to die following the death of a spouse. A promising beginning has been made in this area, and the prognosis for young widows and widowers appears to be less favorable if:

- The spouse's death was unexpected.

- Their pining for the spouse is unusually intense three weeks after bereavement.

- They frequently express suicidal wishes, and a lack of interest in continuing to live.

- Their socioeconomic status is low, as with unskilled manual laborers.

- They have strong, persistent feelings of anger and guilt.

(See Parkes, 1981b). Ideally, research findings like these will lead to the development of improved diagnostic and therapeutic techniques, so that these sufferers can be helped before it is too late.

Helping the Bereaved: Professional and Paraprofessional Therapy

It has been estimated that some 25 percent of the bereaved cannot resolve their grief by themselves. For these mourners, professional or paraprofessional therapy may help to alleviate their emotional pain and suffering.

PROFESSIONAL THERAPY.   During the terminal phase, family members may spend so much time caring for the dying patient that they become overly fatigued, do not follow a proper diet, or have little or no recreation. In such cases, one effective therapeutic measure may simply be to enjoy a good meal, an engrossing movie, or a weekend vacation. As we observed in our discussion of the hospice approach, however, formal therapy may also be appropriate at this time. Such therapy can forestall the emergence of pathological grief by helping the family to release their feelings of guilt, anger, and despair, and to communicate more openly with one another:

A CASE OF TERMINAL CANCER.

Mrs. C. was 34 years old, the mother of a two-year-old girl, and a writer by profession. Her terminal cancer required a mastectomy, a prospect that left her distraught, angry, and depressed. "No one can help me now, since I will die anyway. . . . My husband and I are surrounded by physician friends, and sadly enough, I know the implications of [my] cancer . . . For many years, my husband and I tried to have a child. At long last we conceived, and a beautiful and healthy baby was born. Now both will be robbed of a family." A social worker helped Mrs. C. to understand that her outpouring of feelings, however harsh, was appropriate and needed to be expressed. With the aid of this support, she grew calmer and less angry, and was better able to derive those satisfactions that were available in the time left to her.

Mr. C. was two years older than his wife. Although his appearance clearly reflected his sorrow, he insisted on controlling his emotions. Therapy helped him to realize that expressing his grief was not unmasculine, and that he needed to share these feelings with his wife. "It seems that I'm on a constant seesaw," he observed. "I vacillate between acceptance of my wife's fatal illness and hope for a miracle, especially when she looks fairly well. I walk around with a heavy heart, but it helps so much to talk. We've grown so much closer to each other than ever before . . . I'm so glad there is now."

Only her parents were still alive, and they came from their home in South America to be with her. Because of their grief, and an understandable desire to be helpful, they tended to intrude too much on the dealings between Mrs. C. and her husband. After a family conference with the social worker, they readily agreed to return home, with the understanding that they would be called in case of any emergency. They were present when Mrs. C. died some eight months later, and were of immense comfort to Mr. C. One month after the funeral, Mr. C. decided that he and his daughter would move to South America and live near his inlaws. He had placed his marriage in what appeared to be a healthy perspective. "I will take each day as it comes, and, hopefully, all will turn out fairly well." (Suszycki, 1981.)

At the time of death, therapy may take the form of crisis intervention. Some mourners now experience intense grief, and require appropriate comforting and emotional support. Yet probably those most in need of therapy are the stoics, who remain calm for weeks after the funeral and act as though nothing had happened. This may be due to a misguided belief that outward expressions of an-

guish are a sign of personal weakness, or that they must be strong
for the sake of other family members. But experiencing the loss
emotionally is necessary for the bereavement process to proceed to
a satisfactory conclusion, while denying these feelings is likely to be
the calm before the storm of pathological grief (as we have seen).
These bereaved individuals are therefore encouraged to release their
dammed-up emotions, and to verbalize their feelings of loss, anger,
and sorrow. The therapist may facilitate this catharsis by confront-
ing the mourner with some crucial memento of the deceased, such
as a photograph, item of jewelry, or letter. Or the mourner may be
asked to talk directly to a fantasized image of the deceased, rather
than about the loved one. Or the family may be advised to avoid
excessive denial by having a public funeral with an open casket, and
allowing the children who are old enough to explore the funeral
home and hearse openly and freely. Once an emotional catharsis
has been achieved, mourners are encouraged to escape the trap of
a morbid preoccupation with the past by orienting themselves toward the future. This may involve such activities as acquiring new
friends or pastimes, going back to school, or learning how to drive.
(See, for example, Horn, 1974; Kalish, 1981; Lindemann, 1944; Nichols, 1981.)

In sum: during the terminal phase, professional bereavement
therapy assists the family to function as effectively as possible and
to prepare for the coming tragedy. After the patient's death, therapy helps the bereaved adjust to a world without the loved one and
find ways to make life meaningful and rewarding. Even mourners
who remained grief stricken after several years have been helped to
vent their suppressed emotions through appropriate therapy, and
to bring the bereavement process to a successful conclusion.

PARAPROFESSIONAL THERAPY.   Although professional therapy can
be effective, it may also be too expensive for some mourners. One
increasingly popular alternative is to enlist the aid of formerly bereaved individuals, who have been able to resolve their grief. These
paraprofessionals may serve as group leaders, or the bereaved may
meet in leaderless self-help groups.

How effective is this approach? In one study, some 70 widows
who responded to a request in a local newspaper participated in a
group program for 7 weeks. Some were randomly assigned to self-
help groups, and some to groups with paraprofessional leaders. A
control group did not experience any form of paraprofessional
therapy. Both of the experimental groups subsequently indicated
higher self-esteem, greater optimism concerning their future health,
and a greater ability to feel and express their grief than did the
control group (Barrett, 1978).

Helping the bereaved should not be confused with treating psychopathology; those who suffer from psychological disorders are best advised to consult a trained professional. However, paraprofessional therapy does appear to be an economical way to help alleviate the emotional pain of the bereaved.

FINAL AFTERWORD.   Most of us regard the prospect of death with considerable distaste. Yet research dealing with the bereaved indicates that the process of dying is extremely important, and need not have only ill effects. If the terminal patient suffers unnecessarily, never comes to terms with this condition, cannot relate well to his or her family, and dies embittered, then death may indeed be seen as a defeat. But when the terminal patient accepts the inevitable, welcomes those pleasures that life still has to offer, enjoys a close and supportive relationship with his or her family, and dies peacefully and free of suffering, this final period of life may well be remembered as a fitting and satisfactory ending (Parkes, 1981a).

There are various ways of dying, and the patient and family who rise to the challenge can make something positive out of this otherwise calamitous event. Given the increased prevalence of chronic terminal illnesses, this is a challenge that may well await you in the future.

To die will be an awfully big adventure.
—J. M. Barrie, *Peter Pan*

Summary

THE DEMOGRAPHY OF DEATH

Chronic illnesses have replaced acute illnesses as the major causes of death in our society. As a result, dying is likely to be a fairly drawn-out process for many of us. The leading causes of death in the United States are heart diseases, cancer, and strokes. Conversely, deaths from such communicable diseases as tuberculosis and pneumonia have decreased markedly since 1900.

THE FEAR OF DEATH

Some theorists contend that the fear of death, conscious and unconscious, is the prime motive underlying all human behavior. Among the reasons for death anxiety are the fear of physical suffering, the fear of nonbeing, the fear that we will become cowards in the face of death, the fear of missing out on cherished experiences and goals, the fear of the emotional and economic impact that death will have on our survivors, and the fear of punishment after death. We may also experience these fears in relation to the death of a loved one. Death anxiety also has aspects that are public and conscious, private and conscious, and (very possibly) unconscious. Thus death anxiety is a multidimensional variable. But all too many researchers have treated death anxiety as unidimensional, and have assessed only the public and conscious level.

Perhaps for this reason, relatively few consistent patterns have emerged from the research data. This evidence fails to support the existentialist belief as to the overwhelming importance of death anxiety, but this could be attributed partly or largely to methodological problems. However, serious physical illnesses do appear to be related to an increase in death anxiety. There is also some indication that a significant part of these fears is beyond our awareness, and that some people who claim to have little conscious death anxiety may well be considerably more afraid at an unconscious level.

THE PROCESS OF DYING: THE TERMINAL STAGES OF LIFE

Numerous studies indicate that physicians and nurses have difficulty dealing with terminal illnesses. They may therefore tend to avoid patients who are in the process of dying, or they may behave in other defensive ways. This may be due partly to the personalities of physicians and nurses and partly to their training, which focuses on helping those who can be cured. Although most people want to know the truth, the majority of physicians prefer not to inform patients that their condition is terminal, and usually justify this as an act of kindness. However, some data do indicate that health-care professionals are becoming more aware of the needs of the terminally ill.

According to some theorists, all dying patients proceed through much the same series of emotional stages. Kübler-Ross's pioneering work posits five such stages, based on her clinical observation: denial, anger, bargaining, depression, and acceptance. However, her theory is not supported by the preponderance of research evidence.

For most terminal patients, the single most important need is to alleviate the physical pain which accompanies their illness. This is most often achieved through drug therapy, sometimes through surgery. Also important are the socioemotional needs: to preserve a sense of dignity and self-worth, which is often best accomplished by allowing terminal patients to help plan their own treatment; to receive emotional, social, and spiritual support; and to obtain economic and legal assistance. The hospice approach is an effective and increasingly popular way to satisfy the various needs of the terminally ill. The hospice utilizes an interdisciplinary team of physicians, nurses, social workers, and counselors; drug therapy combined with a loving and caring atmosphere; and a treatment plan that includes both terminal patients and their families.

GRIEF AND BEREAVEMENT

When the death of a loved one occurs suddenly and unpredictably, the psychological consequences are usually more severe than when the death is anticipated. This has been attributed to the inability to express guilt and sorrow through anticipatory grief, and to a perceived lack of control of the environment.

Pathological grief reactions differ from normal grief in duration and intensity, rather than in kind. A certain amount of grief is beneficial and adaptive. The process of normal grieving is a process of learning: the bereaved individual gradually and painfully adopts a new view of the world, one where the loved one is permanently absent. Normal grief typically proceeds through several phases, which may include confusion, shock, denial, emotional numbness, sorrow, weeping, self-reproaches, hallucinations of the loved one, and (eventually) the decision that it is time to concentrate on the future because life must proceed. Pathological grief is often preceded by a period of apparent calm and well-being immediately following the loved one's death. It commonly leads to various physical and psychological disorders, and even to death.

A death in the family significantly increases the mortality rates for close relatives, especially the surviving spouse. This is most probably due to the loss of the will to live, which results from feelings of helplessness and the loss of support from the loved one. Such hopelessness and desolation can lead to a lowered resistance to disease, and to self-destructive behaviors. But the majority of the widowed do recover from their grief, and return to a normal life.

It has been estimated that some 25 percent of the bereaved cannot resolve their grief by themselves. During the terminal phase, professional therapy can help the family to function effectively and to prepare for the coming tragedy. After the patient's death, such therapy can help mourners to release their dammed-up feelings and bring the bereavement process to a satisfactory conclusion. One effective and increasingly popular alternative is to enlist the aid of paraprofessionals, such as formerly bereaved individuals who have successfully resolved their grief.

The process of dying is extremely important, and need not be entirely negative. There are various ways of dying, and the patient and family who rise to this challenge can make something positive out of an otherwise calamitous event. Given the increased prevalence of chronic terminal illnesses, this is a challenge that awaits many of us in the future.

References

ACHTE, K. A., & VAUHKONEN, M. L. Cancer and the psyche. *Omeqa: Journal of Death and Dying,* 1971, 2, 45–46.

ADAMS, B. Mate selection in the United States: A theoretical summarization. In W. Burr, R. Hill, I. Nye, & R. Reiss (Eds.), *Contemporary theories about the family. Vol 1: Research-based theories.* New York: Free Press, 1979.

ADAMS, O, & LEFEBVRE, L. Retirement and mortality. *Aging and Work,* 1981, 4, 115–120.

ADLER, A. *Understanding human nature.* Original publication: 1927. Paperback reprint: Greenwich, Conn.: Fawcett, 1957.

ADLER, A. *The science of living.* Original publication: 1929. Paperback reprint: New York: Anchor Books, 1969.

ALEXANDER, C. Youth and progress. *Journal of Social Psychology,* 1945, 22, 209–213.

ALLPORT, G. W. *Personality: A psychological interpretation.* New York: Holt, 1937.

ALLPORT, G. W. *Becoming: Basic considerations for a psychology of personality.* New Haven: Yale University Press, 1955.

ALLPORT, G. W. *Pattern and growth in personality.* New York: Holt, Rinehart and Winston, 1961.

ALLPORT, G. W. *The person in psychology: Selected essays.* Boston: Beacon Press, 1968.

ALTMAN, I., & TAYLOR, D. A. *Social penetration: the development of interpersonal relationships.* New York: Holt, Rinehart and Winston, 1973.

AMBERSON, J. I., ATKESON, B. M., POLLACK, R. H., & MALATESTA, V. J. Age differences in dark-interval threshold across the life span. *Experimental Aging Research,* 1979, 5, 423–433.

American Psychiatric Association. *Diagnostic and statistical manual of mental disorders.* (3rd Ed., revised.) Washington, D.C.: American Psychiatric Association, 1987.

ANASTASI, A. *Psychological testing.* (4th Ed.). New York: Macmillan, 1976.

ANDERS, T. R., FOZARD, J. L., & LILLYQUIST, T. D. Effects of age upon retrieval from short-term memory. *Developmental Psychology,* 1972, 6, 214–217.

ANDERSON, Y. W., & ROCHARD, C. Cold snaps, snowfall, and sudden death from ischemic heart disease. *Canadian Medical Association Journal,* 1979, 121, 1580–1583.

ANGLEITNER, A. Changes in personality observed in questionnaire data from the Riegel questionnaire on rigidity, dogmatism, and attitude toward life. In H. Thomae (Ed.), *Patterns of aging.* Basel–New York: Karger, 1976.

ANTHONY, J. Children at risk from divorce: A review. In J. Anthony & C. Koupernic (Eds.), *The child in his family: Children at Psychiatric risk.* New York: Wiley, 1974.

ANTONUCCI, T. C. Personal characteristics, social support, and social behavior. In E. Shanas & R. H. Binstock (Eds.), *Handbook of aging and the social sciences.* (2nd Ed.) New York: Van Nostrand Reinhold, 1984.

ARENBERG, D. Regression analyses of verbal learning on adult age differences at two anticipation intervals. *Journal of Gerontology,* 1967, 22, 411–414.

ARENBERG, D. Input modality in short-term retention of old and young adults. *Journal of Gerontology,* 1968, 23, 462–465.

ARENBERG, D. The effects of input condition on free recall in young and old adults. *Journal of Gerontology,* 1976, 31, 551–555.

ARENBERG, D., & ROBERTSON-TCHABO, E. A. Learning and aging. In J. E. Birren & K. W. Schaie (Eds.), *Handbook of the psychology of aging.* New York: Van Nostrand Reinhold, 1977.

ARIETI, S. *Interpretation of Schizophrenia.* (Rev. Ed.) New York: Basic Books, 1974.

ARKIN, A. M. Emotional care of the bereaved. In O. S. Margolis, H. C. Raether, A. H. Kutscher, J. B. Powers, I. B. Seeland, R. DeBellis, & D. J. Cherico (Eds.), *Acute grief: Counseling the bereaved.* New York: Columbia University Press, 1981.

ARKING, G. The elderly widow and her family, neighbors, and friends. *Journal of Marriage and the Family,* 1976, 38, 757–768.

ASH, P. Pre-retirement counseling. *The Gerontologist,* 1966, 6, 97–99, 127–128.

ATCHLEY, R. C. *The sociology of retirement.* New York: Halsted, 1976.

ATCHLEY, R. C. *Social forces of later life.* (2nd Ed.) Belmont, Calif.: Wadsworth, 1977.

ATCHLEY, R. C. Retirement: Leaving the world of work. *Annals of the American Academy of Political and Social Science,* 1982, 464, 120–131.

ATCHLEY, R. C. *Social forces and aging: An introduction to social gerontology.* Belmont, Calif: Wadsworth, 1985.

ATCHLEY, R. C., & MILLER, S. J. Older people and their families. In C. Eisdorfer (Ed.), *Annual review of gerontology and geriatrics.* (Vol. 1) New York: Springer, 1980.

ATCHLEY, R. C., & ROBINSON, J. L. Attitudes toward retirement and distance from the event. *Research on Aging,* 1982, 4, 299–313.

ATKINSON, J. H., & SCHUCKIT, M. A. Alcoholism and over-the-counter-and prescription drug misuse in the elderly. In C. Eisdorfer (Ed.), *Annual review of gerontology and geriatrics (Vol. 2)*. New York: Springer, 1981.

AVERBACH, E., & CORIELL, E. Short-term memory in vision. *Bell System Technical Journal*, 1961, 40, 309–328.

AYLLON, T., & AZRIN, N. H *The token economy: A motivational system for therapy and rehabilitation*. New York: Appleton-Century-Crofts, 1968.

BABCHUCK, N. Aging and primary relations. *International Journal of Aging and Human Development*, 1978–79, 9, 137–151.

BACKMAN, C. W., & SECORD, P. F. The effect of perceived liking on interpersonal attraction. *Human Relations*, 1959, 12, 379–384.

BRADDELEY, A. D. Estimating the short-term component in free recall. *British Journal of Psychology*, 1970, 61, 13–15.

BAILEY, R. C., FINNEY, P., & HEIM, B. Self-concept support and friendship duration. *Journal of Social Psychology*, 1975, 96(2), 234–237.

BALL, K., & SEKULER, R. Improving visual perception in older observers. *Journal of Gerontology*, 1986, 41, 176–182.

BALTES, P. B., CORNELIUS, S. W., SPIRO, A., NESSELROADE, J. R., & WILLIS, S. L. Integration versus differentiation of fluid/crystallized intelligence in old age. *Developmental Psychology*, 1980, 16, 625–635.

BALTES, P. B., & LABOUVIE, G. V. Adult development of intellectual performance: Description, explanation, and modification. In C. Eisdorfer & M. P. Lawton (Eds.), *The psychology of adult development and aging*. Washington, D.C.: American Psychological Association, 1973.

BALTES, P. B., NESSELROADE, J. R., SCHAIE, K. W., & LABOUVIE, E. W. On the dilemma of regression effects in examining ability-level-related differentials in ontogenic patterns of intelligence. *Developmental Psychology*, 1972, 6, 78–84.

BALTES, P. B., REESE, H. W., & NESSELROADE, J. R. *Life-span developmental psychology: Introduction to research methods*. Monterey, Calif.: Brooks/Cole, 1977.

BALTES, P. B., & SCHAIE, K. W. Aging and IQ: The myth of the twilight years. *Psychology Today*, 1974, 7, 35 40.

BALTES, P. B., & SCHAIE, K. W. On the plasticity of intelligence in adulthood and old age: Where Horn and Donaldson fail. *American Psychologist*, 1976, 31, 720–725.

BANDURA, A. Self-efficacy: Toward a unifying theory of behavioral change. *Psychological Review*, 1977, 84, 191–215.

BANDURA, A. Self-referent thought: A developmental analysis of self-efficacy. In J. H. Flavell & L. Ross (Eds.), *Social cognitive development: Frontiers and possible futures*. New York: Cambridge University Press, 1981.

BARON, R., & RODIN, J. Perceived control and crowding stress. In A. Baum, J. E. Singer, & S. Valins (Eds.), *Advances in environmental psychology*. Hillsdale, N.J.: Erlbaum, 1978.

BARRETT, C. J. Effectiveness of widows' groups in facilitating change. *Journal of Consulting and Clinical Psychology*, 1978, 46, 20–31.

BARTON, D., CROWDER, M. K., & FLEXNER, J. M. Teaching about dying and death in a multidisciplinary student group. *Omega: Journal of Death and Dying,* 1979–80, 10, 265–270.

BARTOSHUK, L. M., RIFKIN, L. M., MARKS, L. E., & BARS, P. Taste and aging. *Journal of Gerontology,* 1986, 41, 51–57.

BARUCH, G. K., & BARNETT, R. C. On the well-being of adult women. In L. A. Bond & J. C. Rosen (Eds.), *Competence and coping during adulthood.* Hanover, N.H.: University Press of New England, 1980.

BAYLEY, N., & ODEN, M. H. The maintenance of intellectual ability in gifted adults. *Journal of Gerontology,* 1955, 10, 91–107.

BECK, A. T., WARD, C. H., MENDELSON, M., MOCK, J., & ERBAUGH, J. An inventory for measuring depression. *Archives of General Psychiatry,* 1951, 4, 561–571.

BECK, S. H. Adjustment to and satisfaction with retirement. *Journal of Gerontology,* 1982, 37, 616–624.

BECK, S. H. Retirement preparation programs: Differentials in opportunity and use. *Journal of Gerontology,* 1984, 39, 596–602.

BECKER, E. *The denial of death.* New York: Free Press, 1973.

BEM, D. J., & ALLEN, A. On predicting some of the people some of the time: The search for cross-situational consistencies in behavior. *Psychological Review,* 1974, 81, 506–520.

BENGTSON, V. L., & ROBERTSON, J. F. (Eds.) *Grandparenthood.* Beverly Hills, Calif.: Sage Publications, 1985.

BENNETT, T. S. Divorce. In R. J. Corsini (Ed.), *Encyclopedia of Psychology.* New York: Wiley, 1984.

BENOLIEL, J. Q. Dying is a family affair. In E. R. Prichard et al. (Eds.), *Home care: Living with dying.* New York: Columbia University Press, 1979.

BERGIN, A. E., & STRUPP, H. H. New directions in psychotherapy research. *Journal of Abnormal Psychology,* 1970, 76, 13–26.

BERGIN, A. E., & SUINN, R. M. Individual psychotherapy and behavior therapy. *Annual Review of Psychology,* 1975, 26, 509–556.

BERGLAS, S. *The success syndrome.* New York: Plenum, 1986.

BERGMAN, M. *Aging and the perception of speech.* Baltimore, MD.: University of Baltimore Press, 1980.

BERGMAN, M., BLUMENFELD, V. G., CASCARDO, D., DASH, B., LEVITT, H., & MARGULIOS, M. K. Age-related decrements in hearing for speech: Sampling and longitudinal studies. *Journal of Gerontology,* 1976, 31, 533–538.

BERKMAN, L. F., & SYME, S. L. Social networks, host resistance, and mortality: A nine year follow-up study of Alameda County residents. *American Journal of Epidemiology,* 1979, 109, 186–204.

BERSCHEID, E., & WALSTER, E. Physical attractiveness. In L. Berkowitz (Ed.), *Advances in experimental social psychology (Vol 7).* New York: Academic Press, 1974.

BERSCHEID, E., & WALSTER, E. *Interpersonal attraction.* (2nd Ed.) Reading, Mass.: Addison-Wesley, 1978.

BINET, A., & SIMON, T. Methods nouvelles pour le diagnostic du niveau intellectuel des anormaux. *Annee Psychologigue,* 1905, 11, 191–244.

BIRKHILL, W. R., & SCHAIE, K. W. The effect of differential reinforcement of cautiousness in intellectual performance among the elderly. *Journal of Gerontology,* 1975, 30, 578–583.

BIRREN, J. E. *The psychology of aging.* Englewood Cliffs, N.J.: Prentice-Hall,
1964.

BIRREN, J. E. Translations in gerontology—from lab to life: Psychophys-
iology and speed of response. *American Psychologist,* 1974, 29, 808–
815.

BIRREN, J. E., & MORRISON, D. F. Analysis of the WAIS subtests in relation to age and education. *Journal of Gerontology,* 1961, 16, 363–369.

BJORKSTEN, J. The cross-linkage theory of aging. *Journal of the American
Geriatric Society,* 1968, 16, 408–427.

BLAU, Z. S. *Aging in a changing society.* (2nd. Ed.) New York: Franklin
Watts, 1981.

BLAZER, D. Social Support and mortality in an elderly community sample. *American Journal of Epidemiology,* 1982, 115, 684–694.

BLAZER, D., & WILLIAMS, C. Epidemiology of dysphoria and depression in
an elderly population. *American Journal of Psychiatry,* 1980, 137,
439–444.

BLOOD, R. O., & WOLFE, D. M. *Husbands and wives.* New York: Free Press,
1960.

BLUM, J. E., & JARVIK, L. F. Intellectual performance of octogenarians as
a function of education and initial ability. *Human Development,* 1974,
17, 364–375.

BLUMENFELD, N., LEVY, N. B., & KAUFMAN, D. The wish to be informed of
a fatal illness. *Omega: Journal of Death and Dying,* 1978–79, 9, 323–
327.

BOLLER, F., GOLDSTEIN, G., DORR, C., KIM, Y., MOOSSY, J., RICHEY, E.,
WAGENER, D., & WOLFSON, S. K., JR. Alzheimer and related dementias: A review of current knowledge. In G. Goldstein (Ed.), *Advances
in clinical neurophysiology (Vol. 1).* New York: Plenum, 1984.

BOOTH, A. Sex and social participation. *American Sociological Review,* 1972,
37(2), 183–192.

BORST, B. How women age. *The Denver Post,* Sept. 26, 1982.

BOTWINICK, J. *Cognitive processes in maturity and old age.* New York:
Springer, 1967.

BOTWINICK, J. *Aging and behavior.* New York: Springer, 1973.

BOTWINICK, J. Intellectual abilities. In J. E. Birren & K. W. Schaie
(Eds.), *Handbook of the psychology of aging.* New York: Van Nostrand
Reinhold, 1977.

BOTWINICK, J., & BIRREN, J. E. Cognitive processes: Mental abilities and
psychomotor responses in healthy aged men. In J. E. Birren, R. N.
Butler, S. W. Greenhouse, L. Solkoff, & M. R. Yarrow
(Eds.), *Human aging.* Public Health Service Publication No. 896.
Washington, D.C: United States Government Printing Office, 1963.

BOTWINICK, J., & STORANDT, M. *Memory, related functions and age.* Springfield, Ill.: Charles C. Thomas, 1974.

BOTWINICK, J., WEST, R., & STORANDT, M. Predicting death from behavioral test performance. *Journal of Gerontology,* 1978, 33, 755–762.

BOURNE, L. E., DOMINOWSKI, R. L., & LOFTUS, E. F. *Cognitive processes*. Englewood Cliffs, N.J.: Prentice-Hall, 1979.

BOWER, G. H. Analysis of a mnemonic device. *American Scientist*, 1970, 58, 496–510.

BOYAR, J. I. The construction and partial validation of a scale for the measurement of fear of death. Unpublished doctoral dissertation, University of Rochester, Rochester, N.Y., 1964.

BRADLEY, R. H., & WEBB, R. Age-related differences in locus of control orientation in three behavioral domains. *Human Development*, 1976, 19, 49–56.

BRANCH, L., & JETTE, A. Elders' use of informal long-term care assistance. *The Gerontologist*, 1983, 23, 51–56.

BRANSFORD, J. D., STEIN, B. S., SHELTON, T. S., & OWINGS, R. A. Cognition and adaptation: The importance of learning to learn. In J. Harvey (Ed.), *Cognition, social behavior, and the environment*. Hillsdale, N.J.: Erlbaum, 1980.

BREAUGH, J. A., & DiMARCO, N. Age differences in the rated desirability of job outcomes. Paper presented at the Annual Meeting of the American Psychological Association, New York, N.Y.; 1979.

BREYTSPRAAK, L. M. *The development of self in later life*. Boston: Little, Brown and Co., 1984.

BRODY, E. The aging family. *Annals of the American Academy of Political and Social Science*, 1978, 438, 13–27.

BRODY, E. Women in the middle and family help to older people. *The Gerontologist*, 1981, 21, 471–480.

BRODY, E., JOHNSON, P., FULCOMER, M., & LANG, A. Women's changing roles and help to elderly parents: Attitudes of three generations of women. *Journal of Gerontology*, 1983, 38, 597–607.

BRODY, E., & KLEBAN, M. Day to day mental and physical health symptoms of older people: A report of health logs. *The Gerontologist*, 1983, 23, 75–85.

BRODY, J. A. An epidemiologist views senile dementia—facts and fragments. *American Journal of Epidemiology*, 1982, 115, 155–162.

BROMLEY, D. B. Some experimental tests of the effect of age on creative intellectual output. *Journal of Gerontology*, 1956, 11, 74–82.

BROMLEY, D. B. Some effects of age on the quality of intellectual output. *Journal of Gerontology*, 1957, 12, 318–323.

BROMLEY, D. B. Some effects of age on short term learning and remembering. *Journal of Gerontology*, 1958, 13, 398–406.

BROTMAN, H. *Facts and figures on older Americans, No. 2. The older population revisited: First results of the 1970 Census*. Washington, D.C.: Administration on Aging, United States Department of Health, Education, and Welfare, 1971.

BROTMAN, H. *Every ninth American*. Washington, D.C.: Developments in Aging, United States Senate Special Committee on Aging, 1980.

BROWN, J. A. Some tests of the decay theory of immediate memory. *Quarterly Journal of Experimental Psychology*, 1958, 10, 12–21.

BRUCKNER, R. Longitudinal research on the eye. *Gerontologia Clinica*, 1967, 9, 87–95.

BUCKINGHAM, R. W., LACK, S. A., MOUNT, B. M., MacLEAN, L. D., & COL-LINS, J. T. Living with the dying: Use of the technique of partici-pant observation. *Canadian Medical Assocation Journal*, 1976, 115, 1211–1215.

BUGELSKI, B. R., KIDD, E., & SEGMEN, J. Image as a mediator in one-trial paired-associate learning. *Journal of Experimental Psychology*, 1968, 76, 69–73.

BUHLER, C. Fulfillment and failure of life. In C. Buhler & F. Massarik (Eds.), *The course of human life*. New York: Springer, 1968.

BURG, A. Visual acuity as measured by dynamic and static tests: A com-parative evaluation. *Journal of Applied Psychology*, 1966, 50, 460–466.

BURGESS, A. W., & HOLMSTRUM, L. L. Recovery from rape and prior life stress. *Research in Nursing and Health*, 1978, 1, 165–174.

BURNSIDE, I. M. Sexuality and the older adult: Implications for nursing. In I. M. Burnside (Ed.), *Sexuality and aging*. Los Angeles: University of Southern California Press, 1975.

BURT, J. J., & MEEKS, L. B. *Education for sexuality: Concepts and programs for teaching.* (3rd Ed.) Philadelphia: Saunders College Publishers, 1985.

BURTON, A. The nature of personality theory. In A. Burton (Ed.), *Opera-tional theories of personality*. New York: Brunner/Mazel, 1974.

BUSKIRK, E. R. Health maintenance and longevity: Exercise. In C. E. Finch & E. L. Schneider (Eds.), *Handbook of the biology of aging*. (2nd Ed.) New York: Van Nostrand Reinhold, 1985.

BUSSE, E. W., & BLAZER, D. G. (Eds.) *Handbook of geriatric psychiatry*. New York: Van Nostrand Reinhold, 1980.

BUTLER, R.N., BESDINE, R. W., BRODY, J. A., ET AL. Senility reconsidered: Treatment possibilities for mental impairment in the elderly. *Journal of the American Medical Association*, 1980, 244, 259–263.

BUTLER, R. N., & LEWIS, M. *Aging and mental health*. St. Louis: C. V. Mosby, 1976.

BYRD, E., & GERTMAN, S. Taste sensitivity in aging persons. *Geriatrics*, 1959, 14, 381–384.

CALDWELL, D., & MISHARA, B. L. Research on attitudes of medical doctors toward the dying patient: A methodological problem. *Omega: Jour-nal of Death and Dying*, 1972, 3, 341–346.

CAMPBELL, A., CONVERSE, P. E., & RODGERS, W. L. *The quality of American life: Perceptions, evaluation, and satisfaction*. New York: Russell Sage Foundation, 1976.

CAMPBELL, T. W. Death anxiety in a coronary care unit. *Psychosomatics*, 1980, 21, 127–136.

CAMPBELL, T. W., ABERNETHY, V., & WATERHOUSE, G. J. Do death atti-tudes of nurses and physicians differ? *Omega: Journal of Death and Dying*, 1983–84, 14(1), 43–49.

CANDY, S. A comparative analysis of friendship functions in six age groups of men and women. Unpublished doctoral dissertation, Wayne State University, 1977.

CANESTRARI, R. E., JR. Paced and self-paced learning in young and elderly adults. *Journal of Gerontology*, 1963, 18, 165–168.

CANESTRARI, R. E., JR. The effect of commonality on paired-associate learning in two age groups. *Journal of Genetic Psychology*, 1966, 108, 3–7.

CANESTRARI, R. E., JR. Age changes in acquisition. In G. A. Talland (Ed.), *Human aging and behavior*. New York: Academic Press, 1968.

CANNON, W. G. *Bodily changes in pain, hunger, fear and rage: An account of recent researches into the function of emotional excitement*. (2nd Ed.) New York: Appleton, 1929.

CANTOR, M. H. The informal support system: Its relevance in the lives of the elderly. In E. Borgatta & N. McCluskey (Eds.), *Aging and society*. Beverly Hills, Calif.: Sage Publications, 1980.

CANTOR, M. H. Strain among caregivers: A study of experience in the United States. *The Gerontologist*, 1983, 23, 597–604.

CARPENTER, D. G. Diffusion theory of aging. *Journal of Gerontology*, 1965, 20, 191–195.

CASH, T. F., & DERLEGA, V. J. The matching hypothesis: Physical attractiveness among same-sexed friends. *Personality and Social Psychology Bulletin*, 1978, 4, 240–243.

CASSEM, N.H., & HACKETT, T. P. Stress on the nurses and therapist in the intensive care unit and the coronary care unit. *Heart and Lung*, 1975, 4, 252–259.

CASSILETH, B. R., LUSK, E. J., STROUSE, T. B., MILLER, D. S., BROWN, L. L., CROSS, P. A., & TENAGLIA, A. N. Psychosocial status in chronic illness: A comparative analysis of six diagnostic groups. *New England Journal of Medicine*, 1984, 311, 506–511.

CASTELLI, W. P. CHD risk factors. In W. Reichel (Ed.), *The geriatric patient*. New York: H.P. Publishing Co., 1978.

CATTELL, R. B. A culture-free intelligence test. *Journal of Educational Psychology*, 1940, 31, 161–179.

CATTELL, R. B. Theory of fluid and crystallized intelligence: A critical experiment. *Journal of Educational Psychology*, 1963, 54, 1–22.

CATTELL, R. B. *The scientific analysis of personality*. London: Penguin, 1965.

CATTELL, R. B. *Personality and mood by questionnaire*. San Francisco: Jossey-Bass, 1973.

CATTELL, R. B. *Personality and learning theory, Vol. 1: The structure of personality in its environment*. New York: Springer, 1979.

CATTELL, R. B. *Personality and learning theory, Vol. 2: A systems theory of maturation and structured learning*. New York: Springer, 1980.

CATTELL, R. B., EBER, H. W., & TATSUOKA, M. M. *Handbook for the Sixteen Personality Factor Questionnaire*. Champaign, Ill.: Institute for Personality and Ability Testing, 1970.

CERELLA, J. Information processing rates in the elderly. *Psychological Bulletin*, 1985, 98, 67–83.

CHERLIN, A., & FURSTENBERG, F. F. Styles and strategies of grandparenthood. In V. L. Bengtson & J. F. Robertson (Eds.), *Grandparenthood*. Beverly Hills, Calif.: Sage Publications, 1985.

CHIRIBOGA, D. A. Marital separation in early and late life: A comparison. Paper presented at the meeting of the Gerontological Society, Dallas, November 1979.

CHIRIBOGA, D. A. Consistency in adult personality: The influence of social stress. Paper presented at the 12th International Conference of Gerontology, Hamburg, 1981.

CHIRIBOGA, D. A. Adaptation to marital separation in later and earlier life. *Journal of Gerontology,* 1982, 37, 109–114.

CHRISTENSON, C., & GAGNON, J. Sexual behavior in a group of older women. *Journal of Gerontology,* 1965, 20, 351–356.

CHRISTENSON, C., & JOHNSON, A. B. Sexual patterns in a group of older never-married women. *Journal of Geriatric Psychiatry,* 1973, 6, 80–98.

CHOWN, S. Age and the rigidities. *Journal of Gerontology,* 1961, 16, 353–362.

CICIRELLI, V. G. *Helping elderly parents: The role of adult children.* Boston: Auburn House, 1981.

CIOCCO, A. On mortality in husbands and wives. *Human Biology,* 1940, 12, 508.

CLARK, M. ET AL. A slow death of the mind. *Newsweek,* Dec. 3, 1984, pp. 56–62.

CLARK, M., & SPRINGEN, K. Running for your life: A Harvard study links exercise with longevity. *Newsweek,* March 17, 1986, p. 70.

CLAYTON, P. J. The clinical morbidity of the first year of bereavement: A review. *Comprehensive Psychiatry,* 1973, 14(2), 151–157.

CLAYTON, V. P., & BIRREN, J. E. The development of wisdom across the life span: A reexamination of an ancient topic. In P. B. Baltes & O. G. Brim, Jr. (Eds.), *Life-span development and behavior (Vol. 3).* New York: Academic Press, 1980.

CLOPTON, W. Personality and career change. *Industrial Gerontology,* 1973, 17, 9–17.

COBB, S., & KASL, S. V. *Termination: The consequences of job loss.* NIOSH Publication No. 77–224. Cincinnati, Ohio: United States Department of Health, Education, and Welfare, 1977.

COHEN, G. Language comprehension in old age. *Cognitive Psychology,* 1979, 11, 412–429.

COHEN, J. Some statistical issues in psychological research. In B. B. Wolman (Ed.), *Handbook of clinical psychology.* New York: McGraw-Hill, 1965.

COHEN, K. P. *Hospice: Prescription for terminal care.* Germantown, Md.: Aspen Systems Corp., 1979.

COLBURN, D. Health frauds: Quackery thriving among elderly, ill. *The Washington Post,* July 18, 1985, pp. 1ff.

COLEMAN, J. C., BUTCHER, J. N., & CARSON, R. C. *Abnormal psychology and modern life.* (6th Ed.) Glenview, Ill.: Scott Foresman, 1980.

COLLETT, L., & LESTER, D. Fear of death and fear of dying. *Journal of Psychology,* 1969, 72, 179–181.

COLLINS, K. J., DORE, C., EXTON-SMITH, A. N., FOX, R. H., MACDONALD, E. C., & WOODWARD, P. M. Accidental hypothermia and impaired temperature homeostasis in the elderly. *British Medical Journal,* 1977, 278, 353–356.

COMFORT, A. *Aging: The biology of senescence.* New York: Holt, Rinehart and Winston, 1964.

COMFORT, A. Sexuality in old age. *Journal of the American Geriatrics Society,* 1974, 22, 440–442.

COMPTROLLER GENERAL OF THE UNITED STATES. *Report to Congress: Hospice care—a growing concept in the United States.* Washington, D.C.: General Accounting Office, 1979.

CONTE, H. R., WEINER, M. B., & PLUTCHIK, R. Measuring death anxiety: Conceptual, psychometric, and factor analytic aspects. *Journal of Personality and Social Psychology,* 1982, 43, 775–785.

COOK, T. D., & CAMPBELL, D. T. *Quasi-experimentation: Design and analysis issues for field settings.* Chicago: Rand McNally, 1979.

COOPER, R. M. BILASH, I., & ZUBEK, J. P. The effect of age on taste sensitivity. *Journal of Gerontology,* 1959, 14, 56–58.

COREN, S. PORAC, C., & WARD, L. M. *Sensation and perception.* New York: Academic Press, 1978.

COREY, L. G. An analogue of resistance to death awareness. *Journal of Gerontology,* 1961, 16, 59–60.

CORSINI, R. J. *Current psychotherapies.* (3rd Ed.) Itasca, Ill.: Peacock, 1984.

COSTA, P. T., JR., & McCRAE, R. R. Age differences in personality structure: A cluster analytic approach. *Journal of Gerontology,* 1976, 31, 564–570.

COSTA, P. T., JR., & McCRAE, R. R. Objective personality assessment. In M. Storandt, I. C. Siegler, & M. F. Elias (Eds.), *The clinical psychology of aging.* New York: Plenum, 1978.

COSTA, P. T., JR., & McCRAE, R. R. Still stable after all these years: Personality as a key to some issues in adulthood and old age. In P. B. Baltes & O. G. Brim, Jr. (Eds.), *Life-span development and behavior (Vol. 3).* New York: Academic Press, 1980.

COSTA, P. T., JR., ZONDERMAN, A. B., & McCRAE, R. R. Longitudinal course of social support in the Baltimore Longitudinal Study of Aging. Paper presented at the NATO Advanced Workshop: Social Support Theory, Research, and Application, Chateau de Bonas, France, 1983.

COX, P. R., & FORD, J. R. The mortality of widows shortly after widowhood. In T. Ford & G. F. DeJong (Eds.), *Social demography.* Englewood Cliffs, N.J.: Prentice-Hall, 1970.

CRAIK, F. I. M. Short-term memory and the aging process. In G. A. Talland (Ed.), *Human aging and behavior.* New York: Academic Press, 1968. (a)

CRAIK, F. I. M. Two components in free recall. *Journal of Verbal Learning and Verbal Behavior,* 1968, 7, 996–1004. (b)

CRAIK, F. I. M. Primary memory. *British Medical Bulletin,* 1971, 27, 232–236.

CRAIK, F. I. M. Age differences in human memory. In J. E. Birren & K. W. Schaie (Eds.), *Handbook of the psychology of aging.* New York: Van Nostrand Reinhold, 1977.

CRAIK, F. I. M., & BYRD, M. Aging and cognitive deficits: The role of attentional resources. In F. I. M. Craik & S. E. Trehub (Eds.), *Aging and cognitive processes.* New York: Plenum, 1982.

CRAIK, F. I. M., & LOCKHART, R. S. Levels of processing: A framework for memory research. *Journal of Verbal Learning and Verbal Behavior,* 1972, 11, 671–684.

CRAIK, F. I. M., & MASANI, P. A. Age differences in the temporal integration of language. *British Journal of Psychology,* 1967, 58, 291–299.

CRAIK, F. I. M., & RABINOWITZ, J. C. The effects of presentation rate and encoding task on age-related memory deficits. *Journal of Gerontology,* 1985, 40, 309–315.

CRAIK, F. I. M., & SIMON, E. Age differences in memory: The roles of attention and depth of processing. In L. W. Poon, J. L. Fozard, L. S. Cermak, D. Arenberg, & L. W. Thompson (Eds.), *New directions in memory and aging: Proceedings of the George Talland Memorial Conference.* Hillsdale, N.J.: Erlbaum, 1980.

CRAIK, F. I. M., & TULVING, E. Depth of processing and the retention of words in episodic memory. *Journal of Experimental Psychology: General,* 1975, 104, 268–294.

CRANNELL, C. W., & PARRISH, J. M. A comparison of immediate memory span for digits, letters, and words. *Journal of Psychology,* 1957, 44, 319–327.

CRAPPER, D. R., KIRSHNAN, S. S., & QUITTKAT, S. Aluminum, neurofibrillary degeneration, and Alzheimer's disease. *Brain,* 1976, 99, 67–80.

CROWDER, R. G. Echoic memory and the study of aging memory systems. In L. W. Poon, J. L. Fozard, L. S. Cermak, D. Arenberg, & L. W. Thompson (Eds.), *New directions in memory and aging.* Hillsdale, NJ: Erlbaum, 1980.

CROWDER, R. G., & MORTON, J. Precategorical acoustic storage (PAS). *Perception and Psychophysics,* 1969, 5, 365–373.

CROWDER, R. G., & PRUSSIN, H. A. Experiments with the stimulus suffix effect. *Journal of Experimental Psychology Monographs,* 1971, 91, 169–190.

CROWDER, R. G., & RAEBURN, U. P. The stimulus suffix effect with reversed speech. *Journal of Verbal Learning and Verbal Behavior,* 1970, 9, 342–345.

CUMMING, E., & HENRY, W. E. *Growing old.* New York: Basic Books, 1961.

CUNNINGHAM, W. R., CLAYTON, V., & OVERTON, W. Fluid and crystallized intelligence in young adulthood and old age. *Journal of Gerontology,* 1975, 30, 53–55.

CURTIS, H. J. *Biological mechanisms of aging.* Springfield, Ill.: Charles C Thomas, 1966.

DARLEY, J. M., GLUCKSBERG, S., KAMIN, L. J., & KINCHLA, R. A. *Psychology.* Englewood Cliffs, N.J.: Prentice-Hall, 1981.

DARWIN, C. J., TURVEY, M. T., & CROWDER, R. G. Auditory analogue of the Sperling partial report procedure: Evidence for brief auditory storage. *Cogitive Psychology,* 1972, 3, 255–267.

DASILVA, A., & SCHORK, M. Gender differences in attitudes to death among a group of public health students. *Omega: Journal of Death and Dying,* 1984–85, 15, 77–84.

DAVIDSON, G. W. *The hospice: Development and administration.* Washington, D.C.: Hemisphere Publishing Co., 1978.

DAVIES, P., & MALONEY, A. J. F. Selective loss of central cholinergic neurons in Alzheimer's disease. *Lancet,* 1976, 2, 1403.

DAVISON, G. C., & NEALE, J. M. *Abnormal psychology.* (2nd Ed.) New York: Wiley, 1978.

DELONGIS, A., COYNE, J. C. DAKOF, B., FOLKMAN, S., & LAZARUS, R. S. Relationship of daily hassles, uplifts, and major life events to health status. *Health Psychology,* 1982, 1, 119–136.

DEMMING, J. A., & PRESSEY, S. L. Tests "indigenous" to the adult and older years. *Journal of Counseling Psychology,* 1957, 2, 144–148.

DEMOTT, J. S. New look at the elderly. *Time,* Feb. 18, 1985, 81.

DENNIS, W. Age and achievement: A critique. *Journal of Gerontology,* 1956, 11, 331–333. (a)

DENNIS, W. Age and productivity among scientists. *Science,* 1956, 123, 724–725. (b)

DENNIS, W. The age decrement in outstanding scientific contribution: Fact or artifact? *American Psychologist,* 1958, 13, 457–460.

DENNIS, W. Creative productivity between ages of 20 and 80 years. *Journal of Gerontology,* 1966, 21, 1–8.

DENNY, M. R. Age differences. In R. J. Corsini (Ed.), *Encyclopedia of psychology.* New York: Wiley, 1984.

Department of Health, Education, and Welfare. Monocular visual acuity of persons 4–74 years. *Vital Health Statistics,* 1977, Series 11, No. 201.

DICKINSON, G. E., & PEARSON, A. A. Differences in attitudes toward terminal patients among selected medical specialties of physicians. *Medical Care,* 1979, 17, 682–685.

DICKINSON, G. E., & PEARSON, A. A. Death education and the physicians' attitudes toward dying patients. *Omega: Journal of Death and Dying,* 1980–81, 11, 167–174.

DIENER, E., LARSEN, R. J., & EMMONS, R. A. Person situation interactions: Choice of situation and congruence response models. *Journal of Personality and Social Psychology,* 1984, 47, 580–592.

DOERING, M., RODES, S. R., & SCHUSTER, M. *The aging worker: Research and recommendations.* Beverly Hills, Calif.: Sage, 1983.

DOWSETT, E. G. The dying patient. *Lancet,* 1972, 2, 1416.

DION, K. K., BERSCHEID, E., & WALSTER, E. What is beautiful is good. *Journal of Personality and Social Psychology,* 1972, 24, 285–290.

DOHRENWEND, B. S., & DOHRENWEND, B. P. *Stressful life events: Their nature and effects.* New York: Wiley, 1974.

DOLLARD, J., & MILLER, N. E. *Personality and psychotherapy: An analysis in terms of learning, thinking, and culture.* New York: McGraw-Hill, 1950.

DOLNICK, E. Pioneering research on the aging process yields contradictory theories, prospects. *The Boston Globe,* Dec. 12, 1982.

DOPPELT, J. E., & WALLACE, W. L. Standardization of the Wechsler Adult Intelligence Scale for older persons. *Journal of Abnormal and Social Psychology,* 1955, 51, 312–330.

DOUGLAS, K., & ARENBERG, D. Age changes, cohort differences, and cultural change on the Guilford-Zimmerman Temperament Survey. *Journal of Gerontology,* 1978, 33, 737–747.

DOUVAN, E. Differing views on marriage 1957 to 1976. *Newsletter, Center for Continuing Education of Women* (University of Michigan), 1979, 12(1), 1–2.

Dowd, J. Aging as exchange: A preface to theory. *Journal of Gerontology,* 1975, 30, 584–594.

Drachman, D. A., & Leavitt, J. Memory impairment in the aged: Storage versus retrieval deficit. *Journal of Experimental Psychology,* 1972, 93, 302–308.

Dublin, L. I. *The facts of life—from birth to death.* New York: Macmilllan, 1951.

Dublin, L. I., Lotka, A. J., & Spiegelman, M. *Length of life: A study of the life table.* New York: Ronald, 1949.

Durlak, J. Measurement of the fear of death: An examination of some existing scales. *Journal of Clinical Psychology,* 1972, 28, 545–547.

Eichorn, D. The Institute of Human Development Studies: Berkeley and Oakland. In L. F. Jarvik, C. Eisdorfer, & J. E. Blum (Eds.), *Intellectual functioning in adults. Psychological and biological influences* New York: Springer, 1973.

Eisdorfer, C. Changes in cognitive functioning in relation to intellectual level in senescence. In C. Tibbits & W. Donahue (Eds.), *Social and psychological aspects of aging.* New York: Columbia University Press, 1962.

Eisdorfer, C. Stress, disease, and cognitive change in the aged. In C. Eisdorfer & R. O. Friedel (Eds.), *Cognitive and emotional disturbance in the elderly.* Chicago: Yearbook Medical Publishers, 1977.

Eisdorfer, C., Axelrod, S., & Wilkie, F. L. Stimulus exposure time as a factor in serial learning in an aged sample. *Journal of Abnormal and Social Psychology,* 1963, 67, 594–600.

Eisdorfer, C., & Service, C. Verbal rote learning and superior intelligence in the aged. *Journal of Gerontology,* 1967, 22, 158–161.

Eisdorfer, C., & Wilkie, F. Intellectual changes with advancing age. In L. F. Jarvik, C. Eisdorfer, & J. E. Blum (Eds.), *Intellectual functioning in adults* New York: Springer, 1973.

Eisner, D. A. Developmental relationships between field independence and fixity-mobility. *Perceptual and Motor Skills,* 1972, 34, 767–770.

Ekblom, B. Significance of psychological factors with regard to risk of death among elderly persons. *Acta Psychiatrica Scandinavica,* 1963, 39, 627–633.

Ekerdt, D. J., Baden, L., Bosse, R., & Dibbs, E. The effect of retirement on physical health. *American Journal of Public Health,* 1983, 73, 779–783.

Ekerdt, D. J., Bosse, R., & Levkoff, S. An empirical test for phases of retirement: Findings from the normative aging study. *Journal of Gerontology,* 1985, 40, 96–101.

Ekerdt, D. J., Bosse, R., & LoCastro, J. S. Claims that retirement improves health. *Journal of Gerontology,* 1983, 38, 231–236.

Elias, C. S., & Hirasuna, N. Age and semantic and phonological encoding. *Developmental Psychology,* 1976, 12, 497–503.

Elliott, G. R., & Eisdorfer, C. (Eds.) *Stress and human health.* New York: Springer, 1982.

Elmer-Dewitt, P. Extra years for extra effort. *Time,* March 17, 1986, 66.

ENGEN, T. Method and theory in the study of odor preferences. In J. W. Johnston, Jr., D. G. Moulton, & A. Turk (Eds.), *Human responses to environmental odors.* New York: Academic Press, 1974.

ENGEN, T. Taste and smell. In J. E. Birren & K. W. Schaie (Eds.), *Handbook of the psychology of aging.* New York: Van Nostrand Reinhold, 1977.

ERBER, J. T. Age differences in recognition memory. *Journal of Gerontology,* 1974, 29, 177–181.

ERIKSEN, C. W., & COLLINS, J. F. Some temporal characteristics of visual pattern perception. *Journal of Experimental Psychology,* 1967, 89, 659–667.

EKIRSON, E. H. *Childhood and society.* (2nd Ed.) New York: Norton, 1963.

ERIKSON, E. H. *Identity: Youth and crisis.* New York: Norton, 1968.

EVANS, G. W., BRENNAN, P. L., SKORPANICH, M. A., & HELD, D. Cognitive mapping and elderly adults: Verbal and location memory for urban landmarks. *Journal of Gerontology,* 1984, 39, 452–457.

EVANS, P. A. L., & BARTOLOME, F. The relationship between professional life and private life. In C. B. Derr (Ed.), *Work, family, and the career: New frontiers in theory and research.* New York: Praeger, 1980.

EVANS, R. I. *Gordon Allport: The man and his ideas.* New York: E. P. Dutton, 1970.

EWEN, R. B. Personality theories. In R. J. Corsini (Ed.), *The encyclopedia of psychology.* New York: Wiley, 1984.

EWEN, R. B. *An introduction to theories of personality.* (2nd Ed.) New York: Academic Press, 1985.

EYSENCK, H. J., *The biological basis of personality.* Springfield, Ill,: Charles C Thomas, 1967.

EYSENCK, H. J., & EYSENCK, S. B. G. *Personality structure and measurement.* London: Routledge & Kegan, 1969.

EYSENCK, M. W. Age differences in incidental learning. *Developmental Psychology,* 1974, 10, 936–941.

FARRELL, M. P., & ROSENBERT, S. D. *Men at midlife.* Boston: Auburn House, 1981.

Federal Register. Department of Health and Human Services, Rules and Regulations. Dec. 16, 1983, 48, 243, 56008–56024.

FEIFEL, H. Religious conviction and fear of death among the healthy and the terminally ill. *Journal for the Scientific Study of Religion,* 1974, 13, 353–360.

FEIFEL, H., & BRANSCOMB, A. Who's afraid of death? *Journal of Abnormal Psychology,* 1973, 81, 282–288.

FEIFEL, H., FREILICH, J., & HERMANN, L. Death fear in dying heart and cancer patients. *Journal of Psychosomatic Research,* 1973, 17, 161–166.

FEIFEL, H., HANSON, S., JONES, R., & EDWARDS, L. Physicians consider death. *Proceedings of the 75th Annual Convention of the American Psychological Association,* 1967, 2, 201–202.

FEIFEL, H., & HELLER, J. Normalcy, illness, and death. In *Proceedings of the Third World Congress of Psychiatry.* Toronto: University of Toronto Press, 1960.

FEIFEL, H., & HERMANN, L. Fear of death in the mentally ill. *Psychological Reports,* 1973, 33, 931–938.

FEIFEL, H., & NAGY, V. T. Death orientation and life-threatening behavior. *Journal of Abnormal Psychology,* 1980, 89, 38–45.

FEINLEIB, M. Presentation before the subcommittee on health and long-term care of the Select Committee on Aging of the Untited States House of Representatives. Washington, D.C., Feb. 2, 1984.

FELDMAN, H. *Development of the husband-wife relationship.* Research report presented to the Department of Child Development and Family Relationships, New York State College of Home Economics, Cornell University, Ithaca, N.Y., August 1964.

FELTON, B., & KAHANA, E. Adjustment and situationally-bound locus of control among insitutionalized aged. *Journal of Gerontology,* 1974, 29, 295–301.

FESTINGER, L. A theory of social comparison processes. *Human Relations,* 1954, 1, 117–140.

FIALKA, J. J. Older Americans: What Social Security means to the retired and the about-to-be. *The Wall Street Journal,* Feb. 22, 1989, pp. 1, 16.

FILLENBAUM, G. G., GEORGE, L. K., & PALMORE, E. B. Determinants and consequences of retirement among men of different races and economic levels. *Journal of Gerontology,* 1985, 40, 85–94.

FINCH, C. E. Neuroendocrine and anatomic aspects of aging. In C. E. Finch & L. Hayflick (Eds.), *Handbook of the biology of aging.* New York: Van Nostrand Reinhold, 1977.

FINCH, C. E., & LANDFIELD, P. W. Neuroendocrine and autonomic functions in aging mammals. In C. E. Finch & E. L. Schneider (Eds.), *Handbook of the biology of aging.* (2nd Ed.) New York: Van Nostrand Reinhold, 1985.

FINKLE, T. J., & WALSH, D. A. Sentence and discourse comprehension in young and old adults. Paper presented at the 87th meeting of the American Psychological Association, New York, September 1979.

FISCHER, C. S. *To dwell among friends.* Chicago, Ill.: University of Chicago Press, 1982.

FISCHER, C. S., JACKSON, R. M., STUEVE, C. A., GERSON, K., JONES, L. M., & BALDASSARE, M. *Networks and places: Social relations in the urban setting.* New York: Free Press, 1977.

FISCHMAN, J. The mystery of Alzheimer's. *Psychology Today,* 1984, 18(1), 27.

FISHER, S., & GREENBERG, R. P. *The scientific credibility of Freud's theories and therapy.* New York: Basic Books, 1977.

FISKE, D. W. The limits for the conventional science of personality. *Journal of Personality,* 1974, 42, 1–11.

FISKE, D. W. *Strategies for personality research.* San Francisco: Jossey-Bass, 1978.

FLORIAN, V., & HAR-EVEN, D. Fear of personal death: The effects of sex and religious belief. *Omega: Journal of Death and Dying,* 1983–84, 14, 83–91.

FOLKLMAN, S., & LAZARUS, R. S. An analysis of coping in a middle-aged community sample. *Journal of Health and Social Behavior,* 1980, 21, 219–239.

FOULKES, D. *The psychology of sleep.* New York: Scribners, 1966.

FRANKLIN, P.A. Psychological services for the terminally ill in hospice programs. Paper presented at the 92nd Annual Convention of the American Psychological Association, Toronto, August 1984.

FREDRICK, J. F. Physiological reactions induced by grief. *Omega: Journal of Death and Dying*, 1971, 2, 71–75.

FREDRICK, J. F. The biochemistry of acute grief with regard to neoplasia. In O. S. Margolis, H. C. Raether, A. H. Kutscher, J. B. Powers, I. B. Seeland, R. DeBellis, & D. J. Cherico (Eds.), *Acute grief: Counseling the bereaved*. New York: Columbia University Press, 1981.

FREUD, S. *Mourning and melancholia*. Original publication: 1917. Paperback reprint: *General psychological theory*. New York: Collier, 1963.

FREUD, S. *Three essays on the theory of sexuality*. Original publication: 1905. Standard edition: London: Hogarth Press, Vol. 7. Paperback reprint: New York: Avon Books, 1965. (a).

FREUD, S. *Introductory lectures on psychoanalysis*. (Rev. Ed.) Original publication: 1916–1917. Standard edition: London: Hogarth Press, Vol. 15–16. Paperback reprint: New York: Norton, 1966.

FREUD, S. *The interpretation of dreams*. Original publication: 1900. Paperback reprint: New York: Avon Books, 1965. (c)

FREUD, S. *Introductory lectures on psychoanalysis*. (Rev. Ed.) Original publication: 1916–1917. Standard edition: London: Hogarth Press, Vol. 15–16. Paperback reprint: new York: Norton, 1966.

FRIEDMAN, M., & ROSENMAN, R. Association of specific overt behavior pattern with blood and cardiovascular findings. *Journal of the American Medical Association*, 1959, 169, 1286.

FRIEDMAN, M., & ROSENMAN, R. *Type A behavior and your heart*. New York: Knopf, 1974.

FRIES, J. F. The compression of morbidity. *Milbank Memorial Fund Quarterly*, 1983, 61, 397–419.

FRIES, J. F. & CRAPP, L. M. *Vitality and aging*. New York: W. H. Freeman, 1981.

FROMM, E. *Escape from freedom*. New York: Holt, Rinehart & Winston, 1941.

FROMM, E. *Man for himself: Inquiry into the psychology of ethics*. New York: Holt, Rinehart & Winston, 1947.

FROMM, E. *The forgotten language: An introduction to the understanding of dreams, fairy tales, and myths*. New York: Holt, Rinehart & Winston, 1951.

FROMM, E. *The art of loving*. New York: Harper & Row, 1956. Paperback reprint: New York: Perennial, 1974.

FURRY, C. A., & BALTES, P. B. The effect of age differences in ability-extraneous performance variables on the assessment of intelligence in children, adults, and the elderly. *Journal of Gerontology*, 1973, 28, 73–80.

GALLAGHER, D., & THOMPSON, L. W. Depression. In P. M. Lewinsohn & L. Teri (Eds.), *Clinical geropsychology: New directions in assessment and treatment*. New York: Pergamon Press, 1983.

GALLAGHER, P. Comparative effectiveness of group psychotherapies for the reduction of depression in elderly outpatients. Paper presented at the Annual Meeting of the American Psychological Association, New York, August 1979.

GAMBRILL, E. D. *Behavior modification: Handbook of assessment, intervention, and evaluation.* San Francisco: Jossey-Bass, 1977.

GARDNER, E. F., & MONGE, R. H. Adult age differences in cognitive abilities and educational background. *Experimental Aging Research,* 1977, 3, 337–383.

GARDNER, H. *Frames of mind.* New York: Basic Books, 1983.

GARSTECKI, D. Aural rehabilitation for the aging adult. In D. Beasley & G. A. Davis (Eds.), *Aging: Communication processes and disorders.* New York: Grune & Stratton, 1981.

GATZ, M., & SIEGLER, I. C. Locus of control: A retrospective. Paper presented at the American Psychological Association Meetings, Los Angeles, August 1981.

GELMAN, D., ET AL. Who's taking care of our parents? *Newsweek,* May 6, 1985, 61–68.

GEORGE, L. K., & WEILER, S. J. Sexuality in middle and late life. *Archives of General Psychiatry,* 1981, 38, 919–923.

GINSBURG, H., & OPPER, S. *Piaget's theory of intellectual development: An introduction.* Englewood Cliffs, N.J.: Prentice-Hall, 1969.

GLADIS, M., & BRAUN, H. Age differences in transfer and retroaction as a function of intertask response similarity. *Journal of Experimental Psychology,* 1958, 55, 25–30.

GLASS, D. C., & SINGER, J. W. *Urban stress.* New York: Academic Press, 1972.

GLEITMAN, H. *Basic psychology.* New York: Norton, 1983.

GLICK, I. O., WEISS, R. S., & PARKES, C. M. *The first year of bereavement.* New York: Wiley, 1974.

GLICK, P. C. Future American families. *Washington Cofo Memo,* 1979, 11(3), 2–5.

GOFF, G. B., ROLSNER, B. S., DETRE, T., & KENNARD, D. Vibration perception in normal man and medical patients. *Journal of Neurological and Neurosurgical Psychiatry,* 1965, 28, 503.

GOLDBERG, E. L., & COMSTOCK, G. W. Epidemiology of life events. Frequency in general populations. *American Journal of Epidemiology,* 1980, 111, 736–752.

GOLDE, P., & KOGAN, N. A sentence completion procedure for assessing attitudes toward old people. *Journal of Gerontology,* 1959, 14, 355–363.

GOODE, W. J. *World revolution and family patterns.* New York: The Free Press, 1963.

GOODWIN, J. S. *Suppressor cells in human disease.* New York: Marcel Dekker, 1981.

GORDON, S. K., & CLARK, W. C. Application of signal detection theory to prose recall and recognition in elderly and young adults. *Journal of Gerontology,* 1974, 29, 64–72.

GORE, S., & MANGIONE, T. W. Social roles, sex roles, and psychological distress: Additive and interactive models of sex differences. *Journal of Health and Social Behavior,* 1983, 24, 300–312.

GOTESTAM, K. G. Behavioral and dynamic psychotherapy with the elderly. In J. E. Birren & R. B. Sloane (Eds.), *Handbook of mental health and aging.* Englewood Cliffs, N.J.: Prentice-Hall, 1982.

GOTTSCHALK, E. C., JR. Older Americans: The aging made gains in the 1970s, outpacing rest of the population. *The Wall Street Journal,* Feb. 21, 1983, pp. 1, 20.

GOUDSMIT, J., MARROW, C. H., ASHER, D. M., YANAGIHARA, R. T., MASTERS, C. L., GIBBS, C. J., JR., & GADUSEK, D. C. Evidence for and against the transmittability of Alzheimer's disease. *Neurology,* 1980, 30, 945–950.

GOUDY, W. J. Changing work expectations: Findings from the Retirement History Study. *The Gerontologist,* 1981, 21, 644–649.

GOULD, R. The phases of adult life: A study in developmental psychology. *American Journal of Psychiatry,* 1972, 129, 521–531.

GRANEY, M. J. Happiness and social participation in aging. *Journal of Gerontology,* 1975, 30, 701–706.

GRANICK, S., KLEBEN, M. H., & WEISS, A. D. Relationships between hearing loss and cognition in normally hearing aged persons. *Journal of Gerontology,* 1976, 4, 434–440.

GRAVES, J. P., DALTON, G. W., & THOMPSON, P. H. Career stages: In organizations. In C. B. Derr (Ed.), *Work, family, and the career: New frontiers in theory and research.* New York: Praeger, 1980.

GREER, D., & MOR, V. *A preliminary final report of the National Hospice Study.* Providence, R.I.: Brown University, 1983.

GRIFFITT, W. Attitude similarity and attraction. In T. L. Huston (Ed.), *Foundations of interpersonal attraction.* New York: Academic Press, 1974.

GROSS, A. E., & CROFTON, C. What is good is beautiful. *Sociometry,* 1977, 40, 85–90.

GUIGOZ, Y., & MUNRO, H. N. Nutrition and aging. In C. E. Finch & E. L. Schneider (Eds.), *Handbook of the biology of aging.* (2nd Ed.) New York: Van Nostrand Reinhold, 1985.

GUILFORD, J. P. *The nature of human intelligence.* New York: McGraw-Hill, 1967.

GUILFORD, J. P. Fluid and crystallized intelligences: Two fanciful concepts. *Psychological Bulletin,* 1980, 88, 406–412.

GUILFORD, J. P. Human intelligence. In R. J. Corsini (Ed.), *Encyclopedia of psychology.* New York: Wiley, 1984.

Gurland, B. J. The comparative frequency of depression in various adult age groups. *Journal of Gerontology,* 1976, 31, 283–292.

GURLAND, B. J. The assessment of the mental health status of older adults. In J. E. Birren & R. B. Sloane (Eds.), *Handbook of mental health and aging.* Englewood Cliffs, N.J.: Prentice-Hall, 1982.

GURLAND, B. J., & Copeland, J., Kuriansky, J., Kelleger, M., Sharpe, L., & Dean, L. *The mind and mood of aging.* New York: Haworth Press, 1983.

GURLAND, B. J., & Toner, J. A. Depression in the elderly: A review of recently published studies. In C. Eisdorfer (Ed.), *Annual review of gerontology and geriatrics (Vol. 3).* New York: Springer, 1982.

GUTMANN, D. L. Parenthood: Key to comparative study of the life cycle? In N. Datan & L. Ginsberg (Eds.), *Life-span developmental psychology: Normative life crises.* New York: Academic Press, 1975.

GUTTENTAG, R. E. Memory and aging: Implications for theories of memory development during childhood. *Developmental Review,* 1985, 5, 56–82.

HABER, R. N., & NATHANSON, L. S. Post-retinal iconic storage? Some further observations on Park's camel as seen through the eye of a needle. *Perception and Psychophysics,* 1968, 3, 349–355.

HABER, R. N., & STANDING, L. Direct measures of short-term visual storage. *Quarterly Journal of Experimental Psychology,* 1969, 21, 43–54.

HABER, R. N., & STANDING, L. Direct estimates of apparent duration of a flash followed by visual noise. *Canadian Journal of Psychology,* 1970, 24, 216–229.

HAGESTAD, G. Patterns of communication and influence between grandparents and grandchildren in a changing society. Paper presented at the World Congress of Sociology, Sweden, 1978.

HAGESTAD, G. Continuity and connectedness. In V. L. Bengtson & J. F. Robertson (Eds.), *Grandparenthood.* Beverly Hills, Calif.: Sage Publications, 1985.

HALL, C. S. *The meaning of dreams.* New York: McGraw-Hill, 1966.

HALL, D. T. Pressures from work, self, and home in the life stages of married women. *Journal of Vocational Behavior,* 1975, 6, 121–132.

HAMPE, S. O. Needs of a grieving spouse in a hospital setting. *Nursing Research,* 1975, 24, 113–120.

HANDAL, P. J., PEAL, R. L., NAPOLI, J. G., & AUSTRIN, H. R. The relationship between direct and indirect measures of death anxiety. *Omega: Journal of Death and Dying,* 1984–85, 15, 245–262.

HANDAL, P. J., & RYCHLAK, J. F. Curvilinearity between dream content and death anxiety and the relationship of death anxiety to repression-sensitization. *Journal of Abnormal Psychology,* 1971, 77, 11–16.

HANLEY-DUNN, P., & McINTOSH, J. L. Meaningfulness and recall of names by young and old adults. *Journal of Gerontology,* 1984, 39, 583–585.

HARKINS, S. W., PRICE, D. D., & MARTELLI, M. Effects of age in pain perception: Thermonociception. *Journal of Gerontology,* 1986, 41, 58–63.

HARMAN, D. Free radical theory of aging: Effect of free radical reaction inhibitors on the mortality rate of male LAF_1 mice. *Journal of Gerontology,* 1968, 23, 476–482.

HARMAN, D. The aging process. *Proceedings of the National Academy of Sciences,* 1981, 78, 7124–7128.

HARRE, R., & LAMB, R. *The encyclopedic dictionary of psychology.* Cambridge, Mass.: The MIT Press, 1984.

HARRIS, C. S. *Fact book on aging: A profile of America's older population.* Washington, D.C.: National Council on the Aging, 1978.

HARRIS, J. E., & MORRIS P. E. *Everyday memory: Actions and absentmindedness.* New York: Academic Press, 1984.

HARRIS, L., & ASSOCIATES. *The myth and reality of aging.* Washington, D.C.: National Council on the Aging, 1975.

HARRIS, L., & ASSOCIATES. *Aging in the eighties: America in transition.* Washington, D.C.: National Council on the Aging, 1981.

HARRISON, D. E. Cell tissue transplantation: A means of studying the aging process. In C. E. Finch & E. L. Schneider (Eds.), *Handbook of the biology of aging.* (2nd Ed.) New York: Van Nostrand Reinhold, 1985.

HARTFORD, M. E. The use of group methods for work with the aged. In J. E. Birren & R. B. Sloane (Eds.), *Handbook of mental health and aging.* Englewood Cliffs, N.J.: Prentice-Hall, 1982.

HARTLEY, J. T., HARKER, J. O., & WALSH, D. A. Contemporary issues and new directions in adult development of learning and memory. In L. W. Poon (Ed.), *Aging in the 1980s.* Washington, D.C.: American Psychological Association, 1980.

Harvard Medical School. A look at high blood pressure, Part II. *Harvard Medical School Newsletter,* 1979, 4(9), 1–2, 5.

HATFIELD, C. B., HATFIELD, R. E., GEGGIE, P. H. S., TAYLOR, J., SOTI, K., WINTHERS, L., HARRIS, A., & GREENLEY, N. Attitudes about death, dying, and terminal care: Differences among groups at a university teaching hospital. *Omega: Journal of Death and Dying,* 1983–84, 14, 51–63.

HAYFLICK, L. The limited *in vitro* lifetime of human diploid cell strains. *Experimental Cell Research,* 1965, 37, 614–636.

HAYFLICK, L. The biology of human aging. *American Journal of Medical Science,* 1973, 265(1), 432–445.

HAYFLICK, L. Cell aging. In C. Eisdorfer (Ed.), *Annual review of gerontology and geriatrics (Vol. 1).* New York: Springer, 1980.

HAYFLICK, L. The cell biology of human aging. *Scientific American,* 1986, 242, 58–65.

HAYNES, S. G., McMICHAEL, A. J., & TYROLER, H. A. Survival after early and normal retirement. *Journal of Gerontology,* 1978, 33, 269–278.

HAYSLIP, B., JR., & STERNS, H. L. Age differences in relationships between crystallized and fluid intelligence in problem solving. *Journal of Gerontology,* 1979, 34, 404–414.

HAZZARD, W. R., & BIERMAN, E. L. Old age. In D. W. Smith, E. L. Bierman, & N. M. Robinson (Eds.), *The biologic ages of man.* Philadelphia,: W.B. Saunders, 1978.

HEBB, D. O. On watching myself get old. *Psychology Today,* 1978, 12(11), 15–23.

HEGELER, S. Sexual behavior in elderly Danish males. Paper presented at the International Symposium on Sex Education and Therapy, Stockholm, Sweden, 1976.

HEGLIN, H. Problem solving set in different age groups. *Journal of Gerontology,* 1956, 11, 310–317.

HELLERSTEIN, H. K., & FRIEDMAN, E. H. Sexual activity and the post-coronary patient. *Archives of International Medicine,* 1970, 125, 987–999.

HERON, A., & CHOWN, S. *Age and function.* London: Churchill, 1967.

HERTZOG, C., SCHAIE, K. W., & GRIBBEN, K. Cardiovascular changes in intellectual functioning from middle to old age. *Journal of Gerontology,* 1978, 33, 872–883.

HESS, B. Friendship. In M. Riley, M. Johnson, & A. Foner (Eds.), *Aging and society, Vol. 3: A sociology of age stratification.* New York: Russell Sage Foundation, 1972.

HESTON, L. L., & MASTRI, A. R. The genetics of Alzheimer's disease: Associations with hematologic malignancy and Down's syndrome. *Archives of General Psychiatry,* 1977, 34, 976–981.

HETHERINGTON, B. M. Effects of father absence on personality development in adolescent daughters. *Developmental Psychology,* 1972, 7, 313–386.

HETHERINGTON, B. M., COX, M., & COX, R. Divorced fathers. *Family Coordinator,* 1976, 25(4), 417–428.

HETHERINGTON, B. M., COX, M., & COX, R. The aftermath of divorce. In J. H. Stevens, Jr., & M. Mathews (Eds.), *Mother-child, father-child relations.* Washington, D.C.: National Association for the Education of Young Children, 1977.

HETHERINGTON, B. M., & DUER, J. The effects of father absence on child development. In W. W. Hartup (Ed.), *The young child: Review of research. (Vol. 2)* Washington, D.C.: National Association for the Education of Young Children, 1972.

HEYMAN, D. K., & GIANTURCO, D. J. Long-term adaptation by the elderly to bereavement. *Journal of Gerontology,* 1973, 3, 359–362.

HILLS, B. L. Vision, visibility, and perception in driving. *Perception,* 1980, 9, 183–216.

HINTON, J. M. The physical and mental distress of the dying. *Quarterly Journal of Medicine,* 1963, 32, 1–21.

HIRSCH, B. J. Social networks and the coping process: Creating personal communities. In B. H. Gottleib (Ed.), *Social networks and social support.* Beverly Hills, Calif.: Sage, 1981.

HOCHSCHILD, A. R. Disengagement theory: A logical, empirical and phenomenological critique. In J. F. Gubrium (Ed.), *Time, roles, and self in old age.* New York: Human Sciences Press, 1976.

HOENDERS, H. J., & BLOEMENDAL, H. Lens proteins and aging. *Journal of Gerontology,* 1983, 38, 278–286.

HOERR, S. O. Thoughts on what to tell the patient with cancer. *Cleveland Clinic Quarterly,* 1963, 30, 11–16.

HOFFMAN, L. W., & MANIS, J. Influences of children on marital interaction and parental satisfaction and dissatisfaction. In R. Lerner & G. Spanier (Eds.), *Child influences on marital and family interaction.* New York: Academic Press, 1978.

HOLAHAN, C. K., & GILBERT, L. A. Conflict between major life roles: Women and men in dual career couples. *Human Relations,* 1979, 32, 451–467. (a)

HOLAHAN, C. K., & GILBERT, L. A. Interrole conflict for working women: Career versus jobs. *Journal of Applied Psychology,* 1979, 64, 86–90. (b)

HOLDEN, C. Hospices: For the dying, relief from pain and fear. *Science,* 1976, 193, 389–391.

HOLMES, H. H., & RAHE, R. H. The social readjustment rating scale. *Journal of Psychosomatic Research,* 1967, 11(2), 213–218.

HOLMES, T. S., & HOLMES, H. H. Short-term intrusions into the life style routine. *Journal of Psychosomatic Research,* 1970, 14(2), 121–132.

HOLT, R. R. Occupational stress. In L. Goldberger & S. Breznitz (Eds.), *Handbook of stress.* New York: Free Press, 1982.

HORN, J. Regriefing: A way to end pathological mourning. *Psychology Today,* 1974, 1(2), 184.

HORN, J. L. Organization of data on life-span development of human abilities. In L. R. Goulet & P. B. Baltes (Eds.), *Life-span developmental psychology.* New York: Academic Press, 1970.

HORN, J. L. Human ability systems. In P. B. Baltes (Ed.), *Life-span development and behavior (Vol. 1).* New York: Academic Press, 1978.

HORN, J. L., & CATTELL, R. B. Age differences in fluid and crystallized intelligence. *Acta Psychologica,* 1967, 26, 107–129.

HORN, J. L., & DONALDSON, G. On the myth of intellectual decline in adulthood. *American Psychologist,* 1976, 31, 701–719.

HORN, J. L., & DONALDSON, G. Faith is not enough: A response to the Baltes-Schaie claim that intelligence does not wane. *American Psychologist,* 1977, 32, 369–373.

HORN, J. L., & DONALDSON, G. Cognitive development II: Adulthood development of human abilities. In O. G. Brim, Jr., & J. Kagan (Eds.) *Constancy and change in human development: A volume of review essays.* Cambridge, Mass.: Harvard University Press, 1980.

HORNEY, K. *Our inner conflicts: A constructive theory of neurosis.* New York: Norton, 1945.

HORNEY, K. *Neurosis and human growth: The struggle toward self-realization.* New York: Norton, 1950.

HOUSE, J. S. Occupational stress as a precursor to coronary disease. In W. D. Gentry & R. B. Williams, Jr. (Eds.), *Psychological aspects of myocardial infarction and coronary care.* St. Louis: Mosby, 1975.

HOUSE, J. S., ROBBINS, C., & METZNER, H. L. The association of social relationships and activities with mortality: Prospective evidence from the Tecumseh Community Health Study. *American Journal of Epidemiology,* 1982, 116, 123–140.

HOWELL, D. S., SAPOLSKY, A. S., PITA, J. C., & WOESSNER, J. F. The pathogenesis of osteoarthritis. *Seminars in Arthritis and Rheumatism,* 1976, 5(4), 365–383.

HUGIN, F., NORRIS, A., & SHOCK, N. Skin reflex and voluntary reaction time in young and old males. *Journal of Gerontology,* 1960, 15, 388–391.

HULICKA, I. M. Age differences in Wechsler Memory Scale Scores. *Journal of Genetic Psychology,* 1966, 109, 134–145.

HULICKA, I. M. Age differences in retention as a function of interference. *Journal of Gerontology,* 1967, 22, 180–184.

HULICKA, I. M., & WEISS, R. L. Age differences in retention as a function of learning. *Journal of Consulting Psychology,* 1965, 29, 125–129.

HULIN, C. L., & SMITH, P. C. A linear model of job satisfaction. *Journal of Applied Psychology,* 1965, 49, 209–216.

HULTSCH, D. F. Adult age differences in free classification and free recall. *Developmental Psychology,* 1971, 4, 338–342.

HULTSCH, D. F. Learning to learn in adulthood. *Journal of Gerontology,* 1974, 29, 302–308.

HULTSCH, D. F. Adult age differences in retrieval: Trace-dependent and cue-dependent forgetting. *Developmental Psychology*, 1975, 11, 197–201.

HULTSCH, D. F., & CRAIG, E. R. Adult age differences in the inhibition of recall as a function of retrieval cues. *Developmental Psychology*, 1976, 12, 83–84.

HUNT, E. Mechanics of verbal ability. *Psychological Review*, 1978, 85, 109–130.

HUNT, E. Intelligence as an information-processing concept. *British Journal of Psychology*, 1980, 71, 449–474.

HUNT, E., & HERTZOG, C. *Age-related changes in cognition during the working years.* Arlington, Va.: Office of Naval Research, 1981.

HUNT, M. *Sexual behavior in the 1970's.* Chicago: Playboy Press, 1974.

HYMAN, G. A. Medical needs of the bereaved family. In A. H. Kutscher (Ed.), *But not to lose.* New York: Frederick Fell, 1969.

HYMAN, H. H. *Of time and widowhood.* Durham, N.C.: Duke University Press Policy Studies, 1983.

JAFFEE, L. Sexual problems of the terminally ill. In E. Prichard et al. (Eds.), *Home care: Living with the dying.* New York: Columbia University Press, 1979.

JALAVISTO, E., ORMA, E., & TAWAST, M. Aging and relation between stimulus intensity and duration in corneal sensibility. *Acta Physiologica Scandinavica*, 1951, 23, 224–233.

JARVIK, L. F., & FALEK, A. Intellectual stability and survival in the aged. *Journal of Gerontology*, 1963, 18, 173–176.

JEFFERS, F. C., NICHOLS, C. R., & EISDORFER, C. Attitudes of older persons to death. *Journal of Gerontology*, 1961, 16, 53–56.

JENKINS, C. D. Psychologic and social precursors of coronary disease. *New England Journal of Medicine*, 1971, 284, 244–255; 307–317.

JENKINS, C. D. Behavior that triggers heart attacks. *Science News*, June 22, 1974, 105(25), 402.

JENKINS, C. D. The coronary-prone personality. In W. D. Gentry & R. B. Williams (Eds.), *Psychological aspects of myocardial infarction and coronary care.* St. Louis: Mosby, 1975.

JONES, E. E., & SIGALL, H. The bogus pipeline: A new paradigm for measuring affect and attitude. *Psychological Bulletin*, 1971, 76, 349–364.

JONES, H. E. Intelligence and problem-solving. In J. E. Birren (Ed.), *Handbook of aging and the individual.* Chicago: University of Chicago Press, 1959.

JOYCE, C. A time for grieving. *Psychology Today*, 1984, 18(11), 42–46.

JUNG, C. G. *Psychoanalysis and association experiments.* Original publication: 1905. Standard edition: Princeton, N.J.: Princeton University Press, Vol. 2.

JUNG, C. G. *The association method.* Original publication: 1910. Standard edition: Princeton, N.J.: Princeton University Press, Vol. 2.

JUNG, C. G. *The aims of psychotherapy.* Original publication: 1931. Standard edition: Princeton, N.J.: Princeton University Press, Vol. 16.

JUNG, C. G. *Modern man in search of a soul.* New York: Harcourt, Brace & World, 1933.

JUNG, C. G. *Man and his symbols.* London: Aldus Books, 1964.

JUNG, C. G. *The stages of life.* Original publication: 1930–1931. Paperback reprint: *The portable Jung.* New York: Viking, 1971.

JUNG, C. G. *Two essays on analytical psychology.* Original publication: 1917, 1928. Paperback reprint: Princeton, N.J.: Princeton University Press, 1972.

JUNG, C. G. *Psychological types.* Original publication: 1921. Paperback reprint: Princeton, N.J.: Princeton Universtiy Press, 1976.

KAHANA, B. Social and psychological aspects of sexual behavior among the aged. In E. S. E. Hafez (Ed.), *Aging and reproductive Physiology (Vol. 2).* Ann Arbor, Mich.: Ann Arbor Science, 1976.

KAHN, R. L. *Work and health.* New York: Wiley, 1981.

KAHN, R. L. GOLDFARB, A. I., POLLACK, M. & PECK, A. Brief objective measures for the determination of mental status in the aged. *American Journal of Psychiatry,* 1960, 117, 326–328.

KALISH, R. A. *Death, grief, and caring relationships.* Monterey, Calif.: Brooks/Cole, 1981.

KANDEL, D. B. Similarity in real-life adolescent friendship pairs. *Journal of Personality and Social Psychology,* 1978, 36 306–312.

KANNEL, W. B., & SORLIE, P. Hypertension in Framingham. In O. Paul (Ed.), *Epidemiology and control of hypertension.* Miami: Symposium Specialists, 1975.

KAPLAN, M. F., & ANDERSON, N. H. Information integration theory and reinforcement theory as approaches to interpersonal attraction. *Journal of Personality and Social Psychology,* 1973, 28, 301–312.

KASL, S. Pursuing the link between stressful life experiences and disease: A time for reappraisal. In C. L. Cooper (Ed.), *Stress research: Issues for the Eighties.* New York: Wiley, 1983.

KASL S., & BERKMAN, L. F. Some psychosocial influences on the health status of the elderly: The perspective of social epidemiology. In J. L. McGaugh & S. B. Kiesler (Eds.), *Aging: Biology and behavior.* New York: Academic Press, 1981.

KASTENBAUM, R., & AISENBERG, R. *The psychology of death.* New York: Springer, 1972.

KASTENBAUM, R., & COSTA, P. T. Psychological perspectives on death. *Annual Review of Psychology,* 1977, 28, 225–241.

KASTENBAUM, R., & WEISMAN, A. D. The psychological autopsy as a research procedure in gerontology. In D. P. Dent, R. Kastenbaum, & S. Sherwood (Eds.), *Research planning and action for the elderly.* New York: Behavioral Publications, 1972.

KATZ, S., FORD, A. B., MOSKOWITZ, R. W., JACKSON, B. A., & JAFFE, M. W. Studies of illness in the aged: The index of ADL, a standardized measure of biological and psychosocial function. *Journal of the American Medical Association,* 1963, 185, 914–919.

KAUSLER, D. H. *Experimental psychology and human aging.* New York: Wiley, 1982.

KAUSLER, D. H., & LAIR, C. V. Associative strength and paired-associate learning in elderly subjects. *Journal of Gerontology,* 1966, 21, 278–280.

KAUSLER, D. H., & PUCKETT, J. M. Frequency judgments and correlated cognitive abilities in young and elderly adults. *Journal of Gerontology,* 1980, 35, 376–382.

KAVANAUGH, R. E. *Facing death.* Baltimore: Penguin, 1974.

KAY, D. W. K., & BERGMANN, K. Epidemiology of mental disorders among the aged in the community. In J. E. Birren & R. B. Sloane (Eds.), *Handbook of mental health and aging.* Englewood Cliffs, N.J.: Prentice-Hall, 1982.

KAY, H. The effects of position in a display upon problem solving. *Quarterly Journal of Experimental Psychology,* 1954, 6, 155–169.

KAY, H. Some experiments on adult learning. In *Old age in the modern world.* Edinburgh Scotland: Livingstone, 1955.

KAYLOR, C. Evaluation of home care for the terminal patient: A proposed model. In E. R. Prichard et al. (Eds.), *Home care: Living with the dying.* New York: Columbia University Press, 1979.

KAZDIN, A. E. *The token economy: A review and evaluation.* New York: Plenum Press, 1977.

KEEVIL-ROGERS, P., & SCHNORE, M. M. Short-term memory as a function of age in persons of above average intelligence. *Journal of Gerontology,.* 1969, 24, 184–188.

KELLY, G. A. *The psychology of personal constructs.* (2 Vols.) New York: Norton, 1955.

KELLY, J. The aging male homosexual. *The Gerontologist,* 1977, 17, 328–332.

KELLY, J. B., & WALLERSTEIN, J. S. The effects of parental divorce: Experiences of child in early latency. *American Journal of Orthopsychiatry,* 1976, 46, 20–32.

KENSHALO, D. R. Age changes in touch, vibration, temperature, kinesthesis, and pain sensitivity. In J. E. Birren & K. W. Schaie (Eds.), *Handbook of the psychology of aging.* New York: Van Nostrand Reinhold, 1977.

KERCKHOFF, A. C. Husband-wife expectations and reactions to retirement. In I. H. Simpson & J. C. McKinney (Eds.), *Social aspects of aging.* Durham, N.C.: Duke University Press, 1966.

KESSLER, R. C., & McCRAE, J. A. Trends in the relationship between sex and psychological distress. *American Sociological Review,* 1981, 46, 443–452.

KIESLER, C. A. Psychology and mental health policy. In M. Hersen, A. E. Kazdin, & A. S. Bellack (Eds.), *The clinical psychology handbook.* New York: Pergamon Press, 1983.

KILLIAN, E. C. Effect of geriatric transfers on mortality rates. *Social Work,* 1970, 15, 19–26.

KIMBRELL, G. McA., & FURCHGOTT E. The effect of aging on olfactory threshold. *Journal of Gerontology,* 1963, 18, 364–365.

KIMMEL, D. C. Patterns of aging among gay men. *Christopher Street,* 1977, 2, 28–31.

KIMMEL, D. C. *Adulthood and aging: An interdisciplinary developmental view.* (2nd Ed.) New York: Wiley, 1980.

KING, H. F. An age analysis of some agricultural accidents. *Occupational Psychology,* 1955, 29, 245–255.

KING, W. The case of the missing memory: Special treatment aids the frustrated victims. *The Seattle Times,* Jan. 29, 1982, B1.

KINSEY, A. C., POMEROY, W. B., & MARTIN, C. E. *Sexual behavior in the human male.* Philadelphia: W.B. Saunders, 1948.

KINSEY, A. C., POMEROY, W. B., MARTIN, C. E., & GEBHARD, P. H. *Sexual behavior in the human female.* Philadelphia: W.B. Saunders, 1953.

KIPNIS, D. M. Interaction between members of bomber crews as a determinant of sociometric choice. *Human Relations,* 1957, 10, 263–270.

KIRKWOOD, T. B. L. Comparative and evolutionary aspects of longevity. In C. E. Finch & E. L. Schneider (Eds.), *Handbook of the biology of aging.* (2nd Ed.) New York: Van Nostrand Reinhold, 1985.

KIVNICK, H. Q. Grandparenthood: An overview of meaning and mental health. *The Gerontologist,* 1982, 22, 59–66.

KIYAK, A., LIANG, J., & KAHANA, E. Methodological inquiry into the schedule of recent life events. Paper presented at the annual meeting of the American Psychological Association, Washington, D.C., August 1976.

KLEEGMAN, S. Frigidity in women. *Quarterly Review of Surgery, Obstetrics, and Gynecology,* 1959, 16, 243–248.

KLEEMEIER, R. W. Intellectual change in the senium. *Proceedings of the Social Statistics Section of the American Statistical Association,* 1962, 1, 290–295.

KLEIN, F. C. Older Americans: Actress and ex-Senator believe in conquering age by staying active. *The Wall Street Journal,* March 10, 1983, 1, 10.

KLERMAN, G. L. Problems in the definition and diagnosis of depression. In L. D. Breslau & M. R. Haug (Eds.), *Depression and aging: Causes, care, and consequences.* New York: Springer, 1983.

KLIGMAN, A. M., GROVE, A. L., & BALIN, A. K. Aging of human skin. In C. E. Finch & E. L. Schneider (Eds.), *Handbook of the biology of aging.* (2nd Ed.) New York: Van Nostrand Reinhold, 1985.

KLINE, D. W., & BAFFA, G. Differences in the sequential integration of form as a function of age and interstimulus interval. *Experimental Aging Research,* 1976, 2, 333–343.

KLINE, D. W., & ORME-ROGERS, C. Examination of stimulus persistence as the basis for superior visual identification performance among older adults. *Journal of Gerontology,* 1978, 33, 76–81.

KLINE, D. W., & SCHIEBER, F. What are the age differences in visual sensory memory? *Journal of Gerontology,* 1981, 36, 86–89.

KLINE, D. W., & SCHIEBER, F. Vision and aging. In J. E. Birren & K. W. Schaie (Eds.), *Handbook of the psychology of aging.* (2nd Ed.) New York: Van Nostrand Reinhold, 1985.

KLINE, D. W., & SZAFRAN, J. Age differences in backward monoptic visual noise masking. *Journal of Gerontology,* 1975, 30, 307–311.

KLODIN, V. M. The relationship of scoring treatment and age in perceptual-integrative performance. *Experimental Aging Research,* 1976, 2, 303–313.

KOBRIN, F. E. The primary individual and the family: Changes in living arrangements in the U. S. since 1940. *Journal of Marriage and the Family,* 1976, 38, 233–239.

KOGAN, N. Creativity and cognitive style: A life-span perspective. In P. B. Baltes & K. W. Schaie (Eds.), *Life-span developmental psychology: Personality and socialization.* New York: Academic Press, 1973.

KOLODNY, A. L., & KLIPPER, A. Bone and joint diseases. In W. Reichel (Ed.), *The geriatric patient.* New York: H.P. Publishing Co., 1978.

KOLODNY, R. C., MASTERS, W. H., & JOHNSON, V. E. *Textbook of sexual medicine.* Boston: Little, Brown, 1979.

KRAG, C. L., & KOUNTZ, W. B. Stability of body functions in the aged: I. Effect of exposure of the body to cold. *Journal of Gerontology,* 1950, 5, 227–235.

KRAUS, A. S., & LILIENFELD, A. N. Some epidemiological aspects of the high mortality rate in the young widowed group. *Journal of Chronic Diseases,* 1959, 10, 207–217.

KRIAUCIUNAS, R. The relationship of age and retention interval activity in short term memory. *Journal of Gerontology,* 1968, 23, 169–173.

KRYTER, K, *The effects of noise on man,* New York: Academic Press, 1970.

KÜBLER-ROSS, E. *On death and dying.* New York: Macmillan, 1969.

KUBLER-ROSS, E. *Death: The final stage of growth.* Englewood Cliffs, N.J.: Prentice-Hall, 1975.

LABBY, D. H. Sexuality. In C. K. Cassel & J. R. Walsh (Eds.), *Geriatric medicine. Volume II: Fundamentals of geriatric care.* New York: Springer-Verlag, 1984.

LACHMAN, M. E. Perceptions of intellectual aging: Antecedent or consequence of intellectual functioning? *Developmental Psychology,* 1983, 19, 482–498.

LACHMAN, M. E. Personal efficacy in middle and old age: Differential and normative patterns of change. In G. H. Elder, Jr. (Ed.), *Life-course dynamics: Trajectories and transitions, 1968–1980.* Ithaca, N.Y.: Cornell University Press, 1985.

LACHMAN, M. E. Locus of control in aging research: A case for multidimensional and domain-specific assessment. *Journal of Psychology and Aging,* 1986, 1, 34–40.

LAKE, A. Divorcees: The new poor. *McCall's,* Sept. 1976, 103, 120, 122, 124, 152.

LANGER, E. J., & RODIN, J. The effects of choice and enhanced personal responsibility for the aged: A field experiment in an institutionalized setting. *Journal of Personality and Social Psychology,* 1976, 34, 191–198.

LAO, I. The developmental trend of the locus of control. *Personality and Social Psychology Bulletin,* 1974, 1, 348–350.

LARSON, R. Thirty years of research on the subjective well-being of older Americans. *Journal of Gerontology,* 1978, 33, 109–125.

LARSON, T., SJOGREN, T., & JACOBSON, G. Senile dementia: A clinical, sociomedical and genetic study. *Acta Psychiatrica Scandinavica,* 1963, 39 (supplement 167), 1–259.

LASAGNA L. The doctor and the dying patient. *Journal of Chronic Disease,* 1969, 22, 65–68.

LATHAM, K. R., & JOHNSON, L. K. Aging at the cellular level. In I. Rossman (Ed.), *Clinical geriatrics.* (2nd Ed.) Philadelphia: Lippincott, 1979.

LATTANER, B. A., & HAYSLIP, B., JR. Occupation-related differences in levels of death anxiety. *Omega: Journal of Death and Dying,* 1984–85, 15, 53–66.

LAUER, J., & LAUER, R. Marriages made to last. *Psychology Today,* 1985, 19, 22–26.

LAURENCE, M. W. Age differences in performance and subjective organization in the free recall of pictorial material. *Canadian Journal of Psychiatry,* 1966, 20, 388–399.

LAURENCE, M. W. Memory loss with age: A test of two strategies for its retardation. *Psychonomic Science,* 1967, 9, 209–210. (a)

LAURENCE, M. W. A developmental look at the usefulness of list categorization as an aid to free recall. *Canadian Journal of Psychology,* 1967, 21, 153–165. (b)

LAWTON, M. P. *Environment and aging.* Monterey, Calif.: Brooks/Cole, 1980.

LAWTON, M. P., WHELIHAN, W. M., & BELSKY, J. K. Personality tests and their uses with older adults. In J. E. Birren & R. B. Sloane (Eds.), *Handbook of mental health and aging.* Englewood Cliffs, N.J.: Prentice-Hall, 1980.

LAZARUS, R. S. *Psychological stress and the coping process.* New York: McGraw-Hill, 1966.

LAZARUS, R. S. The concepts of stress and disease. In L. Levi (Ed.), *Society, stress, and disease: The psychosocial environment and psychosomatic diseases (Vol. 1).* London: Oxford University Press, 1971.

LEAF, A. Every day is a gift when you are over 100. *National Geographic,* 1973, 143, 93.

LEE, G. R. Kinship and social support of the elderly: The case of the United States. *Ageing and Society,* 1985, 5, 19–38.

LEE, J. A., & POLLACK, R. H. The effect of age on perceptual problem-solving strategies. *Experimental Aging Research,* 1978, 4, 37–54.

LEFCOURT, H. M. *Locus of control: Current trends in theory and research.* Hillsdale, N.J.: Erlbaum, 1976.

LEHMAN, H. C. The creative years: Oil paintings, etchings, and architectural works. *Psychological Review,* 1942, 49, 19–42.

LEHMAN, H. C. *Age and achievement.* Princeton, N.J.: Princeton University Press, 1953.

LEHMAN, H. C. Reply to Dennis' critique of *Age and achievement. Journal of Gerontology,* 1956, 11, 333–337.

LEHMAN, H. C. The influence of longevity upon curves showing man's creative production rate at successive age levels. *Journal of Gerontology,* 1958, 13, 187–191.

LEHMAN, H. C. The age decrement in outstanding scientific creativity. *American Psychologist,* 1960, 15, 128–134.

LEHMAN, H. C., & GAMERTSFELDER, W. S. Man's creative years in philosophy. *Psychological Review,* 1942, 49, 319–343.

LEMON, B. W., BENGTSON, V. L., & PETERSON, J. A. An exploration of the activity theory of aging: Activity and life satisfaction among inmovers to a retirement community. *Journal of Gerontology,* 1972, 27, 511–523.

LEO, J. Men have rights too. *Time,* Nov. 24, 1986, 87–88.

LEON, G. R., GILLUM, B., GILLUM, R., & GOUZE, M. Personality stability and change over a 30-year period—middle age to old age. *Journal of Consulting and Clinical Psychology,* 1979, 47, 517–524.

LERMAN, S. An experimental and clinical evaluation of lens transparency and aging. *Journal of Gerontology,* 1983, 38, 293–301.

LERNER, M. When, why, and where people die. In E. S. Shneidman (Ed.), *Death: Current perspectives.* Palo Alto, Calif.: Mayfield, 1976.

LESTER, D. Fear of death of suicide persons. *Psychological Reports,* 1967, 20, 1077–1078.

LESTER, D. The fear of death, sex and androgyny: A brief note. *Omega: Journal of Death and Dying,* 1984–85, 15, 271–274.

LEVENSON, H. Activism and powerful others: Distinctions within the concept of internal-external control. *Journal of Personality Assessment.* 1974, 38, 377–383.

LEVINGER, G. A three-level approach to attraction: Toward an understanding of pair relatedness. In T. L. Huston (Ed.). *Foundations of interpersonal attraction.* New York: Academic Press, 1974.

LEVINGER, G. Models of close relationships: Some new directions. Invited address presented at the annual meeting of the American Psychological Association, Toronto, August 1978.

LEVINGER, G., SENN, D. J., & JORGENSEN, B. W. Progress toward permanence in courtship: A test of the Kerckhoff-Davis hypotheses. *Sociometry,* 1970, 33, 427–443.

LEVINSON, D. J. *The seasons of a man's life.* New York: Knopf, 1978.

LEVINSON, D. J. A conception of adult development. *American Psychologist,* 1986, 41, 3–13.

LEVINSON, D. J., DARROW, C. M., KLEIN, E. B., LEVINSON, M. H., & MCKEE, B. The psychosocial development of men in early adulthood and the midlife transition. In D. F. Ricks, A. Thomas, & M. Roff (Eds.), *Life history research in psychopathology.* Minneapolis: University of Minnesota Press, 1974.

LIEBERMAN, M. A. Psychological correlates of impending death: Some preliminary observations. *Journal of Gerontology,* 1965, 20, 181–190.

LIEBERMAN, M. A. The effects of social supports on response to stress. In L. Goldberger & S. Breznitz (Eds.), *Handbook of stress.* New York: Free Press, 1982.

LEIF, H. I., & FOX, R. C. Training for detached concern in medical students. In H. I. Lief & N. R. Lief (Eds.), *The psychological basis of medical practice.* New York: Harper & Row, 1963.

LIEGNER, L. M. St. Christopher's hospice, 1974: Care of the dying patient. *Journal of the American Medical Association,* 1975, 234(10), 1047–1048.

LINDEMANN, E. Symptomatology and management of acute grief. *American Journal of Psychiatry,* 1944, 101, 141–148.

LINDSAY, P. H., & NORMAN, D. A. *Human information processing.* (2nd Ed.) New York: Academic Press, 1977.

LINN, M. W., HUNTER, K., & HARRIS, R. Symptoms of depression and recent life events in community elderly. *Journal of Clinical Psychology,* 1980, 36, 675–682.

LIRETTE, W. L., PALMER, R. L., IBARRA, I. D., KROENIG, P. M., & GAINES,

R. K. Management of patients with terminal cancer. *Postgraduate Medicine*, 1969, 46, 145–149.

LISS-LEVINSON, W. Reality perspectives for psychological services in a hospice program. *American Psychologist,* 1982, 37, 1266–1270.

LITTLEFIELD, C., & FLEMING, S. Measuring fear of death: A multidimensional approach. *Omega: Journal of Death and Dying,* 1984–85, 15, 131–138.

LONG, J. Older Americans: In a retirement town, the main business is keeping yourself busy. *The Wall Street Journal,* March 2, 1983, 1, 17.

LOPATA, H. Z. *Widowhood in an American city.* Cambridge, Mass.: Schenkman, 1973.

LOWENTHAL, M., & HAVEN, C. Interaction and adaptation: Intimacy as a critical variable. *American Sociological Review,* 1968, 33, 20–30.

LOWENTHAL, M., THURNHER, M., & CHIRIBOGA, D. *Four stages of life.* San Francisco: Jossey-Bass, 1975.

LYONS, J. Chronological age, professional age, and eminence in psychology. *American Psychologist,* 1968, 23, 371–373.

MAAS, H. J., & KUYPERS, J. A. *From thirty to seventy.* San Francisco: Jossey-Bass, 1974.

MACHT, M. L., & BUSCHKE, H. Speed of recall in aging. *Journal of Gerontology,* 1984, 39, 439–443.

MAKINODAN, T. Cellular basis of immunosenescence. In *Molecular and cellular mechanisms of aging.* Paris: INSERM, Coll. Inst. Nat. Sante Rec. Med., 1974, Vol. 27.

MANDLER, G. Organization and memory. In K. W. Spence & J. T. Spence (Eds.), *The psychology of learning and motivation: Advances in research and theory (Vol. 1).* New York: Academic Press, 1967.

MARGOLIS, O. S., RAETHER, H. C., KUTSCHER, A. H., POWERS, J. B., SEELAND, I. B., DeBELLIS, R., & CHERICO, D. J. *Acute grief: Counseling the bereaved.* New York: Columbia University Press, 1981.

MARIE, H. Reorienting staff attitudes toward the dying. *Hospital Progress,* 1978, 59, 74–76.

MARKUS, E. J. Perceptual field dependence among aged persons. *Perceptual and Motor Skills,* 1971, 33, 175–178.

MARTIN, G. M. Genotropic theories of aging: An overview. In C. E. Finch & L. Hayflick (Eds.), *Handbook of the biology of aging.* New York: Van Nostrand Reinhold, 1977.

MASLOW, A. H. *Toward a psychology of being.* (2nd Ed.) New York: Van Nostrand Reinhold, 1968.

MASLOW, A. H. *Motivation and personality.* (2nd Ed.) New York: Harper & Row, 1970.

MASON, J. W. A reevaluation of the concept of non-specificity in stress theory. *Journal of Psychiatric Research,* 1971, 8, 323–333.

MASON, J. W. Specificity in the organization of neuroendocrine response profiles. In P. Seeman & G. Brown (Eds.), *Frontiers in neurology and neuroscience research.* Toronto: University of Toronto Press, 1974.

MASON, S. E., & Smith, A. D. Imagery in the aged. *Experimental Aging Research,* 1977, 3, 17–32.

MASSARO, D. W. Perceptual images, processing time and perceptual units in auditory perception. *Psychological Review,* 1972, 79, 124–145.

MASTERS, W. H., & JOHNSON, V. E. *Human sexual response.* Boston: Little, Brown, 1966.

MASTERS, W. H., & JOHNSON, V. E. *Human sexual inadequacy.* Boston: Little Brown, 1970.

MATHISON, J. A cross-cultural view of widowhood. *Omega: Journal of Death and Dying,* 1970, 1, 201–218.

MATLIN, M. W. Perceptual development. In R. J. Corsini (Ed.), *Encyclopedia of psychology.* New York: Wiley, 1984.

MAY, R. Contributions of existential psychotherapy. In R. May, E. Angel, & H. F. Ellenberger (Eds.), *Existence: A new dimension in psychiatry and psychology.* New York: Basic Books, 1958. Paperback reprint: New York: Touchstone Books, 1967.

MAY, R. *Love and will.* New York: Norton, 1969.

MCCARY, J. L. *Human sexuality.* (3rd Ed.) New York: Van Nostrand Reinhold, 1978.

MCCLOSKEY, M., & WATKINS, M. J. The seeing more than is there phenomenon: Implications for the locus of iconic storage. *Journal of Experimental Psychology: Human Perception and Performance,* 1978, 4, 553–564.

MCCONNEL, E., & DELJAVAN, F. Aged deaths: The nursing home and community differential. *The Gerontologist,* 1982, 22, 318–323.

MCCORMICK, K. An exploration of the functions of friends and best friends. Unpublished doctoral dissertation, Rutgers University of New Jersey, 1982.

MCCRAE, R. R., & COSTA, P. T., Jr. *Emerging lives, enduring dispositions.* Boston: Little, Brown, 1984.

MCDERMOTT, J. R., SMITH, A. I., IQBAL, K., & WISNIESKI, M. Aluminum and Alzheimer's disease. *Lancet,* 1977, 2, 710–711.

MCFARLAND, R. A., & DOHERTY, B. M. Work and occupational skills. In J. E. Birren (Ed.), *Handbook of aging and the individual.* Chicago: University of Chicago Press, 1959.

MCGREGOR, D. *The human side of enterprise.* New York: McGraw-Hill, 1960.

MCKINLAY, J. B. Social network influences on morbid episodes and the career of help seeking. In L. Eisenberg & A. Kleinman (Eds.), *The relevance of social science for medicine.* Dordrecht, Holland: D. Reidel, 1981.

MCNEIL, D. N. Mortality among the widowed in Connecticut. New Haven, Conn.: Yale University, M.P.H. essay, 1973.

MACFARLAND, R. A., DOMEY, R. G., WARREN, A. B., & WARD, D. C. Dark adaptation as a function of age: I A statistical analysis. *Journal of Gerontology,* 1960, 15, 149–154.

MEDVEDEV, Zh. A. The nucleic acids in development and aging. In B. L. Strehler (Ed.), *Advances in gerontological research (Vol. 1).* New York: Academic Press, 1964.

MEDVEDEV, Zh. A. Caucasus and Altay longevity: A biological or social problem? *The Gerontologist,* 1974, 14, 381–387.

MEIER, D. E. The cell biology of aging. In C. K. Cassel & J. R. Walsh (Eds.), *Geriatric medicine (Vol. 1).* New York: Springer-Verlag, 1984.

MEISTER, K. A. The 80s search for the fountain of youth comes up very dry. *American Council on Science and Health News & Views,* 1984(9/10), pp. 8–11.

MERTON, R. K. *Social theory and social structure.* (Rev. Ed.) New York: Free Press, 1957.

MEYER, B. J. F., RICE, G. E., KNIGHT, C. C., & JESSEN, J. L. *Differences in the type of information remembered from prose by young, middle, and old adults.* (Research Report No. 5, Prose Learning Series.) Tempe, Ariz.: Arizona State University, Department of Educational Psychology, College of Education, Summer 1979. (a)

MEYER, B. J. F., RICE, G. E., KNIGHT, C. C., & JESSEN, J. L. *Effects of comparative and descriptive discourse types on the reading performance of young, middle, and old adults.* (Research Report No. 7, Prose Learning Series.) Tempe, Ariz.: Arizona State University, Department of Educational Psychology, College of Education, Summer 1979. (b)

MICHAEL, R. T., FUCHS, V. R., & SCOTT, S. R. Changes in the propensity to live alone: 1950–1976. *Demography,* 1980, 17, 39–56.

MIHAL, W. L., & BARRETT, G. V. Individual differences in perceptual information processing and their relation to automobile accident involvements. *Journal of Applied Psychology,* 1976, 61, 229–233.

MILLER, G. A. The magical number seven, plus or minus two: Some limits on our capacity for processing information. *Psychological Review,* 1956, 63, 81–97.

MILLER, G. A., GALANTER, E., & PRIBRAM, K. H. *Plans and the structure of behavior.* New York: Holt, Rinehart & Winston, 1960.

MINKLER, M. Research on the health effects of retirement: An uncertain legacy. *Journal of Health and Social Behavior,* 1981, 22, 117–130.

MISCHEL, W. *Personality and assessment.* New York: Wiley, 1968.

MISCHEL, W. Toward a cognitive social learning reconceptualization of personality *Psychological Review,* 1973, 80, 252–283.

MISCHEL, W. The interaction of person and situation. In D. Magnusson & N. S. Endler (eds.)., *Personality at the crossroads: Current issues in interactional psychology.* Hillsdale, N.J.: Erlbaum, 1977.

MISTLER-LACHMAN, J. L. Spontaneous shift in encoding dimensions among elderly subjects. *Journal of Gerontology,* 1977, 32, 68–72.

MITCHELL, R. E., & TRICKETT, E. J. Social network research and psychosocial adaptation: Implications for community mental health practice. In P. Insel (Ed.), *Environmental variables and the prevention of mental illness.* Lexington, Mass.: D.C. Heath, 1980.

MOENSTER, P. A. Learning and memory in relation to age. *Journal of Gerontology,* 1972, 27, 361–363.

MONGE, R. H. Studies of verbal learning from the college years through middle age. *Journal of Gerontology,* 1971, 26, 324–329.

MONGE, R. H., & HULTSCH, D. F. Paired-associate learning as a function of adult age and the length of the anticipation and inspection intervals. *Journal of Gerontology,* 1971, 26, 157–162.

MOON, M. The role of the family in the economic well-being of the elderly. *The Gerontologist,* 1983, 23, 45–50.

MOR, V., & HIRIS, J. Determinants of site of death among hospice cancer patients. *Journal of Health and Social Behavior,* 1983, 24, 375–385.

MORGAN, L. A. A re-examination of widowhood and morale. *Journal of Gerontology,* 1976, 31, 687–695.

MORRIS, J. N., MOR, V., HIRIS, J., & SHERWOOD, S. Satisfaction with the site of death. Paper presented at the Annual Meeting of the Gerontological Society of America, San Antonio, Texas, 1984.

MORRIS, J. N., & SHERWOOD, S. Informal support sources for vulnerable elderly persons: Can they be counted on, why do they work? *International Journal of Aging and Human Development,* 1984, 18, 81–98.

MORSE, N. C. *Satisfactions in the white-collar job.* Ann Arbor: University of Michigan Survey Research Center, 1953.

MOUNT, B. M. The problem of caring for the dying in a general hospital. *Canadian Medical Association,* 1976, 115(2), 119–121.

MURDOCK, B. B., JR. Recent developments in short-term memory. *British Journal of Psychology,* 1967, 58, 421–433.

MURPHY, C. Age-related effects on the threshold, psychophysical function, and pleasantness of menthol. *Journal of Gerontology,* 1983, 38, 217–222.

MURPHY, C. Cognitive and chemosensory influences on age-related changes in the ability to identify blended foods. *Journal of Gerontology,* 1985, 40, 47–52.

MURRAY, H. A., et al. *Explorations in personality.* New York: Oxford University Press, 1938.

MURSTEIN, B. I., & CHRISTY, P. Physical attractiveness and marriage adjustment in middle-aged couples. *Journal of Personality and Social Psychology,* 1976, 34, 537–542.

MUSSEN, P. H., CONGER, J., KAGAN, J., & GEIWITZ, J. *Psychological development: A life-span approach.* New York: Harper & Row, 1979.

MYERS, G. C., & MANTON, K. G. Compression of mortality: Myth or reality. *The Gerontologist,* 1984, 24, 345–353. (a)

MYERS, G. C., & MANTON, K. G. Recent changes in the U.S. age at death distribution: Further observations. *The Gerontologist,* 1984, 24, 572–575. (b)

NAEIM, F., & WALFORD, R. L. Aging and cell membrane complexes: The lipid bilayer, integral proteins, and cytoskeleton. In C. E. Finch & E. L. Schneider (Eds.), *Handbook of the biology of aging.* (2nd Ed.) New York: Van Nostrand Reinhold, 1985.

National Center for Health Statistics. *Vital and health statistics, Series 20.* Washington, D.C.: United States Government Printing Office, May 1967.

National Center for Health Statistics. *DHHS Pub. No. 83–1232.* Washington, D.C.: United States Government Printing Office, Dec. 1982.

National Center for Health Statistics. *Monthly vital statistics report.* Washington, D.C.: United States Government Printing Office, Oct. 1983.

National Center for Health Statistics. *Health United States.* Washington, D.C.: United States Government Printing Office, 1984.

National Institute on Aging. *Age Page: Aging and your eyes.* Bethesda, Md.: U. S. Department of Health and Human Services, 1983. (a)

National Institute on Aging. *Age Page: Hearing and the elderly.* Bethesda,

Md.: United States Department of Health and Human Services, 1983. (b)

National Institute on Aging. *Age Page: Can life be extended?* Bethesda, Md.: United States Department of Health and Human Services, 1984.

NEALE R. E. Between the nipple and the everlasting arms. *Archives of the Foundation of Thanatology,* 1971, 3, 21–30.

NEISSER, U. *Cognitive psychology.* New York: Appleton-Century-Crofts, 1967.

NEISSER, U. Memory: What are the important questions? In M. M. Gruneberg, P. E. Morris, & R. N. Sykes (Eds.), *Practical aspects of memory.* London: Academic Press, 1978.

NEISSER, U. *Memory observed.* San Francisco: Freeman, 1982.

NESSELROADE, J. R., & LABOUVIE, E. W. Experimental design in research on aging. In J. E. Birren & K. W. Schaie (Eds.), *Handbook of the psychology of aging.* (2nd Ed.) New York: Van Nostrand Reinhold, 1985.

NEUBECK, G. The myriad motives for sex. *Sexual Behavior,* 1972, 2, 50–56.

NEUGARTEN, B. L. Personality and aging. In J. E. Birren & K. W. Schaie (Eds.), *Handbook of the psychology of aging.* New York: Van Nostrand Reinhold, 1977.

NEUGARTEN, B. L., & Associates. (Eds.) *Personality in middle and late life.* New York: Atherton, 1964.

NEUGARTEN, B. L., CROTTY, J., & TOBIN, S. S. Personality types in an aged population. In B. L. Neugarten & Associates (Eds.), *Personality in middle and later life.* New York: Atherton, 1964.

NEUGARTEN, B. L., & GUTMANN, D. L. Age-sex roles and personality in middle age: A thematic apperception study. *Psychological Monographs: General and Applied,* 1958, 17, Whole No. 470.

NEUGARTEN, B. L., HAVIGHURST, R. J., & TOBIN, S. S. Personality and pattern of aging. In B. L. Neugarten (Ed.), *Middle age and aging.* Chicago: University of Chicago Press, 1968.

NEUGARTEN, B. L., & WEINSTEIN, K. The changing American grandparent. *Journal of Marriage and the Family,* 1964, 26, 199–204.

NEWMAN, G., & NICHOLS, C. R. Sexual activities and attitudes in older persons. *Journal of the American Medical Association,* 1960, 173, 33–35.

NEWTON, P. A. Chronic pain. In C. K. Cassel & J. R. Walsh (Eds.), *Geriatric medicine (Vol. 2).* New York: Springer-Verlag, 1984.

NICHOLS, R. V. Sudden death, acute grief, and ultimate recovery. In O. S. Margolis, H. C. Raether, A. H. Kutscher, J. B. Powers, I. B. Seeland, R. DeBellis, & D. J. Cherico (Eds.), *Acute grief: Counseling the bereaved.* New York: Columbia University Press, 1981.

NOBERINI, M., & NEUGARTEN, B. L. A follow-up study of adaptation in middle-aged women. Paper presented at the annual meeting of the Gerontology Society, Louisville, Ky., 1975.

NOYES, R., JR. The art of dying. *Perspectives in Biology and Medicine,* 1971, 14, 432–447.

NYSTROM, E. P. Activity patterns and leisure concepts among the elderly. *American Journal of Occupational Therapy,* 1974, 28, 337–345.

OHRLOFF, C., & HOCKWIN, O. Lens metabolism and aging: Enzyme activities and enzyme alterations in lenses of different species during the process of aging. *Journal of Gerontology,* 1983, 38, 271–277.

OHTA, R. J., & KIRASIC, K. C. The investigation of environmental learning in the elderly. In G. D. Rowles & R. J. Ohta (Eds.), *Aging and milieu.* New York: Academic Press, 1983.

OKIMOTO, J. T., BARNES, R. F., VEITH, R. C., RASKIND, M. A., INUI, T. S., & CARTER, W. B. Screening for depression in geriatric mental patients. *Journal of Psychiatry,* 1982, 139, 799–802.

OKUN, M. A. Adult age and cautiousness in decision: A review of the literature. *Human Development,* 1976, 19, 220–233.

OKUN, M. A., & ELIAS, C. S. Cautiousness in adulthood as a function of age and payoff structure. *Journal of Gerontology,* 1977, 32, 451–455.

OKUN, M. A., SIEGLER, I. C., & GEORGE, L. K. Cautiousness and verbal learning in adulthood. *Journal of Gerontology,* 1978, 33, 94–97.

OKUN, M. A., STOCK, W. A., & CEURVORST, R. W. Risk taking through the adult life span. *Experimental Aging Research,* 1980, 6, 463–474.

OPPENHEIMER, R. Analogy in science. *American Psychologist,* 1956, 11, 127–135.

ORGEL, L. E. The maintenance of the accuracy of protein synthesis and its relevance to aging. *Biochemistry,* 1963, 49, 517–521.

OSARCHUK, M., & TATZ, S. Effect of induced fear of death on belief in afterlife. *Journal of Personality and Social Psychology,* 1973, 27, 256–260.

OWENS, W. A., JR. Age and mental ability: A second follow-up. *Journal of Educational Psychology,* 1966, 57, 311–325.

PAIVIO, A. *Imagery and verbal processes.* New York: Holt, Rinehart & Winston, 1971.

PALMORE, E. The effects of aging on activities and attitudes. In E. Palmore (Ed.), *Normal aging (Vol. 1).* Durham, N.C.: Duke University Press, 1970.

PALMORE, E. *Social patterns in normal aging: Findings from the Duke longitudinal study.* Durham, N.C.: Duke University Press, 1981.

PALMORE, E., & CLEVELAND, W. Aging, terminal decline and terminal drop. *Journal of Gerontology,* 1976, 31, 76–81.

PALMORE, E., CLEVELAND, W., NOWLIN, J. B., RAMM, D., & SIEGLER, I. C. Stress and adaptation in late life. *Journal of Gerontology,* 1979, 34, 841–851.

PALMORE, E., FILLENBAUM, G. G., & GEORGE, L. K. Consequences of retirement. *Journal of Gerontology,* 1984, 39, 109–116.

PALMORE, E., GEORGE, L. K., & FILLENBAUM, G. G. Predictors of retirement. *Journal of Gerontology,* 1982, 37, 733–742.

PALMORE, E., & LUIKART, C. Health and social factors related to life satisfaction. *Journal of Health and Social Behavior,* 1972, 13, 68–80.

PANEK, P. E., BARRETT, G. V., STERNS, G. V., & ALEXANDER, R. A. Age differences in perceptual style, selective attention, and perceptual-motor reaction time. *Experimental Aging Research,* 1978, 4, 377–387.

PARKER, F. Dermatology. In C. K. Cassel & J. R. Walsh (Eds.), *Geriatric medicine: Volume I. Medical, psychiatric, and pharmacological topics.* New York: Springer-Verlag, 1984.

PARKES, C. M. Effects of bereavement on physical mental health—a study of medical records of widows. *British Journal of Medicine*, 1964, 2, 274–279.

PARKES, C. M. *Bereavement: Studies of grief in adult life.* New York: International Universities Press, 1972.

PARKES, C. M. Unexpected and untimely bereavement: A statistical study of young Boston widows and widowers. In B. Schoenberg et al. (Eds.), *Bereavement: Its psychosocial aspects.* New York: Columbia University Press, 1975.

PARKES, C. M. Emotional involvement of the family during the period preceding death. In O. S. Margolis et al. (Eds.), *Acute grief: Counseling the bereaved.* New York: Columbia University Press, 1981. (a)

PARKES, C. M. Psychosocial care of the family after the patient's death. In O. S. Margolis et al. (Eds.), *Acute grief: Counseling the bereaved.* New York: Columbia University Press, 1981. (b)

PARKES, C. M., BENJAMIN, B., & FITZGERALD, R. G. Broken heart: A statistical study of increased mortality among widowers. *British Medical Journal,* 1969, 1, 740–743.

PARKINSON, S. R., & PEREY, A. Aging, digit span, and the stimulus suffix effect. *Journal of Gerontology,* 1980, 35, 736–742.

PARNES, H. S., & NESTEL, G. The retirement experience. In H. S. Parnes (Ed.), *Work and retirement: A longitudinal study of men.* Cambridge, Mass.: MIT Press, 1981.

PAULHUS, D. Sphere-specific measures of perceived control. *Journal of Personality and Social Psychology,* 1983, 44, 1253–1265.

PEARLMAN, J., STOTSKY, B. A., & DOMINICK, J. R. Attitudes toward death among nursing home personnel. *Journal of Genetic Psychology,* 1969, 114, 63–75.

PERLMUTTER, M. An apparent paradox about memory aging. In L. W. Poon, J. L. Fozard, L. S. Cermak, D. Arenberg, & L. W. Thompson (Eds.), *New directions in memory and aging: Proceedings of the George A. Talland memorial conference.* Hillsdale, N.J.: Erlbaum, 1980.

PERLMUTTER, M., METZGER, R., NEZWORSKI, T., & MILLER, K. Spatial and temporal memory in 20 and 60 year olds. *Journal of Gerontology,* 1981, 36, 59–65.

PERRET, E., & REGLI, F. Age and the perceptual threshold for vibratory stimuli. *Eur. Neurol.,* 1970, 4, 65–76.

PERRY, E. K., PERRY, R. H., BLESSED, G., & TOMLINSON, B. E. Necropsy evidence of central cholinergic deficits in senile demential. *Lancet,* 1977, 3, 1981.

PERRY, E. K., TOMLINSON, B. E., BLESSED, G., BERGMANN, K., GIBSON, P. H., & PERRY, R. H. Correlation of cholinergic abnormalities with senile plagues and mental test scores in senile dementia. *British Medical Journal,* 1978, 2, 1457–1459.

PETERSON, L. R., & PETERSON, M. J. Short-term retention of individual verbal items. *Journal of Experimental Psychology,* 1959, 58, 193–198.

PFEIFFER, E. Sexuality in the aging individual. *Journal of the American Geriatrics Society,* 1974, 22, 481–484.

PFEIFFER, E., & DAVIS, G. C. Determinants of sexual behavior in middle and old age. *Journal of the American Geriatrics Society,* 1972, 20, 151–158.

PFEIFFER, E., VERWOERDT, A., & DAVIS, G. C. Sexual behavior in middle life. *American Journal of Psychiatry,* 1972, 128, 1262–1267.

PFEIFFER, E., VERWOERDT, A., & DAVIS, G. C. Sexual behavior in middle life. In P. Erdman (Ed.), *Normal aging II: Reports from the Duke longitudinal studies, 1970–1973.* Durham, N.C.: Duke University Press, 1974.

PFEIFFER, E., VERWOERDT, A., & WANG, H. S. Sexual behavior in aged men and women. I. Observations on 254 community volunteers. *Archives of General Psychiatry,* 1968, 19, 753–758.

PFEIFFER, E., VERWOERDT, A., & WANG, H. S. The natural history of sexual behavior in a biologically advantaged group of aged individuals. *Journal of Gerontology,* 1969, 24, 193–198.

PLECK, J. The work-family role system. *Social Problems,* 1977, 24, 417–427.

PLEMONS, J. K., WILLIS, S. L., & BALTES, P. B. Modifiability of fluid intelligence in aging: A short-term longitudinal training approach. *Journal of Gerontology,* 1978, 33, 224–231.

PLUDE, D. J., & HOYER, W. J. Attention and performance: Identifying and localizing age deficits. In N. Charness (Ed.), *Aging and human performance.* London. Wiley, 1985.

PLUDE, D. J., & HOYER, W. J. Age and the selectivity of visual information processing. *Journal of Psychology and Aging,* 1986, 1, 4–10.

POCS, O., GODROW, A., TOLONE, W. L., & WALSH, R. H. Is there sex after 40? *Psychology Today,* 1977, 11(6).

POLLAK, J. M. Correlates of death anxiety. *Omega: Journal of Death and Dying,* 1979–80, 10, 97–121.

POLLIS, C. Dating involvement and patterns of idealization: A test of Waller's hypothesis. *Journal of Marriage and the Family,* 1969, 31(4), 765–771.

POON, L. W. Differences in human memory with aging: Nature, causes, and clinical implications. In J. E. Birren & K. W. Schaie (Eds.), *Handbook of the psychology of aging.* (2nd Ed.) New York: Van Nostrand Reinhold, 1985.

POON, L. W., WALSH-SWEENEY, L., & FOZARD, J. L. Memory skill training for the elderly: Salient issues on the use of imagery mnemonics. In L. W. Poon, J. L. Fozard, L. S. Cermak, D. Arenberg, & L. W. Thompson (Eds.), *New directions in memory and aging: Proceedings of the George A. Talland memorial conference.* Hillsdale, N.J.: Erlbaum, 1980.

PRENTIS, R. S. White-collar working women's perception of retirement. *The Gerontologist,* 1980, 20, 90–95.

President's Commission on Mental Health. *Report.* Washington, D.C.: United States Government Printing Office, 1978.

PUGLISI, J. T. Semantic encoding in older adults as evidenced by release from proactive inhibition. *Journal of Gerontology,* 1980, 35, 743–745.

QUINT, J. C. *The nurse and the dying patient.* Chicago: Aldine, 1967.

QUIRK, D. A., & SKINNER, J. H. Physical capacity, age, and employment. *Industrial Gerontology*, 1973, 19, 49–62.

RABBITT, P. An age-decrement in the ability to ignore irrelevant information. *Journal of Gerontology*, 1965, 18, 375–378.

RABBITT, P. Age and the use of structure in transmitted information. In G. A. Talland (Ed.), *Human aging and behavior*. New York: Academic Press, 1968.

RABBITT, P. Changes in problem-solving ability in old age. In J. E. Birren & K. W. Schaie (Eds.), *Handbook of the psychology of aging*. New York: Van Nostrand Reinhold, 1977.

RABBITT, P. Some experiments and a model of changes in attentional selectivity with old age. In F. Hoffmeister & C. Mueller (Eds.), *Brain functions in old age: Evaluation of changes and disorders*. Berlin: Springer, 1979.

RABINOWITZ, J. C., CRAIK, F. I. M., & ACKERMAN, B. P. A processing resource account of age differences in recall. *Canadian Journal of Psychology*, 1982, 36, 325–344.

RABKIN, J. G., & STRUENING, E. L. Life events, stress, and illness. *Science*, 1976, 194, 1013–1020.

RAHE, R. H., & ARTHUR, R. J. Life change and illness studies: Past history and future directions. *Journal of Human Stress*, 1978, 4, 3–15.

RAPPAPORT, B. Z. Audiology. In C. K. Cassel & J. R. Walsh (Eds.), *Geriatric medicine: Volume I. Medical, psychiatric, and pharmacological topics*. New York: Springer-Verlag, 1984.

RASKIN, A. Psychopharmacology of depression in the elderly. In C. Eisdorfer (Ed.), *Annual review of gerontology and geriatrics (Vol. 3)*. New York: Springer, 1982.

RAUSH, H., BARRY, W., HERTEL, R., & SWAIN, M. *Communication, conflict, and marriage*. San Francisco: Jossey-Bass, 1974.

RAYMOND, B. J. Free recall among the aged. *Psychological Reports*, 1971, 29, 1179–1182.

REA, M. P., GREENSPOON, S., & SPILKA, B. Physicians and the terminal: Some selected attitudes and behavior. *Omega: Journal of Death and Dying*, 1975, 6, 291–301.

REEDY, M. N. Personality and aging. In D. S. Woodruff & J. E. Birren (Eds.), *Aging: Scientific perspectives and social issues.* (2nd Ed.) *Aging: Scientific perspectives and social issues.* (2nd Ed.) Monterey, Calif.: Brooks/Cole, 1983.

REFF, M. E. RNA and protein metabolism. In C. E. Finch & E. L. Schneider (Eds.), *Handbook of the biology of aging.* (2nd Ed.) New York: Van Nostrand Reinhold, 1985.

REICHARD, S., LIVSON, S., & PETERSEN, P. *Aging and personality*. New York: Wiley, 1962.

REID, D. W. Locus of control as an important concept for an interactionist approach to behavior. In D. Magnusson & N. S. Endler (Eds.), *Personality at the crossroads: Current issues in international psychology*. Hillsdale, N.J.: Erlbaum, 1977.

REID, D. W., HAAS, G., & HAWKINGS, D. Locus of desired control and positive self-concept of the elderly. *Journal of Gerontology*, 1977, 32, 441–450.

REID, D. W., & ZIEGLER, M. Validity and stability of a new desired control measure pertaining to psychological adjustment of the elderly. *Journal of Gerontology*, 1980, 35, 395–402.

REIMANIS G., & GREEN, R. F. Imminence of death and intellectual decrement in the aging. *Developmental Psychology*, 1971, 5, 270–272.

RENNER, V. J., ALPAUGH, P. K., & BIRREN, J. E. Divergent thinking over the life-span. Paper presented at the annual meeting of the Gerontological Society, Dallas, November 1978.

RENO, V. P. Why men stop working at or before age 65. *Social Security Bulletin*, 1971, 34, 3–17.

RENO, V. P. Compulsory retirement among newly entitled workers: A survey of new beneficiaries. *Social Security Bulletin*, 1972, 35, 3–15.

RENSBERGER, B. Sense of smell fades with age, study finds. *The Miami Herald*, Dec. 14, 1984, 1, 10.

RICE, R. W. Organizational work and the overall quality of life. In S. Oskamp (Ed.), *Applied social psychology annual (Vol. 5)*. Beverly Hills, Calif.: Sage, 1984.

RIEGEL, K. F. Personality theory and aging. In J. E. Birren (Ed.), *Handbook of aging and the individual*. Chicago: University of Chicago Press, 1959.

RIEGEL, K. F. Personality theory and aging. In J. E. Birren (Ed.), *Handbook of aging and the individual*. Chicago: University of Chicago Press, 1959.

RIEGEL, K. F., & RIEGEL, R. M. A study of changes of attitudes and interests during later years of life. *Vita Humana*, 1960, 3, 177–206.

RIEGEL, K. F., & RIEGEL, R. M. Development, drop, and death. *Developmental Psychology*, 1972, 6, 306–319.

RIEGEL, K. F., RIEGEL, R. M., & MEYER, G. Sociopsychological factors of aging: A cohort sequential analysis. *Human Development*, 1967, 10, 27–56.

RIMM, D. C., & MASTERS, J. C. *Behavior therapy: Techniques and empirical findings.* (2nd Ed.) New York: Academic Press, 1979.

ROBBINS, S. Stroke in the geriatric patient. In W. Reichel (Ed.), *The geriatric patient*. New York: H.P. Publishing Co., 1978.

ROCKSTEIN, M., & SUSSMAN, M. *Biology of aging.* Belmont, Calif.: Wadsworth, 1979.

RODIN, J. Behavioral medicine: Beneficial effects of self-control training in aging. *International Review of Applied Psychology*, 1983, 32, 153–181.

RODIN, J. Health, control, and aging. In M. M. Baltes & P. B. Baltes (Eds.), *Aging and the psychology of control*. Hillsdale, N.J.: Erlbaum, in press. (a)

RODIN, J. Personal control through the life course. In R. Abeles (Ed.), *Implications of the life span perspective for social psychology*. Hillsdale, N.J. Erlbaum, in press. (b)

RODIN, J., & LANGER, E. Long-term effects of a control-relevant intervention with the institutionalized aged. *Journal of Personality and Social Psychology,* 1977, 35, 897–902.

RODIN, J., & LANGER, E. Aging labels: The decline of control and the fall of self-esteem. *Journal of Social Issues,* 1980, 36, 12–29.

RODIN, J., TIMKO, C., & ANDERSON, S. The construct of control: Biological and psychosocial correlates. In M. P. Lawton & G. Maddox (Eds.), *Annual review of gerontology and geriatrics (Vol. 5).* New York: Springer, 1985.

ROGERS, C. R. *On becoming a person: A therapist's view of psychotherapy.* Boston: Houghton Mifflin, 1961.

ROHLES, R. H. Preference for the thermal environment by the elderly. *Human Factors,* 1969, 11, 37–41.

RORSCHACH, H. *Psychodiagnostics: A diagnostic test based on perception.* Original publication: 1921. Berne: Huber, 1942.

ROSE, M. A. Problems families face in home care. *American Journal of Nursing,* 1976, 76(3), 416–418.

ROSEN, B., & JERDEE, T. H. The nature of job-related stereotypes. *Journal of Applied Psychology,* 1976, 61, 180–183. (a)

ROSEN, B., & JERDEE, T. H. The influence of age stereotypes on managerial decisions. *Journal of Applied Psychology,* 1976, 61, 428–432. (b)

ROSENBAUM, R. Turn on, tune in, drop dead. *Harper's,* 1982, 265, 32–43.

ROSENFELD, M., & OWENS, W. A., JR. The intrinsic-extrinsic aspects of work and their demographic correlates. Paper presented at the Midwestern Psychological Association, Chicago, April 1965.

ROTTER, J. B. Generalized expectancies for internal versus external control of reinforcement. *Psychological Monographs,* 1966, 80 (1, Whole No. 609).

ROUS, J. Effect of age on the functional state of the olfactory analyser. *Ceskoslovenska Otolaryngologie,* 1969, 18, 248–256.

ROUTH, D. A., & MAYES, J. T. On consolidation and the potency of delayed stimulus suffixes. *Quarterly Journal of Experimental Psychology,* 1974, 26, 1–74, 472–479.

ROVEE, C. K., COHEN, R. Y., & SHLAPACK, W. Life span stability in olfactory sensitivity. *Developmental Psychology,* 1975, 11, 311–318.

ROWLATT, C., & FRANKS, L. M. Aging in tissues and cells. In J. C. Brocklehurst (Ed.), *Geriatric medicine and gerontology.* (2nd Ed.) New York: Churchill Livingstone, 1978.

RUBIN, Z. Measurement of romantic love. *Journal of Personality and Social Psychology,* 1970, 16, 267–268.

RUMELHART, D. E. *Introduction to human memory processing.* New York: Wiley, 1977.

RUSSEK, H. I. Emotional stress and coronary heart disease in American physicians, dentists, and lawyers. *American Journal of Medical Science,* 1962, 243, 716.

RUSSEK, H. I. Stress, tobacco, and coronary disease in North American professional groups. *Journal of the American Medical Association,* 1965, 192, 189–194.

RUTTER, M. Protective factors in children's responses to stress and disadvantage. In M. W. Kent & J. E. Rolf (Eds.), *Primary prevention of pa-*

thology: Volume III. Social competence in children. Hanover, N.H.: University Press of New England, 1979.

RYCKMAN, R. M., & MALIKIOSKI, M. Relationship between locus of control and chronological age. *Psychological Reports,* 1975, 36, 655–658.

RYFF, C., & BALTES, P. B. Value transition and adult development in women: The instrumentality-terminality sequence hypothesis. *Developmental Psychology,* 1976, 12, 567–568.

SALES, S. M. Organizational role as a risk factor in coronary disease. *Administrative Science Quarterly,* 1969, 14, 324–336.

Salthouse, T. A. Age and tachistoscopic perception. *Experimental Aging Research,* 1976, 2, 91–103.

SALTHOUSE, T. A. Age and memory: Strategies for localizing the loss. In L. W. Poon, L. S. Cermak, D. Arenberg, & L. W. Thompson (Eds.), *New directions in memory and aging.* Hillsdale, N.J.: Erlbaum, 1980.

SALTHOUSE, T. A. *Adult cognition: An experimental psychology of human aging.* New York: Springer-Verlag, 1982.

SALZMAN, C. Stimulants in the elderly. In A. Raskin, D. S. Robinson, & J. Levine (Eds.), *Age and the pharmacology of psychoactive drugs.* New York: Elsevier, 1981.

SAMUELSON, R. J. The myths of comparable worth. *Newsweek,* April 22, 1985, 57.

SARASON, S. B. *Work, aging, and social change: Professionals and the one life one career imperative.* New York: Free Press, 1977.

SARNOFF, I., & CORWIN, S. M. Castration anxiety and the fear of death. *Journal of Personality,* 1959, 27, 374–385.

SAUNDERS, C. The last stages of life. *American Journal of Nursing,* 1965, 65(3), 70–75.

SCHAEFER, C., COYNE, J., & LAZARUS, R. The health-related functions of social support. *Journal of Behavioral Medicine,* 1981, 4, 381–406.

SCHAIE, K. W. Rigidity-flexibility and intelligence: A cross-sectional study of the adult life span from 20 to 70 years. *Psychological Monographs,* 1958, 72 (Whole No. 462), 1–26.

SCHAIE, K. W. A general model for the study of developmental problems. *Psychological Bulletin,* 1965, 64, 92–107.

SCHAIE, K. W. Methodological problems in descriptive developmental research on adulthood and aging. In J. R. Nesselroade & H. W. Reese (Eds.), *Life-span developmental psychology: Methodological issues.* New York: Academic Press, 1973.

SCHAIE, K. W. Quasi-experimental designs in the psychology of aging. In J. E. Birren & K. W. Schaie (Eds.), *Handbook of the psychology of aging.* New York: Van Nostrand Reinhold, 1977.

SCHAIE, K. W. External validity in the assessment of intellectual development in adulthood. *Journal of Gerontology,* 1978, 33, 696–701.

SCHAIE, K. W. (Ed.) *Longitudinal studies of adult psychological development.* New York: Guilford Press, 1983.

SCHAIE, K. W., & BALTES, P. B. On sequential strategies in developmental research: Description or explanation. *Human Development,* 1975, 18, 384–390.

SCHAIE, K. W., & BALTES, P. B. Some faith helps to see the forest. A final comment on the Horn and Donaldson myth of the Baltes-Schaie position on adult intelligence. *American Psychologist,* 1977, 32, 1118–1120.

SCHAIE, K. W., LABOUVIE, G. V., & BUECH, B. U. Generational and cohort-specific differences in adult cognitive functioning. *Developmental Psychology,* 1973, 9, 151–166.

SCHAIE, K. W., & LABOUVIE-VIEF, G. Generational versus ontogenic components of change in adult cognitive behavior: A fourteen-year cross-sequential study. *Developmental Psychology,* 1974, 10, 305–320.

SCHAIE, K. W., & PARHAM, I. A. Stability of adult personality: Fact or fable? *Journal of Personality and Social Psychology,* 1976, 34, 146–158.

SCHAIE, K. W., & PARHAM, I. A. Cohort-sequential analyses of adult intellectual development. *Developmental Psychology,* 1977, 13, 649–653.

SCHEIDT, R. J., & SCHAIE, K. W. A taxonomy of situations for an elderly population: Generating situational criteria. *Journal of Gerontology,* 1978, 33, 848–857.

SCHIFFMAN, S. Food recognition of the elderly. *Journal of Gerontology,* 1977, 32, 586–592.

SCHIFFMAN, S., & PASTERNAK, M. Decreased discrimination of food odors in the elderly. *Journal of Gerontology,* 1979, 34, 73–79.

SCHLESSINGER, B., & MILLER, G. A. Sexuality and the aged. *Medical Aspects of Human Sexuality,* 1973, 3, 46–52.

SCHMITZ-SCHERZER, R., & THOMAE, H. Constancy and change of behavior in old age: Findings from the Bonn longitudinal study on aging. In K. W. Schaie (Ed.), *Longitudinal studies of adult psychological development.* New York: Guilford Press, 1983.

SCHNEIDER, E. L., & REED, J. D. Modulations of aging processes. In C. E. Finch & E. L. Schneider (Eds.), *Handbook of the biology of aging.* (2nd Ed.) New York: Van Nostrand Reinhold, 1985.

SCHNEIDER, J. *Stress, loss, and grief.* Baltimore: University Park Press, 1984.

SCHNEIDER, W., & SHIFFRIN, R. M. Controlled and automatic human information processing: I. Detection, search, and attention. *Psychological Review,* 1977, 84, 1–66.

SCHOENBACH, V. J., KAPLAN, B. H., FREDMAN, L., & KLEINBAUM, D. G. Social ties and mortality in Evans County, Georgia. *American Journal of Epidemiology,* 1986, 123, 577–591.

SCHOFIELD, J. D., & DAVIES, I. Theories of aging. In J. C. Brocklehurst (Ed.), *Geriatric medicine and gerontology.* (2nd Ed.) New York: Churchill Livingstone, 1978.

SCHONFIELD, D. *Age and remembering.* Duke University Council on Aging and Human Development, Proceedings of the Seminars. Durham, N.C.: Duke University, 1969.

SCHULTZ, N. R., ELIAS, M. F., ROBBINS, M. A., STREETEN, D., & BLAKEMAN, N. A longitudinal comparison of hypertensives and normotensives on the WAIS. *Journal of Gerontology,* 1986, 41, 169–175.

SCHULZ, R. Effects of control and predictability on the physical and psychological well-being of the institutionalized aged. *Journal of Personality and Social Psychology,* 1976, 33, 563–573.

SCHULZ, R. *The psychology of death, dying, and bereavement.* Reading, Mass.: Addison-Wesley, 1978.

SCHULZ, R. Aging and control. In J. Garber & M. E. P. Seligman (Eds.), *Human helplessness: Theory and applications.* New York: Academic Press, 1980.

SCHULZ, R. Emotionality and aging: A theoretical and empirical integration. *Journal of Gerontology,* 1982, 37, 42–52.

SCHULZ, R. Emotions and affect. In J. E. Birren & K. W. Schaie (Eds.), *Handbook of the psychology of aging.* (2nd Ed.) New York: Van Nostrand Reinhold, 1985.

SCHULZ, R., & ADERMAN, D. Clinical research and the stages of dying. *Omega: Journal of Death and Dying,* 1974, 5, 137–143.

SCHULZ, R., ADERMAN, D., & MANKO, G. Attitudes toward death: The effects of different methods of questionnaire administration. Paper presented at the meeting of the Eastern Psychological Association, New York, April 1976.

SCHULZ, R., & BRENNER, G. Relocation of the aged: A review and theoretical analysis. *Journal of Gerontology,* 1977, 32, 323–333.

SCHULZ, R., & DECKER, S. Long-term adjustment to physical disability: The role of social comparison processes, social support, and perceived control. Paper presented at the annual meeting of the American Psychological Association, Anaheim, Calif., August 1983.

SCHULZ, R., & HANUSA, B. H. Long-term effects of control and predictability enhancing interventions: Findings and ethical issues. *Journal of Personality and Social Psychology,* 1978, 36, 1194–1201.

SCHULZ, R., & HANUSA, B. H. Environmental influences on the effectiveness of control and competence enhancing interventions. In L. C. Perlmutter & R. A. Monty (Eds.), *Choice and perceived control.* Hillsdale, N.J.: Erlbaum, 1979.

SCHULZ, R., & HANUSA, B. H. Experimental social gerontology: a social psychological perspective. *Journal of Social Issues,* 1980, 36, 30–46.

SCHULZ, R., & MUNSON, S. Social perspectives on aging. In C. Cassel & J. R. Walsh (Eds.), *Geriatric medicine: Principles and practice (Vol. 2).* New York: Springer, 1984.

SCHULZ, R., & RAU, M. T. Social support through the life course. In S. Cohen & L. Syme (Eds.), *Social support and health.* New York: Academic Press, 1985.

SCHULZ, R., & SCHLARB, J. Two decades of research on dying: What do we know about the patient? *Omega: Journal of Death and Dying,* in press.

SCHULZ, R., TOMPKINS, C. A., & WOOD, D. The social psychology of caregiving: Physical and psychological costs of providing support to the disabled. In press.

SCHULZ, T. H. The economics of mandatory retirement. *Industrial Gerontology,* 1974, 1, 1–10.

SCHULZ, T. H. *The economics of aging.* Belmont, Calif.: Wadsworth, 1976.

SCOGGINS, C. H. The cellular basis of aging. *Western Journal of Medicine,* 1981, 135, 521–525.

SECHREST, L. Personality. *Annual Review of Psychology,* 1976, 27, 1–27.

SEGERBERG, O., JR. *The immortality factor.* New York: E. P. Dutton, 1974.

SEKARAN, U. How husbands and wives in dual-career families perceive their family and work worlds. *Journal of Vocational Behavior,* 1983, 22, 288–302.

SELIGMAN, M. *Helplessness: On depression, development, and death.* San Francisco: Freeman, 1975.

SELYE, H. *Stress without distress.* Philadelphia: Lippincott, 1974.

SELYE, H. The stress concept: Past, present, and future. In C. L. Cooper (Ed.), *Stress research: Issues for the Eighties.* New York: Wiley, 1983.

SHANAN, J., & JACOBOWITZ, J. Personality and aging. In C. Eisdorfer (Ed.), *Annual review of gerontology and geriatrics (Vol. 3).* New York: Springer, 1982.

SHANAS, E. Social myth as hypothesis: The case of the family relations of old people. *The Gerontologist,* 1979, 19, 3–9.

SHANAS, E. Older people and their families: The new pioneers. *Journal of Marriage and the Family,* 1980, 42, 9–15.

SHANAS, E., TOWNSEND, P., WEDDERBURN, D., FRIIS, H., MILHHJ, P. & STEHOUVER, J. *Older people in three industrial societies.* New York: Atherton Press, 1968.

SHANTEAU, J., & NAGY, G. F. Probability of acceptance in dating choice. *Journal of Personality and Social Psychology,* 1979, 37, 522–533.

SHEEHY, G. *Passages.* New York: E. P. Dutton, 1976.

SHERWOOD, S., & MOR, V. Mental health institutions and the elderly. In J. E. Birren & R. B. Sloane (Eds.), *Handbook of mental health and aging.* Englewood Cliffs, N.J.: Prentice-Hall, 1982.

SHNEIDMAN, E. S. *Deaths of man.* New York: Quadrangle/N.Y. Times, 1973.

SCHNEIDMAN, E. S. (Ed.) *Death: Current perspectives.* Palo Alto, Calif.: Mayfield, 1976.

SHOCK, N. W. The physiology of aging. *Scientific American,* 1962, 206(1), 100–110.

SHOCK, N. W. Physiological theories of aging. In M. Rockstein, M. L. Sussman, & J. Chesky (Eds.), *Theoretical aspects of aging.* New York: Academic Press, 1974.

SHOCK, N. W. Biological theories of aging. In J. E. Birren & K. W. Schaie (Eds.), *Handbook of the psychology of aging.* New York: Van Nostrand Reinhold, 1977.

SHOCK, N. W. Longitudinal studies of aging in humans. In C. E. Finch & E. L. Schneider (Eds.), *Handbook of the biology of aging.* (2nd Ed) New York: Van Nostrand Reinhold, 1985.

SHOCK, N. W., & NORRIS, A. H. Neuromuscular coordination as a factor in age changes in muscular exercise. In D. Brunner & E. Jokl (Eds.). *Medicine and sport (Vol. 4).* Basel: Karger, 1970.

SIEGLER, I. C. The terminal drop hypothesis: Fact or artifact? *Experimental Aging Research,* 1975, 1, 169–185.

SIEGLER, I. C. The psychology of adult development and aging. In E. W. Busse & D. G. Blazer (Eds.), *Handbook of geriatric psychiatry.* New York: Van Nostrand Reinhold, 1980.

SIEGLER, I. C. Psychological aspects of the Duke longitudinal studies. In
K. W. Schaie (Ed.), *Longitudinal studies of adult psychological development*. New York: Guilford Press, 1983.

SIEGLER, I. C., & BOTWINICK, J. A long-term longitudinal study of intellectual ability of older adults: The matter of selective subject attrition. *Journal of Gerontology*, 1979, 34, 242–245.

SIEGLER, I. C., & EDELMAN, C. D. Age discrimination in employment:
The implications for psychologists. Paper presented at the meeting
of the Western Psychological Association, San Francisco, April
1977.

SIEGLER, I. C., & GATZ, M. Age patterns in locus of control. In E. Palmore, E. Busse, G. Maddox, J. Nowlin, & I. E. Siegler
(Eds.), *Normal aging III*. Durham, N.C.: Duke University Press,
1985.

SIGALL, H., & LANDY, D. Radiating beauty: The effects of having a physically attractive partner on person perception. *Journal of Personality
and Social Psychology*, 1973, 28, 218–224.

SILVERSTONE, F. A., BRANDFONBRENER, M., SHOCK, N. W., & YIENGST,
M. J. Age differences in the intravenous glucose tolerance tests and
the response to insulin. *Journal of Clinical Investigation*, 1957, 36,
504–514.

SILVERSTONE, G., & WYNTER, L. The effects of introducing a heterosexual
living space. *The Gerontologist*, 1975, 15, 83–87.

SIMPSON, M. A. Planning for terminal care. *Lancet*, 1976, 2, 191–193.

SIVAK, M., OLSON, P. L., & PASTALAN, L. A. Effect of driver's age on
nighttime legibility of highway signs. *Human Factors*. 1981, 23, 59–
64.

SKINNER, B. F. *Science and human behavior*. New York: Macmillan, 1953.
Paperback reprint: New York: Free Press, 1965.

SKINNER, B. F. Intellectual self-management in old age. *American Psychologist*, 1983, 38, 239–244.

SKINNER, B. F., & VAUGHAN, M. E. *Enjoy old age: A program of self-management*. New York: Norton, 1983.

SMITH, A. D. Aging and interference with memory. *Journal of Gerontology*,
1975, 30, 319–325.

SMITH, A. D. Adult age differences in cued recall. *Developmental Psychology*, 1977, 13, 326–331.

SMITH, A. D. Age differences in encoding, storage, and retrieval. In L. W.
Poon, J. L. Fozard, L. S. Cermak, D. Arenberg, & L. W. Thompson
(Eds.), *New directions in memory and aging*. Hillsdale, N.J.: Erlbaum,
1980.

SMITH, A. D., & FULLERTON, A. M. Age differences in episodic and se-
mantic memory: Implications for language and cognition. In
S. Beasley & L. Davis (Eds.), *Communication processes and disorders*.
New York: Grune & Stratton, 1981.

SMITH, D. S. Life course, norms, and the family system of older Americans in 1900. *Journal of Family History*, 1979, 4, 285–298.

SMITH, D. W., BIERMAN, E. L., & ROBINSON, N. M. (Eds.) *The biologic ages
of man*. Philadelphia: W. B. Saunders, 1978.

SMITH, M. L., GLASS, G. V., & MILLER, T. I. *The benefits of psychotherapy.* Baltimore: Johns Hopkins University Press, 1980.

SMITH, P. C., KENDALL, L. M., & HULIN, C. L. *The measurement of satisfaction in work and retirement: A strategy for the study of attitudes.* Chicago: Rand-McNally, 1969.

SMYER, M. A., & GATZ, M. *Mental health and aging: Programs and evaluations.* Beverly Hills, Calif.: Sage Publications, 1983.

SMYTHE, H. Nonsteroidal therapy in inflammatory joint disease. *Hospital Practice,* 1975, 10(9), 51–56.

SOLDO, B. J. The housing and characteristics of independent elderly: A demographic overview. *Occasional Papers in Housing and Urban Development, No. 1.* Washington, D.C.: United States Department of Housing and Urban Development, 1979.

SOLDO, B. J., SHARMA, M., & CAMPBELL, R. T. Determinants of the community living arrangements of older unmarried women. *Journal of Gerontology,* 1984, 39.

SOLNICK, R. E., & CORBY, N. Human sexuality and aging. In D. S. Woodruff & J. E. Birren (Eds.), *Aging: Scientific perspectives and social issues.* (2nd Ed.) Monterey, Calif.: Brooks/Cole, 1983.

SOLOMON, S., & SAXE, L. What is intelligent, as well as attractive, is good. *Personality and Social Psychology Bulletin,* 1977, 3, 670–673.

SORENSEN, R. C. *Adolescent sexuality in contemporary America.* New York: Abrams, 1973.

SPAKES, P. R. Family, friendship, and community interaction as related to life satisfaction of the elderly. *Journal of Gerontological Social Work,* 1979, 1, 279–294.

SPEARMAN, C. E. "General intelligence," objectively determined and measured. *American Journal of Psychology,* 1904, 15, 201–292.

SPERLING, G. The information available in brief visual presentations. *Psychological Monographs,* 1960, 74 (11, Whole No. 498).

STAATS, S. Internal versus external locus of control for three age groups. *International Journal of Aging and Human Development,* 1974, 5, 7–10.

STAINES, G. L., & PLECK, J. H. *The impact of work schedules of the family.* Ann Arbor: University of Michigan, 1983.

STERNBERG, S. High speed scanning in human memory. *Science,* 1966, 153, 622–654.

STERNBERG, S. Memory scanning: Mental processes revealed by reaction time experiments. *American Scientist,* 1969, 57, 421–457.

STERNS, H. L, BARRETT, G. V., & ALEXANDER, R. A. Accidents and the aging individual. In J. E. Birren & K. W. Schaie (Eds.), *Handbook of the psychology of aging.* (2nd Ed.) New York: Van Nostrand Reinhold, 1985.

STEUER, J., LaRUE, A., BLUM, J. E., & JARVIK, L. F. "Critical loss" in the eighth and ninth decades. *Journal of Gerontology,* 1981, 36, 211–213.

STROLLER, E. P. Parental caregiving by adult children. *Journal of Marriage and the Family,* 1983, 45, 851–858.

STOLLER, E. P., & EARL, L. L. Help with activities of everyday life: Sources of support for the noninstitutionalized elderly. *The Gerontologist,* 1983, 23, 64–70.

STONE, J. L., & NORRIS, A. H. Activities and attitudes of participants in the Baltimore longitudinal study. *Journal of Gerontology,* 1966, 21, 575–580.

STORANDT, M. Speed and coding effects in relation to age and ability level. *Developmental Psychology,* 1976, 12, 177–178.

STORANDT, M. Age, ability level, and method of administering and scoring the WAIS. *Journal of Gerontology,* 1977, 32, 175–178.

STOTLAND, E. Stress. In R. J. Corsini (Ed.), *Encyclopedia of psychology.* New York: Wiley, 1984.

STREHLER, B. L. On the histochemistry and ultrastructure of age pigment. In B. L. Strehler (Ed.), *Advances in gerontological research (Vol. 1).* New York: Academic Press, 1964.

STREHLER, B. L. The mechanisms of aging. *The Body Forum,* 1978, 3, 44–45.

STREIB, G. F., & SCHNEIDER, C. J. *Retirement in American society: Impact and process.* Ithaca, N.Y.: Cornell University Press, 1971.

STROEBE, W., STROEBE, M. S., GERGEN, K. J., & GERGEN, M. The effects of bereavement on mortality: A social psychological analysis. In J. R. Eiser (Ed.), *Social psychology and behavioral medicine.* New York: Wiley, 1982.

STRUPP, H. H., & BERGIN, A. E. Some empirical and conceptual bases for coordinated research in psychotherapy: A critical review of issues, trends, and evidence. *International Journal of Psychiatry,* 1969, 7, 18–90.

STUEVE, C. A., & FISCHER, C. Social networks and older women. Paper presented at the Workshop on Older Women, Washington, D.C., September 1978.

STUEVE, C. A., & GERSON, K. Personal relations across the life cycle. In C. S. Fischer et al., *Networks and places: Social relations in the urban setting.* New York: Free Press, 1977.

SUEDFELD, P., & PIEDRAHITA, L. E. Intimations of mortality: Integrative simplification as a precursor of death. *Journal of Personality and Social Psychology,* 1984, 47, 848–852.

SUINN, R. M. Type A behavior pattern. In R. B. Williams, Jr., & W. D. Gentry (Eds.), *Behavioral approaches to medical treatment.* Cambridge, Mass.: Ballinger, 1977.

SULLIVAN, H. S. *Conceptions of modern psychiatry.* Original publication: 1947. New York: Norton, 1953.

SULLIVAN, H. S. *The interpersonal theory of psychiatry.* Original publication: 1953. New York: Norton, 1968.

SUSZYCKI, L. Intervention with the bereaved. In O. S. Margolis et al. (Eds.), *Acute grief: Counseling the bereaved.* New York: Columbia University Press, 1981.

SZAFRAN, J. Psychophysiological studies of aging in pilots. In G. A. Talland (Ed.), *Human aging and behavior.* New York: Academic Press, 1968.

SZILARD, L. On the nature of the aging process. *Proceedings of the National Academy of Science,* 1959, 45, 30–45.

TAGGART, R. *The labor market impact of the private retirement system.* Studies in Public Welfare, Paper No. 11, Washington, D.C.: United States Congress, Subcommittee on Fiscal Policy, Joint Economic Committee, 1973.

TALLAND, G. A. Three estimates of the word span and their stability over the adult years. *Quarterly Journal of Experimental Psychology,* 1965, 17, 301–307.

TALLAND, G. A. Age and the span of immediate recall. In G. A. Talland (Ed.), *Human aging and behavior.* New York: Academic Press, 1968.

TARTER, R., TEMPLER, D, & PERLEY, R. Death anxiety in suicide attempters. *Psychological Reports,* 1974, 34, 895–897.

TAUB, H. A. Method of presentation of meaningful prose to young and old adults. *Experimental Aging Research,* 1976, 2, 469–474.

TAUB, H. A. Comprehension and memory of prose materials by young and old adults. *Experimental Aging Research,* 1979, 5, 3–13.

TAUB, H. A., & KLINE, G. E. Recall of prose as a function of age and input modality. *Journal of Gerontology,* 1978, 5, 725–730.

TEMPLER, D. The construction and validation of a death anxiety scale. *Journal of General Psychology,* 1970, 82, 165–177.

TEMPLER, D. Death anxiety as related to depression and health of retired persons. *Journal of Gerontology,* 1971, 26, 521–523.

TEMPLER, D., & RUFF, C. Death anxiety scale means, standard deviations, and embedding. *Psychological Reports,* 1971, 29, 173–174.

TEMPLER, D., RUFF, C., & FRANKS, C. Death anxiety: Age, sex, and parental resemblance in diverse populations. *Developmental Psychology,* 1971, 4, 108.

THOMAE, H. Cognitive theory of personality and theory of aging. *Human Development,* 1970, 13, 1–10.

THOMAE, H. (Ed.) *Patterns of aging: Contributions to human development (Vol. 3).* Basel–New York: Karger, 1976.

THOMAE, H. Personality and adjustment to aging. In J. E. Birren & R. B. Sloane (Eds.), *Handbook of mental health and aging.* Englewood Cliffs, N.J.: Prentice-Hall, 1980.

THOMAS, L. E. Motivations for mid-life career change. Paper presented at the annual meeting of the Gerontological Society, San Francisco, 1977.

THOMPSON, L. W., EISDORFER, C., & ESTES, E. H. Cardiovascular disease and behavioral changes in the elderly. In E. Palmore (Ed.), *Normal aging.* Durham, N.C.: Duke University Press, 1970.

THOMPSON, L. W., GALLAGHER, D., NIES, G., & EPSTEIN, B. A. Evaluation of the effectiveness of professionals and nonprofessionals as instructors of "Coping with Depression" classes for elders. *The Gerontologist,* 1983, 23, 390–395.

THORNDIKE, E. L., BREGMAN, E. O., TILTON, J. W., & WOODYARD, E. *Adult learning.* New York: Macmillan, 1928.

THURSTONE, L. L. Primary mental abilities. *Psychometric Monographs,* 1938, No. 1.

THURSTONE, L. L. Creative talent. *Proceedings of the 1950 invitational conference on testing problems, Educational Testing Service,* 1951, 55–69.

THURSTONE, L. L., & THURSTONE, T. G. Factorial studies of intelligence. *Psychometric Monographs,* 1941, No. 2.

TICE, R. R., & SETLOW, R. B. DNA repair and replication in aging organisms and cells. In C. E. Finch & E. L. Schneider (Eds.), *Handbook of the biology of aging.* (2nd Ed.) New York: Van Nostrand Reinhold, 1985.

TIERNEY, J. The aging body. *Esquire,* May 1982.

TILL, R. E., & WALSH, D. A. Encoding and retrieval factors in adult memory for implicational sentences. *Journal of Verbal Learning and Verbal Behavior,* 1980, 19, 1–16.

TOLOR, A., & REZNIKOFF, M. Relationship between insight, repression-sensitization, internal-external control, and death anxiety. *Journal of Abnormal Psychology,* 1967, 72, 426–430.

TRIMMER, E. J. *Rejuvenation.* New York: A. S. Barnes, 1980.

TRIPATHI, R. C., & TRIPATHI, B. J. Lens morphology, aging, and cataracts. *Journal of Gerontology,* 1983, 38, 258–270.

TROLL, L. E. Grandparenting. In L. W. Poon (Ed.), *Aging in the 1980s: Psychological issues.* Washington, D.C.: American Psychological Association, 1980.

TROLL, L. E., & BENGTSON, V. Generations in the family. In W. Burr, R. Hill, F. I. Nye, & I. Reiss (Eds.), *Contemporary theories about the family.* New York: Free Press, 1979.

TROLL, L. E., SALTZ, R., & DUNIN-MARKIEWICZ, R. A seven year follow-up of intelligence test scores for foster grandparents. *Journal of Gerontology,* 1976, 31, 583–585.

TROLL, L. E., & SMITH, J. Attachment through the life span: some questions about dyadic bonds among adults. *Human Development,* 1976, 19, 156–170.

TULVING, E. Episodic and semantic memory. In E. Tulving & W. Donaldson (Eds.), *Organization of memory.* New York: Academic Press, 1972.

TULVING, E. *Elements of episodic memory.* New York: Oxford University Press, 1983.

TULVING, E. How many memory systems are there? *American Psychologist,* 1985, 40, 385–398.

United States Bureau of the Census. *Current population reports: Some characteristics of the population.* Washington, D.C.: U.S. Government Printing Office, 1976.

United States Bureau of the Census. *Social indicators III.* Washington, D.C.: United States Government Printing Office, 1980.

United States Bureau of the Census. *Statistical abstract of the United States.* Washington, D. C.: United States Government Printing office, 1981.

United States Senate Special Committee on Aging. *Aging America.* Washington, D.C.: United States Government Printing Office, 1983.

United States Senate Special Committee on Aging. *America in transition: An aging society.* (1984–85 Ed.) Washington, D.C.: United States Government Printing Office, 1985.

United States Senate Special Committee on Aging. *Aging America: Trends and projections.* (1985–86 Ed.) Washington, D.C.: United States Government Printing Office, 1986.

URBERG, K. A., & LABOUVIE-VIEF, G. Conceptualizations of sex roles: A life-span developmental study. *Developmental Psychology,* 1976, 12, 15–23.

VACHON, M. L. S. Type of death as a determinant in acute grief. In O. S. Margolis et al. (Eds.), *Acute grief: Counseling the bereaved.* New York: Columbia University Press, 1981.

VACHON, M. L. S., FREEDMAN, K., FORMO, A., RODGERS, J., LYALL, W. A. L., & FREEMAN, S. J. J. The final illness in cancer: The widow's perspective. *Canadian Medical Association Journal,* 1977, 177, 1151–1154.

VANDENBOS, G., DELEON, P., & PALLAK, M. An alternative to traditional medical care for the terminally ill. *American Psychologist,* 1982, 37, 1245–1248.

VANDERPOOL, H. Y. The ethics of terminal care. *Journal of the American Medical Association,* 1978, 239, 850–852.

VAUPEL, J. W., & GOWAN, A. E. Passage to Methuselah: Some demographic consequences of continued progress against mortality. *American Journal of Public Health,* 1986, 76, 430–433.

VEROWERDT, A., PFEIFFER, E., & WANG, H. S. Sexual behavior in senescence: Changes in sexual activity and interest of aging men and women. *Journal of Geriatric Psychiatry,* 1969, 2, 163–180.

VERZAR, F. The aging of collagen. *Scientific American,* 1963, 208, 104–114.

VINEY, L. L. Loss of life and loss of bodily integrity: Two different sources of threat for people who are ill. *Omega: Journal of Death and Dying,* 1984–85, 15, 207–222.

VROOM, V. H. *Work and motivation.* New York: Wiley, 1964.

WACHTEL, P. L. Investigation and its discontents: Some constraints on progress in psychological research. *American Psychologist,* 1980, 35, 399–408.

WAHL, C. W. The physician's management of the dying patient. In J. Masserman (Ed.), *Current psychiatric therapies.* New York: Grune & Stratton, 1962.

WAHL, C. W. Should a patient be told the truth? In A. H. Kutscher (Ed.), *But not to lose.* New York: Frederick Fell, 1969.

WALFORD, R. L. *The immunologic theory of aging.* Baltimore: Williams & Wilkins, 1969.

WALFORD, R. L. The immunologic theory of aging. *Fed. Proc.,* 1974, 33, 2020–2027.

WALLERSTEIN, J. S., & KELLY, J. B. The effects of parental divorce: The adolescent experience. In J. Anthony & C. Koupernic (Eds.), *The child in his family: Children at psychiatric risk.* New York: Wiley, 1974.

WALLERSTEIN, J. S., & KELLY, J. B. The effects of parental divorce: Experiences of the preschool child. *Journal of the American Academy of Child Psychiatry,* 1975, 14, 600–616.

WALLERSTEIN, J. S., & KELLY, J. B. The effects of parental divorce: Experiences of the child in later latency. *American Journal of Orthopsychiatry,* 1976, 46, 256–269.

WALSH, D. A. Age differences in central perceptual processing: A dichoptic backward masking investigation. *Journal of Gerontology,* 1976, 31, 178–185.

WALSH, D. A. Age differences in learning and memory. In D. S. Woodruff & J. E. Birren (Eds.), *Aging: Scientific perspectives and social issues.* (2nd Ed.) Monterey, Calif.: Brooks/Cole, 1983.

WALSH, D. A., & BALDWIN, M. Age differences in integrated semantic memory. *Developmental Psychology,* 1977, 13, 509–514.

WALSH, D. A., BALDWIN, M., & FINKLE, T. J. Age differences in integrated semantic memory for abstract sentences. *Experimental Aging Research,* 1980, 6, 431–443.

WALSH, D. A., & PRASSE, M. J. Iconic memory and attentional processes in the aged. In L. W. Poon, J. L. Fozard, L. S. Cermak, D. Arenberg, & L. W. Thompson (Eds.), *New directions in memory and aging: Proceedings of the George A. Talland Memorial Conference.* Hillsdale, N.J.: Erlbaum, 1980.

WALSH, D. A., & THOMPSON, L. W. Age differences in visual sensory memory. *Journal of Gerontology,* 1978, 33, 383–387.

WALSTER, E., ARONSON, V., ABRAHAMS, D., & ROTTMAN, L. Importance of physical attractiveness in dating behavior. *Journal of Personality and Social Psychology,* 1966, 4, 508–416.

WALSTER, E., & WALSTER, G. W. *Love.* Reading, Mass.: Addison-Wesley, 1978.

WASOW, M. Sexuality in homes for the aged. *Concern in the Care of Aging,* 1977, 3(6), 20–21.

WATKINS, J. A review of short-term memory. *Psychological Bulletin,* 1974, 81, 695–711.

WATSON, J. D. *The double helix.* New York: New American Library, 1969.

WAUGH, N, & BARR, R. Memory and mental tempo. In L. W. Poon, J. L. Fozard, L. S. Cermak, D. Arenberg, & L. W. Thompson (Eds.), *New directions in memory and aging: Proceedings of the George A. Talland Memorial Conference.* Hillsdale, N.J.: Erlbaum, 1980.

WAUGH, N. C., & NORMAN, D. A. Primary memory. *Psychological Review,* 1965, 72, 89–104.

WEALE, R. What is normal aging? Part XI. The eyes of the elderly. *Geriatric Medicine Today,* 1985, 4(3), 29–37.

WEBER, R. J., BROWN, L. T., & WELDON, J. K. Cognitive maps of environmental knowledge and preference in nursing home patients. *Experimental Aging Research,* 1978, 3, 157–174.

WECHSLER, D. *The measurement and appraisal of adult intelligence.* (4th Ed.) Baltimore: Williams & Wilkins, 1958.

WEG, R. B. *The aged: Who, where, how well.* Los Angeles: University of Southern California, Davis School of Gerontology, 1981.

WEG, R. B. Changing physiology of aging: Normal and pathological. In D. S. Woodruff & J. E. Birren (Eds.), *Aging: Scientific perspectives and social issues.* (2nd Ed.) Monterey, Calif.: Brooks/Cole, 1983.

WEISMAN, A. D., & KASTENBAUM, R. The psychological autopsy: A study of the terminal phase of life. *Community Mental Health Journal.* 1968. Monograph No. 4.

WEKSLER, M. E. The senescence of the immune system. *Hospital Practice,* 1981(10), 53–63.

WELCH, S., & BROTH, A. The effect of employment on the health of married women and children. *Sex Roles,* 1977, 3, 385–397.

WELFOR, A. T. Sensory, perceptual, and motor processes in older adults.

In J. E. Birren & R. B. Sloane (Eds.), *Handbook of mental health and aging.* Englewood Cliffs, N.J.: Prentice-Hall, 1980.

WELFOR, A. T. Psychomotor performance. In C. Eisdorfer (Ed.), *Annual review of gerontology and geriatrics (Vol. 4).* New York: Springer, 1984.

WELKOWITZ, J., EWEN, R. B., & COHEN, J. *Introductory statistics for the behavioral sciences.* (3rd Ed.) New York: Academic Press, 1982.

WHEELER, K. T., & LETT, J. T. On the possibility that DNA repair is related to age in non-diving cells. *Proceedings of the National Academy of Science,* 1974, 71, 1862–1865.

WHITBOURNE, S. K. Test anxiety in elderly and young adults. *International Journal of Aging and Human Development,* 1976, 7, 201–210.

White House Conference on Aging. *Chartbook on aging in America.* Washington, D.C.: United States Government Printing Office, 1981.

WIGGINS, J. S. In defense of traits. Paper presented at the ninth annual symposium on the use of the MMPI, Los Angeles, 1974.

WILKIE, F. L., & EISDORFER, C. Sex, verbal ability, and pacing differences in serial learning. *Journal of Gerontology,* 1977, 32, 63–67.

WILSON, C. W. The distribution of selected sexual attitudes and behaviors among the adult population of the United States. *Journal of Sex Research,* 1975, 11, 46–64.

WILSON, D. C., AJEMIAN, L., & MOUNT, B. M. Montreal (1975)—The Royal Victoria Hospital palliative care service. In G. W. Davidson (Ed.), *The hospice: Development and administration.* Washington, D.C.: Hemisphere Publishing Co., 1978.

WILSON, K., & DESHANE, M. R. The legal rights of grandparents: A preliminary discussion. *The Gerontologist,* 1982, 22, 67–71.

WILSON, K., & SCHULZ, R. Criteria for effective crisis intervention. In M. A. Smyer & M. Gatz (Eds.), *Mental health and aging.* Beverly Hills, Calif.: Sage Publications, 1983.

WINGFIELD, A., & BYRNES, D. L. *The psychology of human memory,* New York: Academic Press, 1981.

WISEMAN, J. P. *Stations of the lost: the treatment of Skid Row alcoholics.* Englewood Cliffs, N.J.: Prentice-Hall, 1970.

WITKIN, H. A., DYK, R. B., FATERSON, H. F., GOODENOUGH, D., R., & KARP, S. A. *Psychological differentiation.* New York: Wiley, 1962.

WOLINSKY, J. Clues found in isolating Alzheimer's disease. *American Psychological Association Monitor,* 1983, 14(8), 26, 28.

WOLK, R. L., & GOLDFARB, A. I. The response to group psychotherapy of aged recent admissions compared with long-term mental hospital patients. *American Journal of Psychiatry,* 1967, 123, 1251–1257.

WOLK, S. Situational constraint as a moderator of the locus of control-adjustment relationship. *Journal of Consulting and Clinical Psychology,* 1976, 44, 420–427.

WOLK, S., & KURTZ, K. Positive adjustment and involvement during aging and expectancy for internal control. *Journal of Consulting and Clinical Psychology,* 1975, 43, 173–178.

WOLPE, J. *The practice of behavior therapy.* (2nd Ed.) New York: Pergamon, 1973.

WOOD, V., & ROBERTSON, J. F. Friendship and kinship interaction: Differential effects on the morale of the elderly. *Journal of Marriage and the Family,* 1978, 40, 367–375.

WOODRUFF, D. S., & BIRREN, J. E. Age changes and cohort differences in personality. *Developmental Psychology,* 1972, 6, 252–259

WORTMAN, C. B., & BREHM, J. W. Responses to uncontrollable outcomes: An integration of reactance theory and the learned helplessness model. In L. Berkowitz (Ed.), *Advances in experimental social psychology (Vol. 8).* New York: Academic Press, 1975.

Wright, J. D. Are working women really more satisfied? Evidence from several surveys. *Journal of Marriage and the Family,* 1978, 40, 301–313.

WRIGHTSMAN, L. S. & DEAUX, K. *Social psychology in the 80s.* (3rd Ed.) Monterey, Calif.: Brooks/Cole, 1981.

YALOM, I. D. *The theory and practice of group psychotherapy.* New York: Basic Books, 1970.

YAMAMOTO, J. Cultural factors in loneliness, death, and separation. *Medical Times,* 1970, 98, 177–183.

YESAVAGE, J., BRINK, T., ROSE, T., LUM, O., HUANG, O., ADEY, V., & LEIRERE, V. Development and validation of a geriatric depression screening scale: A preliminary report. *Journal of Psychiatric Research,* in press.

YESAVAGE, J., & KING, R. Drug treatment of cognitive impairment in the elderly. In C. Eisdorfer (Ed.), *Annual review of gerontology and geriatrics (Vol. 2).* New York: Springer, 1981.

YOUNG, M., BERNARD, B., & WALLIS, C. The mortality of widowers. In T. Ford & G. F. DeJong (Eds.). *Social demography.* Englewood Cliffs, N.J.: Prentice-Hall, 1970.

YURICK, A. G., SPIER, B. E., ROBB, S. S., EBERT, N. J., & MAGNUSSEN, M. H., *The aged person and the nursing process.* (2nd Ed.) Norwalk, Conn.: Appleton-Century-Crofts, 1984.

ZARETSKY, H., & HALBERSTAM, J. Age differences in paired-associate learning. *Journal of Gerontology,* 1968, 23, 165–168. (a)

ZARETSKY, H., & HALBERSTAM, J. Effects of aging, brain damage, and associative strength on paired-associate learning and relearning. *Journal of Genetic Psychology,* 1968, 112, 149–163. (b)

ZEMORE, R., & EAMES, N. Psychic and somatic symptoms of depression among young adults, institutionalized aged, and non-institutionalized aged. *Journal of Gerontology,* 1979, 34, 716–722.

ZILLMER, T. W. Age impact on employee benefit costs is not a major problem for employees. *Aging and Work,* 1982, 5, 49–53.

ZUNG, W. A Self-Rating Depression Scale. *Archives of General Psychiatry.* 1965, 12, 63–70.

ZUNG, W. Depression in the normal aged. *Psychosomatics,* 1967, 8, 287–292.

ZUSNE, L. Age and achievement in psychology: The harmonic means as a model. *American Psychologist,* 1976, 31, 805–807.

ZWISLOCKI, J. S. Theory of temporal auditory summation. *Journal of the Acoustical Society of America,* 1960, 32, 1046–1060.

Index

(Note: Page numbers in *italics* refer to definitions in Chapter Glossaries.)

Fig. 4-8: Anatomy of the Ear: The Middle Ear and Cochlea. Adapted in part S., C. Porac and C. M. Ward. *Sensation and Perception.* Copyright © 1979 Brace Jovanovich, Inc. Reprinted by permission of the publisher. Adapted in part from Lindsay, P. H., and D. A., Norman. *Human Information Processing.* Copyright © 1977 by Harcourt Brace Jovanovich, Inc. Reprinted by permission of the publisher.

Fig. 4-9: Ability to Detect Pure Tones. From Corso, J. "Auditory Perception and Communication." In J. E. Birren and K. W. Schaie. *Handbook of the Psychology of Aging.* Copyright © 1977, Van Nostrand Reinhold, New York. All rights reserved. Modified from Spoor. "Presbyacusis Values in Relation to Noise Induced Hearing Loss." *International Audiology 6.* Used by permission.

Fig. 4-10: Ability to Perceive Speech. Bergman, M., V. G. Blumenfield, D. Cascardo, B. Dash, H. Levitt and M. K. Margulies. "Age-Related Decriments in Hearing for Speech: Sampling and Longitudinal Studies." *Journal of Gerontology 31.* 1976. Reprinted by permission of the *Journal of Gerontology,* Washington, DC.

Fig. 4-11: Typical Hearing Aids (Photo). Rappoport, B. Z. "Audiology." In C. K. Cassel and J. R. Walsh (Eds.). *Geriatric Medicine: Vol. I. Medical; Psychiatric; and Pharmacological Topics.* 1984. Courtesy Springer-Verlag, New York, and the author.

Fig 5-2: Relationship Between Age and Performance on . . . Tasks. Salthouse, T. A. *Adult Cognition: An Experimental Psychology of Human Aging.* 1982. Springer-Verlag, New York.

Fig. 5.3A: Age, Rate of Stimulus Presentation and Errors on a Paired Associate Learning Task. Canestrari, R. E., Jr. "Paced and Self-Paced Learning in Young and Elderly Adults." *Journal of Gerontology 18.* 1963. Reprinted by permission of the *Journal of Gerontology.* Washington, DC.

Fig. 5-3B: Age, Rate of Stimulus Presentation and Number of Trials to Learn a Serial Task. Arenberg, D. "Regression Analyses of Verbal Learning on Adult Age Differences at Two Anticipated Intervals." *Journal of Gerontology 22.* Reprinted by permission of the *Journal of Gerontology,* Washington, DC.

Fig. 5-3C: Age, Prior Associative Strength of Stimuli and Number of Trials to Learn a Paired Associative Task. Zaretsky, H., and J. Halberstam. "Effects of Aging, Brain Damage and Associative Strength on Paired Associate Learning and Relearning." *Journal of Genetic Psychology 112.* Copyright © 1968. Published by Heldref Publications, Washington, DC. Reprinted with permission of the Helen Dwight Reid Educational Foundation.

Fig. 5-3D: Age, Use of Mediators and Number of Errors on a Paired Associate Learning Task, Canestrari, R. E., Jr. "Age Changes in Acquisition." In G. A. Talland (Ed.). *Human Aging and Behavior.* 1968. Reprinted by permission of Academic Press, Orlando, Florida, and the author.

Fig. 5-6. An Experimental Method for Determining the Duration of Iconic Memory. Eriksen, C. W., and J. F. Collins. "Some Temporal Characteristics of Visual Pattern Perception." *Journal of Experimental Psychology 74.* Copyright © 1967 by the American Psychological Association. Adapted by permission of the author.

Fig. 5-7: Aging and Performance on a Speeded Primary Memory Task. Based in part on Anders, T. R., J. L. Fozard and T. D. Lillyquist. "Effects of Aging Upon Retrieval from Short-term Memory." *Developmental Psychology 6.* Copyright © 1972 by the American Psychological Association. Adapted by permission of the author.

Fig. 5-9: The Effect of Improved Organization. Hultsch, D. F. "Adult Age Differences in Free Classification and Free Recall." *Developmental Psychology 4.* Copyright © 1971 by the American Psychological Association. Adapted by permission of the author.

Fig. 6-1: Test Items Similar to WAIS Verbal Subtests. Adapted from Wechsler Adult Intelligence Scale-Revised. Copyright © 1981 by The Psychological Corporation. Reproduced by permission. All rights reserved.

Fig. 6-2: Test Items Similar to Some in the WAIS. Adapted from Wechsler Adult Intelligence Scale-Revised. Copyright © 1981 by The Psychological Corporation. Reproduced by permission. All rights reserved.

Fig. 6-3: WAIS Classic Aging Pattern. Jones, H. E. "Intelligence and Problem-Solving." In J. E. Birren (Ed.). *Handbook of Aging and the Individual.* 1959. Reprinted by permission of the University of Chicago Press.

Fig. 6-4: Changes in Fluid Intelligence and Crystallized Intelligence. Kausler, D. H. *Experimental Psychology and Human Aging.* Copyright © 1982. Reprinted by permission of John Wiley and Sons, Inc., New York.

Fig. 6-5: The Relationship Between Aging and Creative Contributions in Many Academic Disciplines. Lehman, H. C. *Age and Achievement.* Copyright 1953 by American Philosophical Society. Reprinted by permission of Princeton University Press.

Fig. 8-2: Frequency of Sexual Intercourse Among Married Couples. Mussen, P. H., J. Conger, J. Kagan and J. Geiwitz. *Psychological Development: A Life-Span Approach.* Copyright © 1979 by Harper & Row, Publishers, Inc., New York.

Fig. 9-1: Relationships Among Work Variables . . . Modified from Rice, R. W. "Organizational Work and the Overall Quality of Life." In S. Oskamp (Ed.). *Applied Social Psychology Annual 5.* Copyright © 1984. Reprinted by permission of Sage Publications, Inc., Newbury Park, California.

Fig. 9-4: "Financial Status of the Retired," *Newsweek,* April 14, 1986, p. 8; May 5, 1986, pp. 11–12, 14. Copyright 1986 by Newsweek, Inc. All rights reserved. Reprinted by permission.

Fig. 10-1: A General Model of Stress. Elliott, G. R., and C. Eisdorfer (Eds.). *Stress and Human Health.* Copyright © 1982. Used by permission of Springer Publishing Company, New York.

Fig. 10-2: Environmental Demands. Modified from Lawton, M. P. *Environment and Aging.* Copyright © 1980 M. P. Lawton, Ph.D. Used by permission.

Fig. 10-3: Stress Caused by Various Problem Areas . . . Modified from Schmitz-Scherzer, R., and H. Thomae. "Constancy and Change of Behavior in Old Age: Findings from the Bonn Longitudinal Study on Aging." In. R. W. Schaie (Ed.). *Longitudinal Studies of Adult Psychological Development.* 1983. Reprinted by permission of Guilford Press, New York.

Fig. 12-1: A Typical Death Certificate. Courtesy of the Indiana State Board of Health.

Table 1-1: Human Life Expectancy. Lerner, M. "When, Why and Where People Die." In O. G. Brim et al. (Eds.). *The Dying Patient.* 1976. Used by permission of the Russell Sage Foundation, New York.

Table 3-2: Leading Causes of Death in the U.S. as a Function of Age Group. Sterns, H. L., G. V. Barrett and R. A. Alexander. In J. E. Birren and K. W. Schaie (Eds.). *Handbook of the Psychology of Aging,* second edition. Copyright © 1977, Van Nostrand Reinhold, New York. All rights reserved.

Table 3-4: Maximum Recorded Life Spans for Various Species. Modified from Kirkwood. T. B. L. "Comparative and Evolutionary Aspects of Longevity." In C. E. Finch and E. L. Schneider (Eds.). *Handbook of the Biology of Aging,* second edition. Copyright © 1985, Van Nostrand Reinhold, New York. All rights reserved.

Table 3-5: Estimating Your Personal Longevity. Schulz, R. *The Psychology of Death, Dying and Bereavement.* Copyright © 1978. Reprinted by permission of Random House, Inc., New York.

Table 8-1: Attitudes of Middle-Class, Middle-Aged Sample Toward Various Age-Related Characteristics. Neugarten, B. L., R. J. Havighurst and S. S. Tobin. "Personality and

Patterns of Aging." In B. L. Neugarten (Ed.). *Middle Age and Aging.* 1968. Reprinted by permission of the University of Chicago Press.

Table 8-2: Classifying Major Life Events According to Temporal and Statistical Normality. Modified from Schulz, R., and M. T. Rau. "Social Support through the Life Course." In S. Cohen and L. Syme (Eds.). *Social Support and Health.* 1985. Reprinted by permission of Academic Press, Orlando, Florida, and the authors.

Table 8-3: Why Marriages Endure . . . Lauer, J., and R. Lauer. "Marriages Made to Last." *Psychology Today 19.* Copyright © 1985 by the American Psychological Association. Reprinted with permission from *Psychology Today Magazine.*

Table 8-4: Frequency of Sexual Intercourse . . . Pfeiffer, E., A. Verwoerdt and G. C. Davis. "Sexual Behavior in Middle Life." *American Journal of Psychiatry 128* (10). Copyright © 1972, the American Psychiatric Association. Reprinted by permission.

Table 10-1: Stressors Commonly Used in . . . Research. Elliott, G. R., and C. Eisdorfer (Eds.). *Stress and Human Health.* Copyright © 1982. Used by permission of Springer Publishing Company, Inc., New York.

Table 10-3: Stressful Life Events. Holmes, H. H., and R. H. Rahe. "The Social Readjustment Rating Scale." *Journal of Psychosomatic Research.* Copyright © 1967, Pergamon Journals, Ltd., Elmsford, New York. Reprinted by permission of the publisher and authors.

Table 11-1: A Synopsis of DSM III-R, Axis I. Copyright © 1987 American Psychiatric Association. Reprinted with permisson.

Table 11-3: Prevalence Rates (in Percents) . . . by Sex. Kay, D. W. K., and K. Bergman. "Epidemiology of Mental Disorders Among the Aged in the Community." In J. E. Birren and R. B. Sloane (Eds.). *Handbook of Mental Health and Aging.* Copyright © 1980, pages 43, 45. Reprinted by permission of Prentice-Hall, Inc., Englewood Cliffs, N.J.

Table 11-4: Annual Incidence Rates . . . Studies. Kay, D. W. K., and K. Bergman. "Epidemiology of Mental Disorders Among the Aged in the Community." In J. E. Birren and R. B. Sloane (Eds.). *Handbook of Mental Health and Aging.* Copyright © 1980, pages 43, 45. Reprinted by permission of Prentice-Hall, Inc., Englewood Cliffs, N.J.

Table 12-2: Percent of Deaths in and out of Institutions. Adapted in part from Lerner, M. "When, Why and Where People Die." In O. G. Brim, Jr., et al. (Eds.). *The Dying Patient.* 1976. Used by permission of the Russell Sage Foundation, New York.

Quoted material:

Atchley, R. C. From *Social Forces and Aging,* fourth edition. Copyright © 1985 by Wadsworth, Inc., Belmont, California.

Gallagher, D., and L. W. Thompson. Reprinted with permission from "Depression." In P. M. Lewinsohn and L. Teri (Eds.). *Clinical Geropsychology.* Copyright © 1983, Pergamon Press Journals, Ltd., Elmsford, New York.

Kausler, D. H. From *Experimental Psychology and Human Aging.* Copyright © 1982. Reprinted by permission of John Wiley and Sons, Inc., New York.

Lauer, J., and R. Lauer. From "Marriages Made to Last." Copyright © 1985 American Psychological Association. Reprinted with permission from *Psychology Today Magazine 19.*

Long, J. From "Older Americans: In a Retirement Town, the Main Business is Keeping Yourself Busy." *Wall Street Journal,* March 23, 1983. Copyright © 1983 Dow Jones and Company, Princeton, New Jersey. All rights reserved.

Parkes, C. M. From "Emotional Involvement of the Family During the Period Preceding Death." In D. S. Margolis et al. (Eds.). *Acute Grief: Counseling the Bereaved.* Copyright © 1981 Columbia University Press, New York. Reprinted by permission.

Parkes, C. M. From "Psychological Care of the Family After the Patient's Death." In O.

S. Margolis, et al. (Eds.). *Acute Grief: Counseling the Bereaved.* Copyright © 1981 Columbia University Press, New York. Reprinted by permission.

Suszychi, L. From "Intervention with the Bereaved." In O. S. Margolis et al. (Eds.). *Acute Grief: Counseling the Bereaved.* Copyright © 1981 Columbia University Press, New York. Reprinted by permission.

Weg, R. B. From "Changing Physiology of Aging." In D. S. Woodruff and J. E. Birren (Eds.). *Aging: Scientific Perspectives and Social Issues,* second edition. Copyright © 1983 by Wadsworth, Inc. Reprinted by permission of Brooks/Cole Publishing Company, Pacific Grove, California.

Photo Research: Elsa Peterson.